MADDEN

Urban Public Finance
in Developing Countries

A WORLD BANK BOOK

URBAN PUBLIC FINANCE IN DEVELOPING COUNTRIES

Roy W. Bahl
Johannes F. Linn

PUBLISHED FOR THE WORLD BANK

Oxford University Press

Oxford University Press

OXFORD NEW YORK TORONTO
DELHI BOMBAY CALCUTTA MADRAS KARACHI
KUALA LUMPUR SINGAPORE HONG KONG TOKYO
NAIROBI DAR ES SALAAM CAPE TOWN
MELBOURNE AUCKLAND

and associated companies in
BERLIN IBADAN

Published by Oxford University Press, Inc.
200 Madison Avenue, New York, N.Y. 10016

Manufactured in the United States of America
First printing April 1992

The findings, interpretations, and conclusions expressed in this
study are entirely those of the authors and should not be
attributed in any manner to the World Bank, to its affiliated
organizations, or to members of its Board of Executive Directors
or the countries they represent.

*The photograph on the cover is an aerial view of Karachi, Pakistan,
taken by satellite.*

Library of Congress Cataloging-in-Publication Data

Bahl, Roy W.
    Urban public finance in developing countries / Roy W. Bahl and Johannes
        F. Linn. p.   cm.
    Includes bibliographical references and index.
    ISBN 0-19-520805-6
    1. Municipal finance—Developing countries.   2. Local taxation—
Developing countries.   3. User charges—Developing countries.
4. Intergovernmental fiscal relations—Developing countries.
I. Linn, Johannes F.   II. Title.
HJ9695.B34 1992
352.1'09172'4—dc20   91-41999
                                                                CIP

Contents

Foreword

WHEN THE WORLD BANK initiated its research program on urban public finance in the early 1970s, Roy Bahl, Johannes Linn, and I found it difficult to raise much interest in the topic. Indeed, with the exception of the Bank's work, research on public finance then—and in the many years since—concentrated almost exclusively on central governments. Fortunately, over the years, much of the work on urban public finance in developing countries by Bahl, Linn, and their collaborators has reached audiences in academia and developing countries both by finding its way into print in journal articles, conference papers, and World Bank Staff Working Papers, and by being used in the World Bank's operational and training activities. Our main objective all along was to provide these audiences with a structure on which research and operational work could build, rather than to write a book.

The publication of this encyclopedic volume on urban public finance is, however, now very timely. The book distills the lessons learned by the authors during many years of work. After a significant worldwide diminution in concern for urban policy during the 1980s, these lessons will be of great value for policymakers, who more and more are recognizing that urban development is still a major challenge for developing countries. This return to urban policy is reflected in the World Bank's recent policy paper, *Urban Policy and Economic Development: An Agenda for the 1990s* (World Bank 1991b), and in the U.S. Agency for International Development's recent *Urban Economies and National Development* (Peterson, Kingsley, and Telgarsky 1991). What has caused this shift, in the wake of which far more attention has also begun to be given fiscal decentralization and local public finance than has traditionally been paid them?

One reason is that investments by urban local governments in social and physical infrastructure have, however belatedly, come to be recognized as critical. Second, the maintenance of public capital assets in urban areas is now largely the responsibility of local authorities. Third, central government budgets have often been strained in recent years, which has made it politically more attractive to devolve responsibility for public finance to lower levels of government. At the same time, it has become more widely recognized that local authorities, if given unfettered access to central revenues and credits, can drain national resources, with significant macroeconomic implications. Fiscal discipline and reliance on local resources have thus become the watchwords of the 1990s.

There have also been growing demands to involve citizens more directly in governance. This naturally leads to efforts to decentralize responsibility for governance to the lower levels of government, which are closer to constituents. Related to this is the notion that people will pay more taxes, and do so more willingly, if they see a closer relation between what they pay and what they receive in public goods and services. Finally, it appears that urban governments in developing countries have grown able to take on more responsibilities, even though most countries and cities still have a long way to go.

This volume addresses many of these concerns outright. The only treatise of its kind, it provides a policy framework for urban public finance in developing countries. On the basis of an in-depth survey of global experience during the past two decades, it offers detailed guidance on issues of how to design local revenue instruments. But beyond this, it seeks a better understanding of the critical elements that connect urban policy and national economic development, as highlighted in the World Bank's recent urban policy paper:

- The requirements for both citywide policy reform and institutional development
- The relation between macroeconomic policy and the urban economy
- The linkage between fiscal policy and economic development in the cities of the developing world.

In sum, the book provides policymakers at all levels of government with the framework and the evidence to help them relax basic constraints on the growth of urban and thus national productivity. By following the lessons of comparative experience gathered here, cities in the developing world can begin to overcome their governments' failures to provide them with critical physical and social infrastructure, and they can begin to mobilize the financial resources that will sustain their efficient and equitable development.

Douglas H. Keare
The World Bank

Acknowledgments

THIS BOOK draws on the initiative, ideas, and work of many people. Among them we are most indebted to Douglas H. Keare, who provided guidance and support all along, but especially during the critical early years of our research while he served as the chief of the Urban and Regional Economics Division of the World Bank.

Among our close collaborators, Richard M. Bird and Charles E. McLure were foremost in providing us with intellectual insight and friendly critiques. But many others helped us over the years, especially in the preparation of the case studies, on which much of the value of this book rests: Francine Bougeon-Maassen, Pamela Brigg, Hernando Garzón López, Kenneth L. Hubbell, Fernando Montes Negret, Rémy Prud'homme, Roger Smith, Michael Wasylenko, and Hartojo Wignow-ijoto. Carmella Quintos provided invaluable assistance in updating our data base. Deborah Wetzel and Helen Chin were instrumental in putting together the final manuscript. In addition, we drew on the work and advice of numerous World Bank colleagues, especially Bill Dillinger, Robert Saunders, and Jeremy J. Warford.

Of course, the book could not have been written without the assistance of many officials in urban and national government agencies around the globe, who provided us with their valuable time and knowledge so that we might learn from their experience and share it with others. They are too numerous to mention here, but it is largely from them that we gained whatever knowledge underlies this book. Among this group, our late friend Enrique Low Murtra stands out through his intellectual leadership and courage. Our thanks also go to all the faithful people whose minds and hands helped us over the years in pulling together the many facts and figures into a coherent manuscript.

Finally, we dedicate this volume to our families. Their support for us and our work over the past twenty years has been essential in helping us stay the course.

Roy W. Bahl and Johannes F. Linn

Data Sources and Definitions

Data Sources

The data in this study are drawn from many different sources. We began with a series of comparative case studies that followed a similar methodology for Bogotá and Cartagena, Colombia; Ahmadabad and Bombay, India; Jakarta, Indonesia; Kingston, Jamaica; Seoul, Republic of Korea; and Manila, Philippines. We added to this the results of a number of case studies that we either carried out ourselves or gained access to. We also benefited from the results of a number of cross-country analyses done both inside and outside the World Bank.

Finally, and perhaps most important, we relied on World Bank documents to update these data. These World Bank documents include economic reports, background papers for loan negotiations, appraisals, and so forth. Because these are official documents of the Bank, they may not be cited—even though the data they draw on are a matter of public record. The source notes for data from these documents thus simply read "World Bank data."

The sources of data for those tables which do not have a source note are given in an appendix at the end of the book. We realize that this is not wholly satisfactory, but it is probably the easiest way to identify the sources. In the appendix, the sources are listed in alphabetical or numerical order by country, table, city, and year.

Definitions

The expressions "the World Bank" and "the Bank" as used in this book mean both the International Bank for Reconstruction and Development (IBRD) and the International Development Association (IDA).

Unless noted, all dollars are current U.S. dollars.

The symbol "/" in dates, as in "1990/91," means that the period of time may be less than two years but refers to a fiscal year that straddles two calendar years.

1 Introduction: Why Study Urban Public Finance?

THE PROBLEM of urban growth has taken on national significance in most developing countries. There are few governments that do not consider their large cities much too big, and policymakers everywhere seem enamored with regional decentralization programs. Though many students of economic development are more ambiguous in their assessment of the relative costs and benefits of urbanization, there is general concern about both the rapid growth of large cities and the need for policies to manage more effectively urban growth and its related problems of congestion, pollution, slum settlements, and inadequate services and facilities.

Many of those who emphasize the great problems of large cities argue for policies that will slow rural-urban migration. A U.N. survey in the early 1980s reported that more developing-country governments were concerned with internal migration than with overall population growth and that more governments had policies to slow the rate of migration than to reduce the birth rate (United Nations 1982; Standing 1984). Others see significant advantages in large cities: their agglomeration effects lead to higher productivity than in the rest of the country, their more cosmopolitan populations and better educational systems make for a greater potential to develop human resources, urbanization generates an increase in taxable capacity from which additional public resources can be mobilized, and there are economies of scale to be gained from the large investments already made in infrastructure (Hamer and Linn 1987).

Those who emphasize the advantages of city size take the position that large-city problems are a result of an inability to find efficient ways to manage and finance urban growth. They are led to "accommodationist" policies, that is, to the view that the solution to the urban population problem is not to stop migration but to find a better way to deal with the growth which is surely coming. This book, which is about the financing of urban public services in developing countries, is in the accommodationist tradition. The central question we raise is how better to finance public services in large, growing cities and in particular how to capture the benefits of urbanization in order to increase the supply of services.

1

Urbanization and National Planning

The rest of this century is the right time to be concerned with the fiscal health of urban governments. Urbanization will continue to be rapid, and there is a shortage of government revenues to provide the services demanded in growing cities. The prospects are for continued urbanization in developing countries, and there is little evidence that antimigration policies will have a measurable effect on this trend. For the rest of this century, the rate of urban population growth in developing countries is projected to be about 3.5 percent, some three times the rate of rural growth.[1] Whereas in 1960, developing countries had an urban population of 460 million, by 1990 it rose to more than 1.3 billion, and by 2000 it will rise to almost 2 billion (U.N. Center for Human Settlements 1987: 23). In particular, the problems that most concern government planners in developing countries are those associated with very large and rapidly growing cities—the giant cities and the largest metropolitan areas in a country. U.N. projections have indicated that the number of cities with more than 4 million population in developing countries will have increased from 9 in 1960 to 50 in 2000 (10 to 16 in industrial countries) (U.N. Center for Human Settlements 1987: 29).

With projected growth at such rates, the special problems of large cities are crucial national issues in many developing countries. At the head of the list of problems is how to finance and deliver adequate public services in cities. It is inevitable that central government economic planners will eventually accept increasing urbanization and begin to rationalize the role of local governments in accommodating this growth. So far, however, formal policy has progressed very slowly in this direction. For example, of fifty-four development plans examined by the International Union of Local Authorities in 1981, not one explicitly considered the role of local government in the promotion of economic growth (as reported in Cochrane 1983).

The fiscal problems of cities will sooner or later occupy more of the attention of central government policymakers because urbanization will continue to bring pressures on central governments to improve public services in cities. To date, central governments, because of their precarious financial position, have as often ignored as dealt with these pressures. The political and economic constraints on greater taxation are well known, and in fact the mood of the 1980s has been in the direction of reductions in tax rates. In many countries such reductions have caused a large central government deficit financed by an expansion of domestic credit and more external borrowing to support the development of urban infrastructure. The possibilities for further expansion in external debt are quite limited in many developing countries, and there remain substantial pressures to hold the line on tax rates. Against the backdrop of pressing need for a stabilization program and limited potential for greater mobilization of central government revenues, the objective of shoring up the budgets of urban governments has taken a back seat. Moreover, the larger taxable capacity in urban areas can now take on an added significance. A central policy question should be whether (and how) cities can pay their own way.

With migration to urban areas, the formal sector of the economy and overall taxable capacity grow. Some of this capacity, however, is not easily reached by the central government revenue system because its indirect taxes miss many types of transactions, because personal income tax liability begins at quite a high income level, and because urban residents are more likely to resist payment of taxes that do not produce local benefits. Local governments may be better able to reach parts of the urban tax base because they are better able to identify liability for property taxes, automobile-related taxes, business licenses, and user charges, and because resident consumers may be more willing to pay higher taxes to finance local services. Moreover, local governments are in a better position to mobilize more resources through benefit charges for investment in and maintenance of infrastructure. Before all this can happen, however, central governments must help local authorities better understand which taxes they can levy and collect efficiently and must give them the necessary powers and technical assistance to implement such programs. In addition, they must provide better incentives for local governments to improve their fiscal condition, for example, by designing grant programs which stimulate local tax efforts and by instituting credit mechanisms to promote capital formation by local governments.

Objectives of this Book

This book has three objectives. The first is to pull together and interpret what is known about the subject of urban public finance in developing countries and, we hope, to carry the literature another step. The second is to identify and analyze systematically the problems that developing countries have with urban finance. The third is to evaluate options for policy and reform. We hope the book makes two important general contributions: to quantify and describe some of the detail of local fiscal practices in developing countries, and to flag the most common data problems which arise in cross-national analysis.

Improving the State of Knowledge

In pursuing our first objective—to extend the state of knowledge about urban public finance in developing countries—our intent is not simply to describe practices and identify important issues but also to demonstrate the applicability of the techniques of analysis conventionally used in industrial countries. Throughout, we look for parallels between cities in developing and industrial nations.

One has relatively little to build on in studying local government finance in developing countries. For many years, Ursula Hicks's *Devel-*

opment from Below (1961) was the state of knowledge about this subject. In the past two decades, a number of good comparative studies of various aspects of developing-country local finances have appeared.[2] These studies are important because they assemble data and descriptions from disparate sources to describe an "average" practice, and because they extend the framework for analysis from industrial to developing countries. Despite this good work, however, far too little progress has been made in the direction of generalizing about how urban governments in developing countries are financed, what problems and public financing bottlenecks they face, and what successful and unsuccessful practices have improved or worsened their financial position. In short, there is not a good enough feel for what these cities do or how important they are in the scheme of things. A major aim of this research is to fill this gap by providing a substantial amount of description about city government finances in developing countries. A first step toward resolving urban fiscal problems is surely an understanding of the state of the practice.

Insofar as data will permit, we try to describe taxation and borrowing practices, expenditure responsibilities, intergovernmental grant systems, local government structures, and user-charge financing. In some instances, this work is purely qualitative description, but in others we have been able to quantify, identify an average practice (we hope), and explain some of the variation about this average. The data for this comparative analysis come primarily from case studies of individual cities (often unpublished) and give perhaps as good a picture of city finances in developing countries as has been gathered.

Evaluation of the Issues

In pursuing our second objective—to frame the important issues in analyzing urban government finances in developing countries and to offer a way to evaluate them—we face the possibility that the conventional analytic frameworks for studying local government finance (for example, median voter models, general equilibrium incidence analysis, marginal cost-pricing rules) need to be recast to fit the developing-country setting. This recasting, a number of cultural considerations, and a much greater concern with administrative constraints give us not only some new answers to a number of old questions about local public finance but also some new questions.

The full list of specific issues considered in this study is too long to recite here, but these general questions seem to emerge in country after country:

- How can one reconcile the strong advantages of fiscal centralization in developing countries with the need to promote local autonomy?
- How can tax structure and administration be changed to mobilize an adequate share of the growing taxable capacity that comes with urbanization?

- What is the potential for capturing full public investment and service costs from beneficiaries?
- How important are equity effects and allocative impacts as opposed to revenue-raising and administrative issues in formulating local government tax reform?
- Can central grant systems be constructed to provide incentives for local governments to mobilize additional resources and channel the funds to development purposes?

Developing Criteria for Public Policy

Our third objective—to develop some general rules for improved local government financial practices in developing countries, or at least some guidelines for formulating urban finance policy—might be pursued by devising a better approach to evaluating alternative financing practices (for example, by demonstrating how one might choose among alternative grant-in-aid programs). A goal throughout this book is to help urban governments sharpen their formulation of fiscal policy.

Another potential contribution to policy formulation has to do with the transferability of successful experiences. Clearly some important techniques of local government finance may be applicable on a broader scale, for example, land readjustment in the Republic of Korea, valorization in Colombia, municipal development banks in Latin America, and land value taxation in Jamaica and Kenya. These techniques will not work in all settings because of a variety of cultural, legal, and political constraints, but some knowledge of how they have worked in specific settings may improve local public finance in general.

Scope, Method, and Limitations

This study is meant to cover the finances of local government in large cities of developing countries. The questions of what is large and what is a city immediately arise. We define "large" very loosely and concentrate primarily on the larger cities within a country. We are as concerned, for example, with Kenya's two largest cities, Nairobi and Mombasa, as with Calcutta and Bombay, even though the latter two cities have many times more people. On the question of what we mean by "city government," we do not limit ourselves to municipal governments narrowly defined but rather refer to all public authorities operating within an urban area (for example, transportation and water authorities, smaller and adjacent municipalities in the same metropolitan area, and overlapping special districts). States, provinces, departments, and so forth, are not the primary focus of study here, except in the context of intergovernmental fiscal relations, but villages, barrios, and other subcity units are considered. In some places we consider the relation between urban and rural local governments, but the focus is primarily on urban areas.

Unfortunately, there is a shortage of good secondary data; a compendium of local government finances in developing countries does not exist. The newcomer to this area of analysis might expect that one of the international agencies would have begun to gather such data by now, at least for the world's largest cities. This guess would be incorrect. The best comparable data on international public finance are in the International Monetary Fund's *Government Finance Statistics Yearbook*, but this source reports only aggregate, nationwide data from state and local governments. Even in this source, aggregate statistics for subnational governments are not presented for many countries and are incomplete for others. Neither the United Nations nor the World Bank gathers comparable data on local public finance.

The data and information for this study come from a variety of sources. A very important source is a series of case studies of urban public finance in developing-country cities carried out by the authors or under their direction.[3] These studies provide a wealth of fiscal data and information that have been made reasonably consistent, and a substantial amount of qualitative information about tax structures, expenditure responsibilities, and so forth. In each case, the data and information were gathered during field interviews with public officials and from public records, budgets, financial accounts, tax departments, and so forth. Fieldwork rather than home-office analysis is important because accounting methods, budget structures, and fiscal terminology all vary among cities; detail is necessary to bring the data to a common basis.

Case studies of various cities—carried out under a variety of auspices, using different methodologies, covering different years, but asking similar questions—provide the other basic source of information. The statistics in these studies suffer from some lack of comparability, and the supporting details on fiscal operations are not always available. Still, when carefully used they can add significantly to what we know.

Together, these sources of data provide information on more than fifty cities in developing countries and provide as comprehensive a look at developing-country urban government finances as has been taken. There are also important caveats. Some of the data are not comparable in form, different years are used in the comparisons, much of the information is dated, and the sample of cities is not random. We have tried to remedy some of these problems by updating the information where possible and by augmenting the sample where particular types of cities seem underrepresented.

This work also is limited by what we have chosen to study. Many important subjects—budgeting, financial accounting, personnel management, internal organization, political structure—are not covered. We also say far too little about the urban economic base which underlies the fiscal performance of the local government studied here. Population, income, and employment growth are perhaps the major determinants of fiscal health and to a large extent dictate fiscal options. Yet few countries have reliable regional income accounts or employment data, and hence we have only isolated evidence about the relation between the local fisc and the local economy. Finally, this volume—in its focus on *public* finance—has little to say on the role of *private* financing of urban infrastructure. This is a topic that warrants much additional research beyond the scope of this book.[4]

Plan of the Book

This work is organized in four parts. Part I, comprised of the next two chapters, sets the framework for urban fiscal analysis. The structure of urban government expenditure and revenue is described in chapter 2. Chapter 3 discusses how public policy and external events affect the fiscal behavior of local governments in developing countries and explores the relevance of the traditional explanations of public expenditure levels and growth in a developing-country setting.

Part II is about taxation by local governments. Since the property tax in one form or another is the principal generator of revenue in most cities, it is the subject of three chapters. After describing the prevailing practice in chapter 4, we turn to the question of the incidence of the property tax in developing countries in chapter 5 and then to the allocative effects of taxes and charges on land and improvements in chapter 6. The property tax, it turns out, is as justifiably maligned in developing countries as in advanced countries, and its practice is as much in need of improvement. Taxes related to automobiles are given a separate treatment in chapter 7 because of their growing importance and revenue potential and because of the special problems they raise. Finally, chapter 8 analyzes the use, advantages, and disadvantages of taxes on sales and income and of a number of other smaller levies.

Part III is concerned with user charges for urban services. Chapter 9 explores from an analytical perspective the most important of the issues related to the pricing of urban services: the difficult question of reconciling the needs to cover costs and to provide an efficient level of services. The practical issues of pricing public services are reviewed and evaluated in chapter 10, with special attention given to water supply and sewerage charges because of their importance in local budgets and because of their special importance to the quality of urban life. Practical methods of charging for other urban services are analyzed in chapter 11.

Part IV covers intergovernmental fiscal relations: the division of financing and spending powers and responsibilities between central and subnational governments. In chapter 12, the structure of local government in a national setting is considered; that is, what are the economic role and extent of fiscal autonomy of local governments in developing countries, and what common patterns of central-local relations exist? The advantages and disadvantages to fiscal centralization are also considered, and the trend toward centralization is described. Chapter 13 turns to the question of central grants to local governments and attempts to identify the state of the practice and the choices open in designing an optimal grant program. Chapter 14, an epilogue, gives lessons for policy.

A Framework for Analysis

CHAPTER 1 POSTULATED that urban public finance poses important problems and development challenges. Part I provides the basis for this judgment and a framework for analysis. Chapter 2 reviews the available evidence on the trends and composition of urban public spending and revenues and concludes that urban government plays a significant role, especially in larger cities, in raising and allocating public finances relative to other levels of government. Moreover, the functions of urban governments, although varying across and within cities, always give local authorities a large say in how effectively cities grow, especially through their involvement in the provision of urban infrastructure and of social services such as education or health.

On the revenue side, urban governments tend to rely heavily on the property tax, on ad hoc local taxes, and on user charges. Intergovernmental transfers tend to make a relatively small contribution to the revenues of urban governments; local borrowing is rarely a significant source of finance.

Chapter 3 provides a framework for analyzing the role of urban government and the forces that have contributed to the growing discrepancy between expenditure needs and revenue availability, also referred to as the "fiscal gap." It provides a broad outline of approaches that might be followed to close this fiscal gap, both on the expenditure and the revenue sides, and it closes with a discussion of some of the political factors which tend to constrain reform of urban finances.

2 *The Expenditure and Revenue Structure of Urban Governments*

THE INFLUENCE of urbanization on the budget of a local government is dependent on the government's expenditure responsibility, revenue raising authority, and fiscal autonomy. Accordingly, the purpose of this chapter is to describe the fiscal practices of urban governments in developing countries.[1] We begin by trying to gain some perspective on the fiscal importance of the local public sector, that is, to answer the inevitable question of whether the issue is worth studying. We then describe the expenditure responsibilities of local governments, particularly the division of responsibilities among central, state, and city governments and local public enterprises. Lastly, we consider the revenue authority of local governments, their independence in using this authority, and their reliance on external sources of finance. The aim here is primarily to give a picture of the structure of urban government finances; each of these issues is explored in more detail in subsequent chapters.

There is little precedent for this kind of description of city financing practices. Davey (1983) focused on differences in the institutions that govern local finances but did not attempt comparative, quantitative analysis. Smith (1974) used secondary data to compare city government finances in developing countries but did not use the broader definition of local government employed here. Walsh (1969) relied on case studies of selected cities but was not primarily concerned with financing patterns. This book also relies on case studies but differs from earlier works in that the case studies focus on financing, many were designed to produce comparable information, and all use a more comprehensive definition of local government.

The Importance of Local Government in Developing Countries

The expenditure responsibility of local government varies widely across countries. As noted above, accurate data on the finances of individual local authorities are not collected by any central agency for purposes of international comparison.[2] Hence, cross-country comparisons of the degree of fiscal decentralization have usually focused on intercountry variations in the fiscal importance of the entire subnational level of government. On the basis of such evidence, it is possible to obtain some first impressions of the importance of subnational author-

11

ities in developing countries and, to some extent, the importance of local government.

Using fiscal data for 1973–76, a sample of twenty-three industrial and thirty-four developing countries for which data were available, and the expenditure share of subnational governments as the measure of fiscal decentralization, Bahl and Nath (1986) found an average subnational share of 15 percent of all government expenditure in developing countries. Around this average is a substantial variation, with the subnational government sector accounting for up to half of all government expenditures in some countries (for example, Brazil, Chile, and India). To the extent that these figures are reliable, they indicate that state, provincial, and local governments are of substantial fiscal importance in developing countries, though much less so than in industrial nations.[3] It seems clear, however, that fiscal decentralization accompanies development. The subnational average expenditure share for advanced countries in the study mentioned above was 32 percent, and econometric results in Bahl and Nath (1986), Wasylenko (1987), Oates (1972), and Pommerehne (1977) show a significant positive statistical association between the degree of expenditure decentralization and per capita GNP.

There is no clear consensus from past research about whether the expenditure share of subnational government has been increasing. Bahl and Nath's (1986) comparison of twenty-five developing countries for 1960–73 shows an approximately constant share, as does our own comparison of twenty-seven developing countries for 1973 and 1980 using International Monetary Fund (IMF) data.[4]

Such estimates do not necessarily help us understand the fiscal importance of urban local government and how it has changed. In part this is because of the inclusion of state and federal governments, which in some federal countries dominate public financing activities in the subnational government sector. It is also true that local governments in large cities often have more fiscal responsibility than do other local governments because urbanization has pressed them to offer a broader range of services. Many countries in fact have differentiated the fiscal powers and responsibilities of their local governments on the basis of population size. Simple comparisons of subnational expenditure shares do not pick up intercountry variations in these dimensions of the importance of local government.

The problem here is to find a measure which better describes the importance of local government in metropolitan areas. One possibility is to aggregate the expenditures made in the urban area by the central, state, and local governments and to identify the contribution of local government to this total. Unfortunately, few higher-level governments track expenditures according to destination; hence, it is necessary to make some simplifying assumption in order to derive an estimate of total spending within urban areas. We begin with the simplifying assumption that the national (or state) government spends as much on a per capita basis in the city as it does on average throughout the country (or state). To the extent that per capita higher-level government spending is more city-biased, our assumption will understate total government spending in urban areas and will overstate the relative contribution of local government. If biases in higher-level government budgets are toward rural areas and smaller cities, our assumption will overstate the relative importance of higher-level governments.[5]

Using this basis for comparison, and data from a sample of 23 cities in developing countries, estimates of the share of national, state, and local government expenditures in urban areas are presented in table 2-1. For example, all local governments in metropolitan Bombay spent the equivalent of $55 per capita in 1982, which was 43 percent of estimated total (central, state, and local) government spending in the Bombay metropolitan area. (Throughout the text and in the tables, unless noted, all dollars are current U.S. dollars.) As may be seen from the local percentage share column in this table, the median local government expenditure share is about 20 percent, but there is wide variation, and a share of one-third or more is not at all uncommon. Moreover, even this estimate is probably biased downward by the underlying assumption that per capita central (state) government expenditures are equal in the metropolitan area and the rest of the country (state). The right conclusion to draw from this small sample would seem to be that the local governments of many developing-country cities play an important role in the provision of urban services and therefore have an important effect on the economic development of cities. These results should make the case that the fiscal problems of large cities in developing countries deserve more than the little attention they usually are given, and that the popular belief that urban local governments in developing countries play a very minor budgetary role is mistaken.

Table 2-1 (and most of the other tables in this volume) has been constructed to include information from an earlier and a more recent period, usually the 1970s and the 1980s. Accordingly, the data might be used to describe very roughly the changing fiscal importance of urban governments. For example, local governments in metropolitan Bombay increased expenditures by 9.3 percent in the late 1970s and early 1980s while the state and central governments increased spending by 9.3 and 10.2 percent respectively. This would imply that the importance of the local government sector as a provider of public services in metropolitan Bombay has not changed markedly. The data for other cities show a mixed pattern of increasing and declining importance. For example, the rate of growth of local government expenditures in Seoul was significantly higher than that of central expenditures in both periods observed, with the result that the local government share increased by about 2 percentage points. Just the opposite, centralizing tendencies can be ob-

Table 2-1. *Distribution and Growth of Estimated Public Expenditure in Selected Cities*
(dollars)

City, years	Per capita local expenditure[a]	Percentage share in total government expenditure			Percentage growth rate in per capita government expenditure[b]		
		Local	State	Central	Local	State	Central
Bangladesh							
Dhaka, 1980–83	1.5	5.7	n.a.	94.3	0.8	n.a.	8.9
Brazil							
Rio de Janeiro, 1980–84	42.1	13.8	22.9	63.2	−12.4	−5.8	−6.6
São Paulo, 1980–84	56.0	16.1	28.8	55.1	−10.4	−10.1	−6.6
Colombia							
Bogotá, 1970–72	59.5	49.9	n.a.	50.1	20.2	n.a.	21.9
Cali, 1975	51.4	48.8	6.7	44.5	—	—	—
Cartagena, 1969–72	20.0	23.0	8.5	68.4	13.6	15.9	21.9
India							
Ahmadabad, 1965–71	19.7	41.5	49.8	8.7	14.6	9.5	12.5
Ahmadabad, 1977–81	29.6	30.7	34.8	34.5	9.9	13.9	11.2
Bombay, 1963–70	22.0	41.7	31.5	26.9	6.1	12.7	11.5
Bombay, 1975–82	54.5	42.9	30.9	26.2	9.3	9.3	10.2
Indonesia							
Jakarta, 1972–73	8.3	36.9	n.a.	63.1	—	—	—
Jakarta, 1980–81	46.0	21.6	n.a.	78.4	11.2	n.a.	28.1
Iran							
Tehran, 1974	26.2	3.9	n.a.	96.1	—	—	—
Jamaica							
Kingston, 1968–72	20.7	19.4	n.a.	80.6	13.7	n.a.	18.2
Kenya							
Nairobi, 1980–81	58.3	46.3	n.a.	53.7	8.3	n.a.	18.1
Korea, Rep. of							
Daegu, 1976	41.0	23.0	n.a.	77.0	—	n.a.	—
Daegu, 1981–83	174.5	34.2	n.a.	66.0	58.4	n.a.	6.5
Daejeon, 1976	38.4	21.9	n.a.	78.1	—	n.a.	—
Daejeon, 1981–83	90.5	21.3	n.a.	78.7	6.0	n.a.	6.5
Gwangju, 1976	37.8	21.6	n.a.	78.4	—	n.a.	—

Gwangju, 1981–83	141.2	29.6	n.a.	70.4	14.5	n.a.	6.5
Jeonju, 1975	31.0	23.5	n.a.	76.5	—	n.a.	—
Jeonju, 1981–83	128.9	27.7	n.a.	72.3	14.0	n.a.	6.5
Seoul, 1965–71	31.4	36.3	n.a.	63.7	31.5	n.a.	23.0
Seoul, 1981–83	214.4	38.4	n.a.	61.6	16.1	n.a.	6.5
Mexico							
Mexico City, 1966	32.3	18.0	n.a.	82.0	—	—	—
Mexico City, 1980–84	142.2	22.0	78.0	-10.1		0.8	
Nicaragua							
Managua^c, 1972	14.9	15.2	n.a.	84.8	—	n.a.	—
Managua, 1979	15.99	12.4	n.a.	87.6	—	n.a.	—
Peru							
Lima, 1981–82	13.1	6.0	n.a.	94.0	-13.1	n.a.	-14.6
Philippines							
Manila, 1960–70	7.5	30.5	n.a.	69.5	6.5	n.a.	9.7
Manila, 1980–85	5.8	10.0	n.a.	90.0	-12.2	n.a.	-10.3
Thailand							
Bangkok, 1975–77	23.9	25.1	n.a.	74.9	15.7	n.a.	17.4
Tunisia							
Tunis, 1965–70	17.6	17.0	n.a.	83.0	-3.5	n.a.	7.1
Tunis, 1984–85	52.3	10.1	n.a.	89.9	-14.0	n.a.	3.4
Median							
Before and including 1979	23.0	23.0	19.1	76.5	13.7	14.3	12.5
After 1979	54.5	21.7	32.9	68.2	7.1	5.5	6.5

— Not available.

n.a. Not applicable.

Note: The underlying expenditure figures for the local authorities are derived directly from local budgets and financial reports. The spending figures for higher-level governments are, with the exception of Cali and Mexico City, based on the per capita assumption stated in the text. For Cali and Mexico City, direct estimates of higher-level government spending in each city were available. Even these are subject to limitations, however, since the allocation of certain higher-level government expenditures to particular urban areas is necessarily arbitrary.

a. Consolidated expenditure by all local government agencies in the metropolitan area, including (semi-) autonomous local public service enterprise, converted to dollars at the prevailing official exchange rates as shown in IMF (various years, b). The figures are for the terminal year of the period shown in the preceding column.

b. Average annual compound growth rate of per capita expenditures, expressed in dollars at the prevailing official exchange rate.

c. Local revenues are used to approximate the level of local expenditures.

served for Tunis. It is difficult to draw out an average performance from so small a sample and from data that are drawn from so many different combinations of years. The medians presented in table 2-1 suggest that the urban government share of total expenditures has declined over the long run. However, even if this conclusion could be substantiated with a larger and more complete sample of data, it would not suggest a poor fiscal performance by large city governments. Indeed, as we shall show below, some urban governments have done surprisingly well in keeping their expenditures in step with population and inflation.

In table 2-2, we have elaborated on the variation in expenditure growth rates among these cities and have made comparisons with population growth and inflation. As might be expected, there is wide variation in the consolidated expenditure performance of urban local governments. Some city governments have experienced expansions in real expenditure which are substantially above the rate of increase in the city's population (for example, Gujranwala and Seoul). Other cities suffered a decline in real spending (Mexico City and Tunis), whereas yet others show declining real per capita spending (Madras).

One way to read the results presented in table 2-2 is that real per capita expenditures increased in many of the cities in this sample during the periods under consideration. The ability of some local governments to raise per capita expenditures, despite rapid increases in population, limited resource bases, inflation, and constraints placed upon them by higher government authorities, is a remarkable achievement. It suggests a very important conclusion: urban governments can play a significant role in local resource mobilization. Two cautions accompany even this generally favorable evaluation of the fiscal performance of cities. First, expenditure needs still may have gone unmet; that is, although actual expenditures may have kept up with population, they may not have grown enough to hold levels of public service constant. Second, the increase in real per capita expenditures in many cities was probably not sufficient even to dent the existing deficit in services.[6]

One can also read these data as painting a less favorable picture of city finances. Growth in local government expenditure was stronger in the 1970s than in the 1980s for about half the cities studied. This might be attributed to some combination of the aftermath of the oil crisis, a weak world economy, the debt crisis, high rates of inflation, and the low buoyancy of local government revenues in some countries. Many cities show substantial declines in real per capita expenditure in the 1980s, an almost certain sign of fiscal problems and the deterioration of locally provided services.

What Do Local Governments Do?

Another way to examine the importance of local governments in developing countries is to ask what services they provide. How true is the claim that the services provided by local governments are essential to developing the urban economy and to protecting the living conditions of the urban populace, especially low-income families? On the basis of our analysis of urban governments in developing countries, their common functions would appear to be markets, abattoirs, fire protection, street cleaning and lighting, garbage collection, cemeteries, libraries, and minor public disease prevention services. Beyond these common functions, responsibilities vary widely, including—in many cases—the responsibility for major governmental functions. We have attempted to describe this variation in service responsibility for a sample of cities by categorizing local governments as having primary (P), secondary (S), or no (N) responsibility (see tables 2-3, 2-4, and 2-5).[7]

As may be seen from these compilations, many local governments have full or partial responsibility for the provision of physical infrastructure, in particular the construction and maintenance of streets, potable water supply, sewerage, and drainage. In contrast, telephone and electricity services are typically the responsibility of higher-level government agencies, with a few notable exceptions, such as in Colombia. It will be a surprise to many that primary education is frequently controlled by local government in developing countries. Health and welfare services, however, are rarely a local responsibility and are often not provided on a significant scale by any government agency. Local housing programs are of importance in some cities, particularly in former British colonies where the British focus on local public housing has been retained (for example, Kenya and Zambia). Minor local public housing programs are found in many cities; however, they tend to be small relative to national or state housing programs and frequently cater only to municipal employees. Urban mass transportation is frequently the responsibility of a local authority, and sometimes it is managed by private firms which are supervised by local or national authorities. Police protection is almost universally a responsibility of national authorities.

Within developing countries, local governments in the larger cities usually have a greater range of responsibilities than do their counterparts in the smaller cities. One reason is that the largest cities in developing countries, and in particular the capital cities, tend to have a special administrative status combining local and state (provincial) functions and therefore have a greater range of local government responsibilities. This practice is certainly not limited to developing countries; for example, Washington, D.C., is a special district with some of the fiscal functions of both a city and a state.

Cities in virtually all developing countries face an overlap of responsibilities of local, state, and national authorities. Often all levels of government are involved in the provision of a particular service within an urban area, though the intergovernmental arrangement under which responsibility is shared varies widely. For example, various national, state,

(*Text continues on page 23.*)

Table 2-2. *Annual Growth Rate and Composition of Expenditure by Local Governments in Selected Cities*
(percent)

City or state, years	Population growth rate	Growth rate of total local expenditure		Growth rate of recurrent local expenditure in current prices	Share of recurrent total local expenditure[a]
		In current prices	In constant prices		
Brazil					
State of Guabara,[b] 1980–84	1.2	129.1	−1.5	120.6	82.6
Rio de Janeiro, 1967–69[c]	27.0	46.7	16.6	—	71.0
São Paulo, 1980–84	3.7	126.7	−2.5	120.9	35.1
Colombia					
Bogotá, 1963–72	6.6	20.5	9.0	21.8	59.0
Cali, 1964–74	4.4	21.3	7.9	22.9	72.8
Cartagena, 1970–72	5.0	31.0	18.2	31.9	76.4
India					
Ahmadabad, 1965–71	3.3	9.4	3.7	12.2	88.0
Ahmadabad, 1977–81	4.1	12.4	3.9	14.1	81.7
Bombay, 1963–72	3.7	10.5	4.3	11.2	83.7
Bombay, 1975–82	3.7	12.2	6.4	11.3	78.2
Madras (Corp.), 1972–76	3.7	4.3	8.8	9.2	74.0
Madras (Corp.), 1977–79	3.3	−3.4	−4.1	5.9	71.3
Indonesia					
Jakarta, 1970–73	4.6	17.8	9.2	19.4	49.3
Jakarta, 1981–82	6.0	11.9	−0.3	11.1	55.1
Jamaica					
Kingston, 1969–73	2.8	15.3	8.2	11.1[d]	86.5
Kenya					
Nairobi, 1960–76	7.0	17.4	4.6	14.2	70.3
Nairobi, 1980–81	6.0	8.3	−3.1	30.0	53.9

18

Korea, Rep. of					
Seoul, 1963–72	7.6	34.5	20.8	22.5	34.7
Seoul, 1981–83	3.0	27.6	21.2	18.8	35.0
Mexico					
Mexico City, 1980–84	3.6	53.1	–5.1	59.5	35.5
Nigeria					
Lagos, 1979–80	6.5	32.4	18.6	163.6	78.2
Pakistan					
Karachi, 1972–75	5.6	30.2	7.7	26.7	64.2
Karachi, 1981–82	4.3	17.7	11.4	7.9	53.5
Gujranwala, 1971–75	5.8	34.1	16.9	37.6	58.3
Gujranwala, 1983–85	5.8	40.5	32.3	34.1	94.1
Philippines					
Manila, 1960–70	4.9	11.4	6.1	—	—
Manila, 1980–85	3.4	5.2	–12.7	—	—
Tunisia					
Tunis, 1966–72	4.0	–3.2	–6.5	0.0	84.8
Tunis, 1981–82	4.0	–2.3	–9.6	–7.2	74.6
Turkey					
Istanbul, 1960–70	3.9	5.3	–0.6	5.9	86.8
Zambia					
Lusaka, 1966–72	11.3	14.6	5.7	16.8	84.0
Median					
Before and including 1979	4.5	15.0	7.1	14.2	74.0
After 1979	4.0	27.6	–1.5	32.1	54.5

— Not available.
a. For terminal year of the period under consideration.
b. Not including autonomous agencies.
c. 1969 figures are budgeted expenditure.
d. 1966/67—1972/73.

Table 2-3. *Local Public Responsibility for Services in Selected Cities with Extensive Responsibility*

Function	Francistown, Botswana, 1974	Colombia Bogotá, 1970–72	Colombia Cali, 1975	India Ahmadabad, 1971	India Bombay, 1972	India Calcutta,[a] 1977	India Delhi, 1970	Jakarta, Indonesia, 1972	Nairobi, Kenya, 1976	Rep. of Korea Seoul, 1965–71	Rep. of Korea Daegu, Daejeon, 1976; Guangju, Jeonju, 1975
Public utilities											
Water supply	P	P	P	P	P	P	P	P	P	P	P
Sewerage and drainage	P	P	P	P	P	P	P	P	P	P	P
Electricity	P	P	P	N	P	N	P	N	N	N	N
Telephone	P	P	P	N	N	N	N	N	N	N	N
Social services											
Primary education	S	P	S	P	P	P	P	P	P	P	P
Health	S	S	S	P	S	S	S	S	P	P	S
Social welfare	N	S	N	P	S	P	S	S	S	S	S
Housing	S	S	S	S	P	S	S	P	P	S	S
Transportation											
Highways and roads	P	P	P	P	P	P	P	P	P	P	P
Street lighting	P	P	P	P	P	P	P	P	P	N	N
Mass transportation	N	S	N	P	P	N	P	S	N	P	N
General urban services											
Refuse collection	P	P	P	P	P	P	P	P	P	P	P
Parks and recreation	P	P	P	P	S	P	P	P	P	P	P
Markets and abattoirs	P	P	P	P	P	P	P	P	P	N	N
Cemeteries	P	P	N	P	P	P	P	P	P	P	P
Fire protection	N	P	N	P	P	N	N	P	N	P	P
Law enforcement	N	S	N	N	N	N	N	S	N	N	N

Note: P, primary responsibility; S, secondary responsibility; N, no responsibility.
a. Calcutta Corporation.

Table 2-4. *Local Public Responsibility for Services in Selected Cities with Moderate Responsibility*

Function	Cartagena, Colombia, 1972	Madras, India, 1976	Casablanca, Morocco, 1970s	Karachi, Pakistan, 1976	Manila, Philippines, 1980	Bangkok, Thailand, 1974	Zambia Lusaka, 1974	Zambia Kitwe, Ndola, 1974
Public utilities								
Water supply	P	P	P	P	P	P	P	P
Sewerage and drainage	P	P	P	P	P	P	P	P
Electricity	N	N	N	N	N	N	N	N
Telephone	P	N	N	N	N	N	N	N
Social services								
Primary education	S	P	N	S	S	P	N	N
Health	N	S	S	P	S	P	S	S
Social welfare	N	S	S	S	S	N	S	S
Housing	N	S	N	N	S	N	P	P
Transportation								
Highways and roads	P	P	P	P	S	N	P	S
Street lighting	P	P	P	P	S	N	P	P
Mass transportation	N	N	P	N	N	S	N	N
General urban services								
Refuse collection	P	P	P	P	P	P	P	P
Parks and recreation	P	P	P	P	S	P	P	P
Markets and abattoirs	P	P	P	P	P	P	P	P
Cemeteries	P	P	P	P	P	P	P	P
Fire protection	P	P	S	P	P	P	P	P
Law enforcement	N	N	S	N	N	N	N	N

Note: P, primary responsibility; S, secondary responsibility; N, no responsibility.

Table 2-5. *Local Public Responsibility for Services in Selected Cities with Little Responsibility*

									Zaire	
Function	Tehran, Iran, 1974	Kingston, Jamaica, 1973	Lagos, Nigeria, 1960s	Gujranwala, Pakistan, 1975	Lima, Peru, 1982	Davao, Philippines, 1980	Tunis, Tunisia, 1972	Valencia, Venezuela, 1960s	Kinshasa, 1973	Bukaru, Lumbumbashi, Mbuji-May, 1973
Public utilities										
Water supply	S	S	S	S	P	N	N	N	N	N
Sewerage and drainage	S	N	S	S	P	P	P	N	N	N
Electricity	N	N	N	N	N	N	N	N	N	N
Telephone	N	N	N	N	N	N	N	N	N	N
Social services										
Primary education	N	N	P	P	N	S	S	S	N	N
Health	S	S	S	S	S	S	S	S	S	S
Social welfare	S	S	N	S	N	N	N	N	S	S
Housing	S	N	N	N	N	N	S	N	N	N
Transportation										
Highways and roads	P	P	P	S	S	P	P	S	P	S
Street lighting	P	N	P	P	P	P	N	P	P	P
Mass transportation	N	N	S	N	S	N	N	S	N	N
General urban services										
Refuse collection	P	P	P	P	P	P	P	P	P	P
Parks and recreation	P	P	P	P	P	P	P	P	P	P
Markets and abattoirs	P	P	P	P	P	P	P	P	P	P
Cemeteries	P	P	P	n.a.	P	P	P	P	P	P
Fire protection	P	P	P	P	P	P	P	P	P	P
Law enforcement	N	N	S	N	S	S	N	N	N	N

n.a. Not available.

Note: P, primary responsibility; S, secondary responsibility; N, no responsibility.

and local agencies in Cali, Colombia, are involved in providing public housing, public health services, and education (Bird 1980); and in Jakarta the national government and the city government share in the provision of water supply services, public health services, education, and transportation (Linn, Smith, and Wignjowijoto 1976). The different levels of government can also share the responsibility for delivering a service when one level of government controls what another level does. For example, the government of the Republic of Korea replaced the transfer of shared taxes to local government with a more ad hoc allocation which includes project-specific grants and which leads to much greater central control over local investment policies (Smith and Kim 1979). Another means of increasing central control is to create special metropolitan development agencies or autonomous service companies in which the higher levels of government take a more direct role than is the case with regular local government operations. Examples are the metropolitan development authorities in Calcutta, Karachi, and Manila. Overlapping responsibility also occurs where national or state-appointed civil servants carry out local government functions, for example, the manager of an autonomous agency or the local assessor.

Are local governments in developing countries less involved in delivering public services than those in industrial countries? These data do not give us an answer. Because there is so much variation in the scope of local government responsibility, it is difficult to make a statement about differences in the "average" practice. It is generally true, however, that urban mass transportation, health and welfare, and education are provided with greater local government involvement in the industrial nations.[8] And public utility services are more likely to be provided through the private sector in industrial countries. Otherwise, there are some close similarities between developing and industrial countries in the division of expenditure responsibilities. Large cities and capital cities have broader fiscal powers and responsibilities in most countries. Likewise, cities in developing countries are not alone in this pattern of overlapping responsibilities of local and higher levels of government. There is a similar pattern in the industrial nations, and calls for clearer definitions of expenditure responsibilities are heard in virtually every industrial country.[9]

Expenditure Patterns

This section concentrates almost exclusively on expenditures by local authorities. The data are drawn from comparable case studies which give a reasonably consistent and comprehensive view of local government, including the finances of autonomous local public agencies. These bodies have separate budgets and varying degrees of independence from the city government. They may go by a variety of different names, for example, authority, agency, committee, district, and *empresa*. We view them

Table 2-6. *Percentage Contribution of Autonomous Local Agencies to Consolidated Local Government Spending in Selected Cities*

City, year	Number of agencies	Percentage of total expenditure	Percentage of capital expenditure	Autonomous agency functions
Botswana				
Francistown, 1972	2	39.9	—	Water, electricity
Colombia				
Bogotá, 1972	12	79.3	98.5	Public utilities, housing, roads, public transportation, refuse collection
Cali, 1974	4	80.0	90.9	Public utilities, housing, roads, refuse collection
Cartagena, 1972	4	84.1	84.4	Public utilities, roads, refuse collection
India				
Ahmadabad, 1971	3	58.7	32.7	Education, public transportation, milk scheme
Bombay, 1972	1	30.2	19.7	Electricity, public transportation
Bombay, 1982	1	39.2	19.4	n.a.
Indonesia				
Jakarta, 1972	5	23.2	15.9	Water, public transportation, land development, education, abattoir
Jakarta, 1982	4	11.0	n.a.	n.a.
Jamaica				
Kingston, 1972	1[a]	43.4	73.4	Water
Korea, Rep. of				
Daegu, 1975	—	42.2	—	Water, land readjustment, housing
Daegu, 1983	—	35.4	—	
Daejeon, 1975	—	38.4	—	Water, land readjustment, housing
Daejeon, 1983	—	45.4	—	
Gwangju, 1975	—	21.6	—	Water, land readjustment, housing
Gwangju, 1983	—	65.6	—	
Jeonju, 1975	—	36.0	—	Water, land readjustment, housing
Jeonju, 1983	—	40.5	—	
Seoul, 1971	1	23.1	10.3	Education
Seoul, 1983	1	25.5	39.1	n.a.
Nicaragua				
Managua, 1974	1	28.7[b]	—	Water
Managua, 1979	1	25.1	—	n.a.

— Not available.
n.a. Not applicable.
a. Based on revenues.
b. Metropolitan water company administered under central government control. The expenditures and revenues of this enterprise are not included in the other expenditure and revenue tables in this chapter.

24

here as overlapping units of local government. Exclusion of these special districts would have introduced an important error; for example, these bodies contributed more than 80 percent of total local government spending in Colombian cities in the 1970s. It is not at all unusual for an autonomous local government agency to account for more than one-third of total local government expenditures, as suggested by the data presented in table 2-6. Even this consolidation of all local governments and local agencies does not eliminate all the issues of cross-country comparability. There remains the assignment problem, that is, the problem of comparing local government finances when local governments have different sets of responsibilities assigned to them by higher levels of government.

There are wide variations in the distribution of expenditures by service categories (tables 2-7, 2-8, and 2-9). This is to be expected because of the wide variation in urban government responsibilities, the relative severity of existing backlogs in public services, and differing policy objectives. Still, these data show some patterns which are suggestive of the different roles taken on by local governments. Colombian cities spend relatively more on public utilities and relatively less on social services, the transportation system, and general urban services.[10] Because it is a capital district, Bogotá has the combined expenditure responsibilities of a state ("department") and a municipality and therefore directs a relatively high share of its expenditure to education.[11]

For the Indian cities, with the exceptions of Bombay and Calcutta, the picture is reversed: relatively more local spending has been devoted to social services, especially education, and less to public utilities. These cities also have devoted a substantial portion of their resources to the operation of their urban transport (bus) systems. A similar pattern may be observed for the Korean cities, except for Daejon, Gwangju, and Jeonju.

The local authorities in Jakarta and Kingston have in common a relatively very small involvement in public utilities because their national governments carry most of this responsibility. But the similarity between these two cities ends here. Per capita spending in Kingston in the 1970s was two and a half times that in Jakarta, and although spending was spread across virtually all urban services in Jakarta, it was concentrated in social welfare, highways, and refuse collection in Kingston. (There are a few noticeable outliers in this comparison. Lusaka stands out because of its high per capita spending and its relatively heavy involvement in housing and industries, whereas Madras and Karachi spent a relatively high share on health care.)

Finally, it is of interest to return briefly to a review of the role of autonomous agencies in providing urban public services in the cities of developing countries. The data in table 2-6 indicate that in cities where public utilities are provided by autonomous agencies, the central gov-

(*Text continues on page 32.*)

Table 2-7. Percentage Distribution of Total Expenditure of Local Authorities by Function in Selected Cities of Colombia and India

Function	Colombia			India							
	Bogotá, 1972	Cali, 1974	Cartagena, 1972	Ahmadabad, 1971	Ahmadabad, 1981	Bombay, 1971/72	Bombay, 1981	Calcutta,[a] 1974/75	Calcutta,[a] 1982	Madras,[b] 1975/76	Madras,[b] 1984
Public utility	47.9	50.2	36.4	10.2	17.6	24.4	29.6	55.2	26.1	23.0	—[e]
Water supply	26.1	12.3	13.1	5.7	12.0	6.8	10.5[c]	19.9	21.3	23.0[d]	—
Sewerage and drainage	—	—	9.2	4.5	5.6[f]	4.7	6.2	35.3[d]	—	—	—
Electricity	11.0	27.5	14.1	—	—	12.9	19.7	—	4.8[g]	—	—
Telephone	10.8	10.4	—	—	—	—	—	—	—	—	—
Social services	14.0	3.5	1.6	45.1	32.0	25.0	21.8	14.1	12.9	34.0	44.4
Education	10.7	1.1	1.6	16.5	13.2	10.3	7.2	14.1	5.8	10.7	29.3
Health	1.6	1.8	—	7.9	10.6	9.9	10.6	—	5.6	23.3	10.3
Social welfare	1.4	—	—	0.4	4.2[h]	4.8	4.0	—	—	—	4.8
Housing	0.6	0.6	—	0.8	4.0	—	—	—	1.5	—	—
Milk scheme	—	—	—	19.5	—	—	—	—	—	—	—
Transportation	8.5	6.0	5.9	20.0	8.2	21.4	29.0	8.2	10.9	19.7	40.7
Highways and roads	3.9	4.3	5.9	4.4	7.4	5.8	9.5	8.2	7.9	19.7	40.7[i]
Mass transportation	2.1	1.7	—	15.6	—	15.6	19.5[j]	—	3.1	—	—
Other	—	—	—	—	0.8[k]	—	—	—	—	—	—
General urban services	6.4	3.9	12.6	8.4	9.5	7.6	4.9	2.0	20.1	—	3.1
Refuse collection	2.8	2.4	3.9	3.4	5.4	4.3	4.7	—	20.1	—	0.1
Parks and recreation	3.0	—	2.4	1.2	1.5	0.4	—	—	—	—	2.2
Land development schemes	—	—	—	0.8	—	—	—	—	—	—	—
Industries	—	—	—	—	—	—	—	—	—	—	—
Markets and abattoirs	0.3	1.5	4.8	0.1	0.1	1.5	0.2	2.0	—	—	0.8
Fire protection	0.2	—	0.9	1.1	—	0.4	—	—	—	—	—
Law enforcement	0.1	—	—	—	2.5	0.6	—	—	—	5.0	—
Other	—	—	0.6	1.8	—	0.4	—	—	—	—	—

Other expenditure	25.6	36.5	43.5	16.4	32.6	21.8	7.7	20.3	22.1	16.1	3.4
General administration	4.5	18.3	24.7	5.7	9.1	4.5	2.1	17.8	20.4	5.6	—
Employee pensions, health care, and so on	5.8	—	3.1	—	18.9	3.1	—	2.5	—	10.5	—
Debt service	14.3	16.3	14.1	10.7	—	14.2	—	—	—	—	—
Grants and transfers	1.0	1.9	1.6	—	—	—	—	—	—	—	—
Unallocated	—	—	—	—	—	—	—	—	—	—	—
Other	—	—	—	—	4.6[l]	—	5.6	—	1.7	—	3.4
Per capita expenditure (dollars)[m]	59.5	51.4	35.1	19.7	n.a.	26.0	n.a.	6.8	n.a.	1.1	n.a.

— Not available.

n.a. Not applicable.

Note: Except where otherwise stated, the figures include all local authorities within each metropolitan area.

a. Calcutta Corporation.

b. Madras Corporation.

c. Includes general administration of sewerage.

d. Includes night soil and refuse collection.

e. Responsibility for water and sewerage transferred to a local agency (MMWSSB) in 1978/79.

f. Includes maintenance of drainage and roads.

g. Includes street lighting.

h. Includes land management of estates, regulation of buildings, commercial buildings, land acquisition, slum clearance, and urban development.

i. Includes conservancy of buildings and bullock carts.

j. Includes general administration of electricity.

k. Street lighting.

l. Conversion of latrines and public conveniences.

m. Converted at prevailing official exchange rates according to 1986 data from IMF (various years, b).

Table 2-8. *Percentage Distribution of Total Expenditure of Local Authorities by Function in Selected Cities of Indonesia, Jamaica, Korea, and Zambia*

Function	Jakarta, Indonesia		Kingston, Jamaica	Rep. of Korea										Lusaka, Zambia
				Daegu,		Daejeon,		Gwangju,		Jeonju,		Seoul,		
	1972/73	1981	1972	1976	1983	1976	1983	1976	1983	1975	1983	1970	1983	1972
Public utility	7.1	7.5	3.8	18.9	16.4	17.6	14.6	14.6	21.5	23.1	11.3	15.2	9.2	26.9
Water supply	6.4	3.6	3.8	15.2	16.4	11.2	14.6	9.2	21.5	19.2	11.3	11.7	8.1	21.1
Sewerage and drainage	—	3.9	—	3.7[a]	—	6.4[a]	—	5.4[a]	—	3.9[a]	—	3.5	1.0	5.8
Electricity	0.7	—	—	—	—	—	—	—	—	—	—	—	—	—
Telephone	—	—	—	—	—	—	—	—	—	—	—	—	—	—
Social services	20.5	5.1	17.0	35.9	48.0	38.6	12.7	41.7	7.1	32.9	5.1	20.5	40.6	15.4
Education	9.0	—	2.2	21.5	35.4	25.8	—	28.0	—	22.9	—	19.7	25.5	0.7
Health	2.8	—	5.0	1.8	1.6	2.2	—	1.6	—	0.8	—	2.8	0.8	3.3
Social welfare	1.6	—	9.2	6.7	7.1[b]	6.9	12.7[b]	4.9	7.1[b]	7.6	5.1[b]	1.8	10.7[b]	11.4
Housing	—	5.1	0.6	5.9	3.91	3.7	—	7.2	—	1.8	—	8.0	3.7	—
Milk scheme	—	—	—	—	—	—	—	—	—	—	—	—	—	—
Transportation	19.3	17.1	23.5	10.0	0.7	8.1	31.1	15.0	44.2	18.2	29.3	23.2	16.3	5.3
Highways and roads	12.8	9.6	22.2	10.0	0.0	8.1	30.8	15.0	44.2	18.2	29.3	21.2	0.4	4.9
Mass transportation	6.5	7.5	1.3	—	0.6	—	0.3	—	0.0	—	0.0	2.0	15.9	0.4
Other	—	—	—	—	—	—	—	—	—	—	—	—	—	—

General urban services	22.6	2.6	39.4	17.8	16.2	16.6	14.0	9.2	9.7	7.5	10.5	22.6	7.6	20.5
Refuse collection	4.5	—	23.3	—	—	—	—	—	—	—	—	4.0	—	2.1
Parks and recreation	3.6	—	1.7	—	—	—	—	—	—	—	—	—	1.2c	1.9
Land development schemes	6.9	—	—	7.1	15.2	5.7	12.9	5.7	8.3	0.1	9.4	14.7	4.5	—
Industries	2.2	—	—	3.8	1.0	2.2	1.2	1.2	0.3	2.5	1.1	2.5	0.6	13.1
Markets and abattoirs	2.0	2.6	4.4	—	—	—	—	—	—	—	—	—	—	0.3
Fire protection	1.2	—	9.0	—	—	—	—	—	—	—	—	0.3	—	1.8
Law enforcement	0.9	—	1.0	1.0	0.5d	1.1	0.9d	1.7	1.2d	4.8	1.5d	0.3	1.4d	—
Other	0.3	—	—	5.9	—	7.6	—	0.6	—	0.1	—	0.3	—	1.3
Other expenditure	30.4	68.0	16.4	17.3	18.2	19.2	26.7	19.4	17.5	18.3	42.3	7.5	26.3	31.9
General administration	30.4	23.0	10.5	17.3	12.4	19.2	21.7	19.4	15.3	18.3	26.0	7.3	9.7	7.2
Employee pensions, health care, and so on	—	—	—	—	—	—	—	—	—	—	—	—	—	—
Debt service	—	2.3	5.9	—	—	—	—	—	—	—	—	0.2	—	24.7
Grants and transfers	—	—	—	—	—	—	—	—	—	—	—	—	—	—
Unallocated	—	—	—	—	—	—	—	—	—	—	—	—	—	—
Other	—	42.6e	—	—	5.8e	—	5.0e	—	2.3e	—	16.3e	—	16.6e	—
Per capita expenditure (dollars)f	8.3	n.a.	20.7	41.0	n.a.	38.4	n.a.	37.8	n.a.	31.0	n.a.	28.8	n.a.	63.1

— Not available.

n.a. Not applicable.

Note: Except where otherwise stated, the figures include all local authorities within each metropolitan area.

a. Includes night soil and refuse collection.

b. Social welfare includes expenditures on health, cleaning and sanitation.

c. Expenditure on olympic (sports).

d. Includes fire protection.

e. Expenditures on local development work may include tourism and transport. Also includes expenditures on buildings and development of cities.

f. Converted at prevailing official exchange rates according to 1986 data from IMF (various years, b).

Table 2-9. *Percentage Distribution of Total Expenditure of Local Authorities by Function in Selected Cities of Brazil, Kenya, Pakistan, Philippines, and Tunisia*

| Function | Brazil | | Kenya | | Pakistan | | | Manila, Philippines, 1985 | Tunis, Tunisia, 1985 |
	Rio de Janeiro, 1984	São Paulo, 1984	Mombasa, 1981[a]	Nairobi, 1981	Karachi, 1973/74	Karachi, 1982	Gujranwala, 1983		
Public utility	—	26.1	—	—	25.9	21.6	31.8	—	—
Water supply	—	—	—	31.8	18.9	11.6	7.5	—	—
Sewerage and drainage	—	—	—	—	7.0[b]	10.0	8.6	—	—
Electricity	—	—	—	—	—	—	—	—	—
Telephone	—	—	—	—	—	—	—	—	—
Social services	77.0	51.4	64.0	41.0	32.6	30.8	11.6	51.4	8.5
Education	38.2	13.3	30.2	14.3	8.8	6.4	8.7	39.5[c]	—
Health	12.4	8.2	30.1	18.9	23.8	24.4	2.6	7.2	—
Social welfare	8.6	12.1	3.7	3.5	—	—	0.3	4.2	8.5
Housing	1.3	17.8	—	4.3	—	—	—	0.5	—
Milk scheme	—	—	—	—	—	—	—	—	—
Transportation	2.0	18.5	28.0	6.8	19.6	30.7	28.2	0.1	3.5
Highways and roads	2.0	18.5	28.0	6.8	19.6	30.7	26.4	0.1	3.5
Mass transportation	—	—	—	—	—	—	1.8	—	3.0
Other	—	—	—	—	—	—	—	—	—

General urban services	—	—	—	—	20.5	7.4	20.2	12.4	2.1
Refuse collection	—	0.4	—	—	—	—	16.0	—	—
Parks and recreation	—	—	—	—	4.9	6.3	2.3	1.6	—
Land development schemes	—	—	—	—	—	—	—	9.4	2.1
Industries	—	0.1	—	—	—	—	0.1	—	—
Markets and abattoirs	—	—	—	—	1.7	1.1	1.8	—	—
Fire protection	—	—	—	—	—	—	—	1.4	—
Law enforcement	—	0.3	—	—	—	—	—	—	—
Other	—	—	—	—	15.2	—	—	—	—
Other expenditure	21.5	29.8	8.0	20.3	—	9.4	24.1	36.0	82.8
General administration	19.1	29.8	6.4	4.2	—	—	12.7	4.2	18.0
Employee pensions, health care, and so on	—	—	—	—	—	—	—	—	—
Debt service	—	—	0.1	6.0	—	—	11.1	—	3.0
Grants and transfers	—	—	—	—	—	—	—	19.1[d]	—
Unallocated	2.4	—	1.5	10.1	—	—	0.3	12.7	61.8[e]
Other	—	—	—	—	—	9.4	—	—	—
Per capita expenditure (dollars)[f]	42.1	56.0	n.a.	58.3	6.18	n.a.	n.a.	5.8	52.3

— Not available.

n.a. Not applicable.

Note: Except where otherwise stated, the figures include all local authorities within each metropolitan area.

a. Does not include all capital funds.

b. Includes night soil and refuse collection.

c. Includes expenditure on provincial/city libraries.

d. Includes intergovernmental aids, loans, advances and transfers, and aid to nongovernmental entities.

e. Includes personnel expenditures, expenditures on buildings, real estate purchase and expenditures on cars and equipments.

f. Converted at prevailing official exchange rates according to 1986 data from IMF (various years, b).

ernment is less involved in financing capital projects. When capital facilities are not financed through autonomous agencies, central government financing is much more important. The implication is that the
autonomous agency is seen to have a comparative advantage over general
local government financing and implementation, perhaps because of its
autonomy in management or its potential for relying on user charges
(see also chapter 12).

Financing Urban Services

How do local governments in cities of developing countries finance
their expenditures? How much autonomy do they have in structuring
this financing, and what are the basic factors determining their ability to
meet this challenge? This section addresses these questions on the basis
of case studies of selected cities.

Revenue Structures

A first step in analyzing the financing patterns of urban governments
is to distinguish between local and external sources of revenues. The
three categories of local revenue considered here are (a) locally collected
taxes; (b) user charges and benefit charges; and (c) other locally raised
revenues, such as license fees, penalties, stamp duties, and the like. The
external sources of local financing are transfers (grants or shared taxes)
from higher-level governments and borrowing. The distinction between
locally raised and external revenues is important because it describes the
degree to which urban governments draw on the resources generated
by the urban economy.[12] Furthermore, there is a presumption that local
authorities have more discretion in managing their local sources of finance than is the case for external revenues.

The distribution of revenues according to these financing sources is
shown in table 2-10. The share of locally raised revenues in financing
total expenditure has ranged in recent years from 100 percent in Karachi
to an exceptionally low share of 26.9 percent in Kinshasa. More typically,
however, between 60 percent and 90 percent of local expenditure is
financed from local sources, with a median share of about 70 percent.
The locally financed share, however, declined significantly in the 1980s,
as may be seen by comparing the medians reported in table 2-10. These
data also suggest a negative correlation between the ranking of cities
according to the share of locally raised revenues and the ranking according to the share of local government spending in total public expenditure (table 2-1). This supports the hypothesis (Kee 1977) that the
broader the expenditure responsibility of general-purpose local governments, the less they can depend on their own revenue sources, that is,
the more they must rely on external sources which tend to be controlled
by higher-level governments.

LOCALLY RAISED TAXES. Taxes provide more than half of locally raised revenues in the average city, and self-financing revenues contribute about a third. These averages hide a wide variety of local financing patterns and preferences. The large Colombian cities (Bogotá, Cali, and Cartagena) are notable for their relatively limited reliance on local taxes. This is because the governments of these cities provide the most important public utilities (water, sewerage, electricity, and telephones), but it also reflects the relatively heavy emphasis in Colombia on benefit-related charges in financing urban infrastructure.[13] By contrast, Bukaru, Jakarta, Karachi, Madras, and Manila rely heavily on local taxes. This is in part because the governments of these cities provide education, public health services, and other general urban services which do not readily lend themselves to benefit financing. It also may reflect a lack of attention to the potential for benefit and user-charge financing (see Linn, Smith, and Wignjowijoto 1976; Bahl, Brigg, and Smith 1976). Bombay, Francistown, and Seoul appear to have balanced structures of local revenue in the sense that local taxes and self-financing service revenues contribute roughly equal shares to locally raised resources. In Bombay and Francistown the thriving local electricity undertakings contribute substantially to revenues, whereas in Seoul there is an emphasis on benefit and user-charge financing even though the scope for application of such charging systems is limited. Finally, for those cities whose governments have little responsibility, such as Dhaka and Valencia, revenue sources other than taxes or user charges are most important.

Data also were gathered on the percentage distribution of local tax revenues for forty-two cities (table 2-11). Two striking features emerge from an inspection of these data. First, local governments draw on a large variety of taxes. Second, the property tax is levied in virtually all cities and often dominates the revenue structure—the median share in total local taxes is above 40 percent (though it has been declining), pretty much regardless of region or location.

Taxes on motor vehicles and on entertainment are levied in many cities, but with very few exceptions (motor vehicle taxes in Bangkok and Jakarta, for example) neither is of substantial importance for revenue. Industry and commerce taxes (usually a business license or a crude form of sales tax) are common in Latin America and parts of Africa and can account for a significant amount of revenues. For example, this tax contributes approximately one-third of the financing of local government expenditure in Bukaru, La Paz, and Manila. Some other forms of sales tax raise significant revenue in some cities. For instance, the general sales tax levied in Rio de Janeiro and Managua has contributed more than half the financing of total local expenditure in some recent years. Cities of India and Pakistan levy a special type of sales tax called "octroi" on all goods crossing city boundaries. This accounts for a significant share of

(*Text continues on page 40.*)

Table 2-10. *Percentage Distribution of Financing of Local Public Expenditure in Selected Cities by Type of Revenue*

City, year	Locally raised revenue				Revenue from external sources		
	Total[a]	Local taxes	Self-financing services	Other	Total	Grants and shared taxes	Net borrowing[b]
Dhaka, Bangladesh, 1983	113.4	48.9	30.5	34.0	-13.4	34.6	-48.0
La Paz, Bolivia, 1975	97.0	61.9	3.6	31.5	3.0	9.0	-6.0
La Paz, Bolivia, 1985	83.0	46.9	8.8	27.3	17.0	2.0	15.0
Francistown, Botswana, 1972	102.9	46.8	56.1	—	-2.9	1.9	-4.8
Francistown, Botswana, 1986	55.8	33.5	22.3	—	44.2	47.0	-2.8
Rio de Janeiro, Brazil[c], 1967	88.4	74.5	7.2	6.7	11.6	1.7	9.9
Rio de Janeiro, Brazil, 1984	92.2	72.3	12.0	7.9	7.8	0.4	7.4
São Paulo, Brazil, 1984	72.9	62.0	4.2	6.7	27.0	0.4	26.6
Bogotá, Colombia, 1972	62.5	13.7	48.5	0.3	37.5	14.0	23.5
	(72.4)	(23.6)	(48.5)	(0.3)	(27.6)	(4.1)	(23.5)
Cali, Colombia, 1974–77	74.4	15.6	57.5	1.3	25.7	2.8	22.9
Cartagena, Colombia, 1972	70.4	23.3	43.3	3.8	29.6	12.8	16.8
Ahmadabad, India, 1970–71	86.3	38.6	41.8	5.9	13.7	4.2	9.5
Ahmadabad, India, 1981	65.9	60.1	4.5	1.3	34.2	8.6	25.6
Bombay, India, 1970–71	84.6	37.9	38.7	8.0	15.4	1.0	14.4
Bombay, India, 1981–82	81.8	35.8	42.3	3.7	18.2	0.7	17.5
Calcutta (Corp.), India, 1974–75	73.8	64.4	—	9.4	26.2	19.4	6.8
Calcutta (Corp.), India, 1982	61.3	49.0	—	12.3	38.7	54.9	-16.2
Madras, India, 1975–76	69.2	54.5	3.7	11.0	30.8	25.1	5.7
Madras, India, 1979	72.9	58.0	0.6	14.4	27.1	13.7	13.4
	(84.6)	(69.6)	(0.6)	(14.4)	(15.4)	(2.0)	(13.4)
Jakarta, Indonesia, 1972–73	78.8	40.6	15.2	23.0	21.1	21.1	—
	(81.9)	(43.7)	(15.2)	(23.0)	(18.1)	(18.2)	—
Jakarta, Indonesia, 1981	65.7	38.8	17.6	9.3	34.3	39.1	-4.8
	(69.6)	(42.7)	(17.6)	(9.3)	(30.4)	(35.2)	(-4.8)
Tehran, Iran, 1974	46.9	42.8	—	4.1	53.1	45.2	7.9
Kingston, Jamaica, 1971–72	30.1	23.9	2.7	3.4	69.9	67.2	2.7

Mombasa, Kenya, 1981	75.6	75.6	—	—	24.4	32.2	-7.8
Nairobi, Kenya, 1981	80.2	34.1	46.1	—	19.8	13.7	6.0
Daegu, Rep. of Korea, 1983	54.9	25.4	21.5	8.0	45.1	32.9	12.2
Daejeon, Rep. of Korea, 1983	63.2	20.8	34.9	7.6	36.8	32.5	4.3
Gwangju, Rep. of Korea, 1983	41.2	12.4	25.4	3.4	58.8	22.2	36.7
Jeonju, Rep. of Korea, 1983	59.8	13.8	18.8	27.1	40.2	31.0	9.2
Seoul, Rep. of Korea, 1971	80.0	30.3	36.3	13.4	19.9	15.8	4.1
Seoul, Rep. of Korea, 1983	70.1	38.7	26.8	5.5	29.1	22.0	7.0
Managua, Nicaragua, 1979	80.2	45.8	—	34.3	19.8	5.0	14.8
Lagos, Nigeria, 1980	51.2	42.8	0.2	8.2	48.8	48.8	—
Gujranwala, Pakistan, 1983	106.9	82.0	8.5	16.4	-6.9	10.3	-17.2
Karachi, Pakistan, 1974–75	84.1	67.6	2.2	14.3	13.9	2.8	13.1
Karachi, Pakistan, 1982	101.4	93.3	0.9	7.2	-1.5	3.0	-4.5
Lima, Peru, 1982	73.4	27.8	36.1	9.5	26.6	19.0	7.7
Manila, Philippines, 1970	70.0	55.0	10.0	5.0	30.0	30.0	—
Manila, Philippines, 1985	71.6	58.3	6.0	7.4	28.4	24.1	4.3
Bangkok, Thailand, 1977	60.4	47.2	5.3	7.9	39.6	39.6	—
	(84.2)	(71.0)	(5.3)	(7.9)	(15.8)	(15.8)	—
Tunis, Tunisia, 1972	93.9	36.8	7.1	50.0	6.1	0.7	5.4
Tunis, Tunisia, 1985	33.8	24.7	5.3	3.8	66.2	17.1	49.1
Valencia, Venezuela, 1968	90.8	44.8	13.4	32.6	9.2	9.2	—
Bukaru, Zaire, 1971	69.9	67.4	—	2.5	30.1	30.1	—
Kinshasa, Zaire, 1971	26.9	25.4	—	1.5	73.1	73.1	—
Lumbumbashi, Zaire, 1972	90.5	72.8	—	17.7	9.5	9.5	—
Mbuji-May, Zaire, 1971	70.2	66.5	—	2.7	29.8	29.8	—
Kirwe, Zambia, 1975	92.7	35.0	53.1	4.6	7.3	2.2	5.1
Lusaka, Zambia, 1972	78.2	39.3	36.9	2.0	21.8	6.0	15.8
Median							
Before and including 1979	78.5	46.2	13.4	7.9	21.5	11.2	8.7
After 1979	70.1	38.8	17.6	7.8	29.1	22.0	7.0

— Not available.

Note: Figures not in parentheses include shared taxes as a component of grants; figures in parentheses include shared taxes as a component of taxes.

a. Because net borrowing can be negative, this can exceed 100.

b. Net borrowing consists of loan financing minus net changes in financial assets or reserves.

c. Because of the exclusion of autonomous agencies, the contribution of self-financing service revenues are probably understated.

35

Table 2-11. *Percentage Distribution of Local Tax Revenues by Source in Selected Cities*

City, year	Local taxes as percentage of total local expenditure	Tax as percentage of total tax revenues											
		Property	Property transfer	Income	General sales	Octroi	Beer	Gasoline	Entertainment	Industry and commerce	Motor vehicle	Gambling	All other
Dhaka, Bangladesh, 1983	48.9	51.1	8.5	—	—	31.9	—	—	4.3	3.5	0.6	—	—
La Paz, Bolivia, 1975	61.9	5.2	—	—	—	—	7.1	—	1.5	73.8	—	—	12.4
La Paz, Bolivia, 1985	46.7	25.0	—	—	—	—	—	—	—	52.1	22.9	—	—
Francistown, Botswana, 1972	46.8	12.9	—	61.1	—	—	—	—	—	—	—	—	26.0
Francistown, Botswana, 1986	33.5	58.9	—	—	—	—	—	—	—	—	—	—	41.0
Rio de Janeiro, Brazil, 1967	84.4	3.9	1.0	—	89.2	—	—	—	—	—	—	—	5.9
Rio de Janeiro, Brazil, 1984	72.3	15.7	—	—	50.1	—	—	—	—	—	—	—	34.2
São Paulo, Brazil, 1984	62.0	18.7	—	—	50.5	—	—	—	—	—	—	—	30.8
Bogotá, Colombia, 1972	13.7	58.4	—	—	—	—	—	1.8	7.0	18.2	5.1	—	9.5
Cali, Colombia, 1974	23.2	54.0	—	—	—	—	—	—	6.1	27.8	4.3	—	7.8
Cartagena, Colombia, 1972	23.3	61.2	—	—	—	—	—	—	4.4	12.2	2.1	5.8	14.2
Abidjan, Côte d'Ivoire, 1982	—	38.7	—	—	—	—	57.2	—	—	—	—	—	—
Ahmadabad, India, 1971	38.6	43.0	—	—	—	52.0	—	—	—	—	2.0	—	3.0
Ahmadabad, India, 1981	60.1	29.7	—	—	—	68.7	—	—	0.2	—	1.4	—	—
Bombay, India, 1970	37.9	55.6	—	—	—	37.7	—	—	0.3	—	3.7	—	2.7
Bombay, India, 1981	37.4	51.9	—	—	—	46.8	—	—	0.2	—	1.1	—	—

Calcutta (Corp.), India, 1974–75	64.4	64.8	—	—	—	—	—	—	—	—	—	—	8.2
Calcutta (Corp.), India, 1982	73.1	58.5	—	—	—	27.1[a]	—	—	—	6.4	—	—	2.1
Madras, India, 1975–76	54.5	68.9	5.1	—	—	32.9	—	—	16.0	—	—	—	10.0
Madras, India, 1979	69.6	72.0	3.7	—	—	—	—	—	16.7	—	—	—	7.6
Jakarta, Indonesia, 1972–73	43.7	—	—	—	—	—	—	—	16.9	—	50.2	26.9	6.0
Jakarta, Indonesia, 1981–82	42.7	9.5	—	—	—	—	—	—	12.2	—	64.5	—	13.8
Tehran, Iran, 1974	42.8	55.3	—	—	—	—	—	—	9.1	—	10.1	—	25.6
Kingston, Jamaica, 1971–72	23.9	100.0	—	—	—	—	—	—	—	—	—	—	—
Mombasa, Kenya, 1981	75.6	100.0	—	—	—	—	—	—	—	—	—	—	—
Nairobi, Kenya, 1981	34.1	100.0	—	—	—	—	—	—	—	—	—	—	—
Daegu, Rep. of Korea, 1976	n.a.	49.5	21.2	9.1	—	—	—	—	10.4	—	5.4	—	3.5
Daegu, Rep. of Korea, 1983	25.4	27.9	47.8	9.2	—	—	—	—	3.4	0.6	6.9	—	4.1
Daejeon, Rep. of Korea, 1976	n.a.	51.0	20.1	9.7	—	—	—	—	10.7	—	5.5	—	3.0
Daejeon, Rep. of Korea, 1983	24.3	56.3	—	21.9	—	—	—	—	7.1	1.7	12.1	—	0.9
Gwangju, Rep. of Korea, 1976	n.a.	50.3	23.1	13.2	—	—	—	—	6.4	—	4.1	—	2.9
Gwangju, Rep. of Korea, 1983	15.8	58.6	—	22.0	—	—	—	—	4.8	0.9	13.0	—	0.6
Jeonju, Rep. of Korea, 1976	n.a.	52.0	24.4	8.9	—	—	—	—	7.5	—	4.9	—	2.1
Jeonju, Rep. of Korea, 1983	15.6	55.3	—	23.2	—	—	—	—	6.4	1.4	12.5	—	1.1

(Table continues on the following page.)

Table 2-11 (continued)

City, year	Local taxes as percentage of total local expenditure	Tax as percentage of total tax revenues											
		Property	Property transfer	Income	General sales	Octroi	Beer	Gasoline	Entertainment	Industry and commerce	Motor vehicle	Gambling	All other
Seoul, Rep. of Korea, 1971	30.3	20.6	34.8	—	—	—	—	—	16.4	—	22.2	—	6.0
Seoul, Rep. of Korea, 1983	38.7	21.1	51.3	—	—	—	—	—	3.5	0.5	7.6	—	16.1
Monrovia, Liberia, 1982	n.a.	—	—	—	—	—	—	—	—	—	—	—	—
Managua, Nicaragua, 1974	84.3	—	—	—	69.4	—	—	—	2.3	21.1	3.1	—	4.1
Managua, Nicaragua, 1979	45.8	—	—	—	77.1	—	—	—	—	—	—	—	22.9
Ibadan, Nigeria, 1982	14.0[b]	8.6	12.9[a]	—	—	38.8[c]	—	—	—	—	—	—	4.0[d]
Lagos, Nigeria, 1962–63	50.9	100.0	—	—	—	—	—	—	—	—	—	—	—
Lagos, Nigeria, 1980	42.8	99.7	—	—	—	—	—	—	—	—	—	—	—
Maknqdi, Nigeria, 1982	n.a.	—	—	1.7[e]	10.0[a]	—	40.5[c]	—	—	—	2.7[f]	—	54.0[g]
Onitsha, Nigeria, 1982	n.a.	34.1	—	—	—	—	—	36.8[c]	—	—	—	—	19.0[h]
Lima, Peru, 1982	27.8	57.5	—	—	—	—	—	—	20.4	—	—	—	22.2
Gujranwala, Pakistan, 1983	82.1	15.1	9.1	—	—	75.4	—	—	0.2	—	—	—	0.3
Karachi, Pakistan, 1974–75	67.6	46.0	—	—	—	49.9	—	—	—	—	3.0	—	1.0
Karachi, Pakistan, 1982	—	27.3	—	—	—	71.8	—	—	0.1	—	—	—	0.8
Manila, Philippines, 1970	55.0	61.9	—	—	—	—	—	2.2	—	32.1	—	—	3.8
Manila, Philippines, 1985	58.3	59.2	1.0	—	—	—	—	—	7.3	30.7	—	—	1.9
Dakar, Senegal, 1982	—	21.0	20.6[a]	—	—	—	—	—	—	41.0[i]	3.8	—	13.6[a]

Bangkok, Thailand, 1977	71.0	15.4	—	—	—	2.0	—	1.1	42.1	33.3	3.5	2.6
Tunis, Tunisia, 1973	36.8	82.6	12.8	—	—	—	—	4.6	—	—	—	—
Tunis, Tunisia, 1985	24.7	42.4	57.1	—	—	—	—	0.5	—	—	—	—
Valencia, Venezuela, 1968	44.8	21.4	—	—	—	—	—	—	66.7	11.8	—	—
Bukaru, Zaire, 1971	67.4	—	—	3.7	—	87.0	—	—	—	—	—	9.3
Bukaru, Zaire, 1986	—	—	—	—	—	—	—	—	34.0	13.0	—	53.0
Kinshasa, Zaire, 1971	25.4	—	—	14.4	—	62.5	—	—	—	—	—	23.1
Kinshasa, Zaire, 1986	—	—	—	—	—	41.9	—	3.9	10.9	—	—	43.3
Mbuji-May, Zaire, 1971	66.5	—	—	62.7	—	—	—	—	—	—	—	37.3
Kirwe, Zambia, 1972	n.a.	80.0	20.0	—	—	—	—	—	—	—	—	—
Lusaka, Zambia, 1972	39.3	74.6	25.4	—	—	—	—	—	—	—	—	—
Ndola, Zambia, 1972	n.a.	75.6	24.4	—	—	—	—	—	—	—	—	—
Overall median												
Before and including 1979	46.3	54.7	14.4	77.1	43.8	34.8	1.8	6.7	32.1	5.0	9.1	7.6
After 1979	38.7	42.4	12.9	21.9	50.1	46.8	41.9	36.8	4.3	3.5	—	13.8

— Not available.

n.a. Not applicable.

a. Revenue from liquor licenses.

b. Includes rental and plot fees, slaughter fees, and other fees.

c. Includes fees and licenses from business and building inspection, layout development, and other items.

d. Poll and cattle taxes; these were abolished in 1981. Figure for 1982 is arrears collected.

e. Parking fees.

f. Includes ground rent and plot fees.

g. Refers to business taxes and licenses.

h. Includes fees.

i. Includes garbage collection tax collected by central government and other taxes collected by the municipality.

local revenues and where used is a buoyant source of local revenue. In Karachi, more than half of all local spending is financed from octroi proceeds.

Local income taxes are not common but have been important in some African cities, especially in Botswana, Nigeria, Senegal, Zaire, and Zambia.[14] Property transfer taxes are a local tax instrument in a few cities, but only in a few instances—notably the Korean cities—did this source raise a substantial share of local taxes. In Seoul it financed about 20 percent of total local government expenditure. Finally, the category labeled "all other taxes" has contributed a sizable share of local taxes in, for example, Cartagena, Francistown, and Tehran. Usually, however, the taxes falling under this heading comprise a motley collection of nuisance taxes which often are costly to collect and to comply with and which provide little revenue.

The data in tables 2-10 and 2-11 show several quite noticeable changes in the pattern of urban government finance from the 1970s to the 1980s:

- There is a trend toward more or less overall reliance on locally raised revenues.
- Locally raised revenues from charges are increasing in importance, and those from taxes are declining.
- Among local taxes, there appears to be a shift from property-based to consumption-based taxes.

EXTERNAL FINANCING. On average, about 30 percent of all local revenues in these cities are raised from external sources, mostly from grants and shared taxes (see table 2-10). The median share of external financing in this sample is up about 8 percentage points from the previous decade. There is a wide variation around this average, but relatively few cities derive more than half their revenues from external sources and only two in the entire sample get more than half their revenues from grants and shared taxes.[15] This low share flies in the face of popular notions of relatively little self-sufficiency on the part of urban governments in developing countries (Marshall 1969). It also casts some doubt on the common belief that national government policy heavily subsidizes urban as compared with rural dwellers through its fiscal policy. It would appear from these data that if such a subsidy takes place, it is not through transfers to urban authorities. It is not even clear that large cities in developing countries are on average more dependent on grants than are large cities in industrial countries.[16]

Do these results suggest that the share of grant financing in large cities of developing countries is too low? One answer is that it is, and that a way out of the serious problem of urban service deficits in developing countries is to expand the extent of grant and shared-tax financing. Indeed, these data do show an increase in the share of local government expenditure financed from external grants. Another view, however, is that urban local governments in developing countries should receive less intergovernmental assistance than those in industrial countries. This is because public service provision in cities in developing countries tends to have fewer spillovers to the rural hinterlands, and cities in low-income countries do not perform as many central-place functions as do those in industrial countries.[17] Moreover, since cities in developing countries tend to suffer less from jurisdictional fragmentation than is the case especially in the United States, there is less need for equalizing transfers from higher-level government to relieve intrametropolitan fiscal disparities.

Loan financing generally is the smallest revenue source for cities in developing countries, contributing less than 10 percent of total financing. In this respect developing-country cities seem to differ markedly from their counterparts in industrial countries, where capital outlays are largely financed from borrowing (Kaufman and Fischer 1987; Prud'homme 1987). The practice is more possible in industrial countries because capital markets are more highly developed and because higher-level governments are more flexible in their need to control the aggregate level of credit.

A wide variation in the reliance on borrowing may be observed in developing countries (table 2-10). Several cities experienced negative net borrowing during the earlier period under observation, and several others did no borrowing at all. The more important borrowers were the Colombian and Indian cities. For the Colombian cities and for Bombay this may in part be explained by the importance of local public utility operations which (a) require loan financing for their lumpy investments and (b) are relatively good credit risks because they are often run by autonomous local authorities and are heavily financed by user charges. It is also important to note than in Colombia and India the higher levels of government are relatively flexible in permitting loan financing by state and local governments.

Revenue Trends

For a smaller sample of cities, data are available to determine how much each major category of local government revenue has contributed to the financing of the growth in expenditure in recent years (table 2-12). The financing choices of these cities have varied widely. For instance, the Colombian cities have tended to rely more heavily on increases in user charges and borrowing than on increases in grants or local taxes—possibly because of the importance of public utility expenditure in these cities. Bombay and Seoul showed a more balanced expansion in revenues from local taxes and benefit charges but have relied less on external sources of revenues to finance increases in expenditure. In general, however, these data suggest a trend toward increased reliance on external financing.

Table 2-12. Financing of Changes in Local Expenditure in Selected Cities

| City, year | Change in total expenditure (dollars per capita) | Percentage of expenditure change financed[a] | | | | | | |
| | | From locally raised revenues | | | | From revenue from external sources | | |
		Total	Taxes	Self-financed services	Other	Total	Grants and shared taxes	Net borrowing
La Paz, Bolivia, 1983–85	-3.7	-30.4	-5.1	6.0	-31.4	-69.6	-26.2	-43.2
Rio de Janeiro, Brazil, 1980–84	-29.6	-71.5	-58.3	-6.5	-6.7	-28.5	-1.1	-27.4
São Paulo, Brazil, 1980–84	-30.9	-105.1	-76.2	-8.8	-20.1	5.0	-3.2	8.2
Bogotá, Colombia, 1963–72	10.4	48.4	13.4	35.9	-1.1	51.8	7.7	44.1
Cali, Colombia, 1969–72	31.0	68.4	15.8	51.0	1.6	31.6	3.9	27.7
Cartagena, Colombia, 1969–72	2.4	34.5	13.1	25.6	-3.2	65.5	15.6	49.9
Ahmadabad, India, 1965–71	-2.1	-108.4	-38.4	-65.9	-4.1	8.4	-4.3	12.7
Ahmadabad, India, 1977–81	9.3	-25.1	42.8	-0.6	-67.3	125.1	10.6	114.5
Bombay, India, 1963–71	0.4	89.0	48.6	32.8	7.6	11.0	0.4	10.6
Bombay, India, 1975–82	25.3	70.3	26.4	36.0	7.9	29.7	0.4	29.3
Jakarta, Indonesia, 1970–73	3.2	72.5	51.1	1.8	19.6	27.5	27.5	—
Jakarta, Indonesia, 1981–82	4.6	22.4	-7.0	21.6	7.8	77.7	42.9	34.8
Kingston, Jamaica, 1963–72	12.4	17.8	16.4	1.2	0.2	82.2	81.5	0.7
Seoul, Rep. of Korea, 1969–72	17.3	81.8	30.1	38.6	13.1	18.7	11.3	7.4
Seoul, Rep. of Korea, 1981–83	55.2	74.6	41.7	18.9	14.2	25.3	22.6	2.7
Mexico City, Mexico, 1980–84	12.0	-94.6	-32.4	-6.5	-55.8	194.6	-190.8	385.4
Karachi, Pakistan, 1980–81	2.9	73.0	55.9	1.9	15.2	27.0	6.9	20.1
Manila, Philippines, 1960–70	-4.8	-63.6	-51.9	-49.0	-6.8	-36.4	-36.6	-0.2
Manila, Philippines, 1980–85	-5.4	-78.7	-73.6	-3.9	-1.2	-21.3	-24.5	3.2
Tunis, Tunisia, 1966–73	-7.6	-195.0	-30.1	-17.7	-147.2	95.0	102.9	-7.9
Tunis, Tunisia, 1984–85	-8.5	-118.8	-64.7	-50.0	-4.1	18.8	-17.4	36.2

— Not available.
a. Numbers may exceed 100 because some sources may have increased while others decreased, asset positions may have changed, and debt retirements or additions may have occurred.

In fact, a reasonably consistent picture emerges. During the 1970s, for those cities where per capita expenditure increased, locally raised resources were the largest contributors; whereas in those cities where per capita expenditure declined, locally raised resources were the principal culprit associated with this decline. To the degree that one may generalize from such a small sample, it would appear that changes in locally raised resources determine the ability of an urban government to expand its services. Where locally raised revenues fare badly, urban government expenditure suffers; where they do well, urban expenditure thrives. Central government transfers and borrowing play only minor roles either way. The picture is only a little different in the 1980s. Where local expenditure budgets expanded, there generally was a strong local revenue performance, but external financing played a greater role than in the 1970s. Where local revenues did not grow adequately, local expenditure declined or grew slowly, but external financing provided more of a safety net than in the 1970s.

Revenue Authority

In evaluating the capacity of local governments in developing countries to respond to rapidly increasing urban service needs, the degree of local control over revenue sources is of primary importance. Can they adjust tax rates, impose new taxes, borrow to finance capital projects, adjust user-charge schedules, and so forth? An overview of local government revenue authority for selected cities is provided in table 2-13.

The most important of the local taxes, the property tax, is generally not freely controlled by local government. For the cities under consideration here, the setting of property tax rates is almost always constrained by higher-level government, usually by setting a tax rate ceiling to apply to all local authorities. Where property value assessment is a local responsibility it may be freely handled by local authorities (India) or it may be centrally controlled (Korea and Philippines) with national and local agencies cooperating to determine taxable property values. General sales and income taxes are less frequently at the disposal of urban governments, and even then rate setting is usually done by national authorities. There are exceptions. Some specific sales taxes and business taxes are often unhampered by central control, which helps explain their importance in cities where they are levied (especially the octroi in India and Pakistan and the industry and commerce taxes in Latin America and parts of Africa). Motor vehicle taxes, although quite frequently at the disposal of urban government, are usually restricted in use by higher-level government, with Jakarta being a notable exception. The importance of motor vehicle tax revenues in Jakarta points to the significant potential of this tax in the large cities of developing countries (see also chapter 7). Entertainment taxes are often not subject to restrictions by central government but in any case have rarely shown great potential for con-

Table 2-13. *Revenue Authority of Urban Governments by Revenue Source in Selected Cities*

Revenue source	Colombia			India		Jakarta, Indonesia, 1982	Kingston, Jamaica, 1973	Nairobi, Kenya, 1981	Rep. of Korea		Manila, Philippines, 1980	Kitwe, Lusaka, Ndola, Zambia, 1974
	Bogotá, 1972	Cali, 1975	Cartagena, 1972	Ahmadabad, 1981	Bombay, 1981				Seoul, 1983	Daegu, Daejeon, Guangju, Jeonju, 1983		
Taxes												
Property tax												
Assessment	F	—	—	F	F	—	—	F	R	R	F	R
Tax rate	R	R	R	R	R	—	—	R	R	R	R	R
General sales tax	—	—	—	—	—	—	—	—	—	—	—	—
Specific sales tax	—	—	—	F	F	—	—	—	—	—	F	—
Income tax	—	—	F	—	—	—	—	—	R^a	R^a	—	R
Business taxes	F	F	F	—	—	—	—	F	R	R	R	—
Vehicle taxes	R	R	R	F	R	F	—	—	R	R	—	—
Entertainment taxes	R	R	R	F	R	F	—	F	R	R	R	R
Minor taxes and fees	F	F	F	F	F	F	R	F	F	R	F	—
Betterment levies	F	F	F	F	F	F	F	—	F	F	F	—
User charges												
Water and sewerage	R	R	R	F	F	F	—	R	R	R	R	R
Electricity	R	R	—	—	F	—	—	—	—	—	R	—
Telephones	R	R	R	—	—	—	—	—	F	R	—	—
Housing	F	F	—	—	F	F	—	R	R	—	F	F
Public transport	R	—	—	—	F	F	—	—	R	—	—	—
Shared taxes	N	N	N	N	—	N	—	N	N	N	N	N
Grants	N	N	N	N	N	N	N	N	N	N	N	N
Borrowing												
Private capital	R	R	R	R	R	R	R	R	R	R	R	R
Public capital	R	R	R	R	R	R	R	R	R	R	R	R

— Not available.

Note: F = Freely administered at the local level. R = Regulated by higher-level governments. N = No local control.

a. Introduced in 1973.

44

tribution to local revenues. Other minor taxes and fees, somewhat iron- ically, are the sources of local government revenue which are least subject to higher-level government controls and restrictions. In some cities this has led imaginative local officials to design such a wide variety of these minor sources that they add up to a noticeable proportion of total city revenues. But they do not provide a basis for healthy and reliable local revenue collections, and local governments which rely heavily on them usually have serious problems with their revenue structures.

With the exception of the Colombian and Korean cities, betterment levies and related revenue sources rarely account for an important share of revenue.[18] The problem in this case is not central government re- strictions. In fact, virtually all the cities shown in table 2-13 are entitled to use this form of expenditure financing. The problem is partly the reluctance of local authorities to apply these levies and partly their lack of knowledge about implementation.

User charges, like taxes, are often controlled by central authorities. In Colombia, this has taken the form of nationwide guidelines from the National Utilities Tariff Board, which also reviewed and approved all applications for changes in user charges. The board has in the past dis- couraged cross-subsidization between service users, but in general it has been a force supporting the recovery of average long-run costs of public utility services through user charges (Linn 1980a). In other countries and cities, the central control on local user charges has had negative impacts on local revenue-raising efforts. Some Korean cities, for instance, have been unable to raise user fees to levels thought appropriate by local authorities because of intervention by higher-level government. The only sizable self-financing service for which local government has generally been free to set its user charges is the provision of public housing. To the extent that the national government is involved in the planning and design of local housing projects, however, it may also exert influence over the cost-recovery policies in this sector. In any case, in virtually all cities where large housing programs are managed by local government, severe financial problems have arisen (the Zambian cities are a good case in point).

It is not surprising that external revenue sources are even less ame- nable to local control than are locally raised revenues. Local governments rarely have a say in the determination of shared taxes and grants.

Local borrowing is almost always controlled by higher-level authorities in developing countries, but there are variations in the extent of this control. The Colombian Planning Ministry has reviewed and approved all applications for borrowing which exceed a low ceiling, below which local authorities may freely borrow from commercial banks mainly for purposes of cash-flow management (Bird 1980; Linn 1980a). In Kenya and the Philippines, local public agencies have had to receive prior au- thorization for all borrowing activities (Hubbell 1983). In many countries, local authorities may borrow only from higher-level governments. These universal restrictions on borrowing by local governments are no surprise in countries where capital markets are poorly developed and where the national government has to be concerned about the nationwide allocation of public and private savings. Industrial countries do not face such constraints on their capital resources and thus tend to control local borrowing to a lesser degree. It should be noted, however, that the almost unlimited freedom of local authorities in the United States to borrow in private capital markets is exceptional compared with the situations in other industrial countries (Prud'homme 1987). The combination of poorly developed capital markets, savings constraints, and higher-level government restrictions and controls over local government borrowing explains why this source of financing urban services is the least important of all sources of local government revenue, and much less important in developing than in industrial nations.[19]

These constraints on borrowing are particularly troublesome where lumpy investment projects need to be financed by local authorities, especially in the area of public utilities, but also for slum improvement, public housing and sites-and-services projects, school building projects, and the like. Where borrowing is made impossible for these purposes, the investments have to be financed by higher-level grants, carried out directly by higher-level government agencies, or more frequently yet, they will not be made at all.

A comparison of revenue authority with revenue performance suggests that urban governments differ not only in the degree of freedom they possess to raise revenues from various sources but also very much in the ways they use their authority. Ahmadabad, Bombay, and Jakarta have relative freedom to raise revenues but have not used it to the extent one might expect. Jakarta has relied most heavily on its motor vehicle tax, although it has not drawn on betterment levies or user charges to any significant degree. Ahmadabad and Bombay have relied heavily on the octroi, and Bombay has drawn on user charges from electricity services to finance its mass transit system. Colombian cities, in contrast, are more restricted in their use of local taxes and consequently have expanded their use of local taxation very slowly. These cities have used their fiscal autonomy to develop systems of benefit charges, which have led to significant recovery of the costs of providing these services. The government of Seoul, despite the fact that its authority over virtually all revenue sources is limited, has expanded expenditure rapidly with a balanced use of local taxes, betterment levies, and user charges (see table 2-10). The lesson in this comparison of revenue authority and its use is that even cities with comparable degrees of freedom over comparable revenue sources have used them to very different degrees. Furthermore, central government control per se is no guarantee of a more or less successful use of particular revenue sources.

Conclusions: Local Fiscal Performance

Do local governments have enough fiscal importance to warrant study? The evidence would seem to indicate that they do. Subnational governments in developing countries account for an average of 15 percent of total government spending, and an average of about one-third of all urban area spending is financed through local government budgets. Perhaps most important, the expenditure responsibilities of local governments often include major development functions, notably public works, mass transit, and primary education. Together, these findings suggest that local governments have an important impact on the economic development of metropolitan cities.

The trend and pattern of growth in consolidated local government expenditure (general purpose local governments and autonomous agencies) are perhaps surprising: real per capita expenditure increased during the late 1960s and first half of the 1970s. The ability of some local governments to raise per capita expenditure during this period—despite rapid increases in population, limited resource bases, inflation, and constraints placed upon them by higher government authorities—was a remarkable achievement.

The situation changed somewhat in the 1980s. Local revenues were not buoyant enough to cover expenditure needs, and there was a noticeable shift toward central financing of urban services and a slower growth in real per capita local government expenditure. Even so, there is enough evidence here to suggest that urban governments have a significant fiscal potential and that they may make an important contribution to national resource mobilization.

Local public enterprises also are important in providing services in the cities of developing countries. When such an autonomous agency provides a city's public utilities, the central government tends to finance fewer capital projects. And if capital facilities are not financed by an agency, central financing plays a much more important role. The autonomous agency thus appears to have a comparative advantage over general local government in capital project financing, implementation, and management. This advantage may stem from the enterprise's autonomy in management, potential for relying on user-charge financing, and general freedom from the local political process. A major factor determining the importance of the local government sector, then, may be the ability of local governments to create autonomous enterprise activities.

About 70 percent of revenues of metropolitan governments, on average, is raised from local sources, of which the property tax is by far the most important. It will come as a surprise to many that a relatively low average share of financing comes from central government grants and loans, though there is a wide variation in this dependence among the cities studied here.

An examination of changes in local government finances during the late 1960s, the 1970s, and part of the 1980s gives a reasonably consistent picture. In cities where per capita expenditure increased, locally raised resources were the largest contributors, whereas in cities where per capita expenditure declined, a slowdown in locally raised resources was evident. In the 1980s, when real growth in expenditure slowed, growth in locally raised revenues also slowed, and reliance on external financing increased. On the basis of a small sample, changes in locally raised resources appear to have determined the ability of urban governments to increase the services they provide. A fall in locally raised revenues hurts urban government expenditure, and a rise helps it thrive. Central government transfers and borrowing are less important either way—at least for this small sample and for this time period.[20]

Local governments that want to achieve revenue autonomy face severe constraints in choosing their fiscal patterns. Even when they have had substantial freedom of action, however, their existing revenue authority has not always been fully utilized. The revenue instruments which seem most underutilized are property taxation, motor vehicle taxation, betterment levies, and user charges. Thus the degree to which a city's government is able to meet its rapidly rising expenditure requirements depends only in part on its revenue capacity, as determined mainly by the economic base of the city and by the restraints imposed by higher-level governments. It also depends on the revenue effort, that is, the extent to which the local government is using its revenue capacity.

3 The Urban Fiscal Problem in Developing Countries: Issues and Approaches

ANYONE WHO HAS visited a large city in a developing country will have been impressed with the obvious need to improve and expand urban public services. Anyone who has visited a large city in an industrial country will likely have had the same reaction.[1] But the problem is qualitatively different. In the cities of developing countries, the basic services—potable water supply, sewerage, solid waste collection, electricity, telephones, fire protection, health and education facilities—are all in desperately short supply for a majority of the population. Prohibitively large expenditures would be required to eliminate the unmet demand for these services in virtually any developing country.[2] The other main difference from the industrial countries is that resources, particularly for financing capital facilities, are in much shorter supply.

This state of affairs raises two important issues for those concerned with reshaping the fiscal programs of urban governments. First, what are the sources of fiscal pressures on urban governments in the developing world, and how are these pressures (and perhaps fiscal dividends) likely to play out over the next two decades? Second, what are the appropriate policies for responding to the fiscal challenges of urbanization? We begin this chapter by examining these two questions. Next, we consider a theoretical framework for explaining the budget problems of local governments, and we then turn to the evidence on the determinants of urban government revenue and expenditure growth in developing countries. We conclude with a discussion of the scope for urban fiscal reform and the political constraints likely to limit it.

Is There an Optimal Size for an Urban Government's Budget?

It seems clear that local governments in developing countries do not provide adequate levels of service. Does it follow that they underproduce public goods and allow too much private consumption? Discussions about the fiscal problems of local governments in developing countries almost never address the normative question of whether the government's share in economic activity is optimal. The fact of the matter, however, is that urban governments in developing and industrial countries alike have been criticized for allocating resources inefficiently. In some industrial countries it is often claimed that the urban authorities are too heavily involved in the lives of their citizens (overprovision), while in the developing countries urban governments are challenged for not providing enough support (underprovision). The following exposition is meant to put these concerns into some perspective by focusing attention on how fiscal policy can intervene to correct the economic inefficiencies of urban finance systems.

Consider first an ideal urban economy in which the consumption and production of one private good and one government good (or service) is efficient. In diagrammatic terms, the urban economy is located on point A on the production possibility frontier (transformation curve) P in figure 3-1, where the community indifference curve I is tangent to P.[3]

But now assume that instead of efficiently representing community preferences, decisionmakers select consumption points B or C. In the former case, too few publicly produced (government) goods are provided; in the latter, too many. The inefficiency of this allocation of resources is shown by the fact that the new consumption and production points (B and C) lie on a lower community indifference curve (II). Since B and C are still on the production possibility frontier P, the production of private and public goods remains efficient. The misallocation of resources enters on the consumption side through the mistaken choice of consumption along P. In order to get to the optimal consumption point A, an increase in publicly produced goods and a reduction in privately produced goods would have to take place if the consumption point is B,

Figure 3-1. *The Optimal Provision of Government and Private Goods*

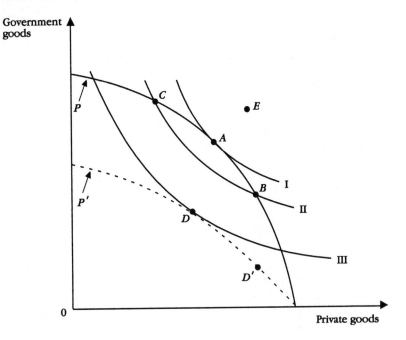

and the converse would have to take place if the consumption point is
C. The concern over excess provision of publicly produced goods and
services may represent a judgment that the city is at a point like C and
that a reduction in the relative size of the public sector is desirable. The
constraints to making such an adjustment in industrial countries are
largely political, although the tax limitation movement in the United
States in the late 1970s showed that such adjustments were in fact quite
possible (Ladd and Wilson 1982; Courant, Gramlich, and Rubinfeld
1980).

In developing countries, one frequently hears the argument that urban
public services are underprovided. This might be interpreted as implying
that the urban economy is situated at a point such as B, and that it is
desirable to shift from privately to publicly produced goods and services
by moving along P from B to A. The constraint to such a movement may
be administrative in that the city cannot collect the additional taxes
needed or does not have the technical capacity to deliver additional services; it may be legal in that the city has very little taxing or borrowing
power to use; or it may be that the central government is providing too
little in grant funds or loan resources.

A different interpretation is also appropriate. If the public sector is
inefficient in its production of goods and services, it is possible to draw
a production possibility frontier P', which lies to the left of and below
P. The efficient consumption point on P' is D, where community indifference curve III is tangent to P'. In this case, the problem is not an
underprovision of publicly produced services caused by a mistaken consumption decision or a binding revenue constraint; rather, the problem
lies in the inefficient production of public services. Its solution must
therefore be found in eliminating the inefficiencies in public production.
This would permit the urban economy to move from D to A by shifting
the production possibility frontier from P' to P. As a result, a larger
amount of publicly produced goods and services would be provided but
private production would not be sacrificed. Better management and
training, use of appropriate low-cost technologies, contracting with the
private sector, more effective coordination of public agencies, and capital-labor substitution are among the methods that can be used to improve
the efficiency of public production.

There are, of course, combinations of these problems. Cities in developing countries may not be at the efficient consumption point D on
P', but they may be at a point such as D', where publicly produced goods
are underprovided along the inefficient production possibility frontier.
A reform of the urban public finance system should therefore aim simultaneously to eliminate the inefficiencies in public production, correct
the present consumption bias in favor of privately produced commodities, and remove the bottlenecks to mobilizing more local resources.

What this analysis suggests is that in theory there is an optimum level of government production and service provision and that it varies from place to place. Because we cannot measure the production possibility or indifference curves, we can never know where this optimum lies, but we can say what reforms might carry us closer to it.

The Fiscal Gap and the Budget Deficit

Whether local governments underproduce or overproduce, they face a financing problem. The more normative definition of the problem is the existence of a "fiscal gap," that is, a gap between perceived service needs and financial resources. It is important for the analyst to distinguish this gap from the budget deficit and to understand how each is pressured by urbanization. We can best understand the nature of this gap by understanding its components and determinants. A useful starting point may be to cast the problem in terms of a set of identities defining the expenditure requirements and revenue constraints of urban authorities.

Expenditure needs or requirements for the ith public service in a particular city may be defined as:

$$(3\text{-}1) \qquad \hat{E}_i = \left(\frac{\hat{E}_i}{\hat{Q}_i}\right) \left(\frac{\hat{Q}_i}{P}\right) P = \hat{e}_i \hat{q}_i P$$

where

$\hat{E}_i$ = required expenditure for service i
$\hat{Q}_i$ = required quantity of service i
P = population
$\hat{e}_i = \dfrac{\hat{E}_i}{\hat{Q}_i}$ = unit cost of required service

$\hat{q}_i = \dfrac{\hat{Q}_i}{P}$ = required quantity of service i per inhabitant.

The actual level of expenditures (E_i) for public service i may be defined as

$$(3\text{-}2) \qquad E_i = \frac{E_i}{Q_i} \cdot \frac{Q_i}{P} \cdot P = e_i q_i P$$

where Q = the quantity of service i actually provided. Local government revenues may be defined as

$$(3\text{-}3) \qquad R = T + C + G$$

where T = taxes, C = user charges and other current revenues, and G = externally raised revenues. The "fiscal gap" $(\hat{D})$ in a city may then be defined as

$$(3\text{-}4) \qquad \hat{D} = \sum_i \hat{E}_i - R = \sum_i (\hat{e}_i \hat{q}_i P) - R.$$

By contrast, the actual budgetary deficit (D) is

$$(3\text{-}5) \qquad D = \sum_i E_i - R = \sum_i (e_i q_i P) - R.$$

This formulation clarifies the distinction between the fiscal gap, which reflects the shortage of revenue available to provide required services, and the budget deficit, which reflects the actual shortfall of recurrent revenues. While budget deficits do not always occur, fiscal gaps are commonplace.

Why Do Urban Government Budgets Grow?

One suspects that urban governments in developing countries produce too little, tax too little, and that virtually all face a fiscal gap. Even so, urban government budgets have been growing—above the rate of inflation and population growth in some cases—and the prospects are for continued pressure to increase expenditures. Since these expenditures must be financed by central and local revenues (or by a larger public deficit), it is important to understand what causes urban government expenditures to grow.

Can theory tell us how population growth and urbanization will affect local government budgets? Economists have long been interested in this question, but they have focused on industrial countries, that is, countries with representative local governments, substantial fiscal autonomy, and the technical expertise to deliver services and collect taxes efficiently at the local level. This research has given a number of theoretical explanations about why government expenditures grow, why budget deficits occur, and why budgets depart from optimal patterns; these are reviewed below. The issue we raise is whether an understanding of urban fiscal problems in developing countries can be based on these theories.

Empirical Theories of Expenditure Growth

A first answer to the question of why local government budgets are growing so rapidly is that the general size of government in developing countries is growing and local governments are simply sharing in this growth. Economists have offered many theses about the relation between economic development and the growth in government expenditures.[4] Wagner's early and much discussed "law" held that a growing government share of output was inevitable (Wagner 1890). Though Wagner's reasoning for the growing share of state activity was not clearly stated, his thesis of a rising government share of expenditure during development has held up—whether examined for industrial or for developing countries (Hinrichs 1966). Most analysts have taken this observed regularity as a starting point and have attempted to construct positive theories of the growth of public expenditure.

Perhaps the most notable theory of long-term expenditure growth is the Peacock-Wiseman displacement thesis, which argued that government expenditures undergo a shift in response to some major crisis or disruption.[5] The displacement thesis as an explanation of the upward shift in government's share has been tested statistically with some success for a number of industrial countries (for example, see Gupta 1967), although it has been challenged on both empirical and conceptual grounds (Bird 1972). This would also seem a plausible explanation for the growth of expenditure in developing countries, given the susceptibility of many developing-country economies to "external" events such as commodity price swings, natural disasters, worldwide recession, and so forth. For a small sample of developing countries, Goffman and Mahar (1971) found evidence of an upward displacement effect, but Bahl, Kim, and Park (1986) estimated a downward displacement for Korean government expenditures between 1961 and 1964, which was caused by changes in government fiscal policy, devaluation, hyperinflation, and internal revolution. Whether upward or downward, the displacement effect puts pressure on local authorities to increase their financing efforts: in the former case, because local authorities may be among the first to feel citizen demands for more public goods and services; in the latter case, because a reduction in spending by the central government is likely to require increases in local public expenditures to offset it at least partially. There has been no testing (that we know of) of the local government dimension of the displacement effect.

A Median Voter, Demand Theory

Another important theory treats the public as a rational consumer of government and private services. This industrial-country model of expenditure determination holds that the fiscal choices of politicians are influenced by the preferences of the median voter. This leads to the development of demand models which link expenditure growth to changes in relative prices of public and private goods, income, and tastes.[6]

The model is roughly described in figure 3-2, in which the indifference curves describe the median voter's preference for government and private goods. If the budget constraint were at AA', the consumer-voter would maximize his welfare by choosing $0G_0$ government goods, $0X_0$ private goods, and a tax rate of $(X_0A)/(0A)$. If the relative price of public goods fell—for example, because of a matching grant—the budget line would pivot to AA'' and the consumer would move to a new equilibrium at X_1G_1 and a higher tax rate. Likewise, an increase in income in the urban area would shift the budget line to a higher level and cause an adjustment in the tax rate, and a change in preferences for public versus private goods would also call forth a response. Using this model, public expenditure demand functions have been estimated, usually on a cross-section basis. The results of the more careful among these studies have

Figure 3-2. *A Median Voter Model for Determining the Size of the Public Sector*

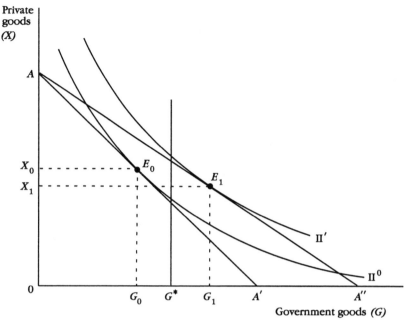

been consistent with theory: price-elasticities were negative, income-elasticities were positive, and "taste" variables usually exerted the hypothesized effects (Inman 1971).

The developing-country situation differs because voters have less chance to express their preferences (local councils are as often appointed as elected) and the chief administrators of the city can be employees of the central government who have substantial autonomy. In addition, the fiscal autonomy of local government is quite restricted; for example, it is common for the central government to place tight controls on the changes in tax rates and borrowing practices of the local government and to impose constraining mandates on service levels. It would seem far-fetched to use the traditional median voter model in a developing-country context. But to say that local fiscal choices in developing countries are constrained is not to say that they do not exist. Indeed, many local councils and mayors are elected, the composition of appointed local councils may reflect local political considerations, and appointed city managers surely do take local preferences into account. Even in centrally planned and politically controlled developing countries, higher bus fares or water rates may cause riots, slum conditions will breed social unrest, tax rate increases may be effectively resisted, unions may press vigorously for higher wages, and more public services may be demanded.

Returning to figure 3-2, we might believe that some preference function does exist in developing-country cities and that there would be some budgetary response to a change in relative prices (or income or preferences) as in this example. The response, however, may be more constrained in the developing-country context. For example, in the case in which the budget constraint pivots from AA' to AA'', a central government mandate or a bottleneck in administering taxes may limit the growth in government services to G_0G^*.[7]

This thinking leads us to hold to a more constrained version of the median voter model. Statistical analyses do give results that support this explanation of expenditure growth. Though there has been a less thorough specification and estimation of such demand models for developing countries, the empirical work available suggests that total public expenditures grow in response to general economic development, population growth, and urbanization (Martin and Lewis 1956; Musgrave 1969; Lotz 1970; Goffman and Mahar 1971; Bahl, Kim, and Park 1986). The extent to which local (as opposed to central) governments are pressured by these factors has not been clearly substantiated, but the importance of urbanization as a determinant of higher total government spending suggests a substantial impact.

In the next sections we turn to the a priori and empirical evidence that urban government expenditures in developing countries are driven by increases in the demand for public services.

EXPENDITURE NEEDS. An important consequence of the urbanization process may be to change the "needs" for public services, such that decisionmakers may have to interfere with or override individual (median voter) preferences in providing certain goods and services. The continuing increase in the number of the urban poor calls for increased social and economic services and perhaps for a different package of public services, for example, serviced sites rather than permanent housing, small health clinics rather than hospital additions, and more public water taps rather than water main extensions.

The growth in the need for public services is most often associated with growth in population. Some would argue that expenditures are required to grow at least in proportion to population in order to maintain a constant level of service. For examples of the argument, theorems on congestion-imposed expenditures are well known: water system expansions may involve increasing marginal costs because of a greater depth required for tubewells or a greater distance to a catchment area. In fact, urban population growth rates in developing countries (see table 3-1) tend to lie well above national population growth rates. Though the projections of urban growth have been revised down somewhat since 1980, the conclusion about the much higher rate of urban versus rural population growth holds. This rapid increase in urban population (P)

Table 3-1. *Urbanization in Selected Developing Countries, 1960 and 1980*

Country	Urban population as percentage of total population		Percentage of urban population in largest city	
	1960	*1980*	*1960*	*1980*
Low-income[a]				
Zaire	26	38	14	28
Tanzania	5	29	34	50
Zambia	23	53	—	35
India	19	27	7	6
Kenya	9	22	40	57
Sudan	13	21	30	31
Pakistan	4	31	20	21
Nigeria	17	33	13	17
Ghana	26	32	25	35
Sri Lanka	20	21	28	16
Indonesia	16	27	20	23
Total	17	30	11	13
Middle-income[b]				
Philippines	32	41	27	30
Egypt	41	48	38	39
Côte d'Ivoire	23	44	27	34
Thailand	13	21	65	69
Jamaica	38	51	77	66
Tunisia	40	54	40	30
Colombia	54	69	17	26
Chile	72	85	38	44
Peru	52	69	38	39
Malaysia	26	40	19	27
Mexico	55	71	28	32
Brazil	50	75	14	15
Argentina	76	85	46	45
Algeria	38	44	27	12
Korea, Rep. of	32	69	35	41
Venezuela	70	83	26	26
Iran, I.R.	37	53	26	28
Total	42	57	28	29

— Not available.
Note: Countries are given in ascending order of per capita GNP from top to bottom.
a. Weighted average for all low-income countries given in World Bank (1981).
b. Weighted average for all middle-income countries given in World Bank (1981).
Source: World Bank (1981).

results directly in larger requirements for urban government expenditures (equation 3-1).

INCOME EFFECTS. The positive and strong relation between urbanization and per capita income in developing countries has been well established in two respects: the more urbanized developing countries tend to have higher per capita incomes (Beier and others 1976; Smith 1974; Renaud

1981), and per capita income in the largest cities tends to be the highest in the country (Linn 1983: chap. 4). There is less objective evidence on the relation between the increase in urban population and the increase in per capita income in urban areas.

Rising per capita income tends to increase the per capita demand for services (q), with the magnitude of the increase being dependent on the income-elasticity of demand for services which are locally provided. Positive income-elasticities for urban services have been observed for water supply, electricity, telephone services, and for solid waste disposal services (Linn 1983). These higher levels of consumption may largely be due to more ownership of water- and electricity-using appliances (washing machines, radios, television sets, and the like), while the greater need for solid waste disposal may be associated with generally higher consumption levels and reduced recycling in the home.

There is also strong evidence that the demand for motor vehicles is highly income-elastic. It follows that the demand for urban highway infrastructure is positively related to per capita income.[8] The demand for schooling is strongly correlated with household income, since the lower the incomes the more likely it is that children are forced to drop out of school in order to seek employment (Beier and others 1976), and the less likely that households are able to bear out-of-pocket education expenditures (Meerman 1979). Similarly, the demand for health care is likely to increase with income, better education, and the growing familiarity with modern techniques of health care.

Increases in per capita income also cause a demand for a higher quality of urban services. This demand may take the form of desires for individual rather than communal water supply and sanitary facilities;[9] for a reduced risk of electricity outage (Munasinghe 1980); for more rapid communication and transportation; and for better health care, education, and fire and police protection.[10]

EXPECTATIONS AND DEMONSTRATION EFFECTS. Another important set of factors which may shift the demand for urban services upward over time are changing tastes and expectations regarding appropriate levels and quality of service. A changing preference for public goods affects the rate at which consumers are willing to substitute private for public goods and also signals a willingness to pay a higher price for public goods. During the development process, preferences may change to reflect the demand for better education services by families whose income has risen above subsistence levels, new societal values such as substitution of welfare and housing services for the extended family structure, the demand for more redistributive actions to offset potential unrest,[11] and the willingness to pay more taxes in order to have government offset negative externalities resulting from the growing underprovision of urban public services. In urban areas of developing countries, changes have been especially observed in the preferences for water- and electricity-using appliances, motor vehicles, and educational achievement, and therefore for the derived demand for related urban services, that is, public utilities, road construction, and education.

The demand for public services, or the translation of this demand by those who set service standards, may be heavily influenced by a "demonstration effect" from more industrial countries. As a result, governments in some developing countries have raised standards rapidly in attempting to attain the levels of quality and technology found in industrial countries. Examples are the often unchecked growth of private automobile ownership; high standards for the use and quality of water supply; water-borne sewerage technologies as replacement for traditional disposal techniques such as nightsoil collection; and incinerator or composting plants for solid waste disposal, replacing conventional recycling techniques. Higher standards can significantly increase expenditures. From World Bank project data it has been calculated that the following cost increases were incurred when providing urban services at higher than minimum levels of quality and quantity in residential areas: for water supply, the cost increases ranged between 53 and 81 percent; for sewage disposal, between 22 and 31 percent; and for circulation and drainage, between 271 and 321 percent. For electricity, a relatively negligible increase of only 5 percent was found (Linn 1983: chap. 5).

MIGRATION AND POVERTY. Local government expenditures also grow because of the migration of people from rural areas to cities. Very often these migrants settle on mountainsides, swamps, floodplains, and so forth where land is cheap and difficult to service. As these settlements become more and more established, servicing them becomes a political and humanitarian necessity for urban governments, and substantial expenditures are required.

Cost and Productivity Factors

Local government expenditures may also rise because the cost of providing any given quantity of public services rises, that is, because of an increase in e_i in equation 3-2. The question at hand is the extent to which these unit costs are pushed up by population growth and urbanization.[12]

Many of the factors pushing up unit costs—such as general inflation and energy price increases—affect all public activities in developing countries, and in that sense are not problems faced exclusively in the larger cities. Yet it is frequently observed that input prices tend to increase with city population size, though accurately measured differentials in the general price levels between larger cities and the rural areas are rare. Thomas (1978) found that the average cost of living in Lima exceeded that in rural Peru by a substantial margin. This may largely be explained by the fact that input prices are differentially higher in Lima than in the rest of the country.

INFLATION. Probably the major factor responsible for unit cost increases is inflation. To the extent that developing countries are generally plagued with higher levels of price inflation than industrial countries, costs of local government will increase more rapidly than in industrial countries.[13] Moreover, as explained below, factors at work in developing countries may cause urban public service input costs to rise more rapidly than the general inflation rate and hence raise the relative cost of the public budget.

Another impact of inflation on public budgets is not often recognized. If government expenditures are more automatically responsive to inflation than are government revenues, the greater the rate of inflation the lower the purchasing power of local government revenue receipts. Inflation may drive up expenditures, but each dollar of revenue is likely to buy less.

Inflation will drive up spending because the cost of materials and supplies will rise, and either there will be pressure to increase the salaries of government employees or "dearness allowances" may automatically be awarded. Revenues, however, are not so automatically responsive: property tax increases (if not indexed) require valuation, local sales taxes are not broadly based, and many local government taxes are imposed on a specific rather than an ad valorem basis.

This situation will push local governments to take discretionary action to restore their lost purchasing power. Inflation may even be a positive force for good government if these actions include improved tax administration, higher tax rates that make better use of existing tax bases, increases in user charges to efficient levels, and the introduction of more cost-effective methods of delivering public services. Unfortunately, local governments may also try to close the budget gap by simply cutting essential services, and central governments may exacerbate the problem by refusing to allow tax rate or user charge increments or, paradoxically, by giving additional subsidies which remove some of the pressure for local government fiscal reform.

CAPITAL COSTS. The provision of public utility services frequently requires investment outlays on a large scale. Urban governments therefore have to rely on foreign credits from international agencies, from the international capital market, or from suppliers. The supply curve for funds is well known to slope upward, and large cities in developing countries are likely to run into increasing costs of capital unless the central government is the primary borrower and passes on the loan funds at subsidized rates to urban governments. The extent and terms of borrowing by urban governments are almost always controlled by the central government, and thus the cost of capital as it is passed on to local authorities is effectively a policy instrument of the central government. The rising cost of capital, however, ultimately is reflected in the public sector as a financial cost, whether at the national or at the local level. Thus the construction of the large, capital-intensive infrastructure projects required by urbanization may well involve higher than average interest rates.

Land prices might be expected to rise rapidly in cities because of fast urban population growth, increased population density, and the resulting scarcity of serviced urban land. Rising land prices tend to have particularly strong impacts on the unit costs of services that are relatively land-intensive: the transport sector, parks and recreation, public housing, schools, and solid waste disposal.

Whether the *relative* price of land increases, however, is an open question. The land rent share of GNP has remained approximately constant in the United States over the long run (Mills 1972). Ingram (1982), working with Korean and Colombian data, found only weak support for the hypothesis that *urban* land rents grow in proportion to output and no support for the hypothesis that land rents grow faster in large cities than in small cities. These findings suggest that the relative pressures of land costs as a determinant of public expenditure increase are less than some have supposed them to be and that the natural buoyancy of the urban property tax base is no more than unity in the long run.

Labor Costs and Productivity

The growth of government expenditure has also been explained in terms of the differential increase in labor productivity in the private and public sectors. If productivity increases less rapidly in the public than in the private sector because of the public sector's high labor-intensity and service orientation, and if there is a "wage rollout" from the public to the private sector so that the wages of public employees increase more rapidly than their productivity, then a continuous increase in the government's share in national income will result (Baumol 1967). This hypothesis is likely to have some validity in developing countries, particularly for local governments whose service package is most labor-intensive. The implication of this theory is that as urban economies become more productive, their public sectors will eat up an increasing share of the income generated. This conclusion only holds, however, if the wage rates in the "less productive" public sector keep pace with those in the private sector.

Consider a simple two-sector urban economy with private and government sectors and demand (D) and supply (S) curves for labor as shown in figure 3-3. Suppose that in equilibrium the public and private wages are equal at W_0. If some increase in demand for the products produced in the private sector shifts the demand for labor to D'_L, then the private

Figure 3-3. *Wage Determination in the Government and Private Sectors*

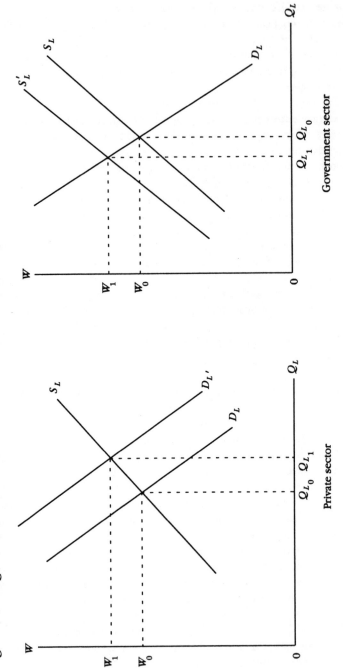

sector wage rises to W_1 and there is need to employ $Q_{L_0}Q_{L_1}$ additional workers. If those workers are all drawn from the government sector, the supply curve shifts back to S'_L and the wage rate in that sector rises to W_1. Since we believe that urbanization is associated with increases in productivity and expansions in export markets, the situation described in figure 3-3 is a reasonable explanation of increasing labor costs during periods of urbanization.

This conclusion may be challenged. The extent to which the competitive wage thesis holds for developing countries depends on the rate of immigration, and all other things being equal a greater rate of immigration will dampen the wage rollout effect described in figure 3-3. The local public sector, as part of the general services sector, is labor-intensive and does not require as skilled a work force as does the industrial sector. Newly arrived migrants swell the numbers of unskilled workers available and hold down the wage rate in the services sector.

One might also argue that public wage rates in urban areas increase more rapidly than the general price level or productivity because of institutional factors. Labor unions for local civil servants are found in some countries and can be extremely vocal in pressing for higher wages.[14] In other cases, local government salaries and wages are determined by the central government. Since it frequently does not bear the brunt of local government salary readjustments, the central government may be quite willing to raise local civil service salaries more rapidly than the general price level.[15]

TECHNOLOGICAL PROGRESS AND ECONOMIES OF SCALE. Technological progress should reduce input requirements per unit of public output, thereby reducing unit cost ($\hat{e}_i$). It is generally recognized, however, that technological progress in most urban services is slow and that developing countries may sometimes adopt modern technologies which are inefficient and excessively costly. Examples are composter facilities for solid waste disposal, water-borne sewer systems and treatment plants, limited-access rapid highways, subways, and premature computerization.

Technological economies of scale may also imply declining unit cost during urbanization. A detailed study of engineering costs for certain urban services in India appears to support this hypothesis (Stanford Research Institute 1968). Similarly, a study of water supply costs for small and intermediate-size cities in Colombia has shown declining unit costs, which are probably largely attributable to technological economies of scale (Insfopal 1975). These economies are likely to be limited to public utilities, however, and it is not clear whether governments in rapidly growing urban areas are always in a position to benefit from such economies.[16]

Moreover, technological economies of scale may be offset by diseconomies of agglomeration, particularly in larger, denser urban areas.

These diseconomies result from problems of congestion, which tend to increase with city size and density and which are especially problematic in the transport sector. Diseconomies may also result from limits in the carrying capacity of the natural environment (for example, air and water pollution) and from the increasing scarcity of natural resources, especially water and energy. Other examples are the increased need for disease control and fire and police protection, which are associated with the large scale and high density of urban living. In all cases, some inputs (space, natural resources, and so forth) grow scarce with increased urbanization, and as a result larger amounts of other inputs (labor, capital, and intermediate inputs in particular) have to be applied to produce equal service levels (clean water and air, good health, and a safe environment).

PUBLIC SERVICE EMPLOYMENT. The costs of urban services may increase if local government is viewed as an employer of last resort. Unfortunately, we have no good data to determine whether local governments are generally overstaffed. Heller and Tait (1984: 8–10) estimate state and local government employment in thirty-five developing countries to average 0.4 percent of total population, as compared with 4.6 percent in sixteen industrial countries belonging to the Organisation for Economic Co-operation and Development. They also report that the average wages of state and local government employees are generally lower than those of central government employees. Even so, the local government share of the total government wage bill can be quite significant: 23 percent in the Philippines, 50 percent in Argentina, and 43 percent in Costa Rica (Cochrane 1983: 23–26).

Although these data indicate the importance of state and local government employment in developing countries, they do not help us understand whether large urban governments do in fact act as employers of last resort. Indeed, any comparable data on municipal employment are not likely to cover the vast amount of part-time casual workers that would be included in public employment programs. Indirect evidence, however, suggests a relation between local government employment and urbanization. Heller and Tait (1984: 15) find a significant positive relation between state and local government employment and per capita GNP; that is, the higher the income level of the country (and presumably the more urbanization), the greater the employment by subnational governments. A second bit of indirect evidence is the International Labour Office (ILO) estimates that the proportion of "urban specific jobs . . . increases with the size of agglomerations, ranging from 9–11 percent for those with 100,000 to 200,000 inhabitants to 10–15 percent for those with 200,000 to 300,000 and 15–20 percent for those with more than one million inhabitants" (Bairoch 1982). The ILO definition of urban-specific jobs—those connected with urban transport, urban administration, traffic police, upkeep of parks, libraries, museums, and general urban services—includes many functions traditionally supplied by local governments.

Are Expenditures Driven by Revenues?

Another explanation for the rising government share of income starts with the assumption that the expenditure level is determined by the availability of revenues (Heller 1954; Please 1970). This theory is consistent with empirical observation, since studies of the relation between the tax share of GNP and stage of development have shown a significant positive association between level of taxation and per capita income (Bahl 1971, 1972; Chelliah 1971). Although these studies do not prove that revenue availability determines expenditures, they do suggest that as development proceeds, countries tend to tax a greater share of GNP, thus permitting greater government spending. The question at hand is whether these increasing revenue shares accrue partly to local governments, either in the form of increased local taxes or increased central grants.

Conclusions: Urbanization and Expenditure Growth

Urbanization involves, or is associated with, many determinants of the level of expenditures. Rapid population growth, increasing per capita incomes, rising productivity and wage rates, greater ability to collect taxes because of better "tax handles," and even displacements caused by war or civil strife are all to some extent associated with the process of urbanization in developing countries. What is more, compared with rural and village life, urban living requires more government intervention. This is because the high population density of cities generates externalities which need to be addressed through public regulation and public involvement in service provision, for example, urban transport and traffic management, infrastructure services, sanitation, public health, and safety. We may begin this study, therefore, with the reasonable expectation that local government budgets will increase with urbanization.[17] The questions we continue to return to are whether and why the expenditure response might exceed the revenue response.

Revenue Constraints and Opportunities

Although it seems clear that urbanization will pressure local government budgets by driving up expenditures, it is less clear whether revenues will be driven up by a commensurate amount. Following equation 3-2 above, total revenues available to finance the growing expenditure requirements of cities may be separated into tax revenues (T), other current revenues, including user charges (C), and external funding (G).

Taxes

The level of total tax revenues of an urban government is determined by a set of factors which may be summarized in the following definitional identity:

$$(3\text{-}6) \qquad T = \sum_j \frac{T_j}{L_j} \frac{L_j}{B_j} \frac{B_j}{Y} \frac{Y}{P} P = \sum_j r_j t_j b_j Y_p P$$

where T = total tax collections, T_j = revenue from tax j, L_j = legal tax liability of tax j for given tax statutes, B_j = base of tax j, Y = total personal income, r_j = collection rate, t_j = legal tax rate, b_j = base-to-income ratio, y_p = per capita income, and P = population. Total revenues of a local authority are therefore determined by (a) the size of the economic base of the city, which in turn may conceptually be divided into the per capita income level (y_p) and the size of population (P); (b) the relation (b_j) between the economic base and the various tax bases (for example, real estate, motor vehicles, sales); (c) the statutory tax rate for each tax (t_j); (d) the collection efficiency (r_j) defined as the ratio of actual tax collection to statutory tax liability; and (e) the mix of taxes selected.

The economic base of a city is probably the most important influence on the level and buoyancy of tax revenues for the city government; that is, it defines the limits to the city's taxable capacity. The size and growth of the economic base, however, is largely outside the influence of the local authorities, in the sense that urban governments have only limited control over the population or economic growth of their jurisdictions.[18]

Other factors in equation 3-6 which determine the level and growth of taxes are more under the control of the local government. In the case of the property tax, for example, the relation between the growth in market value of real estate and the economic growth of the city (b_j) is determined largely by economic forces, although policy intervention may play an important role through regulations such as rent control. Furthermore, the extent to which property values are translated into assessed values (b_j) depends on the property assessment practice. The statutory tax rates (t_j) may be adjusted or held constant, depending on the legal status of the local property tax, while collection efficiency (r_j) is largely a matter of local government practice.

In sum, the tax revenue effects of population and income growth can be substantially enhanced or diminished depending on a number of important factors, only a few of which are under the control of local authorities. Moreover, there is no reason to expect that the exogenous influences of urbanization will call forth a balanced response in revenue and expenditure policies. In fact, the pressures on expenditures are usually greater, and increased urbanization is all but synonymous with increased fiscal gaps.

User Charges

The revenues generated by user charges (C) may be represented as follows:

$$(3\text{-}7) \qquad C = \sum_i \left(\frac{C_i}{Q_i} \frac{Q_i}{P} P \right) = \sum_i (c_i q_i P)$$

where C_i = the user charges collected for urban service i, Q_i = the quantity of service i consumed, c_i = the unit charge for service i, and q_i = the quantity of service i provided per capita. In contrast to urban taxes, user charges for services show a direct link between the quantity of services provided and the revenues generated to finance the provision of these services. Of course, the extent to which user charges cover the cost of service provision will depend on how the average price charged (c_i) compares with the average cost of service provision (e_i).

The evidence on the relation between city size and the c_i/e_i ratio is mixed. On the one hand, autonomous public utility agencies in some large cities seem able to charge rates high enough to cover increasing marginal costs and sometimes to generate a surplus. The same result seems to hold for special assessments on urban landowners, for example, in the Republic of Korea (Doebele 1979) and Colombia (Doebele, Grimes, and Linn 1979). The point is that urbanization creates a demand for these services and a capacity to pay full costs. On the other hand, some services (notably transportation and housing) do not generate enough revenue from user charges to cover full costs. The problem here is that urbanization also generates a great many social costs (for example, congestion and pollution) and poverty problems that may require c_i be held at a level below e_i.

External Funds

Grants and loans (G) are not under the control of local authorities. Rather, they depend on the decisions of higher authorities on how to distribute grants and loans to local governments. Will urbanization bring greater grant assistance to local governments? The answer is that it depends on how the revenue-sharing system operates. For example, if grants are distributed on a straight per capita basis or on the basis of local tax collections, as in a shared tax, urbanization may generate an increased inflow of external resources. The same might be true if grants are made on a cost reimbursement basis.

To help understand the issue, one can write the following functional relationship:

$$G = G(P, Y_p, Q_i)$$

where one would usually expect to find partial derivatives such that

$$\frac{\partial G}{\partial P} \geq 0$$

$$\frac{\partial G}{\partial Y_p} \gtreqless 0$$

$$\frac{WG}{\partial Q_i} \geq 0$$

In other words, grants will tend to vary directly with city population size and with the amount of services provided under a system of per capita grants or cost reimbursement grants. External resource flows may increase or decrease in response to increases in per capita income in the city, depending on the structure of the grant system. A tax-sharing scheme will channel more funds to cities as urbanization proceeds, whereas formula-equalizing grants may have just the opposite effect. These possibilities are discussed in chapter 13.

Reform and the Prospects for Urban Government Budgets

Of all the demand and cost factors discussed above, most act to increase expenditures—actual and required—for urban services. The effects of relative price increases, of technological progress, and of economies of scale could conceivably reduce the expenditure for urban services. But because none of these is likely to have strong cost-reducing effects, one may conclude that public expenditure requirements increase with urbanization in absolute terms, and very probably also in per capita terms.

On the revenue side certain forces—in particular, the growth in population and per capita incomes—work to enlarge the revenue capacity of urban governments. In most cities of the developing countries, however, revenue growth has been hampered by a combination of local governments' insufficient taxing authority and lagging revenue efforts. As a result, revenues often have not kept pace with expenditure needs, and this has led to a severe public service shortage. There is little reason to suspect that this situation will significantly change, unless policy adjustments are made to bring revenue growth more in line with expenditure requirements.

The problem of an urban fiscal gap can in principle be addressed in four different ways: (a) increased local revenue effort with unchanged revenue authority; (b) increased local revenue authority; (c) increased transfers from higher levels of government; or (d) reduced local expenditure responsibility. By asking which combination of these four courses should be chosen, one effectively raises the question of what is an appropriate role for local government budgets in urban areas, or more generally, what is the appropriate degree of fiscal decentralization in developing countries.

The Reassignment of Expenditure Responsibility

In developing countries, one common response of higher levels of government to urban fiscal crises has been to assume responsibility for certain urban services, such as public utilities, roads, education, and health.[19] Arguments for the relief of financial pressures, greater economic efficiency, and more equitable distribution of services are often cited as the justification for such reassignments. In some cases, the rationale is clear: services such as education are too important to nation-building to be interrupted by local revenue shortages. In other cases, it is difficult to measure the gains in efficiency and equity and not easy to justify such reassignments. In any case, two important considerations weigh heavily against this approach to resolving the urban fiscal problem. First, when specific functions are transferred to a higher level of government, the local authority's potential for responding to urban problems is reduced. This is a problem because many urban development activities are interrelated and therefore require an integrated approach to planning and implementation. Local authorities are often better equipped to provide such planning than are national ministries or special-purpose agencies. Second, national governments often assume only the responsibility for making capital investments and leave to the local authorities the tasks of operating and maintaining the facilities. This "turnkey" approach has significant disadvantages in that it tends to burden local authorities with facilities that are often beyond their financial and technical capacity to operate and maintain, and with facilities that may not reflect local preferences. Indonesia is an example of this practice and the problems it raises (Linn, Smith, and Wignjowijoto 1976).

Higher Locally Raised Revenues

Two of the reform options suggested above called for local government to raise more taxes—either by increasing the rates on existing taxes or by receiving central authority to expand their taxing and charging powers. In either case, the reform begs the question of what is the "proper" revenue structure for a city in a developing country. One answer to this question is that it depends in part on the local expenditure functions.

For a given set of expenditure responsibilities, an appropriate revenue mix may be chosen largely on the grounds of efficiency (Bahl and Linn 1983). For publicly provided goods and services from which the benefits accrue to individuals within a jurisdiction and to which the exclusion principle can be applied in pricing, user charges are most efficient. This is the case particularly for public utilities such as water supply, sewerage, power, and telephones, but also for public transit and housing. These services may involve externalities, but most of them are likely to be local and can therefore appropriately be handled either by cross-subsidies among service users or by subsidies from other locally raised revenue sources.

Other local services, such as general local administration, traffic control, street lighting, and security are local public goods whose primary benefits accrue to the local population but to which the exclusion principle in pricing cannot be applied. These are most appropriately financed by taxes whose burden is local so that the electorate is confronted with the true opportunity cost involved (Musgrave and Musgrave 1984: chaps. 1 and 3). Services such as health and education, which have substantial spillovers into neighboring jurisdictions, should receive transfers from state or national government. Purely local financing would lead to underprovision of these services from a regional or national perspective. In the face of interjurisdictional inequalities of incomes, there is also likely to be a need to equalize levels of service across jurisdictions through intergovernmental transfers. Finally, borrowing is an appropriate source of capital for those services which involve investment in long-lasting infrastructure, which is the case particularly for public utilities and roads. Appropriate financing for common local expenditure categories, from the four main types of revenue which have so far been distinguished, is summarized in table 3-2. With these general criteria in mind, we turn to the question of the potential for raising local government taxes and user charges in developing countries.

Higher Local Taxes

The judgment about which taxes are most appropriately allocated to local authorities will depend in part on the perspective of the decisionmaker. From the perspective of the central government, the main goals are to (a) limit competition with local governments for the important national tax bases (broad-based taxes on wealth, income, and expenditure); (b) limit the local use of taxes that are mainly exported to other jurisdictions; (c) provide local authorities with a reasonably buoyant revenue base; (d) avoid local reliance on regressive taxes; (e) encourage the use of taxes that are most easily administered at the local level; and (f) encourage the use of taxes which are closely linked to urban infrastructure and congestion costs, so that some of the externalities prevalent in the urban economy are internalized.

From the local government's vantage, criteria (c) to (f) are likely to be equally relevant, although they may vary in strength. For example, local government is likely to place more emphasis on buoyancy and administrative ease and less emphasis on equity and efficiency. But for criteria (a) and (b)—competition with national tax bases and exported taxes—local authorities are very likely to have priorities exactly the opposite of those of the higher level of government. Since the broad-based taxes tend to be the more buoyant and the most easily tapped, local governments will wish to have access to them. Reliance on taxes which can be shifted to taxpayers outside the jurisdiction will be especially attractive to local politicians.

Table 3-2. *Efficient Assignment of Local Revenue Authority Classified by Type of Expenditure Responsibility*

Services	Local taxes	User charges	Transfers	Borrowings[b]
		Sources of finance[a]		
Public utilities				
Water supply	S	P		A
Sewerage	S	P		A
Drainage	P	P[c]		A
Electricity		P		A
Telephones		P		A
Markets and abattoirs	S	P		(A)
Housing	S	P		A
Land development		P		A
Transportation				
Highways and streets	P	P[c]		A
Public transit	S	P		(A)
General urban services				
Refuse collection	P			
Parks and recreation	P			(A)
Fire protection	P			(A)
Law enforcement	P		S	(A)
General administration	P			
Social services				
Education	P	S	P	(A)
Health	P	S	P	(A)
Welfare	S		P	

a. P = primary source; S = secondary source.

b. A = borrowing is appropriate for major capital expenditures; (A) = borrowing is appropriate for capital spending, but likely to account for small share of total spending.

c. Development charges (that is, special assessments, valorization charges, and so forth) are appropriate for drainage, highways, and streets, especially when their benefits are geographically well defined within a jurisdiction.

Source: Bahl and Linn (1983).

Given these sometimes contradictory criteria, it would appear that the property tax and motor vehicle tax are on balance the most desirable and least objectionable among the major tax instruments that could be delegated to local jurisdictions (see chapters 4–8). From the perspective of central government, they do not compete substantially with national taxes; tax exporting is likely to be limited, particularly for the large cities; and they tend to have salutary effects on revenue, efficiency, and equity.[20] From the local perspective, too, these taxes are largely appropriate. Local access to broadly based taxes on consumption, income, and wealth is generally not granted by national governments (chapter 2) because it is not consistent with central government objectives. "Exportable

taxes"—taxes borne substantially by taxpayers outside the jurisdiction
that levies the tax, such as selective excise taxes, the Indian octroi, tourism, hotel taxes, and the like—are popular among local authorities, but
their use is usually limited if not actually prohibited by the central authorities in most countries. Local use of such taxes is usually tolerated
only because it tends to reduce local governments' claim on national tax
resources.

The empirical evidence on the actual use of taxes by urban governments of developing countries is fully compatible with the tenor of this
discussion (Bahl, Holland, and Linn 1983). The property tax is a major
source of local government revenue in most developing countries, and
some taxes on motor vehicles are common, though not used as extensively as the property tax. The issue raised here is whether the authority
to tax property might be extended to those local governments which do
not now have it and whether motor vehicles might be taxed more generally by local governments. In fact, there would be substantial practical
and political difficulties in transferring additional taxing authority to local
governments. The principal constraint is other national priorities, and
thus the allocation of new revenue authority to local governments simply
may not be in the cards. It may be more realistic to argue for reducing
the central government's limitations on the use of taxes already collected
by local governments in order to develop more effective local tax systems.

User Charges

From the national perspective, an effectively administered set of user
charges should be a desirable source of local revenues. User charges do
not compete with central government revenue bases, are largely nonex-
portable, can have desirable effects on revenue, efficiency, and equity,
and are administratively feasible at the local level. It may therefore come
as a surprise that national governments have sometimes extensively counteracted local authorities' intentions to increase their revenues by raising
user charges in line with costs (see chapter 2). The reasons for these
interventions are generally twofold. First, national governments are concerned about the rate of price inflation and want to limit the rise in
charges for local public services. Second, national governments fear the
political repercussions of price increases for urban services, since consumers are often quite emphatic in their opposition, at times even en-
dangering the political stability of the country through riots and the like.
Local authorities also tend to have mixed attitudes toward raising urban
service fees, partly for the same political reasons as the national government, and partly because they may in the past have come to rely on
central government transfers to finance portions of their public service
investments.

On balance, however, it appears that local service charges have become increasingly important sources of local government revenues. In fact, chapter 2 gave examples of user charges that have been utilized effectively by local authorities in lieu of alternative revenue sources to contribute even to the financing of general expenditures that are not recoverable through user charges. Instead of obstructing user charges, central authorities should give judicious support to their use as a productive way to raise local revenues and close the urban fiscal gap (see chapters 9–11).

Transfers

An increase in the fiscal transfer from higher level to local government is another means of coming to grips with the urban fiscal gap. There are good reasons for developing a system of revenue sharing between different levels of government: to provide central financing for services which are characterized by large externalities, to collect taxes centrally for greater administrative efficiency, to equalize interjurisdictional differences in the revenues of local governments, and to provide incentives for the efficient allocation of local government resources in the presence of externalities. These issues are discussed in chapters 12 and 13. For the large cities, however, it would be unrealistic and inappropriate to expect that transfers could permanently fill the fiscal gap. The pressures on the central fisc tend to be such that transfers to local authorities are among the first programs to be cut when national austerity programs are needed for macroeconomic stabilization. Moreover, there is an ever-present concern that large cities are somehow receiving too large a share of total transfers.

The Prospects for and Politics of Urban Fiscal Reform

Fiscal reforms have been proposed over the years in virtually every major city and in every country to alleviate the serious problems which face urban governments. Although the nature of these proposals has varied from place to place in line with local conditions and with the preferences and background of the study team responsible for the proposals, it is clear from a review of the evidence that major reforms are not commonplace. The countries that have had major reforms in the last twenty years are mainly industrial, for example, Germany (consolidation of communes and reform of revenue-sharing arrangements), Sweden (consolidation of communes), United States (reform of revenue-sharing arrangements and state tax reforms), and Yugoslavia. Among the developing countries the rule would seem to be that fundamental changes in urban finance are very slow and may take decades, if they occur at all.

Much more typical for the developing countries are relatively minor adjustments. These include creating special districts for capital cities with special expenditure responsibilities and revenue authority (as in Manila and Seoul); enlarging metropolitan jurisdictions by annexing adjacent municipalities (Bogotá); gradually developing new revenue sources (betterment levies in Colombian cities, land readjustment schemes in Korea, vehicle taxation in Jakarta, and most recently urban land taxation in China); gradually reforming existing revenue sources (property taxation in Jakarta); reassigning expenditure functions (Kenya and Zambia); and making similar gradual and ad hoc responses to urban fiscal pressures. Major reform proposals have often been shelved or taken up only in very minor respects; for example, proposals for comprehensive local government fiscal reforms in India and Kenya have come to naught. If major adjustments in the fiscal structure of urban governments have occurred, either the higher level of government has taken over important revenue sources previously allocated to local authorities (for example, Islamic Republic of Iran and Kenya); or sweeping political changes resulted in major shifts of national policy priorities (Nigeria, Tanzania, and Uganda); or the fiscal problems have become so unmanageable that some drastic reform was unavoidable (removal of most of the important expenditure responsibilities from rural and small town councils in Kenya in the early 1970s). The lesson from the history of urban fiscal reform is that major proposals rarely have a chance for adoption and implementation. Gradual and stepwise adjustments of the existing structure toward a more desirable state is perhaps the best that can be hoped for.

There are four reasons for this state of affairs. First, policymakers and citizens share an antipathy to the uncertain effects of untested large-scale changes in the economic environment. Second, most major reforms are associated with substantial unexpected losses for relatively few among the urban population—mostly among the elites—while windfalls are likely to be spread over a much larger number of people—mostly among the less well-off. Third, local politicians and officials can be directly linked to a reform and are therefore more accountable to the winners and losers in their constituency. By contrast, individual members of parliament are not as easily identified with national fiscal reforms. We would argue that this makes local tax reform a tougher political sell than national reform. Fourth, although there has been a growing concern in developing countries about how to strengthen the ability of urban governments to come to grips with their tasks, progress has tended to become bogged down in a three-way debate over fiscal decentralization, typically involving the ministry of finance, the ministry of local government, and the administration of the city governments.

The ministry of finance often is in the position of greatest strength and tends to argue in favor of the status quo. It generally refuses to relinquish control over major tax sources or borrowing, arguing that such decentralization would compromise the central government's important fiscal and tax policy programs. On the expenditure side, the finance ministry would rather emphasize central government projects and priorities and is often suspicious of the ministry of local government's ability to regulate the fiscal operations of local governments. The finance ministry will reluctantly agree to a grants system but would prefer that the grant pool be decided year by year rather than take the form of a shared tax. It doubts the management and tax collection abilities of local authorities and believes they can get much more revenue with their existing authority without recourse to new sources of revenue. In general, the finance ministry looks on the local governments, even the largest, as less than junior partners in the fiscal process.

The ministry responsible for local government is often less influential than the finance ministry and in such cases is less well staffed. The ministry of local government usually argues for an extensive grant system and for other regulatory mechanisms which allow a greater measure of control over local government finances. It would prefer that the total grant pool be determined as a fixed share of some national tax, but that the distribution of some or all of these grants be at its discretion. Such a scheme would limit the vulnerability of the grant system to changing priorities in the finance ministry budget and maximize the control of the ministry of local government over local authorities.

The administration of the large city would prefer more independent taxing power and less central regulation of its finances. If there is a grant system, a shared tax based on origin of collection would be the most preferred form, while a grant pool determined by the finance ministry and allocated by the ministry of local government would be the least preferred form.

The competition, suspicion, and lack of mutual confidence frequently characterizing the debate between national and local government authorities in developing countries have jeopardized the success of far-reaching proposals for urban government financial reform. If such reforms are to be passed and succeed, a mutually supportive system of local-central government relations must be established. What is more, in developing such reforms it is important that an overall framework guide the direction of change to ensure that the reform steps are cumulative and mutually consistent in addressing the main problems of urban finance.[21]

PART II

Local Government Taxes

IF URBAN governments are to play a more significant role in the economic development process, they must generate a greater share of total revenues than they do at present. But how? Through new taxing powers or through improved administration? The next five chapters attempt to answer these questions, on the basis of both theory and the past two decades' experience with local government taxation in the cities of developing countries.

The urban property tax, the most important local government revenue source, is the focus of chapters 4, 5 and 6. Chapter 4 reviews the practice in developing countries as regards structure and administration. On the basis of this review, we offer lessons for effective property taxation. Chapter 5 turns to the question of equity, that is, Who pays the property tax? We modify the economic theory of property tax incidence to the developing countries, and we present available empirical evidence to challenge the conventional wisdom that the property tax is regressive. Finally, chapter 6 reviews and evaluates the attempts of developing countries to use property tax policy to influence urban land use or investment in real property.

The subject of chapter 7 is the effectiveness of local governments in using other taxes on individuals and businesses, chiefly income, sales, license, and "nuisance" taxes. Chapter 8 concludes this part by considering local government taxes on the ownership and use of motor vehicles. We think the evidence shows that these are underutilized sources of revenue with considerable potential.

4 Property Tax Systems: Practice and Performance

THE PROPERTY TAX is the single most important local government tax in developing countries. It is, however, not necessarily the best revenue-raising instrument for a city because it is very difficult to administer efficiently, can have undesirable land use effects, and is very unpopular with taxpayers. Yet local governments often have few other sources of revenue, and important strides have been made toward improving the fairness and revenue productivity of property taxation.

In this chapter, we attempt to describe the range of property tax practices in developing countries.[1] We also make some rough estimates of the responsiveness of revenue to increases in income, population, and prices and attempt to identify the major difficulties raised by current administrative practices. Analysis of the equity and allocative effects is left to the next two chapters.

The comparative approach taken here emphasizes the practice in large cities and draws heavily on the results of individual case studies.[2] There are advantages to this focus on individual cities. The alternative, a country survey, is not always useful for comparative urban analysis because there are wide variations among cities within a country in the specifics of the tax structure and its applications. For example, the systems in Bogotá and Cartagena, Colombia, have been markedly different in structure and administration, with the result that the revenue growth is driven by different sets of underlying factors (Linn 1975, 1980b). A general description of property tax practices in Colombia would miss these features. Yet there can be important commonalities within countries, especially where property tax administration is centralized. An analysis of individual city systems without regard for the constraints imposed by higher levels of government would also miss a great deal. So we concentrate most heavily on the practice of individual local governments, but pay close attention to the partnership in property tax administration with the central government and to any legal constraints to discretionary action that are imposed by higher levels of government.[3]

Some general lessons emerge from this review. The first is that policymakers rarely consider reform of the entire property tax system, that is, rate and base structure, valuation principles, and administration. As a result, reform measures sometimes have offsetting effects or unintended side effects and do not lead to the expected increase in revenue. Second, governments have adopted a wide array of property tax practices, and there seems little by way of a pattern to help us understand the determinants of this variation. Third, policymakers tend to overload the property tax with policy objectives—for example, to affect the distribution of land use, to change the distribution of income, or to reward homeownership. Not only does the property tax fail to meet such objectives, but the overload compromises its more basic mission: to raise revenue. Fourth, it is more the quality of administration than the structural form chosen that determines the success of the property tax. Fifth, while the property tax is often a source of revenue for local government, it is almost always controlled to some extent by the central government. Reform of the local property tax in developing countries, it seems, is as much a central as a local matter. We will return to these themes over and over in this chapter.

The Importance of Property Taxation

The importance of the property tax as a source of financing is often overlooked because fiscal analysis usually focuses on central government finances, and in that context the property tax is truly a minor source of revenue. For example, Chelliah (1971) reported that the average ratio of property and wealth tax revenues to gross domestic product (GDP) among fifty-two developing countries was less than 1 percent. More than a decade later, Tanzi (1987) reported that property taxes on land and buildings accounted for no more than 0.2 percent of GDP and 1.2 percent of total tax revenues in forty-nine developing countries. According to these analyses, the property tax is neither an important nor a growing component of aggregate revenue mobilization in developing countries.

These data understate the importance of the property tax as a source of financing for urban services. In part this is because of shortcomings in the data series used. The IMF's *Government Finance Statistics Yearbook*, the basic source, reports little on the finances of those city governments which have the property tax as their mainstay. Measures of the importance of property taxation in financing urban government are also biased downward by a narrow definition of property taxation. The convention proposed here is to consider two kinds of taxes on urban land and buildings: (a) all general taxes on property, including those which are formally designated for certain uses (for example, the water and refuse collection rates in Indian cities and the fire and city planning taxes in Seoul, Republic of Korea); and (b) special assessments, which are levied for a specified purpose and limited to those residents considered to be direct beneficiaries. These special assessments, sometimes referred to as "betterment levies," can become very important for the local budget. For example, in some years of the 1970s, proceeds from the valorization tax accounted for between 2 and 5 percent of all locally raised revenues in Bogotá and Cartagena respectively, and land adjustment receipts for nearly 40 percent in Seoul. This type of tax on property is discussed below in chapter 6.[4]

The property tax takes on added importance if one considers only the financing of public services in urban areas, as shown in table 4-1. The first column of this table refers to the fiscal importance of local governments as reported in table 2-1. The second column shows the contribution of the property tax to financing urban public expenditures. For the large urban areas considered here, the median share of property tax financing in total central, state, and local expenditures in the urban area is 4.6 percent before and including 1979 and 2.8 percent after 1979. If we abstract from the general issue of the relative importance of local and central government expenditures and consider only the share of local expenditures supported by property taxation, quite a different picture may be painted. The third column of table 4-1 shows that it is not uncommon for the property tax to finance more than one-third of all expenditures made by the local government.

We do not have enough data to test rigorously the determinants of intercity variations in the level of property taxation. We can, however, offer some basic hypotheses that appear to be supported by these data. The property tax will be a less important source of finance under four sets of circumstances. The first is that local governments are unimportant relative to the central and state governments in providing services, that is, where the fiscal system is highly centralized (for example, in Kingston and Cartagena local governments accounted for less than 20 percent of urban area financing). The second is that expenditure responsibility has been decentralized but heavy use is made of grants and shared taxes (Nairobi). The third is that expenditure responsibility has been decentralized but the local government finances a major share of its expenditure responsibilities with locally raised nontax revenues (Bogotá and Seoul) or with another local tax (Ahmadabad). The fourth is that the national government collects the property tax and returns a portion of receipts as transfers to local authorities (Jakarta). Since relatively few cities fall under the latter two explanations, one might generalize that where local government taxes play a major role in financing urban public services, the property tax will be an important source of revenue.

One would like to use these data to infer whether the property tax has been increasing or declining as a source of local government finance. Such comparisons, however, are difficult and depend on the sample of cities and the time period chosen. Still, the median share of the property tax in total local taxes fell from 54.7 percent in the pre-1979 period to 42.4 percent in the post-1979 period (table 2-11). Yet it is worth noting that the cities for which we have comparable data for the 1970s and 1980s were as likely to increase as decrease their property tax shares.

A reasonable hypothesis, again supported by these data, is that the property tax had a rougher time of it in the 1980s. This was attributable

Table 4-1. *Revenue Importance of Property Taxes in Generating Revenue to Finance Urban Public Services*

City, year	Percentage of total public expenditures made by local governments	Percentage of total expenditures financed from property taxation	Percentage of local expenditures financed from property taxation
Capital value systems			
La Paz, Bolivia, 1975	—	—	3.2
La Paz, Bolivia, 1985	—	—	11.7
Rio de Janeiro, Brazil, 1980	17.4	2.4	13.8
Rio de Janeiro, Brazil, 1984	13.4	1.6	11.5
São Paulo, Brazil, 1980	17.6	3.1	17.6
São Paulo, Brazil, 1984	16.7	1.9	13.8
Bogotá, Colombia, 1972	49.9	4.0	8.0
Cali, Colombia, 1975	48.8	6.1	12.5
Cartagena, Colombia, 1972	23.0	3.3	14.3
Jakarta, Indonesia, 1970–73	36.9	—	—
Jakarta, Indonesia, 1981–82	21.6	0.9	4.0
Kingston, Jamaica, 1971	19.4	4.6	23.9
Nairobi, Kenya, 1981	46.3	17.2	34.1
Pusan, Rep. of Korea, 1971	33.2	0.6	1.9
Pusan, Rep. of Korea, 1983	21.7	2.8	13.3
Seoul, Rep. of Korea, 1965–71	36.3	2.2	6.2
Seoul, Rep. of Korea, 1981–83	38.4	3.2	8.2
Lima, Peru, 1981–82	6.0	1.4	23.3
Manila, Philippines, 1970	30.5	10.4	34.0
Manila, Philippines, 1985	10.0	3.5	35.0
Lusaka, Zambia, 1971	26.8	7.9	29.3
Annual value systems			
Dhaka, Bangladesh, 1983	5.7	1.5	26.3
Ahmadabad, India, 1965–71	41.5	6.9	16.6
Ahmadabad, India, 1977–81	30.7	5.5	17.8
Bombay, India, 1963–72	41.7	8.8	21.1
Bombay, India, 1975–82	42.9	8.3	19.4
Calcutta (Corp.), India, 1974–75[a]	—	—	41.7
Calcutta (Corp.), India, 1982[a]	—	—	42.8
Madras, India, 1972–76	—	—	50.1
Madras, India, 1977–79	10.1	5.1	50.4
Gujranwala, Pakistan, 1983–85	11.0	3.3	30.0
Karachi, Pakistan, 1972–75	—	—	31.1
Karachi, Pakistan, 1977–82	20.2	17.8[b]	25.4
Singapore, Singapore, 1971	—	—	9.4
Singapore, Singapore, 1983	—	11.5	11.5
Bangkok, Thailand, 1977	25.1	2.7	10.9
Tunis, Tunisia, 1986	10.1	2.4	23.8
Median			
Before and including 1979	33.2	4.6	15.5
After 1979	17.5	2.8	19.4

— Not available.
a. Includes only Calcutta municipal corporation.
b. Excludes state government expenditures.

to several factors: (a) the financing pressures on local governments, which forced the search for new revenue sources, (b) the inelastic response of property tax revenues to income growth and inflation, (c) the legal and administrative difficulties associated with increasing property tax revenues through discretionary actions, and (d) the special difficulties posed by high rates of inflation. The last two factors may be particularly important since discretionary changes in sales tax rates and some user charges are less visible than changes in the property tax and are therefore politically more feasible.

Types of Property Taxation

According to conventional wisdom, there are three basic forms of property taxation. The property tax may be levied on the annual or rental value of the property, the capital value of the land and improvements, or the site value of the land. The annual value form may be seen as an attempt to tax the yearly income from properties, whereas the capital and site value forms are partial wealth taxes. We follow this distinction in most of the following discussion of property tax practices.

This classification of the property tax base is a useful point of departure, but it is an oversimplification and does not necessarily identify all systems. Tax systems are also differentiated by varying coverage, different rate structures, and, perhaps most important of all, different assessment practices. In a sense, each country and each city implants its own style—its cultural values and a unique set of political considerations—on its property tax system. As a result, cities practicing the same basic structural form of property tax do not necessarily implement systems that are even similar. Another reason why this trichotomy oversimplifies is that many systems use both capital and annual value bases. These mixed systems are common in cities of the former French colonies (for example, Abidjan and Tunis), where land is assessed on a capital value basis and improvements on an annual value basis; Mexico levies both an annual and a capital value tax. In Thailand, a capital value basis has been used for vacant land, but an annual value basis for the land and buildings tax (Hubbell 1974). In Turkey, the basic property tax is levied on the capital value of land and improvements, but municipal charges for street cleaning and lighting are based on the rental value of properties (Keles 1972).

Throughout this description and comparison of various applications of urban property taxation, the notion of a "system" is emphasized. This is because the achievement of the desired effects on equity, revenue, and the allocation of resources depends on all aspects of the property tax system—the definition of the tax base, the rate structure, the valuation principles, and the administrative practices. Many of the difficulties encountered with urban property taxation in developing countries have resulted from a failure to consider the total system when making discretionary adjustments. More often than not, the approach to property tax reform is piecemeal, with too little attention paid to whether the components of reform might have offsetting rather than reinforcing effects.

Annual Value Systems

Annual value property tax systems, more or less resembling the British rates, are still used in most of the former British colonies. But inherent assessment problems have prompted many countries to modify their approach to property taxation. Indeed, perhaps the most significant feature of the annual value systems surveyed here is that all resort to some use of capital value assessment.

In an annual value system the base is defined as the expected or notional rental value of a property. An English court has described well the problems of measuring this notional value:

> The rent prescribed by the statute is a hypothetical rent, as hypothetical as the tenant. It is the rent which an imaginary tenant might be reasonably expected to pay to an imaginary landlord for the tenancy of this dwelling in this locality, on the hypothesis that both are reasonable people, the landlord not being extortionate, the tenant not being under pressure, the dwelling being vacant and available to let, not subject to any control, the landlord agreeing to do the repairs, and pay the insurance, the tenant agreeing to pay the rates, the period not too short nor yet too long, simply from year to year. I do not suppose that throughout the length and breadth of Paddington you could find a rent corresponding to this imaginary rent.[5]

Definition and Coverage of the Base

The common feature of annual value systems is property assessment according to some estimate of rental value or net rent. In theory, a discounted stream of net rent payments is equivalent to the capital value of a property; hence, the capital and annual value bases are equivalent. In practice, there is no such equivalence because annual value systems are not based on market rents any more than capital value systems are based on market prices.

There is usually a wide divergence between assessed annual value and net market rent. Though assessment-sales ratio studies are rarely done, some available evidence suggests the extent of underassessment. A survey by the World Bank in Calcutta has estimated the assessment ratio at about 50 percent for central commercial properties and 7.5 percent for outlying industrial estates. Nath and Schroeder (1984) report assessment ratios in the 25 to 35 percent range in Delhi and Madras. The ratio for residential property was estimated at 40 percent in Tunis (Prud'homme 1975) and 50 percent in Dakar. Quite apart from the political and administrative problems that lead to infrequent reassessment, there are three reasons for such divergences: (a) legally allowable reductions in annual value; (b) rent controls; and (c) assessment difficulties, particularly for nonresidential properties.

With respect to the first, the annual value tax base is often adjusted to a basis which is net of maintenance costs. These reductions, however, require no evidence of maintenance expenditures and so are tantamount to a general reduction in the assessment ratio. For example, there was an allowance of 10 percent of annual value in many Indian cities. The allowance in Dakar was 40 percent for residences and 50 percent for businesses.

The presence of rent control confounds the notion of what constitutes a market rent. In theory, the rent control constraints could severely limit both the level and growth of assessed value. The actual level of rent is the controlled amount plus the premium which the renter must pay to secure the lease. The latter component—also called "key money" or a "charge for furnishings"—is indeed a part of market rent but is generally illegal, unreported, and therefore excluded from the base of most tax systems. Where controlled rents are used as the property tax base, assessed value grows only with new construction because controlled rents are rarely increased.[6]

In practice, however, the problem of assessment under rent control has been dealt with in different ways. For example, Bombay, Cairo, Delhi, and Singapore all have had long-standing rent control ordinances, and all assessed property was subject to rent control according to the controlled rent. Ahmadabad ignored the rent control ordinance and assessed at what it deemed market rent—a procedure which has been challenged in the courts.

Two other important points can be made about rent control and the property tax. The first is that rent controls are usually imposed by the state and central governments, which do not feel the pain of the loss of property taxes. The second is the considerable opportunity cost of rent control assessments, in terms of property tax revenues forgone. Mohan (1974) estimated that Bombay's property tax revenues could have been 50 percent higher in the absence of rent controls. Nath (1983) made a similar estimate of property tax loss in Calcutta. Any gains from rent control, which protects low-income families from rent increases, are therefore achieved by sacrificing revenue, and therefore the public services available to these same low-income families may ultimately be reduced.

The third reason for a divergence between net market rents and annual value arises because of the difficulties in defining the tax base for nonresidential properties and for vacant land. In theory, and according to law, it is the annual expected rent, or the amount for which the property could be let; if capitalized, the base is equivalent to the present value of the expected future flow of earnings from the property. In practice,

however, the assessment procedure for such properties usually assumes
that annual rent is equivalent to a fixed proportion of estimated capital
value. But practices in assessing capital value and assumptions about rates
of capitalization vary widely. The same inconsistency appears to exist in
the treatment of vacant land.

The tax base under rental value systems is further reduced by exemptions of certain classes of property and by a range of preferential
assessments. Most annual value systems fully exempt properties of the
government, properties of religious and charitable institutions, and foreign embassies. Another important class of exemption is owner-occupied
properties, as in Abidjan, Bangkok, and Karachi. Where owner-occupied
properties are not fully exempt, preferential assessments are not uncommon; this is the practice in Ahmadabad and Tunis. The underassessment,
relative to comparable rented properties, has been roughly estimated for
selected Indian cities: 60 to 80 percent underassessment in Ahmadabad
(Bahl 1975), 15 to 20 percent in Bombay (Bougeon-Maassen 1976), 10
to 15 percent in Madras, and 25 percent in Delhi (Mohan 1974, 1977).

Rate Structures

There are important differences among cities in the level, structure,
and flexibility of annual value property tax rates. A flat rate structure is
not as common as one that is progressive with respect to property value.
Otherwise, statutory rates may vary according to the location of the
property within the urban area, whether or not the land is developed
and whether or not it is owner-occupied. To give the flavor of the variations in rate structure, some examples are presented in table 4-2.[7] The
problem in reading these schedules is that they may not approximate
real tax rates because of wide variations in the assessment ratio.

Table 4-2. *Statutory Rate Structures: Selected Annual Value Systems*

City, year	Rate[a]	Comments
Ahmadabad, India, 1980	0.120–0.300	Progressive rate with respect to annual value. Exemption limit of 300 rupees.
Madras, India, 1983; ratable value (rupees)		In addition, all properties pay a 3.5 percent lighting tax on ratable value.
Less than 500	0.160	Plant and machinery are not taxed. A
500–1,000	0.220	10 percent depreciation offset is
1,000–5,000	0.240	allowed, and owner-occupied relief of
More than 5,000	0.265	up to 25 percent may be provided.
Bangkok, Thailand, 1980;		The rate is reduced to 0.042 for
House and rent tax	0.125	structures that contain machines for manufacturing activities. Vacant land and unoccupied housing are exempt from tax.

a. Rate for Madras includes general tax, water tax and drainage tax, and education tax.

From an examination of the statutory rate schedules in use in various cities, it might be concluded that two objectives underly their markup. The first is to allocate property tax burdens according to ability to pay. This objective is reflected in the progressive features of statutory rate schedules, as in the cities of India. The second is to allocate property tax burdens according to benefits received, as evidenced by the lower rates on suburban properties (for example, Bombay and Singapore) and on undeveloped properties (for example, Calcutta), where public service levels are thought to be lower, and by the divisions of the total property tax rate into separate rates for water, refuse collection, fire fighting, general services, and the like.[8] From this observation, it would seem that there is more than a little concern about how to make the distribution of the property tax burden more equitable, or at least more fair.

In fact, such attempts to improve the fairness of the property tax may fail because they do not take into account all elements of the property tax system. For example, the equity effects of a graduated rate structure may be offset by preferential assessment of higher-valued properties. A good illustration of this is in Ahmadabad (Bahl 1975), where owner-occupied properties were assessed at as little as one-fifth the level of rented properties. Since owner-occupants were likely to have higher incomes than renters, the intent of the graduated rate structure was defeated by the assessment practice. There was a similar result in Bombay, but in Dakar owner-occupants are taxed at 30 percent and rental units at 15 percent.

Assessment Procedures

Variations across cities in the effective tax rate—the ratio of taxes paid to market rent or market value—are probably as much influenced by variations in assessment practices as by variations in either the definition of the legal base or the statutory rate structure. No matter what the base and rate structure is stated to be, evaluation of the equity, elasticity, and performance of annual value systems must begin with a careful examination of the methods used to determine annual value.

Central to the evaluation of any assessment practice is its potential to keep pace with property values and thereby give some buoyancy to the revenue yield. This in turn means that there must be a system for accurately and regularly determining changes in market value. The assessment procedure should be objective, which means that a manual describing the assessment method should exist, and the procedure should be in some sense horizontally and vertically equitable. Finally, the assessment office should be adequately staffed so that assessment practices match the intent of the stated assessment procedures. Assessment practices under annual value systems in developing countries satisfy few of these maxims. The major problems are an arbitrariness in determining net rent and infrequent reassessment.

RESIDENTIAL PROPERTY. One advantage of rental value systems in urban areas of developing countries is the possibility for mass assessment. This advantage arises if many residential units are rented and if the structures are relatively homogeneous within a neighborhood. Given the substantial understaffing of the assessment office in virtually all cities, mass assessment would be desirable. Available data would seem to support the contention that renting dominates the tenancy arrangement in most cities in developing countries (Lemer 1987: 1–11). The homogeneity case, however, is a much more difficult one to make. Rental value assessment schemes have been criticized in the past on grounds that they ignored variations in the quality of rented premises, such as location by floor in a building or exposure to breezes, factors which surely affect market rent (Manning 1970).

It is possible to gain a better understanding of the strengths and weaknesses of assessment practice under an annual value system by examining some of the detail of the practice. A comparison of the approaches taken in three cities which use mass assessment of rented properties—Ahmadabad (Bahl 1975), Bombay (Bougeon-Maassen 1976), and Singapore (Singapore, various years [1965–73]) can provide this detail.[9] Assessment of rented property in Ahmadabad was based on rents actually realized by the landlord, if such rents were thought by the assessor to approximate a fair market rent. Under this system, both the landlord and the tenant were required to produce a rent payment receipt. If the assessor felt that the stated rent was not a fair one, the estimated average market rent for the neighborhood was used. This neighborhood average was then estimated for a sample of properties on which market rent data were available, and the judgment of the assessor played a major role as these data were combined to reach a neighborhood average. Though a significant proportion of city properties were subject to rent control, assessment was done on the basis of estimated market rents. In the case of Singapore's residential properties, annual values were determined centrally on a basis of comparative rent analysis. Typically, an average rent was estimated for an area—block or neighborhood—and a given type structure, and this average was taken as the assessment of annual value for all similar properties in the area. Actual rents paid varied about this mean, but the residuals were usually ignored on grounds that the proper assessment is on reasonable expected annual rent and that an arithmetic average best approximates the norm. The approach taken in Bombay was similar in terms of mass appraisal, except that controlled rents, where applicable, were taken as the base. For newer properties that are leased, the lease documents were used as evidence of annual rental value.

Because of the great difficulties of imputing rental values to owner-occupied properties and to nonresidential properties, which are typically not rented, the similarities in assessment practice end with rented residential properties. Cities have responded to the problems of assessing owner-occupied and nonresidential properties by developing a wide range of appraisal methods, many of which use elements of capital value assessment.

Owner-occupied residential properties are assessed on a completely different basis than are rented properties. Among the important considerations in determining assessed value are location, the specific amenities of the property, construction material, ventilation, and carpet areas. In Ahmadabad, there were graduated assessment rates (assessed value per square meter) which depended on these considerations but, again, the judgment of the assessor played a major role. Though there was no manual to which assessors strictly adhered, the range of assessment rates which evolved over time were used as a guide. One study estimated that the result of this procedure in Ahmadabad was a substantial preferential assessment of owner-occupied properties, on the order of about one-fifth that for rented properties (Bahl 1975). A similar procedure was followed in Bombay, but the preferential treatment was estimated to have resulted in a reduction to 80–85 percent of ratable value (Bougeon-Maassen 1976).

Mexico assesses owner-occupied properties by a capital value method and rented properties by an annual value method. Both types of properties are subjected to the same capital value rate structure after annual value is converted to rental value using a discount rate of about 15 percent (Garzón López 1989).

COMMERCIAL AND INDUSTRIAL PROPERTIES. Assessment of commercial and industrial properties is generally made on a different basis. Since the direct estimation of expected rent of an industrial or large commercial property is all but impossible, the capital value is estimated and converted to net annual rent with some arbitrarily chosen discount rate. The arbitrary discount rate is inevitably too low; hence, net rents tend to be underestimated. Moreover, since these rents are fixed over time, they dampen the elasticity of the property tax revenue system. As a result, the local government has to negotiate assessment changes with industrialists periodically—a practice which leaves the tax system relatively inflexible with respect to discretionary changes. The practices in Ahmadabad, Bombay, and Singapore illustrate this problem. Ahmadabad (Bahl 1975) used a construction cost approach to estimate the capital value of improvements, a comparative cost method to estimate land values, and a ratio of 6–7 percent to translate this capital value (of land and improvements) to an annual value equivalent. In 1968, the city changed the assessment base from original to current market value and proposed a uniform capitalization rate of 6 percent. Industrialists contested, and after four years of debate property tax liability was increased 25 percent above the pre-1968 levels. When increases in actual property value are considered, large nonresidential firms in Ahmadabad have been assessed at a rate far below market value.

Industrial properties in Bombay (Bougeon-Maassen 1976) fell into two categories: (a) small, traditionally oriented factories and (b) large firms such as textile mills, Bombay Port Trust properties, oil refineries, and railways. In the first group, the properties were usually assessed by a comparative rental value method with the rates varying by location within Greater Bombay. Industrial properties were usually assessed according to some combination of a reconstruction cost basis and negotiation. Under the reconstruction cost method, land values were estimated on the basis of comparative sales and building values on the basis of re-placement cost. To convert the capital value estimates to annual values, rates of 6.5 percent and 9.0 percent, respectively, were used for buildings and land. The textile mills were assessed every five years on a capital value basis by mutual agreement between the city government and the millowners' association.

In the cases of commercial buildings and factories for which rental data are not available or easily estimated, Singapore adopted a somewhat more objective method (Singapore, various years [1965–73]). The sum of (a) a fair return on capital value, (b) a fixed maintenance allowance, and (c) property tax payments was used to approximate gross annual rent. The fair return was computed as 6 percent of the cost of land and buildings. The maintenance cost was computed as a percentage of build-ing costs alone—a figure of approximately 2 percent was used, varying with the type of construction. The tax base, gross annual rent, was then determined by grossing up to include the property tax. In the case of small commercial and business establishments, a comparative rental basis was used to establish annual value. Where subletting occurred and ten-ants paid a large premium for the lease and small annual rents thereafter, annual value was computed on a basis of both the capital sum involved and the smaller monthly rent payments.

VACANT PROPERTIES. In the case of vacant or underutilized properties, a capital value approach is often used. The Singapore experience in this regard is particularly interesting in that the law provided for special as-sessment practices for such properties (Singapore, various years [1965–73]). At the option of the assessor, annual value could be set at 5 percent of the estimated capital value. Valuation practice in Singapore also pro-vided for separate assessment of land and buildings where the use of the land is uneconomic; that is, if the land adjacent to any house or building exceeds some maximum allowable amount fixed by the authorities, the excess land was treated as vacant and its annual value was determined as 5 percent of its estimated market value.

Capital Value Systems

There appears to be much more diversity in practice among cities using capital value systems than among cities using annual value systems. There also are some important common features in assessment practices among capital value systems. The more important of these are (a) a differential tax treatment of land and improvements, (b) an objective assessment practice for residential properties, and (c) a uniform assessment procedure for various types of land. Another common tendency is for capital value systems to involve central and state governments much more heavily in the administration of the tax.

Definition and Coverage of the Tax Base

The tax base is defined as the assessed value of land and improvements, or as only the assessed value of land under the site value version. In fact, most capital value systems in developing countries assess land independent from improvements; hence, the site value approach differs from most other capital value systems only in that it does not tax buildings.

In theory, the legal assessment ratio may vary from 0 to 1, although the assessed value is almost always defined by statute to equal full market value, that is, the value on which a willing buyer and seller would agree in a free market. In practice, however, actual assessed value is generally below market value because of infrequent reassessment and poor assessment practices. Studies of the extent of underassessment are not regularly carried out in cities of developing countries, but evidence from analyses of property tax practices suggests that drastic underassessment is the rule rather than the exception. The ratio of assessed to market value has been roughly estimated at 25 percent in Jakarta (Lerche 1974), 45 percent for Manila (Yoingco 1971), 25 percent in La Paz (Holland 1979), and about 20 percent in the cities of Taiwan (China) (Riew 1987).

In addition to assessment problems, there is a difference between market value and taxable value which results from a number of exclusions from the base. Site value systems (such as in Nairobi and Lusaka) are extremes in excluding all improvements from the tax base. A sweeping reform in Jamaica in the mid-1970s converted Kingston's capital value system to a pure site value tax.[10]

In other cities, improvements are partially exempt. For example, only commercial and industrial buildings were taxed under the previous system in Jakarta (Linn, Smith, and Wignjowijoto 1976), and only residential properties were taxed in Peru before 1983 (Greytak 1983).[11]

Rate Structures

Three important features of capital value rate structures (table 4-4 below) distinguish them from annual value systems: the use of flat rates is more common, there is more frequent use of differential taxation of land and improvements, and the capital value rate structures tend to be more complicated. Some examples are given in table 4-3 to illustrate the variations but, as noted above, these are statutory rates and cannot be used to make inferences about effective property tax rates because there are wide variations in the assessment ratio.

Table 4-3. *Statutory Rate Structures: Selected Capital Value Systems*

City, year	Land		Improvements	Comments
	Vacant	Improved		
Taipei, Taiwan (China), 1986; assessed value class				The tax rate for nonresidential improvements is 3 percent. A preferential rate of 0.5 percent is applied to owner-occupied residential land (if under 300 square meters and within a city planning area or 700 square meters if outside city planning areas), and a flat 1.5 percent rate is applied to all factory sites.
PSV[a]		0.015	0.14[b]	
PSV to (PSV + 500 percent)		0.005		
(PSV + 500 percent) to (PSV + 1,000 percent)		0.010		
(PSV + 1,000 percent) to (PSV + 1,500 percent)		0.010		
(PSV + 1,500 percent) to (PSV + 2,000 percent)		0.010		
(PSV + 2,000 percent) to (PSV + 2,500 percent)		0.010		
More than PSV + 2,500 percent		0.010		
Jakarta, Indonesia, 1986		0.005	0.005	All buildings are given an exemption of 2 million rupees.
Seoul, Rep. of Korea, 1985	0.05–0.10[c]	0.003–0.05[d]	0.003–0.05[d]	All commercial buildings are taxed at the 0.003 rate. Land serving as plant sites is taxed at the 0.003 rate.

Manila, Philippines, 1987		0.02	0.02	The tax code fixes assessment ratios, which may range up to 80 percent. A mandatory 1 percent additional levy is applied in all jurisdictions in the Philippines, with revenues earmarked for education.
Rio de Janeiro, Brazil, 1982	0.005–0.07[e]	0.008	0.006–0.012[f]	Properties with a tax liability less than 0.2 "standard units" are exempted. A standard unit is a reference value fixed by the municipality; it is expressed as a multiple of the price of national treasury bonds. In October 1987, Rio's standard unit was equivalent to $19.50.

a. PSV = progressive starting value. The "progressive starting value" is defined as the average value of 700 square meters and is determined separately for each of the twenty-three local taxing jurisdictions.

b. Applies to all values.

c. The actual rate depends on the holding period.

d. These rates are applied to a graduated structure of assessed values.

e. The rate depends on the location within the city.

f. The rate depends on the floor area of the structure.

These examples do, however, suggest a different emphasis for those designing capital value rate structures (versus those designing annual value rate structures). There is an apparently greater concern with the allocative (land use) effects of the tax under capital value systems than under rental value systems, or at least a concern that there be more flexibility to deal with allocative effects. This is reflected in the differential taxation of improvements versus land, improved land versus idle land, and land in different locations in the urban area. Where tax rates on land and improvements are different, most cities tax land more heavily than improvements; for example, differentially lower rates have been applied to improvements in Bangkok, Francistown, Istanbul, Jakarta, and Tehran. Higher effective tax rates have been applied to improvements in Seoul, Taipei, and Tunis because of higher statutory tax rates, and in Manila because of a higher assessment ratio.[12] Differentially higher tax rates on idle or unimproved land are also common, and in some cases the rate levied, if properly enforced, would be a significant stimulus to develop the land. Bolivia levies a surcharge on idle land—above the basic rate of 0.4 percent of market value—of 2 percent on the land that has access to public utilities and 1 percent that does not. In Honduras, the basic rate is 0.5 percent, but vacant land is subject to a 1 percent rate.

Conversely, the general absence of progressive rate structures implies less propensity to use the property tax to reshape the distribution of income.[13] Rate structures in some cases appear to have been designed to achieve other objectives. The structure in Taipei tends to encourage the breakup of large landholdings because it applies graduated rates to the aggregate value of all holdings of a single owner within the city (Harris 1979; Riew 1987). The Peruvian system also applied a graduated rate structure to all holdings of a single taxpayer within a province (Greytak 1983).

Assessment Procedures

The assessment practices now used in many developing countries were influenced heavily by these countries' colonial heritage but have developed over time into unique systems. Among the cities in this sample which use capital value bases, there is a wide diversity in assessment practices. Each city has introduced its own variations on the basic assessment methods—comparative sales, construction cost, or discounted earnings flow. Indeed, if each of these many variations was applied in the same city, markedly different patterns of assessed value would surely result.

The strengths and weaknesses of capital value systems show up in the application of five features more common to capital value than to annual value assessment: (a) formula-based valuation, (b) separate assessment of land and improvements, (c) multiple sources of valuation information, (d) provisions for reassessment, and (e) centralized assessment.

First, the assessment procedure is often formula-based and is much more complicated than that used in rental value systems. The process typically starts with a classification of land according to its location, amenities, and/or use. Each class of land is then given an assessed value according to a comparative sales analysis. This is done by either computing the average value for a small number of properties (for example, in Bogotá and Seoul), by using mathematical techniques to establish relative property values (Cartagena), or on a judgmental basis (São Paulo).[14]

Even though the actual valuation process differs across cities, and the assessor's judgment plays an important role, the more objective valuation under capital value systems should result in a more uniform treatment than would occur under an annual value system. The more objective the system, however, the more costly it is to administer. Capital value systems are indeed costly to administer. A formula basis for assessing land requires a basic urban plan defining existing and desired land use and a relatively large and skillful staff capable of carrying out comparative sales analyses. Moreover, this technique presumes the existence of an up-to-date property tax roll (that is, an accurate cadastre). The assessment of improvements requires an up-to-date manual of construction costs and substantial fieldwork to record the features of each property. As a result of staff shortages and the high cost of proper assessment, the quality of assessment tends to be compromised, and many of the advantages of the more objective assessment systems are lost. These losses result in disparities between assessed and market values, horizontal inequities, and a failure of the property tax base to keep up with the growth of property value. The first two of these shortcomings cannot be carefully documented (beyond the crude evidence presented above) because few cities in developing countries regularly monitor their assessment-sales ratios. The third shortcoming is evidenced by the slow growth of assessed value relative to income, population, and prices—relations that are discussed below.

A second common feature of capital value systems is the separate assessment of land and improvements. A separate valuation of land and improvements makes possible the application of different assessment ratios and different rates of taxation, and hence can provide authorities with greater flexibility in inducing allocative effects. But there are costs to this approach. Not only is the valuation separate, but the basis of valuation is different. Whereas land is valued on a comparative cost basis and is meant to reflect advantages of location and amenities, improvements are usually valued according to construction costs. The experience in most cities surveyed was that the (construction cost) assessment manuals were out of date and a great deal of judgment crept into the process. This likely reduces horizontal equity and probably results in an undervaluation of improvements relative to land.

A third similarity among capital value assessment systems is their use of multiple sources of information to arrive at an appraised value for a property. Though these data are combined in varying ways to estimate land value, basic land value information is obtained from comparative sales records, realtor and banker opinions, real estate boards, and self-assessment. Improvement values are often based on data provided by the government construction ministry and collected from the private sector. In all cases, the judgment of the assessor plays a major role in adjusting and combining these data.

Fourth, the provision for updating assessed values takes one of three forms. The less frequently used one involves yearly value updates, which are based on a sampling of property sales. This method is used in Seoul. The more common provision is for a specified reappraisal cycle (for example, every five years in Nairobi, every three years in the Philippines). The other possibility is simply to index the property tax base, as has been done in Brazil, Chile, and the United Kingdom.

A fifth area where capital value assessment practices are similar and tend to differ from annual value systems is in the degree to which they are administered centrally for large parts of an economy, if not in fact for the entire economy. The assessment function has been a shared central-local responsibility in Jakarta, Seoul, and Tehran. Bogotá, Nairobi, and Taipei maintained more control over their systems, though other cities in Colombia, Kenya, and Taiwan (China) were subject to more centralized assessment.[15]

Site Value Taxation

Site value taxation[16] is a special case of capital value property taxation,[17] and one that is particularly interesting because of its potential for improving the efficiency of urban land use. The argument for this form of taxation is straightforward: if only the land is taxed, the owner will have no disincentive to developing the land to its most efficient use. Site value taxation has been practiced in a number of developing economies, for example, Barbados, Jamaica, Kenya, and Taiwan (China), and in parts of Australia, New Zealand, and South Africa.[18] Despite the inconclusive results about whether this form of property taxation leads to a better use of urban land (see chapter 6) academic and practitioner interest has remained high.[19]

There are two disadvantages to site value taxation, which many think limit the possibilities for its use in other countries.[20] The first is an assessment problem. There is alleged to be a paucity of evidence on sales of vacant properties, especially in urban areas; hence, sites must be valued by some residual method. That is, first the property value must be determined and then the value of improvements must be deducted. Such an approach makes site valuation less objective than property valuation. Others disagree with this position and can call on some impressive supporting evidence. As is clear from the discussion above, most capital value systems carry out a separate assessment of land and improvements in any case. The implication of the current practice is either that there is no shortage of evidence on transfers of vacant properties[21] or that there are acceptable ways around the problem. With respect to the latter possibility, it is interesting to note that real estate agent opinions, assessor judgments, and consensus are all part of the assessment process in many countries. Indeed, Prest (1982: 386) reads the evidence as showing that site value assessments are quite feasible: "the experience of countries where this tax has operated and general principles lead to the conclusion that valuation is easier, that it can be repeated more frequently, and that there are fewer problems of concealment than if improvements are included in the tax base."

The second frequently discussed disadvantage is that site value alone provides a limited tax base and can produce sufficient revenue only at high rates. Financial officers and politicians of fiscally strapped local government will naturally see downtown office buildings, hotels, and luxury residences—outside the site value base—as legitimate and fruitful objects of taxation. Moreover, there can be no question but that it is politically easier to levy a lower rate on a broader base (one that includes the value of improvements) than vice versa. The rate argument is not easily dismissed. Some countries have made exceptions to the site base to capture this value of luxury improvements. Lent (1974) reports that improvements in Trinidad and Tobago were taxed when the ratio of improvement to land value exceeded 5:1.

On the other side of the ledger, site value taxation has two important advantages, aside from the removal of a disincentive for investing in improvements. The first, paradoxically, is an assessment advantage. It stands to reason that the job can be done more cheaply and uniformly if improvements need not be considered. Moreover, there are much better possibilities for mass appraisal, or even the use of computerized systems, under the land value approach. In an interesting analysis in New Zealand, a former chief valuer estimated the relative costs of assessing a plot under capital, annual, and site value to be 6.7 to 4.3 to 1.0 (Brown 1971). The second advantage has to do with the equity of property taxation. A pure land value tax is likely to be borne proportionately more by owners of the land (compared with a capital value or annual value tax); hence, it should be more progressive (see chapter 5).

Is There an Optimal Property Tax Structure for Developing Countries?

On the basis of this review, could one say that there is an optimal property tax structure for urban local governments in developing countries? Probably not, but we can identify some common trends and reexamine the developing-country experience in light of the supposed advantages and disadvantages of each system. To the extent that there is a trend in property tax practices in developing countries, it is away from the annual value base and toward capital value assessment. This change reflects the fact that, as urban areas modernize, the virtues of the annual value system become less and less important, and the comparative advantages of a capital value system become more apparent.

The move toward a capital value basis implies more than simply a change in the method of assessment. The administration of rental based systems is more likely to be left with the local authority than is the administration of a capital value system. Capital assessment is more difficult and more technical and requires a larger staff of qualified assessors than does rental value assessment as currently practiced. Nearly all the annual value systems studied here were completely administered by the local government, whereas the assessment function tended to be shared or centralized under the capital value systems studied. The movement toward capital value, then, may strengthen the property tax practice, but it also may reduce local discretion.

The horizontal equity of the property tax system is potentially better under capital value assessment because individual property differences are considered in some detail and because an objective assessment manual can be used. A more objective assessment system also can improve vertical equity, and progressive rate structures can be used under either system. Moreover, the assessment of owner-occupied, rented, and nonresidential properties on the same basis (not possible under annual value systems) is likely to improve both horizontal and vertical equity. This is not to say that capital value systems are more equitable in practice, only that they potentially might be.

The capital value basis has the great virtue, as an urban tax, of possibly affecting the intensity and spatial distribution of land use and would also seem preferable on grounds that it can be adapted more easily to affect land use patterns. Differential assessment of land and improvements, and differential tax rates, are common under capital value systems. This differentiation is not possible under the traditional annual value system.

There would seem little room to choose between the two systems in terms of revenue productivity and elasticity. In theory, annual and capital value should grow at the same rate and respond similarly to income and price fluctuations. Annual value is probably more easily reassessed for rented residential properties but is more difficult to determine for commercial and industrial properties (where negotiated settlements seem to be more common than under capital value systems).

The clear advantage to an annual value system is that it is less costly to administer. Fewer qualified valuers are necessary and, where mass appraisal techniques are used, it is not necessary to develop and update a file of particulars for every property. Many annual value systems, however, already rely to a certain extent on capital value assessment, and in some countries and cities annual and capital value systems exist side by side. In these cases, a conversion may in fact reduce duplication, clarify procedures, and increase horizontal equity across different uses of real property.

This cataloging of advantages and disadvantages is of course subject to qualification depending on the application of the tax system in specific cities. Particularly in the case of capital value systems, there is wide variation in the effectiveness of property taxation. Still, with so few advantages to the annual value system, one might raise the question of why it continues to be used so widely. A first reason is simply inertia. Where the system is understood and accepted by the taxpayers and the government, a change appears to be costly and disruptive. Second, the lower cost of assessing annual value is difficult to give up when there are so many other pressures on local government budgets. Third, it is well known that qualified valuers are hard to attract because government salaries tend not to be competitive—a problem which has resulted in some capital value systems working rather badly. Fourth, the rental system is likely to be more palatable to the influential interest groups, such as industrialists and owner-occupiers, and is acceptable to the courts. Fifth, there is a fear that a capital value scheme will lead to centralized assessment and eventually to a loss in local control over the property tax.

These influences notwithstanding, the tide is turning away from annual value systems. Rapid urbanization is placing demands on the local tax system that annual value systems probably cannot meet. In particular there are demands for horizontal and vertical equity, a need to consider land use effects and to raise more revenue, and a desire to capture the land value increments resulting from urbanization. Moreover, the advantages of mass assessment of homogeneous rented properties will continue to diminish as urbanization brings more owner-occupancy and more diversity in the housing stock. On the political side, one would expect more willingness to yield to the pressures for centralization, in exchange for greater leeway in affecting land use and for greater revenues from the property base.

Once the notion of a capital value base is accepted, the question arises as to whether one wants to tax or exempt improvements. The exclusion of improvements would hinge on the interest of the city and country in promoting a more intensive development of land, and on whether the heavy administrative costs of assessing property and collecting a property tax on improvements figure greatly as part of the government's goals. One could not say that there is a groundswell of enthusiasm for site value taxation among local governments in developing countries. Indeed, some of those countries which have adopted site value systems have found ways to tax improvements, for example, the Barbados case mentioned above and the use of a service charge for properties in Johannesburg (McCulloch 1979: 265). Other countries, such as Jamaica and Kenya, have held to more pure land value taxation. There is a clear and dominant trend, however, in the direction of taxing land at a differentially higher rate than improvements. Pure site value taxation may be one step further than most developing countries are willing to go.

Exemptions from the Property Tax Base

Governmental and certain other institutional properties are usually exempt from local property taxes, but there are good arguments for questioning this practice. First, urban services must be provided to workers in these buildings, just as in any other buildings. Second, the absence of a property tax artificially lowers the relative price of a location and may induce a government to choose an inefficient location for certain of its activities. Third, because of the exempted properties, a city with a concentration of government activity (especially a capital) loses a great deal of revenue compared with other cities in the country. Garzón López (1989) estimates that between 25 and 30 percent of the assessed value in La Paz is exempt.

In fact, some central and state governments do make a payment in lieu of property taxes, which is usually negotiated as some fixed percentage of actual property tax liability. This percentage varies substantially by city and by type of institutional property, and there do not appear to be general patterns or procedures. For example, Ahmadabad requested state and central government payments equivalent to 75 percent of the general rate of property taxes, with assessment at 9 percent of a property's original capital value. In Bombay and Singapore, payment was negotiated with each payee (for example, government, railroad, port, and utilities). Even where payments are made, however, they may be small relative to the actual tax liability forgone, are often made only after delays, and tend to be less buoyant than increases in property value. Bombay and Nairobi, among the cases studied here, are cities in which government agencies have been notably delinquent in their payments. In many cities—such as Cartagena, Jakarta, and Seoul—no payments were made.

Institutional properties are but one important class of exemption from the property tax. Another is tax incentives to stimulate construction or increased investment. For example, Singapore used a set of property tax holidays to encourage the development of multistory hotels, and the central government in the Philippines exempted "pioneer industry" firms from local property taxes. Particularly noteworthy about the Philippines case is that the tax loss was not incurred by the level of government granting the exemption. The important issue in the case of these incentive programs is whether they work, that is, whether property tax relief can provide enough cost savings to induce business expansion. Evidence from the United States on this question is inconclusive (see Bartik 1989; Wasylenko and McGuire 1985). In the cities of developing countries where tax rates are even lower, property tax exemptions are even less likely to be effective in stimulating economic development.

Another class of exemptions is for owner-occupancy. The intent is to provide an incentive for homeownership and, presumably, to tax landlords, renters, and nonresidential property more heavily. Full exemption is given in many countries, preferential assessments in others, and preferential rates in yet others. Again, the rate of property taxation may not be high enough to influence the ownership decision. The more pertinent question may well be how the city wants to divide the total property tax bill among various classes of taxpayers; that is, the most important effects of the owner-occupancy exemption have to do with the equity of the property tax. The net equity effects depend on the relative income levels of owner-occupants, renters, and landlords; the extent to which absentee landownership predominates; and the extent to which the property tax may be passed on to renters. One could hypothesize that few governments have based the owner-occupancy decision on a thorough consideration of these issues. Indeed, as we will show in chapter 5, the net effect of this provision probably reduces the overall progressivity of the system.

A third common type of exemption is for low-income families, or at least for low-value properties, such as has been given in Bogotá and Cali; Bombay, Calcutta, and Madras; and in Seoul, Singapore, and Tehran. Whether the primary aim of this exemption policy is to reduce administrative costs or to introduce a progressive element into the tax structure is not entirely clear. Many have argued that such exemptions can lower administrative costs significantly without having much effect on revenue. Mohan (1974) estimated that the exemption of low-income properties in Bombay could reduce the number of taxpayers by 35 percent but tax liabilities by only 5 percent. He reports similar results for Madras. Linn (1980b) reports for Bogotá that the aggregate assessed value of the least valuable 60 percent of properties contributed only 13 percent of total property value in 1972. If these examples are indicative, local governments not giving exemptions for low-valued properties may be incurring a relatively high collection cost for little revenue return. The net revenue cost of such exemptions could be quite low.

Does the Property Tax Generate Adequate Revenue?

The property tax, it is alleged, does not generate enough revenue to satisfy public expenditure demands at any given point in time, nor does it grow as rapidly as do expenditure requirements. This complaint is most forceful in cities which do not have recourse to other taxes or where intergovernmental transfers play an important role in local finances. To examine the adequacy of revenue, we make cross-city comparisons of the level of property tax effort and of the income-elasticity of the property tax. Comparisons of property tax effort can serve as a first approximation to whether there is room to raise additional revenues through discretionary actions. An analysis of the elasticity of the property tax in various cities may also identify international norms, as well as suggest possibilities for improving the responsiveness of the tax to income and population growth in the local area.

Tax Effort

There are conceptual problems with measuring tax effort, that is, the extent to which taxable capacity is actually used (Bahl 1971; Bird 1976a). Interpreting comparisons of effort for particular taxes is even more troublesome; for example, a low property tax effort may mean only that other taxes are used more intensively. For these reasons, we suggest no normative interpretation of the rather mechanical comparisons below—they show norms only in the sense of describing the variation in actual practice.

The ratio of property tax revenue (T) to personal income (Y) is a traditional measure of tax effort. This ratio may be disaggregated for any city as follows:

$$(4\text{-}1) \qquad \frac{T}{Y} = \left(\frac{T}{TL}\right)\left(\frac{TL}{AV}\right)\left(\frac{AV}{MV}\right)\left(\frac{MV}{Y}\right)$$

where TL = the property tax liability, AV = the total assessed value of the property, and MV = the total market (capital or rental) value of the property. The level of effort, then, may be viewed in terms of (a) collection efficiency (T/TL), (b) a tax rate effect (TL/AV), (c) assessment efficiency (AV/MV), and (d) a base effect (MV/Y). The last term, the ratio of the market value of property to income, is beyond the short-run discretionary control of the local government. In fact, in countries where assessment is highly centralized and where tax rate adjustments require central or state government action, local governments may influence only the efficiency of collection. Where there is more local autonomy, the collection, tax rate, and assessment effects may all be subject to manipulation by the taxing local government. This might lead us to the conclusion that, at least in some countries, variations in property tax effort may be attributed in considerable degree to conscious decisions by local governments.

A quantitative comparison of cities according to the four components of equation 4-1 is not as straightforward as it may seem. There are many reasons. Since cities using annual and capital value systems are not strictly comparable in terms of their ratio of property tax base to income, some rate of capitalization must be assumed.[22] Comparable data are not always available to analyze variations in efficiency of collection and assessment. Moreover, actual collections are rarely disaggregated according to how much was collected in relation to any given year's liability; hence, comparisons for a single year may be spurious. Studies of assessment ratios are rarely done in developing countries, thereby making impossible comparisons of assessed and market value across cities. Because of these data problems, we combined the first two terms in equation 4-1 into an effective tax rate (T/AV) and the last two into an effective base rate (AV/Y). If, in a particular city, the effective tax rate is low relative to other cities, the difference may be ascribed either to a low statutory rate or inefficient collection. If the effective tax base is relatively low, underassessment is likely the problem. The effective base and effective tax rates are comparable only among cities using the same base, but the composite measure of property tax effort (T/Y) is comparable across all cities in the sample.

From the small sample available to this study, it is most difficult to infer a normal property tax effort, but the median of property tax collections relative to income of the cities studied was about 2.5 percent in the 1970s and slightly lower in the 1980s (table 4-4). If an effort ratio of 2.5 percent is about average, then Bogotá, Cartagena, Jakarta, Kingston, and Seoul would appear to have made abnormally low property tax efforts relative to their incomes. Because of the very small number of urban areas for which we have data, it is difficult to uncover any systematic relations which may exist between this pattern of effort and the characteristics of the cities.

Something may be learned by analyzing the components of the below-average performance of these five capital value cities. In Seoul, the problem has been a low effective rate, while in Bogotá, Jakarta, and Kingston both the effective rate and the base ratio have been low. This rough comparison squares with policy concerns about the property tax in Kingston and Seoul, that is, Seoul's very low rate and Kingston's long-standing need for overall reassessment before its conversion to site value taxation in the late 1970s. The variations in the tax-to-assessed-value ratio shown in table 4-4 appear to be due primarily to differences in rate level and structure. Variations in the collection ratio (the ratio of taxes collected to tax liabilities) are smaller (table 4-5).

Among the rental value cities, the pattern is less clear. Calcutta and Ahmadabad have made the highest tax efforts, Calcutta because of a high effective rate and Ahmadabad because both the effective rate and the effective base are high.

The wide variation in the base effect observed here could stem from a number of factors, including variations in the composition of the tax base, heavy underassessment, and the level of exclusions. There are many examples of drastic underassessment in these cities, and in virtually every city there was evidence that property is assessed at a rate considerably below true market value. But the reasons for this underassessment vary widely. In some cases it is due to a conscious underassessment of property value, whereas in others it is due to infrequent and dated assessments.

Table 4-4. *Comparative Levels of Property Tax Effort*

City, year	Per capita total property taxes (dollars)	Per capita assessed value (dollars)	Assessed value as percentage of income	Taxes as percentage of value	Property taxes as percentage of income
Capital value systems					
Bogotá, Colombia, 1971	3.49	653	1.260	0.50	0.63
Cartagena, Colombia, 1972	2.76	518	2.040	0.50	1.00
Cartagena, Colombia, 1980	5.43	1,669	1.410	0.32	0.46
Jakarta, Indonesia, 1972	0.35	3	0.020	0.18	...
Kingston, Jamaica, 1971	4.75	90	0.109	0.06	...
Nairobi, Kenya, 1971	12.04	317	0.635	3.80	2.40
Seoul, Rep. of Korea, 1971	2.20	840	1.935	0.30	0.50
Seoul, Rep. of Korea, 1983	17.33	—	0.820	1.00	0.82
Manila, Philippines, 1972	14.20	1,276	2.463	1.10	2.70
Manila, Philippines, 1984	2.13	98	0.170	2.18	0.36
Lusaka, Zambia, 1972	9.60	845	5.709	1.10	6.40
Annual value systems					
Hong Kong, Hong Kong, 1973	15.20	131	0.111	11.60	1.30
Hong Kong, Hong Kong, 1985	289.44	323	0.262	8.95	2.35
Ahmadabad, India, 1972	3.75	15	0.142	24.90	3.50
Bombay, India, 1971	4.80	18	0.068	27.40	1.90
Calcutta, India, 1971	5.73	14	0.080	40.90	3.30
Singapore, Singapore, 1968	14.30	32	0.046	44.40	2.10
Singapore, Singapore, 1985	211.92	593	0.080	35.72	2.86
Tunis, Tunisia, 1971	10.00	143	0.644	18.80	4.50
Median					
Before and including 1979	5.27	137	0.640	2.45	2.00
After 1979	17.33	458	0.262	2.18	0.82

... Negligible (less than 0.10 percent).
— Not available.

Table 4-5. *Property Tax Collection Ratios in Selected Cities*

City, year	Collection ratio (percent)
Dhaka, Bangladesh, 1984	55
Bogotá, Colombia, 1972	84
Cartagena, Colombia, 1972	66
Bombay, India, 1971	82
Calcutta, India, 1971	53
Delhi, India, 1979	68
Madras, India, 1977	65
Jakarta, Indonesia, 1985	53
Dakar, Senegal, 1981	50
Kandy, Sri Lanka, 1983	75

Revenue Growth

Another important question is the adequacy of the growth of property tax revenue. This adequacy is usually measured in terms of the income-elasticity of property tax revenues, with a normative judgment often made that at least a proportionate response is desirable. Such normative statements require qualification. If the property tax were the sole source of local finances and if income were the sole determinant of public expenditure needs, then the unitary income-elasticity argument for property tax revenues might be persuasive. But local governments have recourse to other revenues, and although it may be important that total revenues grow in response to expenditure needs, it is not necessary, or even desirable, that each tax so respond. Moreover, although income growth seems a reasonable basis on which to measure revenue responsiveness, there is nothing magic about an elasticity of 1.0 or 0.8 or 1.2, since it is not at all clear how expenditure needs increase with income. Indeed, one might ask whether it would be good policy, for example, to give up some revenue-elasticity in the short run if an elastic property tax would increase the effective tax burden on the housing sector in the long run and dampen construction activity in the local housing market.

It would be incorrect, however, to ignore the implications of an income-inelastic property tax, especially where the property tax is the principal source of financing for a local government. Income growth is a significant (and elastic) determinant of the demand for public expenditure in industrial countries, and other studies suggest that it may serve as a reasonable proxy for increased wage demands by public employees. To the extent that these patterns hold true in developing countries, a property tax which responds less than proportionately to income growth may substantially reduce the flexibility of a local government to increase public service levels and may force frequent and politically unpopular adjustments to the rate and base.

In fact, the urban property tax in developing countries appears to be income-inelastic. Available data suggest that the growth in property tax revenues has lagged behind the growth in income, and in some cases behind the growth in the general price level; that is, the real property tax yield has fallen. The rates of growth in real and actual levels of property tax revenue and assessed value are described for a sample of cities in the first three columns in table 4-6. There is a wide variation in these growth rates and a normal performance is difficult to identify. Only in about half the cities, however, was there an increase in the intensity of property taxation, that is, in the effective rate.

Ideally, one would like to estimate the long-term income-elasticity of the property tax for each city, but data problems are severe. In particular, data on changes in income are not generally available. Moreover, a major conceptual problem with estimation of the income-elasticity of the property tax is the difficulty in separating the increase in revenue due to automatic growth from that due to changes in the discretionary rate or base. Nevertheless, some estimate of the responsiveness of property tax revenues to urban economic growth is an important element in tax policy planning in general, and in evaluating and adjusting the property tax structure in particular.

In each of the cities studied, some attempt was made to estimate the responsiveness of property tax revenues to growth in the local economy. Because of inadequate data on personal income, we must approximate an upper boundary on the income-elasticity of the property tax. We may derive a revenue-population elasticity, the percentage increase in property tax revenues associated with a 1 percent increase in population, which is equivalent to the income-elasticity of revenue if there has been no change in per capita income. If per capita income has increased, then the population-elasticity exceeds the income-elasticity.

As may be seen in table 4-6, nominal property tax revenues have generally grown two to three times faster than the population. This implies that there has been an increase in per capita property tax revenues, but in real terms this increase has tended to be small or negative. With respect to the cities studied here, the population-elasticity of the property tax exceeds unity in real terms only in Calcutta, Cartagena, Jakarta, and Seoul in the earlier period, and in Cartagena, Seoul, and Singapore in the later period.[23] Though adequate statistics on income growth rates are not available, it seems likely that incomes in these cities have grown at a faster rate than population and that therefore the property tax is inelastic. This conclusion of an income-inelastic revenue response is especially disturbing because we have included discretionary changes in computing revenue increases; that is, these data are an overstatement of the automatic elasticity of the system.

For some cities, income estimates are available, and it is possible to estimate the income-elasticity of property tax revenues and its three

Table 4-6. *The Growth in Property Tax Revenues and the Property Tax Base*

City, years	Annual rate of increase			Population-elasticity[a]			
	Property tax revenue	Assessed value	Prices[b]	Property tax revenue		Assessed value	
				Actual	Real	Actual	Real
Bogotá, Colombia, 1963–72	12.9	19.4	10.5	2.0	0.70	3.7	1.80
Cartagena, Colombia, 1970–72	16.5	22.5	9.0	3.3	1.40	4.4	2.50
Cartagena, Colombia, 1978–80	50.5	23.0	25.6	27.0	1.05	12.30	0.48
Hong Kong, Hong Kong, 1984–86	7.95	2.96	7.9	3.79	0.32	1.41	0.18
Ahmadabad, India, 1961–78	8.88	5.9	6.8	2.17	0.32	1.44	0.21
Bangalore, India, 1961–78	13.46	13.34	5.9	3.64	0.62	3.60	0.61
Bombay, India, 1963–72	8.0	7.2	7.1	2.2	0.20	1.9	0.02
Bombay, India, 1969–78	15.32	7.7	5.8	3.29	0.57	1.66	0.29
Calcutta, India, 1966–78	5.29	4.6	5.5	9.12	1.66	7.98	1.46
Delhi, India, 1961–81	14.61	13.41	5.9	3.14	0.53	2.9	0.49
Madras, India, 1967–77	13.98	9.34	6.1	4.98	0.81	3.32	0.54
Jakarta, Indonesia, 1970–73	120.7	—	13.1	33.6	2.56	—	—
Kingston, Jamaica, 1969–73	6.9	4.7	5.4[c]	2.6	0.47	1.7	0.30
Seoul, Rep. of Korea, 1963–72	38.0	31.0	12.0	4.2	2.50	3.4	1.90
Seoul, Rep. of Korea, 1981–83	16.5	—	5.3	5.5	1.04	—	—
Manila, Philippines, 1974–84	13.8	8.4	18.4	3.8	0.21	2.33	0.13
Singapore, Singapore, 1983–85	12.29	8.99	1.5	10.24	6.69	7.49	4.90
Tunis, Tunisia, 1966–72	4.8	6.8	3.6	1.2	0.30	1.7	0.80
Lusaka, Zambia, 1966–72	16.3	14.8	6.8	1.2	0.60	1.1	0.50
Median							
Before 1979	13.7	9.3	6.5	3.2	0.62	2.90	0.50
1979	12.3	8.4	6.6	3.8	0.68	2.3	0.18

— Not available.

a. Percentage increase in property tax revenues (assessed value) per 1 percent increase in population.

b. The annual increase in price is on a nationwide basis taken from IMF (various years, b) except as otherwise noted.

c. Actual rate of price increase for city.

components (again including discretionary changes). The base-elasticity measures the responsiveness of assessed property value to income changes. The rate-elasticity measures the responsiveness of tax collections to changes in the assessed property value. The collection rate-elasticity indicates the responsiveness of tax collections to changes in tax liabilities. The first component therefore indicates the extent to which property tax revenues respond to changes in the economic base of the city (that is, income) because of changes in the assessed-value base. The second component shows the extent to which increases in assessed value are actually translated into property tax collections, reflecting three factors: the built-in elasticity of a given rate structure, the effect of changes in the rate structure which have occurred during the period of measurement, and changes in collection efficiency. The third component isolates the impact of collection efficiency on changes in property tax collections.

Analysis of these components, as reported in table 4-7, indicates an income-inelastic property tax in most cities, even if discretionary changes

Table 4-7. *Estimated Income-Elasticity of Components of the Property Tax in Selected Cities*

City, years	Elasticity			Total income-elasticity
	Base-[a]	Rate-[b]	Collection rate-[c]	
Bogotá, Colombia, 1962–72	0.71	1.06	1.03	0.77
Cartagena, Colombia, 1961–72	0.70	1.15	—	0.81
Ahmadabad, India, 1961–71	—	0.94	—	—
Ahmadabad, India, 1961–78	—	—	—	0.81
Bombay, India, 1961–71	—	—	1.17	—
Bombay, India, 1969–78	—	—	0.67	0.83
Calcutta, India, 1960–71	—	1.43	0.56	—
Calcutta, India, 1966–78	2.50	0.26	0.38	0.65
Delhi, India, 1966–73	—	—	0.68	—
Delhi, India, 1961–81	1.04	0.98	1.02	1.02
Madras, India, 1961–71	—	—	0.59	—
Madras, India, 1967–77	1.15	0.84	1.20	0.97
Kingston, Jamaica, 1961–72	—	2.33	—	—
Seoul, Rep. of Korea, 1968–71	—	0.89	—	—
Manila, Philippines, 1974–84	—	2.12	1.00	—
Tunis, Tunisia, 1962–72	—	1.56	—	—

— Not available.

a. The base-elasticity is the percentage change in assessed value divided by the change in income.

b. The rate-elasticity is the percentage change in actual tax collections divided by the percentage change in assessed value.

c. The collection-rate-elasticity is the percentage change in actual tax collections divided by the percentage change in tax liability.

are counted. The primary source of growth appears to be the rate-elasticity, likely because of the influence of increases in the statutory rate. These results square with Dillinger's (1988a: 6–8) analysis of the property tax performance in eleven developing countries in the 1980s: seven showed a real decline in property tax revenues.

Property Tax Administration

That the property tax is difficult to administer is an often lamented fact in industrial as well as developing countries. The problems are particularly severe in developing countries because of a shortage of skilled staff and because records of landownership and property transfers are often notoriously bad. Yet urban property values are growing rapidly, and local governments have little option but to make the most of the property tax. It should not be surprising, therefore, that some notable improvements have been made in administering the local property tax in some cities of developing countries.

The administrative constraints to improving the fairness and revenue productivity of the property tax lie in all four facets of property tax administration: identification of property site and ownership, record keeping, assessment, and collection. Reforms that attempt to improve any one aspect without considering the other three are not likely to be successful. Indeed, when the poor revenue performance of the property tax is attributed to administrative shortcomings, the reference may be to any or all of these four areas.

As is discussed below, however, it is difficult to know where to start. Most attempts at reform begin with either property identification or valuation, but Dillinger (1988a) argues that the best place to begin is with collections.

Discovery and Determination of Property Ownership

The problems of identifying ownership and assembling a complete enumeration of properties are perhaps the greatest constraints to efficient administration of the property tax. The basis of a good property tax practice is a full fiscal cadastre. This would involve describing and defining boundaries for every property (cadastral maps), establishing ownership or taxpayer liability,[24] valuing the land, and if necessary describing and valuing all improvements on the land. An estimated 20–40 percent of all urban households in developing countries are living on land to which neither they nor their landlords have legal title. In many cities the figure is much higher (Mayo, Malpezzi, and Gross 1986: 192).

The difficulty of the task is compounded even further because of the poor quality of available information on ownership and sales values. Property title records are in poor shape in developing countries, and a search and interview process to establish ownership for every plot is a very expensive undertaking. Some governments have tried to get around the problem of determining ownership by requiring self-declarations (for example, Guatemala, the Philippines). Such programs do not give the clear-cut results that one would hope for, because of a number of complications: disputes among heirs over ownership, how to treat declarations on occupied properties in illegal and squatter settlements, uncertainties about ownership in regions of land reform, different declared values for family-owned properties, and so forth. One result of required self-declarations in the Philippines, for example, was a large number of duplicate ownership claims (Wasylenko, Bahl, and Holland 1980).

The preparation of cadastral maps is expensive, especially if full aerial surveys are necessary, but these maps are essential to successful valuation and collection. Indeed, the first step toward improved property tax administration is to prepare or update the tax maps. Starting with partial and dated cadastral maps—or better yet, with existing aerial photographs—this procedure establishes (by field survey) a complete inventory of all real property and assigns to each parcel a unique property identification number. This system provides a simple means to keep track of all parcels and to link assessment, billing, and property transfer records. Even this process—which includes no valuation—is expensive; 1980 estimates for the Philippines placed the cost of tax mapping at between $1.30 and $2.60 per parcel, excluding the cost of any aerial photographs (Wasylenko, Bahl, and Holland 1980). Estimates as of 1984 were that the cost per parcel was $2.75, including the assigned overhead cost of the project (Dillinger 1988a: 21). As a result of this relatively high cost and the management and training problems, tax mapping was carried out by only about 20 percent of all Philippine local governments.

The Philippine tax mapping exercise, because it addressed only one phase of the problem of property tax administration, did not necessarily improve the revenue productivity of the property tax. Wasylenko, Bahl, and Holland (1980) studied a sample of 19 tax-mapped municipalities in the Philippines and drew the following conclusions: (a) the total number of parcels increased by more than 10 percent in 11 of the 19 mapped communities, decreased in 4 (because of the removal of duplicates) and remained essentially unchanged in 1; (b) collection efficiency increased in 11 of the 19 but decreased in 8; and (c) assessed value increased in 11 of the 14 for which suitable data were available for analysis. A comparison of 18 mapped with 18 nonmapped but otherwise roughly comparable municipalities showed that the average collection efficiency was 62 percent among the mapped and 57 percent among the unmapped. Yet in 10 of the comparisons, collection efficiency was higher in the nonmapped jurisdiction. Tax mapping may be an important first step to improved property tax administration, but it is only one step in a process. In a later review of the Philippine project, Dillinger (1988a: 46) reports that revenues in the municipalities involved remained stagnant because the project "did not address problems in collection administration and enforcement. In many jurisdictions, reductions in collection efficiency more than offset increases in assessments."

Record Keeping and Records Management

The inadequacy of property tax records is a large problem for administering property tax systems in developing countries. The problem may go back to an incomplete tax roll or inadequate ownership information, but it may also be due to dated information, duplicate records, poor or out-of-date information on improvements, or simply a poor method of maintaining and filing the information. Underlying this problem is a lack of attention by the government responsible and a lack of coordination among the local, state, and central government offices involved.

As a rule, there is an absence of coordination between the office of the assessor, the registrar of deeds, those handling building permits, the public utilities providing services, and the office handling property transfer stamps. It follows that information on changes of ownership, sale prices, and new construction is not recorded promptly by the assessor. Resolution of this problem of coordination lies mostly with the central government, because the office of deeds registration is usually part of a central ministry. Local governments sometimes station an officer in the land registry office to improve the flow of information, but there still remain the problems of the quality of information on deeds and the underdeclaration of sales values. The resolution of all these problems will generally require action by the central government. The problem may reflect the low priority which central governments have assigned to strengthening the local property tax. If that is so, even centralized assessment will not improve matters.

The local government is better able to enforce building permits and regulations and make sure that new improvements are reported to the assessor's office. Improvements require policing to determine that building permits are being obtained and that files describing improvements are being updated. Most local governments simply do not have the staff to carry out such a task, and, as a result, improvements are typically assessed well below their market values.

Brazil has made an attempt to use cross-referencing of information to improve property tax assessment. A system has been developed that requires any approval of subdivision, building or occupancy, permit, or registration of title to be reported directly to the office of the assessor. Brazil's experience with cross-referencing, however, has been somewhat disappointing (Dillinger 1989). In part this is because many of the changes above occur outside the systems of formal permits and registrations—either legally or in violation of the law. Another problem is that the various government agencies are either uncooperative or inefficient in their record keeping.

The organization and handling of the records present other problems.

Procedures for updating are often poor; the design of the records is sometimes inadequate (for example, in Grenada the records were filed alphabetically by owner's name rather than by parcel identification number); quite often all reports are handled manually; and generally not enough clerks are assigned to the job, and they may be unskilled, and have little incentive to carry out a more efficient operation.

Local governments may deal with the records problem in three stages, depending on the level of sophistication of their present system. First, the existing tax records can be sorted manually by neighborhood, duplicates can be eliminated, and some coordination with valuation, billing, and collecting can be established. This option is likely to be most attractive to smaller local governments and to some larger places not yet ready to overhaul their records system. A second stage of reform involves redesigning the format and the content of the information contained on the cards and assigning each parcel an identification number. At this stage, the fiscal cadastre could be updated and a linkage could be established with the titles office to obtain updated information on sales prices. A third level of reform is to computerize the system. This last level is essential, particularly for large cities, but requires specialized technical expertise, careful planning and implementation, and sufficient financial resources. Where these ingredients are absent (as they were, for example, during the 1970s in Bogotá), computerization of property records can cause endless confusion in cadastral administration and property tax collection (Linn 1981). The advent of microcomputers, however, has greatly reduced the problems of computerization and has brought the possibility of efficient and inexpensive computerized record keeping even to small local governments.

Assessment

The largest problems in administering assessments fall under the headings of inadequate staffing, the poor quality of basic information for the valuation process, and the political obstacles to regular reassessment. Qualified valuers are in short supply in nearly all countries, even in the largest cities. In the public sector, wages may be relatively low because of civil service salary schedules, and valuers are often bid away by much more lucrative salaries in the private sector. The shortage of qualified assessors is a story told in nearly every developing country.

Governments might take a number of actions to deal with the staffing problem. The most obvious is to move appraisers out of the civil service schedule so as to offer competitive salaries. This action would produce such a large return in revenue that it is likely to be one of the most lucrative investments open to local governments. It might work for some of the larger cities, but not for all local governments in the nation. Another approach would require something akin to centralized assessment and a centralized training of assessors. A secondment system, whereby senior valuers do a substantial amount of the training, has worked with reasonable success in the Philippines. Yet another approach is to alter the property tax system to make the appraisal job less demanding. Excluding the valuation of improvements can substantially lighten the work load of the valuation staff.

There are problems with the basic data inputs and their use in constructing an assessment manual and instructions. Assessment under all systems is notional; that is, it attempts to determine the value of a property in the market. Yet all systems must rely on some objective evidence in reaching decisions about property values. Unfortunately, the basic data are often badly flawed. In the case of annual value systems, rent receipts may be falsified, or under-the-table payments known as "key money" may be involved if rent control ordinances are in force. The situation is as bad for records of property sales values, because of intrafamily transactions and because sales values may be consciously understated to avoid property transfer and capital gains taxes. The response to these data problems in most developing countries has been to use a combination of sales data and opinions of real estate agents, bankers, and assessors in establishing values or rents. Time may sort out some of the problems. With continuing urbanization, more impersonal or arms-length transactions, greater use of bank mortgage financing, and a tax system that provides incentives for buyers and sellers to state property sales amounts correctly, property sales records may become the more accurate reflections of market values that they are in industrial countries.

The data problems inherent to valuing improvements are the most severe. The valuation is based on estimates of construction costs and building materials, often gathered from the private sector. In most of the cities surveyed here, there did not seem to be a systematic approach that used averaging or formulas, but rather the judgment of assessors was used in developing the manual for assessing improvements. In principle, however, there is no good reason why the appropriate central government ministry could not construct and maintain a reasonably accurate schedule of construction costs.[25]

One important determinant of the accuracy of assessed value and the revenue productivity of the property tax is the frequency of reassessment. Countries and cities vary in their statutory requirement for reassessment, but generally the law states that properties must be reassessed every three to five years. In fact, however, because of the scarcity of assessors and other difficulties of frequent reassessment, the cycle tends to be much longer, more on the order of five to ten years. This is the primary explanation of the low buoyancy of property tax revenues, since in the absence of reassessments the only way for the property tax base to grow is for newly improved properties to be added to the tax roll. Indeed, in the presence of inflation, assessed property values tend to decline in real terms and, even more important, so does the real value of property taxes collected on existing properties. This sets up an unfortunate downward ratchet effect, since property taxpayers get accustomed to the gradual decline in their real tax burden. Thus they will object to a revaluation of their properties and to the resulting sharp upward jump in their tax burdens, even if such a reassessment does no more than reestablish the original value of property and property tax. In the face of such opposition, local authorities often do not find it possible to maintain the real value of their property tax rolls, let alone keep up with the actual increase in real property values.

One solution to this problem, of course, is to carry out regular revaluations. Since administrative costs and political opposition are likely to prohibit this solution, an alternative measure must be found to maintain the real value of property tax burdens and collections between reassessments. One approach is to increase the nominal tax rate between reassessments and roll it back at the time of reassessment, thereby eliminating large jumps in property tax liability. Periodic reassessments would then be used more to maintain accuracy in the relative values of properties than to reestablish tax burdens after long periods of erosion (Bahl and Schroeder 1983d).

Although such explicit and flexible use of the property tax rate would seem to have much to recommend it, it has not been frequently applied in the cities of developing countries (exceptions are Lagos and Nairobi). There are three main reasons for this failure. First, local governments are usually restricted by central and state governments in their liberty to adjust property tax rates. Second, increases in the property tax rate require explicit policy actions which are politically difficult for any level of government. Third, rate increases between revaluations would introduce horizontal inequities to the extent that the values of all properties in the area would not increase at the same rate.

An alternative approach to indexation has been taken in Brazil. Between 1980 and 1987, the inflation rate averaged 160 percent and valuations were indexed to maintain the buoyancy of the property tax. Municipalities were permitted to make increases in valuations, without physical inspection of properties, with the approval of the municipal council; or, the mayor could make these adjustments directly so long as the increase did not exceed the inflation index for treasury bonds (Dillinger 1989). A similar indexing procedure has been followed in Chile and Colombia.

Collection

The last step in administering the property tax, collection, may present the most difficult problems because costs are high and collection efficiency often low. As described above, collection rates (the ratio of collections to collectibles) of less than 75 percent are not at all uncommon.[26] Data problems notwithstanding, these low rates of collection are probably a good indication of the situation. The source of the problem may lie with an inadequate collection procedure, with the structure of the tax itself, with an inadequate set of penalties necessary to enforce the tax, or with the inducements necessary to stimulate collection.

In many cities problems with collection procedures often grow out of a shortage of skilled staff in the treasurer's office. Any number of other problems have been cited: poor coordination between the assessor's and treasurer's offices, no follow-up mailings or field visits to major delinquents, records which do not easily permit an identification of delinquents, and of course inadequate records of property ownership.

High collection costs and low collection efficiency might also be due to the property tax structure. If the tax is thought to be unfair because of horizontal inequity, taxpayers' resistance increases. For example, the high dispersion of assessment ratios was seen as a partial explanation of Jakarta's ability to collect no more than 30 to 40 percent of residential property tax liabilities in the early 1970s (Lerche 1974). In addition, where low-valued parcels are not exempt from the tax base, collection costs may be quite high. In the case of Jakarta, for example, there was a very high concentration of the property tax base: 69 percent of taxpayers accounted for 11 percent of the base, and 7 percent of the taxpayers accounted for 63 percent of the base (Linn, Smith, and Wignjowijoto 1976). Such concentrations and equity objectives have led some cities to exempt low-valued properties from the base. For example, in 1972 Seoul exempted properties with a value less than $300, in 1974 Abidjan exempted properties with an annual rent less than $650, and in the early 1970s Lusaka exempted all squatter settlements.

Two final collection problems are a lack of enforcement and the absence of adequate incentives for prompt and full payment. There are some successes to report in solving these problems, but also many failures. Governments in developing countries have not vigorously exercised their powers to impose heavy penalties on property tax delinquents. In some cases the penalties are adequate but not enforced, in other cases they are quite inadequate. Cash penalties are frequently too low to be effective. For example, the penalty rate in the Philippines (2 percent per month to a maximum of 24 percent) was less than the return on private investments (Bahl, Holland, and Linn 1983), and there has been a poorly enforced lump sum penalty charge of 5 percent in Jakarta (Linn, Smith, and Wignjowijoto 1976). Central governments are hesitant to move to the stiffer penalties (for example, sale of property at auction) for political reasons and also because lengthy court action may be involved. The lack of a special court for the local authority cases has been cited as a serious impediment in Lagos and Nairobi, since the regular courts are unable to dispose speedily of appeals or tax enforcement actions such as expropriation. In court actions, there inevitably arises the problem of determining ownership and the long delay which the local government may face in getting its money. Because of these delays, some Indian cities have in the past negotiated the amounts due (Bahl 1975; Bougeon-Maassen 1976). If contested taxes have to be paid before a court ruling (with the payment refundable), the local government is placed in a much more comfortable position (Mohan 1974). In Anambra State, Nigeria, property tax cases have been dismissed for want of a judge to try the case (Dillinger 1988a: 35).

Other enforcement mechanisms that do not require court action might be effective. In Tehran, where in past years the collection record was good, the electric company cut power to owner-occupied or nonresidential properties that fell two months in arrears. City councils have attached rents in Nigeria (Orewa 1966). Finally, moral suasion is sometimes used: the names of tax delinquents are posted in public places or announced in the news media (Bahl and Schroeder 1983d). One difficulty which inhibits enforcement is that property taxes generally are not levied on the property but on the owner; that is, the tax is in personam, not in rem. This means that the owner must be located and brought to court in order to institute proceedings for nonpayment of taxes. This greatly complicates the collection of the tax, particularly where ownership titles are contested or unclear.

Another possibility to increase collection rates is to provide a set of positive inducements. In many countries (Colombia and the Philippines are examples), cash discounts have been provided for early payment. Unfortunately, these discounts often are well below the market rate of interest. Bangladesh, Indonesia, and Thailand have provided direct incentives to the collectors—village chiefs, neighborhood leaders, and so forth—who participate in the collection process on a commission basis. Alternatively, the incentive might be given to the local government. In the Philippines, 10 percent of the total amount collected has been returned to the neighborhood council (*barangay*) budget. Finally, periodic amnesties have been used in Bogotá, probably to the extent of becoming so expected that the effectiveness of all penalties is reduced (Linn 1980b).

Conclusions

There are three important conclusions here. One is that property tax structure and administration go hand in hand and cannot easily be separated when undertaking a reform. A second is that there are four critical aspects to administration of the property tax—property identification, record keeping, assessment, and collection. Unless all are considered, administrative reform will not necessarily produce a "better" property tax. Both of these conclusions point to the need to view the property tax as a system rather than as a set of independent activities.

A third conclusion is that it is important to monitor and if possible quantify the importance of the property tax in order to plan for effective reform. The major weaknesses in the administrative practices of property taxation can be identified by quantitative measurement of such components as assessment, exemptions, and collection. This approach was developed and applied in Bogotá (Linn 1980b). For 1972, it was found that a ratio of effective to statutory property tax rate of 0.50 was accounted for by a collection ratio of only 0.68, an exemption ratio of 0.87, and an assessment ratio of 0.85. In other words, the 50 percent shortfall of the actual average property tax rate from the legal rate was accounted for by the combination of a 32 percent shortfall in collection below tax liabilities, exemption of 13 percent of all assessed property value, and an underassessment of 15 percent. The low income-elasticity of property tax revenues of 0.77 between 1961 and 1972 was, however, accounted for mainly by the relatively low income-elasticity of market value (0.67). Administrative practices (in particular collection efficiency), exemptions, and assessment practices actually improved slightly over time as indicated by greater than unitary elasticities of tax collections to tax liabilities, taxable assessed value to total assessed value, and total assessed value to market value of property (Linn 1980b). In Bogotá, therefore, administrative practices of property taxation, and especially collection efficiency, left considerable room for improvement. But permanent improvements in the revenue buoyancy should, according to this analysis, not be expected from improved tax administration.[27]

Property Tax Reform

In concluding this chapter, a number of broad findings about property tax policy and administration can be summarized, drawing for completeness on the findings of the next two chapters which, respectively, elaborate on the equity and allocative features of the property tax. There are, we think, some universal lessons about the property tax, irrespective of country setting. There are also some practices that are neither inherently good nor bad, but require countries to make choices and face up to the costs involved.

The Time Horizon

The most important consideration in determining the effect of property tax policy is the time horizon of the decisionmaking process. In the short run, the incidence of the property tax will tend to be neutral; that is, there will be no substantial effect on the allocation of resources or the distribution of income. In the longer run, the allocative and distributive effects are likely to be more substantial, depending on the property tax rate applied.

Whether the short-run or long-run considerations are more important in formulating policy depends on three considerations. The first is the elasticity of factor supplies and the speed of adjustment in response to changes in the property tax. Obviously, property tax effects will vary directly with the elasticity of supply of land and capital and the speed of adjustment. These parameters will differ from country to country, how-ever, and too little is known on this matter. The second consideration is the discount rate of the policymaker, which will determine his tradeoff between policy effects in the near term and in the future. For example, a high discount rate will lead to a preference for a reform that will gen-erate substantial and immediate revenues, even though its long-term effects may be to increase the regressivity of the local tax system. It is important to note in this connection that fiscal planners the world over are notoriously shortsighted.

The third consideration is that the speed with which the allocation of resources adjusts in response to policy depends on past policy. If public policy signals in the past have switched frequently (for example, if policy reversals are the rule rather than the exception), then the private sector is likely to respond more slowly to public incentives. This is because a quick response is likely to be more costly and more risky to the private entrepreneur. For example, a new amnesty is not likely to draw in de-linquent taxpayers if the granting of amnesty has been a frequent practice, and the imposition of new punitive measures for property tax delin-quency is not likely to be effective if old measures were not enforced.

Multiple Objectives

Besides intertemporal tradeoffs as reflected in the need to discount the effects of future policies on particular objectives, choices also have to be made between multiple and sometimes conflicting objectives. The discussion in this and the subsequent two chapters on property taxation makes it clear that there is no magic in property tax policy. The raising of substantial revenues from property taxation will have some undesir-able effects on land use and will burden some taxpayers more than others. This will set in motion a cry for property tax reform and will inevitably lead to piecemeal adjustments to "correct" some of the inequities. These usually well-intentioned adjustments often ignore side effects and lead to further conflict.

There are many examples of this problem. Equity-minded reformers in Peru and Taiwan (China) promoted the application of a progressive rate structure of the total value of an individual's landholdings. Although the burden of the tax may well have fallen heavily on large landowners, this provision encouraged an uneconomic splitting of landholdings in Peru (Greytak 1983) and tax evasion in Taiwan (China) (Harris 1979). Perhaps the principal form of this problem is the tradeoff introduced when the property tax rate is raised—that is, revenue yield is raised—at the possible cost of dampening housing investment.

Sometimes the problem of conflicting goals arises because so many independent actors are involved in formulating property tax policy that it is not always seen as a "system." In particular, the assessment function is often separate from the rate-making and general administrative activities. It is not uncommon to find the local council responsible for establishing taxable values and the treasurer's office responsible for collection, record keeping, and enforcement of penalties. Many problems can arise from such a division of responsibility. For example, in Ahmadabad a graduated rate structure was meant to increase progressivity, but owner-occupied properties were given a preferential assessment and the progressivity effects were thus offset.

There are two important messages here. First, the fact that the property tax constitutes a system needs to be recognized, and rate, base, and administrative decisions need to be made in a coordinated way. Independent decisions about tax structure and administration are as likely to be offsetting as reinforcing. Second, it needs to be recognized that all reforms will not satisfy all objectives. In making policy decisions, it is therefore necessary to assign relative weights to the policy goals so that they can be directly compared and traded off against each other. As important as this may be, it is easier said than done because of problems with measuring the direct tradeoffs between the efficiency and equity implications of various property tax reforms.

Initial Conditions and Transition Costs

Much of this discussion has been cast as if one could start with a clean slate and compare alternative property tax systems. In fact, most countries and cities already have some kind of property tax system, and it is crucial to consider the transition costs from one system to another. Existing systems have the advantage that the start-up costs have already been met. In particular, a fiscal cadastre has been set up and administrators and assessors have been trained. No less important is the fact that property owners will have already capitalized the windfall losses and gains resulting from the development of the existing property tax system. Moreover, taxpayers are familiar with the present system, and a major change will call for reeducating the public and perhaps selling the virtues of the new system. These transition costs may turn out to be quite high.

But one must consider the state of disrepair of the current property tax system. If things have deteriorated too far, the costs of reform may be almost as high as those resulting from the institution of a new system. The relevant considerations, then, are the tradeoffs between the current transition costs and the future benefits of a better system.

Two cases highlight the importance of considering initial conditions and transition costs. Jamaica, after many years of transition, adopted a universal site value tax to replace its capital value tax system, which had not been utilized effectively. Because of the virtual absence of general reassessments for approximately forty years and the resulting weaknesses in the fiscal cadastre and staff, a reform of the existing system probably would have required the same start-up costs as did the introduction of the new site value tax. Considerable efforts were necessary to overcome the political difficulties associated with the higher property taxes collected after the reform (Risden 1979). These difficulties would have been very similar, however, had the old tax system been revised to yield higher revenues. In this sense, then, Jamaica started with something analogous to a clean slate.

An apparently similar set of circumstances prevailed in Jakarta during the early 1970s. The property tax system was producing low yields and was based on an index method which required neither a fiscal cadastre nor substantial administrative skills (Linn, Smith, and Wignjowijoto 1976). Property tax experts recommended a new capital value tax on property. Two years of effort went into the preparation of a land value map and the training of a staff of valuers which, according to the experts, would have permitted a quick transition from the old to the new system and a substantial increase in revenues (Lerche 1974). Despite the existence of this detailed blueprint for reform, authorities decided to maintain the existing tax system and to upgrade its revenue performance through improvements in administration and collection. The start-up costs of the new system were apparently perceived to be too high. Since there appeared to be little disagreement about the facts in this case, the difference between the advice given by the experts and the decision of the authorities must be explained by the higher implicit discount rate used by the latter (thus weighting present costs more and future benefits less than did the experts).

This process was repeated in Indonesia ten years later, but this time the setting was right and a capital value property tax was adopted (Kelley 1986). The base is both land and improvements with a single rate of 0.5 percent. Only a short and conventional exemption list is included, and the government's discretion in giving exemption is dramatically curtailed. The real effective rate is 0.1 percent because the assessment ratio has been set at 20 percent of market value, but it may be raised up to 100 percent by presidential decree. A tax credit of up to 2 million rupiah ($2,597 in 1989) on buildings excludes most low-income and rural housing from the base.

The new property tax in Indonesia, a dramatic improvement over the old, was adopted for many reasons. There had been a chronic revenue shortage in the pre-oil period; the property tax is a central government levy in Indonesia and local government approval of a reform program is not required; the central income and sales taxes were comprehensively reformed in 1984–86; policymakers were in a mood to accept major change in the property tax; and the World Bank provided important finanical assistance in upgrading the government's evaluation and administrative capabilities.

There are many other instances of rejection of major changes in the property tax system. For example, in the mid-1970s the Kenyan government resisted a recommendation to include improvements in its site value system, and Bogotá rejected the advice of an expatriate expert to replace the existing property tax system with a land value increment tax. In both cases, there was a system that already worked toward the goals of the proposed reforms—to raise more revenue in Kenya and to improve resource allocation and equity in Bogotá. Both initiatives were rejected because the transition costs far outweighed the potential benefits.

Generalization about Property Tax Policy

For all the reasons listed so far, it is difficult to draw even broad conclusions in the evaluation of alternative property tax systems and practices. We cannot simply conclude that one country's system is better than another's. The discussion in this volume, therefore, provides an analytical framework and some quantitative methods which can be utilized to study the effects of existing or proposed property tax systems. Examples were provided where possible to illustrate the application of these approaches. Ten generalizations, however, can be helpful in formulating tax reform in cities of developing countries:

1. The property tax should be kept as simple as possible. Exemptions should be kept to a minimum and rate structures kept as uncomplicated as possible. Reform should emphasize improving the general property tax administration rather than adding special features to affect resource allocation or income distribution.

2. The property tax needs to be viewed as a system, and reforms need to be coordinated by all parties involved in structuring and administering the property tax. Decisions about assessment and collection practices, exemption policy, and rate structure design may be the responsibility of different offices but must not be made independently.

3. In general, a flat rate property tax on all real estate is not likely to be regressive in either the short or long run (see chapter 5).

4. The distribution of property tax burdens will be more progressive if the preferential treatment granted to owner-occupants is eliminated (see chapter 5).

5. The exemption of low-value properties or, better yet, granting all taxpayers a deduction from assessed value will make the property tax more progressive, favor low-income housing development, and ease property tax collection problems. The revenue costs will be small (see chapter 5).

6. On balance, it is preferable to tax land more heavily than improvements. Therefore, if increased revenues are to be raised from an existing capital value tax, it is worth considering raising the tax rate only for land, rather than for land and buildings alike (see chapter 6).

7. If a special tax is to be levied on vacant urban land to speed up its development, this tax instrument should be explicitly linked to a land

use development plan rather than applied indiscriminately to all vacant property in the metropolitan area (see chapter 6).

8. A property transfer tax is likely to interfere with the efficient operation of urban land markets and should be replaced by more effective administration, and possibly a higher rate, for the general property tax (see chapter 6).

9. A land value increment tax is not likely to be effectively administered in developing countries. Efforts to raise property tax revenues would do better to focus on improving the administration of existing property tax systems (see chapter 6).

10. The four facets of property tax administration—identification of properties, record keeping, assessment, and collection—must all be improved to make the property tax more productive. Improving collection efficiency alone will increase revenues in the short run but will not provide the broader base necessary for long-run growth.

5 The Incidence of Urban Property Taxation

PROPOSALS TO REFORM the property tax in developing countries have tended to emphasize possibilities for improving revenue performance. The distributive and allocative effects of the tax have usually been considered only in very general terms. Indeed, it would be unusual to find a thorough analysis of these effects in any study of tax reform by urban governments in a developing country. Yet the issues—the equity of the tax and its effects on urban land use—are of great importance in cities of developing countries.

The question "Who pays the property tax?" is very much related to the question "How does the property tax affect the allocation of resources?" Indeed, the extent to which an owner of real estate can shift the property tax burden to others depends on his ability and willingness to reshuffle his asset portfolio. As a result, the relative use of land, capital, and labor may change because of property taxation, as may factor and commodity prices, and thus the distribution of wealth and income.

This chapter focuses on the question of who pays the property tax. We begin with a review of the theory of the incidence of the property tax, drawing extensively on Linn (1979). At least a rudimentary understanding of this theory is required to interpret the results of previous studies of the incidence of the property tax in developing countries. We then turn to an analysis of the distributive effect of a number of policies for adminstering the property tax in order to emphasize that the incidence of the tax is very much influenced by practices in developing countries. We conclude with a brief summary of empirical results.

Conventional Theories of Incidence

The fundamental question regarding the incidence of the property tax is how the tax burden, that is, the ratio of tax payments to personal income, varies with income. If the tax burden is higher for individuals (or families) with higher incomes than for those with lower incomes, then the tax is progressive. If the reverse is true, then the tax is regressive. It is neutral or proportional if the tax burden is the same for all income groups.

The incidence of the property tax is a difficult and interesting problem for study because those who are legally required to pay the tax collector may not ultimately bear the burden of the tax. The taxpayer may simply adjust his demand for or supply of the taxed asset and thereby shift the tax onto someone else. For example, landlords may reduce the supply of rental units, thus increasing the price of rental housing and passing some of the tax burden on to renters. Moreover, to the extent that the after-tax rate of return on investment in housing is reduced as a result of the tax on property, capital owners may reduce maintenance of and new investment in housing and shift their resources to other uses, reducing the rate of return on capital in those uses also, and thus passing some of the burden of the property tax on to all owners of capital. Alternatively, if capital is perfectly mobile internationally, and thus its (post-tax) rate of return is fixed, the capital outflow associated with higher property taxes will reduce the marginal product of labor and the wage rate and thereby pass some of the burden of the tax on to labor. In effect, therefore, the property tax burden may be divided among the owners of taxed land and buildings, all owners of capital, labor, consumers of housing services, and consumers of all goods and services.

Analyzing the incidence of the tax therefore involves two tasks. The first is to determine which groups—land and capital owners, renters, consumers in general, and labor—bear what portion of the tax. The second is to locate the position of these groups in the distribution of income in order to compute the distribution of tax burdens across income groups and thus establish whether the tax is progressive, regressive, or neutral. The theory of tax incidence has addressed mainly the first task in attempting to determine the appropriate tax shifting assumptions, whereas empirical studies of tax incidence usually start out with a set of shifting assumptions and then attempt to trace out the distribution of the tax burden across income groups.

Two dominant sets of shifting assumptions have been debated in the literature on incidence (for a review of the history of this debate, see Aaron 1975 and McLure 1979). The "traditional view" has assumed a fixed supply of land and a perfectly elastic supply of capital. Its conclusion is that a tax on land is borne by the owners of land because they cannot adjust the amount of land which they own, whereas a tax on improvements is borne by the consumers because owners of improvements as a group will reduce the amount of capital embodied in improvements until their post-tax rate of return is restored to its previous level. The resulting reduction in the supply of buildings and improvements will drive up the cost to consumers of goods and services (including housing) that use taxed improvements and structures as an input. According to the traditional view, the incidence of the property tax therefore depends on the distribution of landownership across income groups and on the extent to which the propensity to consume goods and services using taxed improvements and structures in their production varies with income levels.

In contrast to the traditional view, the "new view" of incidence assumes that all factors of production, including capital, are perfectly inelastic in supply in the country as a whole but that capital is perfectly mobile within a country. Under these conditions, any uniform tax on all capital and land in a country will be borne entirely by owners of capital and land, because as a group they cannot shift the use of the taxed assets (Mieszkowski 1972). The incidence of the property tax, then, depends on the distribution of capital and landownership across income groups.

In principle, the new view makes allowance for the fact that property tax rates are not uniform throughout the country. It postulates that, because of perfect mobility, capital will move from high-tax to low-tax areas and activities until after-tax returns to capital are equalized. As a result, the after-tax rate of return is lowered for capital in all its uses and in all regions. But since the capital movements induce changes in relative factor use and therefore in factor returns, and since output prices may be expected to rise for locally traded goods in the high-tax area, tax rate differentials are shifted to land, labor, or consumers in the high-tax areas or activities. In practice, most analysts have judged it extremely difficult, if not impossible, to determine the net countrywide incidence of these so-called "excise effects" (Aaron 1975; Netzer 1974).

A synthesis of the traditional and the new views has emerged in recent years, which may be called the "new orthodoxy." According to this approach the traditional view is appropriate in evaluating a tax change restricted to a particular jurisdiction and the new view is appropriate in analyzing a nationwide change in the effective property tax rate (Aaron 1975; McLure 1979). This synthesis follows directly from two hypotheses regarding capital mobility: (a) for the country as a whole, capital supply is taken to be fixed, as under the new view, and thus a uniform nationwide tax on property must be borne exclusively by owners of capital and land; and (b) for any individual city, capital is assumed to be in perfectly elastic supply. As long as the city's capital stock is small relative to that of the country as a whole, the rate of return on capital will remain unaffected by a tax increase that is restricted to one locality, and the tax will be passed on to other, more immobile factors or to consumers.[1]

Limitations of the New Orthodoxy

The general equilibrium theory of incidence, which underlies the new orthodoxy of property tax incidence just summarized, requires a number of simplifying assumptions: (a) capital, labor, and land are in fixed supply nationwide; (b) capital and labor are in perfectly elastic supply in any jurisdiction (perfect mobility); (c) land is in fixed supply in each jurisdiction; (d) all factor and product markets are perfectly competitive; and (e) all factors are fully employed. Some of these assumptions do not fit the industrial-country context, and even fewer seem applicable in developing countries.

The Elasticity of Aggregate Capital Supply

The new orthodoxy assumes that changes in the rate of return on capital do not affect the nation's capital stock either via international capital flows or through changes in domestic saving. Proponents of the new orthodoxy recognize that savings may respond to changes in the rate of return on capital (Boskin 1978; Tullio and Contesso 1986). It is more generally argued, however, that this is relevant only for the very long run (and thus beyond the immediate concern of economic policy), or that the savings rate is in fact not significantly influenced by the return on capital even in the long run (Aaron 1975; Friend and Hasbrouck 1983). It therefore appears safe to conclude that aggregate domestic saving is not likely to be affected substantially by variations in the rate of return on capital induced by the property tax. There is one major exception to this conclusion: the rate of saving and investment of low-income urban households. Since their saving and investment are mostly in the form of housing, property taxation can have an effect. But such households often face a low rate of property taxation, and the share of this component in total national savings is likely to be small.

Potentially more damaging to the validity of the new orthodoxy is the likelihood that, for a small country with substantial foreign investment and access to foreign capital markets, capital is internationally mobile. Under these conditions, the aggregate supply of capital cannot be assumed to be fixed even in the short run (Bird 1976a; Harris 1976; McLure 1979; Linn 1979b). If one could go so far as to assume a perfectly elastic supply of capital, then this would resurrect the traditional view as correctly applying even to a nationwide property tax; that is, the tax on improvements is passed to consumers, labor, and land. Although there is evidence that foreign investment in developing countries reacts to variations in general profitability,[2] one would go too far to assume a perfectly elastic supply of capital for any developing country. Foreign direct investment is influenced by several considerations other than the rate of return on capital—especially risk and concern for market share.[3] Moreover, it is well known that costs of foreign borrowing rise at the margin for developing countries.[4] And government controls on capital outflows limit capital movements out of the country. Since the onset of the debt crisis in the early 1980s, many highly indebted developing countries have faced, in effect, a near-perfectly inelastic supply of foreign capital.

These arguments do not go much further than to suggest that in many developing countries the elasticity of capital supply is above zero and that it is likely to be higher in the long run than in the short run, whereas in others capital may in fact be perfectly immobile internationally. Thus, much depends on the specific conditions of the country under consideration.

Elasticities of Factor Supply within a Country

The assumption that capital is perfectly mobile among activities, sectors, and regions within a country may also be inappropriate for most developing countries. Such a response of capital to differentials in property tax rates requires that the entrepreneur have perfect information regarding the differentials and the resulting differences in the rate of return. But because in developing countries there appears to be virtually no knowledge of the level of effective tax rates, even among local government officials responsible for them, it would seem difficult if not impossible for entrepreneurs to determine tax rates in different locations or for different activities. Furthermore, given the nature of assessment practices, the variation around the average effective tax rate in any jurisdiction may well be so large as to swamp any interjurisdictional differences.

Other considerations also lead to the conclusion that variations in tax rates play only a minor role in the location decisions of firms in developing countries. In evaluating projects or in making location decisions, firms frequently do not employ procedures that would allow an assessment of the differentials in rates of return induced by property taxation (Townroe 1979); and in any case, facilities and public services are often too inadequate to attract firms anywhere but in the largest cities (Richardson 1977). Furthermore, the fiscal policies followed in many developing countries cause private decisionmakers considerable uncertainty. Frequent policy reversals, uneven application of tax laws, and weak tax enforcement tend to create an environment in which entrepreneurs may perceive adjusting factor use to be potentially more expensive than just sitting tight and attempting to minimize the impact of a tax change.

In sum, differentials in the rate of return induced by variations in property tax rates between regions and cities should not be expected to affect significantly the investment behavior of entrepreneurs in developing countries. It would be more appropriate to assume that capital is internally quite immobile in response to variations in the rate of return introduced by differential increases in the property tax rate. To the extent that these observations on internal capital mobility are correct, any tax on capital, whether nationwide or local, is likely to stay put in the sector or location where it is initially imposed.

Elasticities of Factor Supply within a City

Conventional analysis of the incidence of the property tax postulates that intraurban tax differentials are mainly capitalized into land values because the supply of land is fixed and because "a metropolitan area constitutes a set of reasonably well-connected markets for labor, housing, and most other goods and services" (Aaron 1975: 44). Although U.S. studies tend to confirm this hypothesis, we found no studies of tax capitalization for developing countries. There is, however, some a priori reason to believe that the assumptions of a fixed supply of land, perfect intraurban factor mobility, and well-connected markets are much less appropriate for developing countries. If this reasoning is correct, one should expect less than full capitalization of intracity property tax differentials into land values.

The assumption of a fixed supply of land probably has its origins in a nationwide view of the property tax; that is, to a country as a whole the supply of land is fixed. At the city level, however, the assumption becomes much less convincing, particularly for developing countries. The typical inner city in the United States is hemmed into its land confines by jurisdictional fragmentation, and zoning regulations may limit the expansion of urban land use at a city's perimeter. In contrast, developing-country cities are less troubled by jurisdictional fragmentation and have fewer zoning controls regulating their expansion (see chapter 12). Although the rapid rate of expansion of these cities is not a sufficient condition to prove that the elasticity of land supply with respect to its rate of return is greater than zero, it provides at least an environment in which the supply of urban land may be expected to vary with changes in the rate of return on land as induced, for instance, by changes in the level of urban property taxation.[5]

If the rate of conversion of rural to urban land varies at the margin with the rate of return on land, a higher tax on urban property would, all other things being equal, slow the growth of the urban land area. As a result, some portion of the tax on land may be passed on to other factors or to consumers. As with capital, however, one would also err in assuming that the supply of land is perfectly elastic. The marginal costs of expansion at the urban periphery are certainly rising in the short run (and possibly even in the long run) as cities expand into areas which are costly to service. Some portion of the tax will surely be capitalized.

Intracity capital mobility has generally been assumed to be quite high, especially in industrial countries. The hard evidence to support the assumption of intrametropolitan capital mobility in response to differentials in tax rates is very weak, however, even for industrial countries (see Ihlanfeldt and Martinez-Vazquez 1987). In developing countries, matters are further complicated because capital markets appear to be segmented between the formal and informal urban sectors.

Related to this segmentation of the capital market is the segmentation in the urban housing market. For instance, in Bogotá, Vernez (1973) has observed the existence of two important submarkets between which there is little competition: the first submarket services illegal or "pirate" settlements (mainly low- and lower-middle-income), and the second serves middle- and upper-income renters and owner-occupants. The pirate submarket is characterized by a gradual or staged upgrading of residential construction, which is financed by owners. Given the isolated nature of the informal sector capital market with a fixed capital supply in the short run, the pirate settlement owners will not be able to pass the tax on to other capital owners outside the urban informal sector of the particular city, or to labor or renters. Because the pirate owners see their disposable incomes and the returns to their housing investment reduced by a property tax, however, they may slow down the speed of the phased construction or may even be forced to discontinue expansion altogether. This effect may occur quite quickly, since the savings and investment decisions are effectively identical. As a result, the pirate housing stock will be lower than it would have been otherwise, and thus prices to renters will increase. To the extent that pirate housing construction also involves nonfamily labor, labor earnings in the informal sector are likely to drop. But because the capital stock of pirate housing is also less than it would have been in the absence of the tax, the capital earnings of the entrepreneur are lower and he or she thus still bears part of the burden. These effects depend on the extent to which housing in pirate settlements is reached by the property tax, a subject we take up below.

The effects of a property tax in the formal residential sector depend in part on the elasticity of the supply of capital to that sector from the outside (either from the rest of the country or from international capital flows). To the extent that this elasticity is low, increases in the property tax rate will lead to a reduction in the rate of return on capital in the formal urban sector. This will not result in a reduction in investment activity if the elasticity of investment is low. But if capital is elastic in supply to the formal urban sector, the tax can be passed on to consumers and to labor, as in the pirate sector. To the degree that the lowest income group tends to be heavily involved in the commercial (formal) submarket as renters, they are likely to bear a considerable portion of the property tax levied on the commercial sector.

Market Imperfections

The assumption of perfect markets may also be less applicable in developing countries than in industrial countries.[6] One of the most prevalent market imperfections introduced in the urban housing market in developing countries results from rent control. If rent control is effective and an increase in the property tax cannot legally be passed on to renters in the form of higher rents, then the price of housing is fixed and the incidence of a tax on housing may be treated as if housing were a traded commodity whose price is determined in national or international markets. This would imply that the tax is borne by property owners. If, however, the tax increase can legally be reflected in higher rents and rents are initially kept below the competitive market-clearing level, then owners can pass the tax increase on to renters in the form of higher rents. In that case the burden would fall squarely on the housing consumers.

Before taking these conclusions for granted, however, the analyst must carefully investigate whether rent controls are effectively applied. In Indian cities, for instance, it has been observed that black market payments, or special payments at the outset of a rental agreement (for example, for furnishings), tend to render ineffective the legally imposed rent ceilings (see chapter 4). As a result, the rental market may actually operate quite well, and the usual analysis of incidence applies. Other factors which might impede the functioning of urban land and housing markets are zoning regulations and monopolistic property ownership. However, research on urban land and housing markets in developing countries generally has concluded that zoning and related regulatory interventions tend to be ineffective and that monopoly conditions do not generally prevail (Dunkerley 1983; Linn 1983).

Market imperfections may also result from monopolistic conditions in commodity or factor markets. An important and widespread imperfection in developing countries results from the production of goods and services by state enterprises. In some countries these enterprises account for a significant share of GDP and are often subject to property taxation. The incidence of property taxes on state enterprises will depend on their pricing and investment policies. If their prices are fixed, then the tax cannot be shifted forward to consumers. If, furthermore, investment decisions in these enterprises are not based primarily on rate-of-return criteria—that is, if the primary objectives are social—then a change in the property tax would not induce a shift in factor use from capital to labor, and thus backward shifting to labor would not occur. Under these circumstances the public sector itself will entirely absorb the tax change. If, however, public enterprises produce nontradable commodities (for example, public utilities) and are permitted to pass on a higher property tax in the form of higher prices, then a substantial part of the tax increase (perhaps all of it) will be borne by consumers. If public enterprises are untaxed but compete with private enterprises in the production of nontraded commodities, this would dilute the impact of a change in the property tax on consumers because the taxed private firm would not be able to pass on as much of the tax as they could in the absence of public participation in production.

In summary, if the assumption of perfect competition is not applicable because of public intervention, the incidence of the property tax depends essentially on whether or not output prices are permitted to reflect changes in tax rates. If prices are permitted to change, then consumers will bear the burden of the increased tax. If prices are not permitted to change, then producers (private or public) will tend to bear the burden. Furthermore, where monopolistic conditions prevail in the commodity or labor markets, the private producer tends to bear a greater share of a change in the property tax.

A Framework for a Theory of Incidence
in Developing Countries

Because many of the assumptions which are crucial to the conventional theories of incidence are not applicable in developing countries, it is necessary to alter the conventional approach. An alternative approach that accommodates these differences is presented in figure 5-1.

Assume that there is an urban sector with two cities and a rural sector. Each sector consists of a formal and an informal subsector, and each subsector has residential and business activities. There is assumed to be no capital mobility between the formal and the informal subsectors (as indicated by the absence of any arrows linking these subsectors). But capital is perfectly mobile between the activities (business and residential) in each subsector. Labor is assumed to be fully mobile within the country, and land is assumed to be fixed in supply in the short run in the country as a whole and in each city. In the long run, however, urban land is assumed to be elastic in supply in an individual city but inelastic in the country as a whole. For the formal subsector, intersectoral and international capital mobility are less than perfect but not entirely absent. Capital is more mobile in the long run than in the short run. Each informal subsector is assumed to be entirely isolated in its capital supply from international as well as national sources.

On the basis of this framework a general theory regarding the incidence of property taxation in developing countries can be formulated. A nationwide tax increase will be treated separately from a tax increase restricted to one locality.

A Nationwide Increase in the Property Tax

In the short run, capital is likely to be inelastic in supply in the country as a whole and in each locality. In this case, the increase in the property tax is borne largely by owners of capital and land in each locality. If the tax increase is restricted to the urban sector, there are no spread effects to the rural sector.[7]

In the long run, capital is more mobile both internationally and internally within the formal sector. Assuming, furthermore, that land and labor are quite inelastic in aggregate supply, one finds that in the formal subsectors the tax on structures is shifted to land, labor, and consumers throughout the economy, whereas the tax on land will be borne largely by landowners. Taxpayers in the informal subsectors cannot pass on the tax outside their respective subsectors, given the assumed immobility of capital between the formal and the informal sectors. Within each informal subsector, property owners will bear the tax on land but shift the tax on structures to consumers, renters, and labor by reducing their investment activity.

Figure 5-1. *The Model of Property Tax Incidence*

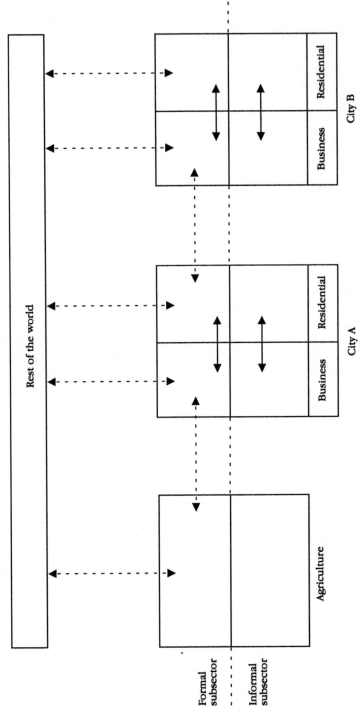

Key: ──────▶ perfect capital mobility;   - - - - -▶ limited capital mobility;   no arrow = no capital mobility.

A Localized Increase in the Property Tax

Given the short-run assumptions employed in the previous paragraphs (an inelastic supply of capital and fixed supplies of land and labor), the incidence of a tax increase by a single local government will parallel that for a countrywide increase, except that the effects will be restricted to the taxing jurisdiction.

Given long-run assumptions (elastic supplies of capital, land, and labor in the taxing jurisdiction), most of the tax on residential properties in the formal subsector will be passed on to renters with only a minor part remaining with landowners. The tax on commercial properties in the formal subsector will be shifted forward largely to consumers: to local consumers in the case of nontraded commodities, especially services, and to national consumers in the case of traded commodities for which local producers dominate the national market and are protected from foreign competition. Within the informal subsectors, the tax burden is shifted to renters and consumers.

Summary and Assessment

The framework presented above emphasizes three important points in assigning property tax incidence: (a) the distinction between nation-wide and localized tax changes; (b) the segmentation of commodity, housing, and capital markets into the formal and informal subsectors; and (c) the time frame in which the incidence of the tax is considered. For a nationwide increase in property taxes, the burden will in the short run be limited to local and subsectoral property owners; that is, it is not spread to all owners of capital. In the long run, a nationwide tax may be shifted away from capital and land to labor and consumers because of international capital mobility. For a localized change in the property tax, most of the burden would again be borne by property owners in the short term but would substantially be shifted to consumers in the long term, including not only the tax on improvements but also that on land.

The distinction between short-run and long-run incidence is thus very important. In the short run property owners largely bear the tax, and they may suffer substantial capital losses as a result of the tax change since property values are likely to be depressed. This may be demonstrated as follows. Assume a property is expected to yield an annual pretax return of $1,000 in perpetuity. Its present value in the absence of a property tax would then be equal to $10,000 if the discount rate is 10 percent. Assume then that an annual tax of $100 is levied in perpetuity; that is, there is a tax rate of 10 percent on the rental stream. If this tax is not shifted by the property owner for a period of ten years but is entirely shifted thereafter, the capitalized present value of the ten years' tax payments amount to approximately $614, or some 60 percent of the total present value of all future tax payments.[8] If the tax is borne

Table 5-1. *Percentage Share of Total Present Value of Property Tax Burden Borne by Property Owner: A Hypothetical Case*

Years borne (n)[a]	Percentage share of owner	Years borne (n)[a]	Percentage share of owner
1	9.1	11	64.9
2	17.4	12	68.1
3	24.9	13	71.0
4	31.7	14	73.7
5	37.9	15	76.1
6	43.5	16	78.2
7	48.7	17	80.2
8	53.3	18	82.0
9	57.6	19	83.7
10	61.4	20	85.1

a. Assuming the tax is fully borne by the owner for n years at a discount rate of 10 percent, applying the equation in note 8 of text.

by the owner for five (two) years, his share in the present value of the tax will be 38 (17) percent (table 5-1). These capital losses will be reflected in a temporarily lower value of the property. The lesson from this example is that property owners are likely to be affected substantially by a change in the property tax rate, even if they eventually are able to shift the burden of the annual tax payment to others. It is not surprising, therefore, that property owners tend to object vigorously to increases in tax rates.

Empirical Estimates of Incidence

The heavy reliance on property taxation by local governments in industrial and developing countries alike has often been lamented on grounds of regressivity. This concern comes partly from an intuitive feel that property taxes are regressive and partly from studies that have confirmed this intuition. In this section we review a number of studies of the incidence of the property tax in developing countries to determine whether, and under what assumptions, they confirm or disprove the common notion that the property tax is regressive.

A number of these studies are summarized in table 5-2. For purposes of comparison, estimates for the United States are also included. Before discussing the nature and implications of these studies, three comments are in order. First, most of the studies deal with the incidence of the property tax in the context of an analysis of the incidence of all taxes in the country on a nationwide basis. Since property taxes generally do not weigh very heavily in the overall national tax system, they are treated rather superficially in some of these studies. Second, with the exception of four studies (numbers 10, 11, 16, and 24 in table 5-2), all these analyses treat the property tax as a nationwide system rather than as city-specific

(*Text continues on page 141.*)

Table 5-2. *Summary of Studies of the Incidence of the Property Tax*

Economy, city	Year	Study number	Type of property tax	Shifting assumptions regarding tax			Elasticity of housing expenditure with respect to income	Income elasticity of consumption expenditure	Distribution of ownership		Allowance for administrative characteristics	Incidence
				On residential properties		On industrial and commercial properties			Of land and improvements	Of all capital		
				Land	Improvements							
Brazil	1976	16	Local property tax in selected cities	Tax borne by property owners		—	—	—	Presumed progressive	—	Implications of differential tax rates and exemptions are discussed qualitatively	Progressive, but not allocated by income classes
Colombia	1961	6	All property taxes, nationwide	¼ of tax is borne by owners (presumably the tax on land) ⅜ of the tax is borne by housing consumers (presumably the tax on improvements)		Tax on commercial and industrial properties is ⅜ of all tax payments and is passed on to consumers in proportion to nonfood expenditure	Unity	Slightly greater than unity	Property owners belong to highest income quartile	—	No	Slightly progressive
	1966	7	All property taxes, nationwide	⅓ (presumably tax on land) is allocated to three highest income groups (approximately 3.8 percent of population) ⅔ (presumably tax on improvements) are allocated according to nonfood expenditure			—	Slightly greater than unity	Highest 3.8 percent of income distribution	—	No	Progressive

(*Table continues on the following page.*)

Table 5-2 (continued)

Economy, city	Year	Study number	Type of property tax	Shifting assumptions regarding tax			Elasticity of housing expenditure with respect to income	Income elasticity of consumption expenditure	Distribution of ownership		Allowance for administrative characteristics	Incidence
				On residential properties		On industrial and commercial properties			Of land and improvements	Of all capital		
				Land	Improvements							
	1970	8	All property taxes, nationwide	Borne by capital owners		Borne by shareholders	—	—	—	All capital: very progressive Share capital: owned by approximately highest 15 percent	No	Very progressive
	1970	9	All property taxes, nationwide	70 percent of the tax is collected from the richest quartile; 30 percent from the second quartile			—	—	—	—	No	Very progressive
Bogotá	1970	10	Urban property tax in Bogotá	Borne by occupants in proportion to housing expenditure		Borne by consumers in proportion to nonhousing expenditure	Approximately unity	Slightly less than unity	—		No	Slightly regressive
Cali	1975	11	Urban property tax in Cali	Borne by owners	Borne by occupants in proportion to housing expenditure	Borne by consumers in proportion to nonfood consumption	Unity for owner-occupants Less than unity for renters	Approximately unity	Progressive	—	Tax rate structure, exemptions collection have progressive impact; assessment is neutral	At least neutral, probably progressive
	1975	12	All property taxes, nationwide	Borne by capital owners		Borne by shareholders	—	—	—	As for study 8	Excise effects resulting from tax rate differences (sectoral and spatial) are progressive	Very progressive

136

Country	Year		Tax	Incidence assumption						Progressivity/regressivity
Jamaica	1963	18	National and local property taxes, nationwide	Tax borne by occupants	—		—		No	Regressive, except for highest income group, which bears a relatively high burden
Korea, Rep. of (Seoul)	1970	24	Taxes on residential properties in Seoul	Entire tax borne by occupants in proportion to actual or imputed rent	—	Less than unity	—	—	Differential rate structure for land and improvements, and for different value classes	Regressive for lower income groups; neutral for middle and higher income groups
Lebanon	1968	21	Nationwide property tax	Allocated to owners according to property income	—	—	Progressive in lower income groups, then neutral	—	No	Highly progressive for lower income groups, then neutral
Malawi	n.d.	23	Nationwide property tax	Borne by owners of dwellings and real estate	—	—	Not specified	Not specified	No	Not allocated
Pakistan	n.d.	22	Nationwide property tax	Not specified	Not specified	—	Not specified	Not specified	No	Progressive
Panama	1969	14	National property tax	19 percent of tax is allocated to urban residential property and is assumed to be borne in proportion to estimated income from owner-occupied housing; 5 percent of the tax is borne by agricultural landowners	76 percent of the tax falls on business property and is borne in line with nonfood consumption	—	Not specified	Not specified	No	Progressive, except for highest two income brackets, for which it declines steeply

(*Table continues on the following page.*)

Table 5-2 (continued)

Economy, city	Year	Study number	Type of property tax	Shifting assumptions regarding tax — On residential properties — Land	On residential properties — Improvements	On industrial and commercial properties	Elasticity of housing expenditure with respect to income	Income elasticity of consumption expenditure	Distribution of ownership — Of land and improvements	Of all capital	Allowance for administrative characteristics	Incidence
Peru	1966	13	All property taxes, nationwide	Borne by property owners in proportion to actual and imputed rental incomes			—	—	All property income, except imputed rent, is assigned to persons with income greater than $1,500 a year. All reported profits, including cash rents, are assigned to the highest 0.1 percent in the income scale. Imputed rents are distributed in proportion to the value of homeownership	—	Lower than average effective tax rates for rural and low-income urban properties are mentioned	Very progressive, except for highest two income groups, for which the tax burden declines but remains above average
Portugal	1973	19	Nationwide rental tax	Tax is borne by occupants in proportion to actual or imputed rental payments		Tax on business borne by consumers of output of business sector	Not specified	Not specified	—	—	No	Neutral except for highest income group, which bears a relatively low burden

Puerto Rico	n.d.	17	All national and local property taxes, nationwide	Tax on owner-occupied properties borne by owners according to expenditure on owned dwelling Tax on rental property borne by consumers in proportion to rental payments	Tax on business land borne by owners and distributed according to dividend receipts Tax on business improvement shifted to consumers		Progressive	—	No	Slightly progressive
Turkey	1968	20	Nationwide property tax	Allocated according to housing expenditure	Greater than unity for all income groups, except the highest; less than unity for the highest two income groups	—	—	—	No	Progressive, except for highest income group, which bears a relatively low burden

(Table continues on the following page.)

139

Table 5-2 (continued)

Economy, city	Year	Study number	Type of property tax	Shifting assumptions regarding tax — On residential properties — Land	Improvements	On industrial and commercial properties	Elasticity of housing expenditure with respect to income	Income elasticity of consumption expenditure	Distribution of ownership — Of land and improvements	Of all capital	Allowance for administrative characteristics	Incidence
United States	1960s and 1970s (various years)	1	All local property taxes, nationwide	No differentiation between land and improvements / Tax on rental property, borne by tenant / Tax on owner-occupied property, borne by owner-occupant		½ passed on to consumers, ½ borne by capital owners	Less than unity	Less than unity	Progressive	Progressive	No	Regressive at lower end of income scale, progressive at top
		2	As for study 1	Tax on rental property, borne by all capital owners / Tax on owner-occupied property, borne by owner-occupant		Borne by all capital owners	—	—	Progressive	Progressive	No	Progressive, but proportional in middle income range
		3	As for study 1	Borne by all capital owners		Borne by all capital owners	—	—	Progressive	Progressive	No	As for study 2
		4	As for study 1	As for study 1		Passed on to consumers	As for study 1	As for study 1	—	—	No	Regressive
		5	As for study 1	Tax on rental property, passed on to renters / Tax on owner-occupied property, borne by owner-occupants		Borne by all capital owners	As for study 1	As for study 1	—	—	No	Regressive at lower end of income scale

— Not available.
n.d. No date.

property tax systems. As the preceding section has made clear, this has important implications for the type of shifting assumptions which are appropriate. Third, out of twenty-three studies, only five (11, 12, 13, 16, and 24) attempt to allow for administrative factors—assessment practices, rate structure, and so on—in the analysis of incidence.

Overall, these studies have used a bewildering variety of assumptions about shifting and assigning the tax burden across income classes. One group assumes that the entire tax is shifted forward to consumers (4, 10, 18, 19, 20, and 24). This set of assumptions approximates the long-run incidence of an increase in the local property tax in the framework developed above. Of the six studies cited, however, only two (10 and 24) actually deal with a local rather than a nationwide property tax. For Colombia (Bogotá), Korea (Seoul), and the United States, these studies show a regressive incidence of property taxation. For the three other countries the evidence is mixed: in Jamaica, the tax is estimated to be regressive except for the highest income group, which bears a relatively high burden. The reverse is true for Turkey, while in Portugal the tax is neutral with the exception of the highest income class, which bears a lower burden than the other income groups. The crucial determinants of the distribution of the tax burden for this set of studies are (a) the income-elasticity of housing expenditure for that part of the tax which falls on residential property, (b) the income-elasticity of total expenditure on goods and services for that part of the tax which falls on industrial or commercial property, and (c) the tax rate schedule.

There is no clear consensus on the income-elasticity of demand for housing in developing countries. Comparative evidence on housing consumption patterns in developing countries is scant. Grimes (1976) and Jimenez and Keare (1984) have concluded that the elasticity of housing expenditure with respect to current income is generally in the neighborhood of unity or slightly below. However, data from surveys of housing expenditure in Peru and the Philippines show income-elasticities of housing consumption greater than unity (1976 World Bank data for the Philippines; Webb 1977 for Peru). Mayo and Gross (1987) have recently concluded that *short-run* income-elasticities of housing demand (based on cross-sectional analysis of household behavior within cities) fall in the range of 0.31–0.88 for renters in selected cities of developing countries (the median is 0.49) and in the range of 0.17–1.11 for owners (the median is 0.46). However, the long-run income-elasticity of housing demand (based on estimates across cities and/or countries) is greater than unity. According to one of their estimates, the long-run income-elasticity for renters is 1.60; for owners it is 1.38.

There are good a priori arguments that the income-elasticity of housing expenditure will not be less than unity in developing countries, especially in large ones. The first argument is that for the poorer segments of the population food is probably the principal essential commodity, whereas

shelter, especially at the lowest levels of income, is much less of a necessity, particularly where the climate permits subsistence with minimal
shelter and where squatting reduces the monetary cost of land occupancy.[9] Second, estimates of the income-elasticity of housing expenditure may be on the low side since they usually refer to current rather
than permanent household income. Although it is doubtful that it is
appropriate to use life-cycle income in analyzing income-elasticities of
housing expenditure in developing countries for the purposes of studying
incidence (Linn 1979b), a longer time horizon than the one frequently
used in surveys of expenditure may be appropriate. As confirmed by
Mayo and Gross (1987), the use of a longer time horizon would lead to
higher income-elasticities of housing expenditure than those estimated
on the basis of current income data because of the averaging of income
fluctuations over longer time spans. In summary, the long-run income-
elasticity of housing expenditure in developing countries is not likely to
be less than unity and therefore would not imply a regressive tax on
residential properties, even where it is assumed that the entire tax is
shifted forward to the occupants.

Most empirical studies assume that the property tax burden on nonresidential properties is shifted forward to consumers of the goods and
services produced on the taxed properties. To approximate the relation
between expenditure and income on these goods and services, the income-elasticity of total consumption is frequently used. This elasticity
is generally below unity. Thus, a regressive element is introduced into
the incidence of the property tax. Since agricultural property often is
not taxed or is taxed at lower rates than urban property, however, it
would be more appropriate to assume that the tax is borne in proportion
to nonfood consumption rather than total consumption. The income-
elasticity of nonfood consumption tends to be above that of total consumption and is probably in the neighborhood of unity (Taylor and others
1965; McLure 1975a). The incidence of the property tax on commercial
properties then would be approximately neutral. The overall incidence
of the tax on residential and nonresidential properties combined is likely
to be at least neutral, and possibly somewhat progressive, if one assumes
a perfectly elastic land and capital supply and thus a complete shifting
of the tax to consumers.

In the next group of studies, four (6, 7, 11, and 14) have estimates of
incidence which apply the traditional view and thus assume that the tax
on land is borne by landowners, whereas the tax on improvements is
assumed to be shifted to consumers. These assumptions approximate the
long-run assumptions about incidence for a nationwide tax increase under
the framework suggested above except that the likely burden on labor
has been neglected. Because in developing countries the ownership of
land is likely to be quite highly concentrated among high-income
groups,[10] under this set of assumptions incidence is virtually certain to

be more progressive than for the group of estimates discussed in the preceding paragraphs. Indeed, with the exception of the Panama study (14), all estimates under this set of assumptions indicate a uniformly progressive incidence.[11]

Only two studies for developing countries (8 and 12) have attempted to apply the new view of incidence and thus assume that the entire tax burden is shifted to the owners of capital.[12] These studies find the property tax to be progressive, as is the case in the United States (see studies 2 and 3). As was argued above, the new view implies that capital is perfectly mobile domestically but perfectly immobile internationally, which is not likely for many developing countries.

Four studies (13, 16, 21, and 23) assume that the entire property tax burden is borne by property owners. This approximates the short-run assumptions about incidence and leads to a conclusion that the burden of property taxation is highly progressive. To the extent that income from real estate tends to be understated in surveys in developing countries, the property tax is probably even more progressive than found in these estimates.[13]

In sum, of nineteen studies of the incidence of the property tax in developing countries or cities, only two found clear evidence of regressivity (10 and 24). In both cases, rather extreme assumptions were made regarding the full shifting of the tax burden to consumers and occupants, and general expenditure patterns were found to be unusually income-inelastic. For the remainder of the studies, incidence varied from neutral to very progressive depending on the precise assumptions made. If the theoretical framework developed above is accepted, then these empirical studies lead to the conclusion that a proportional property tax in developing countries is likely to be very progressive in the short run and at least neutral, if not slightly progressive, in the long run. Therefore, the popular assumption that the property tax is regressive seems inappropriate for developing countries.

Distributive Effects of Structure and Administration

Most studies of the incidence of the property tax assume the application of equal rates to all properties, that is, a tax strictly proportional to property value. Yet in fact the property tax typically is not applied at uniform legal rates, and a great deal of additional variation is introduced by assessment and administrative practices. Indeed, probably more than for any other major tax, the incidence of the property tax depends on its implementation. Unless one takes account of this implementation, it is impossible to determine the distribution of tax burdens.

The features of property tax structure and administration which are relevant to the question of incidence are summarized in table 5-3 for selected cities of developing economies. Typically, these practices can be distinguished by how they affect the appraisal of property values, the

(*Text continues on page 153.*)

Table 5-3. *Structure and Administration of the Property Tax, Selected Developing-Economy Cities*

City, economy, year	Differential treatment by property value		Differential treatment by location or use		Differential treatment of land and improvements	Preferential treatment of owner-occupants	Differential collection practices	Frequency of assessments	Net effect of administrative practices on property tax incidence
	Rate structure	Assessment	Rate structure	Assessment					
La Paz, Bolivia, 1976			Higher tax on vacant urban land (P)						
Francistown, Botswana, 1974			Vacant land is taxed at rates above improved land (P)[a]		Before 1974 only land value was taxed. Since 1974 improvements are also taxed, but at a lower rate than land			Every five years (statutory and actual)	Progressive
Rio de Janeiro, Brazil, 1975			Lower rates for vacant urban land (0.3 percent) than for improved properties (1.3 percent) (R)[b]	Higher assessment ratio for vacant land (80 percent) than for improved properties (55 percent) (P)	For improved properties only, the improvements are taxed, with land exempt (R)	(In some Brazilian cities owner-occupied properties are taxed at lower rates than rental properties)			Regressive
Salvador, Brazil, 1973			Residential properties taxed at lower rate (0.7 percent) than industrial (1.0 percent) or commercial property (1.5 percent).						Progressive

Location, year				Reassessment frequency	Rate structure
São Paulo, Brazil, 1975	*Higher* rates for vacant urban land (3 percent) than for improved properties (0.7–1.5 percent) (P)	Higher assessment ratio in center of city (75 percent); lower on periphery (50 percent) (P)			Progressive
Taiwan (China), 1974	Land value tax: rates increase with assessed land value ("progressive starting values") (P)	*Higher* rate on vacant urban land (2.4 percent) than for improved properties (1.2 percent) (P). Land value tax: penalty rates for nonresidents in each city. Higher taxes on vacant land (P). House tax: higher rates for business structures	Separate tax on land (national land value tax) and improvements (local government house tax)	Land value tax: Preferential treatment for owner-occupiers in residential properties below a certain size	Progressive
Bogotá, Colombia, 1974	Exemption of low-value properties (P)	Rural property taxed at lower rates than urban property. *Higher* tax on vacant urban land (P)	Rotating revaluation by area	About every 5–8 years (unofficially)	Progressive

(*Table continues on the following page.*)

Table 5-3 *(continued)*

City, economy, year	Differential treatment by property value		Differential treatment by location or use		Differential treatment of land and improvements	Preferential treatment of owner-occupants	Differential collection practices	Frequency of assessments	Net effect of administrative practices on property tax incidence
	Rate structure	*Assessment*	*Rate structure*	*Assessment*					
Cali, Colombia, 1975	Partial or full exemption of low-value properties (P)		Rural property taxed at lower rates than urban property	Rotating revaluation by area, concentrating on high-value areas; squatter areas valued on basis of outdated mass appraisals (P)			Discount for early payment of property tax	Every 6–8 years (unofficially)	Progressive
Cartagena, Colombia, 1973	Rate *decreases* with property value (R)		Rural property taxed at lower rates than urban properties	Rapid property value growth of high-income and tourism development areas not captured (R)				1962, 1965, 1967, 1971–72	Regressive
Abidjan, Côte d'Ivoire, 1974			Vacant land, insufficiently developed land, and land owned by cooperatives are taxed at rates additional to basic property tax (P). Temporary exemptions of newly constructed properties (ten years) and of public housing (R)	Relative overassessment of properties in low-income areas (R); assessment ratio lowest for owner-occupied residential properties (20 percent), higher for rental properties (50–60 percent) and of industrial/commercial proper-		Lower assessment ratio for owner-occupied properties (R); longer exemption period for new owner-occupied property (twenty years instead of standard ten years) (R); all owner-occupied properties valued at less than $652 were permanently ex-		Annual assessment by zones, but not keeping in line with property value growth	Regressive

Hong Kong, 1974		ties (50 percent) (R) Refund of "property tax" (but not of "rates") on business property	empted; all owner-occupied housing permanently exempted from Fonds National d'Investissement surcharge (R) Owner-occupants are exempted from "property tax" but not from "rates" (R)		Regressive
Ahmadabad, India, 1973	Rates increase with assessed rental value (P)	— (In some cities in Gujarat State, vacant land is not taxed)	Preferential assessment for owner-occupier (rental properties assessed 3.5 to 5.0 times higher) (R) (similar preferential treatment in other cities of Gujarat State and in Assam State)	Every four years	

(Table continues on the following page.)

Table 5-3 (continued)

City, economy, year	Differential treatment by property value		Differential treatment by location or use		Differential treatment of land and improvements	Preferential treatment of owner-occupants	Differential collection practices	Frequency of assessments	Net effect of administrative practices on property tax incidence
	Rate structure	Assessment	Rate structure	Assessment					
Bombay, India, 1973	Rates increase with assessed rental value (P). Properties with very low rental value are exempt (P). De facto exemptions of squatters on municipal land (P)		Suburban properties taxed at lower rates. Temporary exemptions (ten years) for newly constructed small tenements					Every four years	Progressive
Calcutta, India, 1973	Rates increase with assessed rental value (P). Properties with low rental value are exempt (P)		Vacant land is exempt from taxes (R). Differential tax rates in fragmented metropolitan jurisdictions			Preferential assessment to owner-occupier at 80 percent of full imputed rental value (R)		Every six years	
Delhi, India, 1973	Rates increase with assessed rental value (P)		Higher rates for industrial and commercial properties than for residential properties			Preferential assessment of owner-occupied properties was recently abolished by court order		Every three years	Progressive
Madras, India, 1973	Rates increase with assessed rental value (P). Low-value property is exempted (P)					Informal reduction of 10–15 percent of tax liability for owner-occupants (R)		Every five years	

148

Location						
Jakarta, Indonesia, 1973		Declining assessments (by formula) with increasing distance from city center	Residential improvements are exempt	Infrequent adjustments in index system	Discounts for early payments	Progressive
Tehran, Iran, 1975	Low-value property is exempt (P)		*Higher* rates on land than on improvements	Every five years		Progressive
Kingston, Jamaica, until and 1974	Rate increases with property value (P)	Higher rates in St. Andrews Parish		Last revaluation in 1928		Progressive
Kingston, Jamaica, after 1974	Rate increases with property value (P)	Temporary reductions in site value assessments on appeal where assessed on basis of potential alternative use with higher yield than in present use	Tax on land only	Last revaluation in 1974		
Nairobi, Kenya, 1975		Lower rates for properties in certain suburban locations	All improvements exempt	Every five years (statutory); last revaluation in 1969		
Seoul, Rep. of Korea, 1973	Exemption of low-value properties (P)		Higher rates levied on improvements than on land	Annual		Progressive

(*Table continues on the following page.*)

Table 5-3 (continued)

City, economy, year	Differential treatment by property value		Differential treatment by location or use		Differential treatment of land and improvements	Preferential treatment of owner-occupants	Differential collection practices	Frequency of assessments	Net effect of administrative practices on property tax incidence
	Rate structure	*Assessment*	*Rate structure*	*Assessment*					
Korea, 1975	Property tax rate increases with size of land-holding and value of improvement (P)		Newly built factories in Seoul, Pusan, and Daegu are taxed at five times the regular rate for five years after construction		Assessment ratio is 100 percent for improvements and 60 percent for land. Range of tax rates is identical for land and improvement but varies according to *area* in former case and according to *value* in the latter				Progressive
Karachi, Pakistan, 1976	Rates increase with assessed rental value (P)					Owner-occupied properties exempt (R)			
Manila, Philippines, 1974		For residential properties, statutory assessment ratio increases with property value (P). This may be offset by effective underassessment of market value in some high-property-value areas	Differential rates in metropolitan area due to jurisdictional fragmentation and freedom of local governments to vary rates limited only by nationally legislated maximum values	Higher assessment ratio for commercial and industrial land (50 percent) than for agricultural (40 percent) and residential land (30 percent). Higher assessment ratio for improvements than on land on				To be carried out every five years	Progressive

Country, year						
Portugal, 1976	Rate increases with property value (P); partial or full exemption of low-value residential properties (P)	Rural properties taxed at lower rates than urban properties	commercial, industrial, and agricultural land (up to 80 percent). Assessment ratio varies between jurisdictions in metropolitan area	Exemption for owner-occupied properties up to higher assessed value than for rented property (R)		Progressive
Singapore, Singapore, 1974	Preferential treatment for low-value properties in certain area (P)	Property tax surcharge on foreigners. Temporary reduction in tax rate by 50 percent for twenty years on approved development projects for urban renewal	Lower rates for certain properties in suburban areas			Progressive
Thailand, 1974	Land development tax on land levied at rates which decrease with value class (R)	House and rent tax and land development tax levied only on commercial and industrial properties	Total property tax on land exceeds that on improvements, since land development tax is levied only on former	Preferential treatment for owner-occupiers by partial exemption of taxable land area (R)	Every four years	Regressive

(Table continues on the following page.)

Table 5-3 (continued)

City, economy, year	Differential treatment by property value		Differential treatment by location or use		Differential treatment of land and improvements	Preferential treatment of owner-occupants	Differential collection practices	Frequency of assessments	Net effect of administrative practices on property tax incidence
	Rate structure	Assessment	Rate structure	Assessment					
Tunis, Tunisia, 1978			Separate tax on unimproved land (P). Fifteen-year exemption for newly constructed residential (business) properties (R)	Underassessment of industrial plants	Surcharge on residential housing contributing to National Housing Improvement Fund	De facto underassessment of owner-occupied properties (R)		Every three years	Regressive
Istanbul, Turkey, 1972	Rate on improvements increases with improvement value (P)		Rural land taxed at lower rates than urban land		Urban land taxed at higher rate than buildings	Owner-occupied residential properties taxed at lower rates than other properties (R)			
Zaire, 1973					Differential land and improvement taxes based on land area and floor space respectively				
Zambia, 1976			In Lusaka de facto exemption of squatter areas (P)		Only buildings and infrastructure are taxed			Every five years (statutory); last revaluation in Kirwe and Ndola in 1970	Progressive

a. P = progressive.
b. R = regressive.

structure of tax rates, and collection procedures. Rate structure and appraisal practices in particular may vary with the value, location, or use of the property and differ for land as compared with improvements and for owner-occupants and tenants.

Differential Treatment by Property Value

Property tax structure and administration may discriminate among properties of different values by applying graduated tax rates, by allowing assessment ratios to vary across value classes, or by granting exemption to properties in particular value classes. As was pointed out in chapter 4, two of these practices are common in developing countries. Rate structures are more often graduated than not, and exemptions for owner-occupancy, industrial activity, and low-valued properties are frequently granted. The evidence on assessment bias is less clear. Bahl (1975) found a preferential assessment on owner-occupied properties in Ahmadabad, and we found one city (Manila) in which the statutory assessment ratio increases with property value. Yet another systematic study of assessment ratios by value class in Cali (Linn 1977b; this is the only such study of a developing-country city that we know of) found no statistically significant bias in assessment ratios.

The distributive effects of differential rates or assessment ratios by property value class and of exempting low-value properties are quite straightforward. Since ownership of property and housing consumption tends to vary directly with income, a progressive (or regressive) rate structure, assessment ratio, or exemption policy will also result in a more progressive (regressive) tax incidence than would be the case for a proportional property tax, irrespective of whether the tax falls on owners (short run) or consumers (long run).

Differential Treatment by Location or Use

Cities in developing economies have found numerous ways to discriminate among properties according to use or location. One frequent practice is to apply higher tax rates to vacant lots within the urban periphery (for example, in Abidjan, Bogotá, Francistown, La Paz, Salvador, São Paulo, Taipei, and Tunis). The distributive effect of this policy is likely to be progressive since the burden of the tax differential is necessarily borne by property owners rather than by consumers (even in the long run), and since the ownership of vacant land is likely to be concentrated in the higher-income groups.

Many Indian cities (for example, Ahmadabad and Calcutta) do not tax vacant land. This may be traced to the colonial origins of the Indian property tax: under British rule, vacant lots were not taxed because they were presumed to yield no actual or imputed rental income. This exemption is likely to have regressive effects on income distribution. A special situation appears to have existed in Rio de Janeiro, where lower rates have been charged for vacant than for improved lots but where a higher assessment ratio has been applied to vacant lots. Although these practices partially offset the regressive effects of the undertaxation of vacant land, their net effect is to leave vacant land still relatively undertaxed, at about a quarter of the effective legal rate for improved properties (Richman 1977).[14]

In many countries, rural properties are assessed and taxed on a different basis than urban properties. And even where the same tax is applied to both types of property, different rates are frequently charged. For instance, in the cities of Colombia, Portugal, and Turkey rates within the urban perimeter have been higher than outside. The incidence of this practice is uncertain, but on balance it may heighten the regressiveness of the system. In the long run, much of the tax differentiation may be shifted forward to consumers or to labor, but since the consumers of rural production activities are likely to reside mainly in urban areas and some of the goods and services produced in urban areas are consumed in rural areas, the incidence may be regressive. In the short run, where the tax differential is borne by property owners, the incidence depends on the relative pattern of property ownership of urban and rural land. Since rural land in some countries is owned by wealthy city dwellers, the lower rural rates may again have a regressive impact.

Differential tax rates and assessment ratios are frequently applied to specified locations within cities. For instance, certain suburban areas of Bombay and Nairobi are taxed below the standard rates. In the metropolitan areas of Jakarta, São Paulo, Singapore, and Taipei lower assessment ratios have been applied at the periphery. The explanation frequently given by city officials for these lower effective rates of taxation is that peripheral properties receive fewer urban services and therefore should not be required to pay the same amount of taxes. Even where this criterion is given officially as the explicit rationale, however, it is not always correct, since the favored areas may actually receive the same services as the majority of urban areas taxed at standard rates (for example, in Bombay and Nairobi). Assessment ratios may also differ by area within a city not because of statutory provisions but because of systematic differentials in assessment procedures. In Abidjan and Cartagena, properties in higher-income areas on balance appear to have been assessed at ratios below the standard, whereas in Bogotá and Cali squatters' areas and illegal subdivisions have been favored by lower assessment ratios. Finally, differential tax rates and assessment ratios tend to apply in different sections of metropolitan areas where jurisdictional fragmentation prevails, as in Calcutta and Manila. The distributive effect of all these differential rates and assessment ratios depends on whether they favor high- or low-income areas of the city. In Abidjan and Cartagena it appears that the preferential treatment is given mainly to high-income areas and therefore has a regressive impact, whereas in Bogotá and Cali the reverse is the case.

Tax rates and assessment ratios may also differ according to whether a property is used for residential or commercial purposes. Tax rates have been typically higher for commercial and industrial properties in Salvador (Brazil), Delhi, and the cities of Korea, Taiwan (China), and Thailand. Legal assessment ratios have been higher for the same type of properties in Abidjan and Manila, while the actual assessment ratio appears to have been lower than average for commercial and industrial properties in Tunis. In the short run, higher effective tax rates on industrial and commercial properties may well have progressive effects, since we can assume that owners of commercial property will on balance be in higher-income groups than owners of residential property. In the long run, this pattern of incidence may be reversed. Since the income-elasticity of consumption of nonresidential goods and services may on balance be lower than the income-elasticity for (residential) housing services, the higher tax on commercial properties which is passed on to consumers may well be more regressive (less progressive) than a nondiscriminatory tax. But the precise distributional impact of this differentiation can be established only by careful analysis of surveys of consumer expenditure.

Other, less common administrative features of tax rate and assessment include temporary exemptions for newly constructed buildings in Abidjan, primarily to stimulate construction. The effect on incidence is likely to have been regressive, however, since the poorer segments of the population tend to live in older housing. The tax on their houses would probably only in part be offset by lower rentals resulting from a larger housing stock. Singapore has placed a higher tax rate on foreigners, whereas penalty rates have been applied to nonresidents in the cities of Taiwan (China). On balance these two provisions may well be progressive, although they were probably not instituted for that reason.

Differential Treatment of Land and Improvements

In many cities differential tax rates or assessment ratios are applied to land as compared with improvements. Under site value taxation, improvements are not taxed, for example, in Kingston and Nairobi. More common is the application of a differentially higher tax rate on land, though in some cases improvements are taxed at a higher rate. Two main objectives explain differential taxation of land and improvements. Lower taxes on improvements are justified as providing an investment incentive. Higher rates on improvements are usually supported on the grounds that improvements reflect ability to pay, and thus higher improvement rates are beneficial on equity grounds.

In the short run the distributive impact of differential rates on land and improvements depends on the distribution of ownership of land and structures across income classes, and on the land-improvement ratio. If poorer people tend to own property for which the ratio of land value to structure value is higher than that for property owned by higher-income

Table 5-4. *Assessed Urban Land Values in Colombia as a Percentage of Total Urban Property Value by Property Value Class in Ten Departments (1974) and in Four Departmental Capitals*

Property value class[a]	Land as percentage of total assessed value	Number of properties as percentage of total[b]	Land as percentage of total assessed value	Number of properties as percentage of total[b]
	Bolivar		*Caldas*	
Less than 5	63.5	43.3	60.4	14.9
5–20	54.7	27.0	41.3	36.0
20–50	34.0	16.0	35.2	27.4
50–100	33.7	7.6	37.4	10.7
100–200	38.8	2.9	37.1	6.4
200–500	43.4	2.3	36.6	3.5
500–1,000	47.6	0.7	38.3	0.7
More than 1,000	44.2	0.3	32.9	0.4
Total	42.5	100.0	36.5	100.0
	Norte de Santander		*Quindio*	
Less than 5	71.2	35.7	60.3	13.0
5–20	37.5	33.7	42.1	38.3
20–50	30.9	17.6	34.6	26.3
50–100	32.2	7.0	32.2	12.0
100–200	31.6	4.0	31.1	6.2
200–500	37.2	1.7	35.2	2.9
500–1,000	42.1	0.3	36.5	1.0
More than 1,000	32.3	0.2	25.0	0.3
Total	34.7	100.0	33.1	100.0
	Total (Ten departments)		*Armenia (Quindio) 1971*	
Less than 5	65.4	—	78.3	4.7
5–20	47.3	—	46.6	36.9
20–50	37.6	—	45.2	28.9
50–100	38.3	—	46.1	14.8
100–200	38.0	—	45.2	8.7
200–500	41.6	—	48.8	4.0
500–1,000	44.0	—	44.6	0.7
More than 1,000	39.0	—	31.3	0.7
Total	40.5	—	43.3	100.0

— Not available.
a. In thousands of Colombian pesos.
b. May not add to 100 percent due to rounding.

people, then a lower tax rate on improvements would be regressive relative to a uniform (equal-yield) tax on land.

In the long run it is useful to distinguish between a nationwide application of preferential taxation of improvements and an exclusively local policy charging lower tax rates on structures. In the nationwide case, where it may be assumed that land is relatively fixed in supply, most of the tax on land will fall on landowners. If capital is assumed to be perfectly elastic in supply in the long run, most of the nationwide tax on structures will be passed on to consumers, to labor, and to land. Because landownership is likely to be concentrated among high-income recipients, a preferential treatment of improvements is likely to be more progressive (less regressive) than a uniform tax.[15] For the case of local changes in tax rates, land and capital are assumed to be elastically supplied. This means that much of the tax on land and capital is passed on

Land as percentage of total assessed value	Number of properties as percentage of total[b]	Land as percentage of total assessed value	Number of properties as percentage of total[b]	Land as percentage of total assessed value	Number of properties as percentage of total[b]
Cordoba		Cesar		Magdalena	
72.1	45.0	62.3	33.6	59.2	44.9
54.7	26.9	50.5	34.6	42.1	27.0
42.1	16.4	39.5	17.3	32.3	16.6
42.9	6.5	44.1	6.3	39.5	6.3
44.7	3.2	50.7	2.3	39.6	3.5
45.0	1.5	51.5	0.8	49.8	1.3
48.2	0.4	40.8	0.0	47.4	0.3
38.6	0.2	19.1	0.0	43.1	0.1
45.5	100.0	55.0	100.0	41.5	100.0
Risaralda		Sucre		Santander	
59.6	13.6	65.4	50.0	74.8	17.4
37.0	38.4	58.2	29.7	52.0	31.4
28.8	28.2	42.8	11.7	47.4	28.0
28.8	10.4	41.0	4.8	45.3	13.6
29.0	5.7	40.2	1.9	41.0	6.6
34.9	2.9	38.6	1.3	45.7	2.2
38.2	0.5	33.5	0.2	50.1	0.4
27.9	0.3	35.2	0.0	45.6	0.3
31.3	100.0	43.3	100.0	46.0	100.0
Cali (Valle) 1973		Cartagena (Bolivar) 1972		Pereira (Risaralda) 1971	
93.7	15.1	83.6	—	75.0	5.9
54.9	28.3	71.0	—	45.2	36.2
46.9	20.7	36.7	—	37.2	31.9
48.1	17.2	35.3	—	38.6	13.0
44.7	10.1	42.1	—	42.9	7.6
40.3	6.5	45.2	—	52.2	4.3
47.7	1.1	49.0	—	52.3	1.1
41.6	0.8	47.2	—	30.5	0.5
44.4	100.0	45.1	—	42.1	100.0

Source: Calculated from data obtained from Instituto Geografico "Agustin Codazzi."

to consumers of commodities whose prices are not fixed through national or international trade. Taking the case of residential housing services, the incidence of a preferential treatment of structures relative to land depends on the relative income-elasticities of the expenditure on services from land and structure, respectively. If the income-elasticity of the demand for land services is higher than that for structures, then the lower (higher) rates on improvements are progressive (regressive) relative to a uniform tax rate on all property.

The answer to the question of the tax burden therefore seems to depend on the relative distribution across income classes of ownership of land and buildings (for short-run incidence), and on the income-elasticity of expenditure on services for land and buildings (in the long run). Very little information is available on this question for developing countries. The only source of information we found is a set of data on assessed property values in Colombia. Table 5-4 shows land value as a percentage of total urban property value for eight classes of property value in ten departments (states) and four departmental capitals. If one assumes that there is no systematic change in assessment bias across classes, then the lowest classes show the highest ratio of land value to total property value in all departments and cities. In some cases the lowest ratio is found in the middle value ranges. In other cases the decline in the ratio is uniform as one moves from lower to higher classes. At least for Colombia this provides an important clue for the distributive effect of exempting improvements. Because one can reasonably assume that low-income groups on balance tend to own or rent lower-value properties, the exemption of improvements would have a regressive impact in the short run, whether or not this is done purely locally or nationwide. In the long run it would be regressive if done purely locally by any of the Colombian cities. In any case, as pointed out above, the long-run incidence of a nationwide preferential treatment of improvements would have progressive effects.

In summary, it cannot be assumed automatically that lower (or higher) taxation of improvements will have a progressive effect. If improvements are treated preferentially, as is the case in most cities where differential rates apply, then it should be done nationwide, since this will ensure a progressive effect, at least in the long run.

Preferential Treatment for Owner-Occupants

One of the most common biases in administering and structuring the property tax is preferential treatment of owner-occupied properties. Lower than average tax rates were applied to owner-occupied properties in Abidjan, Istanbul, Karachi, Madras, and three Brazilian cities. In Portugal higher cutoff levels are applied for tax exemptions of low-value property in the case of owner-occupants. In Abidjan, Ahmadabad, Bangkok, Calcutta, and Tunis, preferentially low assessment ratios have been applied to owner-occupied properties. In Abidjan, furthermore, owner-occupants were given larger temporary exemptions from property taxation than was the case for all other types of properties.

In the short run, where all property taxes may be assumed to be borne by owners, this preferential treatment of owner-occupants is not necessarily regressive. In fact, if the distribution of property ownership is such that owner-occupied residential property weighs more heavily in the total taxed property portfolio of lower-income groups than on higher-income groups (as is indeed quite likely), then the preferential treatment of owner-occupied properties is likely to have a progressive impact. In the long run, however, where most of the property tax is passed on to renters and consumers, the exemption of owner-occupied properties is likely to be regressive since rental tenancy is likely to be more common among low-income groups than among high-income groups. Where rental is predominant, the regressive impact will be more important. In countries where rental is relatively important (for example, India, Sri Lanka) the exemption of owner-occupants would be more regressive in the long run than in countries (Colombia and Mexico) where property rental is a less preponderant type of land tenure.

Collecting the Property Tax

Collecting the property tax may introduce further biases into its incidence. In developing countries high-income taxpayers are more successful in evading taxation than are low-income taxpayers.[16] This directly reduces the progressivity of the existing property tax system or worsens its regressivity. It is, however, difficult to quantify the extent to which different income groups benefit from inefficiencies of collection. In Cali, Linn (1979b) measured the relation between arrears and the income level of taxpayers. The evidence indicated the reverse of the usual presumption, in that lower-income taxpayers tended to contribute more heavily to arrears. Evidently the pattern of tax collections by income group may differ from city to city and country to country (and may well differ for different taxes within the same locality). The incidence effects will vary accordingly.

Summary and Evaluation of Administrative Practices

The prevalence of administrative and statutory procedures which tend to distort the incidence of the property tax away from the distributive effect of a proportional tax points to the importance of considering the institutional framework within which property taxes are applied. One of the most extreme cases was found in the city of Abidjan, where a complex system of differential tax rates, differential assessment ratios, and temporary as well as permanent exemptions has made it virtually irrelevant to consider the incidence of the average property tax. In that city, owner-occupants in some past years paid no property tax during the first two years after construction of a building, 1 percent of gross rental value between year three and year twenty, and 6.2 percent thereafter. Rental housing and office buildings paid 6, 9, and 20.5 percent respectively for the same periods. Factories always paid 20.5 percent. Various other statutory provisions and de facto administrative procedures further complicated the picture. Overall, the incidence of this complex set of exemptions is probably more strongly regressive than the proportional tax applied to all properties (1974 World Bank data).

From the broad overview of urban property tax administration in all the cities and countries shown in table 5-3 one can assess to some extent the distributive effects of these practices.[17] In seventeen out of thirty-two cases the overall effect of these institutional aspects is progressive when compared with that of a proportional property tax; in six cases it appears to be regressive. In the remainder of the cases it was either impossible to assign a clear direction to the impact of the administrative practice, or procedures with mutually offsetting distributive effects are being applied (Ahmadabad, Calcutta, Istanbul, Karachi, and Madras). These last examples reflect not only the effect of objectives other than equity, but also the ad hoc way in which distributive objectives are pursued by those who administer the property tax in these cities.

In some countries administrative practices and their net distributive effects differed among cities (for example, Brazil, Colombia, and India). This reinforces the conclusions of the preceding chapter that an analysis of property tax systems at the country level may miss important intracountry differences in property tax practices.

A Case Study of the Effect of Structure and Administration on Incidence

For Cali (Colombia) an effort has been made to quantify the effect of administrative and structural practices on the incidence of property taxation (Linn 1977b, 1979b). The measure used for this purpose is the (cross-section) elasticity of actual property tax payments with respect to income, $E(T_a,Y)$. This elasticity indicates whether tax payments vary more or less than in proportion with income. If the elasticity $E(T_a,Y)$ is less than unity, the tax is regressive. If $E(T_a,Y)$ is unity, the property tax payments vary in proportion with income and the tax is neutral in its incidence. To explain the reasons for any observed pattern of property tax incidence, $E(T_a,Y)$ is broken into a number of component elasticities.

The Model

Five factors determine the actual property tax paid on any particular property: the market value of the property; the assessment ratio applicable to the property, that is, the ratio between the value assessed by the official assessment agency and its market value; the "transmission ratio," that is, the ratio of the assessed value used by the municipal treasury for billing the property tax in relation to the assessed value as appraised by the assessment agency; the statutory tax rate as determined by local or national laws; and the collection ratio, that is, the ratio between actual tax collected and statutory tax liability. In algebraic terms these five factors may be combined and written as follows:

$$(5\text{-}1) \qquad T_a = \left(\frac{t_a}{t_s}\right)\left(\frac{AV_T}{AV_G}\right)\left(\frac{AV_G}{MV}\right)MV$$

[actual tax payment] = [collection ratio] × [tax rate] × [transmission ratio]

× [assessment ratio] × [market value]

where t_a = actual tax payment, t_s = statutory tax liability, t = statutory tax rate = T_s/AV_T, AV_T = assessed value as registered in the municipal treasury, AV_G = assessed value as registered in the assessment agency, and MV = market value. Taking natural logarithms on both sides of equation 5-1 and differentiating with respect to the logarithm of income, one can derive the following disaggregation of the income-elasticity of property tax collections:

$$
(5\text{-}2) \quad E(T_a, Y) = E\left(\frac{T_a}{T_s}, Y\right) + E(t, Y) + E\left(\frac{AV_T}{AV_G}, Y\right)
$$
$$
+ E\left(\frac{AV_G}{MV}, Y\right) + E(MV, Y).
$$

The first four elasticities on the right-hand side of equation 5-2 reflect the administrative and legal framework of property taxation: tax collection, statutory tax rates, transmission of assessment records, and assessment practices. The last is the income-elasticity of the property tax base, which is exogenous to local government policy. For owner-occupants, it is a direct measure of the income-elasticity of housing expenditure. For renters, it is possible to disaggregate the base elasticity $E(MV,Y)$ further, to

$$
(5\text{-}3) \quad E(MV, Y) = \left[1 + E\left(\frac{MV}{R}, R\right)\right] E(R, Y)
$$

where R is the rental payment. The elasticity of the market value of properties with respect to income for renters is therefore determined by the elasticity of rental payments with respect to income, $E(R,Y)$, and the elasticity of the value-rental ratio with respect to rent, $E(MV/R,R)$.

Conventional property tax analysis has concentrated almost exclusively on the housing expenditure conditions reflected in $E(M,Y)$ and $E(R,Y)$ and has generally not separated renters from owner-occupants in the analysis of residential properties.[18] The remainder of this section summarizes the results of a study carried out for the case of Cali, which estimated the sign and size of the various component-elasticities in equations 5-2 and 5-3 and thus derived an estimate of the overall incidence of a property tax change.[19]

Results for Owner-Occupied Properties

For owner-occupants in Cali the estimation results are shown in table 5-5.[20] The elasticity of property tax liabilities with respect to income, $E(T,Y)$, is approximately 1.25 when evaluated at the mean and is significantly larger than unity at the 5 percent confidence level; therefore, the incidence of property taxation in Cali is progressive for this subgroup of taxpayers. In the framework of equation 5-2, this finding may be explained by a combination of a housing expenditure roughly proportional to income, $E(MV,Y) = 1.056$, and a progressive statutory tax rate, $E(t,Y) = 0.207$, while the elasticities of the assessment and transmission ratios with respect to income were found not to be significantly different from zero. The effect of tax collection could not be evaluated in the

Table 5-5. *Incidence of the Property Tax for Owner-Occupants: Linear Regression Equation Results for Cali Household Sample*

$MV = -5.1731 + 16.8274\ Y$ (2.590)	$R^2 = 0.4896$	$E_{MV,Y} =$	1.056^a
$AV_G/MV = 0.4852 - 0.0004\ Y$ (0.0008)	$R^2 = 0.0000$	$E_{(AV_G/MV),Y} =$	-0.005
$AV_T/AV_G = 0.9909 - 0.0041\ Y$ (0.074)	$R^2 = 0.0072$	$E_{(AV_T/AV_G),Y} =$	-0.050
$t = 0.0083 + 0.004\ Y$ (0.0001)	$R^2 = 0.1721$	$E_{t,Y} =$	0.207^a
$T_s = 0.1277 + 0.1043\ Y^2$ (0.0184)	$R = 0.4231$	$E_{T_s,Y}\ ^b =$	1.266

Note: There were 42 observations; elasticities evaluated at the means. Figures in parentheses represent standard errors of the regression coefficients. Y is monthly income and T_s is annual statutory tax liability; both are expressed in thousands of Colombian pesos. In 1975 the official exchange rate was 31.2 pesos to the dollar.
  a. Elasticity is significantly different from zero at the 5 percent confidence level.
  b. Elasticity is significantly greater than unity at the 5 percent confidence level.

framework of equation 5-2 because of insufficient information, but data on arrears indicate that higher-income owner-occupants tend to pay taxes more promptly, thus further strengthening the progressivity of the tax.

Results for Rental Properties

The incidence estimate for rental properties[21] is shown in table 5-6. In contrast to that of owner-occupied properties, the income-elasticity of tax liabilities for rented properties in Cali, $E(T_s,Y)$, is significantly less than unity at the 5 percent confidence level. In order to determine the causes for this divergence in results between renters and owner-occupants, the component elasticities derived in equations 5-2 and 5-3 were estimated. The results indicate that the difference does not lie primarily in any differential legal or administrative treatment accorded to rental properties with respect to statutory tax rates or assessment practices but rather in different housing market conditions. The elasticities reflecting assessment practices for rental properties, $E(AV_G/MV,Y)$ and $E(AV_T/AV_G,Y)$, are not significantly different from zero; and although tax rates on rented properties do not rise significantly with income, the elasticity $E(t,Y)$ is positive. As for owner-occupants, the ratio of property tax arrears to tax liability is negatively related to income, although not significantly. Tax collection is therefore not a major determinant of differences in tax burdens between owner-occupants and renters. In any case, the difference introduced into the elasticity $E(T_s,Y)$ for rental as compared with owner-occupied properties on account of administrative and legal factors is very minor. The conclusion that renters and owner-

Table 5-6. *Incidence of the Property Tax for Renters: Linear Regression Equation Results for Cali Household Sample*

$MV = 67.4197 + 6.2896\ Y$ (3.5816)	$R^2 = 0.0932$	$E_{MV,Y} = 0.325$[a]
$MV/R = 109.2182 - 19.9431\ R$ (13.1747)	$R^2 = 0.0710$	$E_{(MV/R),R} = -0.345$
$R = 0.8211 + 0.1132\ Y$ (0.0333)	$R^2 = 0.02780$	$E_{R,Y} = 0.416$[a,b]
$AV_G/MV = 0.5298 - 0.0070\ Y$ (0.0088)	$R^2 = 0.0208$	$E_{(AV_G/MV),Y} = -0.074$
$AV_T/AV_G = 0.9884 - 0.0008\ Y$ (0.0083)	$R^2 = 0.0003$	$E_{(AV_T/AV_G),Y} = -0.004$
$t = 0.0099 + 0.0002\ Y$ (0.0002)	$R^2 = 0.0390$	$E_{t,Y} = 0.091$
$T_s = 0.3634 + 0.0371\ Y$ (0.0192)	$R^2 = 0.1106$	$E_{T_s,Y} = 0.345$[b]

Note: There were 32 observations; elasticities evaluated at the means; figures in parentheses represent standard errors of the regression coefficients. R is monthly rent expressed in thousands of Colombian pesos.

a. Elasticity is significantly different from zero at the 5 percent confidence level.

b. Elasticity is significantly less than unity at the 5 percent confidence level.

occupants are treated alike is also obtained when comparing average assessment, transmission, and collection ratios, and statutory tax rates for rental and owner-occupied properties. The means of AV_G/MV, AV_T/AV_G, arrears/T_s, and t are not significantly larger for rental properties than for owner-occupied properties.

In contrast, the elasticity of the market value of property with respect to income is significantly below unity for renters. Further disaggregating this elasticity into its two component elasticities $E(MV/R,R)$ and $E(R,Y)$, as in equation 5-3, one finds from the Cali household sample that $E(MV/R,R)$ is negative. From the estimation equations, one finds furthermore that $E(R,Y)$, the elasticity of rental payments with respect to income, is significantly below unity, indicating that rental payments increase less than in proportion to income. The low elasticity of tax liabilities on rental properties with respect to income of renters is therefore explained largely by the declining value-rental ratio as rents increase and by the low income-elasticity of rental payments.

The combined distributive effect of the property tax on owner-occupied and rental property in Cali is estimated to be neutral, mainly since the progressively structured tax rate offsets the regressive impact of overall patterns of housing consumption. An overall progressive collection performance further reinforces the conclusion that the property tax in Cali is approximately neutral in the long run. Assessment practices were not found to introduce a systematic bias into the distributive effect of the property tax.

Summary

Assessing the distributive effect of property taxes is a complex task. A careful determination of tax shifting assumptions must be made. Then a statistical investigation of the distribution of tax burdens—allowing for such important aspects of property tax administration as property assessment and tax collection—must be done. Such an analysis is often not feasible when tax reform is being contemplated. It is therefore useful to summarize the major conclusions of this chapter in the form of several reasonably reliable "stylized facts" regarding the distributive effect of reforming the property tax.

On balance, an increase in the average level of property taxation tends to be progressive in the sense that it burdens higher-income groups more heavily in relation to their incomes. The progressive effect is more pronounced in the short term than in the long term, and more for nationwide property tax increases than for increases restricted to a particular jurisdiction.

The structure and administration of property taxation have a significant impact on the pattern of incidence, and a number of developing countries have introduced structural changes to achieve equity goals. Graduated rate structures and the exemption of low-value properties tend to increase the progressivity of the property tax. Exemption or lower tax rates on improvements, preferential treatment of non-owner-occupants, and tax rate differentials by location may well result in a more regressive (or less progressive) property tax.

These broad guidelines may be useful for reforming the property tax. But it is also appropriate to invest some effort in quantitatively analyzing the distributive effects of reforms that are expected to make far-reaching changes in tax structure and administration and in the level of revenue. The examples in this chapter indicate that this kind of analysis can be carried out effectively and can contribute to an understanding of the distributive effect of the property tax.

6 Allocative Effects of Urban Property Taxation

EFFICIENCY LOSSES ASSOCIATED with raising property tax revenues should be minimized. Few would argue with the importance of adhering to this maxim of good taxation. Urban areas in developing countries are already plagued by a shortage of buildable, serviced land, by high land prices, and by an inadequate housing stock. It would be unwise to allow the property tax to make things worse. In fact, many developing-country governments have adjusted their property tax structures to promote better use of the land resource. Some of these discretionary adjustments have worked, while others have not. This chapter is both a description of this practice and a statement of how the issue of the allocative effects of the property tax might be better addressed.

In the next section we discuss the underlying theory of the economic effects of property taxation and then evaluate the potential of the property tax to affect land use and land prices. Finally, we provide an overview of the various ways in which the property tax has been bent to achieve desired allocative effects.

Property Taxation and Resource Allocation

The imposition of a property tax affects the allocation of resources only if the supply of land and of improvements responds to the imposition of a property tax. To the extent that it does, society may be worse off, for example, if the property tax results in a reallocation of investment from housing to automobiles. Alternatively, society might be better off, for example, if property taxation induces improvements of slums. The question is whether and how the use and price of land are affected by the property tax.

In the short run, if factor supplies are inelastic, no significant resource allocation effects will occur in the wake of changes in the property tax; that is, the property tax will not result in significant losses in efficiency, nor can it be counted on to correct a misallocation of resources. In other words, unless a particular property tax practice is permitted to remain in force for a sufficiently long period, its main effects will be to redistribute income and generate public revenue.

In the long run, if capital is assumed to be mobile within and between countries and if land is flexible between alternative uses, the property tax changes the allocation of resources and thus the efficiency of factor use. As in the previous chapter, it is necessary here to distinguish the economic efficiency effects of a nationwide change from those of a purely local change in the property tax. If the change in the tax is uniform and nationwide, it will not significantly affect the allocation of resources. If the tax on land is purely local or affects only certain land (for example, urban but not rural, or residential but not commercial), then land use may be adjusted by changing it from taxed to untaxed status. Thus a local tax on land in the long run will affect the allocation of resources. Moreover, because the supply of capital will adjust in the long run, a tax on improvements will also affect resource allocation and can result in important losses in efficiency—irrespective of whether a tax on improvements (capital) applies nationwide or only locally.

Property Taxation and Land Use Policy

A review of property tax practices in developing countries indicates that they frequently deviate from a basic proportional tax on the value of property in all uses in order to pursue a wide variety of intermediate policy goals. Sometimes these policies are thought to be related to the ultimate goal of minimizing the losses in efficiency resulting from the use of the property tax as a revenue-raising instrument, sometimes to the goal of correcting preexisting market distortions, and sometimes to promoting social and economic goals. In practice, policymakers and the public see the property tax as being able to help resolve a wide variety of urban ills by increasing investment in construction (or in business), increasing home ownership, speeding up the development of land, discouraging urban sprawl or land speculation, and encouraging lower (or less rapidly rising) land prices (Shoup 1978). These various policy concerns are all somehow related to the goals of promoting a better use of urban land and holding down land prices. The question at hand is whether they can or should achieve either.

Land Use Effects

The assumption that a dense and more rapid pace of urban land development leads to more efficient land use is the basis for discouraging land speculation, inducing early development, encouraging the "infill" development of the urbanized area to a higher density, and encouraging subdivision of land at the periphery. But this assumption may or may not be valid.[1] Unless the government has more accurate information on the private costs and benefits than do private developers, or monopolistic market conditions or externalities prevail, there is little reason to assume that the decisions of government planners would lead to greater efficiency than those of the private sector.

Land Price Effects

A second issue is whether the property tax can and should be used to dampen land prices. There is little to recommend the view that land prices, or the rate of increase in land prices, are "too high" in cities of developing countries. As Walters (1983) has shown, rapid increases in urban land prices may be compatible with normal rates of return on investment in land. Landownership may involve relatively low current yields (especially if the land is not yet fully developed) as well as high risks. As a result, if land is to be held as an asset, that is, if its rate of return is to be comparable to that on other assets, it has to appreciate in value at a relatively high rate. Land speculation with a destabilizing effect may occur if expectations of rising land prices feed on themselves and drive land prices up more rapidly than justified on the basis of normal rates of return and risk-taking propensity (Mohan 1977). There is no apparent reason, however, why the usual law of speculation should not apply to the urban land market, even in developing countries: if speculation is destabilizing (in the sense of reinforcing rather than smoothing out basic fluctuations in market prices), it eventually leads to losses for the speculators.

Much of the concern about the escalation in land prices is probably related to equity and fairness rather than to efficiency. First, it is thought to be unfair that individuals should benefit from unearned increments in land value, that is, the part of the increase which is caused by public investments in infrastructure and for which the landowner does not pay. Second, the rapid rise in land values may price low-income groups out of the land market in the sense that they are unable to raise the necessary capital as a down payment for a land purchase.[2] These are legitimate concerns of land policy, but they should not be construed as showing an inefficiency in the operation of land markets.

There is also some question regarding the factual basis for the assumption that land prices are increasing more rapidly than general price levels or than the relative riskiness of land investments. Biases in land price reporting and estimation would lead one to believe that the average increase in land prices is overstated (Walters 1983). Furthermore, there are few good empirical studies to support the general impression of rapidly increasing average land prices in developing countries. In virtually every city examples of rapid price increases of individual properties or types of properties may be found, particularly at the fringe of urban development or where existing services are upgraded by private or public action. Often, these rapid price jumps occur before actual development or upgrading because expected future benefits are capitalized into current property value. But every city is likely to have areas where land values are stagnant or even declining,[3] and therefore an average change in land value—rather than some exceptional change—should be estimated in analyzing the rate of increase in land values.[4]

Nevertheless, there is some empirical work to support the argument that land prices have not grown faster than inflation and real income in developing countries. Holland and Follain (1990) report an average annual increase in land values in Jamaica of 10 percent between 1974 and 1984, in comparison with an inflation rate of 18 percent. Jamaica had no real income growth during this period. Korea, by contrast, had real income growth of 10 percent per year during the 1960–77 period, and urban land values appear to have increased faster than nonagricultural output during most of this period (Ingram 1982: 107–08). Ingram (1982) estimated that land values grew at about the same rate as ouput in Bogotá during the 1970–78 period, but McCallum (1974), Linn (1980b), and Mohan and Villamizar (1980) found lower rates of increase in land values.

Turning then to the question of whether or not the level of land values is too high, the relevant consideration is "what is too high?" As Walters (1983) points out, there is ample reason to believe that in cities of developing countries actual property value will frequently understate the economic opportunity costs of land in its likely alternative use, let alone in the best possible alternative use. This is the case since market prices of land reflect the private valuation of inputs and outputs involved in generating market rents, since they embody taxes on land, and since they do not fully allow for the social cost of central city congestion. Only monopoly power by landowners or restrictions on land use imposed by the public authorities (such as zoning) are likely to maintain the market value of urban land above its opportunity cost by limiting the supply of various categories of land, for example, by allowing commercial activities only in certain areas or by not permitting expansion of residential use at the urban fringe. Because landownership is frequently dispersed, monopoly power by landowners is not likely to be a major problem in many cities of developing countries;[5] it is not readily apparent that property taxation is the appropriate antidote to high land prices if they are caused by the government rationing the land supply through zoning or not providing urban services. It may be more appropriate to reconsider the use of land-rationing devices.

Thus, as with the growth in land prices, there is reason to doubt an efficiency argument for use of the property tax to reduce land prices. Again, an equity argument may be at the heart of the matter: urban land prices are frequently so high that low-income groups cannot afford to purchase land, given their disposable incomes and the prevailing capital market conditions, which prevent access to mortgage credits at affordable interest rates. To the extent that the revenue from property taxes is capitalized into lower current land values (since the tax reduces the expected future private yield on the land), it partially expropriates landownership rights from the present owner and also constitutes a loan to future owners, who can now acquire the land at a lower price but will have to pay property taxes in the future. If low-income groups cannot buy land because they lack liquidity and access to capital markets, property taxation may be one of the policy instruments to improve their access to landownership.

There is, however, a caveat: when property ownership is clouded by illegal subdivision or squatting on private or public lands, proof that the property tax and related charges (for example, special assessments) have been paid may be taken by private purchasers and public authorities as a sign of relatively well-established claims to the land (Linn 1980a). By increasing the security of tenure, this feature of the property tax tends to offset the decline in property values which would usually be expected to result from the imposition of a property tax.

Allocative Effects and Property Tax Practices

Consideration of the allocative effects of property taxation is complicated by the large number of proxy goals with unclear relations to the underlying efficiency objective and by the large number of property tax instruments used to achieve these goals. This problem is documented in table 6-1, which summarizes the effects of a variety of property tax policies on multiple objectives. The table compares the effect of each instrument with that of a tax on capital value levied at a flat rate and producing an equal revenue yield. It is assumed that capital supplies adjust to changes in rates of return resulting from changed property tax burdens but that the supply of land is fixed; in other words, the long-run effect of a nationwide change in the property tax is reflected in table 6-1. Besides showing the intended direction of the effect of a property tax instrument on a particular goal, the table indicates in parentheses what possible unintended effects may be associated with the use of a particular instrument. The instrument's intended and likely effects on the distributive (equity) and revenue objectives are also shown, as are the places where such instruments have been used.

Three preliminary conclusions may be drawn from these data. First, a large array of property tax instruments has been employed in the cities of developing countries to attain a large number of policy goals. This sometimes has led to conflicts between the goals of equity and efficiency and causes offsetting resource allocation effects. Second, there is a considerable degree of uncertainty regarding the effect of these policy instruments. Third, there is often a difference between desired and actual effects of policies because secondary effects are not explicitly considered or because there is a lack of knowledge regarding the actual effects of a particular policy instrument.

If one takes the effects shown in table 6-1 at face value and does not question the relation between basic objectives and proxy goals, one finds that site-value taxation, land value increment taxation, higher taxes on vacant land, and the exemption of low-value properties have relatively few conflicts between goals and tend to work in the direction of the stated goals. Property transfer taxes, higher taxes on improvements, lower taxes on vacant land, preferential treatment of owner-occupants, and lower taxes on suburban locations also have relatively few conflicts

Table 6-1. *Instruments and Objectives of Property Tax Policy*

	Objective						
Instrument	*Reduce efficiency loss resulting from property tax*	*Increase investment in construction*	*Increase business investment*	*Increase home-ownership*	*Advance timing of land development*	*Discourage urban sprawl, encourage fill-in*	*Discourage land speculation*
Higher effective tax on land than on improvements, including site-value tax (ST)	+	+	+	+	+ (?)	+	+
Lower effective tax on land than on improvements	(−)	(−)	(−)	(−)	(?)	(−)	(−)
Temporary exemption of improvements	+	+	+	+		+	
Higher tax on vacant urban land					+	+	+
Lower tax on vacant urban land					(−)	(−)	(−)
Preferential treatment of owner-occupants	(−)	+ (?)		+		(−)	
Lower tax (or temporary exemption) on industrial and commercial property	(−)		+				
Higher tax on industrial and commercial property	(−)		(−)				
Progressive tax rates	(−)	(−)	(−)			(−)	
Exemption of low-value properties		(+)		(?)		(?)	

Lower land prices	Reduce rate of increase of land prices	Encourage subdivision at periphery	Encourage land assembly in center	Promote more equal distribution of income	Raise higher revenues (elasticity)	Simplify administration	Cities or economies
+ (?)	+ (?)			+		+ (?) for (ST)	Francistown, Botswana; Taiwan (China) (ST); Tehran, Iran; Kingston, Jamaica (ST); Nairobi, Kenya (ST); Thailand; Istanbul, Turkey
(?)	(?)			(?)	+ (?)	+	Rio de Janeiro, Brazil; Singapore; Zambia
				(−)	(?)		Abidjan, Côte d'Ivoire; Bombay, India; Singapore; Tunis, Tunisia
+	+ (−)			(+)	(?)		Buenos Aires, Argentina; La Paz, Boliva; Francistown, Botswana; Salvador and São Paulo, Brazil; Chile; Taiwan (China); Bogotá, Colombia; Abidjan, Côte d'Ivoire; Ecuador; Peru; Senegal; Syria; Tunis, Tunisia; Turkey
(−)	(?)			(−)	(−)		Bahamas; Rio de Janeiro, Brazil; Egypt; Haiti; Hong Kong; India (except Delhi and Madras); Mauritius; Morocco; Sierra Leone; Sri Lanka
				(−)	(−)		Taiwan (China); Abidjan, Côte d'Ivoire; Hong Kong; Ahmadabad, Calcutta, and Madras, India; Karachi, Pakistan; Portugal; Thailand; Tunis, Tunisia; Istanbul, Turkey
				(−)	(−)		Hong Kong; Tunis, Tunisia
				(?)	(+)		Salvador, Brazil; Taiwan (China); Delhi, India; Jakarta, Indonesia; Manila, Philippines; Thailand
(?)	(+)	(+)	(−)	+	+		Taiwan (China); Ahmadabad, Bombay, Calcutta, Delhi, and Madras, India; Kingston, Jamaica; Rep. of Korea; Karachi, Pakistan; Manila, Philippines; Portugal; Istanbul, Turkey
(−)				+	(?)	+	Bogotá and Cali, Colombia; Bombay, Calcutta, and Madras, India; Tehran, Iran; Seoul, Rep. of Korea; Portugal; Singapore; Lusaka, Zambia

(*Table continues on the following page.*)

Table 6-1 *(continued)*

	Objective						
Instrument	Reduce efficiency loss resulting from property tax	Increase investment in construction	Increase business investment	Increase homeownership	Advance timing of land development	Discourage urban sprawl, encourage fill-in	Discourage land speculation
Lower taxes on suburban locations					(−)	(−)	(−)
Land-value increment taxation					(?)		+ (?)
Property transfer tax	(−)	(?)	(?)		(−)		
Rental-value tax					(−)	(−)	(−)

Note: This table refers to the long-term impact of policy instruments used on a nationwide basis. Impact of instrument on the objective: + = positive, − = negative, ? = uncertain. Signs not in parentheses indicate *desired* impact of policy instrument. Signs in parentheses indicate *actual* impact of policy instrument. ST = site value tax.

but on balance move the urban economy away from the stated goals. Some policy instruments, such as progressive rate structures and differential taxation of industrial-commercial and residential properties, have such extensive conflicts in goals that it is impossible to identify their net effects. For policy prescription, therefore, the first category of property tax instruments is useful in promoting an efficient land use; the second set is not; and the third set may be, depending on the relative weights allocated to particular goals.[6]

Having made this general assessment, we turn to a brief study of the prevailing practices in using each of these instruments. If we have learned anything about property taxation, it is that one may not easily generalize about "the prevailing practice."

Differential Taxation of Land and Improvements

Cities in which land and improvements are taxed differentially tend to use lower rates, lower assessment ratios, or exemptions for improvements. There are only a few cases (that we can identify) of improvements being taxed more heavily than land (see chapter 4). The main argument for lower taxation of improvements is to minimize the losses in efficiency associated with property taxation.[7] In the short run, however, there is no such efficiency advantage, since the tax on improvements does not

		Objective					
Lower land prices	Reduce rate of increase of land prices	Encourage subdivision at periphery	Encourage land assembly in center	Promote more equal distribution of income	Raise higher revenues (elasticity)	Simplify administration	Cities or economies
(−)	(+)	(?)		+ (?)ᵃ	(−)		São Paulo, Brazil; Taiwan (China); Bombay, India; Jakarta, Indonesia; Nairobi, Kenya; Singapore
+ (?)	+ (?)	(−)		+		(−)	La Paz, Bolivia; Taiwan (China); Rep. of Korea
(?)	(?)	(−)				(+)	Afghanistan; Taiwan (China); Colombia; Greece; Guatemala; Rep. of Korea; Lebanon; Mexico; Nepal; Singapore
(−)	(+)					+ (?)	Algeria; Egypt; Haiti; Hong Kong; India; Malaysia; Mauritius; Morocco; Lagos, Nigeria; Pakistan; Sierra Leone; Singapore; Sudan; Syria; Tunisia; Venezuela

a. The allocative effect of each tax measure is shown in comparison with the effect of a proportional capital value tax of equal yield on all types of real estate, including land and improvements. The goal is horizontal equity rather than vertical equity.

Sources: Table 5-3; Smith (1979); Lent (1974).

affect resource allocation. It is simply suffered by owners of land and capital. The same is true in the long run if a uniform tax is levied nationwide.

Besides minimizing losses in efficiency from rising tax revenues, higher rates on land and lower rates on improvements are also favored on the grounds that they will force landowners to develop land to its fullest potential and thus will stimulate investment in construction, advance the timing of land development, encourage the "infill" development of underutilized urban land, and discourage speculative landholding practices. The degree to which these will occur has long been debated in the literature. If capital markets operate perfectly, higher land taxes will not stimulate the development of land over and above what would be expected from reduced taxation of improvements. The main effect of a higher land tax will be to lower the acquisition value of land while raising the costs of holding the land, which—in the presence of perfect capital markets—should not affect the decision of anyone considering investing in improvements. To the extent that capital markets are not working perfectly and that site values drop as a result of the higher tax on land, population groups that otherwise are locked out of the land market by their inability to raise the required capital will be able to purchase land and subsequently improve it as a result of higher land taxes. This is, incidentally, also the reason why a higher land tax may be thought to lead to a higher degree of homeownership, which is yet another goal of land policy sometimes encountered in the cities of developing countries.

There are reasons, however, to doubt that higher land taxes accompanied by a decrease in the tax on improvements necessarily lead to lower land values. The higher investment on land, which in the long run results from lower taxes on improvements would raise the productivity of land. As a result, the rate of return to land may rise, and land value will rise to the degree that these changes are capitalized into it (Turvey 1957). But if increased land taxes are not accompanied by reduced taxes on improvements, or to the extent that one is mainly concerned with the price of undeveloped land, higher land taxes will produce the generally expected result of lowered land prices, provided land taxes are capitalized into land values to a significant extent.

To the extent that higher land taxes result in lower land prices, they should not also be expected to lower the rate of increase in land prices. As Shoup has put it succinctly, "the rate of return to landowners is the sum of the rate of return of the land in current use plus the rate of price appreciation of land. For vacant fringe land awaiting development the rate of return in current use may be zero or negative; if so, the rate of appreciation must cover both the supply price of capital (the interest rate) and the land tax. Therefore, to provide the same after-tax rate of return as that on other assets, land prices must increase faster in the presence of an annual land value tax" (1983: 139).

Site Value Taxation

Despite the fact that the debate about site value taxation has been going on for many years, there is little quantitative evidence regarding the effect of the site value tax on urban development and investment in improvements. The debate has mainly been about theoretical considerations and has relied on casual observation of developmental effects. In this section, we make use of some primary data from developing countries to analyze site-value effects. Although it is not possible here to add much new, hard evidence to the debate, some effort is made to evaluate the likely extent of investment incentives generated by alternative forms of property taxation.

In order to analyze the effects of site value taxation on physical development, consider the hypothetical case of a switch from a pure land value base to an annual value base with an equal yield.[8] The inclusion of improvements in the tax base is thought to discourage development by penalizing redevelopment and renovation. Whether this disincentive is an effective constraint, however, depends very much on the level of the property tax rate imposed, that is, on the degree to which the tax reduces the potential return to the investor.

Calculations based on valuation estimates made by the senior valuer of the Nairobi City Council in the mid-1970s provide some evidence of this disincentive effect. Table 6-2 indicates the potential development effects of switching from a site value to an annual value basis. For example, property 17, a modern, high-rise office building in central Nairobi, paid KSh230,000 ($1 = KSh7.4 in 1975) under the site value system, but its liability under a rental value system would have risen to more than KSh412,000, an increase of nearly 80 percent. This increase amounts to nearly 5.2 percent of the estimated yearly rental value of the building. In other words, annual profits were 5.2 percent higher under a site value tax. One might argue that this is enough of an incentive to affect an investment decision.

Conversely, property 20 is an old, low-rise property in central Nairobi whose site value is more than ten times its annual rental value. This property would pay KSh258,750 under a site value rate but only KSh47,160 under a rental system. The 82 percent lower level of taxes is equivalent to about half the annual rental value of the property. Suppose this property were improved by erecting a structure that would yield a rent of KSh3.5 million annually. Taxes under a rental system would exceed those under a site system by KSh365,000, an amount equivalent to about 10 percent of the annual return in the higher use. If the owner bears this higher tax cost, that is, if he cannot pass it on in the form of higher rents, the incentive for redevelopment under a site value tax would appear to be great.

Although these two properties admittedly represent extremes in land use, table 6-2 shows significant changes in tax liability for all commercial properties reported in this sample. By contrast, of the three industrial properties none shows a large increase in tax liability, owing to some combination of the labor-intensive nature of their operations and to rental value assessments which do not adequately take into account the yearly earnings attributable to the use of the property.

Residential properties also show varied effects, which primarily depend on whether the property has multiple units or is for a single family. That is, if intensive use is made of the land, as in an apartment house, the property will fare better under a site value than a rental value tax. In table 6-2 only two properties had a lower liability under the rental value system.

The one vacant plot in this sample—property 15—would experience a drastic reduction in total tax liability under a rental value system. This failure to penalize holding land off the market is often given as a major argument against taxing the total property value—and its converse, as a major argument in favor of a site value system. But the question arises of why, under the present tax system, this plot has remained vacant or, for that matter, why the older commercial property, number 20 in table 6-2, has not been renovated or redeveloped.

Table 6-2. *Tax Liabilities in Kenya under Equal-Yield Site Value and Rental Value Systems*
(Kenyan shillings)

Property number	Use	System Site value (thousands)	System Rental value (thousands)	Site value tax[a] (1)	Rental value tax[b] (2)	(2) − (1)	(2) − (1) as a percentage of rental value[c]
1	Residential	50	65	2,875	7,664	4,789	7.4
2	Residential	60	57	3,450	6,720	3,270	5.7
3	Residential	60	48	3,450	5,679	2,229	4.6
4	Residential	55	28	3,162	3,301	139	0.5
5	Residential	55	48	3,162	5,659	2,497	5.2
6	Residential	56	58	3,220	6,838	3,618	6.2
7	Residential	65	40	3,738	4,716	978	2.4
8	Residential	65	33	3,738	3,891	153	0.5
9	Residential	60	80	3,450	9,432	5,982	7.5
10	Residential	10	40	575	4,716	4,141	10.4
11	Residential	6	12	345	1,415	1,070	8.9
12	Residential	10	15	575	1,768	1,193	8.0
13	Residential	100	10	3,750	1,179	−2,571	−25.7
14	Residential	75	90	4,312	10,611	6,299	7.0
15	Residential (vacant)	200	25	11,500	2,948	−8,552	−34.2
16	Residential	16	36	920	4,244	3,324	9.2
17	Central	4,000	3,500	230,000	412,650	182,650	5.2
18	Commercial	800	180	46,000	21,222	−24,778	−13.8
19	Offices	2,500	900	143,750	106,110	−37,640	−4.2
20	Shops	4,500	400	258,750	47,160	−211,590	−52.9
21	Industrial	1,800	1,500	103,500	176,850	73,350	4.9
22	Industrial	104	56	5,980	6,602	622	1.1
23	Industrial	100	62	5,750	7,310	1,560	2.5
24	Industrial	500	150	28,750	17,685	−11,065	−7.4
	Total[d]	15,247	7,433	874,702	876,370		

a. Tax rate equals 5.7 percent.
b. Tax rate equals 11.79 percent.
c. An approximation of the reduction or increase of the annual returns to the property.
d. Differences in the totals are attributable to rounding the tax rate on rental down to 0.1179.
Source: World Bank data.

176

This small and nonrandom sample does suggest that a potentially large incentive effect will accompany the move from a rental to a site value tax or vice versa. It also suggests a substantial shift of the tax burden from nonresidential to residential taxpayers—a potentially significant disadvantage of site value taxation.

Bougeon-Maassen and Linn (1977) compared a site (unimproved) value tax and a capital value tax, using an even smaller set of data for Kingston, Jamaica. The results are described in table 6-3. Site and capital values for six typical residential urban properties and two hotels were estimated by the chief valuer of Jamaica. The sample is dominated by the two hotels, which have much higher site and capital values than do the residential properties. The results are expected: those properties in which land is used more intensively fare significantly better under the site value system. Because of the much lower level of property taxation in Kingston, however, the investment incentives are not as great as in Nairobi.

In both examples, it was possible to establish only the size of the potential incentive which may be attributed to a site value system. Of equal interest is the question of whether such incentives would actually change the resource allocation. One way to deal with this question is with a model which traces the direct and indirect effects of changes in a property tax system. Such a model has been developed by Grieson (1974) for the urban residential housing market in the United States. It is clearly a dubious undertaking to transfer this model without serious adaptation to cities in developing countries, where factor immobility and market segmentation may be much more prevalent than in the typical city in the United States. No attempt has been made here to replicate, let alone adapt, the Grieson model to developing countries. Instead, we have estimated on the basis of Grieson's model the general equilibrium effects of the abolition of a tax on improvements given some representative parameter values for the Colombian urban sector. Using these simulations, we might suggest some orders of magnitude. On the basis of calculations explained in the appendix to this chapter, the supply of structures would increase by 5 to 7 percent in the long run as a result of the abolition of an annual tax of 1 percent on the capital value of structures with a concomitant increase in the value of land by 10 to 13 percent.

Perhaps the best study carried out on this subject is by Follain and Miyake (1986) for Jamaica. They used a computable general equilibrium model to estimate the effects of replacing part of the national income tax with either a national land value or capital value tax. The results of this analysis can be summarized in four interesting observations:

1. The land value tax cannot be a primary source of central government revenue such as an income tax or general consumption tax. If the land

Table 6-3. *Tax Liabilities in Jamaica under Equal-Yield Site Value and Capital Value Systems, 1977*
(Jamaican dollars)

Property number	Use	System Site value (thousands)	System Capital value (thousands)	Site value tax (1)	Capital value tax (2)	(2) − (1)	(2) − (1) as a percentage of capital value[a]
1	Residential	5	20	250	123	−127	−6.4 (2.1)
2	Residential	10	35	500	216	−284	−8.1 (0.3)
3	Residential	12	45	600	278	−322	−7.2 (1.3)
4	Residential	19	60	850	370	−480	−8.0 (0.4)
5	Residential	28	80	1,400	494	−906	−11.3 (−2.9)
6	Residential	20	75	1,000	463	−537	−7.2 (1.3)
7	Hotel	1,600	13,860	80,000	85,565	5,565	0.4 n.a.
8	Hotel	485	1,100	9,700	6,791	−2,909	−2.6 n.a.

n.a. Not applicable.

Note: The site value tax is assumed to be levied at a flat 5 percent rate. The equal-yield tax rate on capital value is then calculated to amount to 0.62 percent and is used to determine the tax burden on capital value. Rental value is computed at an assumed rate of return of 10 percent on capital value.

a. Figures in parentheses show tax differences when only residential properties are considered in which case the capital value tax rate is 1.5 percent.

Source: Site and capital value estimates provided by the Chief Valuer, Government of Jamaica.

tax were used to replace 20 percent of the income tax in Jamaica, it would amount to expropriation.

2. The efficiency gains associated with a switch to a land value tax from an income tax are quite small in a closed economy with a labor-supply-elasticity of 0.15. The gain amounts to about 0.06 percent of GNP. In an open economy with the same labor-supply-elasticity, the gain is more than ten times larger. The efficiency gains associated with a switch to a capital value tax are equally modest.

3. A land value tax will generate larger ratios of structure to land, relative to a capital value tax. It is less widely recognized that a capital value and land value tax can have different effects on the use of other inputs. This analysis indicates that some of the increase in the intensity of land development associated with a site value tax comes at the expense of employment and investment in equipment. The capital value tax generates a process with smaller buildings that house more labor and machines. The land value tax encourages the construction of larger plants which house fewer workers and fewer machines.

4. The implications for income distribution are that labor gains from a shift to either the land value or capital value tax, and landowners lose from a switch to either. For example, the share of income distributed to landowners declines by 42.3 percent and capital and labor increase their share by about 2.5 percent in the closed economy model when the land value tax replaces 10 percent of the income tax.

Differential Taxation of Vacant Urban Land

The main purpose of higher vacant land taxation is to encourage earlier development of vacant urban land. As Smith (1979) has shown, this objective is likely to be met provided the taxes are levied and enforced at rates which significantly affect the rate of return to vacant urban lots. Evidence from Taiwan (China), where this tax was levied until 1985 and where some of its effects have been studied, suggests that the tax has acted as an inducement to land development in a considerable number of cases (Lent 1977). Another likely effect of higher taxation of vacant land is to lower land values before development and thus to tax away some of the land value increments which precede actual development of a lot as a result of capitalization of expected future increases in yields (Smith 1979). The rate of appreciation in land values is likely to be increased as a result of the vacant land tax, however, for much the same reason that site value taxation is likely to accelerate the rate of increase in land prices. Investors who continue to hold vacant land have to earn a higher proportion of the total rate of return from that investment through capital gains once the yield of the vacant lot is reduced or possibly even turned negative by the vacant land tax.

Surcharges on vacant land are usually of minor revenue importance. Therefore any favorable distributive effects are likely to be unimportant.

The vacant land tax must therefore be judged almost exclusively by how well it achieves its major objective—advancing the timing of development of vacant plots—and to what degree achievement of this goal actually leads to more efficient use of urban land. There is by no means a necessary link between advanced timing of land development and increased efficiency. As Shoup (1983) points out, the tax may also mean that development may occur prematurely or inappropriate structures may be put up in response to the incentives provided by the vacant land tax. And even if in some areas the private sector may be too slow in filling in undeveloped lots in central locations or may not permit rapid enough subdivision at the periphery (this is likely to be the much rarer problem), it is not likely that all vacant urban land will be developed too late. In fact, city officials frequently complain about excessively early development through squatting or illegal subdivision. In order to minimize the distortions generated by a vacant land tax and to maximize its corrective effect, it must therefore be used in coordination with a land development plan designed by the urban authorities to yield the most rational pattern of urban growth. This would require selectively higher taxation of vacant land in certain areas where development is to be accelerated. Such selective vacant land taxation has been employed in Bogotá.

Taxes on vacant land are administratively feasible. With the more extensive use of computers in property tax record keeping, especially in the larger cities in developing countries, it is possible to keep track of liable properties. There remains, however, the problem that it is difficult to provide a watertight definition of what constitutes vacant or underdeveloped land. Such definitional problems, according to Yoingco (1988: 10–11) are a principal reason why the idle land tax sur-rate has never been imposed in the Philippines.

In sum, the vacant land tax can be an effective instrument in advancing urban land development provided it is tied explicitly to existing land use plans, provided it is levied at rates high enough to affect landowners' perceptions of the cost of holding vacant urban land, and provided an unambiguous definition of the tax base is agreed upon. Certainly, there is little reason to tax vacant urban land at rates lower than developed land, although this is done in some countries (see table 6-1).[9]

Preferential Treatment of Owner-Occupants

Many countries provide tax breaks to owner-occupants of residential properties. In the United States, these take the form of income tax deductions for property taxes and mortgage interest payments, and nontaxation of capital gains upon the sale of owner-occupied properties. In many developing countries, owner-occupants tend to receive preferential assessments or outright exemptions, whose immediate goal is to encourage homeownership. This goal does not, however, appear to be related in any direct manner to the basic efficiency objective. Rather, it may be founded on the belief that homeowners provide greater political stability, or it may very simply be intended as a tax break for the middle and upper classes. This last aspect is probably the major actual effect of this preferential treatment, since it has never been established that it has actually led to more homeownership.

Differential Taxation of Industrial and Commercial Properties

Industrial and commercial properties are often more heavily taxed than residential properties. The justification is that owners of these properties have a greater ability to pay than do owners of residential lots; in other words, the main objective is that of equity. In the long run some shifting of the burden will occur and as a result the differentiated tax will become less progressive and may even be more regressive than a flat rate property tax. At the same time, there will be added distortions introduced into decisions about resource allocation and thus a potential loss in efficiency.

If lower taxes are charged to industrial and commercial properties, it is usually with the purpose of encouraging and attracting business investment in a particular jurisdiction. To the extent that tax exemptions are competitive between jurisdictions, they will have no effect on the location decisions of firms; and even if only one jurisdiction were to grant the preferential treatment, the rate differential would have to be substantial and in prolonged existence to have any effect at all. When property tax exemptions for business are pervasive throughout a country, they will result in an added tilt in favor of capital-intensive development, as do subsidized interest rates and other tax breaks for business investment. This is not likely to be a desirable effect in developing countries where capital is a relatively scarce resource.

Progressive Rate Structure

The main purpose of progressively structured property tax rates is to put a higher share of the tax burden on the more valuable properties and therefore presumably on the wealthier population groups. This goal is probably served quite well by this practice. But progressive tax rates also have some allocative effects, which are usually not explicitly considered by policymakers.

As an owner invests in improvements to his property, its value will increase and it will be pushed into a higher tax bracket. This is likely to act as a disincentive to more intensive use and development of the land and as such implies a distortion in the allocation of resources. Conversely, to the extent that increased land value is taxed at higher rates, progressive property tax rates—compared with a flat rate tax—will tend to reduce the rate of growth of land values and will reduce the spread between property values by raising those at the lower end of the spectrum. This effect is probably undesirable on equity grounds, since (given imperfect capital markets) higher land prices for low-value land tend to interfere with the access of low-income groups to the land market.

Exemption of Low-Value Properties

The exemption of low-value properties from property taxation represents one form of progressively structured tax rates. There are two types of exemption. The first, which is the more common, exempts all properties below a certain cutoff value; all properties at or above that value are taxed at the full rate. This system has the great disadvantage of involving a discrete jump in the average tax rate and therefore implying a marginal tax rate of infinity at the cutoff point. As a result, a strong incentive is introduced to falsify property value assessments, so that properties which lie above the exemption limit are actually assessed below it. Furthermore, this structure provides a strong disincentive to invest in improving the property.

Much less distortionary is the second type, under which a certain amount is deductible from taxable property value for all properties. This will result in the full exemption of properties which fall below that value. For properties growing in value above that limit, the marginal tax rate will switch from zero to the basic tax rate. Thus there will still be some incentive for underassessment and some disincentive to investment, but this incentive would be much less than when the marginal tax rate is infinity at the cutoff point. For properties with values above the deductible amount, the marginal tax rate will remain constant while the average tax rate rises asymptotically to equal the marginal tax rate. This has the advantage of distorting investment decisions to only a small extent for a limited number of properties, while at the same time placing higher average tax burdens on properties with higher values, thus continuing the redistribution efforts up to higher property values. Compared with progressively structured tax rates, the deductible method is easier to administer in the absence of computer facilities and does not involve frequent jumps or continuous changes in the marginal tax rate.

Low-value exemptions or deductibles will, like progressively structured rates, raise the value of low-value properties relative to high-value properties. This may again make it more difficult for low-income people to acquire land. Conversely, those low-income people who own land will have more disposable income available for improvements and a greater incentive to make them, since they do not pay taxes on the land and improvements as long as the value of their property remains under the exemption or deductible limit. This would encourage more investment in low-cost housing than would a flat rate tax on all property. Low-value property exemptions would be very simple to administer since the collection costs—as well as the compliance costs—for the many small properties in cities of developing countries are likely to be quite high. This reduction in collection cost should offset to a large extent the loss in revenue resulting from the exemption policy (see chapter 4).

Lower Taxes on Suburban Locations

As mentioned in chapter 5, lower taxes on suburban locations are generally rationalized on the grounds that these properties receive fewer services than inner-city properties and their owners should therefore not be required to pay property taxes at the inner-city rate. This is essentially an argument regarding the horizontal equity of the urban service pricing structure. If the objective of horizontal equity is taken in isolation, this argument is basically correct, although unserviced properties will pay lower property taxes already because the value of these properties tends to be lower than the value of serviced properties. As the appendix to this chapter demonstrates, however, there remains a significant net benefit to properties that have access to public services provided by tax-financed investments.

More problematic in the implementation of differentiated property tax rates is the fact that some areas with lower rates actually have equal or better services than some areas with higher rates. This situation often occurs because of inadequate property tax administration; that is, it takes considerable effort to reclassify particular areas from low- to high-tax status, even after most or all of the public services have been provided. If the property tax is viewed primarily as a benefit charge for services provided, it must be linked explicitly and directly with the quantity and quality of services provided rather than being levied on the basis of an outdated urban-rural classification (as is the case in Colombia and Taiwan [China]) or on an outdated central-periphery dichotomy (as was the case in Bombay and Hong Kong).

One needs to consider the effects of this policy on the timing of development, urban sprawl, speculation, and land prices. Taxing properties at lower rates in specified locations would not tax away any of the speculative gains from holding land vacant before development; it may encourage development of areas outside the high-tax perimeter rather than within the perimeter, to the extent that structures are included in the property tax; and it would leave land prices in the low-tax areas at levels higher than would have existed with equal tax rates applied to all properties.

Land Value Increment Taxation

Land value increment taxation has been promoted on the grounds of equity as well as resource allocation. Perhaps the best-known use of this tax is in Taiwan (China), where it is levied at a progressive rate on the net increment to the value of land at transfer (Riew 1987). Statutory rates range from 40 to 60 percent, and the basis for computing value increments is tied to the wholesale price index. The land value increment tax accounted for about 9 percent of total revenues in Taiwan (China) in 1985 (King 1988: 9–10).

Advocates of this tax claim that it improves horizontal and vertical equity since it taxes away unearned increments in land value which result from public investment. This will tend to equalize benefits from land-ownership, since it helps to eliminate windfall gains from public activity, and it will improve vertical equity, since unearned land value increments are thought to accrue to the landowners, who have higher incomes.

Besides these uncontroversial equity arguments, there are also the intended efficiency effects, measured as usual by the use of proxy goals such as advanced timing of development, reduced land speculation, and lower land prices (or lower land price appreciation). Apart from the question of whether in general it is desirable on efficiency grounds to advance the timing of development or reduce land prices, it is not clear that land value increment taxation will have the desired effect on these proxy goals. As Smith (1979) has argued, the effect of a land value increment tax on the land price depends on whether or not the tax is levied on realized or accrued increments. The latter is the usual practice in developing countries, and it may result in "lock-in" effects (that is, effects which provide a disincentive to sell a property). The stronger these effects, the less likely it is that the price of land will drop as a result of the imposition of an increment tax. Similarly, it is quite uncertain on analytical grounds that a land value increment tax will uniformly affect the timing of development or the rate of change in land prices (Smith 1979). It therefore comes as no surprise to find little strong evidence regarding the effects of this tax on the timing of development or land prices (Grimes 1974).

The main justification for the use of a land value increment tax would therefore appear to depend on its equity effects. These must be balanced, however, against the administrative difficulties of applying such a tax. Land valuation procedures are very imperfect in most developing countries, and it is difficult and costly to refine them with the frequency required to make a land value increment tax work effectively. Furthermore, a standard property tax, if levied at sufficiently high rates, can achieve much the same goal as does a land value increment tax in capturing land value increments. With the framework developed in the appendix to this chapter, it may be shown that a 5 percent tax rate on the site value of land at a 10 percent discount rate captures 50 percent of the increased yield of a property. Any general land value increment tax policy, however, would probably not attempt to recapture much more than 50 percent of estimated increases in land value (given the administrative difficulties of fine-tuning value increment estimates and because some of the land value increases may be due to private, rather than public, action; see Grimes 1974). A site value tax may have much the same equity effects as a land value increment tax. Especially if a reasonably effective property tax system is in place, or if urban services are effectively financed by user or development charges, it would not be good policy advice to argue for a switch from the existing property tax system to a land value increment tax.

Property Transfer Tax

A tax is often levied on the transfer of real estate in industrial and developing countries alike, generally as a proportion of the stated sales price (Smith 1979: 145). In many respects this tax has the characteristics of a true nuisance tax. Its main purpose is to raise revenues, but with few exceptions (for example, in Korean cities) it does not raise significant amounts of resources at either the national or local levels. At the same time, it is likely to affect resource allocation adversely and provides an incentive for understating the sales price of properties, thus weakening the main data base of real estate appraisal for the purpose of other taxes, especially the regular property tax.

The allocative effects of the property transfer tax, like those of any other tax on improvements, would in the long run tend to provide a disincentive to investments in improvement and structures. Whether this is stronger than the case for an equal-yield property tax levied annually depends on the effective tax rates, the owner's expected holding period for the property, and his discount rate. As Smith (1979) has shown, the property transfer tax does not necessarily lead to a lock-in effect in delaying property transfer, but it may delay development if payment of the tax can be avoided or postponed until the owner dies or finds sufficient funds to develop the property himself. These conditions are likely to be typical for many developing countries, and therefore one would expect a lock-in effect to occur. Unfortunately, no empirical evidence is available to verify the conclusion.

Because the post-tax return on property ownership is reduced by a property transfer tax, property values will in general be depressed by the imposition of such a tax. Whether this reduction is more or less than is the case with a flat rate property tax collected annually is difficult to tell in the absence of detailed information on relative tax rates, expected holding periods, and discount rates. Similarly, the relative effect of a transfer tax on the appreciation rates of property values cannot be established without this type of information.

In summary, the property transfer tax can be collected relatively easily if property transfer registration is required in any case; but when levied at rates high enough to provide significant revenues, its effect on land market operations make it a poor substitute for a land tax or even a general property tax. Where both taxes are in operation side by side, as is typically the case, its administrative resources would be saved and distortions avoided if the property transfer tax were removed and additional revenues were raised through a somewhat higher general property tax rate.

Annual Value or Rental Value Tax

A final variant of the flat rate property tax levied annually on the capital value of real estate is the frequently employed tax on the annual or rental value of properties. In discussions of the preferability of one system over the other, two main arguments are usually given. The first relates to the supposed ease of administering a rental tax, which, as was shown in chapter 4, may no longer be a very convincing argument for most developing countries, given changed housing tenure patterns, the difficulties of assessing the nonresidential base, and the difficulties of administration. The second argument relates to the fact that the tax on rental value is based only on the present-use value of a property rather than on the property's development value (that is, that part of the property's current market value which is accounted for by its potential for future development rather than current use). The most extreme form of this practice is found in the nontaxation of vacant urban property under some rental value systems precisely because their current-use value is zero, although their market value, which reflects the capitalized (discounted) stream of expected future benefits from development, may be quite substantial.

To the extent that the property tax is seen mainly as a charge for urban services provided to serviced and improved properties, the exemption of vacant lots, and more generally the taxation only at use value rather than at development value, appears at the surface to be justifiable in terms of horizontal equity. Even in equity terms, however, upon closer inspection it is questionable because a vacant lot in an area which is provided with infrastructure and other urban services unavoidably imposes costs on the service facilities: distribution networks need to be extended to and beyond the property, and excess capacity must be created to allow for future demand resulting from the expected development of the empty lots. In this respect, therefore, taxation of vacant lots is appropriate on equity grounds (sharing costs imposed by lots even before they are developed), and it may be conducive to efficiency in the sense of advancing the timing of development or further improvement. This aspect of capital value taxation—the discouragement of speculation and the creation of incentives for development of vacant urban lots or underdeveloped properties—has been cited as one of the main reasons for preferring capital value over rental value taxation (Lent 1974).

Closely related is the effect on land prices of the alternative property tax systems. Since the capital value tax imposes a higher burden on vacant or underdeveloped land than does the rental value tax, vacant land prices should in general be lower under the capital value tax system. Conversely, in line with the earlier arguments regarding the relations between the level of land prices and their rate of appreciation, the latter will be more rapid the lower the level of land prices in order to compensate for the lower rate of return while the property is still underdeveloped.

Appendix

The Effect of Property Taxes on the Supply of Structures

The following estimation of the effect of a tax on structures is based on the model of the urban housing market developed by Grieson (1974).

As a first step, take Grieson's finding that the elasticity of supply of structures (E_s) may be approximated by the following equation:

$$E_s = \frac{1}{2} \frac{\text{Total property value}}{\text{land value.}}$$

From Colombian data presented in table 5-4, it can be shown by using this equation that the average value of E_s is 1.23, as compared with 2.36 for the United States (Grieson 1974). This finding confirms the expectation that capital is less mobile within developing countries than it is in the United States.

Next, it is possible to estimate the elasticity of the supply of structures with respect to the tax rate (E_{qt}) as

$$E_{qt} = \frac{-1}{\dfrac{1}{E_s} \dfrac{1}{E_d}}$$

where E_s is the supply elasticity of structures as defined above and E_d is the demand-elasticity of structures. This may be set at unity for developing countries as for the United States and therefore, given the estimated value of $E_s = 1.23$ for Colombia, $E_{qt} = -0.55$. And since the elasticity of land value with respect to the tax rate (E_{vt}) may be shown to be equal to $2E_{qt}$, it follows that E_{vt} is -1.10. It is also possible to estimate the elasticity of the total property price with respect to the tax rate (E_{pt}) from the equation

$$E_{pt} = \frac{-1}{1 + E_s} = -0.45.$$

If one then wants to establish the effect of the adoption of, say, a 1 percent annual tax on the value of structures, it is merely necessary to calculate 10 percent of the figures shown above for E_{qt}, E_{vt}, and E_{pt}. The quantitative results indicate that a conversion from a general property to a site value tax would increase the supply of structures by 5.5 percent, land values by 11 percent, and total property value by 4.5 percent. Table 6-4 shows similar changes for alternative assumptions regarding the value E_s. The results conform closely to the theoretical conclusions derived

Table 6-4. *Estimated Impact of the Elimination of the Tax on Improvements in Colombia*

E_s	Supply of structures	Land price	Structure price
0.0	0.0	0.0	10.0
0.5	3.3	6.7	6.6
1.0	5.0	10.0	5.0
2.0	6.7	13.3	3.3
10.0	100.0	20.0	0.0

Source: See text for explanation.

earlier. As the supply elasticity of structures increases (that is, as the time horizon lengthens), the percentage change in structures increases from a low of zero (for $E_s = 0$) to a maximum of 100 (for $E_s = 10$), land value changes from 0 percent to 20 percent, and property value changes from 10 percent when $E_s = 0$, to 0 percent when $E_s = 10$. Taking the range of E_s between 1 and 2, as reflecting the most likely capital market conditions in developing countries, the supply of structures may be assumed to increase between 5.0 percent and 6.7 percent in the long run as a result of the abolition of the tax on structures, with a concomitant increase in land prices between 10.0 percent and 13.3 percent. If, in addition, taxes on land are raised in order to offset the loss from structure taxes, as is likely, additional allocative effects may occur, especially a tendency toward lower land prices offsetting the increase in the price of land observed above.

Property Value Change and Property Taxation

An increase in land value due to improved urban services will be reflected in higher property taxes. This note demonstrates the relation between property value increments and property tax changes on the basis of a simple capitalization model.

Consider two properties, one at the center (property 1) and the other at the periphery (property 2). Property 1 is assumed to command a higher annual yield R_1, due to the availability of publicly provided services, than property 2, which does not benefit from these services and thus has the lower annual yield R_2. The unit value of a property (V) may be expressed as:

$$V = \frac{R}{r + t}$$

where r is the discount rate used to discount the yield stream R, which is expected to remain constant to infinity, and where t is the ad valorem property tax rate, also expected to remain constant to infinity. The tax rate t is defined by the relation $T = tV$, where T is the property tax payment per unit of property. Given this relation, it is then possible to write DV, the difference in property value between property 1 and property 2, as a function of DR, the difference in yield streams:

$$DV = V_1 - V_2 = \frac{R_1 - R_2}{r + t} = \frac{DR}{r + t}.$$

DT, the difference in tax payments between properties 1 and 2, may be written as

$$DT = T_1 - T_2 = t(V_1 - V_2) = tDV.$$

Combining the last two equations, it follows that:

$$DT = \frac{t}{r + t} DR, \text{ where } \frac{t}{r + t} < 1 \text{ for } r > 0.$$

In other words, this last equation shows that there is a difference in tax burdens between properties 1 and 2, which is a constant proportion of the difference in annual yields. However, since the proportionality factor is less than unity whenever the discount rate is positive, the difference in tax burden will in general be smaller than the difference in yields. Taking typical values for t and r, at 1 percent and 10 percent respectively, it may be seen that DT is only 1/11 of DR. Thus there remains a significant net benefit to property 1 from the tax-financed investments in urban infrastructure, whereas property 2, which does not receive this benefit, fails to be compensated by a correspondingly lower tax burden. In this analysis it was assumed that property 2 is not expected to be serviced in the foreseeable future. To the extent that such an expectation exists, however, and that expected higher yields are capitalized into present market values of the property, the tax burden on the still unserviced property will be even higher or, what amounts to the same, the difference in tax burdens DT will be even less than in the case explained above.

7 Automotive Taxation

MOTOR VEHICLE OWNERSHIP and use represent an excellent but much neglected tax base for urban governments in developing countries. A city's number of automobiles often grows faster than its population (see table 7-1), automobile ownership and use are easily taxable, and the burden of automobile taxes is likely to fall on persons with higher incomes. The case for greater use of such taxes is strong: in addition to possibilities for yielding revenue, the growing number of automobiles requires more expenditures to maintain roads and imposes the costs of congestion and pollution on the urban environment. This chapter identifies and evaluates the various fiscal instruments which urban governments might develop to utilize this important revenue base and to control the high costs of urban vehicular congestion.

The Case for Automotive Taxation

There are three possible arguments for taxation of the ownership and use of automobiles:

- To take advantage of a rapidly growing tax base
- To recapture the costs of public expenditures required because of automobile use
- To control the social cost of automobile use.

In this section, we explore each of these arguments.

Table 7-1 shows the degree to which the growth in the number of registered automobiles has exceeded that of the population in a sample of cities in developing countries. (The overwhelming proportion of the total urban motor vehicle fleet is made up of automobiles.) Furthermore, comparing automobiles and populations in urban areas with national totals shows that car ownership is heavily concentrated in the largest cities of developing countries.[1] For example, in 1970, Bangkok had 8 percent of Thailand's population and 83 percent of its cars. Comparable figures are 7 and 57 percent in Seoul, 15 and 65 percent in Tunis, but 17 and 16 percent in Paris. These trends of growth and concentration in developing countries are likely to persist, and thus—along with the continued growth of urban populations and of income—make the case for automobiles as an important part of the urban tax base.

Associated with the growth of the urban motor vehicle fleet is the greater expenditures required to maintain road and street infrastructure

Table 7-1. *Rates of Growth of Population and Number of Automobiles,
Selected Cities*

City	1960–70		1970–80	
	Rate of growth of population	Rate of growth of number of automobiles	Rate of growth of population	Rate of growth of number of automobiles
San José, Costa Rica	5.4	10.9	3.5	—
Hong Kong, Hong Kong	2.9	7.1	2.5	7.4
Bombay, India	3.7	8.2	3.7	6.1
Calcutta, India	2.2	7.2	3.0	5.6
Madras, India	4.5	5.8	3.5[a]	2.4[a]
Jakarta, Indonesia	5.3	8.8	4.0	9.8
Seoul, Rep. of Korea	8.5	22.0	5.0	11.7
Beirut, Lebanon	2.9	9.1	—	—
Kuala Lumpur, Malaysia	6.5	11.3	2.5	40.0
Mexico City, Mexico	5.8	10.5	5.0	11.5
Lagos, Nigeria	7.9	15.5	7.6	− 5.2[b]
Singapore, Singapore	2.6	6.7	1.5	6.8
Bangkok, Thailand	6.2	12.0	9.1	7.9
Tunis, Tunisia	2.5	6.0	3.1	2.6[c]
Istanbul, Turkey	6.0	12.2	—	—
Caracas, Venezuela	5.4	8.3	—	—

— Not available.
a. Growth in population is for 1970–86; for automobiles, 1970–84.
b. 1983–85.
c. 1980–83.
Source: World Bank (1986).

and to manage traffic. That more cars will create more pressure for more
expenditures is only half the story. The unit costs of these services are
also likely to rise with the growth of congestion and land prices in central
urban areas, and the growth of the relative price of materials (for example, asphalt and concrete; World Bank 1975c).

Besides these two reasons for taxing motor vehicles—the base is there
and greater numbers of cars generate a need for more road expenditures—there are the strong efficiency arguments for controlling the use
of motor vehicles in urban areas. Traffic congestion and air and noise
pollution in many cities of developing countries are either as bad as or
worse than in industrial nations.[2] And although higher levels of congestion and pollution may be more acceptable in developing than industrial
countries, actual congestion and pollution in most of the large developing-country cities have almost certainly far exceeded tolerable levels.
Perhaps most important, things are likely to get worse in the years ahead.

The potential gains from reducing the growth of automobile use are
substantial—time savings, health benefits from cleaner air, reduced expenditures on roads and streets—but structuring automobile taxes to
achieve them is not easy. Consider three observations about taxation and

road congestion. First, the costs imposed by an additional vehicle using an urban roadway are external to the operator in that other road users bear most of the additional costs in terms of time.[3] The private cost of operating a vehicle on congested urban streets therefore diverges from the social cost, and the result is an inefficient use of urban streets. One of the aims of urban motor vehicle taxation should be to reduce this discrepancy between private and social cost by charging road users the marginal social cost of operating their vehicles. This would reduce urban street congestion and increase the efficiency of urban road use. Second, buses and commercial vehicles are likely to be affected more seriously by congestion than are automobiles because of the high proportion of labor costs in their total operating costs, their lesser degree of flexibility in timing and road choice, and the losses of efficiency associated with uncertainty in bus schedules and delivery times (World Bank 1975c: 27–29). Third, congestion varies according to the time of day and the location in the city. Any road user charges designed to account for the external costs of congestion should therefore be restricted to the times and places at which congestion occurs; otherwise the use of uncongested roads would be overpriced and reduced to inefficiently low levels.

Which level of government should tax motor vehicles? A strong case can be made that urban governments, rather than higher-level authorities, should be permitted and required to deal with the social costs of the rapid growth in the number of urban motor vehicles. Urban residents bear most of the negative externalities, such as congestion and pollution, and are therefore likely to be most interested in countering these costs through appropriate fees and taxes. Furthermore, local authorities are often responsible for constructing and maintaining much of the urban road infrastructure and are frequently responsible for regulating city traffic and for providing public transportation (see chapter 2). Local governments in metropolitan areas should therefore be given authority to control congestion with fiscal instruments and to provide for urban infrastructure commensurate with an optimal expansion of motor vehicle traffic.[4] This does not imply that higher-level governments should not levy any taxes on motor vehicle ownership and use. In fact higher authorities should levy automotive taxes (over and above standard sales or value added taxes) to meet three goals: to recover (approximately) the variable maintenance costs of uncongested rural and interurban highways, to recover some of the capital costs of the interurban and rural road network, and (perhaps) to tax consumers of luxury cars more highly in the interest of income redistribution. Fuel taxes—and probably quite low ones—would serve the first goal, sales and license taxes on motor vehicles would serve the second and third. Import tariffs on automobiles would serve to protect domestic production of automobiles and limit imports for balance of payments reasons. In most cases, however, such protection is likely to be a second-best instrument of national economic policy.[5]

Local Automotive Tax Practices in Developing Countries

Despite the strong case for local government taxation of urban motor vehicle ownership and use, particularly in large metropolitan areas, urban governments in developing countries are not universally authorized to levy such charges. For instance, in Manila local authorities have been expressly enjoined from levying any taxes or fees on motor vehicle registration (Bahl, Brigg, and Smith 1976). And local governments that can impose taxes on motor vehicles or fuel consumption generally have not made a large effort to tap this revenue source at its full potential. Only in two of the approximately thirty developing-country cities discussed in chapter 3 have automotive taxes contributed more than 10 percent of total local revenue (Jakarta and Guatemala City), and only in five cities has the share of these taxes in total local tax revenue exceeded 10 percent (Guatemala City, Jakarta, Seoul, Tehran, and Valencia). The example of Jakarta especially underlines the fact that automotive taxation, if turned over to local authorities and if given sufficient attention, can make a major contribution to local revenues even in a city not otherwise noted for its fiscal or administrative achievement.[6] In all cities for which detailed revenue and expenditure data could be assembled, the expenditure on urban roadways exceeded revenues from automotive taxes. In Jakarta the reverse held true, with motor vehicle tax revenues exceeding road-related expenditures by 220 percent (table 7-2).

A careful look at the practices in selected countries and cities reveals that local automotive taxation consists of a very heterogeneous set of levies (Linn 1979a). Most cities impose some form of annual license taxes

Table 7-2. *Revenues from Local Automotive Taxation as a Percentage of Total Local Expenditure on Urban Roadways, Selected Cities*

City, year	Revenue
Cartagena, Colombia, 1972	7.2
Ahmadabad, India, 1972	19.2
Ahmadabad, India, 1981	19.4
Bombay, India, 1971	19.0
Bombay, India, 1982	4.1
Jakarta, Indonesia, 1973	220.2
Jakarta, Indonesia, 1982	286.9
Kingston, Jamaica, 1971	0.0
Seoul, Rep. of Korea, 1970	36.2
Seoul, Rep. of Korea, 1983	18.3
Manila, Philippines, 1970	0.0
Tunis, Tunisia, 1973	0.2

on all motor vehicles whose owners reside in the particular taxing jurisdiction, some levy a one-time tax on the registration of motor vehicles,
and two cities levy a local fuel tax. Only in Singapore has an effort been
made to apply restrictive licenses according to time and area of road
usage within the city. Singapore also appears to be the only city in the
sample in which parking fees have been introduced and collected at more
than a nominal level. Tolls on urban roads do not appear to be levied
in any of the cities surveyed for this study.[7]

Local license taxes fall into three major categories. In Guatemala City,
Ahmadabad, and the Honduran municipalities, flat annual taxes have
been levied, differentiated only by type of vehicle. In Colombian and
Korean cities and in Jakarta and Bombay, the tax has varied not only by
type of vehicle but also according to weight, cylinder size, or age. In
addition, there are "special features" in a number of cities: in Korea, the
local license tax was lower for business than for nonbusiness use, and
for large cars the tax varied with axle distance; in Bombay, higher taxes
applied to vehicles not equipped with pneumatic tires; in Bogotá, the
license tax declined with the age of the vehicle; and in Colombian and
Korean municipalities buses were charged according to the number of
seats.

In contrast to annual license taxes, registration fees and transfer taxes
were levied whenever the title to the motor vehicle changed hands (Bogotá, Cartagena, Jakarta) or only once at the time of the initial registration
(Tehran). In Colombia the registration fee appears to have been nominal
(less than $1 in the mid-1970s) and was presumably intended to reflect
only the administrative cost of registration. In Jakarta and Tehran, however, the registration "fees" were clearly more in line with the nature of
taxes. They amounted to a sizable proportion of vehicle value in Jakarta
(10 percent for initial title transfer and 5 percent for any subsequent
transfer) and in Tehran a flat charge of approximately $44 was required
for the initial registration of cars, taxis, and buses (half that amount for
trucks).

Where local fuel taxes applied, they were usually levied on a specific
basis (in Bogotá, Guatemala City, and Singapore) and generally applied
only to gasoline.[8] The case of Singapore is exceptional since the fuel tax
is a combination of a local and national tax, and Singapore had one of
the highest national gasoline tax rates in a sample of forty-eight developing countries surveyed by Smith (1974). In the Philippines, cities and
municipalities could (before 1974) impose a tax on gasoline of up to 25
percent of the national gasoline tax. In the Manila metropolitan area,
different percentage rates applied in the various local jurisdictions, varying from 0 to 25 percent of the national tax.

Singapore is even more exceptional since it is the first city in the world
(that we know of) to make a significant effort to restrain central city
congestion through the application of area- and time-specific licenses and

parking charges. The scheme was initiated in June 1975 and was monitored extensively by local officials and by World Bank staff (Watson and Holland 1978). In essence, a restricted zone in the city was defined to include the most congested portion of the central business district, covering 62 hectares with twenty-two entry points. Between 7:30 a.m. and 10:15 a.m. entry into this restricted zone by private automobile was permitted only if the vehicle exhibited a license which cost $26 a month or $1.30 a day (in 1976). Buses, commercial vehicles, motorcycles, and car pools (that is, cars carrying four persons or more) were exempt. This scheme was supplemented by a drastic increase in public and commercial parking fees. In addition, fringe parking lots and park-and-ride schemes were offered.

In sum, local governments in developing countries have had a range of experiences with automotive taxes, but with few exceptions these taxes are underutilized. Considering the potential scope of these taxes for raising local revenues, improving the allocation of resources, and more equitably distributing income, a careful review of them is important. The remainder of this chapter is devoted to this task.

Objectives of Automotive Taxation

Automotive taxes may serve multiple objectives, and various tax instruments can be used to emphasize one objective over another. Economic efficiency, distributive equity, buoyant revenue performance, administrative ease, and political acceptability are common goals of automotive taxes.

The efficiency goal takes on special significance because of the frequently encountered divergence between the private and social costs of operating a motor vehicle. In an assessment of automotive taxation, therefore, an important issue to address is how well various taxes are able to approximate the difference between the marginal social and private costs of automobile use. The marginal social cost includes the variable maintenance and pollution costs and the marginal congestion costs, that is, the additonal cost of vehicle operation, lost time, and noise and foul air that the vehicle operator imposes on others by putting an additional vehicle on the road. If automotive taxes exactly equal these marginal costs, they will produce an efficient use of roads. If, however, these taxes exceed or fall short of the marginal social cost, road use will be inefficiently restricted or expanded, provided only that the demand for road space is responsive to the cost borne by the user. The marginal social costs of road use cannot be measured exactly, but they can be approximated closely enough to generate a set of guidelines for tax rates.

Variable maintenance costs of road use, whether in rural or urban areas, depend mainly on the type of road surface and are significantly higher on unpaved than on paved roads.[9] Therefore, the use of unpaved roads should be taxed at a higher rate than the use of paved roads. The proportion of unpaved roads can be significant in cities of developing countries. Officials in Cali estimated in 1974 that approximately 50 percent of its streets were unpaved. In Guatemala City the proportion of unpaved streets in the late 1960s was 51 percent, and in San Jose 21 percent.[10] Congestion costs vary with time of day and location in the city, and efficient charges for urban road users would have to vary accordingly.[11] Air pollution costs are directly related to the amount of fuel consumed, but also to the state of repair of the car and to climatic conditions, in particular, wind and precipitation.

Even if these costs could be measured precisely it is unlikely that any single tax instrument could be structured so as to reflect the full marginal social costs. Moreover, when one considers other criteria, such as revenue performance, equity, and administrative ease, the possibilities of finding a single best tax are even more remote. The implication is that more than one tax instrument will have to be used to attain the multiple policy goals and that each instrument should be aimed at the goal it is most likely to attain. It is therefore important to consider each form of automotive tax carefully and to review its impact on the policy objectives. On the basis of this analysis, a strategy for urban automotive taxation might be developed.

Two important caveats are in order. First, no practicable tax design is likely to achieve all objectives; in particular, some efficiency gains will have to be traded off against some efficiency losses. Moreover, better revenue performance, greater administrative ease, and equity will involve some efficiency losses, whatever tax instruments are chosen. Much will therefore depend on the circumstances of a city, as well as on the weights attached to the various objectives. Second, existing tax policies, and more generally the existing institutional framework in any given city, will influence the desirability and feasibility of automotive tax policy. Of particular importance are higher-level government actions, since they may significantly interfere with the ability of local government to design a rational automotive tax policy. This interference can occur either because higher-level government regulations prohibit local motor vehicle taxes or because higher-level government has "used up" the automotive tax base.

Fuel Taxes

In order to focus on the issue of local government fuel taxes, let us assume that higher-level governments impose a fuel tax at a rate which covers the variable maintenance costs of interurban paved highways.[12] The question is then whether and to what extent governments of large cities in developing countries should levy an additional fuel tax over and above this national tax, and whether and how national fuel taxes might be adjusted to capture the externalities associated with road use.

From the point of view of economic efficiency, the national fuel tax would provide the appropriate charge for road use on uncongested paved urban roads and for pollution. Fuel taxes are less appropriate for approximating congestion charges, since it is not feasible to vary fuel taxes by the time of day or the extent of congestion at a location. One alternative is to set the fuel tax high enough to approximate congestion costs at peak hours and risk restricting vehicle use on uncongested streets.[13]

The efficiency losses resulting from this action may not be very great for three reasons. First, the elasticity of road use with respect to changes in the fuel price is likely to be low.[14] Second, to the extent that congestion occurs mainly on paved urban roads but uncongested traffic is more typical for unpaved roads, the higher fuel taxes on uncongested urban road use would reflect the substantially higher variable maintenance costs imposed by the users of unpaved roads. Third, more fuel is used on congested than on uncongested roads, although the differential is not high (World Bank 1975c). Therefore a fuel tax would fall less heavily on operators in uncongested traffic than in congested traffic.

According to most estimates, fuel taxes set at rates designed to cover the variable maintenance costs of unpaved urban streets would fall considerably short of the tax necessary to recover peak congestion costs (by a factor of three, according to Smith 1975). These figures indicate that although fuel taxes are not likely to represent a good instrument for controlling urban congestion, a much higher tax rate would result in efficiency losses only to the extent of encouraging vehicle use on uncongested paved streets. Such a tax would go some way toward controlling congestion.

But the degree to which fuel taxes can be set higher in metropolitan areas than in the surrounding nonurban districts is limited by the fact that "fuel carrying" from low-tax to high-tax areas may become worthwhile. Some regional fuel price differentials exist without apparently resulting in major fuel-carrying activities. In fact, fuel prices tend to be lower in the cities and higher in the outlying rural areas. The reasons for this reverse differential include the cost of transporting the fuel to the outlying areas and the natural monopoly position of the fuel retailer in isolated rural areas. Higher fuel taxes could therefore be imposed in most urban areas at least at a level which would reverse the existing price differential, without resulting in undue fuel carrying activities.

This tax falls short, of course, of approximating the cost of unpaved urban roads, let alone a peak congestion levy. From the point of view of efficiency, therefore, this tax is not likely to be particularly harmful or beneficial. It would neither restrict congestion substantially nor impose a significant burden of variable maintenance costs of urban unpaved streets on the vehicle operator; nor would it significantly distort traffic on uncongested urban streets.

To the extent that one is particularly concerned about the distorting effects of higher urban fuel taxes on commercial vehicles and buses, one could consider excluding diesel fuel from the fuel tax, as is done in Bogotá, Guatemala City, and Singapore. Because generally there are more diesel-powered trucks and buses than automobiles, this would favor commercial vehicles and buses. Furthermore, where bus operators receive subsidies from the government (as in Bogotá), these subsidies can be adjusted to offset any higher fuel costs resulting from the tax increase.

The undesirable efficiency effects of local fuel taxes are thus likely to be negligible. The effect on revenue, however, could be substantial. For instance, in Guatemala City an increase of the fuel tax from the actual rate of $0.02 to $0.10 per gallon in 1971 would have made the fuel tax the largest local tax, exceeding in importance the local property tax, and would have increased local tax revenues by about 50 percent. In Bogotá in the early 1970s, an increase of the local gasoline tax from $0.016 to $0.10 per gallon would also have made the gasoline tax the most important local tax, with revenues almost double that of the property tax, and would have raised local tax revenues by more than 100 percent. The revenue-elasticity of this tax depends crucially on whether it is levied at a specific rate or on an ad valorem basis. In the case of a specific rate, tax revenues are likely to be quite income-inelastic, especially if inflation erodes the real value of the specific tax and if gasoline consumption does not grow. In the ad valorem case, however, tax revenues will rise if the price of fuel rises. Ad valorem taxes also have the advantage of not distorting the price-cost relation for fuels (Walters 1968: 211).

Besides their excellent revenue potential, fuel taxes have the great advantage of being relatively easy to administer, especially if the production and wholesale distribution of fuel is in the hands of a government-owned enterprise, as in a number of developing countries. Ad valorem taxes are more difficult to administer than specific levies because of the possibility of evasion, especially at the retail level (Walters 1968). This explains the general preference for national and local specific fuel taxes in developing countries.

In terms of equity, urban fuel taxes are likely to be progressive, especially if a substantial portion of commercial vehicles benefit from an exemption of diesel fuel. Automobile ownership and use are highly concentrated among higher- and middle-income groups in all developing countries (World Bank 1975c), and thus a tax on fuel is likely to be highly progressive.[15]

A local fuel tax, in sum, is usually an excellent financing source for local government in terms of revenue performance, social equity, and administrative ease. Any efficiency losses are likely to be minimal, and to the extent that they would arise could be more than offset by efficiency gains resulting from the tax's effectiveness in helping to curb congestion and lessen the inefficient use of unpaved urban streets. The principal limitation is the possibility that higher urban fuel taxation will lead to fuel carrying; however, this is not likely to be a problem at the tax rates suggested here. Perhaps the central question is whether higher-level governments are likely to allow local authorities to share in such an important revenue source. The fact that very few local governments levy this tax may lead to some skepticism on this score. In 1969, Jakarta imposed a fuel tax of approximately $0.01 per gallon. Other local governments in Indonesia followed suit, but within a year the national government had taken over the tax (Linn, Smith, and Wignjowijoto 1976). In 1989, however, the government was again considering proposals by the provinces to impose a fuel tax.

Sales and Transfer Taxes on Motor Vehicles

Sales and transfer taxes on motor vehicles increase the cost of cars for purchasers. This increase has two effects. First, it restricts ownership to the extent that the demand for automobiles is price-elastic. In this way, road use might be indirectly limited. Second, it raises the annual cost of a car for the purchaser and, to the extent depreciation is linked to use, the cost of its use.

Consider first the implications for efficiency of higher depreciation. Because depreciation is not likely to be significantly higher if the vehicle is used on congested rather than on uncongested roads, a sales tax could cause substantial losses in efficiency if it were set at a level to raise user costs to equal social costs on congested streets. This is because one would expect as much reduction in motor vehicle use on uncongested as on congested streets. For moderate increases in depreciation costs caused by a higher sales tax, however, the response of vehicle use is likely to be low and will probably cause neither large gains in efficiency by reducing congestion nor losses in efficiency on uncongested streets.

Of greater importance may be the effect of the sales tax on the decision of whether or not to own a vehicle at all, since the price of new (and used) vehicles would be raised by approximately the amount of the tax. To the extent that private automobiles are used mainly for commuting, a reduction in automobile ownership could have a significant effect on urban congestion, even if it did not much affect the use of automobiles by those who continue to own them. The decline in automobile ownership—or, more likely, the slowdown in its growth—also means a loss of welfare to those who would have owned and used the vehicles on uncongested streets, and in that respect again results in some inefficiency. As with fuel taxes, the efficiency effects of a vehicle sales tax operate in opposite directions, and the net effect cannot easily be quantified.

Two other considerations are important. First, sales taxes are more easily structured than fuel taxes to discriminate between commercial vehicles and buses, on the one hand, which are operated mainly on intercity highways and whose use one may not want to discourage, and automobiles, on the other hand, which are operated mainly on urban roads and are generally seen as the main cause of urban traffic congestion.[16] Second, it is likely to be quite difficult to administer higher local sales taxes on automobiles in urban areas because the potential for evasion is considerable. Automobiles may be purchased in lower-tax jurisdictions or out-of-town addresses may be given if the tax is linked to the residence of the purchaser rather than to the place of residence. The incentive for evasion is likely to pose a much greater problem in the case of sales taxes than for the annual license tax discussed below if the two are set at rates to produce equal annual revenues. This may explain why local governments generally have been given access to license taxes on automobiles, but only in rare cases to sales taxes.

One such case is Jakarta, where both transfer and license taxes are levied by the provincial government, including Jakarta.[17] In fiscal 1987, the transfer tax accounted for 44 percent of locally raised revenues in Jakarta and the license tax for 33 percent.

Both of these taxes are plagued by high rates of evasion. Bastin and Hadiprobowo (1987) report that neither tax grew at as high a rate as regional GNP. He estimates that if the 10 percent of motor vehicles which are unregistered in Jakarta could be brought onto the tax rolls, revenues would have increased over actual 1987 amounts by about 13 percent.

Thus while the revenue potential of a local automobile sales or transfer tax could be substantial, and its tax incidence would likely be quite progressive, a problem arises with regard to the horizontal equity of the automobile sales tax. As the tax is imposed or increased, current vehicle owners experience a windfall gain since the values of their vehicles increase as a result of the tax on new automobiles. This problem does not arise with annual license taxes, which are considered next.

Unrestricted Annual License Taxes

Unrestricted annual license taxes are levied annually on the ownership, rather than on the transfer or use of the motor vehicle. This tax, therefore, does not affect the use of a vehicle once it has been purchased; however, as in the case of the transfer tax, the decision to own a motor vehicle is affected by the license tax, since the expected annual net return from the vehicle will decrease as a result of the license tax. The question is whether license taxes are likely to be imposed at a rate sufficient to affect the ownership decision. In theory, the greater annual depreciation may indirectly affect the use of roads, and in particular a license tax on cars may reduce urban traffic congestion to the extent that automobiles are used in urban areas predominantly for the purpose of commuting to and from work. Again, of course, a license tax which is high enough to reduce traffic congestion to acceptable levels would also lead to a loss in efficiency because of the decline in the use of uncongested roads. The net effect on efficiency of the unrestricted annual license tax is therefore uncertain, and it is not necessarily superior or inferior to fuel or vehicle sales taxes on efficiency grounds.

Much depends on how the license tax is structured. In practice, commercial vehicles and buses are generally taxed at lower rates, relative to vehicle value, than are automobiles. This practice perhaps recognizes that the price-elasticity of demand for these vehicles may be higher than that for private cars, that the marginal social cost of their use in urban traffic is less than that of automobiles, or that they make a larger contribution to development objectives. Differentiation of the unrestricted annual license tax according to weight or tire type may reflect (apart from ability-to-pay considerations) the realization that vehicles with higher weight or nonpneumatic tires tend to impose higher variable maintenance costs than vehicles with lesser weight or pneumatic tires. Engine capacity, which also is a criterion for differentiating license taxes, is seen as a proxy for fuel use, but of course there is only an imperfect correlation between engine capacity and fuel use and between fuel use and the social costs imposed by the motor vehicle. Thus in practice none of these typical discriminating features of the annual license tax—with the possible exception of lower taxes on commercial vehicles and buses—is likely to produce significant gains in efficiency. For instance, light and less powerful vehicles may be encouraged by taxing according to weight and engine capacity.

Instead of attempting to affect the allocation of resources by differentiating among vehicles, it might be more desirable to primarily use the annual license tax to raise revenue. It would then be more appropriate to vary the tax with the value of the automobile since this reflects ability to pay as well as the extent to which different users derive consumer surplus from the use of the road system. This form of license tax is in fact directly comparable to the personal property taxes levied on automobiles in many jurisdictions in the United States.

As with the local fuel tax and the motor vehicle sales tax, the problem of evasion arises. Owners may escape the annual license tax by registering their vehicles in low-tax jurisdictions. This limits the degree to which license taxes can differ, especially between adjoining jurisdictions. There are two reasons to believe, however, that some differentiation without major evasion is feasible. First, in the United States, insurance rates differ considerably between locations without any apparent large-scale attempts at evasion by the insured (Walters 1968). Second, with a combination of vigorous enforcement and sizable penalties, compliance may be expected to be good. The example of Jakarta tends to confirm this conclusion. Penalties of 100 percent of tax liability were applied and enforced—if necessary through confiscation of the vehicle where other means of enforcement had failed (Linn, Smith, and Wignjowijoto 1976). In recent years, enforcement efforts for automobile registration have declined, and thus so has the collection efficiency for the registration tax. In Bogotá it is claimed that many residents register their vehicles in surrounding jurisdictions. The main reason for this does not appear to lie with higher license taxes in the city than in the rural areas, however, but with the long waiting times and the amount of red tape associated with obtaining the annual license in Bogotá. This emphasizes the importance of compliance costs and therefore the need for more effective vehicle registration and licensing procedures. For instance, permitting registration and tax payment by mail rather than in person may make a considerable difference in the degree of compliance.

A good motor vehicle registration and licensing system is not only in the interest of better tax collection but also essential to curbing motor vehicle theft, which in some cities (for example, Bogotá) has reached epidemic proportions, and necessary for identifying and prosecuting traffic offenders. Once a good registration system is in place it is relatively easy to tax motor vehicle ownership.[18] Assessment of the tax can proceed by schedules designed either according to the physical characteristics of the vehicle (such as weight and engine capacity), or according to the assessed value of the car.

Annual motor vehicle license taxes can be important sources of local revenue in cities of developing countries. In Jakarta, motor vehicle license taxes accounted for approximately 33 percent of all local taxes during fiscal 1986, and in Seoul for 7.7 percent during 1982. The level as well as the buoyancy of revenues depend very much on how the tax is administered. In Jakarta and Seoul, where administration was good and rates were regularly adjusted to allow for changes in the general price level, high and buoyant revenues were generated. In Seoul the buoyancy amounted to about 1.2 (Bahl and Wasylenko 1976). In Jakarta, the buoyancy was estimated at 1.5 in the 1970s (Linn, Smith, and Wignjowijoto 1976), but it was well below unity for the 1979–84 period (World Bank estimates). In Bogotá, per capita revenues collected from the motor vehicle license taxes declined in real terms through the 1970s, thus implying a very low buoyancy, whereas in Cartagena vehicle tax revenues expanded rapidly and exhibited a buoyancy of about unity (Linn 1975). In Bombay and Ahmadabad revenues collected from the local motor vehicle taxation remained approximately constant in real per capita terms and thus showed a buoyancy of very probably less than unity (Bougeon-Maassen 1976; Bahl 1975). The main lesson from these widely divergent revenue experiences is that the motor vehicle license tax can be a major revenue source for urban governments only if it is well-structured and aggressively administered. The rapid growth in the base will ensure a certain amount of revenue growth, but evasion and inflation are likely to cut heavily into this growth if administration is poor and specific tax rates are not regularly increased to keep pace with changing prices.

With regard to the question of incidence, there can be little doubt that the motor vehicle license tax is progressive, especially because commercial vehicles and buses are usually taxed at concessional rates. This conclusion is confirmed by studies of tax incidence covering vehicle taxes in various developing countries.[19]

The summary verdict on motor vehicle licenses is therefore that they are an excellent tool for raising local revenue in terms of potential performance and equity. But the administration of these taxes needs to be designed and implemented carefully to reap their potential benefits. No large losses or gains in efficiency should be expected from the imposition of annual license taxes, and indeed there is probably little reason for the tax structure to be as complex as it often is in the cities of developing countries, for gains in efficiency are likely to be negligible while administrative costs are likely to rise. It might be preferable to develop a reasonably accurate and flexible method of assessing the approximate value of the motor vehicle, since this is likely to enhance the equitability and buoyancy of the tax.

Congestion Charges

The principal goal of all local automotive taxes is to raise public revenue equitably and simply. Efficiency is usually a secondary concern, and justifiably so, for these taxes have an uncertain and, at moderate tax rates, probably unimportant effect on automobile use and purchase. Still, traffic congestion in the central city remains one of the major problems of urban life, and automotive taxes and user charges could be designed to address this problem. Some local governments have responded to this possibility.

Three major types of congestion charges will be briefly evaluated here: area- and time-specific vehicle licenses, parking charges, and tolls.[20] All of these are suited for local government administration, provided that local governments pay enough attention to design and that they are given the legal authority to levy the appropriate charges.

Restricted Licenses

The success of any pricing scheme depends on its ability to distinguish between congested and uncongested areas and times and to a lesser degree on the extent to which various types of vehicles contribute to congestion.[21] Specific vehicle licensing schemes achieve this goal by requiring that road users exhibit special licenses while operating in prescribed zones of the city at specified times of day. For the efficient allocation of urban resources, this type of scheme is preferable to any of the other forms of automotive taxes discussed above.

The licenses are purchased daily or monthly at prices that approximate the marginal social cost of vehicle use in the congested areas. In order to be administratively feasible, the number of zones that are differently priced must be kept small and clearly defined. This of course limits the fine-tuning that may be expected from a restricted licensing scheme and therefore the degree to which differing conditions of congestion may be approximated.

The system is likely to be more easily applied if congestion is largely confined to one central area of the city and if the peak times of congestion are well defined and restricted to no more than two a day. If there are several subcenters and multiple daily peak times, the restricted licensing scheme is likely to be more difficult to apply. Bogotá is a good case in point. It has at least two main nodes of congestion—the central business district and the commercial district in the north of the city—and four peak traffic times because the city's citizens return home during the long lunch hour. An area licensing system would therefore be very difficult to install.

Another problem is that because congestion costs are difficult to measure precisely and the response of motorists to congestion pricing is not easily predicted, the initial charges may be too high or too low to provide the optimal rationing of road space. Authorities must therefore be prepared to vary the charges if after some lapse of time they appear to restrict traffic too much or too little.

To date, Singapore is the only city that we know of with a system of restricted motor vehicle licensing. It is an invaluable example of the feasibility and effect of this type of scheme and has been carefully monitored since its inception. Singapore is special in four ways. First, it is a city-state with a strong, dynamic executive branch not hampered by higher-level government controls or intrametropolitan jurisdictional fragmentation. Second, the metropolitan management and administration can attract highly qualified staff, whereas in many other cities, local authorities are typically not able to compete effectively with higher-level governments for scarce talent. Third, the metropolitan authorities for a long time had been concerned with the rapidly rising number of privately owned automobiles, growing congestion, and potential environmental deterioration and had demonstrated their willingness to take strong measures to deal with these problems. Fourth, the pattern of congestion in Singapore was amenable to the application of a restrictive licensing scheme because prime congestion was limited to a readily identifiable central area and to one morning and one evening rush hour.

For a detailed description and evaluation of the Singapore scheme and its effects, see the excellent study by Watson and Holland (1978). Here only the five major conclusions are summarized. First and most important, the scheme has proved to be technically, administratively, and politically feasible. And although Singapore's special circumstances certainly favored a successful outcome, its experience can serve as an example for other cities.[22]

Second, the major objectives of the scheme were achieved, at least in the short term, and there is little reason to expect a reversal as the scheme continues. Central city congestion has been reduced substantially by inducing motorists to use alternative forms of transportation, in particular public transport and car pools. As a result, all transport users reported improvements: traffic moved faster, and there was less pollution and fewer traffic accidents. Commercial operations apparently were not negatively affected, although an existing trend toward increased decentralization of commercial location decisions may have been somewhat reinforced.

Third, major problems affecting the efficiency of traffic operation were limited. Initially, the scheme induced congestion on the ring road encircling the restricted area and created minipeaks in congestion immediately before and after the restricted hours. The former problem was alleviated by minor improvements in traffic management and engineering, the latter by extending the restricted hours.

Fourth, administration, enforcement, and public acceptance of the scheme proceeded smoothly. This was at least partly due to the large-scale publicity campaign which started a year before the scheme began, the gradual introduction of the scheme, and the rigorous enforcement of the license regulations and the application of stiff penalties.[23] The capital costs of the scheme were small in comparison with the high cost of central city street construction and related mainly to a park-and-ride scheme introduced simultaneously.[24]

Fifth, the revenue and equity implications of the scheme, although not of great scope, are on balance favorable. Annual revenues net of operating costs, when compared with revenues collected from other taxes on motor vehicles or from property taxation, are not substantial (approximately 2 percent of motor vehicle taxes and 1 percent of property taxes), but at least the system does not constitute a net drain on the public purse and compared with other tax measures it has a low ratio of administrative costs to revenues (less than 1 percent). The overall incidence of the scheme has not been fully assessed because there are no relevant figures on income distribution and the effect of shifts in transport modes is difficult to evaluate. Given the concentration of motor vehicle ownership and use among high-income groups, however, there is reason to believe that the financial cost of the scheme is borne mainly by these groups.[25]

One may therefore conclude that the area license scheme in Singapore has proved to be a successful instrument for pricing central city road use and for limiting congestion, without major negative administrative, revenue, or equity implications. Although this is no guarantee for the success of similar schemes elsewhere, the Singapore example indicates that area license schemes must be taken seriously as a potential instrument for improving the efficiency of urban road use. Any attempts to follow the Singapore example should note the various practical aspects which helped make the system work: adequate study and preparation, including an extensive publicity campaign; simplicity of regulation and flexibility in implementation; preexistence of an effective vehicle registration system and a clear commitment to the enforcement of the scheme; and unfettered authority by the metropolitan government to impose whatever scheme was regarded as the most appropriate.

Parking Fees

Parking fees and taxes have been suggested as one alternative to charging motor vehicle operators directly for the use of congested urban streets (for example, McLure 1971a: 795; Churchill 1972: 145; Walters 1968: 203). The argument, first, is that parking spaces are demanded by the same commuters who use automobiles during rush hour; and second, that because on-street parking interferes with the use of the roads by moving traffic, parked vehicles should be charged the cost of these interferences. The parking tax would have two components: a tax on commercial and private parking facilities in congested central city areas, and fees for on-street parking collected either by attendants (as in Jakarta; Linn, Smith, and Wignjowijoto 1976) or by parking meters (as in Central American cities; Churchill 1972).

Taxes on off-street parking facilities were not encountered in any of the cities surveyed here with the exception of Singapore.[26] (In fact, at least one city, Cali, has employed a perverse policy that encourages the construction of central city parking facilities through a blanket exemption of them from municipal taxes for a period of ten years.[27]) Public authorities apparently fail to realize the need for taxes on parking facilities, and there is also a problem with administration, particularly if the tax is to be levied on an ad valorem base of parking rates, as suggested by McLure (1971a). It may be administratively simpler to levy a property tax surcharge on central city parking facilities. This would discourage use of central city space for private or commercial parking facilities and discourage the use of existing commercial parking lots because parking lot operators would presumably pass on the higher taxes to their customers.

Fees for on-street parking are potentially more troublesome because they require expensive metering and labor-intensive attendant and enforcement. Rough cost-benefit calculations can determine whether parking meters should be used in any particular case.[28] Collection and enforcement of parking fees, if properly administered, do not necessarily lead to insurmountable problems. In Guatemala City, for instance, about 4,500 parking meters, as well as parking regulations, were apparently successfully administered and strictly enforced (Churchill 1972). Similarly in Cali, a well-trained and highly motivated team of municipal transit police kept a tight rein over moving and stationary traffic in the city center, to the great lament of many motorists. The administration of on-street parking, however, is likely to be quite costly.[29] It may be preferable to forbid on-street parking altogether on congested streets during peak periods, for even one single parked car may seriously impede traffic flow (Churchill 1972). Furthermore, parking meters and prohibitions are more easily administered if the congestion is confined to relatively small contiguous central city areas and a few main thoroughfares. If congestion is wide and dispersed, as in some of the large metropolitan areas, on-street parking fees and regulations are less likely to provide an effective control over the use of central city streets. As Churchill (1972) has observed, at going wage rates in developing countries it may be worthwhile to hire chauffeurs rather than pay the parking fees, thus possibly increasing traffic congestion.

The upshot of this discussion is that parking taxes and fees by themselves are not likely to solve central city congestion, although they at least work in the right direction. To ensure a reasonable degree of equity and effectiveness it would be necessary to cover all forms of parking in the prescribed area, including on-street parking as well as commercial and private off-street parking.

Tolls

Only a couple of points need to be made about tolls for the control of urban traffic, for they clearly are not the appropriate tool for implementing a system of congestion pricing. First, for a toll system to be operable, entry and exit points on the roadway must be limited in number, which is typically not the case for congested urban streets, with the exception of a few limited-access expressways. Second, toll collection is costly to administer and may itself contribute to congestion by creating a bottleneck at the tollgate. Tolls therefore should not be considered efficient instruments for congestion pricing in most circumstances. They may be adequate for financing special urban expressways through charges levied on users. But careful consideration first needs to be given to their efficiency and administrative cost.

Summary and Evaluation of Local Automotive Taxation

The main arguments in this chapter regarding the objectives of economic efficiency, equity, revenue-raising potential, and ease of administration may be summarized as follows. For economic efficiency, restricted area license charges and parking fees and taxes are the most desirable, because they can be designed to approximate the excess of social over private cost of using congested streets without restricting the use of uncongested streets. All other automotive taxes also affect the allocation of resources to some extent, but the direction of the net effect is uncertain, and efficiency gains and losses may occur side by side. The unrestricted license tax probably affects resource allocation least of all.

For equity, all forms of automotive taxation are likely to improve the distribution of income, and most are fair in the sense of horizontal equity. One exception is the motor vehicle sales tax, which results in windfall gains for the present owners of vehicles because the value of these automobiles tends to increase after the tax is imposed.

For revenue performance, local fuel taxes and unrestricted license taxes can be expected to do well in yield, buoyancy, and stability. These taxes should be levied ad valorem if buoyancy is to be preserved in the absence of frequent rate changes. Automotive sales and transfer taxes are likely to be less effective in their revenue performance because of the narrower tax base and the greater likelihood of year-to-year variations in the base. Congestion levies also tend to have a relatively narrow revenue base and are often costly to administer.

For ease of administration, fuel taxes are probably most easily handled, whereas congestion levies are likely to be most troublesome. But the examples referred to in the preceding sections have shown that restricted licenses and parking taxes and fees are administratively feasible if carefully designed and implemented.

The extent to which the various taxes require coordination with higher-level government is likely to be an important element in the local government's ability to impose them. On this account, fuel and sales taxes are the weakest candidates, since the overlap with national or state taxing authority is likely to be substantial. In contrast, license taxes and congestion charges in most cities can probably be imposed without serious interference from higher-level governments.

Political acceptability is a crucial constraint on local tax policy. Differential fuel taxes may be relatively easy to impose because they tend to be hidden in the sales price of the fuel. Tolls are likely to be acceptable since they affect relatively few taxpayers and are clearly linked in the public's mind to the benefit derived from the use of the roadway. At the other end of the spectrum are restricted license taxes and high parking fees. The problems here are that the principle of congestion pricing is not well understood by policymakers and the public and that significant changes in choice of travel modes would be induced by these measures. This combination of lack of experience and unwillingness to consider fundamental changes is a very powerful deterrent to policy action.

The optimal course of action in automotive taxation in the large cities of developing countries is likely to include some combination of the instruments reviewed here. Unrestricted license taxes and differential fuel taxes can make major contributions to local revenue without causing major efficiency losses. Restricted license taxes and parking fees and taxes could then be imposed mainly to constrain urban congestion. Singapore is a showcase for this kind of comprehensive approach to the problem of automotive taxation. Although the city is favored with a number of special circumstances, which have greatly facilitated the design and implementation of a rational urban automotive tax structure, it is well worth careful study by experts and practitioners in urban finance and management.

8 Other Urban Taxes

APART FROM PROPERTY and automobile taxes, local governments can and do make use of a large number of other taxes and licenses. Although these alternative sources of revenue are not always easily administered or free from unwanted efficiency or equity effects, and although they tend not to be as revenue-productive as local governments would like, they have the very great advantage of being available. If local governments were starting with a clean slate with no existing taxes and no restrictions on the bases they could use, these residual revenue sources would probably not be chosen. However, this is not the case, and despite their second-best nature, many of these smaller taxes give local governments some opportunity to tap the growing taxable capacity of urban areas.

Local governments in developing countries typically have one major nonproperty tax. Usually it is an income or poll tax, some form of indirect tax on local trade or business activity, or an automobile-related tax (see table 2-11). In a few cases, these governments have made general use of a sales tax. They also usually have a large number of "miscellaneous" local taxes and fees that add relatively little to total revenues.

In most cities, the structure of the nonproperty tax system tends to be antiquated. One reason for this is a virtual absence—usually for many years—of comprehensive local tax reform. Tax structures that may have been appropriate for smaller towns fifty or even a hundred years ago persist and are adjusted ad hoc and piecemeal to attempt to deal with the rapidly rising revenue needs which characterize the larger cities of today. There seems to be little concern with how changes in individual taxes affect the overall goals of the local tax system; practitioners rarely get beyond the question of how to raise another thousand rupees, shillings, or pesos. A second reason is simply that local governments lack good alternative choices when they carry out a reform. Higher-level governments have preempted the use of most, if not all, of the more productive taxes (import tariffs and broadly based income and sales taxes). Local governments, and especially those in the larger cities, therefore have been forced to look to what was left. Moreover, even in the use of these residual sources, they are often inhibited by central government legislation regarding tax base, rate structure, and enforcement procedures.

The situation need not be so dismal. Local governments in developing countries can reasonably impose a productive set of nonproperty taxes: a large number of excises (for example, sumptuary taxes, various taxes on business activities, and gambling and entertainment taxes); a set of taxes which very aptly have been characterized as "nuisance taxes" (occupation charges, stamp duties, and the like); and, where the law permits, even more narrowly based income and sales taxes. The trick is to find a reasonable way to structure these taxes and to combine them in a coherent tax system that meets the objectives of the local government. This chapter describes the use of these taxes in the cities of developing countries and discusses the possibilities for a more rational use of them.

Policy Objectives

The policy objectives to be considered in formulating the system of nonproperty taxes may be subdivided into the usual four broad goals of revenue policy: economic efficiency, fairness, revenue performance, and low administrative cost. Our analysis of nonproperty taxes will center on the relative importance of these goals in different settings and on the tradeoffs a local government might be willing to make in certain circumstances. A consideration of these basic objectives leads us to a set of tax rules or at least to criteria for evaluating the effects of particular taxes.

According to traditional public finance theory, the efficiency goal implies that a tax instrument which creates unwanted distortions in resource allocation would have a negative effect on economic efficiency, whereas a tax which corrects any preexisting malallocation of resources due to market failure would have a positive effect on it. Of course, all taxes have some effect on economic activity, and it would be useless to suggest that policy reforms should center on finding "neutral" taxes. A more sensible approach here is to consider the strength of these effects for various taxes. In some cases, policy may simply ignore efficiency effects on grounds that local taxes are levied at too low a rate to make much of a difference. In other cases, adjustments in tax policy might be called for. For example, a sales tax or an increase in market stall rental fees may drive shoppers or vendors from the local area. In still other cases, the tax may be intended to change patterns of consumption or production (for example, sumptuary taxes), and the issue is whether or not the tax can achieve the desired objective.

In analyzing equity concerns, one can usefully distinguish between horizontal and vertical equity. The former has to do with the equal treatment of equals (however defined) and in that sense may be equated with the common concept of fairness, and the latter represents the goal of improving an existing maldistribution of income in the city.[1] One question we grapple with below is whether the nonproperty tax system can have enough of an effect on the distribution of local incomes to make equity a guiding (or even a relevant) concern in formulating local government tax policy. Particularly when the low effective tax rates, the failure to cover the informal sector, and the effects on the incidence of expenditure are considered, the effects of changes in local nonproperty taxes on the distribution of income may be a secondary consideration.

Generally, the most important criterion for the success of local government tax reform is revenue-productivity. Three issues are important here. The first is defining a nonproperty tax system that is capable of raising adequate revenue for the local government. The small size of some tax bases—for example, signboards, nonmotorized vehicles, slaughter activities—and their concomitant limited revenue yield, explains the proliferation of local taxes in many cities. The second issue is the income-elasticity of the tax: the degree to which the revenues of a tax grow more or less in proportion with the level of general economic activity in the area. Because expenditure needs would seem to grow more or less in proportion to personal income and prices, one might argue that local government revenues should be equally buoyant. The third issue is stability: the extent to which revenues are sensitive to yearly fluctuations in economic activity. Hence, a high income-elasticity is good, but it can be too good in making the yield of the local tax system unstable and erratic. Similarly, revenue structures that are heavily reliant on a single firm, industry, or crop are vulnerable.

Finally, there is the important criterion of low administrative cost. If the tax cannot be effectively collected at reasonable cost, it will be of little use to the local government. Perhaps the major problem with nonproperty taxes is that local governments are unable to collect the taxes they are permitted to levy. Often these taxes are badly designed and thus all but impossible to administer because of, for example, shortages of staff or the very high compliance cost placed on taxpayers. The goal of low administrative cost suggests a number of sub-objectives in designing the nonproperty tax system: compliance costs as well as government administrative costs should be considered, the liability for and methods of payment should be clearly known, penalties should be sizable enough to induce payment and should be enforceable, and interference with higher-level government taxation should be minimized.

In sum, the reform and redesign of local nonproperty tax systems in developing countries are and will continue to be motivated by revenue-raising concerns and constrained by administrative feasibility and restrictions imposed by higher-level governments. Efficiency and equity effects are in most cases not important concerns. Yet urban local governments have done much less with these taxes than they could have, and they often have not taken the opportunity to design away some of the undesirable efficiency and equity effects and administrative costs. One is struck by how little attention has been given to integrating nonproperty taxes into a system of local government finance. Concerns about efficiency and equity effects are in most cases not important.

Local Income Taxes

Income taxes are an important source of local tax revenue in a number of industrial countries, for example, Japan, the Scandinavian countries, and the United States.[2] Local income taxes in developing countries, though more widespread than might be expected, tend to be narrower in coverage, more basic in structure, and often quite primitive in administration (see table 8-1).

The limited coverage of local income taxes in developing countries is due to a number of factors: the narrow coverage of the central government income taxes, legal constraints imposed by the center out of a fear of tax base competition,[3] and administrative weaknesses. The result is that local "income taxes" end up as some combination of a poll (head) tax, a wage tax, and a limited income tax shared with higher authorities. In Guatemala City, an ad valorem tax levied on all public employees distinguished among three income groups.[4] In Zambia, a similar system has been applied, except that there are seven income classes taxed at different specific rates. In Zaire, local authorities were permitted to levy what amounts to a local wage tax at approximately proportional rates, and a specific tax on traders and professionals, but only for those income earners who are exempt from the national income tax. Nigerian cities have levied poll taxes on those not subject to state income taxes, and Dakar (Senegal) collects substantial revenue from a "withholding" poll tax on all workers. Korean cities have combined a tax on heads of households (and on corporations) with a 7.5 percent surtax on all tax liabilities of the national personal income tax, the corporate income tax, and the farmland tax.

Effects on Efficiency

Local income taxes may affect the allocation of resources in urban areas in a number of ways, not all of them beneficial. Theory tells us that if the tax is levied only on wages in the formal sector, employment in that sector will be discouraged, pretax wages will tend to rise, and a more highly capital-intensive development (of the modern urban sector) will be favored. Whether or not this basically undesirable effect on local employment is realized depends on a number of factors: the level of the tax rate, the possibility for capital-labor substitution in the modern sector, and factor mobility between the modern and traditional sectors. A combination of the low tax rates we know to exist and the low elasticities of factor substitution which are believed to exist in the formal sector in developing countries leads us to conclude that the efficiency effects of an increase in the local income tax are likely to be quite marginal.

A second kind of efficiency cost is the result of individuals and firms making location decisions that differ from those they would have in the absence of the tax. This is not likely to be of as much concern in developing as in industrial countries (Wasylenko and McGuire 1985) because there is less variation in the tax rate among local governments and because the occupational and regional mobility of the labor force is limited. Local taxes are not likely to be a principal determinant of the choice of location of business in developing countries (Hamer and Linn 1987).

Higher urban tax rates and the location choices they generate may also be viewed in a positive light as a way to raise the relative price of urban living and hold back migration to large cities. But whether the higher taxes levied in large cities would be enough to offset the attractiveness of large cities, especially the capital city, is doubtful. Moreover, because these higher tax rates are levied by the local government, they may be used to purchase a greater quantity of those amenities that attract firms and induce the migration of households.

This leaves us with little to say about the efficiency effects of local income taxes. A good argument can be made that urban areas are preferable to central-local government transfers biased in the direction of urban areas. At present tax rates, and with limited factor substitution, the magnitude of any distortions of resource allocation is likely to be inconsequential.

Effects on Equity

Local income taxes in developing countries are by their very nature unfair. As head taxes or as taxes limited to wages in the modern sector, they do not treat all income earners the same. Those in the informal sector and those with nonwage incomes face a lower effective tax rate. Even where local income taxes are more broadly based in law, they are usually unfair in the sense that not even all wages and salaries are being taxed; that is, withholding schemes are easily evaded by employers in smaller enterprises, in the service sector, and by the self-employed. Such horizontal inequities are an obvious flaw in local income taxation, and they are not easily dealt with because of administrative constraints.

Another question is vertical equity; that is, what is the effect of a local income tax on the distribution of income? One answer is that it will have very little effect because effective tax rates typically are very low. Consider the case of Seoul's surtax on income tax liability or Dakar's withholding-poll tax. In both cases, most of the burden is likely to be borne by the modern sector because the mobility of factors between the modern and the traditional sectors is limited, and because the supply of capital and land is relatively inelastic, even in the long term (Bird 1977a). Since employees and the owners of capital in the modern sector are on the average likely to have higher incomes than owners of productive factors in the untaxed traditional sector, a local tax on modern sector wages should improve the relative income position of the poorest seg-

Table 8-1. *Local Income Tax Structures, Selected Developing Countries*

City, country, date	Base	Rate — Monthly income	Rate — Annual tax	Exemptions	Level of government with collection responsibility
Guatemala City, Guatemala, 1979	All male inhabitants of the city (and all women in public sector employment)	Under Q50: Q50–200: More than Q200: ($1 = Q1)	Q1 (0.3) Q2 (0.1) Q4 (0.1)	None	Local
Calcutta, India, 1977	All professions, trades, and salaried persons	Rs15–500, depending on trade or profession		All taxpayers earning less than Rs8,000	Local
Pusan and Seoul[a], Rep. of Korea, 1977	*Head tax:* all heads of household, and corporations with domiciles or offices in each city *Income tax:* tax liability for personal income tax, the corporate income tax, and the farmland tax	*Head tax:* 4,000 won per household ($1 = won 484) 40,000 won per corporation *Income tax:* 7.5 percent of personal income tax, corporate income tax, and agricultural land tax		*Head tax:* heads of household with annual income below 360,000 won are exempt *Income tax:* none	Local

Ibadan, Nigeria, 1982	Males of 16 years of age or older with annual earnings less than N600 (= $1,100)	N7.50 per person ($11)	Anyone paying state income tax	Local
Dakar, Senegal, 1982	All persons over 14 years of age	Rates vary from S2 to S17 depending on income level	Students, military	Central
All local authorities, Zaire, 1973	Residents over 18 years of age, whose income is below Z240 annually. ($1 = Z0.5)	*For wage earners:* Approximately 4 percent of wage income. *For traders or professionals:* Z9.6 a year. *For others:* Z4 a year in Kinshasa, Z3 a year in other cities, Z2 a year elsewhere	None	Local
All local authorities, Zambia, 1976	All personal earnings of individuals 18 years or older	*(see table below)*	All income below K20 is exempt; income of women below K300 is exempt; housing allowances are exempt	Local

Annual earnings	*Annual tax*
K120–200:	K1.25 (0.8)
K200–300:	K2.25 (1.0)
K300–400:	K4.00 (1.1)
K400–600:	K8.00 (1.6)
K600–800:	K12.00 (1.7)
K800–1000:	K16.00 (1.8)
K1,000 and above:	K20.00 (1.0)

Note: Q = quetzales, Rs = rupees, N = Nairas, and S = Senegalese francs, Z = zaires, K = kwachas.
a. In other Korean cities and counties identical taxes are levied, except that for the head tax lower rates apply in cities and counties according to size.

ment of the population. A positive distribution effect may be augmented by a judicious policy of exemption of the lowest levels of earnings, as is done in India. Other considerations would lead us to expect a lessening of progressivity. In particular, higher-income residents fall out of the taxpaying population if administrative difficulties allow the self-employed and those who receive substantial nonwage income to avoid the tax. A flat rate structure, or the use of specific rates, also tends to dampen the progressivity of the national income tax.

In some cases, however, income tax structures have been designed specifically to capture lower-income workers. Personal taxes in Ibadan, for example, have covered only those with incomes below a certain level. This is done to get around a central government limitation on the use of local income taxes and, while the principal goal of the tax is to raise revenue, there may also be a desire to extend the coverage to low-income groups in order to expand participation in the governmental process. In view of the negative income distribution effects of such a policy, as well as its potentially high administrative and compliance costs, the wisdom of such extensions of the tax is questionable.

Revenue Performance

The potential yield of a local income tax depends very much on the coverage of the tax and rate structure, and the actual yield depends on the effectiveness of assessment and collection. Of the six systems examined here, the systems used in Dakar and by the Korean and Zambian cities would seem to hold the greatest revenue potentials because of their relatively broad coverage. The inhabitant tax accounted for about 16 percent of local government tax revenue in Seoul in 1982 (Chun, Kim, and Lee 1985), up from 10 percent in 1976, and for 12 percent in Pusan in 1985. The withholding version of the poll tax in Dakar yielded about 19 percent of local government revenues in 1982 (Dillinger 1988a). In the Zambian Councils of Ndola, Kitwe, and Chingola, the personal tax accounted for between 6 and 10 percent of total local government revenue in 1976; and in the Nigerian cities of Ibadan and Onitsha, the poll tax raised about 4 percent of local revenues in the early 1980s.

Unfortunately, there is relatively little information on which to base an estimate of the income-elasticity of these taxes; one would, however, expect a greater responsiveness from income-based than from head-based taxes. If income-elasticity is high, the yield of the tax will keep in better step with the demand for local government expenditures, but also it will be less stable because revenues will tend to vary directly with the ups and downs of the business cycle. According to World Bank data, in both Zaire and Zambia the revenues from the local income tax were subject to severe fluctuations in response to national economic conditions, which caused local authorities to have considerable difficulties with fiscal management. Conversely, the more local income taxes approximate poll taxes, the less is the scope for revenue raising and the less buoyant is the revenue yield, but the more stable will be the revenue growth.

Administrative Costs

Local income taxes in developing countries have a narrow coverage because of the problems of controlling evasion and avoidance. Monitoring payroll deductions for an income tax is a difficult enough job for a local government, but collection of income from nonwage sources and from the self-employed is nearly impossible. In fact, the income tax is so difficult for local governments to administer that a simple alternative such as a head tax seems attractive. The tradeoff is clear: the broader the coverage of the tax and the more progressive its rate schedule, the better its revenue potential and the less bothersome its equity implications, but the higher its administrative costs and the lower its collection efficiency.

The main problem is that local governments simply do not have the skilled staffs to assess and collect income taxes. An approach to overcoming this problem is to coordinate the assessment and collection of local and central government income taxes. The easiest procedure would be to define the local tax as a surtax on the central tax, as in Korea, and leave tax administration to the higher-level government. The drawback of this solution is that it tends to reduce local autonomy with regard to policies for rate structures and exemptions. Still, a surtax might be viewed as a local tax (rather than as an intergovernmental transfer) if the local government has some discretion in setting the tax rate.

A second version is to accept whatever base the central government taxes and collect the local government tax by withholding at the source. This could make the administrative and compliance costs of local income taxes acceptable, and very probably no higher than for any other typical local revenue source. The experience with such a wage tax in Dakar is quite encouraging. The local rates are quite different in structure than the central rates (see table 8-1), but the same base is taxed. Approximately 96 percent of all local income taxes in Dakar are collected by withholding at the source. The problem with this approach is that for the informal sector and the self-employed, for which withholding is not possible, evasion of the tax becomes relatively simple and overall resistance to the tax will inevitably grow. For example, Dakar is able to collect virtually nothing from these groups, even though they are technically subject to tax.

Administrative costs may become quite high when the local income tax is extended to nonwage sources. In this particular respect, the track record of income taxes in Guatemala, Zaire, and Zambia is dismal. Even where a poll or head tax is substituted for the pure income tax on traders and professions, taxpayer evasion is generally widespread.

The other approach is pure local administration. Where this is done the poll tax is not usually a viable proposition. The typical approach is to construct a roll of eligible taxpayers; require a payment as a condition for receiving tax clearance for a business license, property transfer, and so forth; and make use of patrolling inspectors to enforce the tax. This rarely works. Low-income taxpayers may have little need for clearance, the patrol method invites corruption, and many local governments cannot keep a proper roll in place. The implications of this approach for collection efficiency are predictable. In Kinshasa, for instance, it was estimated (1973 World Bank data) that the actual revenue collected was equal to about one-tenth of the estimated total statutory tax liability. The comparable number is about 15 percent in Ibadan and Onitsha (1984 World Bank data). Moreover, administrative costs associated with broadening the base can be very high. World Bank estimates for 1982 indicate that the payroll cost of inspectors to collect the poll tax in Onitsha was equivalent to about half of the revenues collected.

Tax Base Competition

The threat of competition with central and state government taxation limits the potential for income taxes as a source of local revenue in developing countries. Central governments have been reluctant to grant local governments access to the income tax base or even to offer the possibility of administrative coordination. The assumption seems to be— in some cases perhaps with justification—that if any more can be squeezed out of the income tax base, it belongs to the center.

Reservations about tax base competition led the central government in Kenya to abolish quite a lucrative local income tax, the graduated personal tax. Moreover, in cities where powers have been granted to local authorities to raise income taxes (for example, in Korea), they have been so tightly circumscribed that the local authorities have little freedom to vary the rate, base, or exemptions.

Conclusions

The scorecard for how well the local income tax meets the objectives of local tax policy is thus mixed. If its administration is somehow piggy-backed onto the central income tax, it becomes a more viable revenue-raising proposition. The cost in this case is that local discretion is limited; the tax begins to take on many of the features of an intergovernmental transfer. If administration is left to the local governments, however, the goal of revenue-productivity is likely to be compromised. In terms of economic efficiency and equity, there is little to say about local income taxes because the effective tax rates are so low that any effects are likely to be small.

General Sales Taxes

Very few city governments in developing countries are permitted to levy broad-based sales taxes.[5] Typically, this potentially important source of local revenues is reserved for higher-level governments. In the quite substantial review of the practice undertaken for this study, only Rio de Janeiro and Managua were found to derive a sizable share of their substantial revenues from a local sales tax. Its success in these cities, however, attests to its considerable revenue potential (see table 2-11) and so it is not surprising that general sales taxes have sometimes been proposed in prescriptions for the fiscal reform of local government. A municipal retail sales tax was proposed for Colombia by the Musgrave Tax Reform Commission (Musgrave and Gillis 1971: 119–21).

Local governments in developing countries will "grow into" the use of general sales taxes, in the next decade in many cases. As the business sector modernizes and the enforcement of proper bookkeeping for most firms becomes possible, many cities will graduate from the makeshift sales taxes and business licenses that they now use. It would seem useful, therefore, to examine the principles that might guide the design of urban government general sales taxes in developing countries even though the current pratice is quite limited.

An examination of the possibilities might begin by noting that there are five basic types of sales taxes: the turnover tax is levied on every sale; the manufacturer's sales tax is levied at the stage of production; the wholesale sales tax is imposed on transactions between wholesaler and retailer; the retail sales tax is imposed on the sale to the final consumer; and the value added tax is levied on each transaction but is based only on the additional value generated by the establishment selling the good or service.[6] From the point of view of administration, the turnover and the retail sales taxes are likely candidates for a local tax.

Single-stage manufacturer's and wholesale taxes are not good candidates for local taxes because substantial exporting of the tax burden is possible, and because the yield will be measurably higher in large cities with greater shares of a nation's commerce and industry. This raises problems of fairness (because consumers in other locations might be paying the tax indirectly but reaping little of the local public service benefits as a result).

A value added tax (VAT) would in theory be no less appropriate as a source of local tax revenue than the turnover or retail sales tax, but it is unlikely to be administratively feasible at the local level.[7] If a VAT is chosen, the best bet is for local governments to receive a nationally determined proportion of collections, as is done in Brazil and Mexico.

Although the retail sales tax and the turnover tax are not without problems, they remain the best candidates for general local sales taxes.

An analysis of the possibilities for local sales taxes in developing countries therefore must be concerned mostly with the merits of these two forms. On grounds of economic efficiency, the retail sales tax is clearly superior to the turnover tax. It results in a uniform ratio of taxation relative to consumer spending if applied uniformly to all retail transactions and does not distort the production or distribution of goods and services. The turnover tax, in contrast, results in differing ratios of tax to consumer spending depending on the markups for various commodities and the degree of vertical integration in production and distribution. The difference in distortion effects, however, may not be serious because of the typically low rates of local turnover taxes and large number of exemptions likely to be given under a retail sales tax.

A more serious concern about the local sales tax is that it may bias retailers and shoppers against choosing to do business in higher-taxing local jurisdictions that have it. This is more likely to be an issue in industrial than in developing countries for two reasons. First, the problem arises only where there is geographic fragmentation of governments in the metropolitan area—a situation less common in developing than industrial countries (see chapter 12). Second, because private ownership of automobiles is still much less prevalent in the cities of developing countries, the mobility of shoppers is considerably lower. Large distortions thus are not likely to arise from a general local sales tax.

In terms of vertical equity, local government general sales taxes are likely to be regressive. This is because the marginal propensity to consume tends to fall with income, and because services are likely to be exempt. This regressivity can, however, be alleviated by exempting basic necessities and foodstuffs, by exempting very small retail establishments, and by gearing up the tax administration to capture goods and services consumed by high-income groups—for example, automobiles, electrical appliances, and restaurant and club services. Of course, there is no guarantee that local governments will utilize these means of increasing the progressivity of the sales tax. A fair question is whether it is worth the administrative cost involved to improve the vertical equity of income distribution. Local sales tax rates will in all probability be so low that the potential effects on the distribution of income will be insignificant.

The potential revenue performance of the local sales tax is its principal attraction and justifies its typically higher collection cost. In Managua, the local sales tax contributed 70 percent of local tax revenue and financed almost 60 percent of total local expenditure in the mid-1970s. The revenue-elasticity of the tax is also likely to be good because the tax is levied ad valorem and revenues thus increase with general economic activity and inflation. In terms of revenue stability local sales taxes may be found wanting, because collections expand and contract in proportion to general business conditions—although the consumption base of a sales tax is not likely to be as unstable as that of an income tax.[8]

A sales tax is revenue-productive for the local government only if it can be adequately assessed and collected, and a retail sales tax is not a good bet in this regard for low-income countries. The administrative difficulties of a retail sales tax stem from the small formal sector and from the preponderance of small retail establishments, even in the modern sector—for example, ambulatory salesmen and small shops set up in residences. An attempt to levy a retail sales tax on these enterprises would pose tremendous administrative costs. Small retail establishments would almost certainly have to be exempt. Such a limited local retail sales tax could be more easily administered because a considerably smaller number of firms would be covered. For Bogotá, Gillis estimated that a retail sales tax with such an exclusion would lead to a reduction in the number of taxpayers from about 40,000 to about 6,000–9,000 (Gillis 1971: 654). Because the number of taxpayers is relatively small under such a system and because most larger merchants are keeping accounts anyway, the added compliance costs are likely to be negligible. The base would be so narrow, however, that statutory rates would have to be quite high—perhaps dampening consumption in the modern sector and stimulating it in the informal sector, which could encourage tax evasion and certainly provoke political opposition by making the tax more visible. The alternative is that the tax rate could be kept low and revenue-productivity would be limited.

This quandary has led the few cities in developing countries that impose general sales taxes to opt for the more broadly based turnover tax. Even here, there remains considerable scope for evasion due to the difficulty of auditing small firms, and even some of the larger ones. Record keeping is not good, even by medium-size firms, and there is little hope that local government staffing will permit a thorough accounting of gross sales (turnover) for all firms. Particularly for smaller firms, local turnover taxes may be based largely on voluntary declarations, or a flat fee may be assessed. The assumption in choosing a turnover tax over the retail sales tax is that what is lost in ability to assess is made up for in the larger number of firms covered and the lower statutory tax rate for each firm.

In all developing countries, sales taxes are levied by higher levels of government. This raises the question of how a local tax could be piggybacked onto the central tax—that is, assessed and collected by the higher level of government but with a share of revenue remitted to the local authority where the tax was collected. Two arrangements are possible. First, the local tax could be a sur-rate on the central tax, and the central government could act as collection agent. The local government would set the local rate, determine special exemptions, and so forth, and pay the central government a collection charge.[9] Local autonomy would be sacrificed only in that the central government would choose the tax base and determine how to collect the tax efficiently. The problem with this arrangement is competition for the tax base. The central government (or state governments in some federations) is not willing to share this very lucrative source of revenue with local authorities.

The second arrangement would consist of pure tax sharing. The central government would return a percentage of what it collected in a locality to the local authority, thereby providing revenue with no administrative cost but also with no local autonomy. For example, municipalities in Brazil receive a guaranteed share of state value added tax collections, but distribution is by formula and local governments have no say in rate or base determination. This is an intergovernmental transfer rather than a local tax. The problem with such tax sharing is that local governments might not trust the higher-level tax collectors to turn over revenues during budget squeezes.[10] If the sharing arrangement is constitutional and if local tax receipts do not enter into the national (or state) budget but are paid directly to the local government accounts, the problem is not likely to be serious. But this is rarely the arrangement under a purely shared tax (see chapter 13).

A final criterion for evaluating the local sales tax is its political acceptability. Because indirect taxes can be hidden in the purchase price of goods and services, they are less likely than direct taxes to raise taxpayer resistance and grassroots political opposition. This is especially true for local government taxes on gross receipts, which are likely to have a very low rate and which will be buried in sales at several levels of production and distribution.

In summary, the main advantage of the local sales tax is its substantial potential for raising revenue. The main problems are administration and regressivity. The first step toward resolution of these problems is exemption of food and small retailers.

As development proceeds and the modern sector grows, general sales taxes will come to be seen as much more feasible. Even the largest cities in some developing countries are, however, many years away from the conditions necessary to levy a retail sales tax effectively. The best option is probably some combination of a shared sales tax with the state or center and a makeshift sales tax, levied locally, that captures the portion of the base that is presently not reached by the central system. It is to these makeshift sales taxes that we now turn.

Local Taxes on Industry, Commerce, and Professions

Taxes on industry, commerce, and professions are a common source of local revenue, particularly in Latin America. The data in table 2-11 show that these taxes have accounted for as much as 67 percent of local taxes in Valencia and for 74 percent in La Paz. In the Philippines about 40 percent of municipal revenues come from the business license tax. Dakar and Abidjan each receive about a third of total revenues from the business tax or *patente*.

The nature of this local tax varies widely among countries and even among cities within a country. In Colombia, five types of local taxes have been called "industry and commerce taxes." A turnover tax was used in Armenia, Bogotá, Medellín, and Monteria. A tax on the value of gross business assets was levied in Barranquilla, Cali, and Cartagena, among other cities. Some cities levied a tax on the value of fixed assets of the firm located in the taxing jurisdiction (Neiva and Popayan), others on the rental value of the business establishment (Cucuta). Finally, most smaller municipalities imposed specific levies by type of enterprise. Thus, although all municipalities imposed a tax with the same name, it was actually a sales tax in some cities, a tax on business capital in others, an annual value tax on business real estate in yet others, and in most small municipalities nothing but a business license.

In other countries the business and commerce tax has been more uniform than in Colombia, but its form may vary widely by type of business. In San Salvador, most commercial establishments were taxed according to the value of their assets, but some were taxed at specific rates according to the type of enterprise (Avenarius and others 1975). The business tax in Abidjan and Dakar has two components: a fixed amount based on type of activity and an ad valorem rate based on the annual value of the business's real estate (1984 World Bank data). To reach the service sector, provincial and city governments also tax various occupations at a flat rate, but this is a much less important source of revenue. In Kingston, trade licenses are based on the valuation of the premises in which the commercial activity takes place. The municipalities of Brazil levy a service tax on a federally defined base of the gross value of "municipal" services. In practice, the tax is levied on self-declared values of gross receipts for most firms and according to a notional reference value for self-employed occupations (Silveira 1989).

In theory any tax on industry and commerce will impose efficiency costs by taxing business capital more than other capital—or, probably more important, by applying various rates to different types of enterprises. But in Brazil it is argued that since the local service covers a part of the base that is missed by the state value added tax, the efficiency effects are positive (Silveira 1989). In most countries, however, the tax rates are very low and so, one would guess, are the price distortions. For the same reason, adverse effects on equity may not be important.

Nevertheless, one might speculate about the potential effects on equity of a tax on industry and commerce. If the tax is shifted forward to consumers (as for a gross receipts tax), it will tend to be regressive. If it is not shifted forward (as is likely in the case of a tax on business capital), vertical equity may depend on the rate structure. For example, a proportional tax on business capital or on the rental value of business property may well be progressive because it mainly affects the high-income modern sector. In contrast, a flat charge for business licenses is likely to be regressive because large and small establishments pay equal taxes, even though the latter belong to the low-income traditional sector. But once one allows for graduated rate structures, which are common, the issue becomes more complicated. For instance, in the Philippines the tax rate declined with the level of gross receipts, in Cartagena and San Salvador rates declined with the value of business assets, and in Yumbo (Colombia) the rate increased with the value of assets. Yet assessment of the tax on smaller firms can be much more lax, and effective rates may be lower; in the Philippines small firms have paid a flat charge which is likely below the normal rate.

The potential revenue yield of business taxes can be quite substantial. With urbanization, the number and size of businesses grow, and so does the taxable base. Although the base may be inadequately assessed, the tax yield can grow quite rapidly. An analysis of the Philippines business license tax shows that even with quite poor assessment and collection practices, the income-elasticity of the tax yield can be greater than unity (Bahl and Schroeder 1983a). Dakar reports the same growth experience in the late 1970s, but there has been a revenue-inelastic response in Abidjan (1984 World Bank data). The local services tax in Brazil benefits from inflation adjustments and has an estimated income-elasticity greater than unity (Silveira 1989: 10–11).

Taxes on industry and commerce are difficult to administer. The shortage of skilled staff makes it difficult for local governments to assess business capital, gross receipts, or rental value, especially for very small firms which do not keep proper accounts. Moreover, it is very difficult to get a complete enumeration of taxable firms within an urban area. As a result, there is a high degree of evasion. For example, a 1971 study by the municipal authorities in Cartagena revealed that 60 percent of businesses were operating without valid business licenses and thus were evading the industry and commerce tax. At the same time, it was estimated that exempting as many as 70 percent of all businesses because of small size would lower gross tax liabilities by only 1.2 percent (Linn 1975).

Urban governments have tried to resolve the problem of assessment and collection in various ways. A flat charge eliminates the need to assess small firms and self-employed professionals and leaves only a collection problem. How to assess larger firms remains a difficult issue, however, which has been addressed in different ways. In many cases, the tax is self-assessed; in effect, it is a voluntary levy. These declarations are often accepted, and only the larger firms are asked to support their declaration. Special problems arise when the base of the business tax is rental value. In such cases, appropriate coordination with cadastral authorities might reduce assessment costs. This was the situation in Dakar. But assessment data gathered for the property tax are likely to be useful for the business tax only if the property tax is an annual value tax. Under the capital value or site value tax system, usually no effort is made to collect information on rental incomes from properties. In Kingston, where trade license taxes were imposed in relation to the value of the premises in which the commercial activity was carried out, property tax assessments were not used. Instead, local officials made separate assessments for the purpose of issuing trade license taxes (Bougeon-Maassen and Linn 1977).

The business tax is also plagued by serious collection problems. For example, delinquency rates were 30 percent in Côte d'Ivoire (1984 World Bank data), which probably represents a strong performance. Two ways to improve the efficiency of collection have been tried. First, in Abidjan, the tax was collected from larger firms by the central government and from smaller firms by patrolling tax collectors (who are also responsible for assessment). About 12 percent of 1981 collections were made by these field inspectors. Second, tax collection and other government actions can be coordinated—for example, by requiring proof of payment of business taxes before issuing a permit of operation. In some Philippine cities, proof of property and business tax payments has been required for the issuance of the mayor's business permit. In Brazil, about 70 percent of the local service tax due is actually paid, although this percentage may vary widely across cities.[11]

In summary, the main problems with these types of business taxes is that, to make them a permissible revenue source for local governments, they must be contrived to differ from central government sales taxes. For example, the business license tax in the Philippines was really a gross receipts tax on all businesses, but its administration and design were kept quite separate from central government sales taxes. As a result, the local business tax is rarely designed to reflect the four common objectives of a "good" tax. It is usually meant to tax firms according to the level of their activities but rarely does so, either because local governments cannot easily tax turnover or value added or because they are legally barred from taxing sales and resort to a proxy sales tax or a property tax on businesses. Even with these flaws, industry and commerce taxes tend to be acceptable politically, in the sense that local politicians are generally willing and able to convince their constituents that local business should contribute a fair share to the fiscal health of local government. And there is not usually much resistance to it from the business community because substantial amounts can be passed on or evaded.

The typical business tax has either inconsequential or unfavorable effects on efficiency. Its effects on equity depend on local practice, and its administrative costs are high. One therefore justifies a business tax on the grounds that it can raise substantial revenues, that its rate and base adjustments will largely be unfettered by higher-level government restrictions, that it will be relatively costless politically, and that it often has no suitable alternative. Given the weight local politicians usually attach to its revenue-raising advantages and the mild political resistance to it, analysts might best be concerned with what if anything can be done to alleviate its relative inefficiency, uncertain equity, and administrative shortcomings.

The path must vary according to a country's and jurisdiction's stage of development. The more modern the local economy, the more persuasive is the case for switching to a formal sales tax. The legal framework may permit a relatively easy changeover, as witnessed for instance by the adoption of a turnover tax in Bogotá (which still, however, is called a business and commerce tax). Or such a reform may necessitate changes in the legal framework and hence the support of higher levels of government. But given the aversion of these higher levels to sharing their control of income and sales taxes with local government, the outlook for a modern local sales tax is not very good. In such cases, the best strategy is to improve administration of the present levy.

In smaller jurisdictions and in those with less modern economies, the path must be a simple one. For administrative reasons, more modern sales taxes, for example a turnover tax, are out of the question. The emphasis must be on improving administration and on structuring a tax that can be easily administered. Two rules are more or less universal. First, a flat rate should be adopted, because a graduated rate structure would unduly complicate administration. Second, administration can be simplified by exempting smaller establishments or taxing them a flat charge. This reduces collection problems, increases efficiency (at least if license taxes are used), and very probably improves the vertical equity of the tax with relatively little loss of revenue.

"Terminal" Taxes

Terminal taxes are levied on goods, vehicles, or passengers entering or leaving a local jurisdiction. The most important form is the octroi, which is an important source of revenue for local governments in India and Pakistan. There is also some use of local terminal taxes on intercity passenger traffic, both air and surface.

The Octroi

The octroi is a tax levied on goods entering a city for the purpose of local processing or final consumption.[12] It is found in many local jurisdictions in India, Pakistan, and (until 1981) Bangladesh.[13] Despite the revenue success enjoyed by the octroi in India and Pakistan, there are strong movements afloat to abolish this tax. It has been condemned regularly by analysts of local government finance, including numerous Government of India Study Commissions. Gujarat, Karnataka, and Madya Pradesh states in India have all abolished octroi. In Calcutta, however, where the octroi was more recently adopted, it was introduced by the state for the entire metropolitan area, with its revenues to be shared among the various local bodies and the Calcutta Metropolitan Development Authority.

The base of the octroi is the value, weight, or number of items entering a local jurisdiction by road, rail, sea, or air. In Bombay, for instance, the tax has been imposed according to value for some commodities, according to weight for others, and on a specific basis for oil entering the city via a pipeline. In Karachi, the tax has been imposed by weight for commodities entering on roads but by value for commodities entering via the city's port. Rates varied according to complicated schedules, and some types of commodities and goods in transit were exempt. The taxes were collected at octroi stations: checkpoints on roads at the jurisdictional borders and at railway stations, airports, and docks. In Ahmadabad, for instance, there were 34 stations in 1973—18 rail, 15 road, and 1 air. There was usually no assessment problem when the levy was specific; however, an invoice was required and had to be examined at the octroi station. Ahmadabad assessors were equipped with a manual of market values which they used to double-check the invoiced amount. The taxes were collected directly from the driver by the attending clerks (Bahl 1975).

A major problem with the octroi is that it may greatly increase transport time and cost, and therefore the price of "imported" goods. Many have estimated these costs as being quite substantial. A good example of the magnitude of lost time is the estimate from the Mysore Taxation Enquiry that "between Bangalore and Mangalore, about 800 km, a vehicle has to stop for 36 hours and 40 minutes at checkposts" (Rao and Rao 1977: 32).

Other complications of the octroi, such as bribery of octroi staff by operators and spoilage of merchandise, are frequently mentioned. Nanjundappa (1973) estimated that in India the total nontax cost of reduced utilization at border crossings was approximately 25 percent of variable vehicle operating costs. Not all of these costs could be directly ascribed to the local octroi, but the magnitude of the figure indicates that considerable losses in efficiency may be imposed.

The octroi therefore gives locally produced commodities a pricing advantage over commodities imported from outside the metropolitan area. If a metropolitan area has grown beyond the boundaries of taxing jurisdictions, the octroi may curtail even intrametropolitan trade. And as the final irony, the tax can provide a cogent disincentive for metropolitan integration under an areawide authority, because consolidation of fragmented local authorities would automatically reduce the octroi tax base by detaxing intrametropolitan commodity flows. From the standpoint of efficiency, the octroi is therefore an unmitigated disaster.

In terms of equity the picture is more complicated and depends on local practice. In the cities of Pakistan, attempts have been made to structure the tax in such a way that it does not fall heavily on food and other essentials consumed mainly by low-income groups, and to tax especially luxury items. In Ahmadabad and Bombay, where in the past less emphasis has been put on a progressive octroi rate structure, the octroi was regressive and probably more so than state sales taxes (Bahl 1975).

In view of its many problems—costs of administration are considerable, the degree of collection efficiency is unknown but likely to be poor, and the method of collection invites corruption—why does the octroi continue to be used by local governments on the Indian subcontinent? There are three reasons. First and most important, the octroi can produce substantial revenue for local authorities. In fact, in many Indian and Pakistani cities, it dominates the revenue structure. For example, in Karachi the octroi accounted for 80 percent of total taxes in 1986. The corresponding statistic in Ahmadabad was 70 percent in 1984. This buoyancy is caused in part by the underlying automatic growth in the base as intercity trade expands in value and volume, and in part by the efforts of local authorities to increase revenues by raising and restructuring octroi rates.

A second reason for the growing reliance on the octroi is the absence of a good alternative. Other potential sources, such as automobile taxes, income or sales taxes, and user charges, are generally of only minor importance in the revenue structures of cities in India and Pakistan. Moreover, the central and state governments of India and Pakistan have not provided sufficient grants or subsidies to enable local governments to move away from the octroi. The fact is that the octroi is the only major tax base (besides property values) not claimed by higher-level authorities. Indeed, in Bangladesh and in those Indian states where the octroi was abandoned, it was not replaced by an equally productive and buoyant revenue source. A third reason for the continued popularity of the octroi is that, in the Indian and Pakastani fiscal tradition, the octroi has been politically more acceptable than user charges, and this has tended to reinforce its use.

For these three reasons, belaboring the disadvantages of the octroi is not a very useful approach to resolving the fiscal problems of Indian and Pakistani cities. As long as no other productive and buoyant source of revenue is offered and accepted, the octroi will remain a prime source of funding for urban governments.

Other Terminal Taxes

Besides the octroi, some Indian local authorities have levied taxes on intercity vehicle and passenger transport by charging according to the vehicle or the number of passengers entering the city. Cities in other countries have comparable charges, but these appear to be linked mainly to the provision of public bus terminal facilities (in Jakarta and Kingston) and to airport taxes (in Jakarta). In evaluating these taxes one must distinguish between taxes related to road transport and to air travel.

If a terminal tax covers the marginal cost imposed by each bus or passenger using the public bus station, it is efficient. If it exceeds the marginal cost, it will introduce a bias in favor of the private automobile and reduce overall passenger traffic. The extent of such losses in efficiency depends on the price-elasticity of demand for intercity transport. Even if this elasticity is relatively low and the efficiency losses are minimal, there is little reason to use this tax base. The tax base is narrow and subject to fluctuations, administration is difficult, and in the best of cases revenues will be negligible. Higher automotive taxation would be a much better alternative on both efficiency and revenue-raising grounds. Moreover, automotive taxation is likely to be less regressive because high-income people tend to use automobiles but low-income people are restricted to buses, if they engage in intercity travel at all.

A local terminal tax at airports presents a somewhat different situation. It is likely to generate little distortion in resource allocation and is quite progressive: the price-elasticity of demand for air travel is likely to be low, and the income-elasticity is high. Furthermore, because most cities have only one major civilian airport, usually managed by a higher-level public authority, the collection of a local airport terminal tax is in principle quite simple. It can be collected directly from the airlines on a per passenger or per airplane basis, from the airport operator, or from passengers. In any case, the proceeds from local airport taxes are not likely to weigh heavily in the local budget.

Local Sumptuary Taxes

Taxes on beer, liquor, and tobacco—usually referred to as "sumptuary taxes"—are widely used in developing countries. In some countries, local authorities are entitled to levy such taxes or to share in the revenues. For example, in Zairian cities the local tax on beer consumption has been the most important source of local tax revenues (see table 2-11); in Guatemala City local taxes on liquor, beer, and cigarettes contributed about 8 percent of local tax revenues in the early 1970s; in San Salvador a local tax on liquor contributed 15 percent and in La Paz a local beer tax contributed 7.1 percent, both in the mid-1970s. In Bogotá the national tax on beer consumption, of which 40 percent was shared on a derivation principle with departments (states) and the city government, in 1979 raised 14.4 percent of all local revenues (excluding local autonomous agencies). The government of Bogotá also derived revenues from a local tax on foreign cigarettes and a shared tax on all tobacco products.

On the surface, local sumptuary taxes seem to have three advantages. First, there is a perceived moral advantage stemming from the traditional justification for these taxes: the paternalistic concept that commodities thought to be harmful to society should be taxed. In developing countries the argument is at times heard that consumption of liquor, beer, and cigarettes is not in the interest of national development and should therefore be discouraged. The second argument is that these taxes can generate substantial revenues. Third, sumptuary taxes are relatively easy to collect, although smuggling and evasion impose rate limits.

Three considerations, however, should dampen the enthusiasm with which sumptuary taxes are sometimes viewed by local or national authorities (Due 1988; McLure and Thirsk 1978). First, consumption of sumptuary items tends to be quite inelastic with respect to price changes. This implies that the moral objectives of sumptuary taxes are not likely to be well served. Indeed, at lower income levels a rise in the price of beer, liquor, or tobacco products may lead to a reduction in the consumption of other essential or nutritious goods. If this is so, even the moral argument that those who indulge in the vices of liquor or tobacco ought to pay for them may be quite misguided because often it may be the children of drinking and smoking household members who are paying the tax in terms of reduced consumption. Thus, inadvertently, sumptuary taxes may reduce health standards and interfere with efficiency.

Second, because the consumption of beer, liquor, and tobacco is quite inelastic with respect to income, sumptuary taxes are highly regressive. In Bogotá it has been estimated that low-income families paid about 2.5 percent of household income in local sumptuary taxes, which accounted for about 70 percent of their local tax burden in the early 1970s. High-income families, in contrast, paid only 0.2 percent of household income in sumptuary taxes, less than 20 percent of their local tax burden (Linn 1980a).[14] This regressivity is lessened in many countries by taxing locally produced liquors at lower rates than imported brands.

Third, in the long term the income-elasticity of sumptuary taxes is likely to be quite low—unless real tax rates are continuously increased—because of the low income-elasticity of liquor and cigarette consumption. The beer tax in Bogotá, which was one of the success stories of revenue performance, actually maintained its share in overall city government revenues from 1963 to 1972. But this was a time when the most important source of local revenue, the property tax, remained quite stagnant in real terms, thus depressing the overall growth of revenues. The income-elasticity of all local taxes in Bogotá during this period was a dismally low 0.142 (World Bank data).

In sum, sumptuary taxes can raise a substantial and steady amount of local revenues with relatively little administrative complexity, minor political costs, and no major efficiency loss, except for the possible but largely unproven reduction of nutritionally important items in a family's food basket. The main drawback of these taxes is therefore their distributional effect, which is potentially quite regressive. This drawback causes us to ask about the distributive implications of expenditures financed by these sumptuary taxes.

To answer this question, one must carefully consider the expenditure policies of the local taxing authority. If expenditures are primarily directed toward the population—such as primary education, basic health care and disease prevention, infrastructure provision for low-income neighborhoods, and community development—then additional revenue generation, even through a regressive tax on beer, liquor, and tobacco, may improve the overall distribution of income. Cursory observation of the activities of the local government in Bogotá (excluding autonomous agencies) suggests that indeed this may have been the case. Nevertheless, the property tax in Bogotá, which is clearly more progressive than the beer tax, decreased in importance in the 1970s, although the beer tax at least maintained its share. Thus quite possibly the total distributional effect of local government activities in Bogotá has deteriorated (see Linn and others 1984).

Entertainment Taxes

Local governments in many developing countries commonly levy taxes on various forms of entertainment: restaurants and hotels, theaters, movies, other public events, and betting and gambling. Lotteries operated by local governments might also be thought of as an entertainment tax. Most commonly, taxes are levied on theaters and movies, sometimes at specific rates per show, sometimes as recurrent license fees, and in yet other cases as a proportion of gross receipts or of the value of the tickets sold. Rates can be quite high, as for instance in Jakarta during the early 1970s, where they ranged up to 45 percent on the gross receipts of the better movie houses.

In most countries, local governments assess and collect the entertainment tax and in many cases may freely alter the rate and base. In some Indian states, however, it is a shared tax with state assessment, collection, and rate-base determination. Ninety percent of collections in Karnataka, for example, were assigned to local bodies on the basis of origin (Malhotra 1986).

Local taxes on betting and gambling may be a particularly important source of revenue, especially where a racecourse or casinos provide readily identifiable tax opportunities (as in Cartagena, Jakarta, and Seoul). Arrangements between local authorities and casino operators typically involve a considerable amount of bargaining and at times even take a contractual form (Cartagena). To what extent this practice also invites under-the-table payments is difficult to establish, but in some cases it leads to poor budgetary management and control. For instance, unexplained discrepancies between contractual obligations and actual payments occurred in Cartagena in the early 1970s. At the same time in Jakarta, a substantial part of the revenues from gambling taxes and licenses did not enter the official accounts of the local authorities but was channeled into a separate fund under the exclusive control of the governor (mayor) of Jakarta and was used without formal accountability for various local projects.

In many respects the common arguments for entertainment taxes are similar to those for sumptuary taxes. Entertainment is not regarded as essential consumption, and it is believed that those being entertained deserve to pay heavily for it and to support the public purse. As with sumptuary taxes, there is little evidence that the price-elasticity of demand for entertainment is high or that these taxes significantly restrict the consumption of luxury goods. If people intend to play, an entertainment tax probably will not deter them. Indeed, the greater danger may well be that for gambling operations and other more dubious forms of entertainment, local officials may get too closely involved with operators while bargaining for and collecting taxes and thus incur the risk of losing their credibility as impartial administrators.

In contrast to sumptuary taxes, however, entertainment taxes may be structured so as to be quite progressive. Taxes on restaurants and hotels, as well as those on theaters and movies, frequently vary with the type of establishment, such that more luxurious establishments are taxed at higher rates than those providing cheaper fare. The distributive effect of gambling taxes depends on the type of gambling covered. In Colombia, for instance, various types of betting cater heavily to low-income groups. Conversely, casino gambling tends to be restricted to high-income groups, including tourists. Therefore, unless these taxes fall especially heavily on forms of entertainment enjoyed by the low-income classes, such as cheap movie houses and some common types of betting, the distributive effect of these taxes is likely to be quite progressive. Indeed, entertainment is one type of luxury consumption that can be taxed quite effectively at the local level (as in Bogotá, Cartagena, and Seoul).

The revenue performance and administrative sides of entertainment taxes are somewhat less favorable. Assessment and collection can be difficult, as in Jakarta and Seoul, but it is also possible for the central government to act as the collection agent, as in Bangkok.[15] Revenues are generally not substantial, although their buoyancy can be considerable. For instance, entertainment tax revenues in Jakarta and Seoul had a buoyancy greater than unity in the 1970s, and in many of the other cities revenues from these taxes were among the most rapidly growing of all local taxes.

Except for public lotteries, which are a rather special way to raise local revenues, entertainment taxes represent a relatively desirable form of local taxation, although their administration may cause some concern. But these taxes cannot be relied upon to provide a major source of financing for urban governments. Jakarta was exceptional in two respects: first, the base for entertainment taxes was particularly large; and second, other local revenue sources, with the exception of motor vehicle taxes, were not very well developed. Thus the contribution of entertainment taxes, which appeared large when considered in relation to all other revenues, was less impressive on a per capita basis or relative to income in the city.

Public lotteries deserve special consideration because they are not coercive and do not distort resource allocation. Common objections are that they encourage gambling, that by making betting a matter of public policy they undermine the moral fiber of society, and, most important, that they divert consumer spending away from necessities—especially among low-income groups. But lotteries can make quite a substantial contribution to revenue. For instance, Bogotá's lottery raised 11 percent of all local tax revenue in 1982.

At first glance, the incidence of lottery ticket payments might seem quite regressive, but much depends on how one views it. Lottery revenues do not compete with other forms of taxes, simply because they are not perceived as taxes by the public or by policymakers. Rather, their revenues are often viewed as a financial resource which could not have been raised in other ways. Another way to look at the problem is that the lottery tickets would have been purchased in a private game had there not been a local government lottery; hence, there is only a transfer effect and no harm to the income distribution. In addition, there is the question of how the money is spent. Lottery proceeds are often earmarked for socially worthy causes. In Bogotá the statutes governing lottery operations required that 75 percent of the net proceeds be spent on basic public health and general welfare measures, with the remainder going to help the large number of homeless children stranded on the streets of the city. At least in this case, the overall distribution effect of the local lottery might be quite favorable. Providing that lotteries are acceptable on ethical and political grounds, they may present a useful supplement for local finances in the large cities of developing countries. They bring in some revenue and have few bad side effects.

Minor Local Taxes, Licenses, and Fees

One of the most striking features of the tax systems in most cities of developing countries is the proliferation of minor revenue sources.[16] These are mostly selective excise taxes and a variety of license taxes, fees, stamp taxes, and poll taxes. Although any one of them does not contribute much to revenues, they may jointly weigh quite heavily on the overall financial structure, making wholesale abandonment quite difficult (see table 2-11).

There are three good reasons for the continued existence of these taxes. The most obvious is the lack of other options for raising revenue. The second is simply inertia: these miscellaneous sources have "always been there." Comprehensive local government tax reforms are very rare, though not unheard of; hence, there is no particular occasion to abolish these taxes. Their abolition can occur, however. In the past, Buenos Aires relied on a large number of minor nuisance taxes, but these were abolished and replaced by a tax on commercial and industrial activities (Mouchet 1972). The third reason for using these taxes is the desire to include as much as possible of the local population in the taxpaying community. This can be a costly process, but there may be important social benefits to be gained from expanding the public's involvement in government.

For some combination of these reasons, it is thus not unusual to find as many as two dozen different local taxes. Of 20 local taxes in Managua, only 3 yielded as much as 3 percent of total local revenues in 1974. In Cartagena, 28 of 32 local taxes contributed less than 5 percent (in aggregate) to locally raised revenues in 1972 (not including revenues of local autonomous agencies). In Jakarta, of the 11 largest local taxes, only 3 yielded more than 5 percent of total local revenues in 1974. All local governments in Indonesia are eligible to impose more than 100 taxes, but together these yield less than 20 percent of local governments' own source revenue.

In general, these minor taxes are difficult and costly to collect, and compliance costs are high. In Cartagena the cost of assessing and collecting all local taxes, with the exception of the property tax, amounted to approximately 15 percent of receipts from taxes and licenses. In many cases the taxes are poorly understood and enforced by local officials, and they may amount to little more than voluntary contributions by those who choose not to evade them.[17] Each individual tax source yields little revenue and shows little buoyancy or predictability, although some cities, notably Jakarta, have been able to increase revenues through more aggressive collection efforts and by increasing the number of minor taxes. The effect on efficiency and equity varies widely with the particular tax concerned, but on balance they tend to interfere with consumer choice and business activity and are likely to be quite inequitable horizontally as well as vertically. The size of these effects, however, is likely to be minimal.

There is an almost endless variety of these minor taxes. The following five types are the most common. First, local governments frequently have taxed advertisements (Bangkok, Bogotá, Cali, Cartagena, Jakarta, Tehran). These taxes are imposed on specific types of advertisements (for example, signboards) and are characterized by complicated rate schedules, considerable collection and compliance costs, and small revenues.

Second, taxes on construction activity also abound. Typically, they are levied on building permits (in the cities of Colombia and Zaire and in Valencia), but in some cases on building materials (Managua, Tehran). These taxes interfere with construction activity and thus can lead to inefficiency in the building sector. Building permits could conceivably be used to tax luxury construction in the interest of equity and resource allocation, but this is generally not done. In Cartagena, where it was possible to analyze carefully the local construction tax, it was found that the tax rate was inversely related to the value of the structure. In any case, administration and enforcement of this type of tax are likely to be difficult and costly, unless this type of tax can be combined with a well-administered property tax. Unfortunately, coordinated administration of these two taxes is the exception rather than the rule.

Third, nonmotorized vehicles are frequently taxed by local authorities, as in Colombia, India, and Indonesia. These taxes generally are designed to recover the cost of road and street construction and maintenance, and they usually take the form of annual license fees. As the discussion of automotive taxation in chapter 7 indicated, license fees cannot approximate the marginal cost of road use. If the costs imposed by nonmotorized vehicles are believed to be excessive (for example, in a heavily congested city center), it may be preferable to restrict their use through more direct means. As a revenue raiser, taxes on nonmotorized vehicles are ineffective, given the difficulties of assessment and collection and the low value of the tax base. Furthermore, on equity grounds, these taxes are quite objectionable because they tend to burden mainly low-income operators and users.

Fourth and much less common are local excise taxes on public utilities. In Cali, the local public utility—which provides water, sewerage, electricity, and telephone services—was required to pay 4 percent of gross revenues to the general account of the local government. In Cartagena in the 1970s the local government levied a tax on telephones. In Tehran, a local tax was levied on the sale of electricity, but for most uses this tax was only nominal; instead of collecting a tax on electricity sales, the municipality received free electric services from the electric company. Elsewhere, implicit taxes (or subsidies) are frequently levied on (granted to) the users of local public utility services through utility pricing practices. These are discussed further in chapters 9, 10, and 11.

The main feature of interest here is that in some cities public utility operations have been explicitly recognized and utilized as a local tax base. Of the three major types of public utility services (water, power, and telephones), telephones are probably the most promising source of local revenues. Residential telephones, in particular, are a luxury consumption item restricted mainly to high-income groups that can be the base for a progressive local tax. The tax is easily administered and can raise quite substantial revenues. In Cartagena a tax of $5 per telephone connection per month (compared with the fees of $0.15 actually in place) would have increased tax revenues of the local authority by 120 percent as of 1972. In Bogotá a similar tax would have increased tax revenues by approximately 80 percent during the same year. This type of tax is uniquely suited for the larger cities of developing countries, in which telephone ownership is heavily concentrated. Because excess demand for telephone connections is frequently encountered in cities of developing countries and because the price-elasticity of demand for telephone connections is likely to be quite low, the efficiency losses from a residential telephone tax are probably minimal.[18] More problematic are taxes on water supply and electricity. The equity argument is likely to be less strong in this case, and the efficiency losses may be more serious.

Fifth, local governments typically employ a whole host of stamp duties, licenses, and fees. In the least, they are merely bothersome for tax administration, as for instance the stamp duty on salaries and wages of local government employees in Cartagena. Usually, however, they interfere with the efficiency of local government (for example, by setting up an incentive for evading local regulatory actions such as health and sanitary inspections) or they impede the administration of other taxes (for example, by subjecting bank checks or receipts to stamp taxes and thereby encouraging the use of cash in transactions and reducing actual evidence for sales and income tax administration and enforcement; Due 1988).

Selective license taxes and fees are generally intended to recover the cost of issuing licenses or providing minor government services (for example, building inspections), or to limit public nuisance caused by private actions (for example, pet ownership or the obstruction of sidewalks by scaffoldings). To the extent that these charges are actually linked to administrative or nuisance costs, this can be a reasonable basis for taxation, provided that costs of administration and compliance do not outweigh gains in revenue and efficiency. But most of the licenses and fees actually applied in developing countries are likely to be way off the mark in this respect, and a careful review with an eye toward reducing the number of charges usually levied would be appropriate.

Summary and Evaluation

Local taxes fall into five broad categories. The first group includes property taxes, vehicle license taxes, and entertainment taxes. These taxes are generally uncontroversial on efficiency grounds, with the exception of the issues of the taxation of buildings, and tend to improve the distribution of income. Most important, each of these sources can raise substantial local revenues at relatively low administrative cost.[19] Although they may require some coordination with higher-level authorities, local authorities are given a relatively large degree of freedom to manage these taxes. Finally, these taxes tend to be quite well established and accepted by politicians and taxpayers alike as fair and reasonable bases for local revenue generation, provided that their administration is moderately effective in avoiding unnecessary horizontal inequities and compliance costs. These are, therefore, the taxes which should generally be expected to finance a major share of urban expenditures.

The second group of taxes includes industry and commerce taxes, terminal taxes, and sumptuary taxes. The main reason for their existence is that they can raise substantial amounts of revenue in politically and legally acceptable ways and with little need for coordination with higher-level authorities. But they potentially distort the allocation of resources in production and consumption, they can be regressive and usually involve horizontal inequities, and almost invariably they have considerable administrative and compliance costs (sumptuary taxes excepted). These well-known drawbacks are given little weight by local legislators and administrators, for whom the expanded use of these taxes offers a path of least resistance in meeting revenue objectives. More important, all possible modifications must be made in the structures of these taxes to reduce distortions, inequities, and administrative costs; and less costly alternative local taxes or revenue sources must be explored.

The third group of taxes includes income taxes and general sales taxes. The major problem with these taxes is that their success requires a large degree of coordination between local and higher-level authorities and that the higher level frequently does not accept them as suitable instruments of local taxation. The efficiency losses and horizontal inequity associated with local income taxes and general sales taxes are likely to be small, and although revenue yields may be large and buoyant, they are likely to fluctuate considerably with business activity.

The fourth group of taxes consists of what may best be called nuisance taxes (selective excises, licenses, stamp duties, poll taxes, and so forth), most of which are highly inefficient and inequitable, perform poorly in raising revenue, and have high administrative costs. They continue to exist because their use is generally unencumbered by higher-level governments and because they are a conventional and thus politically accepted source of local revenues in many countries. To the extent which is feasible, they ought to be abolished, simplified, or integrated into other less harmful local taxes.

This leaves the fifth group, those charges which are primarily intended to increase efficiency. The main examples discussed so far are the various forms of congestion charges on motor vehicles in urban areas. They are also generally desirable on grounds of equity, revenue performance, and the relatively low need for coordination with higher-level authorities. Their main problems are difficulties with administration and political acceptability, although the admittedly limited experience in Singapore indicates that congestion charges are feasible and effective. User charges for urban services are the most important source of urban revenues whose collection can help improve, not worsen, the efficiency of resource allocation. We turn to these charges in chapters 9, 10, and 11.

PART III

User Charges for Urban Services

URBAN GOVERNMENTS in developing countries rely on a large variety of charges which are directly related to the provision or use of urban public services. These charges include public utility tariffs, special assessments to recoup the costs of infrastructure investments, fees for education and health services, and, more generally, all the types of charges which are levied on urban residents on the basis of some benefit received or cost imposed on account of service provision and use.

The extent to which these charges contribute to urban fiscal resources varies widely between countries and cities (see chapter 2 above), but in many places service-related charges have contributed significantly to the level and growth of revenues of urban government. Considering that user charges can raise substantial revenues in a fair and publicly acceptable manner, increase the efficiency of allocation of existing service capacity, and help guide investment decisions, it is surprising how often their role in financing urban services in developing countries is neglected.

The purpose of the following chapters is, therefore, to direct attention to the principles and practices of user charge financing in the cities of developing countries. The services discussed here include the main public utilities (water supply, sewerage, electricity, and telephones), solid waste disposal, public transport, road construction, and housing. Education, health, public markets, cemeteries, and abattoirs will be dealt with only in passing, whereas police, fire protection, and recreation will largely be ignored on the grounds that either the scope for user charge financing of these services is severely limited in developing countries (for example, police and fire protection), or that the services do not have the prominence which they tend to have in the cities of the more industrialized countries (for example, recreation).

Chapter 9 discusses the basic principles of user charge finance as they apply, to a greater or lesser extent, to all major urban services. Chapter

10 deals in detail with water supply and sewerage services. The reasons for this emphasis are twofold. First, these services are almost universally a responsibility of the local authorities in developing countries, and they lend themselves particularly well to user charge financing. Second, the empirical evidence on these services is quite rich, thus providing a good basis for a case study of the issues involved in user charge financing of urban services. Chapter 11 discusses briefly the major issues and the evidence available on the pricing of each of the other urban services.

9 Issues in Pricing Urban Services

THIS CHAPTER PROVIDES an overview of the most important issues arising from an analysis of the pricing of urban services. The complexity of the matter warrants a careful exposition of how the same basic analytical arguments apply to various services. Without this exposition, the impression could be given that different principles apply to different services. In fact the opposite is the case: the same basic principles apply to all services, provided one allows for the specifics of supply and demand and for the varied institutional situations.

This chapter is organized in four sections dealing with four concerns in pricing urban services: efficiency, fiscal constraints and their implications for financial viability, equity and growth, and political and administrative feasibility. Although economists are prone to emphasize efficiency, all four concerns need to be considered if one is to arrive at a reasonable compromise among them. This chapter treats each concern to show how tradeoffs among them are made for various services.

The Efficiency Argument for User Charges

Efficiency is clearly not the only objective for which user charges are levied or designed; indeed financial, administrative, and equity objectives tend to dominate policy decisions regarding the level and structure of user charges.[1] Although these objectives can and should not be forgotten, it behooves the economist to begin the discussion from the vantage point of efficiency because "he is likely to be a lone voice for efficiency (in a chorus of shouts for inefficiency) in order to achieve this or that desired social or political goal."[2] The efficiency argument for user charges begins with the simple but much debated rule of marginal cost pricing for public enterprises, which requires considerable amendments before it can be applied to any specific service.

The Marginal Cost Pricing Rule

The basic rule of efficient pricing states that the price of a public service should be set equal to the marginal cost of producing the service. The justification of this rule is that welfare is maximized when the benefit of an additional unit of the service to the consumer—which is reflected by his willingness to pay the price—is equal to the cost of producing this additional unit, that is, its marginal cost. As long as price is above marginal cost, a reduction in price and the resulting additional consumption of the service will lead to an increase in net benefits because total costs will increase by less than total benefits. If price falls short of marginal cost, however, then consumers will value the last unit consumed at less than the cost of producing it, and therefore net benefits will be increased by raising the price and reducing consumption.[3] The rule thus allocates resources efficiently in that it identifies the level of output that produces the greatest net benefit from service provision.

The marginal cost concept of relevance here is short-run marginal cost, that is, the cost incurred by producing an additional unit while keeping productive capacity constant. To the extent that capacity can be expanded in small installments, long-run costs will equal short-run marginal costs in an efficiently managed plant. This is because the plant will always operate at the level at which the cost of producing an additional unit with existing capacity is equal to the cost of expanding capacity to provide the additional service. Matters are more complicated if capacity can be expanded only in "lumpy steps," as is the case for many urban services— for example, the construction of a dam, sewage treatment plant, highway, school, or hospital. Unless service shortages are endemic, the service system will possess excess capacity after a new (large) unit of capacity has been added. As long as this is the case, in principle all that should be charged for an additional unit of the service consumed is the variable cost of increasing service output at that time. To determine this cost, one should be guided by the causal relationship between output and costs. For instance, an additional unit of potable water may require additional pumping and treatment expenses but not much else. An additional passenger on a half-empty bus or an additional student in a half-empty schoolroom may impose virtually no additional cost. Therefore, on a strict interpretation of the principle of marginal cost pricing, whenever there is excess capacity, the charge should be very low, possibly even zero, because the marginal use of excess capacity imposes virtually no opportunity cost.

There will also be times when existing service capacity is fully utilized, however, and this is frequently the case for urban services in developing countries. A corollary of the marginal cost pricing rule then applies: whenever capacity is fully utilized, the price should be set so that it will cause demand for the service to adjust to equal the capacity to supply it. This prescription is based on the principle that using price to ration a scarce commodity is more efficient than other means of rationing (for example, waiting lines or administrative fiat). Price rationing is superior to other forms of rationing because it allocates the scarce commodity or service among users according to the highest marginal valuation; it saves administrative costs; and it may prevent losses associated with over-crowded public facilities, such as low pressure in water pipes caused by excess demand, and the like.

The implication of this corollary to the marginal cost pricing rule is that, whenever extension of capacity is feasible only in lumpy stages, price will fluctuate over time. Price would equal short-run marginal cost as long as there is excess capacity, and thus it would be set low or possibly at zero. But as full capacity is reached, price would increase to equalize demand and capacity supply. Investment in new capacity would be appropriate if consumers were willing to pay the long-run marginal cost of system expansion, that is, if price equaled the opportunity cost of expanding the system to provide the additional unit demanded. Ideally, then, the marginal pricing rule can also guide the investment decision because consumers are made to reveal their preferences for the additional output and thus provide a measure of the marginal benefit of system expansion which can be compared with its cost.[4]

This scenario of the "pure" marginal cost rule of pricing a publicly provided service may strike the reader as rather unreal for a number of reasons, not the least of which is that wide fluctuations in price may be quite impractical, and indeed costly. In fact, application of the pure rule requires a number of restrictive assumptions:

- The demand for the service should respond to price changes; that is, it should not be perfectly price-inelastic.
- There should be perfect information on the part of the users regarding future cost and price changes.
- No externalities should result from the provision or consumption of the service.
- There should be no distortions anywhere else in the economy.
- The prices of inputs to the production of the service, and the prices of substitutes or complements to the service, should not be distorted by taxes, subsidies, or externalities.
- Whenever the rule results in a financial surplus or deficit for the service, nondistorting subsidy or tax schemes should be available so that it will be possible to absorb the surplus or deficit without affecting the allocation of resources in the economy.
- There should be no administrative or transaction costs associated with implementing the rule.
- Production of the service should be efficient in that the costs of producing a given unit of it are minimized.

These assumptions represent a formidable array of limitations on applying the rule. Their effect will be further assessed below. Even under most modified pricing rules, however, five implications of the marginal cost principle remain relevant. First, the marginal cost principle is not concerned with sunken or historical costs but with opportunity costs incurred by greater use of a service. These may or may not equal historical costs, and in many cases they will not, because economies or diseconomies of scale, technological advances, natural resource constraints, shifting factor prices, changed service standards, and the like will change the marginal costs of service provision over time. Factors that lead to changes in marginal cost include economies of scale in public utility services, advances in telecommunications technology, limitations on energy and water resources, improvements in educational or health standards, and increases in labor costs.

Second, consumers should be charged equal prices for the services consumed unless they impose differential marginal costs on the system. Rising (or falling) block rates commonly encountered in public utility services usually cannot be justified on efficiency grounds because it is the cost of the last or additional unit consumed by any user (large or small) that must be matched by the price.[5] Quantity discounts or surcharges can sometimes be justified on efficiency grounds, however, because of (dis)economies of scale or externalities associated with the extent of an individual's use of the service.[6]

Third, marginal cost prices need to be adjusted frequently during inflationary periods. If the underlying real cost structure does not change over time and if a user charge has been correctly set at a particular time, rapid inflation means that after two or three years the nominal user charge may diverge considerably from the efficient charge. User charges thus share the fate of excise taxes in that their real value erodes during periods of general price inflation unless an effort is made to maintain it through frequent (and often politically difficult) upward adjustments. We could find only a few cases in which frequent attempts were made to keep user charges in line with the rise in the general price level.[7]

Fourth, only if the demand for the public service shows some price-elasticity will efficiency be affected by whether or not the service is priced at marginal cost. If the demand for a service is perfectly or almost perfectly inelastic, the quantity consumed will not change in response to a change in price. Therefore, the use of economic resources will not be affected by the price, and no loss or gain in efficiency will result from setting prices above or below marginal cost. Demand does not have to be very elastic, however, before the effects of price setting on resource allocation become important. For instance, Ray (1975: 12–15) develops a simple example of a bus transit system in which he assumes that the elasticity of demand is as low as -0.3 (that is, demand for the service falls by 30 percent as price is raised by 100 percent). He then shows that even for such a low demand-elasticity a welfare loss of 6–58 percent can occur for every unit of additional revenue generated by an increase in transit fares. The exact amount depends on the response of operating costs to the reduced demand for public transit. Thus the efficiency losses or gains from incorrect or correct pricing may not be negligible, even at low demand-elasticities.

Fifth, developing and industrial countries differ in the reasons for their concern about user charges. In industrial countries there are two main reasons for more efficient user charges. One is to limit the excess provision of public services, which is encouraged by pricing policies geared to satisfy such noneconomic objectives as the desire of public service managers to increase their sphere of influence via even an inefficient expansion of the service (Bird 1976b). The other is to control environmental hazards, in particular water and air pollution. Pricing policy is seen as one way of promoting an efficient use of natural resources (Kneese and Schultze 1975).

In developing countries the problem is perhaps less one of an overextension of the public sector, although here, too, charging for public services is a way to ensure that public and private providers compete on an equal footing. Rather, a policy for user charges should discipline planners and users to limit service standards so users are able and willing to pay for their costs, permit the replicability of services, and raise resources for the expansion of services required by rapidly growing large cities. The role of user charges in controlling the environmental damage caused by economic development is so far still largely undetermined, mainly because many developing countries have not made a priority of environmental conservation. As environmental issues take on more importance in developing countries, however, the possibility of limiting environmental damage through appropriate pricing policies is becoming a major concern. These perceptions of the differing potential roles of user charges in developing and industrial countries reflect large differences in resource endowments and preferences. In rich and poor countries alike, however, user charges set equal to marginal cost can increase the efficiency of urban growth and development.

The remainder of this section, which takes economic efficiency in resource allocation as the dominant objective of pricing policy, explores further implications of the marginal cost pricing rule and critically reviews the assumptions on which it is based. Two kinds of refinements need to be made before the rule can be applied. The first is a more careful specification of the dimensions of cost and output of a service and a recognition that the cost may vary across space, time, and consumer classes. This consideration leads to a more complex formulation of the rule without, however, affecting its basic validity. The second refinement is to amend the basic rule because one or more of the assumptions on which it is based do not hold. This particularly relates to the problems of lumpiness of investment, lack of perfect information among consumers, administrative and transaction costs, externalities and distortions elsewhere in the economy, and the fact that nondistorting taxes or subsidies generally are not available to finance deficits or absorb surpluses that may result from an application of the rule. These refinements are discussed below.

Refinements of the Rule

DIMENSIONS OF PUBLIC SERVICE OUTPUT AND COSTS. In applying the marginal cost pricing rule the first question which arises is, What aspect of service provision is being considered? Is it the *consumption* of a service output such as potable water, electricity, waste disposal, education, or health? Is it *access* or *connection* to a service such as water, electricity, or telephones? Or is it the *opportunity to use or to connect* to a service? For each of these three dimensions, different private decisions and marginal costs are involved.

The decision to demand or not to demand an additional unit of a publicly provided good or service involves consideration of the short-run marginal costs of public production and distribution, that is, the additional inputs required to produce the added service unit. These may include the wear and tear from use and stock depletion. For example, the consumption of an additional unit of drinking water may involve marginal costs of treatment and pumping, of wear and tear on machinery, pipes, and so forth, and of depletion of storage tanks.

The decision to connect or not to connect to a service (that is, gain access to a service) involves two types of costs. First, there is the cost of the infrastructure work to connect a customer to the arteries of the distribution (or collection) network, including any recurrent costs of maintaining service. The costs of any extension of the network required to hook up a customer (piping, electric lines, earthworks, and so forth) and of maintaining it, the costs of metering equipment and of maintaining it, and the costs of reading meters and billing customers could thus be attributable to the connection decision. Second, with the connection of an additional customer the public authority in charge of the service often incurs a requirement of "readiness to serve" whatever amount of the service the customer demands. This requirement may mean that capital investment must be made to provide productive capacity related to the number and type of connections rather than to actual use.

For some services actual connections do not determine the need for capital investment. Rather, enough investment must be made to give people who decide to settle at a particular location the opportunity to connect. For instance, if people move from the countryside to the city or from one part of the city to another the public sector must provide service capacity (education and health facilities, production and distribution facilities for public utilities, and so forth), whether or not any one migrant decides to utilize a service. For example, public utility mains and the urbanized area of a city must expand together. A property owner may decide not to connect to a service or may decide to send his children to private school; the public authorities must nevertheless (within margins set by experience) provide service capacity.[8]

These different private decisions and costs are important because the main function of an efficient service pricing structure is to ensure that each individual has to weigh the marginal costs of each decision against its benefits. Therefore a use-related price should reflect the marginal cost of production and distribution, a connection charge should reflect the marginal connection costs (capital and recurrent) and the capacity costs related to the need to be ready to serve those who are connected, and a location charge should reflect the costs of being ready to serve the population which are not taken care of in the connection price.

The use-related decision, and its associated cost and price, exist for virtually all urban services. The connection-related decision, cost, and price exist mainly for site-specific services which require a hookup to distribution or collection networks (especially public utilities). The location-related decision, cost, and price are particularly important for services that are not site-specific, such as public education and health. But they are also applicable to the distribution (and collection) mains, major storage facilities, and productive capacity required for public utilities, to the extent that these are linked not only to connection but also to the locations of potential consumers or connections in particular service areas.

For the optimal provision of the services related to each type of decision, their prices need to be set equal to their marginal costs. Multiple service charges may therefore be required for efficiency, even before financial viability or equity is considered. The application of these considerations to several urban services and their implications for pricing structures will be discussed in chapters 10 and 11.

VARIATIONS IN COSTS ACROSS SPACE, TIME, AND CONSUMER CLASSES. The marginal cost pricing rule requires that each individual pay the marginal cost he generates. Hence, differences in service costs—across space, time, and customer classes—should be reflected in a refined pricing structure. This concern must be tempered by consideration of the higher costs of administering and processing the transactions required by these refinements. This section briefly describes possible spatial, temporal, and consumer-group service cost differences without weighing these transaction costs explicitly.

There are three kinds of spatial cost differences: sectoral (rural and urban areas compared), interregional (one region or city compared with another), and intraregional (neighborhoods within a region or city compared). First, sectoral differences may occur because the marginal cost of providing public services to rural consumers may be higher than for urban consumers, mainly because rural areas have lower population densities and thus higher costs of distribution or collection. The smaller-scale operations that tend to be found in rural areas, especially public utilities, may also have higher unit costs for providing certain services.

Second, interregional differences may occur because of variations in natural resource availability, input costs, technologies, or size of operations. Much of the argument about optimal city size has revolved around the question of whether it is more costly to provide public services in larger than in smaller cities.

Third, intraregional or intracity differences result mainly from variations in density of population and topography. In general, densely populated areas are cheaper to service because less needs to be spent on the distribution or connection network per consumer or per connection, particularly for public utilities and for road and street construction. The negative relation between density and per unit service costs is, however, not a necessary phenomenon. Higher density may require higher-cost technologies (underground electric cables instead of overhead lines, waterborne sanitary sewerage systems instead of septic tanks, and so forth) and may be associated with higher input costs, especially for land. Topographical cost differences result mainly from the fact that many of the larger cities in developing countries have rapidly expanded into such areas as steep mountainsides, swamps, and floodplains, which are difficult and therefore costly to service. In such areas, the construction of roads, the laying of service pipes, and even the construction of schools and health facilities may require larger capital outlays (and possibly higher operating costs, for example, special pumping of water) than in areas of flat and dry ground.[9]

An efficient system of service prices should reflect these location cost differentials. If marginal service costs are not reflected in service prices and are instead averaged across locations, then use and extension of the service will be overly encouraged in costly areas and discouraged in cheaper areas. Nevertheless, if the service is provided by a suprasectoral or regional authority, costs are frequently averaged across sectors (that is, rural-urban differentials) and regions. And intraregional cost differentials are often neglected by local and higher-level government agencies alike. The reasons for this averaging and neglect differ from case to case. Sectoral averaging is often a deliberate policy pursued for equity reasons, that is, an attempt to redistribute income from the more prosperous urban sector to the poorer rural sector, where without some subsidization the provision of services might not otherwise be feasible because of rural consumers' lack of ability or willingness to pay.[10] Interregional averaging often has a similar cause, but it may also be part of an explicit policy of encouraging the development of lagging regions for reasons other than interregional equity (for example, in order to offset biases in favor of the development of central or leading regions, which exist for various reasons in many developing countries).

Very often, however, there is simply not much knowledge about, or attention paid to, cost differentials, not least because of a pervasive philosophy that public services should be provided as a right to consumers, all of whom may be expected to pay the same price because "a gallon of water [or whatever] is a gallon of water," whenever or however consumed. If such a philosophy prevails, there is no incentive to compute differential intersectoral, interregional, or intraregional costs, let alone apply different charges based on different costs. The following chapter will report the results of research on locationally differentiated marginal costs for water supply and sewage services in Cali and Nairobi which indicate that at least for these services intracity cost differentials can be quite significant.

Demand and supply change not only across space but also over time. On the demand side, many public services are characterized by seasonal, weekly, or even daily peaks in consumption. Seasonal demand peaks especially affect water supply. During the dry season(s) more water may be demanded due to the absence of private substitutes and the increased need to water gardens and lawns. Weekly and daily peaks occur for virtually all public services, but especially for electricity, telephones, and urban transportation. The main point about intertemporal demand variations is that, although excess capacity exists, during off-peak periods peak demand typically runs into capacity constraints beyond which supply cannot be expanded or can be expanded only at the cost of increased crowding and congestion (for example, longer telephone waiting times, low water pressure, electrical brownouts or power outages, and crowded buses and congested highways[11]). Service prices should therefore vary with demand.

During off-peak periods, price can be set equal to short-run marginal cost (provided excess capacity exists). During peak demand periods, the principle of efficient pricing requires that the price be set equal to the higher marginal cost which applies at the peak, including costs of crowding or congestion. Moreover, when an absolute capacity constraint is reached during peak periods, then the service should be rationed by price (rather than by other methods, such as waiting).

Another reason to charge different prices at different times is to reflect changes in costs. This phenomenon is often linked to seasonally changing climatic conditions. Water, for example, may become more expensive during dry seasons when it requires additional pumping or treatment. Another example is electricity: the supply of hydropower may vary across seasons, and more expensive sources of power may have to be used during periods of low hydropower supply.

A failure to charge differential prices over time may cause not only efficiency losses from over- or underconsumption but also mistaken investment decisions. Excess demand is commonly taken to mean it is time to invest in new capacity, but if this demand is due to a failure to apply peak-load pricing the investment is likely to be premature. The extension of capacity is appropriate only if the discounted expected benefit of the new capacity exceeds the cost of providing it. Though this investment rule is not directly related to the question of peak-load pricing, the application of an effective pricing system can help establish consumers' willingness to pay and thus assist in forecasting private benefits.

There is one other important aspect of intertemporal pricing. In the preceding examples, the dimension of service provision which was assumed to be affected by intertemporal variations in demand and cost was the use of a service, not access or connection to it. This reflects the fact that intertemporal variations occur mainly in the context of use rather than access. In other words, it is not the demand for service connections which shifts according to season, week, day, or time of day but rather the use of the service by those who already have access to it or are already potential customers.[12] The private decision which must be affected by the intertemporal price variations is the decision of how much to consume at any particular time, not whether to seek access to (stay on) the system. The implication of this point is that peak charges should be applied to service use during the peak so as to reflect peak-time use-related costs, or so as to ration peak-time demand in line with available supply. It would be inefficient to try to deal with the intertemporal pricing problem by, say, changing the price of access to the service.

Figure 9-1 may be used to demonstrate this argument and some of its implications. Panel A describes the price and quantity of service use, and panel B describes the demand for, and cost of, service connections. Panel A shows intertemporally shifting demand curves D_1 and D_2 (which describe off-peak and peak periods, respectively) and a marginal cost curve which rises beyond Q^*. Following the analysis in the preceding paragraphs, optimal prices would be P_1 in the low-demand period and P_2 in the high-demand period. Now assume that the price for connections shown in panel B is raised above the optimal level P_c to P_c'—thus reducing the demand for connections from C to C' and leading to an efficiency loss in terms of consumer surplus forgone, as shown by the shaded triangle in panel B. The reduction in the number of connections leads to a downward shift in the use-related demand curves in panel A, as shown by D_1' and D_2'. The seasonal "problem" is now reduced, in the sense that if P_1 is charged during the high-demand period, the actual quantity consumed lies below the quantity consumed if price P_1 had been charged with the original demand conditions (that is, Q_2' versus Q_2''). There is still, however, an efficiency loss in this case during the peak times because marginal cost still lies above price (the efficiency case is shown by the shaded triangle in panel A). Only if the demand curve D_2' is shifted even further to the left so that it intersects with MC in the horizontal stretch (that is, to the left of Q^*) would this efficiency loss be eliminated. However, elimination of this efficiency loss in panel A is connected with the efficiency loss in panel B, which could be even greater than the one shown for the initial distorted price of connections, P_c'. Whether the pricing system which attempts to deal with the peak-load problem by changing connection prices leads to a net gain in efficiency as compared with a system that does not recognize the peak-load problem at all cannot be said a priori. In any case, both pricing systems are suboptimal when compared with a true peak-load pricing system which deals with the problem in the proper output, cost, and price dimension.

Figure 9-1. *The Case of Misguided Peak-Load Pricing*

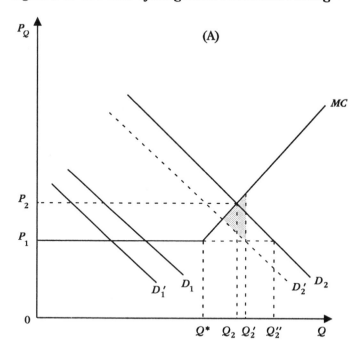

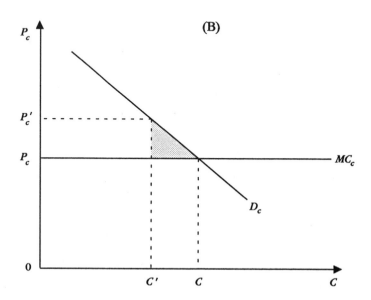

The problem of addressing the peak-load pricing problem in the wrong dimension arises quite frequently. The problem is seen as "an attempt to allocate the utility's fixed or capacity costs to user groups on the basis of their contribution to, or responsibility for, the peak loads that necessitate a given level of system capacity" (Mann 1968: 41). Often this is carried out by differential fixed charges, that is, charges not varying with use but with some other characteristic of the service, for example, maximum load capacity for electricity, connection or meter rental fees for water supply, and automobile license fees for urban street congestion. In any case, it is not appropriate to view the peak-load problem as one of capacity-cost allocations between users; rather, it should be viewed as a problem of how to achieve the most efficient use of existing capacity if demand fluctuates intertemporally.[13]

When service providers are able to discriminate among relatively homogeneous groups of consumers, they frequently charge varying prices. Public utilities, for instance, frequently have different rates for residential consumers and for industrial or commercial consumers. In aiming for efficiency, there are two possible situations in which different consumer groups should be charged different prices for what may appear to be the same service. First, the kind of service provided, and thus marginal service costs, may differ between groups. Second, even if the service provided is the same, groups' consumption patterns and thus elasticities of demand may differ sufficiently to warrant different prices.

In the first situation of differences in service provision, it is clearly in the interest of economic efficiency to charge different prices. For instance, industrial consumers may be using untreated water that is less costly to produce than treated water used by residential consumers. This lower (marginal) cost should be reflected in a lower price. Conversely, residential sewage, may require less treatment than industrial effluents, and residential waste disposal consumers should therefore, for reasons of efficiency, be charged a lower price. In the case of garbage collection, removing and disposing of residential refuse may cost considerably less than removing industrial and commercial waste. Again, different prices would be appropriate on the grounds of efficiency.

In a special case, what amount of different services are provided to different consumers, relates to the administrative and transaction costs of pricing. It is frequently cheaper to measure per unit consumption by large consumers than by small consumers, and costly metering devices therefore become efficient only when fairly large volumes of service use are reached. Thus for sewage disposal, the strength of sewage may be measured; and for electricity, meters with timers that capture varying peak and off-peak usage may only become cost-effective for large, that is industrial, users. (The question of optimal metering decisions is further discussed below.) Therefore different prices are appropriately charged for different consumer groups depending on whether or not individual or timed meters are in place.

The second situation in which different user groups should be charged differing prices relates to the users' varying elasticities of demand. Industrial users, for instance, may have a lower demand-elasticity for water than residential users. In this case the public utility can act as a discriminating monopolist and extract a higher price from the industrial users by applying the principle of charging "what the traffic will bear."[14] Similarly, rich residential customers in particular may have a very inelastic, possibly perfectly inelastic, demand for access to public utility service, in which case a high fixed charge on these users would not result in significant efficiency losses. In contrast, poor residential consumers may be kept off the system if they have to pay high fixed charges (that is, they have more elastic demand for access), and efficiency losses would result.

In summary, varying charges for different consumer groups are appropriate on efficiency grounds only if different costs (of metering, administration, and so forth) apply or if some consumer groups have a perfectly inelastic demand and others do not. In many cities of developing countries, however, different prices do not follow cost or demand differentials. At times this may be explained by the equity goals of the public service agency or by other political objectives. In many cases, however, there has simply been a failure to consider carefully the principles of efficient pricing.

Amendments to the Rule

In the preceding discussion of refinements of the basic rule of marginal cost pricing—marginal cost equals price—the rule itself was not at issue; rather, some of the intricacies of its application were highlighted. In the following paragraphs a number of amendments to the basic rule will be introduced. They are related to the fact that the assumptions on which the basic rule rests are often not satisfied. In those cases the rule must be amended if efficiency in resource allocation is to be achieved by public service pricing.

EXTERNALITIES. The basic marginal cost pricing rule assumes that there are no external benefits or costs associated with the private decision to consume or seek access (connection) to an urban public service. "Externalities" are benefits and costs which are not received by the service user but by other members of society, and which are therefore not taken into consideration by the user in deciding to consume or seek access to the service. As a result over- or underconsumption of (or insufficient or excessive connections to) the service occurs if service prices are set equal to private marginal cost. The basic implications of externalities for public service pricing are well understood. In the present context, however, a deeper analysis of externalities is desirable in order to consider clearly the various dimensions of urban service costs and benefits, in particular service use and access.

Assume that a user's consumption of a service conveys benefits not only directly to him but also to others.[15] This is shown in panel A of figure 9-2 by the curve D_s. It lies above the individual's demand curve D_p, which in turn reflects the consumer's willingness to pay, and thus the private benefits derived by him from the consumption of the service. Examples of such a discrepancy between private and social benefits of service consumption are, for instance, water and sewerage services or primary education, for which the consumption of a unit of service confers a benefit on society at large. The common prescription for service pricing in these cases is to charge a price below marginal cost (such as P'_Q) so that consumption is stimulated to a socially optimal level (Q_s), at which the marginal *social* valuation of using the service equals the marginal cost of producing it.

The conventional analysis of externalities ends here, but it needs to be carried one step further in the present context. As a result of the reduction in the price of the service from P_Q to P'_Q, private consumer surplus associated with service consumption increases, and thus additional consumers may be induced to connect to the service. This is shown in panel B of figure 9-2 by a shift of the demand curve for connections from D_c to D'_c, leading to an increase in the number of connections. A subsidized connection charge set at P'_c would attract the optimal number of consumers (C'_p). But each consumer would not use the optimal amount of the service Q_s at the unsubsidized use-related price P_Q, and there would thus be an efficiency loss as shown by the upper shaded triangle in panel A.

If, however, the connection to, rather than the use of, a service conveys external benefits, as in the case of telephone services, then it would be efficient to provide a subsidy to connections rather than to use of the service.[16] Assume, for example, that in panel B of figure 9-2, D'_c reflects the social demand for connections. Then the efficient connection charge would be P'_c, leading to C'_p connections. If, conversely, the subsidy were placed on service use, and the charge was P'_Q in panel A rather than P_Q, then each user would make excessive use of the service and there would be an efficiency loss as shown by the lower shaded triangle in panel A. Therefore it is crucial to analyze in which dimension of service provision externalities occur. If the externality is use-related, the subsidy should be related to use; if it is connection- or access-related, then the subsidy should be too.

There are three special considerations. First, assume that external benefits exist but only for relatively low quantities of use, which at marginal cost prices are exceeded by all users, as may well be the case for water

Figure 9-2. *Public Service Pricing in the Presence of External Benefits*

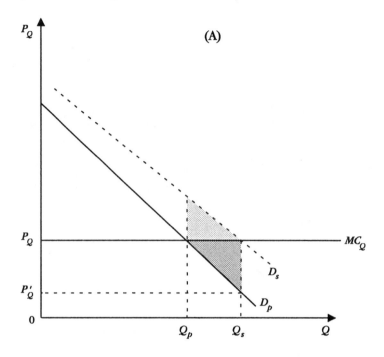

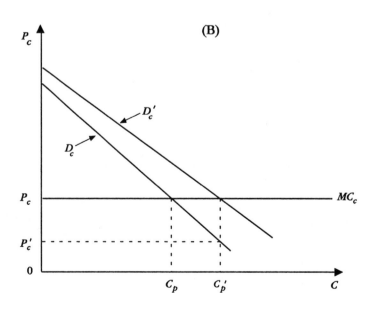

supply. This is shown in panel A of figure 9-3, where marginal social benefits exceed marginal private benefits only up to relatively small quantities of consumption (Q^*). Given the prevailing marginal cost MC_Q, and assuming that price P_Q is set equal to marginal cost, consumption is at Q in excess of Q^*. Thus no subsidy (that is, price below MC_Q) is required in the use dimension of the service. But because potential consumers do not incorporate the social benefits from consumption of the service into their benefit-cost calculations when deciding on whether or not to connect to it, the private marginal valuation of benefits from connection lies below the social valuation. This is shown in panel B of figure 9-3 by the curves D_c and D_c', respectively. In order to achieve an optimal number of connections to the service, the price for connections should be set at P_c', that is, below the marginal connection cost, MC_c.

Second, another means of achieving the optimal consumption or connection level in the presence of external benefits would be to require compulsory use of the service or compulsory connection to it at the optimal level, depending on whether the externalities are use- or connection-related. The feasibility of this method depends on the type of service under consideration. For instance, in the case of water supply, if the conditions shown in figure 9-3 hold and if the total number of potential connections lies at or to the left of C_s in panel B, then all potential users (households) would be compelled to connect. The connection charge then is of no relevance in achieving efficiency because the private (compelled) connection decision is no longer influenced by the connection price.[17] The efficient price for service would, however, be equal to marginal cost MC_Q in panel A. For other services, such as garbage collection and disposal, compulsory connection may not be sufficient if, as shown in figure 9-2, external benefits accrue over the entire range of service use. In that case, it would be necessary to compel also the optimal level of service use, Q_s in panel A of figure 9-2, or to combine a compulsory connection with the subsidization of service use.[18]

Third, sometimes, despite external benefits, no reduction in service charges below the marginal cost price is appropriate. This occurs if there is excess demand for either use or connections on service capacity. For example, the capacity for production of water may fall short of demand at a unit price equal to marginal cost. Or the substantial excess demand for telephone service connections which exists in many developing countries may not be satisfied at marginal cost prices. Figure 9-4 demonstrates this case for both service use and connections. Given the capacity constraints, $\overline{Q}$ for service use and $\overline{C}$ for service connections, demand-rationing prices P_Q' and P_C' above marginal costs MC_Q and MC_c have to be levied despite the existence of external benefits. Otherwise, excess demand will occur and allocation of existing capacity will be inefficient. In other words, the corollary of the basic pricing rule—that demand

Figure 9-3. *Public Service Pricing in the Presence of External Benefits: A Special Case*

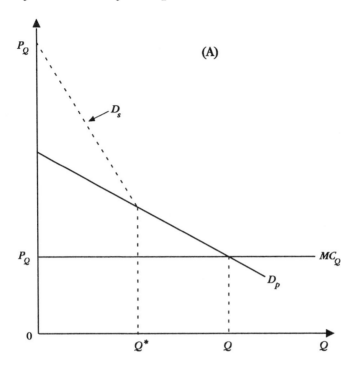

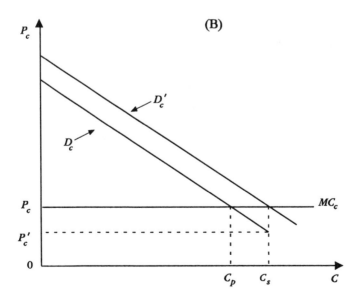

Figure 9-4. *Public Service Pricing in the Presence of External Benefits and Capacity Constraints*

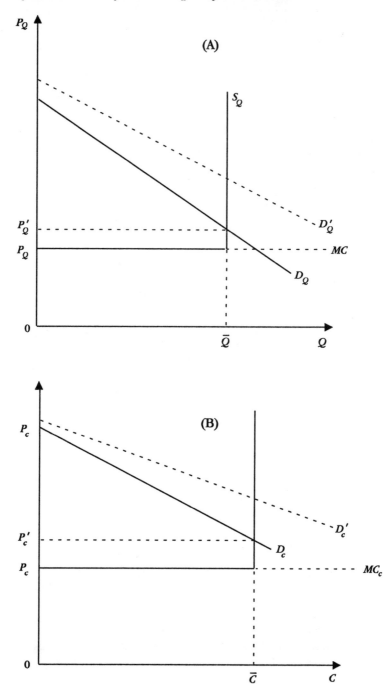

should equal supply—remains in force despite the existence of external benefits.

In summary, it is not sufficient merely to cite the likelihood of external benefits in arguing for subsidized provision of services. One also needs to know which dimension of service provision is conveying the externalities; the extent of externalities, in at least rough quantitative terms; and whether there are capacity constraints which require price rationing. Because of these practical difficulties and because of the natural tendency of actual and potential users or their political representatives to clamor for service charges below marginal costs, one should be very cautious in accepting arguments for a digression from marginal cost pricing of urban services on account of external benefits.[19]

DISTORTIONS IN INPUT AND OUTPUT PRICES. Distortions in input and output prices have long confounded marginal cost pricing. They lead to the problem of the "second best." In its most extreme form this was interpreted to mean—if the marginal conditions for efficient allocation of resources are not satisfied in some part of the economy (for example, if taxation prevents the marginal rate of transformation from equalling the marginal rate of substitution in consumption for any good or factor)—that setting the price of a good or service equal to marginal social cost will not necessarily lead to an increase in welfare. In fact, welfare might be increased if the marginal cost condition were systematically ignored. These arguments have led some analysts to the agnostic view that because many distortions exist in all economies, and particularly developing ones, no clear guidance can be given to policymakers on how to price public services. A less radical, now widely accepted view of the second-best problem is that distortions in the factor and product markets need to be accounted for but often do not matter much, and that there are ways to adjust the basic marginal cost pricing rule to allow for the distortions that affect the pricing decision for a service.[20]

Beginning with distortions in input markets, the methods of shadow pricing which have been developed extensively for cost-benefit analysis apply to setting user charges. The concept of marginal cost therefore should be reinterpreted as meaning not a service's marginal market cost but its marginal opportunity cost to society, that is, the cost of output forgone in providing an additional unit of it.[21] Shadow pricing requires adjusting the relative prices of all tradable commodity inputs by eliminating any tariff and tax distortions to which they may be subject and evaluating nontradable inputs—in particular primary factors of production such as land, labor, and capital—in terms of the opportunity cost of output forgone by their use in the context of the provision of the service. A well-known example is the shadow wage set below the market wage in the presence of underemployment.

Somewhat more complex, and in general less explored, is the question of how to allow for distortions in the prices of products which substitute for, or compete with, a service. The common advice is to neglect these distortions unless they affect close and important substitutes or complements of the service.[22] If service A has a close and important substitute which is underpriced (or overpriced), then service A should be priced below (above) marginal cost. If, conversely, a close and important complement to the service is underpriced (overpriced), the service ought to be priced above (below) marginal cost. There are only a few services to which these rules apply strongly and for which allowance should therefore be made in pricing for distortions in the output market. One is urban public transportation, in particular commuter bus and rail services, which compete with the private automobile.

As long as the operators of automobiles do not have to pay the full social cost for their use of urban roads, and thus as long as automobile use is priced below social marginal cost, it may well be inefficient to price public mass transportation at marginal cost, for this would bias the choice of traffic modes toward the socially more costly mode of the automobile. The scope for such subsidization may be limited by financial constraints. But as long as the first-best policy of marginal social cost pricing for all road users is not feasible, second-best pricing may well put optional public transportation fares below marginal cost.

Another example of second-best pricing is access to sanitary sewer systems. If these systems were priced at full marginal cost, potential users might be induced to switch to (or stay with) individual latrines, which would be cheaper for them but possibly more costly for society given the external costs of pollution caused by septic tanks in high-density urban locations. Because the external costs of septic tanks cannot usually be priced adequately, it would be appropriate to subsidize connections to the sanitary sewage system by setting connection fees below marginal cost.[23]

One important question arises in the discussion of second-best pricing issues: To what extent should urban authorities be expected to correct, through their own pricing policies, inefficiencies introduced by higher levels of government? Distortions in input prices caused by trade tariffs are an example of a situation in which local governments have no power to take direct corrective action and in which they may run into financial difficulties when pricing their services at rates below marginal cost in order to reflect social opportunity cost rather than financial cost. On efficiency grounds, urban governments should be encouraged or required to employ such a second-best pricing policy, but they will generally be able to do so only if higher levels of government support such pricing policies, particularly by providing local authorities with the necessary financial aid if the second-best pricing principle leads the local authorities into financial difficulties.

IMPERFECT CONSUMER INFORMATION. The basic marginal cost pricing rule presupposes that consumers have at their disposal all the information required to understand the effect of all current price structures and to forecast changes in prices that will occur because of their consumption decisions. For instance, if the cost structure for a service requires a complex system of charges which change by type of service, location, time of use, or user class, consumers should always be aware of what price applies in a particular situation for each of their decisions. Moreover, consumers sometimes have to make capital investment decisions which will affect the level of their service use for a considerable time (for example, decisions about consumer durables, which use water or electricity; about production processes and capital goods for manufacturing, which utilize water or electricity; and about local infrastructure, which determines the pattern of use for the transportation system). If consumers are guided in their decision mainly by current and recent prices and are not able to accurately forecast changes in relative prices, then they may be induced to make costly mistakes by installing overly service-intensive equipment—if future service prices are above current prices—or insufficiently service-intensive equipment—if future service prices are below current prices. In other words, optimal pricing policy must consider that current prices affect consumer expectations and that these expectations in turn affect current private investment decisions, which affect future consumption. If consumer expectations are mistaken, then current private decisions are suboptimal, that is, inefficient.

The existence of imperfect consumer information implies two things. First, all pricing systems work more efficiently if they are accompanied by an effort to improve consumer information on the pattern of current prices and on likely future prices. Public service authorities are usually in a better position to forecast future costs than are consumers, for it is part of their task in planning and programming for expansion to estimate the cost of providing the service for some years ahead. Thus, if marginal costs are expected to rise or fall over the planning horizon (for example, due to a constraint on capacity or excess capacity after a large capital investment), then consumers should be informed of these projected price trends.

Efforts to inform the consuming public are not costless, however, and the utilization of such information is not always costless to the consumer. Certainly, many consumers are not able or ready to digest this information; hence, there may continue to be a misallocation of resources as long as complex pricing formulas are used. In other words, because of information costs, a systematic application of the basic marginal cost pricing rule could well result in an efficiency loss. Efficiency gains, therefore, may be derived from a simplification of the pricing structure to capture only the main elements of cost differences among consumers of different types of services, at different locations, and at different times. Furthermore, if private consumers do not adequately take future cost and price developments into account in their current decisionmaking because they lack information or are unable to utilize it fully, some information on future prices may need to be built into the current pricing structure; that is, current prices could be raised (or lowered) above (below) current marginal costs if projected marginal costs are substantially above (below) current marginal costs.

Another complication relates to a supposed inability of consumers to fully appreciate the benefits or costs of a service, for example, the effect on health of such public services as water supply and sewerage, immunization, health care, and family planning. How might one deal with the undervaluation of benefits, and with the consequent unwillingness to pay full marginal cost? One avenue is to provide better information. Another is to assume that information costs are too high and that a subsidy should be provided to the beneficiaries. Although one should be wary about using lack of consumer information as a strong argument for service subsidies, a potentially useful practice is to apply promotional service tariffs, which temporarily subsidize new consumers. The assumption here is that their initial demand falls short of reflecting the full benefit received but that, once they have learned to appreciate the full benefits of the service, they can be charged the full marginal cost price with actual use.

ADMINISTRATIVE AND TRANSACTION COSTS. Related to the problem of imperfect consumer information is the problem of administrative and transaction costs, which was assumed away in the derivation and refinement of the basic marginal cost pricing rule. As mentioned above, the provision of information by the public authority, and the collection and use of information by consumers, may have significant costs. These costs must be weighed against the benefits derived from a very finely tuned marginal cost pricing structure.

Probably even more important are the public administrative and transaction costs associated with measuring (metering) precisely the level of service consumption according to location, time, and type of consumer, as well as the costs of billing and collecting charges under a highly complex pricing scheme. Furthermore, calculating a full profile of marginal costs for all aspects of service provision may be a costly exercise and not warranted by the benefits that could be derived from a more refined pricing scheme.

The basic principle which should be used to make each additional refinement of the pricing structure is simple cost-benefit analysis; that is, all expected additional current and future costs of a more refined pricing structure should be compared quantitatively with the benefits of the improvement in the allocation of resources which the structure would bring. If the net present value implied by this cost-benefit calculation is positive (negative) then the refinement should be implemented (re-jected).[24] But only qualitative judgments are feasible in most instances. One of the best-explored cases of the cost-benefit analysis of improved pricing schemes is that of metering the water supply.[25] The details of this experience are reviewed in the next chapter.

In most cases it is difficult to weigh the costs and benefits of improved pricing structures. The main difficulty is that little is known about the demand-elasticities which determine the benefits derived from a refined structure. This should not, however, deter the public service authorities from attempting to apply the principle of efficient pricing, at least in broad terms, especially if metering has already laid the administrative foundation for an efficient pricing scheme. Particularly if costs are quite variable and differential pricing is not overly costly to administer and implement (for example, strong seasonal or locational variations in de-mand for water and high congestion costs of urban traffic in the centers of large cities), a refined application of the marginal cost pricing principle may be called for.

Refined pricing and metering schemes are generally more appropriate for large consumers than small ones. For large ones, administrative and transaction costs are likely to be low relative to the benefits of an im-proved pricing structure; the reverse is true for small ones. Thus it is often defensible to have a simple set of charges for the large number of small residential consumers (that is, not differentiating by location, time, or type of service) while applying a more refined set of prices to large industrial consumers (for example, peak-load pricing for electricity, or pricing treatment of sewage according to effluent strength).

CAPITAL INDIVISIBILITY. The simplest model of the marginal cost pricing principle is based on the assumption that total cost is a continuous, single-valued, monotonic function of output of the public service. Output is usually defined in terms of some measure of the quantity or number of units of service consumed (for example, gallons of water or kilowatts of electricity; Saunders, Warford, and Mann 1976: 20). In practice, how-ever, public service cost functions are characterized by a multidimen-sionality of output and are affected by capital indivisibility, that is, lum-piness of investment.

Production capacity and the distribution network of most public ser-vices can generally not be extended in smaller increments to meet changes in demand for the services. Instead, larger units of production and distribution capacity need to be built, frequently meeting existing backlogs in demand while building ahead of the growth in demand ex-pected in the foreseeable future. The reasons for this capital indivisibility are frequently technological; that is, the existence of technological econ-omies of scale for many aspects of public service provision make the continuous addition of capacity in small increments uneconomical.[26] Another factor explaining capital indivisibility, especially in developing countries, is that financing for capital construction frequently needs to be secured in the form of large loans or grants from higher levels of government or from international lending agencies. If this is the case, investment projects may have to be carried out on an even larger scale than may be warranted on purely technological grounds.

The result of such capital indivisibilities is that the short-run marginal cost (SRMC) pricing rule could result in considerable fluctuations in user charges. Strict application of SRMC pricing would require, during periods of excess capacity, that prices be set equal to variable operating costs. During periods when the capacity constraint is reached but new investment in capacity is not yet appropriate, prices would rise above the variable operating cost so as to equate demand and supply. Three possible caveats to the optimality of SRMC pricing must be raised in a situation of capital indivisibility: consumers must have perfect foresight of the future changes in user charges, the adjustments must be feasible with zero administrative or transaction costs, and frequent and large changes in user charges must be acceptable to political or other institutions.[27]

As noted above, lack of consumer information regarding future changes in user charges may cause consumers to make incorrect decisions. This problem may be complicated by capital indivisibility, especially if nonreversibilities are involved. For instance, during periods of excess capacity, when user charges are low, consumers may be led to invest in complementary (service-using) appliances or machinery on the mistaken assumption that charges will remain low indefinitely, or at least over the planning horizon. Then, when service prices actually rise because of capacity constraints, these investment decisions turn out to be mistaken and cause losses to the consumers and the economy.[28] Another type of possible mistake in consumer decisions concerns location choices. Cities that have excess capacity to provide services, and whose service prices are therefore lower than those of cities that have capacity constraints, may be particularly attractive to private investors. Again, however, this advantage may only be short-lived, and therefore shortsighted; poorly informed location decisions may be mistaken (but largely irreversible) in the longer term. In any case, future consumption is affected by today's price, and thus future costs must be taken into consideration in setting today's price.

Administrative costs are an important constraint on frequent fluctuations in user charges. Depending on the type of service and the extent of the capital indivisibility, considerable administrative effort may be required on the part of the public service agency to compute the varying SRMC prices and to bill consumers accordingly. What is more, because of political considerations, increases (or decreases) in future prices may in part be limited by today's price.

On the basis of considerations such as these, virtually all advocates of marginal cost pricing have recognized that some method must be employed to average out cost and thus price variations over time. This provides consumers with some information regarding future prices and thus assists them in making correct investment and location decisions. It also reduces administrative costs and permits efficient user charges in the long term. The criterion for the selection of the optimal smoothing device should be that the costs (losses from mistaken investment decisions and additional administrative costs) saved by the averaging should just equal the losses (consumer surplus forgone or non-price-rationing costs) which arise if the SRMC principle is not applied.[29]

The computation of an optimal average price path would of course require a considerable amount of information on the present and future cost structures of a service, present and future demand, the incidence and costs of investment and location decisions, the price of nonprice rationing, and the costs of administering alternative pricing systems.[30] It is therefore not surprising that a number of shortcuts or rules of thumb have been applied in attempting to approximate the true optimal path. These pricing schemes have generally been dubbed "long-run marginal cost pricing" and vary with the type of service. Some of them are discussed in the following two chapters.

EFFICIENCY IN PRODUCTION. The marginal cost principle is based on the assumption that production efficiency prevails in that the service is produced at the lowest feasible cost per unit. This requires that as much emphasis be placed on ensuring efficiency in production (that is, the plant is operated effectively and new investments represent the minimum-cost solutions given particular demand forecasts), as is placed on setting the correct price for consumers. There is, however, likely to be a link between marginal cost pricing and production efficiency: when consumers have to pay the marginal cost of a service they are more likely to exert pressures on managers and politicians to provide the service efficiently, that is, at minimum cost.

Of course, the efficiency objective is not the only goal to achieve in setting public prices. Financial, fiscal, and equity concerns may be just as important. The ways in which these objectives alter pricing decisions are discussed in the following sections.

Fiscal Considerations and Full Cost Pricing

The application of the basic marginal cost pricing rule may cause deficits for at least two reasons. First, because average costs decline with service growth, marginal costs of service expansion lie below average historical costs, particularly for those services for which economies of scale are important or whose technological progress is rapid (for example, telecommunications). A second common reason is capital indivisibility, which means the SRMC falls below average financial or accounting costs during periods of excess capacity. During periods of a shortage of capacity the reverse would be the case, and the price would be set above average accounting costs to ration existing capacity. Once capacity has been extended, however, the SRMC price again drops below accounting costs. In fact, SRMC prices tend to have a financing pattern just the reverse of the typical pattern for prices set equal to average accounting cost. After expansion of capacity, financial costs tend to be highest because loans and interest charges have to be repaid, whereas the SRMC price is lowest at that point. After some years, when loans have been repaid, financial cost tends to drop off. With the growth of demand and greater shortages in capacity, however, the SRMC will have risen and SRMC prices should be set higher to ration available capacity. Under conditions of capital indivisibility, financial and efficiency requirements thus tend to be out of phase. If capital markets were perfect (and if, over the long term, SRMC pricing would meet financial requirements), then these temporary deficits would not be problematic. But capital markets are not perfect; that is, the borrowing capacity of public service enterprises is limited. Furthermore, the application of SRMC pricing may in the long term even lead to deficits and may require either alternative ways to finance the resulting deficit or an amendment to the basic pricing rule.[31]

Various alternative ways to finance deficits have been discussed in the literature.[32] Three common ones are general fund financing, that is, financing the deficit out of tax or revenue sources totally unrelated to the service; multipart tariffs, that is, recovering all service costs from service users, not exclusively through use-related charges but through charges related to connection, access, or the like; and single-part tariffs set so as to satisfy the financial requirements, and thus diverging, at least from time to time, from marginal cost. These three alternatives will be discussed in turn.

General Fund Financing

General fund financing of a deficit would be desirable, even on efficiency grounds, under the following conditions: (a) if a deficit still prevails after marginal cost prices have been applied to all dimensions of service provision (that is, use, access, and location); (b) if general funds can be raised without distortion to resource allocation for the taxed activities or assets; and (c) if the management and investment decisions in public service provision are not affected negatively by the existence of a financial deficit. These are the efficiency considerations that must be accounted for before resorting to general fund financing of financial deficits resulting from marginal cost pricing. In addition, of course, it is often argued on grounds of fairness that it would be inequitable to subsidize beneficiaries of a service with a high proportion of fixed costs relative to total costs at the expense of general taxpayers.

Virtually no device for raising public revenue is entirely free of distortionary effects. Automotive taxes, sales taxes, income taxes, and property taxes all distort consumer choices in some way. The local tax which is most commonly proposed as being free of allocative effects is the pure and general land value tax.[33] But even if one fully accepts the land tax as nondistortionary, it is generally recognized that the revenue capacity of land taxes is limited for practical and political reasons, and it is illusory to expect in practice that all general fund revenue requirements can be met from taxes on land.[34] In practice, the revenue sources that finance local government activities include a mix of taxes, as described in chapter 2.

General fund financing will thus result in some distortions, and the critical question is whether greater or lesser distortions are induced by financing the deficit from user charges which exceed marginal cost or from general fund financing.[35] As a general rule one can state that public service charges should exceed marginal cost up to the point where the cost of the distortions in resource allocation induced by this pricing policy just equal (at the margin) the cost of the distortions resulting from raising one additional unit of general fund revenue. It is worth noting that this rule applies whether or not a public service operates at a deficit. As long as a public service price is one of the revenue instruments of government, and as long as funds are fungible between service accounts and general accounts, the allocation of resources is efficient only if the marginal cost of raising public revenues (in terms of administration costs, distortions, and so forth) is equal for all revenue instruments. Note also, however, that the application of this fiscal principle does not necessarily mean that full costs of service provision are covered, although price may be set above marginal cost. A deficit may still persist, which would then—in the absence of other considerations—be most efficiently met from general fund revenues.

An important consideration that is frequently used to argue for full cost pricing, rather than permitting the possibility of covering deficits from general account, has to do with the effects of financial deficits on management and investment decisions.[36] In practice, these decisions do not take place in a context in which an exclusive concern for efficiency in resource allocation can be expected from decisionmakers. Therefore, it is argued that public service managers may need the discipline which is imposed on them by the application of a full cost pricing rule. The acceptance of deficits in public enterprises is believed to eliminate an important yardstick for the evaluation of the effectiveness of management. It is also thought to lull managers into neglecting many aspects of effective management, and thus is taken to result in a general decline in efficiency of the operations of the service.[37] It has also been argued that investment decisions are likely to be distorted if service users and managers are not made aware of the opportunity cost of the scale of operations. This happens because service beneficiaries would tend to outvote—or, depending on the relative electoral strength or influence of the users' lobbies, be outvoted by—nonbeneficiaries in the allocation of investment funds to a particular service. This would result in an overprovision—or underprovision, as the case may be—of the particular service.[38] This argument presupposes that public service investment decisions are to a large extent based on the relative political strength of prospective beneficiary groups, rather than on pure economic cost-benefit criteria. In the presence of general account deficit financing of public services, the beneficiary groups have a stronger incentive to attempt to bend the provision of the service in their own favor than is the case with full cost financing, under which beneficiaries have to bear, as a group, the full burden of service provision and nonbeneficiaries do not bear any burden.[39]

Of particular importance for the provision of urban services in developing countries is the relationship between the pricing of services and the standard quality and technology of service provision. Total fiscal resources are very limited in developing countries, and high-standard (and thus high-cost) methods of public service provision will therefore not go far in actually providing services to urban populations. At high standards and costs only relatively few families can be serviced and, especially if these families are poor, it is not possible to extract from them a substantial contribution to the cost of service provision. This in turn limits the ability of the public authorities to provide services to others. The requirement of full cost pricing has the advantage that the project analyst is forced to consider the beneficiaries' ability to pay and to choose design standards with costs (and prices) that they can afford. The resulting lower service standards will make it possible to provide a greater number of households with services at any given time and with a given amount of investment resources. Moreover, it makes it possible to provide a greater number of households with the service in the future, as additional fiscal resources are made available from the repayment of service costs by the beneficiaries.

All of these arguments against general fund financing of deficits resulting from marginal cost pricing are in essence concerned with the efficiency of resource allocation. Indeed, the gist of these arguments is that the implementation of marginal cost pricing can lead to inefficiency in the allocation of resources and that alternative pricing rules, and in particular the full cost pricing rule, can result in less serious distortions. A different type of argument against general account financing of deficits relates to the question of fairness or equity.[40]

Consider the principle of horizontal equity, which postulates that "he who benefits ought to pay," and which is usually a powerful and popular argument for full cost pricing. In fact, as a normative criterion the benefit argument is neither linked to the question of economic efficiency nor to the common objective of improving the (vertical) distribution of income.[41] As a normative criterion this principle of benefit-related charges may well stand in conflict with efficiency and income distribution considerations, but to the extent that underpricing of public services is the norm, rather than the exception, in many developing countries, a greater emphasis on the principle of horizontal equity may well serve to improve the efficiency and distribution of urban services in developing countries.

In considering the relationship between user charges and general account finances of the government, it was assumed that marginal cost pricing results in a deficit. It is, of course, also possible that marginal cost pricing—either in its pure form of SRMC pricing, or in some form of long-run marginal cost (LRMC) pricing—may result in a financial surplus.[42] Full cost, rather than marginal cost, pricing in this case would lead to excess demand in the short term, given capacity constraints, and to overextension of the service in the long term, as service managers move to meet this demand through increased investments. On efficiency grounds it would be preferable in such a situation to apply marginal cost prices and to channel the resulting surplus to the general account of urban governments. Institutionally, it may still be desirable to retain separate management and accounting units for general purpose government and for special public service authorities. Nevertheless, it is possible to extract the surplus from these autonomous public service agencies through appropriately scaled taxes levied by a general purpose urban government on the special service authorities. Such taxes are found quite frequently in the cities of developing countries, whether as de facto transfer requirements or as de jure taxes, and these could therefore become part of the pricing policy of public services in developing-country cities.[43]

Multipart Tariffs

One of the most frequently proposed alternatives to general fund financing of the deficits that result from marginal cost prices is multipart tariffs.[44] The primary idea of multipart tariffs is that the marginal costs incurred as a result of service use can be charged by the appropriate application of SRMC prices related to service use, and any deficit may be covered by levying fees or charges which fall exclusively on the users but which are unrelated to the extent of their actual use of the services, for instance, flat monthly fees and lump-sum access charges.

The discussion of the multidimensionality of urban service provision at the beginning of this chapter has contended that for many public services multipart marginal cost tariffs are appropriate on efficiency grounds quite apart from the question of financial constraints. In fact, the question of financial viability should be raised only after all dimensions of marginal cost pricing have been explored. If the application of the multipart marginal tariff results in financial deficits, then it may be desirable to consider how any particular component, or possibly all components, of this multipart tariff should be amended to improve the overall efficiency or fairness of the pricing system.

The price elasticities of demand for the various service dimensions (use, access, location) are of course one of the basic criteria for selecting the tariff component(s) which is (are) to be priced above marginal cost in order to meet financial requirements.[45] For instance, if access or connection to a service is statutorily required, as is the case for urban water supply and sewerage systems in some developing-country cities, and this requirement is effectively enforced, then charging access or connection fees (either as a recurrent or as a lump-sum basis) above marginal cost would not affect the allocation of resources. Where compulsory connection is not the rule, however, or where enforcement of such a rule is not effective, the price-elasticity of demand for service connections may be considerable. This is especially likely to be the case for low-income consumers, for whom the satisfaction of essential needs such as food, clothing, and shelter must be of primary concern, and for whom clean water, safe waste disposal, education, health, and the like are luxury commodities with a high price-elasticity. In contrast, for high-income earners, access to clean water supply, sanitary sewage and garbage disposal, health, and education are much more in the nature of essentials; that is, the demand for access to these services tends to have a low price elasticity. The lesson to draw from this observation of differential price elasticities of demand for service access by different income groups is as follows: for high-income groups, connection or access prices may be set considerably above marginal cost without large losses caused by misallocation of resources; while for low-income groups, such a pricing policy would involve considerable efficiency losses since many potential consumers would be kept outside the service system altogether.[46]

In designing multipart tariffs to meet a given financial constraint, one needs to bear in mind the possible existence of capacity constraints in one or the other dimensions of the provision of a particular service. Especially in developing countries many services are characterized by the existence of capacity constraints in one dimension of the system (for example, constrained access due to a limited distribution network) while there exists excess capacity in another dimension (for example, due to the existence of excess capacity in the production of the service). In this case, the application of the SRMC pricing principle would require price rationing in the first dimension, while a low SRMC price would be appropriate in the other dimension. The financial surplus generated by the access component of the service may then be utilized to finance (at least partially, and possibly totally) the deficit of the use component of the service.

Uniform Tariffs

A final possibility for meeting deficits resulting from the application of marginal cost pricing is to abandon this pricing principle altogether and adopt a uniform use-related charge equal to average historical or accounting cost, which is designed to meet the financial requirements of a public service authority.[47] Although this pricing method is not generally advocated by experts of public service pricing as optimal, it is frequently found in operation. A common practice is to ignore the multidimensionality of service provision in the actual design of user charges and to focus exclusively on only one dimension of service provision—service use or connection (access). When this is done, a pricing system designed to meet financial or historical accounting costs of a public service must, by definition, charge average historical cost per unit of consumption. This type of approach is generally easiest to implement, since it represents a simple extension of financial analysis which is generally accepted as an important method for evaluation of public enterprise performance. It does, however, forgo the opportunity to improve the allocation of resources through a restructuring of the pricing system.

Income Distribution Considerations

Policymakers virtually everywhere are concerned not only with the efficiency of resource allocation but also with the objective of improving the distribution of personal income. But is this objective a proper concern in the context of urban service pricing? Could it not be better pursued by other public policies, particularly general tax policy at the national level?[48] Local governments cannot make personal transfer payments to equalize incomes; the tax base would be driven out, and lower-income families would be attracted. And although local property taxes may be progressive, local tax rates are too low to redistribute much personal income. Yet this does not mean that local budgets cannot significantly affect the distribution of income or that public service pricing cannot aid in redistribution. The structure and level of user charges may in fact determine the extent to which low-income people make use of services such as water, sewers, electricity, and buses.

Pricing policy, then, can play an important part in achieving national income redistribution. In developing countries conventional national tax instruments have a very limited capacity to improve income distribution, and more extensive consideration must be given to the potential use of public service expenditure and pricing policies at all levels of government.[49] Moreover, in many countries urban service provision and pricing are under the direct or indirect tutelage of the national government and can therefore be utilized to better distribute income nationally.

Judging from the redistributive intent of public service tariffs, many decisionmakers in developing countries accept income redistribution as a goal of public service pricing policy. But how and to what extent should the rule of marginal cost pricing be modified to allow for income redistribution? A number of theoretical models which try to answer this question are reviewed in this section. Although none provides a universally

Table 9-1. *Summary of Selected Public Service Pricing Models*

Source of model	Number of services	Budget constraint	Cross-subsidization	Tariff structure Use-related	Tariff structure Access-related	Price-elasticity of demand for access	Summary of optimal pricing rules
Munasinghe and Warford (1978)	1	Variable; premium on public revenue	Among users of same service and general taxpayer	Differential rates among users of same service	None	n.a.	$P \begin{Bmatrix} > \\ < \end{Bmatrix} MC$, if consumer $\begin{Bmatrix} \text{above} \\ \text{below} \end{Bmatrix}$ "critical income level"
Feldstein (1972b)	2	Fixed deficit or surplus	Between users of different services and general taxpayer	Uniform rate for each service	None	n.a.	Users of a service with a relatively high income-elasticity but low price-elasticity should subsidize users of a service with a low income-elasticity but high price-elasticity
Feldstein (1972a)	1	Balanced budget	Among users of same service	Uniform rate	Uniform access charge	Zero	$P > MC$
Munk (1977)	1	Balanced budget	Among users of same service	Uniform rate	Variable access charge (related to income or property value)	Zero	$P < MC$, provided income-elasticity of income or property tax is greater than the income-elasticity of service demand
Ng and Weisser (1974)[a]	1	Balanced budget	Among users of same service, but without reference to incomes	Uniform rate	Uniform access charge	Less than zero	$P > MC$

n.a. Not applicable.
a. No consideration was given to income distribution.

applicable framework, together they offer insights into the complexity of the question and point toward practical suggestions for policymakers.

Table 9-1 summarizes these models. They differ from each other mainly in the number of services they consider; the budget constraint assumed; the type of cross-subsidization permitted; whether they include only user charges or also access charges; and, if access charges are imposed, whether or not the demand for access is responsive to the charges. All the models (except Munasinghe and Warford 1978) assume a social welfare function in which an additional unit of income in the hands of the poor is valued more than an additional unit in the hands of the rich.

The first model (Munasinghe and Warford 1978) considers one service with a variable budget constraint and any deficit financed from general fiscal resources. The opportunity cost of these resources is explicitly incorporated by applying a shadow price (premium) on public funds. The tariff structure permits only a user charge, which may, however, be differentiated according to the income of the user, thus permitting cross-subsidization among users. No access charges are included. Under these conditions, and assuming a redistributive weighting system favoring lower-income groups, the optimal user charge may be calculated. This calculation shows that, in general, the optimal service price will differ from the efficient (marginal cost) price, even if such considerations as externalities and distortions in input or output prices are not allowed for. Moreover, the optimal user charge should differ among consumer groups according to their incomes. The direction and extent of divergence of the price charged to each consumer (group) from marginal costs depends on the shadow price of public revenue, the income of the consumer and its weight of income distribution, and the price-elasticity of demand. Given a noninferior demand for the public service, the socially optimal price will lie above (below) the marginal cost price, as long as consumers are above (below) a level of income (the "critical income level") at which public revenue is judged equal in value to private income. The greater the premium given to public revenue, the higher should be the optimal price; and the greater the dispersion in weights of income distribution, the greater will be the dispersion of optimal prices across different consumer groups.

Another tack is taken by Feldstein (1972b), who postulates a framework in which two services are produced and there is a uniform user charge for all consumers of each service. He assumes no access-related tariff structure and permits interservice cross-financing but postulates an overall budget constraint for the two services combined by specifying a target surplus (deficit), which in turn implies a particular shadow price for public income. He further specifies a marginal social utility function very similar to that of Munasinghe and Warford, on the basis of which (at least implicitly) one can derive income distribution weights.[50] Using these assumptions he is able to derive the optimal price of each good, and thus the optimal extent of cross-financing between prices.

According to the Feldstein model, the optimal tax (subsidy) on each service depends on its relative own-price-elasticity, its income-elasticity, the size of the target surplus deficit, the distribution of income, and the parameters of the social utility function. For given distributional conditions and financial targets, the model gives the following interesting results:

- The higher the income-elasticity and the lower the price-elasticity of a service, the greater the tax on it ought to be.
- The users of a service with a relatively high income-elasticity but a low price-elasticity should cross-subsidize the users of a service with a relatively low income-elasticity but a high price-elasticity (or if a large target surplus is postulated, at least the former group should be made to contribute a greater share to the financial surplus than the latter).
- If a higher target surplus (that is, a higher premium on public income) is assumed, then the price of the service which is relatively more heavily consumed by lower-income groups (that is, which has the relatively lower income-elasticity) tends to rise relative to the price of the other service.
- The greater the income inequality and the greater the weight given to income redistribution, the greater the tax (subsidy) on the service with the relatively high (low) income-elasticity.

The institutional and normative context postulated by Feldstein is applicable if a single public agency supplies two (or more) services and operates under a fixed budget constraint. This is quite typical in many cities of developing countries. For instance, in Cali one local public enterprise provided water, sewerage, electricity, and telephone services and was required to transfer annually a fixed percentage of its revenues to the general account of the municipal government. Interservice transfers also take place, particularly from electricity and telephones to water supply. In Bombay one local public enterprise extensively subsidized bus transportation with revenues from electricity and urban services. Other examples could be cited. The model proposed by Feldstein provides a framework for evaluating financing arrangements, given the basic context it postulates, which in practice often cannot be changed.

These two models of optimal service pricing presume that only use-related prices may be charged. Other models have explored optimal two-part service pricing, and some have considered explicitly income distribution. One such model, devised by Feldstein (1972a), assumes that one service is produced by a public enterprise operating under the requirement of a balanced budget. Any discrepancy between total cost and total revenue which arises with the application of a user charge must in this model be met by a uniform fixed charge for all consumers. As in the previous two models a marginal social utility function is assumed, with a declining marginal utility of income as income rises. On the basis of these assumptions, the optimal user price of the service lies above marginal cost.[51] In Feldstein's words: "The logic of this is clear: charging more than marginal cost makes higher-income families pay a larger share of the fixed cost. The inefficiency loss due to not charging marginal cost is outweighed by the gains in distributional equity" (Feldstein 1972a: 178). Furthermore, the higher the income-elasticity of demand for the service, the higher should be the optimal price and the lower the fixed charge. The greater, in absolute terms, the price-elasticity of demand for the service, the lower should be the optimal use price and the higher the fixed charge. Finally, the more severe the imbalance in income distribution, or the greater the weight placed on income equality, the higher should be the use-related price and the lower the fixed charge.

The results of this model require two crucial assumptions: (a) the non-use-related charge is uniform for all consumers, and thus not related to income, and (b) the demand for service access is not affected by the access charge. The first of these assumptions is relaxed by Munk (1977), who concludes that if the access-related part of the two-part tariff is an income or property tax whose distributional characteristics are more favorable than the distributional effects of the tax on service use (that is, a charge over and above the marginal cost),[52] then the Feldstein result is reversed; that is, the optimal commodity price lies below marginal cost. This is a classic example of the importance of "counterfactual" assumptions in (balanced budget) differential incidence analysis: Feldstein assumes that the counterfactual is financing through a poll tax on all service users; Munk explores the importance of alternative counterfactuals, that is, the income tax or the property tax.[53] The other limitation of the Feldstein model of a two-part tariff system, namely the assumption of a fixed demand for service connections, has been investigated by Ng and Weisser (1974), who do not, however, consider income distribution. They assume a price-elasticity for access of less than zero and find that optimal commodity price should exceed marginal cost.[54] Furthermore, the higher the price-elasticity of commodity (that is, use-related) demand (in absolute terms), the greater the excess of optimal price over marginal cost and the lower the fixed charge.

The conclusions of Feldstein (1972a), Munk (1977), and Ng and Weisser (1974) together suggest that the optimal two-part tariff will depend on the relative own-price-elasticities of demand for access and use, and on the income-elasticities of the consumption of the service relative to the income-elasticity of the access-related component of the tariff. The precise relations for this general case remain to be worked out, but the following conclusions are plausible in light of the partial models reviewed.

If the demand for access has a high price-elasticity and if access is little related to income, a higher proportion of an enterprise's budgetary requirements should be met by use-related prices. Thus, if prevailing access fees are lump-sum charges on all consumers (as is frequently the case for meter rental fees with water supply tariffs), and if many consumers are kept off the system by high access fees (as may be the case particularly for low-income consumers of public services in developing countries), then it would be appropriate to keep access or connection charges quite low and attempt to meet financial requirements through user charges set above marginal cost.[55] If access fees can, however, be designed to fall more heavily on wealthier consumers and if demand for access is quite inelastic for the relevant range of access prices, whereas demand for commodities is highly price-elastic but not highly income-elastic, then it would be appropriate to extract a relatively large proportion of financial requirements from access charges. This result for the two-part tariff is quite similar to that derived by Feldstein (1972b) for the case in which two services are provided by one enterprise under a single budget constraint. Conceptually, one can define access as one commodity and actual service use as the other, both of which are provided and priced by the public enterprise.[56]

A general solution to the problem of multipart tariffs in the presence of fiscal and income distribution considerations would build on the Munasinghe-Warford model, in which a shadow price for general government revenue is taken as given and variations in price by consumer group are envisaged. This model could be extended by formulating demand and cost functions for the dimensions of service provision, that is, service use, access, and location. If it is assumed that the private demand decisions about the dimensions are unrelated, the Munasinghe-Warford model may be reformulated directly for each dimension.[57] The problem becomes more difficult to solve if the demands for the dimensions are interrelated, for example, if the expected level and structure of user charges affect the decision of whether or not to connect a service.

Five analytical and practical problems must be considered before the models can be used. First, becauses all models in some way make a tradeoff among the objectives of efficiency, growth (public revenue), and income distribution, and because efficiency gains or losses depend crucially on the price-elasticity of service demand, it is necessary to know the price-elasticities of consumer demand for different consumer categories and for different dimensions of public service. Price-elasticities of demand for public services are, however, notoriously difficult to estimate.[58]

Second, the final incidence of public service benefits and charges must be identified. This problem is most readily apparent when services are intermediate products rather than items of final consumption. In the intermediate products case, the tax (or subsidy) on any particular commercial user of a service would burden or benefit owners of land or capital, labor, or the consumers of the products produced.[59] The exact incidence of such a tax (subsidy) therefore depends on the factor supply-elasticities to the service-using activities, and on the price- and income-elasticities of the final product. Thus, for services such as public utilities, for which intermediate usage represents a sizable proportion of total use, one has to be careful in specifying who bears the final burden of any service-related tax or subsidy. Even when the service is used by final consumers, as with residential use of public utilities, care needs to be taken in presuming that they ultimately bear the service tax (subsidy). Some of the gain or loss in consumer surplus may be capitalized into land value at the time of initial imposition of the subsidy (tax) and thus may create a benefit (burden) mainly for the owners of land at that time rather than for any subsequent owner or renter. The extent to which such capitalization occurs is not well established for developing countries, but some capitalization takes place, especially when these service-related taxes or subsidies have existed for some time. Another problem occurs with transportation pricing. Some of the benefits from subsidized public transportation may accrue to employers rather than employees if wages can be lowered as transportation costs go down.

Third, once the final incidence of service-related taxes or subsidies has been determined, it is necessary to calculate the social weights and shadow prices. Squire and van der Tak (1975) have provided some guidelines for the derivation of these weights, and some applications of their methodology exist in a number of developing countries.[60] Feldstein (1972a) applied his optimal pricing rule to the U.S. electricity sector. Nevertheless, the use of these weighting systems remains experimental.

A fourth problem is how to differentiate commodity prices by user group, if it is assumed that each group, categorized by income, is charged a different (and optimal) price. It may be possible to do this to a limited extent, for example, by differentiating access charges according to the value of the property which is connected, charging higher prices for users living on higher-valued properties. Another possibility, particularly for certain public utilities, is to let prices vary with the amount consumed. This can take either the form of multiple block rates (prices rising with larger and larger blocks of consumption) or simple two-block rates (the first block is charged at relatively low levels, and the remaining use in excess of the basic allowance is charged at a higher, but flat, fee per unit of consumption).[61] Yet another possibility is to vary service charges by area, on the assumption that households of comparable income groups tend to live in relatively easily identifiable homogeneous neighborhoods. All of these differentiating measures are of course only of limited accuracy because the correlation between income levels and assessed property values, or consumption or locational characteristics, is never perfect. The extent to which attempts have been made to introduce progressive, or income-redistributive, features into service charges and their likely effectiveness will be discussed in the following chapters.

A fifth criticism of the models concerns the manner in which they introduce redistribution of income. All of the models base their analyses on an assumed social welfare function in which an additional unit of disposable income in the hands of the rich is valued less than an additional unit in the hands of the poor. This notion and its implied distributional weights, although quite familiar to economists, have been criticized for not adequately reflecting the altruism of individuals, which in turn is reflected in the political decisionmaking process (Harberger 1978). Harberger has asserted that altruism and its manifestations in economic policy should instead be taken as an externality of consumption that applies only to individuals consuming to satisfy their "basic needs" (1978: 9). He compared the implications of distributional weights with those of basic needs and showed that they are indeed fundamentally distinct (1978: 12).

These arguments need not be elaborated on here. Instead, figure 9-5 shows the essence of the basic needs approach and its implications for

Figure 9-5. *Basic Needs and Public Service Pricing*

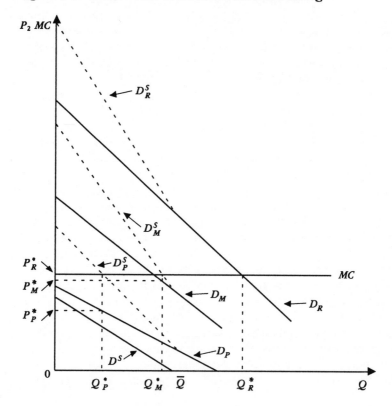

urban service pricing. The three curves, D_P, D_M, and D_R, show the demand for a particular public service by poor, middle-income, and rich consumers, respectively. Assume, moreover, that external benefits accrue to society from individual consumption as shown by the curve D^S.

The social demand curves, D_P^S, D_M^S, D_R^S, corresponding to the private demand of each consumer group, are then derived by vertical addition of D^S to the private demand curves. D^S is drawn so as to reflect the view that altruism implies that an additional unit of consumption of a particular service is valued more highly by society the less a particular individual is actually consuming. Beyond the level of consumption $\overline{Q}$ no benefits at all are derived by society over and above the consuming individual's private benefits.

Optimal pricing policy is then easily shown. For a given marginal cost curve, MC, the price for each consumer group ought to be set where the social demand curve intersects with the marginal cost curve. This implies a subsidized price P_P^* for poor consumers, who without this subsidy would not consume the service at all. For middle-income consumers a small subsidy is also appropriate (as these curves are drawn). For rich consumers, whose unsubsidized consumption falls beyond $\overline{Q}$, the marginal cost price (P_R^*) is the optimal price.[62] The importance of this for equity is that only specific items of consumption are viewed as being of social concern, whereas a general increase in individual welfare as measured by consumer surplus is not, per se, believed to be of concern for policy. Moreover, external benefits of consumption are viewed as accruing to society only up to some point—not, however, from marginal consumption beyond a certain level.

Externalities of consumption based on altruism are difficult to measure—as are all externalities—although the general argument makes considerable sense on the basis of common value judgments. As Harberger puts it, "The rest of society wants the recipients of welfare payments to spend more on feeding and clothing their children, not on what are judged to be sumptuary or trivial items" (1978: 9). Many public programs are designed to enable consumers to satisfy their basic needs rather than "frivolous wants" (for example, the frequent earmarking of "sin" taxes for spending on education and health).

This way of determining an optimal price requires value judgments, which of course are not simply right or wrong. One may, however, argue about how common values are, how they are to be measured, and how they are to be incorporated into the economist's analytical framework. All three aspects need more attention in analyses of both distributional weights and basic needs value systems. In fact, it is quite likely that in most societies both systems are espoused at the same time. Clearly, there is a need for more analysis of the equity objective in public service pricing. At present, only rather general guidance can be obtained from the models discussed above. The models, however, do provide insights about considerations for the pricing decision, can guide experimental designs of tariff structures, or can be used for sensitivity analysis to test the effect of alternative value judgments on the optimal design of service tariffs.

The Politics and Institutions of Public Service Pricing

Like all instruments of public policy, service prices are set in a context of a multiplicity of objectives pursued by a multiplicity of actors. User charges therefore are the product of interactions among these actors and are influenced by the political power of each interested group as well as by the institutional setting for the pricing decision. A realistic assessment of the political and institutional context is essential to any analysis of how to reform public service pricing. This concluding section of the chapter will consider the typical actors and their various, frequently conflicting objectives, the institutional setting, and the influence the history of pricing practices may have on the degree of flexibility for present pricing decisions.

The Politics of Public Service Pricing

Six interest groups are usually involved in and affected by decisions regarding user charges. To understand how patterns of user charges have come into being, how each group is likely to react to proposals for change, and what kinds of obstacles need to be overcome in introducing tariff reform, it is helpful to look at the groups. The first group, the recipients or beneficiaries of a public service, naturally have an interest in paying as little as possible for all dimensions of service provision, provided they do not perceive a link between the quantity or quality of the service supplied and the service price. Especially if services are customarily provided free of charge and are financed by general funds, the perception of a link between user charge and benefit may easily get lost.[63] Conversely, if users see a necessary connection between price and quantity and quality of service, they are likely to accept the system of user charges and moreover will exert pressure on managers and politicians to increase production efficiency.

The second group, the nonbeneficiaries of a public service, are—to the extent that they are general taxpayers—naturally interested in service prices which cover costs or, even better, permit a contribution to general funds or a cross-subsidization of services which they themselves tend to consume more intensively. These general taxpayers are frequently not well organized politically, especially if they have low incomes. Furthermore, the pricing arrangement for a service in isolation may not have large enough tax effects on the general fund to produce a well-orchestrated reaction by nonbeneficiaries. In some industrial countries, especially in North America, well-publicized popular movements have developed to restrain the local taxes which finance subsidized urban services.[64] To date, they appear not to have spilled over into developing countries.

The third group, the managers of public services, are likely to espouse multiple and possibly conflicting objectives—to the extent that they are free from direct political pressure from either the beneficiaries or other political actors (in particular local politicians or higher levels of government). It is in their general interest to expand service as rapidly as possible in order to increase their influence, follow their professional-technical ethics, and meet with public approval. If service demand is price-elastic, a manager would therefore want to set user charges as low as possible. He is constrained, however, by the financial viability of his service unless he receives grants or subsidies. Within the limits of his financial constraints, he will therefore try to set prices as low as possible while attempting to extend services, particularly to higher-income groups, which have the greatest willingness and ability to pay. These motives and constraints commonly lead the manager to resist avidly any attempt to generate a surplus for his service that will be used to support the general fund or another service not under his control.[65] Yet another motive commonly attributed to the manager is that of wanting to "maintain a quiet life." Again, he will be led to a compromise between staying within the financial constraints of the agency and maintaining prices so as to minimize complaints or other angry reactions from consumer groups.[66]

The fourth group, local politicians, generally tends to favor free provision of as many public services as possible with general fund financing. This arrangement maximizes their ability to provide patronage, at least as long as they have a say in where, to whom, or how the service is provided. Only if a politician has no real say in the provision of the service and is out to capture the support of a well-organized group of taxpayers is he at all likely to argue for raising user charges to match costs. In any case, he will attempt to maximize financial support from outside the local jurisdiction in order to minimize the burden of both general local taxes and local user charges. Moreover, he will aim to minimize the burden on those groups from whom he receives most political support or from whom he expects most trouble. For instance, it is not surprising that in the early 1970s politicians in Bogotá in general favored low use-related (commodity) charges for water supply for the large number of low- and middle-income water users while they favored retaining financial viability for the municipal water company by levying very high commodity charges on the relatively very few high-income users and charging high connection fees for the relatively few new consumers joining the system each year.

The fifth group, higher-level authorities, frequently take some interest in the prices local governments charge for urban public services. Their objectives may, however, vary quite widely, and their influence on setting local prices will thus differ from case to case. The goal of controlling inflation will often lead them to keep local authorities from raising user charges. Restraints on the level of user charges may also reflect the goal of keeping local authorities under tight national (or state) control by limiting their ability to use their own sources of local revenue.[67] Conversely, if national governments want to strengthen the fiscal structure of local authorities in order to minimize the drain on national resources, they can be counted on to work toward prices approximating the cost of service provision.[68] National authorities may also pursue income redistribution by encouraging such redistributive tariff structures as graduated rates and life-line rates.[69]

The efficiency concerns of national governments are usually limited to encouraging free or subsidized provision of services if positive externalities are thought to weigh heavily, especially in the case of public education and health. Few governments have paid much attention to the level or structure of marginal cost in service provision, although this may begin to change as they are made more aware of the importance of efficiency.

The sixth group, the international institutions that provide grants or loans and technical assistance to developing countries, has become an important part of the process of determining urban service charges. In early years they tended to look mainly at the financial viability of public service enterprises, especially in the utility and transit sectors. Since the 1970s, they have also begun to consider efficiency and redistribution (Julius and Alicbuson 1989). For example, virtually every public service project financed by the World Bank includes extensive exchanges between Bank staff and country officials (both national and local) regarding the level and structure of prices. These discussions are very important for preparing, approving, and supervising a project. Thus it is not entirely surprising that in recent years developing countries have begun to develop and apply user charge systems which tend to conform much more with the concerns of the economist for a reasonable balance of efficiency, equity, and financial feasibility than is common in many industrial countries.

The Institutional Setting

The ways in which interest groups can intervene in the process of setting user charges are mostly determined by the institutional setting. The role of higher levels of government in determining urban service charges depends largely on intergovernmental fiscal relations. If national authorities provide services directly, they also usually carry direct responsibility for setting user charges (for example, national electricity or telephone companies in many developing countries). Of course, national authorities are by no means homogeneous. The national public service company is likely to have considerably different goals than the ministry of finance.

Even if national authorities do not directly provide a service, they often build facilities for it, which are then handed over to the local authorities for operation. The local authorities typically try to avoid any financial responsibility for the facilities; their share of costs is determined by bargaining. There is usually a grant, which means that the charges for the service do not reflect its full costs and that cross-subsidization between the national taxpayer and the consumer has been introduced.

Intergovernmental financial flows can also exert considerable influence on the pricing decisions of urban authorities. If financial transfers are structured to provide incentives for raising local resources, user charges are more likely to be applied than if there are no such incentives. Repayable loans and matching grants provide stronger incentives for cost recovery than do grants with no strings attached. In some countries, for example Colombia, nationally provided or insured loans to local authorities were linked with a review of pricing practices by the national planning authority to ensure adequate financing from local resources, in particular user charges.

National authorities also frequently reserve the right to review local decisions regarding the level and structure of service charges, regardless of whether financial assistance is provided. The effect of this review depends on the objectives of the national government. During inflationary periods, local authorities are often prevented from raising user charges in line with inflationary pressures because it is believed that increases in service charges contribute to inflation.[70] Even if this effect is recognized as negligible, national authorities often cannot resist the temptation to suppress increases in public service charges in the interest of short-term political gains. Such interference with local decisionmaking is usually predicated on either the existence of established legal and institutional channels for national government review of local pricing decisions or financing arrangements under which national authorities are not directly and negatively affected by their refusal to accept increases in service charges.

Other special institutional conditions may affect price setting. More than one agency may provide a service. For example, in Colombia the National Telephone Company provides long distance lines and service, and in most big cities local or regional agencies provide local service, including telephones. Similarly, in Cali a local public agency distributes electricity but a regional authority generates power. In these institutional circumstances, there inevitably arise conflicts between agencies over how to allocate joint costs and over who should bear the political brunt of unpopular increases in user charges. Each agency will try to shift much of the burden to the other, which leads to the danger that none will make the hard decision to raise prices adequately and that the resulting financial difficulties will inhibit the maintenance and expansion of services. In such a context clear, binding pricing rules coupled with cost sharing agreements can go a long way toward preventing harmful stalemates, particularly if higher authorities enforce them. Nevertheless, if various agencies share responsibility to provide a service, conflicts are likely to occur. Although this does not necessarily argue for integrated provision of services, it is one of the costs of administrative decentralization.

The opposite case is also common. If more than one service is provided by a single agency, cross-subsidies between users of different services may occur. These multiservice agencies may be problematic if systematic pricing rules are not applied. And if common fund accounting is used, as is frequent in developing-country cities, the financial and economic management of all services may begin to suffer because "each tub doesn't have to stand on its own bottom." Yet integrating various services under one administrative umbrella does have the advantage of permitting more sophisticated pricing systems, such as those discussed in the preceding section, as long as managers are responsible and sympathetic to efficiency objectives.

These examples show the importance of the institutional setting for pricing mechanisms. There is no ideal institutional setting for an ideal pricing structure, mainly because many actors pursuing many conflicting objectives are involved in providing and benefiting from urban services, and because compromises need to be made among actors as well as objectives.

The Importance of Past Pricing Practices

Past as well as present pricing practices influence the desirability and feasibility of changes in pricing schemes. It is important to know whether administrative and technical conditions permit the introduction of a scheme. For example, if water meters are generally in use, a marginal cost pricing rule is more readily implemented than if water charges have been based on other criteria, such as property or rental value as in many Indian cities. Or recovering sewage system investment costs from property owners through betterment levies is likely to be a good deal easier if there is an administrative framework for assessing and collecting levies, as in many Colombian cities. What is more, new pricing practices may require legal changes that may involve cumbersome legislation. Past pricing practices, therefore, influence to a considerable extent how well and how fast user charges can be reformed.

Besides these technical and administrative aspects, there are three further problems. One is the fact that many people have come to accept past practices as a norm, particularly if services have been free or highly subsidized. Subsidized services may have come to be accepted as a right people are not willing to give up easily. Matters are often complicated because subsidies have been capitalized into property values or because people expect continued subsidies and have locked themselves into location or investment patterns which may be difficult and/or costly to reverse in the short term. Sudden and far-reaching changes in pricing may thus lead to considerable windfall losses, which in turn cause resentment and even political upheaval.

The second problem is the perception of unfairness, which occurs when a new pricing system requires payment for services which were free or heavily subsidized. The third problem is that failure to operate services efficiently and to charge effectively for them often makes the agency providing the service financially weak, which in turn leads to poor service. In these circumstances it is extremely difficult to introduce an effective charging system because users' willingness to pay is likely to have been seriously eroded by bad service. A vicious circle is thus established: charging systems cannot be improved if services have not been improved first, and services cannot be improved if charging systems have not been improved first.

To break this circle, it is necessary to work simultaneously at all aspects of urban service provision: to introduce measures that improve production efficiency, including those that improve the institutional framework and incentive system for managers, and gradually to implement a pricing system which provides a reasonable balance of efficiency, financial feasibility, and equity. As the following two chapters will demonstrate, the tradeoffs among these objectives are less severe than they may at first appear. In fact, urban service prices can often be structured to achieve all of them.

10 Charging for Urban Water Services

THE SUPPLY of potable water and the sanitary collection and disposal of residential and industrial wastewater are among the most essential urban services. Centralized systems to provide these services improve health, save money, and give more personal comfort (World Bank 1980a). Important advances have been made in providing access to these services (table 10-1), but much remains to be done. For example, in many towns and cities of developing countries, many people still do not have access to safe water; those who do often suffer service interruptions, and at times receive contaminated water. Although access to the services has risen, the quality of service in many urban areas has declined over the years (Hamer and Linn 1987).

One of the main constraints on more rapid extension and improvement of urban water services is limited financial resources. The tremendous resources needed for the services far exceed the capacity for resource mobilization. As might be expected, this needs-resources gap is greatest in the poorest countries, in which it is especially important to adapt investment strategies and service standards to affordability. In the poorest nations of Africa and South Asia, investments in neighborhood water systems and low-cost wastewater disposal systems are likely to be most feasible (Linn 1983). In the wealthier nations of Latin America, the Middle East, and East Asia, however, it may well be feasible to cover urban households fully with water services and even piped sewer systems. Pricing and financing policies must also be designed with these different circumstances in mind; and as noted above, appropriate pricing policies can assist in the development of better investment strategies.

Besides affecting the programming, planning, and financing of urban water supply and disposal systems, pricing can have important effects on the efficient use of national and regional water resources, on urban land use, and more broadly on the allocation of the economic resources of a country or region. Water charges can also significantly affect the spending patterns of the urban poor, as is shown in table 10-2, which reflects estimates of shares of household incomes spent on water in selected cities.[1] The variation across cities is considerable both in terms of the shares of the income spent on water and sewer charges in any income quintile and of the extent to which the shares increase or decline when moving from low- to high-income quintiles. To the extent that water and sewerage pricing systems can shift the burden of service financing from

Table 10-1. *Water Supply and Sanitation Coverage, by Region, 1983*
(percentage of population served)

	Water supply		Sanitation	
Region	Urban	Rural	Urban	Rural
Africa[a]	57	29	55	18
Western Asia[b]	95	50	93	21
Asia and the Pacific[c]	67	44	48	9
Latin America and Caribbean[d]	85	49	80	20

Note: No comparative data are available for the region of the U.N. Economic Commission for Europe and North America.
 a. Members of U.N. Economic Commission for Africa.
 b. Members of U.N. Economic and Social Commission for Western Asia.
 c. Members of U.N. Economic and Social Commission for Asia and the Pacific, excluding China.
 d. Members of the U.N. Economic Commission for Latin America and the Caribbean.
Source: U.N. Center for Human Settlements (1987).

low- to high-income groups, or vice versa, the distributive effect of these charges can be quite significant.

A further consideration which makes the pricing and financing of water services an important issue for this volume is that water supply and sewerage systems in large and medium-size cities are generally managed by the local government even though they are often the administrative re-

Table 10-2. *Estimated Monthly Water Charges as a Percentage of Estimated Monthly Household Income, by Income Group, Selected Cities*

	Income group (and consumption category in thousands of liters)				
City, year	Lowest 20 percent (7)	Second 20 percent (15)	Third 20 percent (27)	Fourth 20 percent (36)	Highest 20 percent (40)
São Paulo, Brazil, 1970	4.71	2.28	3.35	2.85	0.90
Bogotá, Colombia, 1971	0.67	0.70	1.04	0.83	1.51
Cartagena, Colombia, 1971	0.97	0.84	1.23	1.25	0.62
Addis Ababa, Ethiopia, 1972	8.70	7.89	7.70	6.17	2.46
Kingston, Jamaica, 1971	1.76	3.04	6.05	3.75	0.81
Nairobi, Kenya, 1970	6.80	5.51	6.00	3.93	1.88
Seoul, Rep. of Korea, 1972	0.36	0.32	0.55	0.61	0.49
Mexico City, Mexico, 1970	0.41	0.33	0.38	0.29	0.17
Lima, Peru, 1971	4.96	2.34	1.25	1.41	0.56
Manila, Philippines, 1970	9.27	1.67	1.65	1.50	0.72
Bangkok, Thailand, 1972	0.49	1.12	2.19	2.20	0.86

Note: Water charges (which include drinking water and sewerage) are estimated from tariff schedules and estimated water consumption figures for households in the individual cities.
Source: Computed by K. Hubbell from survey data. Cited in Saunders and Warford (1976: 188).

Table 10-3. *The Provision of Urban Water Services in the 1970s*

Region and economy	City	Institutional structure
Latin America		
Colombia	Bogotá and others	Local autonomous agency
Costa Rica	San José and others	National autonomous agency
Ecuador	Large cities	Local autonomous agency
Jamaica	Kingston	National autonomous agency
	Other towns	National autonomous agency (separate)
Mexico	Mexico City	Local autonomous agency
Panama	Panama City and others	National autonomous agency
Africa		
Côte d'Ivoire	Abidjan	National government
Ethiopia	Addis Ababa	Local autonomous agency
Kenya	Nairobi and others	Local government
	Mombasa	Regional autonomous agency
	Small cities	National government
Nigeria	Lagos and others	State autonomous agency
Sudan	Khartoum	National government
Uganda	Kampala	National government
Zaire	Kinshasa and others	National government
Zambia	Lusaka	Local government
Asia		
Afghanistan	Kabul and others	Local government
Bangladesh	Dhaka, Chittagong	Local autonomous agencies
Burma	Rangoon	Local autonomous agency
Taiwan (China)	Taipei	Local autonomous agency
India	New Delhi and others	Local autonomous agency
Indonesia	Jakarta	National autonomous agency
Korea, Rep.	Seoul	Local government
Nepal	Kathmandu	Local government
Pakistan	Lahore, Karachi	Local autonomous agencies
Philippines	Manila	Local autonomous agency
Middle East		
Algeria	Algiers	National government
Israel	Tel Aviv, Haifa	Local government
Jordan	Amman	Local autonomous agency
Tunisia	Tunis	National autonomous agency

Source: Based on a review of World Bank reports carried out by Prabhas Sharma. Cited in Bird (1980: table 4).

sponsibility of autonomous or semiautonomous local agencies (table 10-3; also see chapter 3). Spending on the services usually accounts for a sizable portion of total urban government expenditure (table 10-4). The pricing of water supply and sewerage disposal is thus often one of the main fiscal decisions at the local level. This chapter reviews charges commonly found in cities of developing countries and discusses the design of water tariffs in terms of the general principles of user charges laid out in the preceding chapter.

Table 10-4. *Percentage Share of Water Services in Total Expenditure of Urban Governments, Selected Cities*

City, year	Percent
Francistown, Botswana, 1972	14.7
Bogotá, Colombia, 1972	26.1
Cali, Colombia, 1974	12.3
Cartagena, Colombia, 1972	22.3
Ahmadabad, India, 1971	11.2
Bombay, India, 1971–72	11.5
Calcutta, India, 1974/75	55.2
Madras, India, 1975–76	23.0
Jakarta, Indonesia, 1972–73	6.4
Kingston, Jamaica, 1972	3.8[a]
Daegu, Rep. of Korea, 1976	18.9
Daejeon, Rep. of Korea, 1976	17.6
Gwangju, Rep. of Korea, 1976	14.6
Jeonju, Rep. of Korea, 1975	23.1
Seoul, Rep. of Korea, 1970	15.2
Karachi, Pakistan, 1973–74	25.9
Lusaka, Zambia, 1972	27.0

a. Does not include expenditure by the nationally run water and sewerage agency for the Kingston metropolitan area.

Pricing Water Supply Services

Water charges may be grouped into four categories:

1. A lump-sum development charge, which may be determined by the capital cost of infrastructure and by lot size, frontage, or value of properties lying in the area provided with community water supply; this charge applies whether or not the lot is actually connected to the water main
2. A lump-sum connection charge, which may be determined by the size of the connection or by characteristics of the consumer related or unrelated to his water use
3. A periodic fixed payment determined by consumer characteristics related or unrelated to, but not varying directly with, water use
4. A periodic payment determined by metered water consumption; the rate per unit of water consumed may vary with the amount consumed, with the season, or with property value, type of consumers, and so forth.

In the following discussion, category 4 will be referred to as a "consumption charge" or "use-related fee." Lump-sum connection charges and periodic fixed payments (categories 2 and 3) are often treated together under the term "connection fee," because both types of charges are related to the consumer's decision to connect to the system. In principle, any recurrent charge can be capitalized into an equivalent lump-sum charge, or any lump-sum charge annuitized into a recurrent charge at the prevailing rate of interest. In practice, however, because of the many imperfections of capital markets in developing countries, lump-sum and periodic fees may have quite different effects.

After a brief review of common systems of water charges in developing countries, this section will discuss how to design a system of water charges that can meet goals of efficiency, financial viability, and equity. Allowance will also be made for institutional factors which may influence the feasibility of pursuing these goals through an appropriate set of water charges.

Existing Systems of Water Charges

Table 10-5 summarizes some salient characteristics of existing systems of water charges in selected cities of developing countries.[2] Emphasis is placed on the differential treatment frequently given to commercial and industrial users, and on users drawing water from public taps.[3] Although table 10-5 is quite limited in its coverage of countries and somewhat dated in its information, it includes countries and cities in all major regions of the developing world and therefore is reasonably representative. It does not contain a column for development charges because according to the available information no such charges were levied in any of the cities listed.[4] The typical structure of water charges, however, appears to include one or more of the remaining three types of charges.

With the exception of Ahmadabad, all the cities listed levied a charge related to the metered consumption of water for those house connections with working meters. The proportion of metered connections varied, however, from city to city. In more than two-thirds of the cities the use-related rates rose with the amount of water consumed, in two or more steps or "blocks" (up to eight blocks in Guayaquil). Rate differentiation by characteristics other than metered water use has also been quite common. In Bombay rates varied with a property's size of lawn or availability of swimming pools, presumably as a way to catch luxury consumption and possibly to pass on capacity costs to seasonal users (especially sprinkler demand). The fact that declining block rates are not commonly found in the developing countries is remarkable only because of the frequency with which this system of water charges has been used in industrial countries, particularly in the United States and Canada, despite long-standing objections to this as an inefficient practice (Bird 1976b). Only in three cases studied here did declining block rates occur. They were applied to residential users in Cameroon and in Gabon; in Abidjan (Côte d'Ivoire), declining block rates were in force for industrial and commercial users, whereas residential rates were structured in rising blocks.

Fixed monthly fees have been very common, although they have taken on many different shapes. In many cities minimum monthly fees have applied for metered consumers, but these were often supplemented by so-called meter rental fees or other fixed monthly charges. These charges usually increased with the size of the meter or diameter of the pipe connecting the consumer to the distribution main, or they were positively related to the value of the connected property (Colombia). Unmetered users were usually charged monthly fees varying with diameter of the connecting pipe, or at times varying with the value of the connected property (India).

Connection fees have been quite common, but again have varied across countries and cities. A flat charge related (at least historically) to the cost of installation has been most common. In some cases (for example, Colombia), additional charges were levied when a property was connected and were determined as percentage rates of assessed property value. In other cases (Bangkok and Jakarta), the diameter of the connecting pipe determined the connection fee. Finally, in some cities returnable deposits were required at the time of connection. Industrial and commercial users were in most cities charged at levels above those of residential users with some notable exceptions, such as Abidjan and Tunis, where industrial and commercial customers were given favorable treatment.

The information available on rates charged to users of standposts is quite limited for the cities listed in table 10-5. In Colombia, India, and Thailand the use of water from public taps in the cities appears to have been free of charge, whereas in Jakarta, Nairobi, and Seoul higher rates were charged to users of public taps than to most users with in-house connections. The relatively high cost of water from public sources or from street vendors is further demonstrated in tables 10-6 and 10-7. The tables show, respectively, the charges levied at standpipes in selected cities and a comparison of the price of water from in-house connections with the price paid for water from carriers. Especially considering the private costs of hauling water (the time and effort spent in carrying the water from the source to the site of use), it is clear that users with in-house connections generally face much lower unit prices than users of public taps or carried water.

Efficient Charges

For water supply, as for any other urban service, it is useful to begin a discussion of pricing strategies by focusing on the goal of efficiency.[5] Other policy goals and constraints are then brought into the analysis.

DEMAND. If the demand for a service does not respond to price changes, the efficiency of resource allocation is not affected by the selection of service charges. In discussing the price-elasticity of water demand, that is, the degree of responsiveness of water demand to changes in user charges, it is important to remember that more than one dimension of service demand is relevant. These dimensions are related respectively to three separate decisions: (a) whether, where, and at what density and

(*Text continues on page 296.*)

Table 10-5. *Water Tariff Structure in Selected Cities*

Country, year, state or city	Lump-sum connection charge	Fixed monthly fee	Consumption charge	Standpipe charge	Industrial and commercial charges relative to residential charge
Brazil, 1974					
Belo Horizonte Minas Gerais	n.a.	Flat rate	n.a.	—	Higher
	n.a.	Minimum charge	Two blocks (rising)	—	Higher
Bujumbura, Burundi, 1966	By pipe diameter and length of pipe	Meter rental fee (for five years)	Two blocks (rising); rising with dwelling area and declining with family size	—	Higher
Cameroon, 1975	Flat charge	Minimum charge; flat fee where unmetered	Three blocks (first rising, then falling)	Rate charged	Equal
Colombia					
Bogotá, 1979	Rising with property value and cost of installation	Minimum charge rising with property value	Five blocks (rising); rising with property value	Free	120–130 percent of residential tariffs
Cali, 1978	Rising with property value and cost of installation	Minimum charge rising with property value	Five blocks (rising)	Free	Consumption charge equal to residential monthly fee, approximately equal to mean residential fee
Cartagena, 1973	Rising with property value and cost of installation	Minimum charge rising with property value and meter rental charge rising with property value and pipe diameter	Three blocks (rising)	Free	Lower, if using untreated water

292

Abidjan, Côte d'Ivoire, 1975	n.a.	n.a.	Two blocks (rising)	—	Lower; three blocks (falling)
Guayaquil, Ecuador, 1974	n.a.	Minimum charge; meter rental fee rising with pipe diameter	Eight blocks (rising)	—	Higher
Addis Ababa, Ethiopia, 1972	Cost of installation; deposit rising with pipe diameter	Meter rental rising with pipe diameter; flat fee where unmetered	—	—	—
Libreville, Gabon, 1973	n.a.	n.a.	Five blocks (first rising, then falling)	—	—
Accra/Tenna, Ghana, 1974	n.a.	Minimum charge	Flat rate	—	Higher
India					
Ahmadabad, 1973	n.a.	General property tax	n.a.	Free	—
Bombay, 1978	Charge rising with meter size	Minimum charge and meter rental fee rising with meter size; tax on property value for unmetered users; special low rate for slums	Flat rate; higher rate for properties with large lawns or swimming pools	Free	Higher
Indonesia					
Jakarta, 1973	Charge rising with pipe diameter	Meter fee increasing with diameter of pipe	Two blocks (rising)	Rate equal to highest residential rate	Higher
Malang, 1974	Flat charge	Minimum charge	Flat rate	—	Higher rising; block rates

(Table continues on the following page.)

Table 10-5 *(continued)*

Country, year, state or city	Lump-sum connection charge	Fixed monthly fee	Consumption charge	Standpipe charge	Industrial and commercial charges relative to residential charge
Kingston, Jamaica, 1975	—	Rate varying with meter size; low-value properties are exempt	Six blocks (rising)	—	Highest residential tariff
Kenya Mombasa, 1975	Flat charge	Meter rental rising with diameter; flat rate for nonmetered users	Two blocks (rising)	—	Lower
Nairobi, 1975	Connection fee and returnable deposit	Minimum charge and meter rent	Flat rate	Private operators charge unit rate five times official rate for house connections	Equal

Malaysia				
Kuala Lumpur, 1973	n.a.	Minimum charge	Flat rate	—	Higher
Penang, 1973	—	Minimum charge	Two blocks (rising)	—	Higher
Mexico City, Mexico, 1973	n.a.	For nonmetered users flat charge rising with pipe diameter	Six blocks (rising)	—	Equal
Kathmandu, Nepal, 1970s	Flat charge	For nonmetered users flat charge rising with pipe diameter	Two blocks (rising)	—	Equal
Tunis, Tunisia, 1973	—	n.a.	Flat rate	—	Lower
Seoul, Rep. of Korea, 1972	—	Flat minimum charge	Five blocks (rising)	Higher than low-use residential fees	Higher
Lahore, Pakistan, 1973	Flat charge	Minimum charge rising with pipe diameter; meter rental charge	Flat rate	—	Higher minimum charge
Bangkok, Thailand, 1975	Charge varying with pipe diameter	n.a.	Six blocks (rising)	Free	Equal

— Not available.
n.a. Not applicable.

Table 10-6. *Water Charges at Public Taps in Selected Cities
of Developing Countries*
(dollars per cubic meter)

Country and city	Charge
Burkina Faso	
Ouagadougou	0.30
Bobo Dioulasso	0.30
Cameroon	
Douala	0.20
Yaoundé	0.26
Gabon	
Libreville	0.50
Port Gentil	0.50
Lambarene	0.50
Indonesia	
Jakarta	0.70
Kenya	
Nairobi	0.13

Note: This is the price charged by the water supply organization for water supplied to the public hydrants. Actual consumer prices may be higher because of resale. No date is given in source.
Source: Vlieger and others (1975: 46).

service levels to develop a tract of urban land (assuming that each lot in the tract will have the option to connect to the water distribution network but will not necessarily choose to connect); (b) whether to connect to the distribution network or not, and with what size or length of connection pipe; and (c) how much water to consume once connected to the system. The crucial question then becomes whether any of these decisions is affected by the prices or sets of prices which a utility may choose.

Table 10-7. *Costs of Public and Private Water Supply in Selected
Developing Countries*
(dollars per cubic meter)

Country or city	In-house connection (public utility)	Water carrier (private vendor)
Burkina Faso	0.30	1.0–1.5
Ghana	0.10	1.3–2.5
Nairobi, Kenya	0.20	1.4–2.1
Senegal	Free	1.6–2.4
Kampala, Uganda	0.33	1.3–3.0

Note: Ratios of private to public water costs in additional locations are: for Abidjan, 5 to 1; for selected cities in Indonesia, between 2 to 1 and 10 to 1 (World Bank data); for Karachi, 10 to 1 (USAID 1976); and for Lima, between 16 to 1 and 25 to 1 (Thomas 1978).
Source: Linn (1983), based on Vlieger and others (1975: 48).

Evidence about the demand-elasticity of water use is scant for developing countries. Probably the most careful study was done for Nairobi by Hubbell (1977). On the basis of a stratified random sample of 400 households, a linear regression equation was estimated for pooled cross-section, time-series data to determine the effect on the demand for water of a change in water tariffs and differences in user rates at any particular time, holding constant other determinants such as household income, site value of property, family size, and ethnic background. The results show a price-elasticity of -0.5. Another study estimated the effect of a water price change in Penang (Malaysia) purely on the basis of intertemporal changes in the quantity demanded (Katzman 1977). The estimated elasticities fell in the range of -0.1 to -0.2. Less reliable estimates were made for Bogotá, where changes in water tariffs were associated with drops in consumption indicating a range of price-elasticity between -0.35 and -0.50 (Linn 1976b), and in selected Colombian cities, where elasticities fell in the range of -0.1 to -0.6 (World Bank estimates). These results, and in particular Hubbell's elasticity estimate, fall within the range of estimates for the United States. A survey of U.S. studies concluded that "a rough estimate of about -0.5 seems a reasonable compromise for the American data" (Gorman 1980: 1–3). To what extent the price-elasticity varies with income level is not well researched in developing countries, although for the United States the evidence appears to indicate that the demand for water is less price-elastic among the poor.

The implication of these findings is that because the demand for water is moderately responsive to price changes, efficiency considerations should not be neglected in setting user rates. This conclusion is strengthened for the case of metered versus unmetered use. The available evidence unequivocally indicates that metering has quite considerable effects on consumption. Saunders (1976) estimates that in Bangkok the elimination of meters on average would lead affected households to consume 40 percent more water. White, Bradley, and White (1972) report on a study in Uruguay showing a strong inverse relationship between the proportion of households metered and daily use of water. Similar evidence is available for the United States (White, Bradley, and White 1972). The implications of these findings are that efficiency considerations are very important for metered user prices and can substantially guide the metering decision itself.

Evidence for the other dimensions of water demand—connection and access—is much less readily available. For water connections, the price-elasticity in principle can be reduced to zero by requiring connection to the distribution network. In practice, however, this regulation may not always be enforceable, particularly in low-income neighborhoods. Evidence for Colombia suggests that a significant number of urban households will choose not to connect to the public water systems despite legal

connection requirements (Selowsky 1979). One reason for this failure
to connect may well have been the steep connection fees (Linn 1980a).
The ease with which illegal connections to the water system can be made
is another major consideration in determining the elasticity of connection
demand. In Bogotá and Jakarta, for example, illegal connections have
been quite common in poor neighborhoods, apparently in response to
sizable connection fees (Linn 1976c; Linn, Smith, and Wignjowijoto
1976). The choice not to connect to an existing water system is likely
to be of interest mainly to low-income families who demand small quantities of water and therefore can effectively satisfy this demand from
communal water taps or carriers, or from rivers and creeks. For higher-
income groups, whose demand for water tends to involve much larger
quantities, private sources of supply are generally a less acceptable substitute. The connection demand is therefore likely to be much more
price-elastic for low- than for middle- or high-income consumers.[6] The
connection demand for industrial and commercial uses may be quite
price-elastic, particularly where groundwater is readily available. Evidence of use of private wells for industrial and commercial users in response to high user charges or connection fees was, for example, found
in Bangkok (Saunders 1976).

Does the level of charges affect the location or access demand for
water services? Evidence on migration appears to indicate that utility
pricing is not a significant determinant of the rural-urban or urban-urban
migration decision (Findley 1977). To what extent this is also true for
industrial location decisions, and therefore for the possible indirect effects which utility pricing may have on migration, is more debatable.
There does not appear to be any conclusive evidence on this subject for
developing countries. Nor is there good information available on the
effect of spatial differences in utility pricing on intraurban location decisions; this is not surprising, however, considering that such cost differentials are rarely considered in setting urban water prices.[7]

Finally, the effect of pricing on other land use decisions, especially
those concerned with density of development, also appears not to have
been carefully investigated. It has been argued, however, that if government agencies are required to charge the real cost of providing a
service to actual or potential beneficiaries, the agencies are forced to
consider the standards of service for which the prospective beneficiaries
are willing and able to pay (World Bank 1980b). This implies that service
demand, defined in terms of the development decision, is effectively
price-elastic. Again, for water supply it is quite likely that this elasticity
is higher for low-income groups than for middle- or high-income groups,
which are more likely to select their housing solutions without particular
attention to water supply accessibility or its cost, except that they will
want to ensure what they see to be a minimum standard of water service:
multiple-tap in-house connections with sufficient capacity to service

showers, flush toilets, and water-using appliances such as washing machines. Within reasonable boundaries, changes in the water development charge will not lead to changes in the demand for this standard package among those who are better off.

In sum, one may conclude that the demand for water consumption is moderately price-elastic, but possibly less so for low- than for high-income groups. In contrast, the demands for water connections and access opportunity are likely to be more elastic among lower-income households, and especially among the very poor, but show very little price-elasticity for higher-income groups. This last set of conclusions is highly conjectural, and considerably more analysis is required to confirm the findings. Overall, however, one must conclude that for at least some types of users the efficiency of the level of water charges is likely to matter in all of the three dimensions of water demand. From the point of view of economic efficiency it is therefore important to consider the resource costs of water provision and to attempt to link the structure of water charges to those costs.

COSTS OF SUPPLY. The basic rule of efficient public service pricing is to set price equal to marginal cost. In the case of water supply, possibly more than for other urban services, it is important to consider carefully the service dimensions to which the marginal cost price or prices are applied.

All three dimensions used previously—use, connection, and access—are of relevance here. As regards use, the incremental cost of producing and transmitting water includes the short-run operating and maintenance costs incurred by the utility in producing and transmitting potable water (such as material costs of treatment, energy costs of pumping, and maintenance requirements caused by wear and tear on the plant during operation) as well as labor costs directly related to the level of production at which the facilities operate. It is relatively easy to estimate these costs from the financial data of a water enterprise.

More difficult is the treatment of incremental capacity costs of water production and transmission, for which investments are generally lumpy. One method of estimating incremental capacity costs in the water supply sector has in recent years been frequently applied in developing countries. This method draws on the concept of average incremental cost (AIC), which "is calculated by discounting the incremental costs which will be incurred in the future to provide the estimated additional amounts of water which will be demanded over a specified period, and dividing that by the discounted value of incremental output over the period" (Saunders, Warford, and Mann 1976: 15).[8]

The purpose of pricing on the basis of AIC is to provide a smoothing of price fluctuations, which the application of the pure short-run marginal cost (SRMC) rule would entail, while permitting price signals to guide

Figure 10-1. *Schematic Comparison of AIC, SRMC, and AC Trends over Time*

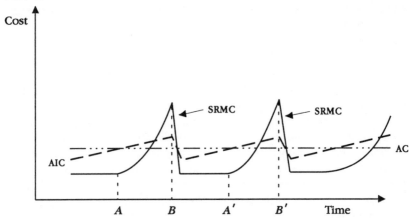

Key: —— ··· —— AC, average cost per cubic meter; — — — AIC, average incremental cost per cubic meter; ———— SRMC, short-run marginal cost per cubic meter.

investment decisions.[9] Figure 10-1 schematically compares the AIC cost or price trend over time with that of SRMC or price, assuming constant long-run costs of capacity expansion.[10] Points A and A' reflect times at which the capacity constraint is reached and SMRC begins to rise until capacity expansion becomes appropriate at points B and B', respectively. At that time SRMC drops again to its previous levels in a sharp reversal of the previously rising level. AIC, in contrast, exhibits an initially higher level than SRMC but a more gentle rate of increase, so that it eventually falls short of capacity-rationing SRMC. At the time of capacity expansion AIC also drops, but less markedly than SRMC. AIC pricing thus represents a compromise between, on the one hand, the perfectly smooth price trend of an average cost pricing rule reflected in the AC (average cost) line in figure 10-1, and the highly volatile price trend shown by SRMC. The shorter the intervals between capacity expansion the smoother will be the AIC trend line, and when applied to a rising long-run cost trend, the declines in AIC may actually vanish altogether (Saunders, Warford, and Mann 1977).

AIC cost estimates have been extensively applied in recent years in water supply projects financed by the World Bank and have been used to inform pricing decisions of the public utility agencies involved. In such practical applications of AIC estimates, care must be taken to include only those costs which are incremental with respect to present or future consumption. In fact, numerous cost items should not be included in an AIC calculation.

One set of such cost items concerns the decision to connect to the water supply system and typically includes the material and labor costs of installation (excavation, pipes, plumbing, and meter). In addition to the costs of initial installation, clerical and other labor costs may be incurred when occupants of a property change. More important, there are recurring administrative and clerical costs associated with a water connection, including meter reading and maintenance, record keeping, and billing. All of these costs are related to an individual consumer's decision to connect to the service but do not vary with the amount of water consumed. On efficiency grounds, these costs should be charged to each connection as a flat periodic fee unrelated to the quantity of water consumed. To the extent that these costs reflect the capital cost of installation, a lump-sum connection charge would also be appropriate. As mentioned earlier, under certain conditions lump-sum charges and flat periodic fees are equivalent, since the former can be annuitized or the latter capitalized.

Returnable security deposits can be interpreted as providing merely insurance against willful tampering with meters or other parts of the water connection. They may also, however, imply a real charge if any interest rate paid on the deposit held by the utility falls below the rate of interest that the consumers could earn on this money in other uses. The extent to which such an implicit charge is related to the actual cost of connection will depend on each case but should be of concern, particularly if the deposits are large and inflation rates are high.[11] Again, this cost is unrelated to the quantity of water consumed.

Finally, there are the development or access charges for the cost of installing the necessary distribution and retriculation network. This cost is not directly related to the amount of water consumed, although expected consumption per connection may influence the diameter of the distribution pipes. Costs of water distribution are related more closely to the density of development: the distribution cost per connection varies inversely with the density of development, as is shown in table 10-8 for a sample of neighborhoods in Cali.[12] The costs of the distribution system may also vary between areas of a city because of different geological conditions. Efficient private development decisions as regards timing, location, and density of development as well as standard of demand for service will be encouraged by charging developers and lot owners the incremental cost of water distribution networks. What is more, public development decisions will be improved by the need to take into consideration the willingness of private beneficiaries to pay for the costs associated with the public supply of water. In principle it is inefficient to charge development costs through connection fees, because once the distribution network has been constructed, the marginal cost of connecting to the system is restricted to the installation and related cost

Table 10-8. *Relation between Water Distribution Costs and Density in the Neighborhoods of Cali, Colombia*
(thousands of Colombian pesos)

Neighborhood	Density (connections per hectare)	Costs per hectare	Costs per connection
Conquistadores	88.6	348.7	3.9
Leon XIII	48.8	129.0	2.7
Quiroga I	48.0	237.0	4.9
Doce de Octubre	47.8	118.0	2.5
Alfonso Lopez V	41.9	88.4	2.2
Cotraval	41.7	67.4	1.6
Sindical	40.3	104.3	2.5
San Judas Tadeo	40.3	38.6	1.0
Atanasio Girardot	37.2	138.2	3.7
Alfonso Lopez VI	33.9	84.5	2.5
Union Vivienda Popular	33.6	64.7	2.0
El Rodeo	33.0	88.2	2.7
Los Cambulos	26.4	80.4	3.1
Jorge Eliecer Gaitan	22.6	51.4	2.4
Terron Colorado	22.0	37.6	1.8
Siloe Lleras	19.6	99.8	5.1
Camino Real I	12.8	86.8	6.4
Leonar III	5.6	85.5	15.3
La Merced VIII	2.0	85.7	42.9
Average	34.3	107.1	5.7
Median	37.2	88.2	2.7

Note: June 1975 prices. Regression equation relating cost per connection to density: $\ln (C/S) = 3.88 - 0.80 \ln (S/A)$ $R^2 = 0.66$, where C/S is the cost per connection and S/A is the number of connections per hectare. The coefficient of $\ln (S/A)$ is significant at the 0.1 percent level of confidence.

Source: Linn (1976b: table 7, p. 24).

discussed earlier. Indeed, charging development fees only at the time of connection will restrict the connection decisions to inefficiently low levels. The development charge should be levied on all property owners at the time the system is built whether or not a particular owner chooses to connect to the system at that particular time.

GEOGRAPHICAL AND SEASONAL VARIATIONS IN COST. Following the general principle of efficient pricing, water users should be charged equally if they impose equal marginal costs on the system but should be charged differentially if marginal costs differ. Costs of water supply commonly differ between cities within the same country due to differences in system size, water resource availability, geological conditions, or possibly input prices. Table 10-9 indicates the considerable variations between urban areas in Colombia. Uniform national or regional tariffs, as were found in some countries (for example, Malaysia and Tunisia[13]), certainly would be inefficient under these conditions.[14]

Table 10-9. *Comparison of Long-Run Cost and Average Tariff for Selected Colombian Cities, 1974*
(Colombian pesos per cubic meter)

City	Actual average tariff[a]	Long-run cost[b]	Percentage shortfall of actual tariff from long-run average cost
Armenia	1.54	2.19	29.7
Barranquilla	2.53	3.32	23.8
Bogotá	1.84	3.60	49.9
Cali	2.16	3.06	29.4
Cartagena	1.95	4.44	56.1
Cucuta	1.40	2.82	50.4
Medellín	1.40	1.79	21.8
Neiva	1.38	1.45	4.8
Tulua	1.30	2.30	43.5
Average			34.4

a. Total revenue from sale of water (including sewer surcharge) divided by quantity sold.
b. Sum of operating costs plus depreciation plus 8 percent of revalued net fixed assets, divided by quantity sold.
Source: Linn (1980a: table 9).

Intrametropolitan differences in costs are also common, although not generally explored by water companies or researchers. Two case studies in Cali and Nairobi commissioned for this volume have found cost differentials within these cities by estimating AICs for selected areas in the water distribution systems. Table 10-10 summarizes the findings for these two cities. In Nairobi, the cost differences resulted from supplementary pumping requirements to convey water from a low-elevation source to high-elevation users. The AIC estimates reflect differences in planned investments in pumping facilities. In Cali, low-elevation areas experienced (in general) higher costs, because planned expansion of the

Table 10-10. *Geographical Water Cost Differentials in Cali and Nairobi*

Area	Average incremental cost	Average incremental cost as percentage
Cali, Colombia, 1977	In Colombian pesos per cubic meter	Of high level
High elevation	0.818	100
Low elevation	0.903	110
Siloe Lleras	1.054	129
Terron Colorado	1.080	132
Nairobi, Kenya, 1975	In Kenyan shillings per thousand gallons	Of low level
Low elevation	8.80	100
Central	9.25	105
High elevation	11.60	132

Sources: For Cali, Linn (1976a: table 16). For Nairobi, McLure (1977: table 14).

pumping system in these areas required investments in water mains attributable only to the low-level area. For Cali and Nairobi, AIC in the highest-cost area was approximately one-third above AIC in the lowest-cost area.

The capital costs of water distribution may also vary substantially among areas of a city, mainly in relation to the density of development, but also because of differences in soil conditions, accessibility, or distance to the distribution main. Table 10-8 describes the extent to which such differences can exist. Differential development charges by area are therefore important to signal to potential new customers the resource costs incurred as a result of their location and land use decisions.

Variations in spatial service costs within cities are rarely reflected in water charges. There are, however, examples of efforts to do so. In Cali, a surcharge on water use was applied for some time in two high-lying areas, Siloe Lleras and Terron Colorado, to reflect supplementary pumping costs. In 1975, however, this surcharge was only about 40 percent of actual short-run marginal costs of supplementary pumping (Linn 1976b). In Kingston, Jamaica, surcharges of 50–75 percent over the base charge were in the past applied to consumers living in areas requiring supplementary pumping (Bougeon-Maassen and Linn 1977). These examples indicate that it is possible not only in principle but also in practice to vary water fees by area.

Seasonal cost differentials may also be important in the case of water supply. During dry periods supply may drop and demand may increase to such an extent that constraints on capacity are reached. It may then be more efficient to ration available supplies through price increases rather than to permit pressures to drop or to provide water only intermittently.[15] In Cali, for example, dry-period declines in the water source serving high-lying areas led to seasonal pumping requirements and resulted in a doubling of short-run marginal cost (Linn 1976b). In one region of Tunisia it was found that water consumption during the summer quarter exceeded the yearly average by about 50 percent (World Bank estimates). In a city in Paraguay per capita water consumption more than doubled between seasons, but in many other cities seasonal demand changes are not significant (White 1974). In Lahore, peak-season consumption was between 30 and 40 percent above off-peak season consumption (Turvey and Warford 1974). Because of added pumping requirements during the peak season, marginal peak consumption costs exceeded marginal off-peak consumption costs by about 40 percent. For the Tunisian region previously mentioned, World Bank estimates indicated that peak user cost was forty times off-peak cost. This estimate was based on attributing all costs of incremental increases in capacity to peak users because peak consumption necessitated the planned expansions in capacity to produce water.

The need to reflect seasonal cost differentials in designing water tariffs depends on the extent of cost differences and on the administrative feasibility of applying differential rates at different times of the year. Turvey and Warford (1974), for example, advised against seasonal price differences in the case of Lahore because of the difficulties likely to be encountered in timing meter readings to accurately reflect the switchover from one season to another. In any case, there can be seasonal variations in charges only if meters are in use. For nonmetered connections, it is inefficient to vary charges seasonally. There have been no seasonal differences in water prices in the cities surveyed for this study, although in Kingston higher water prices were charged during droughts (Bougeon-Maassen and Linn 1977).

EXTERNALITIES AND OTHER "SECOND-BEST" CONSIDERATIONS. Water supply works are commonly justified by the health benefits for the community of reducing the incidence of water-borne diseases. Research has shown that 20–40 liters per capita per day (lcd) of readily available water, if accompanied by adequate waste disposal facilities and sound hygienic practices, are sufficient to attain the main health benefits of water use (Kalbermatten, Julius, and Gunnerson 1982; World Bank 1980a, 1980b, 1980d). Additional consumption is also beneficial, but mainly because of the direct convenience to the user. The external benefits from water use are thus likely to be restricted to the range of consumption below 40 lcd. Consumers therefore should be given an incentive to consume at least this amount of safe water if they are not willing or able to do so at their prevailing incomes and marginal cost price. This has been one of the major reasons for the introduction of so-called life-line tariffs in many developing countries.[16]

Life-line tariffs consist of a heavily subsidized low tariff for an initial consumption block equivalent to, say, 20–40 lcd, whereas consumption beyond this amount is charged at full marginal cost. Because water consumers with house connections typically use more than 40 lcd even at low incomes (table 10-11), the subsidy provided by the life-line tariff in practice is inframarginal to consumption but acts as an incentive for connection to the system. This is indeed desirable, because consumption from public taps, the main alternative source of safe water, often is at the lower limit of the amount required for maintaining good health (table 10-11).[17] The corollary to this argument is that it is not desirable to limit water consumption from standpipes by charging high fees. Ways should be found, however, to limit water waste arising from unnecessary spillage, which may include charging a nominal fee.

Distortions in market prices of inputs to public water provision can be allowed for by shadow pricing inputs in the computation of costs. In particular, it is important to cost imported capital goods at border prices, rather than at financial cost, if tariffs are levied on such inputs.[18] More generally, shadow pricing should be employed to price all tradable inputs

Table 10-11. *Daily Water Consumption from Community Water Supplies*
(liters per capita per day)

World Health Organization region	Urban			
	House connections		Public standposts	
	Minimum	Maximum	Minimum	Maximum
Algeria, Morocco, Turkey	65	210	25	40
Africa	65	290	20	45
Central and South America	160	380	25	50
Eastern Mediterranean	95	245	30	60
Southeast Asia	75	165	25	50
Western Pacific	85	365	30	95
Average	90	280	25	58

Note: Average daily consumption rounded to nearest 5 liters.
Source: Saunders and Warford (1976: table 5-4).

directly at border prices and to price all nontradable components indirectly at border prices following, for example, the shadow pricing methodology developed by Squire and van der Tak (1975).[19] In practice, water tariff studies appear to have been limited to netting out all duties and taxes directly applying to purchased inputs, and in some cases, to using a shadow exchange rate to adjust the foreign exchange component of capital costs.

The sensitivity of water charges to shadow pricing apparently has not been widely explored. Linn (1976b) found that the application of a 20 percent shadow exchange rate premium increased AIC in Cali by only 7 percent. Also of possible importance is the discount rate applied in deriving AIC, reflecting the real rate of interest. For the case of Cali, AIC increased by approximately 10 percent when the discount rate was raised from 8 to 12 percent (Linn 1976b). In Bangkok similar results were obtained by Saunders (1976). Shadow pricing foreign exchange at a 25 percent premium raised AIC by about 6 percent, whereas raising the discount rate from 8 to 12 percent increased AIC by 30 percent. Water costs and efficient price estimates therefore do not appear to be very sensitive to the shadow pricing of any particular set of inputs, although cumulatively the failure to shadow price (or to use the correct discount rate) may well lead to substantial errors when attempts are made to set water prices at efficient levels.

One particular input which should be carefully priced at its economic cost is electric power used to provide water. Water utilities often receive electricity at special rates from the power company. Or, if electricity is internally generated, water companies often fail to cost the use of electricity in water production and transmission at the rate they could sell it to their customers. In Cali, to calculate marginal cost an upward adjustment of about 30 percent in the price of energy used for pumping was required in 1975 because of underpricing of internal use of electricity by the Cali public utility agency. This adjustment resulted in an increase in the estimated short-run marginal cost of about 13 percent (Linn 1976b).

On the output side, distortions in the price of substitutes for publicly supplied water may cause problems and result in inefficient water use; a case in point is household use of water from financially cheap but contaminated sources, such as rivers or shallow groundwater wells. The true cost of using the cheap substitute is not apparent or relevant to users, either because they are not aware of the damaging implications to their health or because the costs are borne by others because of lower levels of community health. This is, of course, directly related to the health externality discussed in earlier paragraphs, except that it is now viewed in terms of a distortion in the price of a competing product. The solution remains the same, particularly for low-income households: lifeline tariffs or subsidization of connections, and subsidized water consumption from public taps. For wealthy consumers who might feel inclined to use a private but contaminated source of water, compulsory connection to the public water system is a more appropriate solution.[20] Industrial and commercial consumers similarly should be compelled to connect to the public water system or be charged a special tax on their consumption of water if they are not connected to the public system and if the private cost of drawing water does not reflect fully the social cost. This is of particular importance where substantial use is made of scarce groundwater. The withdrawal of groundwater by one user lowers the groundwater level for other users, and then deeper wells and more pumping are required. In Bangkok, Saunders (1976) estimated that large private consumers could supply their own water at a financial cost of only about a third of the total economic cost imposed. The same author cites Mexico City, Taipei, and Tokyo among other cities for which this may be a serious consideration.

ADMINISTRATIVE CONSIDERATIONS. Administrative considerations cannot be neglected in the design of water tariff structures. A basic issue is whether or not metering is efficient. The considerable cost of metering goes beyond the mere capital cost of the meter and its installation and includes meter inspection, reading, repairs, accounting, and billing (White, Bradley, and White 1972). All of these costs need to be weighed against the benefits expected to be derived from metering: a reduction in production costs, an improved capacity to monitor water production and consumption and thus to detect sources of leakage, and reductions in costs associated with nonprice rationing when capacity constraints cause service interruptions, low pressure, and contaminated supplies.[21]

Careful analyses of the metering decision have been carried out for Lahore and Bangkok. For Lahore, where metering was uncommon,

Turvey and Warford (1974) found that to reduce production costs to the point where the costs of metering would just have been offset, water production would have to fall by 80 percent.[22] Such a reduction was judged to be unlikely, especially for small consumers, for whom metering costs weigh much more heavily relative to the cost of water consumption. It was therefore tentatively concluded that metering should not be introduced in Lahore, except for a few large industrial consumers. In contrast, Saunders (1976) used similar analyses for Bangkok, where metering was much more common, and concluded that it was likely to be justified. The main reason for the different results was that the cost of providing water in Lahore was significantly below that in Bangkok. Generally speaking, metering is usually justified if water is scarce and thus has a high cost, or if extensive treatment is required before it is safe for household use. As Saunders (1976) points out, however, it may be unwise to attempt metering for small and poor consumers even under conditions such as those in Bangkok because of the difficulty of reading and maintaining meters in slum neighborhoods; flat periodic rates may be preferable. In setting charges for unmetered connections, it is possible to reflect the different requirements for production capacity that are associated with different levels of expected consumption by linking the periodic connection fee to the pipe size of the connection. This, however, will affect only the connection decision, not the consumption decision, except insofar as it limits consumption to maximum flow levels at any time. Another way of approximating expected consumption levels without metering is to link the periodic charge to the number of taps in a house. As Turvey and Warford (1974) point out, however, there are numerous difficulties in implementing and enforcing such a pricing policy.

This set of considerations raises an essential point: efficient water tariff structures can achieve their purpose only if administered effectively. If a large percentage of all meters do not function properly, as is often the case in developing countries, tariffs based on metered consumption are not likely to be very effective. The same result holds if charges, even if properly metered, are not effectively collected.[23] Finally, if infrequent price adjustments allow inflation to erode the real value of user charges, an initially efficient charge can quickly become a considerable subsidy to water users. In Bogotá and Cartagena in the early and mid-1970s, the failure to adjust user charges for inflation led to a rapid decline in the real value of charges that was not supported by changes in the underlying real cost structure (Linn 1975, 1976c). In other cities, in contrast, regular rate adjustments were evidently feasible and prevented a similar slide in the real value of water charges (for example, Jakarta and Kingston; see Linn, Smith, and Wignjowijoto 1976 and Bougeon-Maassen and Linn 1977). One way to deal with this problem is to make regular small adjustments in water rates, say, in monthly installments. In the 1970s, this practice was increasingly applied in Colombian cities. In Cali water consumption charges were increased by 1.5 percent every month and less frequent but more sizable changes were made in the entire tariff structure in line with the financial and economic requirements of the water operations.

Public water taps present special problems for administration, not only in pricing, but also because of the difficulties encountered in preventing vandalism, wastage, and surcharges by attendants. To provide water from public taps at subsidized rates, if not free of charge, raises the problem of wastage unless an attendant is continuously posted. Attendants, however, may be costly, and they may add monopolistic (and usually illegal) surcharges. Flow-limiting devices are subject to tampering and vandalism and often lead to greater wastage if malfunctions are not quickly corrected. A reading of the discussions in Vlieger and others (1975) and Saunders and Warford (1976) concerning alternative flow-limiting devices leads one to conclude that no ideal method has yet been found. Much appears to depend on local customs and on the ability to develop community participation in and a sense of community responsibility for maintaining a well-functioning, wastage-free system of public water taps.

AN EFFICIENT STRUCTURE FOR CHARGES. A three-part water tariff is likely to be required for the efficient pricing of water. First, a consumption charge should be related to the quantity consumed and set equal to average incremental cost. AIC should be calculated for the systemwide marginal costs of operation and maintenance and of projected capital expenditures in water production and transmission. AIC represents, however, only an approximation of the truly efficient consumption price, because it only roughly balances the efficiency benefits of a highly volatile price set to equal short-run marginal cost and those of a smoother, more predictable price trajectory. A consumption charge requires metering of water use, which is likely to be appropriate in all those countries where potable water is not in abundant (and thus cheap) supply. For small residential consumers, however, particularly if only one tap is installed in a dwelling, the costs of metering may well outweigh the benefits. Second, a connection charge should be levied to reflect the marginal capital cost of connection, including meter reading, billing, and so forth. This connection charge may be a lump-sum charge upon initial connection, or it may be a fixed periodic fee. The former is probably most appropriate for the installation costs, the latter for the recurrent costs of maintaining the connection. Third, a development charge should be applied to cover the marginal cost of the distribution (reticulation) system. This charge should be prorated for each plot—whether or not it is immediately connected to the system—depending on the incremental capital costs of installing the system.

In calculating efficient charges, four refinements may be required. First of all, inter- and intraurban spatial variation in costs should be accounted for in all three types of charges. Second, seasonal variations in costs and demand should be reflected if they are significant and if meters can be carefully read at the time of transition between seasons. Third, shadow pricing may be necessary for inputs and in setting the discount rate for calculating AIC. Fourth, externalities should be allowed for by setting life-line tariffs for residential users and by compelling all large users, especially industrial and commercial enterprises, to convert to the public system.

Once an efficient system of user charges has been designed, its real level must be maintained by frequent, though mostly small, adjustments to reflect the effect of inflation and changing real costs. Moreover, effective metering and collection are necessary if the charges are to serve their purpose of encouraging the efficient use of resources. Water used at public standposts in most cases is best provided free, but care needs to be taken to encourage community initiative to prevent wastage, damage to pipes or flow-limiting devices, and illegal charges. Finally, setting price equal to AIC makes sense only if the production and investment decisions reflect least-cost conditions. Therefore, quite apart from price setting, it is essential to ensure that production and investment costs are indeed minimized for any level of projected demand.

Fiscal Considerations

One of the primary concerns of this volume is how to mobilize fiscal resources for urban development. Financial considerations are therefore of great importance in assessing alternative systems of water charges.

Self-financing urban water supply systems are very attractive for six reasons. First, there is a sense of fairness in having people pay for what they get, in having "each tub stand on its own bottom." This is particularly true in developing countries, where there is a suspicion that urban areas have an unfair advantage over rural areas and large cities over small ones when it comes to service provision. Second, self-financing avoids the need to raise revenues from other sources and the risk of the distortions in resource allocation associated with most taxes. Third, self-financing helps to avoid the need to encroach on the taxing territory of higher levels of government and thus lays a foundation for local autonomy. Fourth, self-financing avoids the need to rely on uncertain transfers from higher levels of government and thus provides greater certainty and efficiency in planning investments and in operating and maintaining waterworks. Fifth, self-financing can encourage appropriate standards in service provision because the beneficiaries' ability to pay cost-covering charges needs to be taken into account in designing investment programs. Sixth, because of the incentives for the efficient management of public utilities thought to be associated with self-financing operations, financial self-sufficiency is a guiding principle of national policy for the water sector in some developing countries and a common objective of international lending institutions.

In principle, no conflict arises between the objectives of efficiency and financial self-sufficiency if average historical costs (commonly defined to include operational and maintenance costs, debt service, depreciation, and an adequate return to capital) are below marginal cost or demand rationing price, or below AIC—if average incremental cost is taken as the guiding principle for pricing decisions. In these cases a financial surplus can be generated by charging an efficient price. The surplus can be used selectively to subsidize classes of consumers if the subsidies are efficient and equitable. In particular, life-line tariffs for small, poor consumers, subsidized connections in poor neighborhoods, and subsidized provisions of water from public taps would likely be efficient uses of surplus funds. If a water enterprise still has surplus funds after all efficient investment programs have been carried out, it may be appropriate to transfer funds from the enterprise to finance other urban services or water systems in parts of the country where financial self-sufficiency cannot be achieved.

Such transfers are not uncommon. In Cartagena funds generated from water operations have supported deficits in the operation of public markets and slaughterhouses in some years (Linn 1975). In Cali a 4 percent municipal tax on public utility operations, including the water supply, has generated resources for the general account of the municipal government (1978 World Bank data). In Jarkarta, the local water company made regular transfers to the general local government in the early 1970s (Linn, Smith, and Wignjowijoto 1976). In Nairobi, water operations have produced a cash surplus in past years; these were "borrowed" for use in the financially strapped general account of the Nairobi City Council (1978 World Bank data).

Only in Nairobi, however, were average historical costs below marginal cost or AIC and consumption charges set to approximate AIC. But life-line tariffs and subsidized consumption at public taps, which could be justified as efficient because of externalities, were not in force in Nairobi before 1978. In the other cities mentioned, the transfers out of the water account were partly, if not totally, made up by transfers into the water account from other sources. In Cartagena loan finance was used in some years to finance recurrent expenditure (Linn 1975). In Cali the water account was heavily financed from transfers out of other service accounts, especially electricity and telephones (1978 World Bank data). In Jakarta all capital works in water production were financed by national government funds and not recovered through user charges (Linn, Smith, and Wignjowijoto 1976).

These financial patterns reflect the frequently haphazard nature of intergovernment financial relations in developing countries. User charges often are set not to be efficient and financially viable but to meet short-term financing needs, which are the result of complex and confused intergovernmental financial flows. Nevertheless, these examples demonstrate that mechanisms can be set up to transfer surplus funds from water charges to other uses. Such transfer mechanisms, however, are likely to be feasible only if continuing financial surpluses are expected.

If surpluses are only the temporary result of AIC pricing during periods of capacity shortage, and are followed by deficits during periods of excess capacity, it is preferable to keep aggregate consumer bills relatively constant. This may be done by lowering the flat periodic fee to offset rises in the consumption charge before capacity expands and by raising the periodic fee after expansion when AIC is low (see figure 10-2). The flat periodic fee can then be used essentially as the balancing item to keep the water enterprise financially sound and total consumer bills relatively

Figure 10-2. *A Time Profile of the Consumption Charge and Periodic Connection Fee under a Rule Ensuring Self-Financing of the Water Supply*

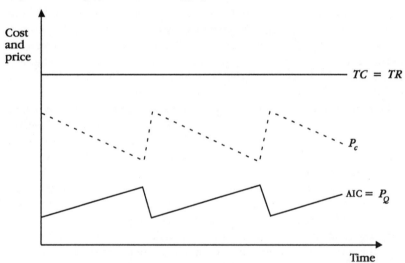

Key: AIC = average incremental cost per cubic meter of water (Q); P_Q = consumption charge per cubic meter of water (Q); P_c = periodic charge per connection (C); TC = total (financial) cost including debt service and return on invested capital; TR = total (financial) revenue.

Note: Pricing rule for P_c : $TC = TR = (\text{AIC} \times Q) + (P_c \times C)$; therefore, $P_c = [TC - (\text{AIC} \times Q)]/C$. Dimensions of variables differ; therefore, the figure is only representative of time trends. TC and TR are measured in dollars (or other monetary units); P_c is measured in dollars per connection; AIC and P_Q are measured in dollars per cubic meter of water consumed. It has been assumed for simplicity that long-run costs are constant.

steady while permitting a variable consumption charge in accordance with AIC. For this pricing rule to be efficient, the demand for connections must be highly price-inelastic. This inelasticity may be the result of an intrinsic insensitivity to price changes, which is likely for middle- and high-income consumers or if connection is compulsory. Such compulsion, however, is not likely to be effective in low-income neighborhoods.

If a rising long-run cost structure prevails—as is likely for most urban water systems because of the growing difficulty of finding plentiful, clean sources of water close by—times of surplus will tend to prevail (Saunders, Warford, and Mann 1977). Examples are Bangkok, Lima, Mexico City, and Nairobi. Falling long-run average costs for water are likely to be rare, although in Lahore plentiful groundwater has resulted in marginal costs lying below average costs but rising with increased water consumption (Turvey and Warford 1974). In this case permanently elevated fixed periodic fees would cover the deficits resulting from marginal cost pricing. More typically, marginal costs (AIC) are likely to be below average historical costs only temporarily after large expansions of the system (which may even be based on overestimates of growth in demand) cause excess capacity. This occurred during the 1970s in Bogotá and Cali (1978 World Bank data). A conflict arises between the objectives of efficiency and financial self-sufficiency, unless—as proposed above—flat periodic fees are used to ensure financial self-sufficiency by raising fees above marginal costs of connection to the point where they cover the deficit arising from a strict application of the marginal pricing rule.

Other methods of financing deficits include transfers from general municipal funds, as occurred in Bombay until 1973 (Bougeon-Maassen 1976); national government financing of major capital works, as in Jakarta during the early 1970s; and cross-subsidies from other urban services, as in Cali during the early and mid-1970s. The problem with such transfers is that they tend to become accepted policy for the long term and may be retained even when they are no longer appropriate. This is particularly true if investments are lumpy and marginal costs thus fluctuate. Efficient pricing policies during periods of capacity shortage, which would require raising prices and generating surpluses, would be inhibited because of the ingrained practice of external transfers to the water operation and political pressure to keep water bills low.

A pricing strategy for urban water supply systems which aims to balance efficiency and financial self-sufficiency therefore usually has four components. First, water operations should be financially self-sufficient. Second, a consumption charge should be set equal to AIC and vary over time with recurrent cycles of shortage and excess in capacity to produce water. Third, a flat periodic charge should be levied on water consumers to reflect recurrent connection costs. This charge would be adjusted upward to generate the financial resources required to ensure financial self-sufficiency during the periods when AIC falls below average historical

costs, and it would be adjusted downward to absorb any financial surpluses during periods of capacity shortage when AIC exceeds average
historical cost. Fourth, capital costs of development and connection
should be reflected in some combination of life-line consumption
charges, subsidized periodic fees, and connection and development
charges for the neighborhoods of low-income consumers. Consumption
from public taps would also be subsidized. For these financial subsidies
to be compatible with financial self-sufficiency, the fixed periodic charges
may be adjusted upward for consumers who do not generate any externalities, that is, middle- and higher-income residential consumers and
industrial and commercial consumers. All these consumers will likely
seek connection anyhow and consume quantities above the minimum
required for good public health.

The main features of this pricing structure are multiple prices, the
allowance for external benefits, a consumption charge set equal to AIC,
and a periodic charge which varies over time to ensure financial self-
sufficiency but does not vary with the consumption of any individual
consumer. The first two features are now commonly accepted in water
pricing in developing countries. Calculations of AIC are standard practice
in all World Bank appraisals of water projects as a measuring rod against
which to evaluate existing water tariffs. Consumption charges are not
necessarily set equal to AIC, however, usually because of considerations
of financial viability or equity. The failure to price water use efficiently
is usually accompanied by a failure to be more flexible in the use of
periodic connection fees to achieve financial (and equity) objectives.

To illustrate these pricing rules, inefficient water tariff structures may
be contrasted with efficient, financially viable structures. Table 10-12
compares estimates for AIC in Bogotá, Bombay, Cali, and Nairobi with
actual consumption charges. Bombay and Nairobi had capacity shortages,
whereas Bogotá and Cali had excess capacity. Accordingly, AIC is relatively high in Bombay and Nairobi but low in the other two. Only in
Nairobi were actual consumption charges set equal to AIC (with the exception of a life-line rate for low consumption) and fixed periodic charges
set so as to ensure financial self-sufficiency and permit subsidized water
consumption at public taps. The periodic charges were, however, quite
low (in comparison with Cali) because the high level of AIC was expected
to generate adequate financial resources. In contrast, the actual consumption charges in Bogotá and Cali were set at levels considerably
higher than AIC for most, if not all, consumers.[24] But periodic fees were
set quite low for most consumers, especially in Bogotá, in comparison
with the periodic fees which would have been required to ensure financial
self-sufficiency for water operations while charging consumers a low consumption fee equal to AIC.

The case of Bombay is somewhat more complex because of the cross-
subsidies from industrial and commercial consumers to residential con-

Table 10-12. *Water Cost and Tariff Comparisons in Four Cities*

City, year	Average incremental cost (AIC) (dollars per cubic meter)	Consumption charge as percentage of AIC		Fixed periodic charge (dollars per year)[a]	
		Residential	Industrial and commercial	Residential	Industrial and commercial
Bogotá, Colombia, 1978	0.06	90–361	108–469	2.1–4.5 (1.1–0.0)	2.5–5.6 (1.3–0.0)
Cali, Colombia, 1977	0.04	155–184	176–209	1.8–88.4 (6.6–0.2)	36.2 (—)
Bombay, India, 1978[b]	0.21	22	171	— (0.80)[c]	— (0.80)[c]
Nairobi, Kenya, 1977	0.45	70–100	70–100	1.2–21.0 (—)	1.2–21.0 (—)

— Not available.

a. Figures in parentheses show fixed periodic charge expressed as a percentage of the assessed capital value of the connected property.

b. Charges for Bombay are combined water supply and sewerage fees and taxes.

c. The tax on rental value has been translated for purposes of comparison into an equivalent tax on capital value, assuming a capitalization factor of 10 percent.

Source: World Bank estimates.

sumers. Consumption charges for industrial consumers were significantly above AIC whereas charges for commercial consumers were significantly below AIC. At the same time, residential and nonresidential consumers were charged a periodic water (and sewer) tax which was quite high in relation to the fixed periodic fees in the other three cities and probably above the recurrent costs of connection.

Neglecting for the moment any distributional and possible political or institutional considerations, there is no apparent reason why the water tariff structures in Bogotá, Bombay, and Cali could not have been adjusted to reflect the basic principles proposed above. For Bombay, this would have implied increased consumption charges for residential users, except as modified by a life-line block, and lower consumption rates for industrial and commercial consumers.[25] The periodic charges could then have been adjusted to make up for any possible shortfall in revenues, possibly by a progressively structured tax on property values.[26] For Bogotá and Cali much lower consumption charges would have been efficient, whereas the fixed periodic charges should have been increased for middle- and high-income residential consumers and for industrial and commercial consumers in order to ensure financial self-sufficiency.

Equity Considerations

Equity considerations are frequently embodied in water tariff structures in developing countries. The methods used to build redistributive effects into pricing schemes vary widely from country to country and even from city to city. The following methods are the most typical (see also table 10-5):

- Rising block rates
- User fees or periodic connection charges linked to the value of connected property
- Financing through a general property tax
- Charges that vary with the socieconomic characteristics of neighborhoods
- Higher charges for industrial and commercial consumers than residential consumers
- Cross-subsidies with other urban services
- Interregional or urban-rural cross-subsidies
- Transfer between national and local general-fund accounts
- Charges that vary according to line size or number of taps
- Subsidized consumption from public taps.

In determining the redistributive effect of a user charge, it is important to be clear about the point of reference. Here that point is an efficient pricing structure, which—in the absence of externalities—consists of marginal cost prices for the consumption, connection, and access dimensions of the service. Subsidies and taxes are defined as departures from this marginal cost pricing structure. A subsidy occurs if the actual price is set below the efficient price, and a tax is imposed if the actual price is set above the efficient price.[27] The redistributive effect has to do only with the excess (or shortfall) relative to the marginal cost price. Alternative financing instruments can then be ranked by how much of a burden of taxes they put on high-income groups and as compared with the subsidies they create for low-income groups. With these preliminaries in mind, the redistributive financing methods listed above can be compared for efficiency and difficulty of implementation.

RISING BLOCK RATES. As was pointed out above, rising block rates, and in particular life-line tariffs, may represent an efficient tariff structure if external benefits are derived from increased water consumption at low levels of consumption. Because a life-line tariff also provides cheaper water to low-income customers than a flat-rate water tariff, redistribution and efficiency do not work at cross-purposes.

If, however, block rates are designed to charge high-volume consumers more than marginal cost and low-volume consumers less than what would reflect the external benefits of their consumption, then the losses in efficiency that are incurred at both ends of the scale must be balanced against the redistributional benefits. The redistributive effect of rising block rates is, however, subject to three limitations. The first is a behavioral limitation, and the other two are related to implementation.

The first limitation is the income-elasticity of the demand for water.

In the extreme case, if water demand has a zero income-elasticity, that is, water demand does not increase with income, then rising block rates will have no systematic redistributive effect but will result in inefficient patterns of consumption. Conversely, if the demand for water is highly elastic, then there is considerable scope for redistribution through rising block charges without having to differentiate prices substantially. In practice, it appears that water demand has quite a low income-elasticity. Katzman (1977) estimated income-elasticities in the range of 0.0–0.4 for consumers in Penang, Malaysia. Hubbell (1977) found an income-elasticity of 0.36 for Nairobi; an income-elasticity of 0.30 for Cali was estimated for 1976.[28] In a cross-sectional analysis of thirty-eight cities in Africa, Asia, and Latin America, Meroz (1968) found an income-elasticity of about 0.40. These estimates are compatible with results obtained for U.S. studies of water demand, although the latter appear to show on balance a somewhat higher income-elasticity of about 0.50 (Gorman 1980). Therefore, the scope for redistribution through rising block rates without serious losses in efficiency is limited. In Kingston, it was estimated that the proportion of household income spent on water was more than twice as high for the poorest 30 percent of the population than for the richest 10 percent. This situation prevailed despite highly progressive block charges, which meant that the block consuming the most was charged five times more per unit of water than the block consuming the least (Bougeon-Maassen and Linn 1977).

The second limitation is that the per capita income of the connecting household (or households) is not the only variable influencing consumption per connection. Other variables, in particular family size and the number of families per connection, may partially or even fully offset the income effect. Katzman observed for Penang that there is a much higher correlation between family size and water consumption per family than there is between income and water consumption and found that "only 40 percent of the poorest families fall entirely into the lowest rate class, while fully 10 percent of the wealthy families fall into that class" (1977: 179). Similarly, in Cali, household income explained less than 20 percent of the variation in the quantity of water consumed per household. Household size performed about equally well as an explanatory variable. Rising block rates may therefore be more of a burden for larger rather than richer households. To the extent that household size and incomes are negatively correlated, the redistributive intent of rising block rates may be thwarted.

The third limitation is the fact that in many cities more than one household is frequently drawing water from a single residential connection. In Bombay the average number of persons per connection in 1976 was thirty (1978 World Bank data) because of the large proportion of apartment buildings and single-room tenements. To the extent that multiple-household connections are prevalent among low-income households, the redistributive effect of rising block rates may have the opposite of its intended effect.[29]

For these reasons, the scope for redistribution through rising block rates is limited. Careful consideration should be given not only to the loss in efficiency resulting from deviations in setting the consumption price equal to marginal cost but also to the often very tenuous relation between consumer income and consumption per connection.

USER FEES LINKED TO PROPERTY VALUES. As an alternative to, or in conjunction with, rising block rates, user fees have been linked directly to property values. In Bogotá in the 1970s, consumption charges varied with assessed property value and with the amount consumed. More commonly, monthly periodic fees are designed to rise with property values, as in Cali during the 1970s (table 10-13).

Linking consumption charges to property values is another way to vary consumption charges with the income of the consumer. The hypothesis is that higher-income families both consume more water and tend to live on more valuable properties.[30] The practice of stratifying consumers by property value has some apparent advantages over a rising block tariff.

Table 10-13. *Minimum Monthly Fee for Residential Water Supply in Cali, 1977*
(Colombian pesos)

Assessed property value (thousands)	Minimum monthly charge[a]	Implicit annual property tax rate (percent)[b]	Average minimum price of water per cubic meter
0–2	5.50	6.6	0.34
2–5	7.00	2.4	0.43
5–10	10.00	1.6	0.76
10–20	12.50	1.0	1.00
20–35	18.00	0.8	1.44
35–50	29.00	0.8	2.32
50–100	40.00	0.6	3.20
100–150	63.50	0.6	5.08
150–200	84.00	0.6	6.72
200–300	117.50	0.6	9.40
300–500	192.00	0.6	15.36
500–1,000	244.00	0.3	17.92
Over 1,000	269.00	0.2	21.52

a. For the minimum charge each connection obtains a minimum quanity of water at zero marginal cost. This column shows the average cost of this initial block per cubic meter of the amount of water allocated to each tariff category. For the categories of property value Col$0–5,000, this amounts to 26 cubic meters per month; for the next category, 21 cubic meters per month; for all others, 20 cubic meters per month.

b. Evaluated at the midpoint of each property value range; last category evaluated at Col$1.5 million.

Source: Empresas Municipales de Cali.

First, the relation between property value and income tends to be more elastic than the relation between water consumption and income and thus provides a better way to structure consumption charges. For example, it is accepted that the income-elasticity of housing demand, although perhaps no more than 0.5 in the short term, tends to be significantly greater than 0.5 in the long term (see chapter 5). In Cali the income-elasticity of market value of property estimated for the sample of households mentioned above was 0.6, and more than 30 percent of the variation in income could be explained by variations in households. The elasticity of market value with respect to income was higher for owner-occupants than for renters. The association between these two variables is closer for the former than for the latter, as indicated by a considerably higher correlation coefficient between market value of property and income for owner-occupants than for renters (0.49 compared with 0.09; Linn 1977b). Thus, although the use of market values of properties, rather than consumption, is a better way to discriminate between water consumers, this method for determining graduated charges nevertheless has difficulties in practice.

The market values of properties must be approximated by their appraised values, which rarely match market values because of poor assessment techniques and failure to update assessment rolls. (These problems were discussed extensively in chapter 5.) The main relevant effect of poor assessment practices is that there generally is less correlation between income and assessed property value than between income and market value. Assessment practices may also introduce biases by underassessing properties of high-income groups more than low-income groups. In Cali the correlation coefficient of income and assessed values used by the public utility company for structuring user charges was only 0.19, whereas that for market value was 0.31. As it turned out, the elasticity of market value with respect to assessed property value was only 0.40, considerably below the income-elasticity of market value.[31]

The same practical difficulties also apply if property values are used to structure progressively the periodic monthly charge for each water connection. Clearly, the progressivity of any particular rate structure is weak when the correlation between income and market value of the property is low, assuming that the charge is fully passed on to the occupant or consumer rather than being borne by the property owner.[32] Compared with rising block rates or consumption charges that rise with property value, however, progressively structured periodic charges have the advantage of being less likely to affect individual consumers' decisions and are thus less likely to cause losses of efficiency. As previously discussed in the context of the review of demand-elasticities, this assumption presumes that the connection-elasticity among middle- and high-income groups is very low or can be made to be so by making connection a compulsory requirement.

Periodic water fees which vary with property value may, however, affect the decision to invest in housing, just as a property tax on improvements may do so (see chapter 6), and this may result in a loss of efficiency. It would therefore be preferable, in principle, to link periodic charges only to land value, not to the value of land and improvements. In practice, however, this is difficult to do if land values are not appraised separately from total property value.

The redistributive effect of periodic charges depends on the progressivity of the rate structure. How one defines progressivity is important here. Take as an example the rate structure of Cali in 1977 (see table 10-13). The periodic monthly charge (in the second column of the table) is highly progressive in absolute terms. The charge for the highest rate category is almost fifty times that for the lowest. The progressivity appears even stronger in the last column of table 10-13, which shows the fixed charge expressed in terms of the average "price" paid for the basic amount of water to which the fixed monthly charge entitles the consumer.[33] The average price of water increases more than sixty-three-fold from the lowest to the highest rate category.[34] But if the fixed monthly charge is expressed as a percentage of property value, the picture looks very different (see the third column in the table). For the lowest category the implicit "tax" rate is 6.6 percent of property value. For the highest category it is only about 0.2 percent, the exact percentage depending on the base point taken for calculation in this open-ended category. This comparison is instructive because it emphasizes the need for a point of reference in discussing the distributive effect of user charges. If the monthly charge as structured in table 10-13 is compared with a flat monthly fee (reflecting recurrent connection costs) that applies equally to all consumers, then the actual rate structure in Cali is highly progressive. If, conversely, the monthly charge is compared with a proportional property tax, then the monthly fee structure appears highly regressive. Therefore, in distributive terms, the rate structure in Cali is more progressive than fixed uniform periodic fees but less progressive than a proportional property tax.

Continuing for a moment with the example of Cali, it is not surprising to find that in 1976 the payments for the fixed monthly charge, despite its apparent progressivity, declined when expressed as a percentage of income. Similarly, despite rising block rates, the ratio of consumption charge to income was found to decline. Or, to put it differently, a 10 percent increase in household income was associated with only a 5.7 percent increase in the household's payment for water services. To the extent that consumption charges are fully borne by the household, they are therefore less progressive than a proportional income tax and probably also considerably less progressive than a proportional property tax. If we remember, however, that the income-elasticity of water demand in Cali was on the order of 0.30 percent, the rising block rate structure in Cali resulted in a consumption rate considerably more progressive than a uniform consumption charge producing an equal amount of revenue.[35]

Similar results were observed by Katzman (1977) for Penang. A flat-rate consumption charge would have imposed a (somewhat) higher burden on the poor consumers than the actual rising block rates. An earmarked property tax, however, would have put a smaller burden on the poor. When expressed as a percentage of income, the effect does not appear to be large in either case: the switch from a rising block rate to a flat consumption rate reduces incomes of the poorest income group in Penang by less than 0.1 percent; the switch to (partial) property tax financing increases the incomes of the poorest by about 1.4 percent. Even when similarly redistributive pricing policies are applied to all major urban services (water, sewerage, electricity, telephones, and garbage disposal), as in Colombia, the cumulative effect on the distribution of income is not necessarily very substantial (table 10-14).

Indeed, table 10-14 reflects one of the potential hazards involved in focusing too much attention on cross-subsidization among existing consumers of a service. The effect of life-line or rising block rates and progressively structured monthly fees, which tend to encourage connection, may be counteracted by high lump-sum connection fees, which tend to discourage connection. This appears to have been the case in the early and mid-1970s in Colombia, as is reflected in the fact that in table 10-

Table 10-14. *Public Service Subsidies (Taxes) as a Percentage of Income by Population Group and Change in Gini-Coefficients, Four Cities of Colombia, 1974*

Population decile	Bogotá	Barranquilla	Cali	Medellín
0–10	0.18	—	0.20	1.3
10–20	0.40	0.12	1.90	1.6
20–30	0.34	0.92	1.50	3.1
30–40	1.95	0.61	1.40	3.7
40–50	1.47	0.26	1.10	2.4
50–60	1.18	0.22	0.80	1.9
60–70	0.70	(0.02)	(0.03)	1.5
70–80	0.24	(0.44)	(0.07)	1.2
80–90	(0.42)	(0.56)	(0.30)	(0.5)
90–100	(1.24)	(0.66)	(1.50)	(0.7)
Gini-coefficient of income distribution				
Without charges	0.5103	0.4145	0.4308	0.4593
With charges	0.5070	0.4129	0.4261	0.4533

— Not available.

Note: Figures without parentheses are subsidies; those in parentheses are taxes (negative subsidies).

Source: Linn (1983).

14 the two lowest income deciles were estimated to have benefited very little from the internal cross-subsidies since they were mostly not connected to the utilities.[36] Cali is an exception, because there the local water company had long engaged in an aggressive program of system expansion, with subsidized connections in low-income neighborhoods ensuring a near-universal effective demand for connections.[37] As a result, utility service coverage was high in Cali and the cross-subsidies on service use reached down very low in the income distribution. This serves as another reminder that the entire tariff structure of an urban service must be considered when framing a tariff policy. Again, the case of Colombia is instructive. Explicit statements of tariff policy were drawn up by the Colombian National Tariff Board for the major public utility services, but although these statements devoted much attention to the structuring of consumption charges and periodic fixed fees, no attention was given to the structuring of lump-sum connection or development charges (Linn 1980a).

In developing countries, especially for low-income groups it may matter considerably whether connection charges are levied on a lump-sum or recurrent basis. A lump-sum connection fee which needs to be paid out of savings or borrowing may present an insurmountable barrier to the poor, who have extremely limited access to capital markets. But they may well be able to afford the annuitized equivalent of the lump-sum charge by drawing on their recurrent earnings. Thus for poor consumers, a recurrent charge is virtually always preferable to an equivalent lump-sum charge.

It is of interest to note in concluding this section that since 1983 water and other utility charges in Colombia have been delinked from property values on the grounds that linkage inhibited the development of an accurate valuation of properties for property tax purposes because an increase in assessments was also directly mandated into higher user charges. In principle, of course, this would not be necessary if the autonomous urban service enterprises were willing to adjust their tariff rates downward as property assessments were increased. It should also be noted that despite the delinking of user charges from property values and express policy statements by the government aimed at improving property assessments, progress in updating property valuation had not been substantial by early 1989. One may thus hypothesize that the user charge system prevailing before 1983, which linked water (and other utility) charges to property values, was not the critical obstacle to better property valuation.

A GENERAL PROPERTY TAX. General property taxes are used to finance municipal water supply systems in some countries, especially India, sometimes in conjunction with consumption charges for metered connections (Bombay) and sometimes as the sole source of financing (Ahmadabad). Where the latter practice applies, two inefficient effects must be balanced against potentially favorable redistributive effects: first, the loss in efficiency due to the underpricing of water and (possibly) connections, and second, the disincentive to private investments in improvements of property due to the property tax.[38] The property tax is one of the more progressive local sources of revenue for financing water supply. If the tax is restricted to properties with access to the distribution network—whether or not they are actually connected—it can quite closely resemble a development charge reflecting the varying costs of development at different levels of density. To the extent that the tax is more steeply structured than the degree to which costs of development rise with rising incomes and declining densities, its net effect is likely to be quite progressive and is not likely to create strong locational or land use incentives or disincentives. The redistributive effect of a general property tax, compared with a more restrictive tax on developed areas, may be less advantageous if the undeveloped or unconnected properties are owned or inhabited mainly by low-income groups. More of the burden of a general tax than of a property tax restricted to connected customers is likely to fall on low-income groups.

Administrative difficulties apply to the property tax, as to all taxes and charges based on property values (see chapter 4). Besides the general difficulties of accurately assessing property values, there is also the problem of exemptions or other favorable assessments given to certain categories of property. Although these special provisions may be serving other fiscal goals, they may not serve the objectives of financing the water supply. For example, in Ahmadabad owner-occupied housing has been appraised at lower effective rates than rental housing. This carries over also to the property tax, which is levied to finance water charges although there appears to be no clear indication that policymakers have consciously opted for this solution as a desirable way to finance the water supply, especially because rental housing is more likely to be occupied by low-income groups than owner-occupied housing (Bahl 1975).

CHARGING BY SOCIOECONOMIC AREA. To what extent an area-specific pricing structure which is introduced for redistributive reasons conflicts with the criterion of efficiency depends on the variation of costs, if any, across space and between neighborhoods. In Nairobi the areas which could be served at lower cost were also the areas where the low-income groups were concentrated (McLure 1977). In Cali the reverse appears to have been the case (Linn 1976b). Cali may well be more representative than Nairobi, for poor neighborhoods usually are heavily concentrated in areas where land values are low due to difficult physical access (for example, on steep mountainsides) or other undesirable features (swamps, marshland, and so forth), all of which tend to be associated with particularly high costs in providing infrastructure. Nonetheless, the example of one Colombian city (Cucuta) indicates that it is possible to structure user charges according to homogeneous areas within a city, whether the differentiating principle is efficiency—to reflect accurately the geographical differences in marginal costs—or one of redistribution—to reflect accurately the differences in the standard of living. Area-specific pricing of the second type presupposes that neighborhoods are internally quite socioeconomically homogeneous. This may be more true in many Latin American cities than in Asian cities.

One further dimension of area-specific tariff structures concerns the metering decision. It was pointed out above that for small consumers, metering is not efficient unless water costs are quite high. To the extent that consumers of very small volume belong mainly to low-income groups, and these groups live clustered in relatively homogeneous neighborhoods, it may be most efficient and equitable not to meter connections in most low-income areas of a city. It would be quite difficult to meter selectively the few large consumers living in a poor residential area, and probably quite costly to read and maintain the meters.

CHARGING BY CONSUMER CATEGORY. Industrial and commercial water users are commonly charged at higher rates than residential consumers (see table 10-5), often on the grounds that this serves to improve the distributive effect of user charges. The loss in efficiency caused by charging industrial consumers higher than marginal cost prices may not be serious if the price-elasticity of demand for industrial and commercial water is particularly low, as indeed it may well be. To the extent that the industries in question have to compete in international markets (for export or input substitution), however, the high water (and other utility) charges may well negatively affect their ability to compete. Moreover, if these higher rates are used to cross-subsidize residential consumers, as was done in Bombay (see table 10-12) at rates below marginal cost, residential consumption will be inefficient. And overall, an inefficiently large demand for water may lead the water company to invest prematurely in expanding capacity.

The distributive effect of a cross-subsidy from industrial and commercial to residential users is, despite the common assumption of progressivity, not at all clear. Ultimately, the higher charge must be borne by the consumers of the firms' products, by labor, or by capital. The first of these three patterns of incidence will tend to be important if the products are nontradable beyond the local market or beyond the national market. This pattern, which is likely to be important only for such local services as hotels, restaurants, and swimming pools, will likely put most of the burden on local consumers. And given that these services are likely to be consumed mainly by better-off local inhabitants or (probably well-off) visitors—the effect of the subsidy is likely to be progressive.

If, however, the commodities are nationally but not internationally traded, and local producers have a national monopoly (as is often the case, for example, in the beverage industry, which tends to use water heavily and be highly concentrated in the large city or cities of a country), then much of the tax on this industrial use of water is exported to consumers outside the city. This may well have a regressive effect, particularly if—as in the case of beer—consumption is heavily concentrated among low-income groups and if the subsidies to residential users are not channeled specifically to aid the lowest-income groups. For internationally traded or nationally competitively produced products, the burden of the tax on industrial and commercial use of water will be shared among capital and labor, the precise distribution depending on the relative international mobility of labor and capital. To the extent that capital is more mobile than labor, particularly in the long term, the tax may fall quite heavily on labor; therefore, its distributive effect, combined with that of a subsidy for residential use of water, may be regressive.

For these reasons, the incidence of higher charges for industrial and commercial users than for residential users may not be progressive. When this fact is combined with the inefficiency of such a cross-subsidy, water pricing along these lines does not appear to be appropriate.

CROSS-SUBSIDIES WITH OTHER SERVICES. Subsidies to or from other urban services apparently are not common in developing countries.[39] Such cross-subsidies have been made in Cali, where water supply users appear to have been subsidized by telephone and electricity users (1978 World Bank data), and Cartagena, where water users have subsidized the beneficiaries of public markets and slaughterhouses (Linn 1975). In both cases the financing patterns probably had progressive distributive effects. It can be argued that power and telephone consumption in Cali are likely to exhibit a higher income-elasticity than water consumption and that therefore transfers from the former to the latter services are redistributive. In fact, the transfers were channeled mainly into extending the water (and sewerage) network to the low-income areas of the city at subsidized connection fees. This most certainly increased the redistributive effect of the transfer and was probably not associated with important losses in efficiency. In Cartagena, municipal markets and slaughterhouses served mainly the poorer segments of the urban population, whereas the tariff structure was heavily redistributive among water users (Linn 1975). The overall effect of the transfer was thus probably to provide a subsidy to low-income users of public markets and meat consumers, which was paid for by a tax on the water use of high-income groups. It is doubtful, however, that this type of cross-subsidy was more pro-poor than a policy of subsidized water connections for poor consumers.

SUBSIDIES FROM GENERAL FUND ACCOUNTS. Subsidies or transfers from general fund accounts to or from urban water users are not typically implemented for purposes of income redistribution. Nevertheless, such transfers are likely to have distributive implications when compared with the self-financing of water services.

In the case of cross-subsidies of water services with local general fund accounts, the relevant issue is the incidence of the set of local taxes which must be raised or lowered to accommodate transfers to or from the water account. If property taxes are the dominant local tax source, transfers to the water account can have progressive effects on the overall distribution of income, whereas the reverse is true for transfers from the water account; regressive effects are especially pronounced if transfers from the water account are financed by an adjustment in a flat rate water consumption fee.[40] If, however, local taxes are on balance very regressive, as might be the case with poll taxes, beer taxes, and so forth, then a transfer to the water company from the local general account could be regressive, whereas a transfer to local general account from water users could be progressive.[41] Local taxes would, however, have to be more regressive than a tax on water consumption over and above marginal cost, which is no mean feat, given the low income-elasticity of demand for water. Even if water connections are heavily biased in favor of higher-income groups, it is very likely that subsidies financed from a surcharge on use of water could be more effectively channeled to low-income groups by subsidizing investments in standposts and house connections in low-income areas than to provide tax relief to local taxpayers. On balance, therefore, it will be a rare occasion where transfers from a local water operation—financed from water prices above marginal cost—to the local general account are equitable.[42] The reverse, however, is not the case. Transfers to the water account from the general local account may well be progressive.

For transfers from the central government to urban water operations, the same general conclusions hold: because studies of national incidence show central government taxes to be more or less neutral in relation to the distribution of income, and because low-income households generally fall outside the net of most central taxes, a cross-subsidy from national taxpayers to water users would be progressive. But this progressivity is not likely to be any stronger than if there is a switch from a flat user fee to property tax financing, because property taxes on balance also tend to be neutral. For efficiency (in particular that of intermunicipal location decisions) and for reasons cited earlier in the discussion of financial considerations, however, local financing, and especially self-financing, is preferable to transfers from the central government.

REGIONAL AND URBAN-RURAL CROSS-SUBSIDIES. Water users in large and medium-size cities in developing countries often subsidize water services in small towns and rural settlements. Rural water services require considerable subsidies because of high system costs and the relatively low ability to pay of rural beneficiaries. Under such circumstances uniform regional or national tariffs, such as were found in Tunis, will yield cross-subsidies from urban to rural users (Prud'homme 1975).[43] Of course, the reverse may also occur: if urban water costs are particularly high, uniform water rates will yield a cross-subsidy for urban consumers.

If cross-subsidies from urban to rural water users are not financed by surpluses resulting from efficient pricing in urban areas but by taxes on water users over and above efficient water tariffs, they are likely to be progressive—provided that rural beneficiaries are not predominantly among the richest rural inhabitants and that the urban water tax is not primarily borne by the urban poor. These conditions imply that the rural subsidy should be devoted primarily to subsidize capital works that improve the access to rural water supplies rather than to provide subsidized prices (below short-run marginal costs) to those already enjoying access to rural water supply. In urban areas, the water tax should preferably be a progressive, fixed periodic charge.

SUBSIDIZED CONSUMPTION FROM PUBLIC TAPS. Subsidized consumption from public taps benefits the community's health. This is thus yet another case in which efficiency and equity are mutually reinforcing. Because public taps are used almost exclusively by the poor and very poor, this subsidy would be strongly progressive with little possibility for spillovers to high-income groups. The one possible caveat is that legal or illegal distribution monopolies could be set up, and water salespeople could extract high monopoly charges. This qualification aside, under most circumstances water should be provided free at public standpipes. Users of public taps should not have to pay unit charges equal to or in excess of charges for water supplied at in-house connections (as they sometimes do—see tables 10-6 and 10-7).

The capital and recurrent costs of public taps can be financed in various ways. Property taxes applied to neighborhoods with taps is one way to recover the costs, but would eliminate many of the redistributive effects. General local taxes, especially property taxes, financial surpluses derived from rising block water tariffs, or better yet, progressively structured fixed periodic fees would provide resources for financing subsidies for taps without reducing their benefits.

Of course, there is a tradeoff between subsidizing house connections and subsidizing public taps. In cities of low-income countries, large proportions of the population are often not served even by standposts within reasonable proximity to their houses, and only middle- or upper-income groups can afford to pay for subsidized house connections. Because subsidized connections in these cities benefit relatively high-income groups and reduce the resources available to provide standposts, in-house connections should not be subsidized to improve health and alleviate poverty. In contrast, in middle-income developing countries (such as many Latin American countries), in-house water connections are available to a high percentage of the population and the rest is well served by standposts. Subsidized connections for low-income households thus are a primary concern for redistribution and even public health (and therefore efficiency).

Institutional Considerations

In principle, water pricing systems can be designed to provide services that are efficient, financially viable, and equitable no matter what their institutional context. For example, urban services do not need to be integrated under a single local authority to permit cross-subsidies between services; taxes on users of one service could be earmarked for another service. Similarly, a service does not need to be under an autonomous agency to achieve financial self-sufficiency. Vertical integration of a service—one agency in charge of all aspects of service provision, including production, transmission, and distribution—is not required to introduce a pricing structure which approaches the norms of efficiency, financial viability, and equity. Regional integration of water supply services under one institution is not required to permit cross-subsidies between, say, urban and rural users. Effective pricing structures can theoretically thus be designed regardless of the institutional setting, and transfer mechanisms could ensure the desired cross-subsidies.

In practice, however, the institutional framework cannot be so easily disregarded. It has an important influence on the strategy for financing and pricing the urban water supply. Different kinds of institutions develop different objectives. The managers of a multifunctional public service agency are likely to consider the tradeoffs of integrating vertically and horizontally to provide and finance the services concerned. In contrast, the managers of an institution with only a single service function are likely to consider tradeoffs only within their narrower range of responsibility and authority. Therefore we encounter what appear to be systematic relations between institutional setting and pricing structures, although we do not have the data to quantitatively test this association. Even without such qualitative verification, however, the design of institutions should fit the goals of pricing. The remainder of this section elaborates on this issue.

HORIZONTAL INTEGRATION. Metropolitan integration of various urban services under a single service agency permits and may encourage cross-subsidization among various services. Autonomous service agencies, in particular water companies, tend to be financially self-sufficient. Cross-financing between services is not ruled out under autonomy, but it is made considerably more difficult to institute and maintain, given the focused opposition by the managers of the agency providing the net funds for transfer.

The Colombian cities shown in table 10-15 are especially interesting because of the variation of institutional arrangements within a single country. In Bogotá water and sewerage services were provided by a local financially self-sufficient water company. (The same had been the case for some years in Seoul.) Cross-subsidies or transfers between services were difficult to implement in Bogotá, as was demonstrated in an acrimonious debate between that city's local water and power companies about how to share the financial burden of the construction of a major dam which increased capacity for water and power production. In Cali, where a single agency provided water, sewerage, electricity, and telephone services, revenues from power services subsidized water operations. In Cartagena water and sewerage services were provided in conjunction with solid waste collection, markets, and slaughterhouses, with water services subsidizing the other services in some years; however, no transfers occurred from the regional power company or from the municipal telephone company to the municipal water account.

Bombay is also of interest. Until 1973 its water and sewerage functions were fully integrated with other municipal services under the chief executive officer of the Bombay municipal government, and transfers from general funds to water and sewerage services were common. (A similar situation existed in Ahmadabad.) With the introduction of a water and sewerage department with separate financial accounts, the water and sewerage services became financially self-sufficient. In Cameroon, a similar phenomenon existed on a regional basis. A central government ministry operated eight water systems in the Northwest and Southwest regions of the country, which subsidized users at substantial losses. An autonomous, financially self-sufficient national water company provided unsubsidized water services to users in most of the rest of the country.

These examples confirm that institutional autonomy goes hand in hand with pricing practices that result in financial self-sufficiency. But institutional autonomy is no guarantee of sound financial management, efficient pricing, or the absence of interagency transfers. In Bogotá, the operating expenses of the autonomous water company exceeded its operating income for many years, and the resulting recurrent deficit was financed from capital account receipts (Linn 1976a). In the late 1970s a pricing structure was designed to achieve long-term financial stability, but it did not price resources as efficiently as it might have within the constraint of financial self-sufficiency. The contrast between Bombay and Nairobi also demonstrates that the autonomy of an institution is not necessarily an incentive for more efficient pricing. Nairobi granted less autonomy to water services, but it achieved a more efficient pricing structure than did Bombay, despite its greater autonomy.

The financial self-sufficiency of urban water systems is certainly not

Table 10-15. *Institutional Setting and Financial Policies for Water Supply in Selected Cities*

City or state, year	Institutional setting	Financial and pricing policy
Cameroon		
Northwest and Southwest, 1975	National government ministry	Subsidization of water users
Rest of country, 1975	National autonomous agency	Financially self-sufficient
Bogotá, Colombia, 1973	Autonomous water and sewerage company	Financially self-sufficient
Cali, Colombia, 1978	Autonomous agency for water, sewerage, power, and telephones	Transfers from power and telephones to water; transfers from all utilities to general municipal account
Cartagena, Colombia, 1973	Autonomous agency for water, sewerage, solid waste disposal, markets, slaughterhouses, and so forth	Transfers from water account to other services provided by the agency
Ahmadabad, India, 1973	Fully integrated in general purpose local government	Transfer from general account to water
Bombay, India		
Before and including 1973	Fully integrated in general purpose local government	Transfer from general account to water
After 1973	Semiautonomous water department	Financially self-sufficient
Jakarta, Indonesia, 1973	National ministry in charge of investment in productive capacity; local autonomous agency in charge of operations and distribution	Ministry finances capital works from general revenues; local autonomous agency does not share cost or charge users accordingly, but makes small transfers to general local account
Nairobi, Kenya, 1978	Fully integrated in general purpose local government	Transfers ("borrowing") from water to general account
Seoul, Rep. of Korea, 1965–71	Semiautonomous water company	Financially self-sufficient, except for small transfers from general local government account
Korean medium-size cities, 1976	Local government agencies in charge of investment and operations, national government controls setting rates	National government has restricted rate increases
Lagos, Nigeria, 1960s	National agency for metropolitan region in charge of all water production, and for distribution in unincorporated areas of metropolitan Lagos; city council in charge of distribution within city	In Lagos city, water charges collected by Lagos City Council at below cost, payments from city council to national water agency for water purchase are negotiated and generally below cost
Tunis, Tunisia, 1974	National autonomous water company	Uniform water tariffs for entire country
Valencia, Venezuela, 1968	National government agency provides water; local government shares responsibility for setting user charges	Charges not sufficiently frequently adjusted to permit adequate service expansion

the only goal of decisions on pricing and institutional structure. Other goals, in particular equity and efficiency, may well be in serious conflict with financial self-sufficiency or institutional autonomy. In Cartagena the financial self-sufficiency of the municipal public service agency, whose main functions were water supply and sewerage services, made it unwilling to invest in a program to supply water and extend sewerage to poor areas (Linn 1975). A similar problem was observed by Vlieger and others (1975) in discussing the reluctance of autonomous water agencies to increase the number of taps which provide free or highly subsidized water. By contrast, in Cali the ability of the water agency to draw on the financial resources of the municipal power and telephone operations enabled it much more aggressively to extend water and sewerage service to poor neighborhoods.

Another consideration may be important. The creation of an autonomous water agency may leave behind an ineffectually managed, insufficiently funded municipal government. There are, moreover, problems with functional fragmentation, especially a possible lack of coordination in investment planning among otherwise interdependent agencies.

In conclusion, creating functionally and financially autonomous urban water systems is likely to encourage pricing policies which meet the goal of financial self-sufficiency. But these reforms must be placed in a broader context of reforms in urban finance to result in efficient and equitable pricing mechanisms.

VERTICAL INTEGRATION. The vertical integration of responsibility for water service has two aspects: first, the integration of responsibilities for either investment and operation or production and distribution; and second, the integration of the responsibility to provide service and set prices. In Jakarta national authorities were responsible for planning, implementing, and financing investments in water production and transmission, and the local water company operated the production facilities and the distribution network. The effect on local pricing policies was that capital costs were neglected by the local water agency because these costs did not show up in its accounts (see table 10-15). A somewhat similar sharing of responsibility occurred in the Lagos metropolitan region. The Lagos City Council distributed water in the city itself and a national government agency, the Lagos Water Supply Company, produced water for the rest of the region and distributed it in the unincorporated districts surrounding the city. The city council collected the water charges and paid the supply company an annually negotiated sum below the cost of water production (Williams and Walsh 1968).

The absence of vertical integration of production and distribution in these two cases encouraged pricing which very likely did not serve overall allocation goals. Of course, if the authority in charge of water production had charged the local distributing agencies an efficient price for the service provided in the case of Lagos, the city council would have had an incentive to pass this price along to its consumers. Similarly, if in Jakarta the national agency had been able to pass along the capital costs of building facilities to the local agency, this would have provided an incentive for the local agency to recover the full cost from beneficiaries. Therefore, although the fragmentation of responsibilities for production and distribution—or for investment and operation—does not preclude efficient, financially sound pricing, the integration of these functions is a much more effective way to encourage such pricing.

Another common kind of fragmentation is the separation of responsibility for providing water from that for setting prices. Typically, central, state, and regional government authorities intervene in local pricing decisions. For example, in Colombia the National Tariff Board, an agency of the National Planning Ministry, reviewed all proposals for changes in utility charges. It had developed guidelines and attempted to enforce these, albeit with some flexibility (Linn 1980a). Parallel to this institution, a 1979 presidential decree froze all utility prices for some months, ostensibly to help stabilize inflationary tendencies in the country.

Similar reasons account for the limits placed by central government on increases in user charges desired by local authorities in medium-size cities in Korea in some recent years (Smith and Kim 1979). A somewhat different situation was reported for Valencia (Venezuela), where a national agency was responsible for service provision but the municipal authorities were able to exert some control over the setting of tariffs. In all these cases—with the exception of the general policy guidelines for setting utility tariffs in Colombia—separation of operational responsibility and authority to control user charges have had quite detrimental effects on the ability of the operating agencies to provide services effectively. To provide the most efficient and effective service, responsibilities for operations and for setting rates should be integrated as far as possible. Central authorities may, however, want to retain the prerogative to review practices for setting rates to ensure compliance with broad criteria of performance, particularly when they provide heavy financial support or guarantees (for example, if utilities borrow funds from international agencies).

REGIONAL INTEGRATION. Regional or national integration of water service allows relatively easy transfers from one user group within the region or nation to another, for example, from urban to rural users or from large to small towns (as has been the case in Tunis; Prud'homme 1975). This may be desirable if other means of financing the expansion of rural service are not readily available. Tax instruments could be designed to extract the same resources from city dwellers as an earmarked revenue source for rural water programs, but such instruments are likely to be difficult to use.

Regional integration of water systems may be more readily feasible. But the financial and equity rationale for such integration is not the only relevant one. Regional water companies may be less responsive to the specific needs and preferences of population groups in various locations; and administration may be more effectively carried out at the city or town level. Again, however, no unequivocal advice can be given on this score; if regional redistribution through water investment and charges is a goal of water policy, a regionally integrated organization would facilitate it.

Sewerage and Drainage

Obviously, the use of potable water and the disposal of wastewater must be considered jointly. This has important implications for planning investments in water and sewer services, for organizing institutions to provide the services, and for pricing the services. For investment planning, water and sewerage services must be expanded simultaneously to avoid unsanitary disposal of wastewater and to ensure proper functioning of sewer systems.[44] For the institutional setup, the linkage between water and sewer systems implies that it is desirable to combine responsibility for them under one agency. For pricing policy, the relationship between water and sewer services implies that the marginal cost of disposing of wastewater can be charged jointly with the marginal cost of providing potable water. Moreover, in deciding whether to meter water use, the resulting cost savings in reduced water disposal should be considered together with the cost savings from reduced water provision.

There are, of course, limits to the linkage. First, leakages occur in water use; that is, not all water used is passed into the sewer system. This is especially true for lawn sprinkling and other horticultural uses, and for such industrial uses as the production of beverages. Second, the cost of wastewater disposal and treatment depends not only on the quantity of wastewater but also on the nature and degree of contamination. In particular, industrial effluents are likely to be more toxic than residential effluents. These differences need to be considered in setting sewerage tariffs.

Important linkages may exist between drain and sewer systems. Although requirements for investment in drainage vary with climatic, geographical, and geological conditions and with the additional runoff resulting from urban development, drain systems were often developed jointly with sewer systems. Newer investments tend to provide for separate sewer and drain systems (for example, in Bogotá, Cali, and Nairobi). Neighborhood drainage networks generally are constructed jointly with roads and streets.

When considering appropriate pricing strategies for sewerage and drainage, it is therefore useful to consider the following separately: first, residential sewerage pricing, which is closely related to water pricing;

second, industrial sewerage pricing, which depends more on the degree and type of contaminants than on the amount of water used; and third, the pricing of drainage services, which has no relation to water use but may be related to the development of infrastructure for sewer systems and roads.

Pricing Residential Sewerage

Table 10-16 summarizes residential sewerage tariffs in selected cities. The structure of tariffs is very similar to the structure of water tariffs in the same cities, except that development charges or earmarked property taxes and transfers from general government funds are more common for sewerage than for water.[45] The most common practice in pricing sewerage appears to be levying surcharges on water-use fees and on periodic charges unrelated to the use of water. Although not reflected in table 10-16, there is commonly also a difference between charges for connections to piped sewer systems and those for other sanitary methods of waste disposal (septic tanks, conservancy tanks, night soil collection, and so forth). In discussing charges for residential sewerage, it is useful to treat the pricing of piped sewerage separately from that of other sewer systems.

CONVENTIONAL PIPED SYSTEM. Piped sewer systems require investment, operation, and maintenance of the following components: internal plumbing in the house; connection to the neighborhood collection network; and trunk collectors. In addition, pumping and treatment facilities may be required. In all cases, minimum water consumption of 50–100 liters per capita each day is required for the use of cistern-flush toilets (World Bank 1980c: 19). As a result of these requirements, private and public costs are incurred which need to be considered when sewerage services are priced.

Some of these costs are related directly to the quantity of water used—in particular, transmission, pumping, and treatment costs. These costs can therefore be reflected in the price charged for water use, after allowing for the estimated household leakage of water not returned to the sewer system. Because investments in sewerage are, like those in water, frequently quite lumpy, the average incremental cost method is an accurate way to calculate the marginal cost of residential wastewater disposal associated with incremental water use. In Nairobi, the AIC for sewerage was 43–57 percent of the AIC of water supply in 1975 (McLure 1977), whereas in Bogotá the AIC of sewerage and water supply were approximately equal in 1978 (World Bank data). The difference is explained largely by the fact that the AIC of water production and transmission in Nairobi was more than seven times that in Bogotá during these years (see table 10-12), whereas the AIC for sewage disposal in Nairobi was only about twice that in Bogotá (McLure 1977; World Bank

1979). Although it thus appears that water production costs in general equal or exceed sewage transmission and treatment costs, the reverse relation generally applies to connection and development costs. In Nairobi the cost of connection and neighborhood collection costs for sewerage in 1975 were about 70 percent higher than the connection and reticulation costs for water (World Bank data).

As with charges for water supply, residential sewerage tariffs are structured efficiently if they reflect the marginal cost of sewage disposal through a connection fee and the marginal cost of the neighborhood collection system through a development charge. A sewer charge which varies with the quantity of water consumed can be applied only where water meters are installed. Commonly, this charge is expressed as a fixed percentage of the water fee (table 10-16). This practice is not likely to be appropriate over extended periods of time, however, because in general water supply and sewerage investments are not made at the same time and therefore do not have parallel AICs. It is more appropriate to recompute the AICs separately at regular intervals, say once a year, in line with changing investment plans and operating conditions and to set the water-use-related price accordingly for each service.

If sewerage development costs vary mainly with the density of development, a system of charges related to front-footage or lot size is most likely to reflect the marginal costs imposed by a developer's land-use and subdivision decision. Installation charges can be directly related to the cost of installing each connection.

In setting efficient sewerage tariffs, an important consideration is the benefits for a household connecting and using the sewer system. Although connection is not a necessary or sufficient condition for improving community health conditions (World Bank 1980c), the introduction of such a system, where no adequate system existed, is generally justified on this basis. These external benefits are likely to be concentrated most heavily in the immediate neighborhood but may also affect the entire urban area or region. In terms of financing, therefore, subsidizing sewage collection systems and connections is efficient, at least for low-income families who would choose not to connect at a marginal cost price. These subsidies are appropriately financed by cross-subsidies that draw on the fiscal resources of a neighborhood or an urban area rather than of an entire region or country. Property tax financing is particularly appropriate in this context. Because improvements in a neighborhood's environment are likely to be reflected to a considerable extent in higher property values, a part of the subsidies for building and connecting the sewerage network is actually paid for by the community through the resulting automatic increase in property taxes.[46] The citywide benefits are also appropriately captured by the property tax. Transfers from the national treasury for the construction of urban sewer systems in general would not be required for efficiency. Given shortages of national fiscal

Table 10-16. *Residential Sewerage Tariffs in Selected Cities*

Country and city or state, year	Development charge	Connection fee (Lump-sum or periodic)	Water-use charge	Transfers
Colombia				
Bogotá, 1979	Valorization tax for development costs; requirement that developer builds neighborhood collection systems	Periodic water charge of 30 percent	30 percent of water fee	n.a.
Cali, 1978	Front footage fee to collect costs of neighborhood collection systems; requirement that developer builds neighborhood collection system; valorization tax for trunk collectors	Periodic water charge of 60 percent	60 percent of water fee	Transfers from telephone and power accounts
Cartagena, 1973	Sewer tax of 0.4 percent on assessed capital value of all built-up properties, whether sewered or not; 0.8 percent tax on vacant lots	Periodic water charge of 50 percent	50 percent of water fee	Capital works grants from central government
Abidjan, Côte d'Ivoire, 1975	—	—	Surcharge on water fee	—
India				
Ahmadabad, 1973	Conservancy charge (surcharge on general property tax)	n.a.	n.a.	Partially financed from municipal revenues
Bombay, 1973	Property tax of 3 percent on annual rental value (ARV) of all urban connections	Sewerage tax of 4 percent on ARV of unmetered and unsewered properties	Surcharge of 50 percent on water fee for metered and sewered connections	n.a.

336

City				
Uttar Pradesh cities, 1975	—	n.a.	n.a.	Financed from municipal revenues
Kingston, Jamaica, 1975	Property tax on land within 100 yards of sewer line	n.a.	n.a.	Deficit grants from national government
Nairobi, Kenya, 1978	Development charge recovering sewer collection capital costs in development area according to plot size (payable over up to ten years at 8 percent interest)	Lump-sum connection fee; minimum periodic sewer charge	Surcharge on water fee	n.a.
Kuala Lumpur, Malaysia, 1976	—	—	Surcharge on water fee	Property tax financing
Mexico: medium-size cities, 1976	—	—	Water surcharge proposed	Mostly subsidized from municipal revenues
Lahore, Pakistan, 1976	—	Property tax for unmetered connections	Surcharge on water fee for metered connections	—
Tunis, Tunisia, 1975	—	—	n.a.	Property tax and other general municipal revenues
Yugoslavia Dubrovnic, 1975	—	—	Surcharge on water fee	n.a.
Sarajevo, 1976	—	—	Surcharge on water fee	n.a.

— Not available.
n.a. Not applicable.

resources and the fact that large cities are generally wealthier than rural areas and small towns, it would also be difficult to justify such transfers on the grounds of fiscal feasibility or equity.[47]

Considerations of equity may influence the tariff structure for sewerage services. In particular, there are likely to be cross-subsidies from wealthy to poor households through a progressive structuring of the connection and the development charges and through the application of a life-line tariff in the water-use-related sewer charge. Considerations of efficiency already will lead to a tariff structure which, because of density-related cost differentials and externalities, will impose higher charges on the wealthy than the poor areas of a city. Further accentuation of these differences is possible; in particular, connection and development charges related to property value, rather than front-footage or lot size, will tend to result in a more progressive set of sewer tariffs that will not only reflect property size but also higher land values. Another way to redistribute is to modify the area- or front-footage pricing system; for example, in Colombia valorization charges have been used to finance sewerage investments in Bogotá.[48]

The scope for financing sewerage investments through cross-subsidies or from general urban taxes is limited by the high cost of piped sewer systems. In 1980 the total annual cost per household for investing in conventional sewerage was estimated at about $400 (table 10-17), which is not only beyond the ability to pay of most families in developing countries but is also well beyond the fiscal capacity of all but the richest cities in developing countries. Financial viability, reinforced by considerations of efficient resource allocation, therefore dictates the search for lower-cost safe disposal of wastewater in many, if not all, cities of the developing world.

LOW-COST METHODS. Low-cost methods—listed in table 10-17—can provide acceptable disposal of residential wastewater in most urban areas, with the exception of the high-density downtown districts (Kalbermatten, Julius, and Gunnerson 1982). Because of the lower public expenditure requirements per household and the relative affordability of these alternative waste disposal techniques, urban governments may be able to use them to serve many more households than with conventional sewer systems.[49]

A public agency may finance its expenditures on low-cost sanitation services in various ways. One is to include the capital cost in plot-development charges for new publicly developed low-income settlements, for example, sites and services projects. Another is to charge the capital costs as an annuity that is part of the periodic fees for water supply. This practice would also cover the recurrent costs of maintenance and operation. Finally, a general or property tax is also conceivable.

If low-cost services are subsidized from tax revenues, a tradeoff will

Table 10-17. *Total Annual Cost per Household and Affordability of Alternative Sanitation Technologies, 1980*

Technology	Mean cost (1978 dollars)	Percentage of income of average low-income household[a]
Low-cost		
Pour-flush toilet	18.7	2
Pit latrine	28.5	3
Communal toilet	34.0	9
Vacuum-truck cartage[b]	37.5	4
Low-cost septic tank[b]	51.6	6
Composting toilet	55.0	10
Bucket cartage	64.9	6
Medium-cost		
Sewered aquaprivy[b]	159.2	11
Aquaprivy	168.0	16
Japanese vacuum-truck cartage	187.7	15
High-cost		
Septic tank[b]	369.2	29
Sewerage[b]	400.3	26

Note: Costs include appropriate shadow prices for unskilled labor, foreign exchange, and capital.
a. Assuming average annual per capita income of $180 and six persons per household.
b. Suitable for urban areas.
Source: Linn (1983), based on Kalbermatten, Julius, and Gunnerson (1982, tables 3-1 and 3-11).

have to be made between financial viability and replicability on the one hand and efficiency and equity on the other. For efficiency, there would very likely need to be some subsidy on the grounds of the external health benefits if poor households are not willing to pay the full cost. Equity also would favor a subsidy because the benefits would mainly reach low-income groups. Property tax financing may be an appropriate intermediate route if newly serviced properties are revalued to reflect the increase in value resulting from the improvement. The direct beneficiaries will bear some of the cost of the project through higher property tax payments, whereas the remainder of the financing will be drawn from the other urban residents roughly in proportion to their incomes. If, however, full recovery of the cost from the immediate beneficiaries is selected to ensure the replicability of the investments, then at a minimum this policy should also apply to those sections of the city which are served by piped systems. It would not be financially viable, efficient, or equitable to require low-income households to pay for low-cost systems while high-cost sewerage is financed from general tax revenues.

Pricing Industrial Sewerage

Small industrial or commercial sewerage connections are probably best treated like residential connections, unless there is reason to suspect that large amounts of pollution or noxious matter are being discharged into the general sewer system. In contrast, medium-size and large industrial enterprises which emit substantial quantities of effluent should be subjected to careful scrutiny. Consideration should be given to the possibility of measuring effluents, either regularly through metering or intermittently through sampling, and of pricing effluent according to its quantity and strength. A crucial aspect of this consideration is the costs imposed by the industrial polluter. These include the cost to the public of treating effluent either in the same city or further downstream, the cost of lost opportunities for downstream fishing, recreation, and so forth, and the cost of health and other environmental hazards.[50] These costs will vary with the quantity of effluent and the amount of pollutants such as BOD (biochemical oxygen demand), phosphorous, nitrogen, and other suspended solids that it contains.

The cost of metering or sampling must then be compared with the benefits of any reduction in pollution achievable through pricing effluent. Industrial pollution seems to be quite elastic with respect to charging systems (Bird 1976b; U.S. Department of the Interior 1969). If marginal costs of pollution—in particular downstream treatment or economic losses—are clearly identifiable, measuring and pricing the treatment of pollution for large industrial polluters are appropriate. Alternative ways of attempting to limit the detrimental effect of industrial pollution (for example, regulating pollution and subsidizing investments in controlling pollution) have been shown to be less effective and efficient than a system of effluent charges.

One advantage of charges on pollution is that they encourage industrial polluters to install their own control devices, thus reducing the need for public spending. If they do not provide their own control devices, the effluent charges provide a financial resource for making the necessary expenditure.

Financing Drainage Systems

The need for drainage is generally not linked to residential or industrial water use but to the runoff of rainwater. This runoff in turn is a function of physical factors, such as climate, geography, and geology, and of factors related to urbanization, in particular the density of development. The higher the density, the greater the runoff and therefore the greater the need for and cost of drainage canals per hectare; but the lower the cost per household. In setting charges for investments in and maintenance of drainage, these cost relations must be borne in mind.

One method for allocating drainage costs approximately in line with marginal costs is to subdivide the city into relatively homogeneous drainage areas according to density and the need for drainage—for example, swampy, low-lying areas are likely to involve more costly drainage works—and to compute drainage service costs per hectare for each area.

The marginal cost of drainage per lot may then be approximated by a charge distributing the total area cost according to the front-footage or area of each lot. This type of charge would give developers the marginal drainage cost of their development decision in terms of location and density. This approach would be efficient and could easily be levied along with development charges for other works carried out simultaneously. General or property tax financing would share the financial burden more widely and might be more equitable, provided the beneficiaries of the drainage works are in low-income groups. In determining the extent to which low-income groups actually benefit, it is important to consider the ownership of the land which is being better served—and thus having its value improved—as a result of the drainage system. Although low-income groups may occupy the affected areas, high-income landowners may effectively reap the benefits from increases in rents and land values. A development charge thus may be more progressive than a general tax or property tax.

Summary

The proper pricing of water supply and sewerage in urban areas of developing countries is of importance not only for the goal of financial viability but also for those of efficiency, equity, and administrative viability. Five general rules are:

- First, consider the design of an efficient pricing structure. Then modify this preliminary structure in a way that pursues the other goals with the least possible losses in efficiency.
- Second, to design an efficient pricing structure, estimate the marginal or incremental costs of providing a service, adjusted to reflect externalities and apply shadow prices if market prices are distorted.
- Third, in designing an efficient pricing structure, consider the entire structure of service charges—development, connection, and user fees. When a departure from efficient pricing appears desirable for reasons of financial viability or equity, that part of the tariff structure should be selected where private demand response (elasticity) is likely to be least.
- Fourth, regularly update the tariff structure to reflect changes in the general level of prices caused by inflation as well as changes in the underlying cost structure of the service. During a period of inflation a simple monthly adjustment may be made to keep tariffs approximately unchanged in real terms. This could be supplemented by more in-depth reviews of the structure of real tariffs at less frequent intervals, say, once a year.
- Fifth, collect water and sewerage tariffs effectively from all users. Compare costs of administration and collection against expected benefits from service charges when selecting a particular method of charging, for example, metering.

The remainder of this section briefly summarizes this chapter by out-lining a framework for tariff structures for urban water, sewerage, and drainage services for developing countries. The framework leaves con-siderable flexibility to permit necessary adjustments in line with the con-ditions prevailing in any particular country or city.

Water Supply

The first decision to be made in designing a system to supply water is whether to meter consumers. The reduction in the cost of providing and disposing of water must be measured against the cost of metering. For large consumers, in particular large industrial consumers, metering is almost always efficient; for small consumers, in particular households in poor areas of a city, it is usually not.

For metered residential users, a three-tiered charging system is likely to be efficient. First, a use-related charge should be set equal to the average incremental cost of incremental water production and transmis-sion. This charge will, however, have a life-line tariff for the initial con-sumption block equivalent to a daily consumption of 20–40 liters per capita. The charge may vary across areas within the city or across seasons if there are sufficiently strong cost differences. It also should vary over time to reflect changing levels of AIC as a system moves from excess capacity to a shortage of capacity and back to excess capacity in line with its investment cycle.

Second, residential water users should be charged a periodic fee that does not vary with water use. For low-income consumers this charge should be set at or below the sum of marginal recurrent costs associated with a connection (meter maintenance and reading, billing, and so forth) and the annuitized cost of installing the connection. The extent of the subsidy to low-income households depends on the strength of the re-distributive goal and on whether an internal cross-subsidy is possible. It also depends on alternative claims on the financial resources—especially for standposts. To generate the financial resources required to permit cross-subsidies—such as for standposts—the periodic connection fee for middle- and high-income consumers should be set at or above the mar-ginal recurrent costs of connection. This will permit cross-subsidies and maintain the overall financial self-sufficiency of the water operations as the use-related charge varies over time with changes in AIC. Installation costs could be charged to high-income groups on a lump-sum basis, pos-sibly with brief financing periods at the market rate of interest.

Third, a one-time development fee should be designed to recoup the capital cost of the retriculation network in proportion to the front-footages of privately subdivided properties. (This fee can be avoided if private developers are required to install this network themselves.) In areas of predominantly low-income property owners it may be equitable to reduce the fee below cost and impose higher connection charges on high-income owners. A way must then be found to distinguish owners according to income. If property valuation systems are accurate, a proportional property tax on residential lots with water connections could work. This tax would have to be varied over time to reflect changes in the use-related fee. If property valuation is inaccurate, differential connection fees could be charged in different parts of the city. Rising block rates—except for the life-line—would generally not work because the relation between consumption per connection and the per capita incomes of consumers is limited and because the use-related fees may be inefficient.

For unmetered residential consumers, a proportional tax on property or land would be equitable. Fees might also be charged according to the size of the pipe connecting the lot to the distribution network. This charge would be set to ensure the financial self-sufficiency of the water operation and would allow for the revenue from development charges.

Consumption at public taps should be free. The taps must, however, be supervised to avoid water wastage. The funds to operate the taps should first come from water users with individual connections. General tax revenues should only be used if cross-subsidies among water users are ruled out for political reasons. Therefore, there is in effect a hierarchy of uses of funds that are extracted from high-income users for purposes of cross-subsidy. These subsidies should first go toward installing taps and supplying free water from them. Once the need for the taps has been fully satisfied, the cross-subsidies can be extended to individual households with connections. The reason for this sequence is that the households without access to even taps are the poorest households, while tap users are the poorest consumers. Subsidization of taps and of water consumption at them is therefore equitable and has very little, if any, leakages to middle- or high-income beneficiaries.[51] What is more, the benefits for public health of the increases in consumption from subsidized taps are likely to exceed those from subsidized in-house connections.

Industrial and commercial consumers should be charged a use-related price equal to AIC. Connection and development fees can be set for the high-income residential consumers, provided the charges above costs are not passed on—especially to low-income consumers or wage earners. Beer and other popular beverage industries require particular caution on this score.

This proposed tariff structure should lead to self-financing of water supply operations with a minimal loss in efficiency and with attention to redistribution. It would probably be implemented most easily by a vertically integrated water authority operating autonomously from other service agencies. Local and national authorities should merely oversee the broad adherence to the basic pricing—and investment—principles outlined above. Autonomy and vertical integration are not necessary preconditions for implementing this structure; in their absence, however, special efforts would have to be made to ensure that water operations are self-financing and that all relevant costs have been considered in setting charges.

Sewerage

Three types of users of sewerage services must be distinguished: residential users connected to a conventional piped sewer system, households which employ low-cost alternative sewage disposal methods, and industrial users.

For residential users of piped systems who have water meters, a feasible tariff structure should be parallel to that for water and should have the following elements:

- A water-use-related charge equal to the AIC of sewage transmission and treatment, and of any additional downstream costs imposed on other individuals
- A periodic fee unrelated to water use reflecting marginal connection costs but adjusted for income distribution and financial considerations much as water fees would be
- In high-income areas, a development charge levied on a front-foot basis to recover the costs of the collection network
- In low-income areas, a local property or general tax to finance the system.

Unmetered residential water users would be charged a periodic fee (perhaps linked to property value), coupled with a development charge for metered users.

Residential users of low-cost sewage systems (in contrast to high-cost, piped systems) should be charged the actual cost as part of a development fee for general upgradings, or—if local fiscal capacity permits—should be subsidized by a general property tax to finance the expansion of these systems. As with water, there is a hierarchy of subsidization: connection to piped sewer systems should not be subsidized until all households not connected to piped systems are served by safe, low-cost methods.

Large industrial enterprises which generate large quantities of polluted wastewater or highly toxic effluents should be charged fees for the costs of their pollution. These fees, which are preferable to other measures of pollution control, require estimation of costs and repeated measurement of effluent quantity and strength.

Given the close linkage between the two services, it is most appropriate to combine the provision of and pricing of water and sewerage in one agency. Provision and pricing by separate agencies seriously complicate the development and maintenance of efficient and equitable pricing policies.

Drainage

Front-footage charges should be levied to recover the cost of neighborhood drainage works. They can be levied jointly with other development charges for water, sewerage, or road construction. Poor neighborhoods should be charged a general property tax to finance drainage works if local financial resources permit. Property tax financing can also be used to finance the construction of large canals to better drain an entire city, and for the maintenance cost of drainage systems.

11 Charging for Other Urban Services

THIS CHAPTER ANALYZES the pricing of electricity, telephone services, solid waste collection, bus service, and housing. The last section reviews two general development charges, land readjustment and valorization.

The discussion does not cover such other important urban services as health, education, fire and police protection, markets, slaughterhouses, and cemeteries. User charges, although they can help finance some of these services, tend to make a smaller contribution because of externalities and distributional considerations. For these services, it is more useful to rely on the overall system of financing, including local taxes, charges, and intergovernmental grants. An additional complicating factor is that many of these services, especially health, education, and police protection, are controlled by national or provincial authorities. Pricing for them requires considerations that go well beyond urban government finance.[1]

As in the preceding chapters, the discussion here applies pricing and financing principles to selected public services in the light of experiences in developing countries. Complementary policy issues, such as the role of the public sector and allocation and management decisions for investment and recurrent expenditure, are treated only in passing. See Linn (1983) for a more comprehensive treatment of these issues.

Electricity and Telephone Services

Urban governments in developing countries have little if any responsibility for electric power and telephone services, which are usually supplied by national or regional public agencies. It has been seen as desirable to centralize these services because of the savings in costs to the systems of building nationwide interconnections, planning investments, standardizing service components, managing scarce technical human resources, and dealing with foreign suppliers of advanced technical hardware and financiers.[2] Centralization also permits urban-rural cross-subsidies—an important consideration, because customer service costs tend to be significantly higher in rural than in urban areas, whereas the capacity to pay of the average rural resident is considerably lower than that of the average urban resident (World Bank 1975b).

Arguments to decentralize power and telephone services are less frequent and less convincing than in the case of other services. In some countries, however, urban agencies are involved in providing power and telephone services. For power, a national or regional agency typically provides bulk supply and local agencies are responsible for distribution. For telephones, local agencies typically are in charge of the local telephone network and service. If such local agencies exist, the pricing of services is part of the overall problem of urban finance and can be an important issue for revenue. More and more, the privatization of power and telephone system components and agencies has been identified as an option to improve the efficiency and reduce the fiscal burden of these public utilities (World Bank 1988: chapter 8).

Pricing Electricity

The organization and pricing of power service in selected developing countries and cities are surveyed in table 11-1. Although dated, the patterns shown are representative of the arrangements found in developing countries, which cover a wide spectrum from (a) entirely local responsibility for generation, transmission, and distribution in Bogotá, through (b) regional generation and transmission but local distribution in Bombay and Cali, through (c) regional generation, transmission, and distribution in Cartagena, to (d) entirely national responsibility in Seoul and Tunis.

Service charges for residential consumers of electricity typically consist of so-called energy charges, that is, a rate per kilowatt-hour which commonly rises in blocks with the quantity of power consumed. Only limited data are available on residential connection fees, but the flat minimum monthly charges in some cities act as a recurrent connection or access charge. For industrial and commercial consumers, electricity tariffs usually consist of flat energy rates either in the middle or upper range of residential energy charges, supplemented either by capacity-related or peak and off-peak tariffs. Capacity charges are rates per kilowatt of installed capacity. Peak load pricing is achieved by charging higher energy rates during hours of high system demand. Regional or nationwide uniform tariff policies are usually encountered if electricity is distributed by a regional or national agency. Such a policy generally leads to an implicit system of cross-subsidies from low-cost urban to high-cost rural users. Other cross-subsidies also are quite frequent. Large-quantity residential consumers tend to subsidize small residential users because of rising block rates, and industrial and commercial users tend to subsidize residential users. In Cali there have been subsidies from urban power to water (and sewerage) service users.

The sample of power tariff systems shown in table 11-1 does not necessarily represent the full range of tariff structures in developing countries, but it serves as a reference point in the following discussion of electricity pricing. As with water and sewerage pricing in the preceding chapter, we will first consider the main considerations for deciding on

Table 11-1. *Tariff Structure of Electric Power in Selected Countries and Cities*

| Country, city, and year | Service responsibility | | Structure of residential charges | | | Industrial and commercial charges | Load pricing | Tariff policies | Cross-subsidies |
	Generation and transmission	Distribution	Capacity charge	Energy charge	Connection charge				
Colombia Bogotá, 1978	Local	Local	No	Rising block rates	Flat minimum monthly charge	Flat energy rates, higher than residential	Yes, for industrial users	No	Industrial and commercial, residential, large and small consumers
Cali, 1975	Regional	Local	No	Rising block rates	Flat minimum monthly charge	Flat energy rates, in middle level of residential rates; plus capacity charge for industry	No	—	Industrial and commercial, residential, large and small consumers, electricity and water

Cartagena, 1973	Regional	Regional	No	Rising block rates	—	Flat energy rate, higher than residential for commercial, lower for industrial (plus capacity charge)	No	Equal regional prices	Industrial and commercial, residential, large and small consumers
India Bombay, 1973	Regional	Local	No	Flat rate	Meter rental fee	Flat energy rate higher than residential rate, plus capacity charge	No	—	Industrial and commercial, residential
Korea, Rep. of Seoul, 1976	National	National	No	Rising block rates	—	Declining block energy charge plus capacity charge	No	Equal rates nationwide	—
Tunisia Tunis, 1974	National	National	Yes	Declining blocks	—	Lower rate for medium than for low voltage	Yes, for medium voltage	Equal rates nationwide	Urban and rural

— Not available.

efficient power tariffs. Then we will consider equity, financial viability, and institutional options.

EFFICIENCY. Electricity demand tends to be quite price-elastic, judging at least from estimates of demand functions in the United States. According to Halvorsen (1975) the long-run price-elasticity of demand for electric power in the United States is approximately unity for residential users and significantly greater than unity for industrial users. The case for the efficiency of marginal cost pricing is thus quite strong, because the welfare losses from deviations from the efficient price can be quite substantial for price-elasticities in this range.

The cost structure of electric power is dominated by significant and lumpy capital costs (capacity costs), which are usually incurred in generating power and transmitting it to the area of consumption (Munasinghe 1979). Marginal operating costs of energy generation depend very much on the type of generating capacity. For hydropower these costs are likely to be low or negligible, particularly if an ample water supply is available. In contrast, for thermal power stations the marginal energy cost will be substantial largely because of the cost of fuel. In a mixed hydrothermal system, the thermal plant is typically used to satisfy marginal changes in customer demand; hence the marginal energy cost of the thermal plant represents the marginal energy cost for the entire system. The lower marginal costs of the hydropower plant are inframarginal to the system as a whole and thus irrelevant for efficient pricing. Also important in the cost structure are a number of consumer costs. These include the one-time cost of installing each consumer's power hookup and meter and recurrent costs of meter reading, billing, and related administrative tasks. Finally, there are the capital costs of developing the distribution network for each service area.

As is typical for public utility pricing, the pricing of capacity costs creates the greatest analytical difficulties because of the lumpiness of the investment pattern. Long-run marginal cost pricing has been found efficient for electric power. The long-run marginal cost here is defined as the cost of "advancing the commissioning date of future plant or inserting new units such as gas turbines or peaking hydro plants" (Munasinghe 1979: 28). For transmission and distribution capacity costs, an average incremental cost concept similar to the one described for the water and sewerage sector in the preceding chapter may be used (Munasinghe 1979: 30).

Increases in power generating, transmission, and distribution capacity are usually caused by increases in peak period demand, and therefore the costs of these capacity increases should be reflected only in the tariffs charged to peak consumers. This can be done either on the basis of the maximum kilowatt demand imposed by each user on the system during the system's peak period or on the basis of the kilowatt-hours consumed during system peak hours. Both approaches signal to the user the variable marginal costs of using the system during peak and off-peak periods and are an incentive to utilize the system more efficiently. But a general capacity charge not linked to maximum peak period demand is only a second-best peak-load pricing instrument for electricity because it penalizes capacity installation irrespective of whether or not it is utilized during peak periods. Peak-load pricing for industrial consumers in Bogotá and for medium-voltage consumers in Tunis conformed to the first-best pricing principle, whereas the general capacity charges in the other cities were second best (table 11-1). Of course, first-best peak-load pricing requires time-dependent metering devices likely to be justifiable only for relatively large consumers, in particular, industrial consumers.[3]

Another factor which needs to be considered in the context of capacity cost estimates is the difference in distribution costs for high-, medium-, and low-voltage consumers. Voltage reductions require investments in substation capacity whose incremental capital costs need to be computed and charged to the appropriate consumer group. The lower the voltage, therefore, the higher the cost of power distribution. Because residential users typically have the lowest voltage requirements, their capacity cost is highest. The common practice of charging industrial users more than residential users is therefore inefficient; rather, the reverse would be required.[4]

Higher rates for low-voltage users should not be confused with declining block rates which have been common in the United States and less common in developing countries. These rates are lower per kilowatt-hour at given voltage levels. A higher rate per kilowatt-hour for one small initial consumption block is in essence identical to a fixed recurrent connection charge, if all consumers can be expected to exceed the initial high rate block. Further rate decreases in declining blocks are, however, not generally efficient because at a given voltage level marginal costs across consumers are not likely to differ according to quantity of energy consumed. In fact a perverse pattern is set up for each consumer, as individual peak consumption is encouraged rather than discouraged. If individual peaks are coincident with system peaks, a reverse peak-load pricing system is thus employed. Finally, declining block rates run counter to common social objectives in power pricing, which will be further discussed below.

Two other aspects must often be considered in calculating efficient power pricing. The first is seasonality in capacity and energy costs. For example, power tariffs should fluctuate if hydropower supply is reduced during dry as compared with wet seasons, and power demand is exceptionally high because of air conditioner usage during the dry (or hot) season. Second, as with water supply, shadow pricing of inputs is appropriate, and distortions in the prices of competing energy products must be considered. If, for example, a subsidy is applied to kerosene as a means of subsidizing energy use of low-income households, then it would likely be appropriate also to provide electric power at a tariff below marginal cost to the same consumer groups in order to avoid inefficient biases in the selection of different energy sources. These issues are discussed in greater detail in Munasinghe and Warford (1978) and Munasinghe (1979).

By way of example of what are likely to be representative cost structures, data for the cities of Bogotá, Cali, and Medellín in Colombia are of interest. Table 11-2 summarizes the results of four cost studies carried out in 1979 by the power companies in each of these three cities and one by the Colombian national power interconnection company. The structure of costs in each city fell into two broad components: energy costs and capacity costs. Energy costs were about 50 percent higher in the dry than in the wet season, increased slightly with declining voltage, and, during the wet season, were approximately 20 percent higher during peak than off-peak hours. Capacity costs apply only to peak period demand. They were significantly above energy costs—while high-voltage energy costs were only on the order of 3 cents per kilowatt-hour, capacity costs were on the order of 1–2 dollars per kilowatt-hour. In contrast to energy costs, capacity costs varied quite extensively with voltage level: low-voltage capacity costs typically were 50 percent or more than high-voltage costs. Shadow pricing (not shown in table 11-2) increased energy costs 2.4–2.7 times above the levels shown in table 11-2, mainly because of the domestic underpricing of fossil fuel input at the time of measurement.

In summary, a set of efficient power tariffs for large (especially industrial) users has these components: an energy charge per kilowatt-hour reflecting the short-run marginal cost of energy generation, possibly varying by season and between peak and off-peak hours; a capacity charge per kilowatt-hour of consumption or per kilowatt of maximum demand during system peak periods; and a fixed monthly fee reflecting recurrent connection (consumer) costs and a lump-sum connection fee reflecting the capital costs of installation. Finally, it may be appropriate to charge a development fee for industrial lots, for example, in an industrial park whose lots are not immediately connected to the system network but may be at the time of development. Because time-dependent metering is not likely to be cost-effective for most small (especially residential) consumers, a simple energy charge per kilowatt-hour of consumption is appropriate. This charge should be derived as a weighted average of peak capacity energy costs and off-peak energy costs and allow for the price-elasticity of demand as well as the amount demanded during each period. To determine an optimal charge, the daily load factor of different types of small consumers and the elasticity of demand at peak and off-peak periods need to be estimated. Charges should also be levied on the residential consumer for connection costs and—possibly—on the developer of housing for the capital costs of the distribution lines to residences.

Table 11-2. *Summary of Long-Run Marginal Cost Estimates for Three Colombian Cities, 1979*
(U.S. cents per kilowatt-hour)

Voltage level (kilovolts)	Dry season (January–June) Energy cost			Wet season (July–December) Peak energy cost			Off-peak energy cost			All seasons Peak capacity cost		
	Bogotá	Medellín	Cali	Bogotá	Medellín	Cali	Bogotá	Medellín	Cali	Bogotá	Medellín	Cali
115	2.7	2.5	2.5	1.8	1.7	1.7	1.5	1.4	1.4	148.7	118.9	115.3
34.5	2.7	2.5	2.6	1.8	1.7	1.7	1.6	1.5	1.5	183.0	131.3	131.2
13.2	—	2.6	2.7	—	1.7	1.8	—	1.5	1.5	—	182.5	132.7
Secondary distribution[a]	—	2.7	—	—	1.8	—	—	1.6	—	—	—	211.4
Low voltage												
Urban	2.8	2.7	2.8	1.9	1.8	1.9	1.6	1.6	1.6	222.3	198.9	144.0
Rural	3.1	—	—	2.1	—	—	1.8	—	—	3,034.7	—	—

— Not available.

Note: January 1979 prices, without shadow pricing; preliminary estimates.

a. Underground urban network.

Sources: Compiled by Colin J. Warren on the basis of reports by F. Ochoa, Orlando Solano, Carlos Velez, and Cesar Molinares presented at the Second Latin American and Caribbean Power Seminar, Brasília, Brazil, July 27–August 2, 1980.

NONECONOMIC GOALS AND CONSTRAINTS. With rapidly growing demand for electricity service and a general pattern of long-run rising costs in the sector, marginal cost pricing will generally lead to financial surpluses in the urban power sector (Munasinghe 1979).[5] In Bogotá the average tariff (which provided approximate financial balance) as of December 1979 was 3.12 cents per kilowatt-hour as compared with (average) marginal cost of 6.05 cents per kilowatt-hour, or 9.47 cents per kilowatt-hour when shadow pricing inputs (especially fossil fuels); in Medellín an average tariff of 2.10 cents per kilowatt-hour was in line with financial requirements, but was well below an (average) marginal cost of 4.88 cents per kilowatt-hour. In Thailand it was found that the national power company would have made large profits had it applied marginal cost pricing, for two reasons. "One reason is that the marginal cost of energy is an oil cost, while much of the energy comes from hydroelectric plants. The other reason is that the marginal cost of new oil capacity is higher than the average accounting cost of existing capacity, which was acquired at a lower price" (Anderson and Turvey 1974). Thus there is no inherent conflict between efficiency and financial goals, except that past emphasis on financial self-sufficiency has sometimes led to power prices significantly below marginal costs. Conversely, there are various ways to absorb the surplus resulting from efficient power pricing: to levy taxes on the power company or to require general budgetary contributions, as, for example, in Bombay and Cali during the 1970s (see table 11-1).[6]

Another way to use the financial surplus from power operations is to subsidize poor power consumers. This can be done in two ways. One is to charge, as is common in developing countries, rising block rates and, in particular, life-line rates. An initial low rate consumption block is followed by a marginal cost rate at consumption levels exceeding the life-line block.[7] A second method is to subsidize the capital and recurrent costs in low-income areas. If the life-line block is set so that even the poorest consumers—once connected—consume more than the minimum amount, the subsidy becomes inframarginal and acts essentially as a subsidy to connection on consumer costs. This is as it should be, because it is equitable to encourage the poorest population groups, which are not connected to the system, to get connected. Gains in equity from subsidizing the consumption of poor residential consumers are not likely to be great, because power charges tend to be a relatively small share of total household expenditure. But the poor may benefit substantially from the consumers' surplus which may be derived from being connected to the system in the first place.

This principle of equitable cross-subsidization also applies to urban-rural cross-subsidies, which are common in regionally or nationally integrated systems. Table 11-2 shows an estimate of rural as compared with urban supply costs in Bogotá that reflects the considerable cost differentials.[8] Geographically uniform pricing thus can result in considerable cross-subsidization, typically running from wealthy urban to poor rural consumers. Because average costs are likely to be below marginal costs in urban systems but above them in rural systems, this is an efficient method of redistribution.

Yet other ways have been found to deal with power service surpluses. In Cali they have been used in past years to finance water and sewerage extensions at subsidized rates in poor neighborhoods. In Bombay they have financed deficits in the operations of the public municipal bus service. These examples underline the importance of the institutional framework in which service provision and pricing take place. Local autonomy of the municipal power company, as in Bogotá, tends to encourage financial self-sufficiency at the expense of efficient pricing and limits the scope for efficient cross-subsidization. Locally integrated provision of urban services provides scope for interservice cross-subsidies but not for urban-rural subsidies, which national and regional integration fosters. A mixed system, as in Bangkok, Bombay, and Cali, in which national or regional authorities generate electricity and supply it in bulk to municipal utility companies in charge of distribution, may well provide an optimal degree of flexibility. The national or regional power company should set urban bulk prices at efficient levels, which commonly would mean that it would reap considerable financial surpluses which could be utilized to subsidize rural supply agencies. Urban power authorities can also use efficient pricing of power distribution to generate financial surpluses. These surpluses can be used for internal cross-subsidization to benefit low-income power consumers, subsidize other urban services, or contribute to general local government. In fact, however, the scope for such redistribution at the city level is likely to be limited because it is the marginal cost of power generation, rather than of distribution, which tends to exceed average cost and thus generates most of the financial surplus. This, of course, would be skimmed off by the national or regional power-generating agency.

The introduction of an efficient power tariff system may require considerable changes in the existing structure of power tariffs and substantial increases in the average level of tariffs. These changes are likely to be difficult to introduce in a single step and may require gradual adjustment. Alternatively, power tariffs might be revised as part of a comprehensive reform of the urban financing system. In this case, some of the fiscal effects of higher power tariffs could be offset by reducing public revenues from other sources. In any case, major tariff reforms in this, as in any other urban service sector, need to be carefully analyzed, planned, and supported by public relations efforts. What is more, in inflationary periods power tariffs need to be continuously kept in line with general price increases through regular, small, and virtually automatic tariff adjustments which do not require major political decisions.[9] To satisfy the requirements of political control—and to check on the adjustment mechanism—the tariff structure should be regularly reviewed in the light of changed economic, social, and political conditions.

Pricing Telephone Service

Telephone service is important to urban development since it permits rapid communication over short or long distances at low cost.[10] In only a few countries, however, is this service provided by local agencies. One is Colombia, where fifty agencies are responsible for local telephone operations in as many municipalities. The issue of how to charge for urban telephone service therefore arises more broadly as a question of how to manage urban public service and—in a few countries—how to finance urban government.

Urban telephone service in developing countries is commonly characterized by excess demand for new telephone lines (also referred to as direct exchange lines) and congested exchanges for existing lines during peak hours. This is quite different from the industrial countries, in which at prevailing telephone tariffs there is usually no backlog in demand for lines and congestion in telephone traffic is restricted to a few special holidays.[11] This has major implications not only for telephone service investment policy—the area toward which public attention is usually directed—but also for telephone pricing. Under conditions of excess demand the role of efficient prices is to ration demand to permit the use of scarce capacity by those placing the highest value on the service and to avoid the costs of nonprice rationing, which in the case of telephone traffic congestion can be substantial. The appropriate pricing strategy, therefore, is first to calculate the incremental costs of developing, connecting, and using the service, and second to raise fees for these tasks to the point at which demand in each dimension approximately equals supply. The willingness to pay the demand-rationing price will also provide a basis for judging the desirability of new investments in relation to costs. For telephone service charges the most important components are, first, the fixed monthly fee, which reflects consumer costs and (if necessary) rationing demand for lines; and second, a call charge, which varies by time of day. Modern telephone exchange technology can handle the time-dependent billing of calls quite cheaply. Not only long-distance calls but also local calls can be billed on a call basis by time of day.[12]

Commonly, there are biases in telephone rates against long-distance calls and in favor of local calls: long-distance calls are charged at rates above costs when there is no excess demand, whereas charges for local calls are often below costs in the face of strong congestion (Saunders and Warford 1977). This pattern needs to be revised. In addition to being more efficient, such a reversal would also likely meet long-term development goals in developing countries, where the growth of secondary cities and backward regions is frequently impeded by the high cost of communication, including that of long-distance telecommunication.

Another common bias is against industrial and commercial subscribers and in favor of residential subscribers.[13] The rationale is likely to be the belief that the demand for access to the lines of industrial and commercial users is less price-elastic than of residential users. But if industrial and commercial users generally face the choice of how many lines to install rather than whether or not to install a line at all, this may not actually be the case. There is, moreover, a link between an insufficient number of lines for heavy-use subscribers and the problem of congestion of exchanges. Industrial or commercial enterprises tend to create heavy traffic. Thus, discouraging them from installing a sufficient number of lines, by levying high monthly charges per line, is likely to worsen congestion costs for all system users during peak hours. Preferential rates for residential as compared with industrial consumers are also not likely to be socially and economically beneficial. This is because residential subscribers are likely to belong to high-income groups in most developing countries, whereas the high charges for industrial and commercial telephone service are likely to be passed on to consumers of the goods and services produced—a substantial proportion of whom would probably be poor consumers—or to labor. In addition, excessively high industrial and commercial user charges will tend to harm the international competitiveness of domestic industries and commerce.

Apart from this issue, the question of the equity of telephone service does not loom as large as for water supply or electric power. Explicit structuring of fixed monthly charges and also rising block rates have been in use in some countries and cities.[14] The extent of redistribution achievable through such practices is minimal, however, because of the limited access to and use of telephone service by low-income groups.[15] What is likely to be particularly beneficial to low-income households is the provision of public telephones in poor neighborhoods. Subsidization of these facilities would increase efficiency (because of positive externalities of more rapid communication during emergencies, fires, and so forth) and would increase equity (because of the direct benefit to the low-income groups).

During shortages of telephone capacity, efficient pricing policies of the type suggested above are likely to lead to financial surpluses. These can be utilized for system extensions where cost-benefit analysis shows that such investment is warranted either in the specific area where the surpluses are generated (usually large cities) or in areas where costs commonly exceed revenues (that is, in the less densely populated and remote areas of the country). Alternatively, the revenues generated by telephone operations can be channeled to the government as special telephone taxes (for example, in Cartagena) or as cross-subsidies to other urban services (for example, in Cali). Permitting local authorities to tax local telephone users, if the tax is collected jointly with telephone charges by the local, regional, or national telephone company, is quite an attractive local tax

Table 11-3. *Financing of Solid Waste Collection in Selected Cities*

City, year	Refuse charges		Financial status
	Residential	Industrial/Commercial	
Bogotá, Colombia, 1973	Property tax surcharge (earmarked)	Tax on business value and volume charge for collection above minimum volume	Deficit
Cartagena, Colombia, 1973	Property tax surcharge (nonearmarked)	Property tax surcharge (nonearmarked)	Deficit (tax less than expenditure for refuse collection)
Ahmadabad, India, 1972	Conservancy tax (nonearmarked property tax surcharge)	Conservancy tax	Deficit (tax less than expenditure for refuse collection)
Bombay, India, 1974	Conservancy tax (nonearmarked property tax surcharge)	Conservancy tax	Deficit (tax less than expenditure for refuse collection)
Jakarta, Indonesia, 1973	None	Private collection and disposal, except where special contract with public agency	—
Kingston, Jamaica, 1974	None	None	—
Seoul, Rep. of Korea, 1973	Flat monthly charge varying with household space, monthly income, and property value	Flat volume charge	Deficit
Singapore, 1974	Flat monthly charge, except in public housing, where no charge	Commercial—flat monthly charge plus volume surcharge for collection above minimum volume; industrial—private collection, with free disposal at public sites	Deficit
Tunis, Tunisia, 1974	Sanitation tax (nonearmarked surcharge on rental tax)	Sanitation tax (nonearmarked surcharge on rental tax)	Deficit (tax less than expenditure for refuse collection)

— Not available.

instrument in developing countries for improving revenue yield, efficiency, equity, and administrative feasibility.

In countries where the supply of telephone capacity has caught up with demand at marginal cost prices,[16] the telephone tariff issues change rather drastically. This is not likely to be a common situation in most developing countries, however. Suffice it to say, therefore, that the main issue becomes the existence of externalities in telephone service. There are two kinds of externalities: the benefit to the recipient of a telephone call, and the benefit to existing telephone subscribers when a new subscriber joins the system because they can now call and receive calls from an additional subscriber.

With externalities, efficient telephone pricing may require charges below marginal cost. Moreover, if long-run cost curves are declining either due to economies of scale or, more likely, to technological advances, marginal costs will tend to lie below the average historical cost of telephone systems, causing deficits if efficient pricing rules are adopted (Munasinghe, Saunders, and Warford 1978). Telephone operations may thus turn from net contributors of fiscal resources to a net drain on government budgets. This scenario is likely to be sufficiently far off in the future for most developing countries, however, so as not to constitute a major concern for the financing of urban development at this juncture.

Collecting and Disposing of Solid Waste

In industrial countries, collecting and disposing of solid waste in cities is frequently the responsibility of private enterprises regulated by the public sector.[17] In the cities of developing countries, it is much more common for local governments to assume responsibility for this service because it would be difficult for them to regulate and enforce private collection at a level of charges that covers average costs—particularly in low-income residential neighborhoods. But public provision of this service commonly poses considerable financial and managerial problems. The financial problems are reflected in table 11-3. In all nine cities listed, charges for collection either did not exist or did not cover average costs. In Colombia, collection and disposal services in twenty out of twenty-seven cities surveyed in 1975 experienced financial deficits (Colombia 1976). The managerial difficulties are also common and result from two labor aspects of the service. First, the service is highly labor-intensive, and therefore there is much scope for political influence in hiring. Second, the staff have relatively low prestige and financial incentives.

These problems are compounded by the fact that service requirements tend to rise rapidly with the growth of urban population and income. Table 11-4 gives a cross section of this association for cities of different sizes and countries at different levels of per capita income.[18] Increases over time have also been precipitous: in Jakarta, the amount of refuse collected almost tripled between 1966 and 1972 (Linn, Smith, and Wign-

Table 11-4. *Per Capita Income and Per Capita Solid Waste Generation in Selected Countries and Cities*

Country and city	Per capita income, 1973 (dollars)	Solid waste generation (kilograms per capita per day)
Bolivia	230	
Cochabamba		0.650
La Paz		0.750
Santa Cruz		0.440
Brazil	760	
Porto Allegre		0.500
Rio de Janeiro		1.000
Salvador		0.550
Ecuador	380	
Cuenca		0.500
Quito		0.920
Hong Kong	1,430	0.660
India	120	
Deshapera		0.318
Nicaragua	540	
Managua		0.370
Peru	620	
Piura		0.611
Singapore	1,830	0.540
Sweden	5,960	0.925
United Kingdom	3,060	0.890
Yugoslavia	1,010	0.650

Source: Compiled by Alfredo Sfeir-Younis on the basis of data collected by the Pan American Health Organization and Gilbert Associates.

jowijoto 1976). The financial requirements to provide adequate collection and disposal thus tend to rise quite rapidly in the cities of developing countries, and sources of revenue must be found to cover the costs.

The evidence available for nine cities on the type of charges levied specifically to finance collection and disposal is summarized in table 11-3. In a number of cities property tax surcharges have been imposed to support the residential collection service; in no city is there a volume-related charge on residential refuse. For collection from industrial and commercial premises, volume-related charges were encountered in three cities; the remaining cities have a variety of charges unrelated to volume. No city listed attempted to relate collection charges explicitly to density variables or distance from disposal site.

In discussing appropriate pricing methods for collection and disposal, it is useful to consider first the basic cost elements of the service. Disposal costs consist primarily of the labor and capital costs of collecting refuse from residences and industrial or commercial premises. The collection is done by handcarts or motorized vehicles. Sometimes temporary storage requirements are also involved. Collection costs tend to vary directly with the volume and weight of refuse collected, frequency of pickup, and distance from the disposal site and vary inversely with the density of the settlement. Disposal costs vary with quantity and type of refuse, technology chosen (simple or sanitary landfill, composting or incinerating plants, and so forth), opportunity cost of land required for disposal, and the land and capital inputs required for disposal. If lumpy investments are involved, as for example in the construction of composting or incineration plants, the average incremental cost method can be used to derive long-run marginal cost estimates, as with water supply and sewerage services.

In any case, it is important to calculate all costs net of benefits which may result from waste disposal. The generation of electric power and recovery of scrap metal by incineration plants are common benefits. In Singapore it was estimated in 1974 that the net total annual cost of an incinerator plant with 19 megawatts of power generation was only a bit over one-third of the gross total cost, that is, unadjusted for the value of power and scrap metal derived from the operation of the incinerator plant (Saunders and Shipman 1975). Other less common benefits include feeding refuse to livestock and raising the development potential and the value of previously unutilizable urban land by using it as landfill.

In setting user charges for this service, it is important to distinguish between residential and industrial or commercial wastes. For residential waste, a charge related to the quantity (volume or weight) and type of refuse collected is generally not enforceable: how would one stop private individuals from discarding refuse on streets, in canals, or on other illegal dumping grounds? The private costs to the individual of such disposal are minimal, but the social costs can be substantial. Therefore, in this case it is clearly appropriate to "charge" a price, which is below marginal cost, at zero for quantity.

For fiscal and equity reasons, however, some form of service charge for residential collection is likely to be desirable. If collection costs vary with distance from the disposal site and with residential density, flat monthly charges may be differentiated by area in the city and by front footage of a lot, respectively. Such charges would not provide any incentive for households to dump refuse illegally, nor would it encourage presorting and recycling at the household level, but it would tend to encourage efficient decisions on location and development. A surcharge on the property tax is quite an imperfect instrument to finance garbage collection and disposal: it does not necessarily reflect factors of distance or density relevant for collection costs, although in principle it has the advantage of being equitable and financially sound. The property tax surcharge is equitable in that it tends to fall more heavily on those producing more garbage and is probably more progressive than a charge for quantity. In any case, to provide a ready means of enforcement, resi-

Table 11-5. *Public Mass Transit Operations and Pricing in Selected Cities*

City, year	Type of service	Level of government in charge of service	Structure of fares	Extent and source of subsidies	Private involvement in bus service
Bogotá, Colombia, 1980	Buses	Autonomous local agency	Flat rate (higher for night and weekend service)	Subsidy from national and local government budget	Most bus service provided by private operators
Ahmadabad, India, 1973	Buses	Semiautonomous municipal company	Varies with distance; concessional fares for students, children, and the disabled	Revenues below operating costs and debt service requirements; transfer from general municipal account	—
Bombay, India, 1976	Buses	Semiautonomous municipal company	Varies with distance and type of service (express buses at higher fare); discounts for children	Operational deficits financed from surplus in electric power operations	No
	Suburban railways	National autonomous agency	Varies with distance	Deficit	n.a.
Calcutta, India, 1980	Buses	State-owned autonomous agency	Varies with distance	Deficit financed from state government (open-ended subsidy)	2,000 private buses and minibuses, compared with 1,000 public buses
	Tramways	State-owned autonomous agency	Varies with distance	Deficit financed from state budget	n.a.
Jakarta, Indonesia, 1973	Buses	Autonomous local agency	Flat rate	No subsidy	75 percent of buses run by private operators
Jakarta, Indonesia, 1980	Buses	Autonomous local agency	Flat rate	Subsidy to cover operating costs	—
Seoul, Rep. of Korea, 1973	Buses	Semiautonomous local agency	Flat rate (higher for seated than for standing passengers)	Subsidy to cover operating costs financed by transfers from local government account	—
Tunis, Tunisia, 1974	Buses	National autonomous agency	Varies with distance; discounts for children and students	No subsidy	—

— Not available.
n.a. Not applicable.

dential refuse charges or taxes are best collected jointly with water and sewerage (or possibly electricity) charges. When property tax surcharges or other fees to finance collection have been linked to the collection of utility tariffs, the problem of uncollected bills has generally been significantly lower than when it is linked to the basic property tax in the same city (for example, in Bogotá; Linn 1976c).

The marginal cost pricing rule can be more usefully applied to industrial and commercial refuse because their disposal methods are easier to control. The tariff includes a basic volume charge reflecting the net average incremental cost of disposal and a volume charge reflecting the cost of collection. The volume charge is differentiated according to distance from disposal site and density of establishments. If private collection and transport to disposal sites is the rule (as in Singapore), only a disposal charge is levied. The disposal charge would reflect the net average incremental cost of disposal, including the opportunity cost of land. Free dumping of waste in cities where land has a high opportunity cost involves considerable losses in efficiency. In Singapore the disposal cost was about 40 percent of the total collection and disposal cost in 1974 (Saunders and Shipman 1975).

In principle, marginal cost charges for collecting and disposing of solid waste lie above average financial costs for two reasons. First, the financial cost of public land used for disposal generally fall below the land's opportunity cost. Second, unit costs are likely to rise as the city grows because readily accessible landfills are likely to be exhausted first, leaving more distant and therefore more costly disposal sites, and perhaps requiring relatively expensive investments in composting or incineration plants (as, for example, in Singapore). Thus it is probable that marginal cost pricing of refuse collection and disposal will yield financial surpluses. Because such pricing is unpopular, however, and because it is practically impossible to charge residential users tariffs based on quantity, deficits have been frequent.

Mass Transit

Some salient features of the organization and financing of public mass transit in selected cities of the developing world are shown in table 11-5. Subsidization has been the rule, and what is more, most public transit enterprises have been beset by difficulties in management, operations, and financing. Operating costs and the requirements for subsidies are usually higher for public transit than for private competitors (table 11-6). Indeed, there has been considerable debate as to whether mass transit systems should be publicly rather than privately owned. Policymakers have frequently seen public ownership and management of bus operations as a means to rationalize an apparently chaotic urban transit system, but in recent years transport analysts have begun to favor strongly the

Table 11-6. *Bus Transit Tariffs, Costs, and Subsidies in Selected Cities*
(dollars)

City	Service	Date	Tariff	Total cost per passenger	Subsidy per passenger
Buenos Aires, Argentina	Private bus	1979	0.15–0.23	0.15–0.23	0.0
Santiago, Chile	Private bus	November 1980	0.167	0.17	0.0
Bogotá, Colombia	Private bus	July 1980	0.05	0.09	0.04
	Public bus	April 1979	0.048	0.156	0.108
	Private minibus	December 1980	0.15	0.15	0.0
Paris, France	Public bus	July 1980	0.43	1.62	1.19
Jakarta, Indonesia	Public bus	July 1980	0.08	0.16	0.08
Tokyo, Japan	Private bus	June 1970	0.41	0.41	0.0
	Public bus	June 1970	0.50	0.56	0.06
Lima, Peru	Private bus	November 1980	0.108	0.108	0.0
Istanbul, Turkey	Public bus	1977	0.10	0.25	0.15
	Private minibus	1977	0.10	0.10	0.00

Source: Urrutia (1981: table 3).

364

privatization of public urban bus transit operations (Roth 1973; World Bank 1975c, 1986; Walters 1979; Urrutia 1981).

There exists ample evidence that cities served by private buses tend to have better transit service at substantially lower costs to transit users and to government alike than ones served by public buses (table 11-6). The primary problem of public companies appears to be management-labor relations because strong union pressures lead to excessively labor-intensive operations. Moreover, there tends to be a lack of an incentive structure for management and drivers to provide efficient services. The transfer of private operations into public management frequently has led to a quick erosion of service quality, whereas the reverse has been true for privatized operations (Walters 1979; Urrutia 1981). In particular, minibus franchises have met with notable success in a number of cities. In Kuala Lumpur a decision in the mid-1970s to permit minibuses led to the operation of a hundred vehicles within nine months. Private mass transit thus appears to be a viable alternative to public buses.

The issue of pricing mass transit tends to arise, however, as a public policy question, whether the transit system is public or private. This is because fares are almost invariably regulated by government agencies, frequently at the national level. In principle, the economic justification for such control is linked to the question of whether there is free entry into the mass transit sector by operators. If there is, competition among operators ought to keep prices in line with costs. If there is not, monopoly or oligopoly pricing might result, leading to calls for public intervention (Roth 1973). In fact, in many cities, unless free entry is prohibited by government (which it frequently is), urban bus service is a free-entry market with a high degree of competition among many small owner-operators. Nevertheless, price control is the rule and is often linked to the political sensitivities of the national government, which tend to be articulated as equity arguments that fares should be kept low so as not to hurt the poor. Before turning to these, however, it is necessary to review the arguments which can be made for the efficiency of subsidized prices.

The efficiency case for subsidies of mass transit is based on the view that the absence of congestion charges is a strong incentive for the use of the private automobile. It is well known, however, that mass transit subsidies are a second-best alternative to congestion pricing (Churchill 1972; Gomez-Ibanez 1975; Roth 1973; Walters 1968; World Bank 1975c). If congestion is a serious problem it would be preferable to deal with it directly, as was done in Singapore (see chapter 7). What is more important, particularly in developing countries, is that shortages of public resources generally do not permit large-scale subsidization. Subsidized transport systems therefore are underfinanced and tend to become de-capitalized, resulting in a lower level and quality of service. Subsidies also encourage low-density development and urban sprawl, which in turn tend to increase the cost of many services, including transport (Linn 1983). In sum, therefore, the efficiency argument for mass-transit subsidies is quite weak, especially if considered along with the difficulties that arise from protracted subsidization.

Once service quality has dropped and residential settlement patterns have become established, it is very difficult to raise fares. First, those benefiting from the subsidies will object to the loss of a "free ride," especially if quality is so low as not to deserve higher payments in the eyes of the users. Second, increases in fares are highly visible policy measures which affect a large number of city dwellers who are locked into their existing locations at least over the short term and may sustain considerable losses because the higher charges may reduce the value of land and housing in the most affected areas. The only way to deal with these difficulties and the resulting political barriers to bus fare increases is to combine changes in pricing policies with immediate improvements in the level and quality of mass transit services. Fares may need to be raised gradually to permit individuals to adjust to inevitable transition costs.

The equity argument for subsidized bus fares, which supposes that low-income groups are the primary beneficiaries of the subsidy, also has limitations. First, there is the question of static incidence: a substantial portion of subsidies may "leak" to wealthy landowners, transport operators, employers, and nonpoor consumers (Linn 1979). Second, the poor, especially in low-income developing countries, frequently cannot afford to pay for even subsidized mass transit and thus do not benefit from the subsidy. Third, many middle- and high-income people also use mass transit (Zahavi 1976)—especially subways—thus further reducing the redistributive effect of subsidies. Last and not least, as noted above, the decapitalizing effect of subsidies tends to lower the level and quality of service for the poor. Thus those who are excluded from service lose not only the subsidy but also the benefit of even unsubsidized transit.

These equity arguments against subsidies depend, however, on a number of factors, the most important being the level of income in the country or city. In middle-income countries all except the very poorest people can afford some form of mass transit at reasonably small subsidies, and general tax resources may be more readily available to maintain an extensive network of service. Subsidies may thus reach down quite far in the income distribution without overly deleterious effects on the efficiency of the system. Bogotá is a good example: its largely private bus system receives subsidies from the national government and provides efficient, low-cost service to even the poorest areas of the city (Urrutia 1981). In low-income developing countries, however, a large proportion of the urban poor cannot afford even subsidized transport. Furthermore, financial resources tend to be very scarce, and thus the system is bound to suffer. The net effects tend to be that subsidies do not reach the poor and that the system loses passengers at both ends of the income scale because of a declining quality of service. At the high end, people switch to automobiles or intermediate forms of motorized traffic such as mini-buses, increasing congestion and lowering the efficiency of the system. At the low end, people drop out or were never served in the first place because services were cut in established neighborhoods or were not provided in new areas.[19]

In addition to the questions of levels of fares and subsidies, there is the question of the structure of fares. Basically, the fare structure should reflect variations in relative marginal costs, which should allow for differences in distance traveled, peak and off-peak ridership, and type of service. The factor of distance is relatively straightforward, and there should not be large administrative problems in charging fares that vary with distance, as is done in some cities and countries (table 11-5). At the same time, publicly regulated bus fares in most countries are flat fares that do not vary with distance. Differences between peak and off-peak relative costs are more complicated. During peak hours, costs per vehicle mile tend to be higher due to congestion, but costs per passenger mile may not be that much higher due to substantially larger passenger loads in peak than in off-peak hours. What is more, peak (commuting) hours tend to be the times when one would most want to lure automobile users out of their cars and into mass transit use. For this reason, it is much more important to subsidize peak than off-peak use of mass transit (in the absence of congestion charges). An efficient fare structure would thus vary fares with distance, charge higher fares for most costly service (such as minibuses or express buses), and permit higher fares during nights and weekends.

The issue of setting fares for mass transit must be placed in the larger context of policies to organize and finance it. Even more broadly, it must be seen in the framework of the managment of the transport sector, which allows consideration of the relative costs and benefits—private and social—of alternative transport modes. This comprehensive view is essentially desirable, although few cities have been able to attain it. In Singapore an effort has been made to combine congestion pricing (including area license fees and parking charges) with policies to regulate pricing and public investment that are jointly designed to develop an efficient transport system.

Housing

Public authorities in developing countries are even less well equipped to be involved in the construction of shelter than in mass transit, particularly if the goal is to serve the urban poor. In fact, four factors stemming from broad experience suggest that the construction of public shelter does more harm than good.[20]

First, given the heterogeneity of people's preferences for a kind of shelter and the speed at which they can or want to improve its quality, it is not surprising that public housing projects often do not fit the housing preferences of the poor (for example, high-rise apartment buildings constructed for the poor in Caracas and Rio de Janeiro have not met traditional preferences and needs). Second, public investment in shelter substitutes for, and tends to impair, private savings and investment activities. Low-, middle-, and high-income groups alike appear to be willing and able to finance private housing construction commensurate with their ability to pay, provided that complementary inputs into housing (tenure, space, and services, and to some extent capital) are readily available. The public resources spent on housing construction could be better used to provide these complementary inputs. Third, public housing units are usually preempted by high- and middle-income households, who then benefit from the subsidies provided. These subsidies further tie up scarce public funds that could otherwise have been used to provide serviced land. And to the extent that public housing construction programs bid up material prices, they tend to harm the self-help, low-cost, low-income construction sector. Fourth, public housing projects in the past were often accompanied by the razing or "eradication" of slums, which actually reduced the supply of housing and demolished the investments of poor households, frequently without substituting feasible alternative housing.

The most notable exceptions to this generally negative experience with public shelter construction are the low-income housing programs of Hong Kong and Singapore. A number of factors contributed to their success in providing a significant improvement in housing for the poor: (a) quality standards were chosen at levels low enough to permit high-rise construction at costs affordable by the poor without substantial subsidies; (b) contrary to the experience in many other countries, high-rise units were culturally and socially acceptable to the households in these two cities; (c) the programs were on such a large scale that they induced general rent reductions and thus had an important "trickle-down" effect; (d) relatively high per capita incomes in these two cities provided the fiscal basis for such a large-scale program and made standards affordable; (e) the lack of readily developable land in these two cities had led to high densities and high land prices and made high-rise construction necessary for any large-scale housing program; (f) both cities possessed the necessary managerial and technical resources as well as strong metropolitanwide governments which permitted the implementation of such housing programs.

A similar combination of circumstances does not exist in other cities in developing economies, with the possible exception of Korea and Taiwan (China). In fact, incomes are often so low as to exclude the possibility of large high-rise public programs, which in any case generally are not accepted among the poor. Finally, public managerial expertise is very scarce in most developing countries, and developable land tends to be at the metropolitan fringe. Thus the experiences of Hong Kong and Singapore, although tremendous achievements, are not blueprints for other cities of developing countries.

This evaluation of public construction of housing in the cities of developing countries is not meant to imply that urban governments have no rationale for intervention in the housing market. On the contrary, there is much room for public involvement in several aspects of the housing supply, including land development, investment in on- and off-site infrastructure, and even interventions in the market for housing finance.[21]

Yet for better or worse, urban governments in some countries play a much larger role in the construction of shelter by subsidizing housing consumption or setting housing prices through rent control. In Nairobi in the early 1970s about a third of the population lived in public housing. Public agencies in the city, mostly the local government, constructed approximately half of the new housing units produced by the formal housing market (that is, the market minus squatter and other illegal housing construction; World Bank data). In Singapore 230,000 public housing units were built between 1960 and 1975, and by 1980 approximately 70 percent of the population lived in public housing (Laquian 1980). In Zambia almost the entire housing stock is owned by public institutions, and about 90 percent of all Zambian public employees receive some form of housing subsidy (Valverde and Bamberger 1980). Finally, in many cities of developing countries, particularly on the Indian subcontinent, public rent control is used to affect the prices of private housing. The direct or indirect financial implications of these policies for urban governments are substantial, and the policies therefore need to be reviewed at least in summary fashion. The issues to be discussed include the desirability and feasibility of housing subsidies; the pricing of two important inputs into housing, namely land and financial capital; and rent control.[22]

In conventional economic terms, subsidies distort private decisions on consumption unless demand is perfectly price-inelastic; they thus result in inefficient allocation of resources unless economies of scale, externalities, or other market imperfections exist which require correction through a subsidy.[23] This argument applies to housing, for which demand-elasticities are known to be significantly larger than zero and market imperfections are generally unimportant. Subsidized housing thus leads to overconsumption of housing relative to other goods and services. Moreover, subsidies encourage overly ambitious expectations for housing standards among both public and private decisionmakers because the full resource cost is not borne by the beneficiaries. Thus subsidies tend to result in mistaken investment decisions.

What is more, housing subsidies do not address the crucial limitations generally facing the housing market: housing shortages do not exist because of limits on effective housing demand but because of limits on housing supply. Indeed, the fact that public resources are channeled into housing subsidies generally limits the government's capacity to finance the essential components of housing supply, urban infrastructure, and services, for which it usually has sole responsibility. To take an extreme case, in Zambia in 1978 total estimated housing subsidies by the central and local governments and the parastatal sector amounted to 16 percent of total government consumption (as defined in the Zambian national accounts).[24] Indeed, the almost universal experience with public housing subsidies in developing countries has been that they very quickly run up against the fiscal resource constraint of both local and national authorities alike and that they therefore cannot provide housing of the desired standards for a large share of the population.

Housing subsidies are often considered to be equitable. But here also arise a number of serious problems. Subsidies tend to favor middle- and higher-income groups, either because public housing is preempted by members of these income groups even if intended for low-income groups or because subsidy schemes heavily favor high-income groups. Table 11-7 shows that conventional public housing in five developing countries typically has not reached down below the fiftieth percentile in the income distribution, a finding which is supported by evidence for other countries as well (Linn 1983). In Zambia, the bottom 50 percent in the income distribution were estimated to have received only about 10 percent of the total housing subsidy, whereas the top 10 percent received about 50 percent (Valverde and Bamberger 1980). As a result, it has been estimated that if the housing subsidy is counted as part of household income, the income distribution is more equitable than if these subsidies are not included in income estimates.[25] The negative distributional effect of public housing subsidies tends to be reinforced by the resulting shortage of financial resources for other urban services—services which could help lower housing costs for the poor by either increasing the overall stock of serviced land or providing services for the poor.

Another question is how to price the land components in these development projects. It is tempting either not to consider cost at all or to value land at its cost to government, which may be well below its opportunity cost because of various special circumstances. For example, the government may own the land already, or it may be able to expropriate it at a cost below what it would fetch in the private market. For efficiency, however, it is important to estimate the opportunity cost of land. This opportunity cost should then be the basis for calculating efficient charges for publicly developed land. If it is then thought desirable to subsidize development costs, the distributive and longer-term financial implications of such subsidies should be carefully considered. For example, although a first project may be able to draw on financially cheap public land, follow-up projects may have to purchase land at commercial prices from private owners. In that case the replicability of the first project—if it heavily relies on subsidized land costs—is in doubt; and even if it is replicable, a problem of fairness and political acceptability arises when beneficiaries of follow-up projects are charged the full commercial cost of the land.

A further issue is the charge for capital supplied by public agencies. One common means of subsidizing public housing programs is to provide financing at terms below the real long-term cost of capital. Judging from the nominal interest rates charged in the conventional public housing programs listed in table 11-7, a large number of countries have employed such subsidies. The problem with this type of subsidy measure, however, is that it tends to hide the full extent of subsidization unless explicit present-value accounting is carried out; and it limits both the cost recovery of public projects and their replicability. Explicit subsidies, if they are thought desirable at all, are more appropriate than implicit subsidies through low-interest charges. If—during inflationary periods—standard fixed-payment mortgage schedules tilt the real value of payments more heavily toward the early years of the life of a mortgage, this may hurt the ability of low-income groups to acquire housing. In this case an indexed lending scheme may be preferable, if the real rather than the nominal value of mortgage payments is kept (approximately) constant over the life of a mortgage.

A final issue is the question of rent control, which is an attempt to reduce the real cost of housing.[26] Rent controls have existed in Egypt, El Salvador, and India. These controls are imposed ostensibly to restrain rents that have risen rapidly as a result of urban growth and of the failure of housing supply to keep up with housing demand. This is a particularly unfortunate attempt to solve a problem by limiting its symptoms, thereby making matters worse. Although rent controls are frequently circumvented by illegal payments between owner and renter, the return to housing investment and maintenance still becomes less certain as a result of them, and if owners do adhere to the law, the return is lowered in absolute terms. Therefore, the willingness of owners to invest in new buildings or maintain old structures tends to be reduced. Furthermore, in many cases the mobility of households is reduced because once installed in a low-rent home a household stands to lose the benefit of the low rent by moving, or it must forfeit the "key money" which is frequently charged by landlords as a way to recapture part of the economic rent forgone as a result of rent control. In any case, many low-income households do not have access to the capital to pay these lump sums which are required to get access to rent-controlled housing. Another problem arose in El Salvador, where low-income households were frequently evicted because rent control laws permitted higher rents only when tenants change.

Finally, in countries that levy property taxes on rental values, the con-

Table 11-7. Comparison of World Bank Housing Projects with Conventional Public Housing Programs

Project and date of presentation to Board of World Bank	Effect on poverty: lowest percentile of population reached			Percentage of shelter costs recovered[a]			Interest rate (percent)[b]		World Bank projects	
	Sites and services (1)	Upgrading (2)	Conventional public housing[c] (3)	Sites and services (4)	Upgrading (5)	Conventional public housing (6)	World Bank project (7)	Conventional public housing (8)	Charges as percentage of household income (9)	Cross-subsidization (10)
Sub-Saharan Africa										
Botswana I, 1974	27	21	—	—	—	—	7–8	—	14–23	Yes
Botswana II, 1978	26	5	60	81	100	—	8.25–9	8	15–20	Yes
Burkina Faso, 1978	—	—	—	100	100	—	8.5	8.5	22	No
Côte d'Ivoire, 1976	14	5	—	70	50	—	9–13	13	25–32	No
Kenya I, 1975	22	n.a.	—	100	n.a.	—	8.5	6.5	25	Yes
Kenya II, 1978	24	1	—	100	90	—	8.5	6.5	30	Yes
Senegal, 1972	47	n.a.	—	100	n.a.	—	7	11–13	8	n.a.
Tanzania I, 1974	31	14	—	100	—	—	6–9	6	15	Yes
Tanzania II, 1977	20	5	—	75	75	—	6	8	15	Yes
Zambia, 1974	17	15	—	80	80	—	7.5	6.25	25	Yes
Low-income Asia										
India										
Calcutta I, 1973	n.a.	—	—	n.a.	100	—	5	5	—	No
Calcutta II, 1977	20	n.a.	—	100	n.a.	—	8.5	8.5	20	Yes
Madras, 1977	9	8	n.a.	100	100	—	12	10–11	13	No
Indonesia I, 1974	12	1	—	—	0	50	12	8–9	20	—
Indonesia II, 1976	n.a.	About 0	30–40 (50)[d]	n.a.	0–30	35	n.a.	—	n.a.	—

Middle-income Asia										
Korea, Rep. of, 1975	19	n.a.	—	100	n.a.	—	12	8	25	No
Philippines, 1976	33	22	>50	100	100[e]	56–84	12	6–8	26	Yes[f]
Thailand, 1978	25	11	—	100	80	—	12	15	13–30	Yes
Latin America and Caribbean										
Bolivia, 1977	10	2	—	78	100	50	10	3–6	32–50	No
Colombia, 1978	16	8	—	63	63	—	13.8	14–18	24	Yes
El Salvador I, 1974	17	n.a.	—	100	n.a.	—	6–8	5–10.5	25	Yes
El Salvador II, 1977	18	9	—	83	100	—	6.4	2–3	10–20	No
Guatemala, 1976	10	n.a.	—	100	n.a.	—	4	8–11	20	No
Jamaica, 1974	30	11	—	—	—	—	8–12	11	33	Yes
Mexico, 1978	17	7	75	98	81	—	15	6–8	20	No
Nicaragua, 1973	15	n.a.	—	100	n.a.	—	5	6–14	20	Yes
Peru, 1976	14	7	—	100	100	65	12	10–12	20	No
Europe, Middle East, and North Africa										
Egypt, 1978	23	22	90	100	100	25	7	3	7–20	No
Morocco, 1978	20	5	—	67	79	—	7	9	25	Yes

— Not available.

n.a. Not applicable.

a. Excluding all nonshelter costs (see note in table 6-1).

b. Nominal interest rate, not allowing for inflation or different payment periods.

c. Including subsidies.

d. Without subsidies on structures and not including land costs.

e. Not including land costs.

f. Higher charges for lots on corners and major roads; approximately one-third of total project cost borne by commercial and industrial properties.

Source: World Bank data and information compiled by C. Clifford.

trolled rents may be used as a basis of tax assessment. This reduces significantly the level and buoyancy of tax revenues and thus limits the ability of local authorities to expand public services. The housing shortage and high housing costs, which were initially the reasons for the introduction of rent control, are as a result only aggravated further.

In sum, public agencies should generally steer clear of direct involvement in the construction of urban shelter, although they may have an important role to play in providing essential service inputs to the housing market. If an urban government is actually involved in the supply of housing, however, it should avoid large-scale subsidies, which generally do not effectively serve to increase the efficiency or equity of urban development in general or of the housing sector in particular.[27] Such subsidies tend to impose heavy fiscal burdens and limit the scope and replicability of housing programs. Land and financial capital should be charged for at economic rates, and any subsidies should be made explicit in a full cost accounting for a project rather than implicit by not calculating its full incremental cost. Finally, rent control is not an effective tool to deal with the commonly perceived problems of housing shortages and high housing costs in the cities of the developing world.

Development Charges

We now turn to a set of charges which may broadly be classified as development charges. They have different names in different countries and, to some extent, serve different purposes and involve different practices. These are "special assessments," "contributions for betterment," "land readjustment," "valorization contributions," and so forth. Their principal feature is that they are lump-sum charges designed to recoup the public costs of developing urban infrastructure from the beneficiaries. They may cover only quite limited projects for a particular service (for example, a neighborhood paving scheme or the construction of a sewage canal[28]), or they may cover the full development of new urban areas in a city or even of entire new towns. They are usually imposed on the owners of property in the areas which are improved by public action rather than falling directly on the occupant of a property or the user of a service.

These charges are usually levied for three reasons. First is the goal of increasing the financial resource base of urban governments by tapping a source of finance where the benefit and the charge are very closely linked in the mind of the beneficiary, and the beneficiary's willingness to pay for it would therefore be higher than for general taxes.[29] Second, an efficiency argument can be made for the charges because they pass the public costs of development on to the individual making the development decision in terms of location, density, and standards of service demanded. Third, it is generally believed that it is equitable to charge those who benefit from the investment in infrastructure, that is, the urban landowners. The redistributive effect of the charges depends, however, on what other financing mechanisms would have been employed in their absence and thus on the structure of tax and user charges in a country or city.

These arguments in favor of development charges are of course parallel to the more general arguments advanced in chapter 9. This section explores two types of these charges which have been used successfully for some years: land readjustment systems, which are most common in East Asia; and valorization systems, found predominantly in Latin America. These two systems indicate the potential for broadening the use of development charges beyond their quite narrow, often partial application in many countries and cities.

Land Readjustment

In a typical urban land readjustment system, a public agency assembles numerous small parcels of raw land at the urban periphery without paying monetary compensation to the owners. This land is serviced and subdivided for urban use and then returned to the original owners in proportion to the value of their land contribution. Some of the land is retained by the public authority for infrastructure (roads, green spaces, and so forth). And some is retained to finance development by being sold at market prices in commercial transactions or auctions. Although the system is usually managed by public agencies, especially at the local level, in some economies it has also been under private development associations, usually subject to public regulation and supervision.[30]

A readjustment system has been in use in Germany for a hundred years, and it is used in one Australian city, Perth.[31] Similarly, one was introduced in Japan in 1899, and the Japanese introduced it in Korea during their occupation of the country. By 1976 6,395 projects covering 261,785 hectares had been carried out in Japan under such a system. Korea has used it for virtually all large residential urban developments in 49 cities and towns, which by 1976 involved 186 completed projects covering 18,102 hectares; another 88 projects in progress at the time covered 17,538 hectares of land. Land readjustment has been applied in Taiwan (China) since the early 1950s, initially in rural areas. Between 1969 and 1978 about 2,000 hectares in 49 areas were developed in this way.

The Korean system has been quite extensively analyzed. Its importance is documented by Doebele and Hwang (1979), who found that in 1976 almost seven times as much urban land was developed through land readjustment as through the private market. Furthermore, in 1970, 15 percent of all expenditure by the government of Seoul was for readjustment schemes, and almost a quarter of all capital spending by the Seoul metropolitan authorities was devoted to these schemes (Bahl and Wasylenko 1976). Between 1963 and 1970 spending increases for readjustment accounted for 16 percent of the increase in total spending by the local authorities. The importance of readjustment activities was thus quite considerable, in both their contribution to overall development in Seoul and their contribution to local spending. Moreover, the activities were largely self-financing and thus were not a drain on other sources of local finance. Doebele and Hwang (1979) report that the cost of borrowing in some cases was not fully borne by the readjustment scheme but by local government. These implicit subsidies, however, are not likely to have been very important relative to total spending. The same authors have also observed that readjustment schemes are often quite limited in the services they explicitly provide and finance. They sometimes do not cover even such essential services as water supply and generally do not cover the cost of investments in off-site infrastructure required for development. Some of the implicit costs of development therefore need to be recouped through other taxes or charges.

Land readjustment schemes in Korea appear to have contributed efficiently to the development of new land at the urban fringe. But Doebele and Hwang (1979) conclude from their analysis of urban land markets in Korea that municipal authorities may have restricted the expansion of urban land below the rate that would have stabilized land values and below rates that an unrestricted market would have generated. Moreover, they observe that incomplete servicing in some cases, and speculative ownership of land in others, has led to significant vacant landholdings after land readjustment. Despite these reservations about the efficiency of readjustment schemes, most of which are lacking thorough quantitative foundation, Doebele and Hwang (1979) conclude that the system has been quite an effective development mechanism that deserves replication.

In terms of equity, the readjustment schemes in Korea were a mixed blessing. On the one hand, they did ensure that the urban development costs were borne by beneficiaries of the investments; on the other hand, the substantial capital gains after readjustment accrued primarily to middle-income landowners (Doebele and Hwang 1979). The relatively poor farmers who originally owned the land generally could not hold on to it long enough to reap these capital gains, and indeed they may have suffered losses from the cutoff of farming opportunities because of compulsory development schemes. Moreover, the schemes have generally not increased the housing stock for poor urban households. To the extent that the schemes did not supply land in step with the growth in demand and to the extent that private development was restricted, especially among the poor, they may even have worsened the housing shortage of the poor.[32]

Readjustment schemes require fairly sophisticated methods of public land management, including effective land registration and cadastral records and land redistribution formulas. In East Asia these have been developed and implemented over time and may not be readily transferable elsewhere. Nevertheless, the administrative feasibility of the schemes has been amply demonstrated. Improvements may well be desirable, particularly in the rate at which land is developed, in the amount of capital gains extracted for public benefit, and in the access of low-income groups to the benefits of the schemes. For example, Doebele and Hwang (1979) suggest that the financial surpluses frequently reaped in Korean cities in implementing schemes be used to cross-subsidize low-income residential development instead of being used to reimburse the landowners or to improve further the project areas from which the surpluses were generated.

Valorization

In contrast to land readjustment programs, which are used mainly in developing new urban areas at the fringes of cities and towns, the valorization system has principally been used to finance improvements in the physical infrastructure in already subdivided or built-up urban areas. The basic principle underlying the valorization system as commonly found in Latin America is to recoup the cost of infrastructure projects, especially road construction and improvement, by levying one-time lump-sum charges on the owners of surrounding land.[33] A valorization system differs therefore from a land value increment tax because it does not attempt to tax the increase in land value per se but aims to allocate infrastructure costs across benefiting properties. An increment tax is closer in nature to a capital gains tax (Bird 1976), whereas a valorization levy or special assessment is a development charge, linked—in principle—directly to the cost of providing services.

The method of allocating costs to specific properties varies from country to country and city to city. Generally, however, it consists of three steps. First, the infrastructure project is designed and costed out. To this direct cost a margin is frequently added to allow for indirect costs of administration, thus yielding a total budget for the project. Second, an area surrounding the project is defined as the zone of influence; this is the area within which most of the benefits of the project are thought to be limited, and over which the costs of the project are to be distributed. For example, this zone may include only the properties immediately adjoining a neighborhood road that is being improved, or in the case of an arterial road it may go significantly beyond this to include properties in a much larger area. Third, the total cost of the project is allocated among the properties included in the zone of influence. The system of allocation varies widely from country to country, but these methods are typical (Bird 1976b): allocation according to a property's length of frontage, location by subzone within the zone of influence, land area, value, or direct benefit estimated for the project.

The frontage method is appropriate for distribution networks and access roads because it approximates quite closely the costs attributable to each property, which are likely to vary directly with the length of the project passing the property. The subzone method may be appropriate if costs vary significantly among subzones (because of geological conditions or quality differentials) or if there is a clear gradation in benefits received because properties differ in their access to the project (for example, if the project is a park or a street). No clear cost-benefit rationale appears to exist for the land area and property value methods of allocation, except perhaps that large or highly valued properties are likely to reap a greater proportion of benefits than small or less valuable properties. This link is likely to be quite weak, however. Finally, it is virtually impossible to allocate costs in proportion to direct benefit because it has proven to be very difficult to estimate accurately the increase in land value attributable to a particular improvement in infrastructure. Several of these methods are often combined, for example, costs may be allocated by land area but vary with distances from the project.

Before reviewing the experience with valorization in Colombia, where it has been most extensively applied, the system can briefly be evaluated on the basis of the four criteria of financial yield, efficiency, equity, and administrative ease. Valorization systems generally have not been notable for a great contribution to urban fiscal resources (Macon and Merino Mañon 1977). Colombia is the exception: in Bogotá valorization expenditures in 1968 contributed 16 percent to total consolidated expenditures of all urban government agencies, and valorization revenues in 1969 amounted to two-thirds of the revenues raised by the property tax (Doebele, Grimes, and Linn 1979). In principle, therefore, valorization payments can significantly help to raise financial resources, particularly during periods of rapid expansion of urban infrastructure. As regards efficiency, valorization has the advantage of imposing the cost of urban infrastructure on the largest beneficiaries, and it thus tends to make both beneficiaries and public decisionmakers more cost-conscious. Location decisions by individuals and investment decisions by government are thus likely to be more efficient than if infrastructure investments are financed from general funds. In terms of equity, much depends on the application of the system and the available alternative means of financing the expansion of urban infrastructure. Equity tends to be fostered if valorization replaces financing through regressive local taxes, or if the introduction of valorization permits public investment to be directed to poorer neighborhoods than was previously the case, thus allowing the poor to benefit from public services instead of continuing to rely on inadequate and costly subsidies. Administratively, valorization systems can range from the extremely simple to the extremely complex. Administrative simplicity reduces costs but also makes it more difficult to convince taxpayers that they have been treated fairly. Administrative complexity, conversely, makes the system costly to implement and may hamper its development if there are not enough adequately trained administrators. A middle course should therefore be steered between the type of project and the human resources available.

In order to give the reader a better impression of some of the advantages of the valorization system, but also of some of its pitfalls, the remainder of this section will briefly review how the system has been applied in Bogotá.[34] In essence, valorization in Bogotá follows the steps outlined above. The most important refinement is that costs are allocated to specific properties within the zone of influence. Most commonly, a system of coefficients is used which attempts to reflect the effect of the project on each property by allowing for such factors as the property's distance from the project, shape, topography, use, neighborhood socioeconomic composition, and so forth. An overall coefficient per square meter of land is derived by combining for each property the coefficients for each of these factors. Project costs are then allocated in accordance with the area of the property, weighted by the overall coefficient. This method of cost allocation thus combines a number of the "pure" methods described above, including area, zone, frontage, and at times property value and (estimated) increase in value. More important, as has been documented in Doebele, Grimes, and Linn (1979), the cost allocation system has varied tremendously from project to project. It has been tailored to the size and nature of each project, especially the extent to which costs and beneficiaries in the zone of influence are homogeneous. This flexibility in applying the basic method has undoubtedly contributed to the relative success of the system, as has the fact that during the 1960s Colombia built up a considerable body of technical expertise, both among public agencies carrying out valorization projects and among private consulting agencies specializing in studies of feasibility and cost allocation for municipal valorization programs.

At its height, the valorization system contributed significantly to the mobilization of fiscal resources in Bogotá. It appears that valorization revenues were complementary to other sources or revenue, rather than substituting for them (Doebele, Grimes, and Linn 1979: 85). At the same time, the valorization system made possible extensive infrastructure works which have given the city's inhabitants relatively high access to road transport in most areas, including poor neighborhoods, and high access to sewerage. The system has thus contributed to an equitable and efficient infrastructure.

A number of difficulties arose, however, which are somewhat representative of the difficulties encountered throughout Colombia in the use of valorization. The existence of such difficulties is manifested in the drastic decline of valorization during the 1970s compared with the second half of the 1960s (see table 11-8). The decline in the relative share of valorization spending and revenues for 1969 through 1974 continued even after 1974. Whereas in 1974 the agencies in charge of valorization

Table 11-8. *Valorization in Bogotá, 1959–74*

Year	Total per capita valorization expenditures in 1959 prices (pesos)	Valorization expenditures as a percentage of total local authority spending	Valorization contributions as a percentage of property tax revenues
1959	16.4	—	—
1960	14.8	—	—
1961	17.1	—	5.9
1962	10.8	—	19.5
1963	12.0	3.2	41.9
1964	14.1	5.8	20.7
1965	12.4	5.5	21.6
1966	13.3	6.6	29.7
1967	36.4	14.3	59.2
1968	49.1	15.9	60.2
1969	35.3	10.3	66.9 (68.0)[a]
1970	21.7	6.8	62.0 (75.4)
1971	17.8	5.1	44.6 (57.6)
1972	15.2	4.2	31.0 (38.8)
1973	9.8	—	22.0 (27.5)
1974	16.9	—	18.2 (34.1)
Average			
1961–66	13.3	5.3[b]	23.2
1967–70	35.6	11.8	62.1 (65.7)
1971–74	14.9	4.7[c]	29.0 (39.5)

— Not available.

a. Figures in parentheses show the percentage of valorization charges relative to property tax revenues when the valorization revenues from the Sewerage Master Plan are included.

b. 1963–66.

c. 1971–72.

Source: Doebele, Grimes, and Linn (1979: table 2).

works still contributed 8.6 percent to total consolidated expenditure of all local government agencies, this share dropped to 3 percent by 1979. Similarly, although valorization charges in 1971 still were about 5 percent of the consolidated revenue of all government agencies, their share had dropped to 2.5 percent in 1979. There were four important reasons for this decline.

First, the system did not manage to recoup the full cost of the projects it was supposed to finance. This led to serious liquidity problems for the agency in charge of it. Negative real interest rates on outstanding valorization debts, lagging collection efforts, legal prohibition of double taxation of individual properties affected by more than one valorization project, the failure of many public agencies to pay valorization charges, and subsidies to property owners in poor neighborhoods all helped create a shortfall of revenues. Frequent difficulties in acquiring land and other causes of delay in implementation often resulted in serious cost overruns without, however, resulting in new calculations of valorization charges. The cost overruns thus had to be absorbed entirely by the agency carrying out the project. Financial matters were made worse when, during the mid-1970s, support from general tax revenues to the system was cut by the general purpose local government.

A second reason for the decline of the valorization system during the 1970s was the failure of local authorities to continue a systematic program of investments in urban road infrastructure, which would have attracted loan financing and could have continued to yield financial resources from valorization charges. Third, the system has been vested in an autonomous local agency; this was in part responsible for the lack of integrated planning of development in the city.

Fourth, during the 1970s the system appears to have lost the extensive support which policymakers had given it during the preceding decade. Thus its problems were not given the attention they deserved. Efforts have been made to remedy some of the financial problems, but their success remains to be seen. In principle, there is little reason why many of the troubles cannot be overcome by appropriate measures: more realistic interest rates on term payments; effective penalties for late payments; integral service development at the neighborhood level and thus avoidance of double taxation; better methods of acquiring land, of avoiding cost overruns, and of passing them on to the taxpayer where unavoidable; and—to the extent that less than full cost recovery is adopted as a policy—steady support from general tax sources.

Summary

Land readjustment systems in East Asia and the valorization system in Colombia have demonstrated the varying potential of development charges. Although the systems are not directly transferable to other countries, a serious consideration of development charges is likely to be appropriate. The limitations and difficulties encountered with land readjustment in Korea and valorization charges in Colombia should not be downplayed or neglected. On the contrary, they provide useful clues to the pitfalls which may be encountered when development charges are used. For readjustment, besides the need for a rather sophisticated administrative system, the main problems arise in improving established urban areas as against new areas and in aiming to benefit low-income groups. For valorization programs, financial viability and program development are among the main problems. In designing improved systems of development for any city in developing countries, the experiences in Korea and Colombia should prove valuable.

PART IV

Intergovernmental Fiscal Relations

THE TWO PRECEDING parts of this book drive home the lesson that urban local governments must become more of a partner in the revenue mobilization process. But even with heroic advances in the importance of local taxes and user charges, most developing countries will continue to operate with a very centralized fiscal structure. It is essential, therefore, that central governments define a set of fiscal relationships with their local governments, especially those of their rapidly growing cities, that enable them to find the right balance between their needs for decentralization of governance and control over resource allocation.

The subject of chapter 12 is fiscal decentralization, an issue that is on the economic planning and political agenda in most countries. We first look at theory to identify the factors that push countries to exercise more or less control over fiscal instruments, and then at the various ways in which the relations between central and local governments are arranged in developing countries. Chapter 12 also takes up the subject of the structure of metropolitan government, and it reviews the relative merits of metropolitanwide government versus a fragmented local government structure.

Intergovernmental transfers in developing countries are taken up in chapter 13. Shared taxes, formula grants, and subsidies are reviewed and evaluated. Both experiences with these systems and theory are called on to establish principles for designing systems of intergovernmental transfers.

12 The Structure of Urban Governance

IN INDUSTRIAL and developing countries alike, there is much disagreement about the proper way to organize the public sector to finance and deliver services. The debate centers on questions about which level of government should provide which services, how much managerial and fiscal autonomy the local governments should have, whether the revenue base given to local governments is commensurate with their expenditure responsibilities, and how much fragmentation in the structure of local government within urban areas should be allowed. This chapter seeks to develop a framework for answering such questions in the context of developing countries.

The questions we raise here by no means exhaust the list of important concerns. Among the important issues not discussed in any detail are mandated expenditure requirements by higher levels of government, the legal limits on interactions among governments, the elective process, the relation between the national and local civil services, and a host of very important management and administrative topics.[1] Perhaps the most important omission is a direct discussion of the influence of politics on the choice of structure for local government. As in earlier chapters, we are concerned both with what theory tells us about how the intergovernmental system should be structured and with current practices.

Fiscal Decentralization

The current structure of local government in developing countries—and that which will emerge in the future—reflects the commitment of central governments to decentralization.[2] Indeed, the rhetoric on this issue is strong: the decentralization of population and economic activity is a common goal for developing-country governments and the international agencies which advise them. A development strategy of decentralization, however, does not necessarily mean that local governments will finance and deliver more services. Some countries limit their concern to population, that is, to seeking a better balance in size and economic well-being between rural and urban areas or between large and small towns. Others want to decentralize government operations, for example to pass decisionmaking authority to the regional branches of central government ministries. Still others may view the lowest levels of subnational government (municipalities and counties) as inconsequential to decentralization and go no further than to consider central-provincial relations. Bird and DeMello give us two good statements of this view:

> One of the most interesting features of the governmental structure in Papua New Guinea is that by far the largest city in the country, with a population greater than that of most provinces and a budget and public service establishment which is also much larger than that in most provinces, has apparently never been taken explicitly into account in any of the interminable discussions over the last decade about the relationship between national and provincial governments [Bird 1983: 56].

> As a rule, national development plans in Latin America do not explicitly include local governments as part of their strategies . . . no Latin American development plan has come down, for example, to the establishment of a national system of cities or to a blueprint for the redistribution of functions among the several levels of government, as a means to enhance economic and social development [De Mello 1977: 28–37].

Conversely, many countries have come to realize that strengthening local governments by granting them some fiscal autonomy is an important component of decentralization. The evidence for this concern is a rash of government commissions on allocating fiscal responsibilities to local governments, restructuring intergovernmental grant systems, and solving the special fiscal problems of large cities. The role of local governments in the development process is in general less often spelled out in national plans than included in administrative and legislative actions that become part of the planning process.

Three general arguments might be given in support of fiscal decentralization:

- If the expenditure mix and tax rates are determined closer to the people, local public services will improve and local residents will be more satisfied with government services.
- Stronger local governments will contribute to nation-building because people can identify more closely with local than central government.
- Overall resource mobilization will be increased because local governments can tax the fast-growing parts of their economic base more easily than can the central government.

The third argument is particularly important and ultimately may make the strongest case for fiscal decentralization. As the economies of rural areas and secondary cities develop, their taxable capacity and willingness to purchase public services will also develop. It will be very difficult for central governments to capture much of this fiscal surplus because neither central government income nor consumption taxes typically reach small firms, workers in smaller firms or outside the larger cities, or marketing activities; local government business and occupation licenses, sales taxes, permits, and property taxes have a much better chance.

With this set of general arguments for fiscal decentralization as backdrop, and because decentralization policies are followed by many developing countries, we turn now to a more systematic inquiry into the merits and demerits of the practice. Several questions call for answers:

- What does the theory of public finance suggest about the optimal assignment of functions among levels of government?
- How can fiscal decentralization be measured?
- How far have developing countries gone in decentralizing their fiscal activities?
- What population and economic characteristics make some developing countries stronger candidates for fiscal decentralization than others?
- What policy changes are likely to lead to more fiscal decentralization?

The Theory of Fiscal Assignment

Economic theory cannot lead to firm conclusions about the best division of fiscal responsibilities between central, state, and local governments, that is, about optimal fiscal decentralization. It can only suggest the considerations relevant in making the best fiscal assignments. "Best" of course varies from country to country and depends on the institutional setting, history, and most of all politics.

Musgrave's view that the purposes of government budgets are to stabilize growth, redistribute income, and allocate fiscal resources has long been the starting point for discussing the division of taxing powers and responsibility for expenditure.[3] The stimulation of stable economic growth and the distribution of income, he argues, are appropriate budget objectives of the central government. The mobility of capital and labor rules out local government success with policies in either area. This leaves allocation as the main role for local governments, that is, the decisions about how much to spend for each service and how to finance these expenditures. Subnational governments, it is said, are closest to voter-consumers and are in the best position to read local preferences for public services and for various kinds of taxes and user charges. The proper degree of decentralization, then, will depend on how the efficiency gains achieved by getting government closer to the people compare with the advantages which result from giving central governments more discretion to pursue fiscal policy.

THE CASE FOR CENTRALIZATION. The arguments for fiscal centralization are stronger in developing than in industrial countries. Because low-income economies are less diversified and therefore more exposed to international fluctuations in commodity prices, natural disasters, wars, worldwide recession, and so forth, stabilization is especially important for them. This argues for central government control of the main tax and borrowing instruments. In developing nations, a policy for economic growth is also an argument for fiscal centralization because investment capital is scarce and must be controlled by the central government to maximize returns. If local governments are given access to major tax bases, they may compete with the central government and therefore limit the amount available for the central tax. As a corollary, centralization allows the national government to allocate fiscal resources to goods and services with national benefits, whereas local autonomy would inevitably lead to greater expenditures on those services that have more local benefits.

Several arguments for income distribution also support fiscal centralization. The most important is that regional (and rural-urban) disparities in income and wealth may be accentuated by fiscal decentralization because wealthier urban governments will benefit most from greater taxing powers. Centralization allows the national government more discretion in shaping regional differences in levels of public service and taxation, which is an especially important consideration for governments that intend to use tax and subsidy policy to shape the spatial distribution of economic development.

The final argument is that central governments have superior abilities to administer taxes and manage the delivery of public services. Local governments in almost every country have very weak administrative practices, and less local autonomy means less chance for local governments to mismanage finances. A corollary to this argument is that skilled fiscal managers—analysts, accountants, valuers, and collectors—are too scarce in developing countries to be shared between the central and local governments.

THE CASE FOR DECENTRALIZATION. One might counter the above justifications of centralization with these good arguments for decentralization:

- Cities could levy higher taxes and could thereby charge residents the full marginal cost of urbanization. A more efficient size distribution of cities could result.
- Local governments could adjust budgets to local preferences, and a more efficient distribution of local public services could result.
- Local governments might be able to tax some sectors of the urban economy more easily than could the central government. A higher rate of national resource mobilization could thus occur.

Are these arguments really valid? Can local governments actually respond to citizens' preferences for more or fewer local services, or to a willingness to pay more tax to receive local services? In fact, the efficiency case for fiscal decentralization is much stronger in industrial than developing countries. Consider first the notion that moving service provision closer to the people can lead to gains in the welfare of consumer-voters. Because the theory of fiscal assignment was developed in industrial countries, it was heavily influenced by democratic processes of budgetmaking, for example, the median voter theories of public expenditure determination. In this model, the level of tax effort and the expenditure mix in local areas are responsive to changes in relative prices and income, and the potential losses in efficiency caused by interference from a higher level of government can be substantial (as can the potential efficiency gains from the greater fiscal autonomy of local government). Although the model is based on a number of questionable assumptions, empirical research has shown that the behavior of U.S. state and local governments more or less squares with it.[4]

The model does not so easily fit developing countries, however, and the efficiency gains from decentralization therefore may not be so great in developing countries. This is partly because voter preferences are not as readily translated into budget outcomes as in industrial countries. Local councils are often not elected, chief officials are often not locally appointed, and adjustments in the allocation of local resources are often severely constrained by central government controls. These controls include approval of the budget, central appointment of chief local government officers, central government regulation of tax administration, mandates as to salary levels of local government employees, and the general absence of a mechanism by which local voters could reveal their preferences for a larger or smaller government. In this setting—where the devolution of revenue authority and expenditure responsibility is not accompanied by a relaxation of central government control over local fiscal decisionmaking—there is less to be gained from decentralization of taxes and expenditure than would be the case in industrial countries. (The standard constrained maximization approach, adapted to developing countries, is presented in the appendix to this chapter.)

Given this state of affairs, the situation in a developing country which could give maximum gains from a more decentralized local government structure would include: (a) enough skilled labor, access to materials, and plant capital to expand public service delivery when desired, (b) an efficient tax administration, (c) a taxing power able to capture significant portions of community income increments, (d) an income-elastic demand for public services, (e) popularly elected local officials, and (f) some local discretion in shaping the budget and setting the tax rate. These conditions are most likely to exist—or are likely to exist to the greatest degree—in large cities in developing countries. This important point is not likely to excite those who see decentralization as a strategy for improving the relative well-being of small municipalities and rural local governments.

Measurement

To what extent is the theory of fiscal assignment predictive? Is fiscal decentralization more prevalent in industrial countries, and have some types of developing countries chosen more decentralization? A first step toward answering such questions is to devise an index of fiscal decentralization, an exercise fraught with conceptual as well as empirical problems.[5] First, there is the issue of what dimension of fiscal decentralization one wants to measure and then the problem of constructing the index. As always, the difficulties are best resolved by a careful thinking through of the questions being asked, and by accepting at the outset that some degree of subjectivity will be involved. All measures of decentralization will be flawed in some ways, and the "best" choice will depend ultimately on which questions are the most important.

The fiscal importance of subnational government might be measured in terms of the share of revenues generated or the share of expenditures made. The revenue measure would help determine the extent to which local governments are mobilizing public resources through their systems of taxes and user charges and could indicate the relative claim of local governments on total national income. This measure, however, would understate the total involvement of local governments in public activities because it would ignore the possibly greater final responsibility of local governments for the delivery of expenditure and services. The alternative is to measure the share of expenditures made by subnational levels of government and ignore the question of the level of government at which the funds are raised.[6] Indeed, a larger share of expenditure at subnational levels might indicate increasing fiscal decentralization, even though revenue-raising authority remains highly concentrated at the central level. Such a result could occur if there were substantial intergovernmental grants.

We have chosen the share of total government expenditure made by subnational government as the index of fiscal decentralization. This index has three limitations as a comparative measure. First, even though a subnational government is responsible for a particular expenditure, it may or may not be fiscally autonomous. Musgrave has pointed out that local governments which act as spending agents of the central government do not reflect true decentralization of expenditure, just as centrally collected but shared taxes do not constitute true revenue decentralization (Musgrave 1959: 342). The measure of expenditure decentralization used here does not allow one to determine whether a high subnational government share of expenditure is a result of the constitutional assignment of functions, a statutory delegation of expenditure powers, or a division of fiscal functions "just for the sake of administrative convenience."

A second problem that reduces the comparability of the index across countries is that two countries may have the same share of subnational expenditure but a different number of participating local governments. More governments, all other things being equal, imply more fiscal decentralization. Moreover, the index will not pick up the difference between a subnational government share of expenditure concentrated in one or a few cities and an even distribution across all cities. A third problem is that the inclusion of defense expenditures in the denominator of the measure may artificially overstate the degree of centralization. Countries at war, or close to it, are more centralized. Bahl and Nath (1986) have estimated a significant negative relation between decentralization of expenditure and the share of defense in the central budget.

Determinants

Why does fiscal decentralization occur in developing countries, and to what extent does it occur? The voices in many countries calling for more fiscal autonomy for subnational government suggest the overwhelming importance of political considerations. These voices state the needs for more participation in the governmental process, for larger incentives to finance local public services, for recognition of regional diversity, and for an untying of the red tape that seems to characterize big government. One would not have to stretch too far to understand why politicians and even higher-income urban residents would be sympathetic to these needs: the majority of the voting age population lives outside the largest city in most countries, greater involvement in government might mean less opposition to government, better local government services might slow the rate of migration to big cities, and many politicians have their roots if not their constituencies outside large urban areas.

The political advocates of centralization are less vocal but possibly more persuasive. Centralists see decentralization as creating a power base for political rivals and as promoting factionalism. Bureaucrats also want to limit decentralization because stronger local government would drain away some of their budgetary control. As Bird has noted, though perhaps too strongly, "to sum up this discussion of political objectives, no clear conclusion emerges: there are political reasons why centralization may be desirable and equally good reasons for decentralization. On the whole, however, it seems likely that the main political objective in most countries—national unity—is centralizing in nature and that the theoretical merits of decentralization receive little weight in practice" (Bird 1978: 46).

Economic and managerial considerations also seem stacked against decentralization. Indeed, the review of the merits of decentralization above suggests significantly less decentralization in developing countries than in industrial countries. Decentralization more likely comes with the achievement of a higher stage of economic development. This is because per capita income growth is usually accompanied by an increase both in urbanization and in the local government tax capacity implied by urbanization; by a greater degree of local administrative capacity, improvements in the implementation skills of local governments; and perhaps by the desire to eliminate gross regional disparities in the quality of public services.

This hypothesis appears to be borne out by an analysis of 1973 U.N., World Bank, and IMF data conducted by Bahl and Nath. Using a sample of twenty-three industrial and thirty-four developing countries and the share of expenditure of subnational governments as the measure of fiscal decentralization, they found clear evidence of the greater dominance of central governments in developing countries. On average, subnational governments in industrial countries accounted for 32.2 percent of all government expenditures, compared with 14.9 percent in developing ones. Moreover, only four developing countries (all in Latin America) had a ratio of fiscal decentralization above the average for industrial countries. Further, they find that this pattern did not change during the 1960s and early 1970s. In fact, between 1960 and 1973, the subnational government share of total government expenditures increased more in the industrial than in the developing countries. A more recent analysis using 1980 data finds little change in this measure since 1973 for either developing or developed countries (Wasylenko 1987).

The question of what types of countries are most likely to decentralize fiscal activity has been subject to empirical testing using econometric models. This literature suggests three main determinants of the decentralization of expenditure. Cross-sectional studies have shown that the stage of development, measured as per capita GNP or urbanization, is associated with a significantly greater subnational share of expenditure.[7] A second influence on fiscal decentralization is country size: the larger the country, the more decentralization. In some cases, the size effect has led to the choice of a federal system of governance, whereas in others it has led to the delegation of more fiscal responsibility to subnational governments.[8] Fiscal management in very large countries becomes unwieldy and, all other things being equal, leads to a much stronger role for subnational government. This is not to say that smaller countries do not struggle with the question of the optimal degree of decentralization; for example, the question has very recently come under government study in Papua New Guinea (Bird 1983), Ecuador (Greytak and Mendez 1986), and Burkina Faso (Miner and Hall 1983).

Finally, there is the "crisis effect," that is, a propensity to give less discretionary powers to local governments in countries where there is a continuing threat of social upheaval. This possibility was raised in Peacock and Wiseman's displacement theory of the growth of government expenditure (1961). It has been supported by at least one cross-section study of developing countries which shows a negative association between fiscal decentralization and the central government share of expenditure devoted to defense (Bahl and Nath 1986). There are many examples of this effect. In the aftermath of civil war, Zaire considered complete abolition of local government (Prud'homme 1973), and Bolivia and Honduras abolished their municipal councils in the late 1970s, as did Jamaica (Kingston's) during the economic crisis of the early 1980s. Fiscal centralization may also be stimulated by a revenue "bonanza effect." One example is the growth of the Nigerian public sector during the period of increase in the price of oil. The revenues did not pass through—the state government share of total federal revenues fell from 40 percent in 1970 to 15 percent by 1973.

Conclusions and Implications

Theory and empirical analysis point to three reasons why subnational governments in developing countries receive varying amounts of public expenditure. First, there appears to be a direct relation between level of expenditure and level of economic development. Development stimulates demand for services provided by local governments in addition to increasing the local tax base. Second, countries with larger populations are more decentralized, perhaps because central provision of many government services becomes all but impossible. Third, countries whose budgets carry less of a defense burden and that have not faced social upheavals are more able to decentralize.

These results suggest three hypotheses about how government policy can strengthen the local fisc. First, fiscal decentralization may well accompany economic development, but the threshold level of economic development—beyond which countries decentralize government as per capita income rises—appears to be quite high. The implication of this observation is that government policies to promote fiscal decentralization are more likely to be effective for middle- and high-income countries. For the lowest-income countries, decentralization may be limited to rhetoric.

The second implication for policy is that the benefits of fiscal decentralization are most likely to be received by devolving fiscal authority to large cities. The primary gains from decentralization are thought to be gains in efficiency from allowing locals to choose their own levels of taxes and expenditure and the greater revenue mobilization that will result from letting local governments "get at" their growing tax bases. Large cities are more likely to capitalize on these potential benefits.

Third, as central governments raise more money, the subnational government share of expenditures falls—taxes stick where they hit. The implication of this "flypaper effect" is that the best route to decentralization of expenditure is to assign local governments particular revenue bases or to guarantee them shares of particular central taxes. Otherwise, larger central tax revenues will not be shared proportionately with subnational governments and more fiscal centralization will result.

The National Structure of Urban Government

The theoretical extremes in the national structure of urban government are complete centralization—a single central government—and complete decentralization—no central government. There appear to be no examples of complete decentralization, whereas Singapore and some West Indian nations come close to approximating the former. Most countries lie between these extremes with varying degrees of decentralization in revenue raising authority, expenditure responsibility, and local autonomy in deciding on the mix and level of services to be produced.[9] As noted above, we would expect developing countries to tend toward centralization.

The actual amount of fiscal decentralization in a country is not a straightforward, one-dimensional characteristic. Some local governments may be given more responsibility for expenditure than others, taxing powers may be broad or limited, borrowing may be permitted or prohibited, and so forth. To try to develop a reasonable taxonomy of local autonomy or local self-governance, we might think of a country's "intergovernmental arrangement"; this would include the delineation of levels of government, a definition of the formal relations these levels may have with each other in a national setting, and the degree of autonomy given to each subnational level of government. In short, what is the place of local governments in the national setting?

Typically, the structure of government in a developing country provides three degrees of autonomy for its local governments. Small, rural local governments are thought to have less wherewithal to plan and manage their fiscal affairs, and they have the least fiscal autonomy. Therefore the rural system of local government is often managed directly by the central government (in Kenya) or through provincial governments (in the Philippines). Municipalities—large urban governments—are given more autonomy and a broader range of revenue-raising powers and fiscal discretion. These governments often have the status of both municipal and provincial governments (in the Philippines and in China). The largest cities are treated differently from other municipalities and are usually given even more fiscal discretion. In short, the degree of autonomy given local governments varies within a country and depends largely on the size of the local government.[10]

Although this general pattern holds true in most developing countries, there is still a great deal of variation. Is one structure of local government and set of intergovernmental arrangements somehow best? Theory will not give us an answer. There are tradeoffs in choosing more or less autonomy for local governments and political considerations will weigh heavily in the choices eventually made. This leads us to turn to a more positive analysis, that is, consideration of the choices regarding local government structure which governments of developing countries have actually made. If there is some rationality in these choices, we might be able to identify those factors which appear to lead to the granting of more or less fiscal autonomy to local governments.

How do the varying degrees of local fiscal autonomy come about? One possibility, suggested by empirical research, is that a federal structure tends to be associated with a strong subnational government. Accordingly, knowledge of why some countries have a federal and others a unitary system is a useful starting point. A second possibility is that central versus subnational control of government fiscal affairs, rather than constitutional versus statutory provision of subnational fiscal powers, most delimits local fiscal autonomy. These two possibilities are taken up below.

Alternative Systems

Two common models of intergovernmental arrangements have emerged in developing countries. Under a unitary system, state (or provincial) and local governments are statutory bodies defined by the central government; their fiscal powers are a matter of central policy and are not guaranteed by any constitutional provision.[11] Under a federal system, the powers, duties, and responsibilities of state governments are defined in the constitution, and local governments usually are creations of the state government. Their fiscal powers may be changed often by the state, or they may be given residual fiscal powers. Therefore in a federal system, central-state relations normally are defined by the constitution, whereas state-local relations are organized as in a unitary state. This is the situation in India. Another version is for local governments to be full partners in the federal system with their financial powers and responsibilities provided for in the constitution. This is the case in Brazil and Nigeria.

The struggles for more autonomy between national and state governments and that between state and local governments are very different, especially in countries with strong intermediate governments or at least strong regional differences. The central-state struggle is usually over political autonomy and grows out of historic regional power bases; movements for independence; and ethnic, linguistic, and cultural differences (for example, the ongoing debates in Colombia, India, Indonesia, Mexico, and Nigeria). The central government resists too much subnational independence in the name of retaining the cohesion of the country or resisting dominance by a particular region, state, elite, or culture. By contrast, the central-local and state-local government struggle tends to center on the allocation of fiscal resources and the desire of local governments for autonomy in providing services. This relatively new conflict has arisen primarily because of the population growth of large cities. Of course, there is overlap: central-state relations also involve purely fiscal aspects, and central-local relations can also involve issues of independence, political power, and culture.

FEDERAL SYSTEMS. Many developing countries have chosen a federal system to structure the relation between central and subnational governments, for example, Brazil, India, Malaysia, Pakistan, and Nigeria.[12] This system, typically but not always, transfers control of city finances from the central to an intermediate level of government.[13] There are strong arguments for and against an intermediate level government with substantial budgetary control. In populous, large countries where preferences are likely to vary widely, for example Brazil and India, it enables the central government to avoid direct dealings with a large number of diverse urban governments. For example, the central government can use grant formulas to recognize broad differences in needs and preferences without having to take into account the needs of individual cities, or it can simply assign responsibility for local finances to the state government. Imagine the problems a country such as India would have in attempting to allocate grant funds or approve tax rate increases on a city by city basis.

Advantages and disadvantages aside, urban governments in a federal system generally depend on the state government to provide some services directly, pass through central grants, approve borrowing plans and increases in tax rates, appoint chief government officers, and assign expenditure responsibility and taxing power.[14] Under this system, the central government essentially gives the responsibility for local finance to state governments. The degree of local autonomy that results depends on how state governments interpret their powers.

There are disadvantages to this approach. The federal structure creates an intermediate level of decisionmaking that complicates the implementation of any national urban plan; that is, it is necessary to rely on state governments to pass central funds through to targeted urban and rural governments. If state governments are relatively autonomous in their fiscal and economic planning, the resulting allocation may not match central goals. For example, in the 1960s and 1970s the U.S. government watched states follow policies that increased the fiscal disparities between low-income central city governments and high-income suburban governments.[15] This inequitable attitude is not restricted to state governments in industrial countries. Adamolekun, Osemwata, and Olowu (1980: 98) report that in Nigeria, "the overall attitude of the state governments was to take whatever financial allocations the Federal government made to local governments and disburse same on their own terms, with little or no regard for what the Federal government requested them to do with such allocations."

To counter such disadvantages, some federal countries have taken the position that a viable system of local government requires direct central-local relations. Direct federal-local relations have become more important in Brazil and Mexico (De Mello 1977: 28–37), and in Nigeria the new constitution in 1979 recognized "the existence of local governments as a distinct third level of government within the national federal governmental system" (Adamolekun, Osemwata, and Olowu 1980: 97).

Are local governments given more or less fiscal latitude in a federal structure? The answer is by no means clear. Data on expenditure responsibility and revenue mix are reported for a number of developing-country cities in chapter 2 (tables 2-7, 2-10, and 2-11). Although the fiscal responsibility and importance of these local governments is far greater than has been generally supposed, there is a wide variation in their importance, and a pattern is not easily found. In one test, the cities were grouped according to their location in federalist and unitary countries and average values were calculated for the share of property taxes, grants, and borrowing in total revenues. There was little difference in any of these measures between the two groups. By the same procedure, there was little pattern in the distribution of responsibilities for expenditure. Some local governments do very little (Kingston), whereas others have a broad range of responsibilities (Seoul). Whether there is a federal or nonfederal structure does not appear to be the key to understanding this variation.

UNITARY SYSTEMS. A second form of intergovernmental arrangement links larger local governments directly to the center. Because local governments are statutory bodies, they are subject to direct control by the central government and may be abolished at its pleasure.

An intermediate level of government may still lie between the central and local governments under a unitary system. This is the case in Korea and the Philippines, where provincial governments act as the agent of the central government in regulating the finances of the smaller local units. In the case of urban governments, these provinces do not exert regulatory control or lend financial assistance.[16]

There are advantages to the unitary system. The central government can target aid flows more easily to particular local governments, and local governments can be made more accountable for their fiscal actions. Substantial national variation in the size and structure of local government budgets is also allowed. A major disadvantage is that it is administratively difficult for the central government to deal directly with a great number of local governments which may vary widely in service needs, fiscal base, and capacity to provide services. But as Henderson (1980) has shown, the unitary developing countries tend to have fewer large cities.

Central Regulation and Fiscal Autonomy

Local governments appear to spend relatively more under federal than unitary systems, but this may occur mostly because federal countries are larger. But there may not be any more urban fiscal autonomy under federal than unitary systems.

The important issue here is fiscal autonomy, the control over sufficient resources to plan and manage the provision of local public services without continuous interference from higher authorities.[17] In trying to understand whether a federal system somehow gives large city governments more fiscal autonomy than does a unitary system, we might raise the following questions about the differences between the two systems:

- Do structures of revenue and responsibility for expenditure differ?
- Is there more latitude in revising tax rates under one system than the other?
- Are borrowing powers equally circumscribed?
- Does the degree of budgetary monitoring differ?
- Does the process of selecting the council and chief officers vary?

Because comparable information on the above measures is not readily available, it is not possible here to compare and contrast all cities in the world. What we can do is piece together the fragmentary evidence on fiscal performance presented in chapter 2, the information on government structure provided in the case studies which underlie this book, and other available data on the practice. These materials do not yield a random sample for econometric testing; they only lead to many examples and anecdotes. But they do give some sense of the relation between local fiscal autonomy and intergovernmental arrangement. Two overriding conclusions may be drawn: the fiscal activities of local government are very tightly controlled, and there is as much variation in fiscal autonomy and practice within the unitary and federal groups of cities as between them.

FISCAL DISCRETION. Two city governments may raise or spend the same amount but have very different degrees of autonomy in their fiscal actions. The central question here is not the size of the budget but the discretion which the local government has in the disposition of the budget.[18] In fact, the authority of local government to adjust tax rates and to enact new taxes is limited in virtually every developing country. National or state law normally prescribes the tax bases available (or unavailable) to local governments and sets maximum rates within which they must operate. These restrictions usually hold even for large cities. When the rate ceilings are binding, as is often the case, local governments have little discretion and must depend on the center to approve every revenue proposal. A similar arrangement holds for increases in user charges for most primary services, for example, water rates, bus fares, and rents. The issue then becomes whether the central or state government will approve the requested increases. Practice varies, but some countries have consistently refused requests for local increases; for example, cities in Bangladesh were held at 1960 property tax rates despite repeated requests for incremental increases (Schroeder 1985a: 33, 55). All countries, however, are not subject to such stringent controls. In

Brazil and Venezuela municipal laws are not subject to approval by higher levels of government, though some tax changes do require approval by a central agency (De Mello 1977: 6–16).

In developing countries most central or state governments have approval powers over local government budgets. The extent to which this process reduces local fiscal autonomy depends on the tightness of the review process. The experience in this regard varies widely. Nairobi has faced a line-by-line review of expenditures by the Kenyan Ministry of Local Government, but the Ministry of the Interior in Indonesia generally accepts the proposal of a metropolitan council.[19] The budget autonomy of local government may also be hampered by central government mandates. For example, nearly 50 percent of the budgets of Philippine municipal governments are earmarked for specific purposes, giving them only a very limited latitude to adjust the budget to respond to local demands (Bahl and Schroeder 1983c: chap. 2). Less permanent but unexpected central government mandates may also have dramatic and direct effects on the level of local government spending. For example, in the 1970s the Kenyan central government mandated an increase in local government employee emoluments, ordered the provision of free drugs and dressings by local authorities, and abolished local school fees. A common form of mandate which local governments in developing countries face is a hiring freeze, a reaction by the central government to what it sees as irresponsible management.

The borrowing powers of local governments are quite limited in most developing countries. Though credit is made available to local governments under a variety of schemes (see chapter 13), most local governments are given little discretion over the amount or purpose of the loan, the source of the funds, or the terms of repayment. The issuance of debt is tightly controlled by central governments on the grounds that expansion of total domestic credit is an important stabilization issue and that the allocation of scarce credit among regions and purposes must conform closely to the national development plan. Still, some local governments have been given more autonomy than others in the planning and issuance of debt. For example, the Calcutta Metropolitan Development Authority may borrow in the open market (from banks and provident funds) subject to a limit tied to its tax revenues; the Nairobi City Council may sell bonds in the market, but Ministry of Finance approval is required; and local governments in many countries are allowed to engage in short-term borrowing from commercial banks.

LOCAL COUNCIL AND OFFICERS. Perhaps the most important issues of all in establishing local autonomy have to do with how local council and chief administrative officers of the city are selected, and with the definition of the powers of the council and the administration. For example, it may matter little that local governments have a broad range of fiscal powers if all local decisions about financing and governance rest in the hands of centrally appointed officials. Again, a broad range of practices is followed. At one extreme are very centralized systems (such as those in Bangkok, Seoul, and Tunis), in which the head of the city government is appointed by the president. At the other extreme the local council and mayor are elected (as in Brazilian cities and Colombo, Sri Lanka). In between are many shades of centralization and decentralization. For example:

- Under the presidency of Ferdinand Marcos, the mayors of the Manila region's cities and municipalities were elected, but the councils and the governor of the Metropolitan Manila Authority were appointed by the president.
- Malaysian local government councils are appointed by the state government.
- One-hundred-fifty members of the Karachi Metropolitan Corporation are elected, and the other sixteen are appointed by the state government.

If the political and managerial systems of a city are separate, there is the issue of the status and appointment of the local public administrators, that is, the municipal commissioner or town clerk, treasurer, assessor, and so forth. Again, there are many variations. Though local councils are popularly elected in the Indian federal system, the chief administrative officer is a state appointee; in Mexico City, which has state and city status, he is a federal appointee. Chief officers may be seconded from the federal or state service in Nigeria, and the local assessor and treasurer are actually central government employees in the Philippines. In many Latin American countries, the municipal chief executive also represents the central government in the municipality.

There is the provision, in most developing countries, for the central government to dissolve the local council. Again, however, what these provisions mean for local autonomy depends on the degree to which the government exercises its powers. For example, Kingston's local council is elected but may be abolished by the central government if the latter finds evidence of an abuse of power. In fact, the Kingston–Saint Andrews Council has been abolished four times since 1923; the latest occurrence was in 1984 because of "financial irresponsibility" and "gross mismanagement." Manila's local councils were abolished during martial law, Bangkok's experience is similar to Manila's, Karachi's council was abolished in 1971 but restored in 1979, and local councils in Bolivia and Honduras were abolished in the late 1970s.

The Special City

The position of the city in a national system of urban governance may be modified to take account of special problems, needs, or national goals.

In almost every country, the capital city is afforded special status, and more often than not it is given more fiscal autonomy than other cities in the nation. Several factors have led to this special treatment. First, the machinery of government, and therefore a disproportionate amount of tax-exempt property, is in the capital. Second, because both the services provided and the local administration are highly visible, local government finance is inevitably a national political issue. Third, and perhaps most important, the capital city tends to be the primate city. As such, it usually offers a wider range of public services than other local governments in the country. Moreover, because it offers more employment opportunities and induces a greater rate of immigration, there are great pressures of urbanization and congestion on public services.

Nearly all countries have responded to these special needs by creating, by one name or another, a national capital district. For example, Bogotá and Jakarta are national capital districts with both city and provincial powers, Nairobi was for many years the only chartered city in Kenya, Seoul is a special city under the office of the president and has both city and provincial status, and Kingston is an amalgamation of two parishes. Though in most cases the status of special city is reserved for the capital city, there are situations in which other large cities in the country are afforded similar treatment. Pusan is a special city in Korea, but under the Ministry of Interior; Rio de Janeiro is a special city; Chittagong and Mombasa have become the second municipal corporations in Bangladesh and Kenya, respectively; and Beijing and Shanghai have provincial status in China. In many countries, the criteria for special treatment are less ad hoc, and cities are usually differentiated according to population size.[20] Large cities are given more taxing powers and expenditure responsibilities, and in some countries the chief local officers are paid at a higher rate. The most important of these extra powers is typically the authority to tax at a higher rate.

The status of special city in effect creates a separate intergovernmental system. This has both positive and negative features. Placing the city directly under the nation's president, the common model, has the potential to enable more effective coordination of various ministry activities within the urban area and allow for special treatment of cities which are qualitatively different from other urban areas in the country because of their function, size, and development. It does not allow, however, for the development of a unified intergovernmental system which might establish a role for local government as a sector.

Conclusion

Empirical analysis suggests that about 15 percent of total government spending in developing countries may be attributed to subnational governments. But the aggregate statistic understates the fiscal importance of urban local governments. The contribution of local government to the financing of public services in the larger metropolitan areas is much higher—as much as a third to a half. This is perhaps of more substantial fiscal importance for local governments than many would have expected. But do these fiscal shares indicate a commensurate degree of fiscal autonomy? The answer to this question depends on the way in which countries organize themselves to finance and deliver services at the regional and local levels.

One hypothesis is that subnational governments under federal systems are given more fiscal powers. This seems true for state governments, but we cannot find evidence that the greater fiscal autonomy given to states is usually extended to local governments. The choice of a federal or unitary system, by our reckoning, is not a principal determinant of the degree of fiscal autonomy of local government.

In fact, the main difference among countries turns out to be the degree to which the central or state government controls the everyday operation of the local governments. As noted above, central governments can control the fiscal operations of local authorities in many ways: local budgets and borrowing may have to be approved by the center, the principal local administrative officer may be appointed or approved by the government, all or a portion of the local council may be appointed by the central government, and local units may be restricted in what revenue sources they may tap. The real issue, however, is the degree to which the higher level of government chooses to exercise these controls. Two local governments may have responsibility for providing primary education services. In one instance decisions about the number and compensation of schoolteachers may be made locally. In the other these decisions may be a responsibility of the education ministry, allowing relatively little local autonomy. The same kind of situation arises if increases in local tax rates must always be approved. In some countries rate increases are granted freely once the local council requests them, in others increases need no approval at all up to certain limits, and in still others the central government strongly resists increases.

The contrast between Kingston and Nairobi is a useful example of different approaches to limiting the fiscal autonomy of local government in two cities not too dissimilar in size or colonial heritage. Before its two-year abolition beginning in 1984, the Kingston–Saint Andrews Corporation (KSAC) had little responsibility for expenditure aside from that for a few basic urban services. The central government in Jamaica provided and maintained all primary social services and infrastructure either directly, with autonomous agencies, or through franchises to the private sector. For all practical purposes, the KSAC had no taxing powers. The city of Nairobi, conversely, has a full range of responsibilities for expenditure, the power to tax property and (until 1975) even income, and some authority to borrow funds. But in Kenya the central government aggressively exercises its rights to approve and amend the budgets of local governments, control the amounts and sources from which local governments can borrow, and approve all increases in tax rates. Though such controls exist in most countries, they are not always applied with such fervor.

In the last analysis, what really matters is the will of the central government to allocate more fiscal autonomy to local governments. The signs are not strong that the will is there. The subnational government share of fiscal activity is not increasing, and one is hard-pressed to find examples of local governments being given substantially increased taxing powers, especially access to the buoyant income and consumption tax bases. Three examples illustrate how central governments have backed away from granting more local autonomy. The central government in Kenya unilaterally abolished an income-elastic local income tax in 1975 and replaced it with a grant of a fixed amount. The octroi, the main source of city revenue, was abolished in Bangladesh in 1981 and replaced by a grant of a fixed amount. Federal and state governments in Nigeria abolished the local government's cattle and poll taxes.

The Structure of Large Metropolitan Areas

The division of fiscal responsibility between central and local governments is the vertical dimension of fiscal decentralization. The horizontal dimension is the way large metropolitan cities organize themselves to finance and deliver services within their areas. The issue takes on special significance when one remembers that some of these cities are larger than many countries and that some account for a significant fraction of national population.

Metropolitan cities almost always have more fiscal autonomy than other cities in a country, but the similarity ends there. Some deliver services and levy taxes and charges primarily through an areawide general purpose government, others use autonomous (decentralized) agencies, and still others rely on a fragmented system of many small municipalities. The choice of one of these systems of horizontal fiscal relations implies a tradeoff between the various advantages and disadvantages of each. Again, it is not a question of a best way to do things, but rather of the weights attached to the efficiency and equity benefits.

At issue here are the fiscal implications of the three general models of urban governance: centralized metropolitan government, under which a single local government has responsibility for all or nearly the full range of local functions and has a service boundary that includes the entire urban area; functional fragmentation, under which the provision of services is areawide but is split between the general purpose local government and autonomous agencies; and jurisdictional fragmentation, under which responsibility for the same local functions lies with many local governments operating in the area. The structure of urban government in most areas is a hybrid of these, though one form is usually dominant.

To illustrate the practice of urban governance in developing countries, we describe the systems used in several representative metropolitan areas before turning to an evaluation of the implications for equity and efficiency.

Centralized Metropolitan Government

The most common form of local government in developing countries is areawide general purpose local government, that is, centralized metropolitan government. Under this form most of the basic services provided in the metropolitan area are the responsibility of the city government, and no other general purpose local government (municipality) operates within the urban area. But the urban service area is usually overlapped by one or more special purpose districts, for example, a water supply authority or a bus company. Seoul, Kingston, and Jakarta have more or less representative forms of centralized metropolitan governance.

SEOUL. The Seoul city government, the only general purpose local government operating within its urban area, is responsible for a wide range of services.[21] It is far from an autonomous local government: Seoul is a special city under the direct control of the central government. The chief administrative officer is the mayor, who is appointed by the president and can exercise broad decisionmaking and executory powers with little or no check at the local level. One exception to this centralized administration is school finance, which is administered by a semiautonomous Board of Education composed of six members appointed by the president, with the chairman being the mayor of Seoul. The Board of Education is responsible for educational planning, including decisions on expenditure, in conjunction with the Ministry of Education. Although the education budget does not have to be approved formally by the city government, it is recorded as a special account in the Seoul city budget.

There is little decentralization in fiscal decisionmaking, either in terms of other local government bodies operating within the metropolitan area or in terms of influences at the neighborhood level on expenditure decisions. The city is divided into nine administrative wards, or *gu*, whose boundaries appear to be more the result of history or accident than of design for planning purposes.[22] These *gu* are large enough that one would not expect them to hold a more homogeneous population than does the city as a whole. In point of fact, these administrative units serve as channels through which information on neighborhood problems can be transmitted to the central administration, as units for tax assessment and collection, and as centers for issuing licenses, permits, registrations, and so forth. Decisions regarding the level and functional distribution of expenditures within any given neighborhood remain at the city level.

In terms of horizontal fiscal relations, Seoul is perhaps as centralized as any city we have studied. This gives it the advantage of ease in co-ordinating activities and in implementing plans. There is less chance for duplication of services than under other systems, and the size of the city should allow for the capture of economies of scale in the provision of some services. But because the local government is quite large, it is difficult to manage, and there is no ready mechanism for responding to intracity differences in demand for the package of public services to be delivered.

KINGSTON. The KSAC is a general purpose local government with area-wide responsibility for the delivery of services.[23] Three institutions make up the structure of public administration: the Municipal Council, the Municipal Administration, and the Water Commission.

The Municipal Council is responsible for all local public services with the exception of water supply. The council (elected every third year) consists of thirty-two popularly elected councillors and a mayor, who must be a councillor and who is elected by the council. The mayor, although having no special authority over the other council members, has particular weight in policy matters having been elected by, and thus able to speak for, the majority of councillors. The council prepares the budget and can raise revenues, determine tax rates, and borrow, always subject to approval by the central government. These powers may seem broad, but it must be remembered that the KSAC has been given limited access to revenue bases and little responsibility for expenditure. In 1984 it raised only 1.5 percent of total revenues from its own sources.

The KSAC administration is headed by the three statutory municipal officers: the town clerk, the city treasurer, and the city engineer. All are appointed by the council, and all can be removed from office by the council with the approval of the central government. The clerk is the chief administrative officer and has disciplinary powers over nonmuni-cipal officers. The treasurer works in close collaboration with the clerk, although the treasurer is also separately responsible to the council. The engineer reports directly to the clerk.

The Water Commission is a semiautonomous body whose functions are to provide water and sewerage services in the corporate area. It is administered by a board of nine members appointed by the Ministry of Public Utilities for five years and recallable at any time by the minister. In 1973 the mayor of the KSAC was put on the board for the first time since 1965, when the statutory requirement for local government par-ticipation on the board was abolished. The commission reports directly to the Ministry of Public Utilities, and its annual budget must be ap-proved by the ministry.

By comparison with Seoul, Kingston allows for a good deal more cit-izen participation in making the budget. Conversely, the KSAC has very little responsibility for expenditure by comparison with Seoul and must coordinate all its activities with the central government and autonomous water company. Other than the locally elected council, there is no provision for allocating resources to neighborhoods or otherwise decentralizing fiscal decisionmaking powers.

JAKARTA. The city (district) of Jakarta (DKI) delivers a broad range of areawide services (Linn, Smith, and Wignjowijoto 1976). There is some degree of functional decentralization, in that a number of semiautonomous metropolitan public service enterprises exist; however, their autonomy is limited to day-to-day management. Governmental authority at the local level is shared between the metropolitan council and the governor. The governor is appointed by the president, three-quarters of the forty members of the metropolitan council are popularly elected, and the remaining members are appointed by the minister of the interior. The council's main functions are approval of the city budget, as proposed by the governor; review of the activities of the executive branch; and enactment of legislation concerning tax structure, rates and implementation, and orders regulating city affairs. In this last obligation, the council shares responsibility with the governor, who may also issue regulations through executive decrees. The executive of the DKI is headed by the governor, who is assisted by four deputy governors and a general secretary. The general secretary (sometimes also referred to as town clerk) coordinates the daily business of the executive agencies.

The DKI administration supervises the activities of several semiautonomous local public enterprises—which are in charge of particular service functions—and commercial corporations that are owned partly or entirely by the DKI. The budgeting and accounting procedures of these agencies are not subject to review by the metropolitan council or the minister of the interior, but they must be approved by the governor. Moreover, the governor has the authority to appoint the manager and staff of each.

An interesting feature of the structure of urban governance in Jakarta is the attempt to decentralize fiscal affairs to the neighborhood level. The city is divided into 5 municipalities, each of which is headed by a mayor. These municipalities are further partitioned into 27 districts, each administered by a district head. The districts in turn consist of 200 villages led by village heads, and the villages are further subdivided into neighborhood and family associations. These submetropolitan agencies are extensions of the governor's office. They are meant to serve as two-way channels of communication and control at the regional level to relay information from the grass roots to the governor's office and back. These sublocal administrative units have less autonomy than the lower-level local government units in the rest of Indonesia (that is, the municipalities, districts, and villages). In the DKI, sublocal officials are appointed by the governor or the general secretary, and the sublocal authorities do not have their own revenue, expenditure, and budgeting authority. The sub-local authorities are included in the general DKI budget, but their expenditures cover only staff salaries and office-related equipment.

Jakarta, then, is highly centralized like Seoul in that considerable power is vested in an appointed governor and in that a wide range of public services is delivered. It differs, however, in two important respects: a partially elected metropolitan council provides some citizen participation in making the budget, and there is a mechanism for reflecting neighborhood preferences in the mix of public services.

Functional Fragmentation

In functionally fragmented metropolises, the municipal government's responsibilities for services are limited, and basic functions are delegated to autonomous local bodies. The difference between centralized metropolitan governance and functional fragmentation is largely a matter of degree, because almost all urban areas are overlaid by some special districts; for example, water supply and sewerage are commonly provided by separate companies. In some metropolitan areas, however, this functional fragmentation has gone so far that local public enterprises have been created to finance and deliver even some of the traditional services of municipal government.

The advantages of functional fragmentation are easily seen. The delivery of services may be separated from political influence; a higher-paid, more professional staff might be secured if the regular government pay scales can be bypassed; and dedicated revenues from user charges form a basis for financing capital expansions that might not be available to a general purpose government. But it also has important disadvantages. The more autonomous the agencies that operate within a metropolitan area, the greater is their potential for duplication of efforts, the harder it is to coordinate urban development, and the less possibility there is to finance one service with the surplus generated through the provision of another. The experience with functional fragmentation in Cartagena illustrates some of the potential advantages and problems of this form of metropolitan governance.

The Republic of Colombia is a unitary democracy, organized on a national, departmental (state), and municipal level. Each department is headed by a governor appointed by the president, and each municipality by a mayor who is in turn appointed by the governor. The mayor shares political responsibility with the elected municipal council and is the link between the municipal administration and the autonomous statutory bodies that provide most local public services to a municipality. These statutory bodies have their own sources of revenue (from earmarked taxes and/or service charges) and are independent in their day-to-day operations as well as in their fundamental policy choices. In fact, this independence from legislative control is often cited as the main reason for the existence of such agencies. On the one hand, the agencies' freedom from the political process enables them to achieve a high level of management and strategic planning. On the other hand, their freedom from the budgetary control of the legislative bodies has made these agencies attractive tools in the hands of the president, governors, or mayors, who use them to pursue particular policies.

The municipal council's functions in Cartagena (Linn 1975) consist primarily of approving the municipal budget, determining tax rates and service charges, appointing the chief local government officers, and appointing the auditor for the principal autonomous agency, the Municipal Public Service Company. The functions of the municipal government are narrowly prescribed and almost entirely restricted to representative, general administrative, and coordinating activities. This explains why the mayor's position is not a full-time job. In summary, the municipal administration of Cartagena is primarily a tax collection agency.

The Municipal Public Service Company (EPM) provides the majority of local public services. The functions of the EPM include water supply, sewerage, the construction and maintenance of roads, fire protection, the administration of markets and slaughterhouses, the maintenance of parks, the collection and disposal of refuse, and the cleaning of streets. The EPM is governed by a board of directors, which determines the statutes of the enterprise, selects its general manager, approves its budget and important personnel decisions, decides (within legal limits) on the service charges and taxes to be levied by the company, and in general supervises the financial and economic development of the enterprise. The board of directors consists of six members, including the mayor of Cartagena, a representative of the president of the republic, two members selected by the municipal council, one representative of the local chamber of commerce, and one representative of the central bank. The board selects its own president. The general manager of the EPM is responsible for the day-to-day management of the company as well as for its long-term planning. He presents the EPM budget to the board for consideration and approval and selects the personnel of the enterprise, subject to approval by the board. He participates in the deliberations of the board but has no vote. There are three other major decentralized municipal agencies in Cartagena organized similarly to the EPM: the telephone company, the Valorization Department, and the Tourism Promotion Bureau.

The system of governance in Cartagena possesses some clear advantages over the systems of metropolitan government described above. The management and operation of the EPM and the other municipal enterprises can be more professional and detached from the political process, and financing through user charges is more easily accomplished than general tax increases. Conversely, coordination of activities has proven to be a problem with the autonomous agencies, despite their overlapping boards of directors. Moreover, the dedication of revenues from an activity (for example, telephones) solely to that activity is a rigid arrangement that may lead to overinvestment in that activity. This kind of earmarking can be avoided under a centralized structure of metropolitan governance.

Jurisdictional Fragmentation and Two-Tier Systems

A third approach to urban governance, jurisdictional fragmentation, allows many general purpose local governments to exist within the same urban area. This structure of local government is most often associated with the United States, where single metropolitan areas may house dozens or even hundreds of local governments with taxing power. But fragmented structures of local government are not uncommon in developing countries. For example, four cities and thirteen municipalities operate within metropolitan Manila; thirty-one of São Paulo's municipalities have populations in excess of 100,000; and Tunis is comprised of thirteen communes (municipalities). Many other developing-country cities use this form of governance: Dhaka, Lagos, Lima, Madras, Medellín, and Rio de Janeiro are examples. It is important to understand the crucial difference between the origins of functional and jurisdictional (geographic) fragmentation. Functional fragmentation is often a deliberate and rational decision; for instance, the functions of Colombian cities were split up among autonomous agencies mainly to enhance managerial and financial soundness. In contrast, geographic or jurisdictional fragmentation often is just a natural consequence of urbanization—the expansion of metropolises beyond old core cities into surrounding minor centers and formerly rural areas without changes in jurisdictional boundaries.

The advantage of a fragmented government structure is that it moves government closer to the people by creating smaller local government bodies. The disadvantages may be that it gives up the possibility of capturing economies of scale and may breed disparities in tax burdens and public services among local governments within the urban area. To deal with these disadvantages while retaining the inherent advantage of small local governments, overlapping metropolitan governments have been created. The strengths and weaknesses of this two-level governance might best be understood if one example, Manila, is considered and several metropolitan development authorities are described.

MANILA. The Manila metropolitan area is governed by nineteen local bodies: four chartered cities (including the city of Manila), thirteen municipalities, the Metropolitan Manila Commission (MMC), and an autonomous Metropolitan Water and Sewer Authority. In practice, the governance of this system is highly centralized. The MMC chief executive, the governor, is appointed by the national government, as are all local councils and the chief officers (for example, treasurer, assessor, and engineer) of each municipality and city. Since the lifting of martial law, however, the mayors and deputy mayors have been popularly elected.[24]

The size and wealth of local governments in urban Manila vary widely, from Manila City's estimated 1980 population of 1.6 million to Pateros municipality's 42,000. The MMC was created in 1975 to coordinate, integrate, and unify the services within metropolitan Manila. It does this by providing some services directly and by exercising direct supervision and control over local governments. The MMC derives about a third of its resources from taxes and about half from contributions by constituent local governments.

There is a formal structure for decentralized decisionmaking in the form of the barangay—a grouping of about 200 families who choose a chairman and six council members. The barangays, which have no independent taxing power but receive recurrent grants, have a range of minor responsibilities for public services. In the city of Manila alone, there are more than 900 barangays.

METROPOLITAN DEVELOPMENT AUTHORITIES. Metropolitan development authorities (MDAs) have been a popular way to solve the problems resulting from the geographic fragmentation of local governments in metropolitan areas. This approach has been especially popular on the Indian subcontinent. The following paragraphs give some idea of the form which MDAs have taken in Bombay, Calcutta, Karachi, Madras, and Tunis.

• The Bombay Metropolitan Regional Development Authority is mainly a financing agency which passes on loans to local authorities in the Bombay metropolitan area. It also has some responsibility for the capital budgeting and programming of metropolitanwide investment plans.

• The Madras metropolitan area contains three municipalities, one cantonment, and twenty-four town panchayats. The core city of the metropolitan area, the Madras City Corporation, contains approximately 75 percent of the population, but only 11 percent of the metropolitan land area. The Madras Metropolitan Development Authority was established in 1974 to prepare metropolitanwide development plans and to initiate and monitor their implementation. It also has a mandate to provide services and to improve employment opportunities for low-income groups. It employs a rolling five-year capital budget complemented by annual capital budgets.

• The Calcutta Metropolitan Development Authority (CMDA) was set up as a planning, supervisory, and coordinating agency, with some executive functions, in a highly fragmented metropolitan region. Its executive responsibility is generally limited to the investment stage—responsibility for operation and maintenance remain with the local authorities. This division of responsibilities leads to an inadequate provision for recurrent expenditure needs because of the limitations of the local authorities' technical capacity to operate and maintain new facilities. The CMDA lacks a true fiscal base of its own and is dependent mainly on loans and transfers from higher levels of government.

• The Karachi Development Authority is a state body responsible for all land development and for planning and authorizing new development projects. It does not have an independent source of revenue, except for proceeds from bulk sales of water, which are constrained by the unwillingness of purchasers at lower levels of government to pay the set rates in full. Similar MDAS were set up in 1974 for Islamabad, Lahore, and Peshawar. In all cases the MDAS had responsibility for master planning and project preparation and execution throughout the metropolitan area and were under the direct control of provincial (state) governments.

• In 1972 the Tunis District was set up as a metropolitan authority. Its main functions are to coordinate, plan, budget, and supervise all public investments in the Tunis metropolitan area. Its staff is under the control of the governor-mayor of Tunis. A planning board of local representatives chaired by the mayor can suggest program and planning initiatives; but a supervisory council consisting of the prime minister and other ministers retains effective decisionmaking authority.

It is difficult to judge the success of metropolitan development authorities because the returns from efforts to plan and coordinate are not easily measured. Nevertheless, a number of general observations may be made. First, metropolitan development authorities are likely to be necessary and useful only if a substantial number of local governments operate within an urban area. In other cases, annexation or amalgamation of jurisdictions, interlocal compacts, or selective metropolitanwide provision of services by existing enterprises may be preferable.

Second, at least in India and Pakistan, the setting up of MDAS by state governments has usually implied some loss of local autonomy. Third, MDAS need to have executive functions and fiscal autonomy (resources) if they are to coordinate the delivery of services within metropolitan areas and provide certain services with areawide benefits. A planning agency with only advisory powers cannot effectively play this integrative role. Typically, MDAS have not been given such powers and as a consequence their effectiveness has suffered.

Fourth, MDAS often fail to combine development (investment) and operating responsibility and thus create the typical turnkey problem: the agency responsible for the capital outlay and planning does not allow sufficiently for the preferences and the technical, managerial, and financial capacity of the operating agency. The result is that local facilities deteriorate for lack of adequate maintenance.

Evaluating Experiences with Alternative Structures

How does one evaluate the structure of local government in a metropolitan area? What goals should be most aggressively sought in any reform of the structure? Which of the commonly used forms of horizontal relations best satisfies the norms for a good structure? In fact, each primary form of metropolitan government has advantages and disadvantages. One could make the case for each form being optimal, depending on the criteria used for evaluation and on whether one views the situation from the vantage point of central or local government. The norms for a good structure typically considered in such an evaluation are economic efficiency, technical efficiency, equity, cost containment, and autonomy of local government (Bahl and Campbell 1976). The paragraphs below describe these norms and survey the efforts of various countries to capture the advantages and offset the disadvantages of alternative systems of urban governance.

Economic Efficiency

One criterion used in evaluating government structures is whether resident preferences can be reflected in the local budget. The desire to increase the welfare of the population, what we will call the concern for economic efficiency, would seem to point toward more decentralized structures and smaller units of local government. The core of the argument is clear: the closer government is to the people, all other things being equal, the more likely a household is to have some effect on the budget and to receive something closer to the package of public services and taxes that it desires. Individual preferences are most likely to be satisfied if the size of the decisionmaking unit is smaller, local preferences are more homogeneous, and more fiscal autonomy is given to local governments.[25]

A fragmented structure of local government—many municipalities operating in the same urban area—would at first glance seem the best way to give resident consumers significant control over fiscal matters. But does the existence of smaller urban governments alone guarantee that government will be close to the people? The evidence suggests not. As noted above, most developing countries are not voting democracies, and therefore the decisionmaking process of local government may not reflect citizen preferences. For example, until recently the councils of Manila's eighteen cities and municipalities were appointed by the president. Even if the councils were popularly elected, there remains the possibility that the local government's fiscal activities would be so tightly regulated by the center (or state) that the demands of local residents would be partly neutralized. More damning is the fact that even local governments operating under a jurisdictionally fragmented system still may be too large to allow any significant measure of decentralized decisionmaking. For example, the core metropolitan jurisdictions of Calcutta and Manila have well over 1 million residents each. Finally, the smaller the local government, the less efficient its administration is likely to be and the less able it will be to provide a package of services that reflects the demands of citizens.

Gains in economic efficiency thus are the product of a system of governance in which governments are small enough to give local residents a choice, the political process allows local voters to reveal their preferences, and the local government has the fiscal autonomy and technical capability to reflect voter preferences in its budget and service delivery. These conditions are met in few developing countries.

Another important issue for economic efficiency that arises in connection with the fragmented structure of government is that some public services are characterized by externalities: the social benefits and costs of these services are different from those realized by the local community. As a result, the local community—left to its own devices—may underproduce or overproduce these goods, and there may be some losses of economic efficiency when government is brought closer to the people.

Here lies the efficiency tradeoff. Under a large metropolitan government, fiscal decisionmaking is far from the people and there are losses of economic efficiency by comparison with more jurisdictionally fragmented systems. Yet fragmented structures might better capture the preferences of local voters but could lead to overall losses in consumer welfare if they attempt to deliver and finance services whose benefits and costs are areawide.

In fact, governmental structures in metropolitan areas have reacted to the problem of economic efficiency in a predictable way. The accommodation in jurisdictionally fragmented areas—where one would guess there is the most commitment to fiscal decentralization—has been to assign functions characterized by significant externalities and economies of scale to the regional or central government and to assign the remainder to local governments. The system of local governments in the Manila metropolitan area is an example of a jurisdictionally fragmented structure in which an upper tier was created along these lines. The MDAs on the Indian subcontinent described above are another.

Metropolitan government removes fiscal decisions farthest from citizens. Hence the accommodation of creating small, subcity governmental units which could facilitate more citizen participation is not an unexpected development in some cities. In some cases, the subunits have been given control over some, albeit very limited, resources (earmarked taxes or grants) and the authority to select projects. The *alcaldes menores* (jurisdictions of minor mayors) of Bogotá, the municipalities of Jakarta, the barangays of Manila, and the *juntas communales* (common councils) of Panama are examples of the actual devolution of resources. For example, Philippine barangays are supposed to receive a 10 percent share of local property taxes, a national grant, and a grant from the local government. Still, there is no evidence to suggest that the result of this devolution has been a substantial influence by neighborhoods on the package of services. In some cases, the decentralized structure is created, but there is no provision to pass resources to the subcity unit. Typically, this results in no more than an administrative decentralization of the metropolitan government; the *gu* subdivisions in Seoul, wards in Bombay, and districts in Bangkok serve such a purpose.

Citizen participation is not restricted to situations in which formal neighborhood governance exists. Informal organizations such as neighborhood associations and community boards have sprung up in many of the slums and squatter settlements in cities of developing countries, especially in Latin America. Their functions are to articulate citizens' demands, offer judicial and law enforcement services, and even provide some social services (often through cooperative self-help efforts). In some Latin American cities, this development is now being integrated with the formal structure of local government. One well-documented example is the valorization process in Colombia, in which the municipal community boards are an integral part of the decisionmaking process (Doebele, Grimes, and Linn 1979).

What we make of the current practice is that the trend is not in the direction of decentralization to capture gains in efficiency. Witness the creation of MDAs in cities which have decentralized structures of local government. Similarly, one does not sense much movement by metropolitan governments to assign fiscal responsibility to neighborhoods or to set up new subcity budgets. There are some decentralized municipal structures, but these exist primarily for administrative and perhaps political purposes. In the case of the functionally fragmented structures, the emphasis is so strongly on management and coordination, and on capturing the advantages of specialization and centralization, that there seems little attention left for the goal of economic efficiency. Satisfying citizen preferences with public budgets may be a noble goal for developing-country fiscal planners, but it would appear to be low on their list of priorities.

Technical Efficiency

Higher on their list is technical efficiency, that is, finding a method of delivering adequate public services at the lowest unit cost. A popular notion is that the cost per resident of delivering a public service declines as the number of residents increases; hence, gains in technical efficiency are the result of economies of scale. Such an argument would lead to a preference for areawide delivery of services, that is, for metropolitan government or functional fragmentation. Jurisdictional fragmentation would be the least preferred form of metropolitan governance.

Certainly the argument for economies of scale has much intuitive appeal. If one large government replaces many smaller governments, there are bound to be savings from the elimination of duplication of services, and with more size may come a greater possibility for cost savings through capital-labor substitution. These savings may be particularly important for metropolitan cities because of the superior ability of large local units to finance additions to the capital stock of local government. Because the consolidation of local governments increases the taxable capacity of the financing unit, it also increases the ability of local units to borrow and recover operating and capital costs through user charges. The construction and operation of markets and slaughterhouses, and even telephone and power companies, are examples of this.

To what extent does the argument for economies of scale hold up for developing countries? The literature seems clearly to show that there are economies of scale for such "hardware" services as public utilities and transportation (see chapter 3). These economies may be captured if the government is large enough to make the substantial capital investment required—for example, to build the proper-size sewage treatment plant, to extend the water distribution system, or to buy the fleet of buses. Jurisdictionally fragmented structures are at a disadvantage here in that they are not large enough to make the capital investment necessary to lower the unit cost of output. This is why in cities with fragmented structures, such as Calcutta and Manila, responsibility for capital-intensive services has been shifted to special purpose, areawide financing districts or has been assumed by a higher level of government. Capital-labor substitution is not the only way gains in technical efficiency might be captured by large local governments. Small governments probably cannot efficiently handle secondary education, hospital services, and even tax administration because of the construction and equipment costs involved and because specialty services might only be justified for large client populations. In the latter category might fall large markets, slaughterhouses, municipal sport stadiums, fire-fighting equipment for higher buildings, detective services, vocational schools, and hospitals with a broad range of services.

There is much less evidence that economies of scale exist in the provision of other public services. This is because many such services—for example, primary education, clinics, and street cleaning—are labor-intensive and have little room for capital-labor substitution.

In conclusion, if local government has significant responsibility for capital-intensive services, the advantages for the centralized metropolitan governance and functional fragmentation models will be greatest. Moreover, areawide provision may also capture the spillover costs and benefits of such services.

Equity

A third standard for evaluating a government structure is the pattern of geographical equity it produces. Specifically, the question is whether the government structure per se leads to disparities in tax burdens and service benefits between similar households living in different parts of the metropolitan area. This problem usually arises with jurisdictionally fragmented structures. It leads to the following kind of situation. High-income families will be pulled toward those jurisdictions with good public services and (because of the concentration of wealth) relatively low tax rates. Low-income families, zoned-out of these areas by high property values, will tend to cluster in jurisdictions which have become less wealthy and have higher tax rates and lower public service levels. The more municipalities within the metropolitan area, the greater the potential for this problem.

Do such disparities actually occur, and do people really vote with their feet in this manner? Certainly this has been the case in the United States, where a fragmented government structure has led to sizable fiscal disparities between city and suburban jurisdictions (ACIR 1977, 1981).

There is not a great deal of evidence on this question in developing countries. A World Bank analysis of metropolitan Manila revealed a wide variation in efficiency of tax collection, tax effort, and per capita expenditures among the seventeen constituent local government units (Bahl, Brigg, and Smith 1976). For example, Makati, the wealthiest of municipalities, contained about 2 percent of the total municipal population in 1975 but accounted for about 41 percent of municipal revenues. Among the four chartered cities in the metropolitan area, Manila city's per capita revenues are several times larger than the average of the other three, and Manila city's tax burden appears well below the average of all local governments in the metropolitan area (Bahl, Brigg, and Smith 1976). Prud'homme (1975) reports a similar result from a study of 1973 data on metropolitan Tunis: per capita revenues in the commune of Tunis were 1.6 times higher than the average in the other twelve communes.

Areawide governments are a better choice on the grounds of geographical equity because taxes are levied on a uniform basis. There may still be disparities in service levels within the urban area—low-income neighborhoods with less ability to pay for services may not have the same access to these services as do high-income neighborhoods. Linn (1976c) found evidence of such disparities in Bogotá with a correlation analysis between neighborhood income level and an indicator of level of services, and Bahl, Brigg, and Smith (1976) found similar results with an empirical analysis of disparities in levels of public services among neighborhoods in Manila city.

Cost Containment

A number of general management issues might be lumped under the heading of cost containment; that is, is one structure of local government more amenable than the others to control the growth in government spending? Local government expenditures might grow faster under a more highly centralized, metropolitan system of governance for several reasons. First, a large city will be more willing to take on the construction and expansion of capital facilities because of its broader revenue base and its broader discretionary taxation and borrowing powers. Such capital expenditures have a multiplier effect on total expenditures because they require future maintenance costs, and because they may occasion complementary costs (for example, the construction of a new municipal roadway probably also requires changes in traffic control, street lighting, street cleaning, bus routing, and so forth). Moreover, capital projects carry an interest cost in addition to the project costs.

A second reason why more centralized, areawide governments exert an upward long-term pressure on expenditures is that more revenues can be mobilized by larger than by smaller local governments. Larger urban governments are more likely to use income- and price-elastic consumption and income-type tax bases, and property tax administration is likely to be better in larger cities. Third, there is more political flexibility at the level of the metropolitan area than at the level of the submetropolitan jurisdictions to make discretionary changes in tax rates or user charges. This is because local tax increases can be more closely identified with particular elected officials than can areawide changes, which suggests that politicians will be more willing to make unpopular tax decisions at the metropolitan level than at the "neighborhood" level. As a result, greater reliance on areawide tax bases could raise the long-term growth rate of expenditure.

A functionally fragmented system also has features which might push up the cost of providing services. First, the budget-maximizing technocrat in charge of the autonomous agency may try to maximize the size of his operation rather than expand and allocate resources according to community needs.[26] Second, areawide, special purpose authorities may dedicate revenues from user charges (for example, water rates) to finance capital expansions. Because some utility operations generate a surplus under marginal cost pricing, more resources and hence expenditure growth might be expected. Third, autonomous agencies may raise taxes and charges outside the usual constraints faced by local governments in making fiscal decisions, and a faster rate of expenditure growth might occur.

This is not to say that a jurisdictionally fragmented system does not also have features which may stimulate costs. First, because economies of scale cannot be captured, costs may be higher. Second, administrative duplication may make costs higher, all other things being equal, under a more decentralized system. Third, planning and coordination are more difficult under a decentralized system, and as a result costs may not be contained as well. Fourth, a more decentralized system is less likely to make use of modern, cost saving management skills and technology.

It is difficult to draw a firm conclusion about the relationship between cost containment and government structure. Moreover, a particular system may contain costs better in one developing country than in another. Again, it depends on the functions, taxing powers, and general fiscal autonomy given to local governments. All other things being equal, however, the view here is that the growth in expenditures is likely to be greatest under more centralized systems.

Autonomy of Local Government

There does seem to be some relation between the structure of local government within a metropolitan area and the degree of fiscal independence given to local government. Functional fragmentation seems more consistent with greater local autonomy. By setting up special purpose districts or agencies, local governments may gain back a measure of the autonomy taken away by central regulation. It has long been a practice to create separate water and transportation authorities to make possible a more professional (and less political) management, to avoid civil service regulations in employment practices, and to create more autonomy in taxing, pricing, and investment decisions. The use of autonomous agencies in Colombian cities is one good example of this practice—the public *empresas* in Bogotá (which provide street cleaning, telephones, power, and the water supply) have proven to be effective in circumventing central controls on personnel policy that would have been binding had these services been delivered through general purpose local governments. Some provinces and cities in the Philippines have used local public enterprises to deliver and finance public and commercial services such as markets, slaughterhouses, and even a convention center. This separation from general government has enabled various pricing adjustments to be made (and avoided what might have been cumbersome civil service regulations) and even permitted the contracting out of management services (Greytak and Diokno 1983).

Conclusions: Reforming the Structure of Local Government

A jurisdictionally fragmented structure of local government seems to be least suited to the cities of developing countries. Theoretically, it offers a structure wherein consumer-voters can segregate themselves into groups with like preferences and can affect the mix of public services. But this efficiency advantage is rarely captured in developing countries because local governments have so little autonomy to make fiscal decisions, because the decentralized municipalities themselves are quite large, or because the local governments do not have the technical wherewithal to produce the package of services desired. Moreover, the costs associated with a geographically fragmented structure of local government—fiscal disparities, diseconomies of scale, planning and coordination problems—may be substantial. The trend in developing countries is clearly not in the direction of fragmented structures of metropolitan governance, perhaps because the cost of moving government closer to the people is perceived as being too high.

In many cases where jurisdictional fragmentation exists, or where the metropolitan area has spilled over into adjoining jurisdictions, reforms have been proposed to deal with the problems of coordination, uniform planning, and service provision. The most popular reform seems to be the creation of a metropolitan development authority. Other approaches to dealing with the problem are annexation (in Bogotá), the formation of municipal associations (in Medellín), and the creation of a metropolitan tier of government (in Manila). Remedies for geographic fragmentation are more easily found in developing countries than in industrial countries because the central (or state) governments in developing countries tend to have much more sweeping powers to set municipal boundaries, and because in general there is much less of a tradition of autonomous local governments to stand in the way of amalgamation. There are exceptions, of course. In Calcutta, there is a very strong political base at the municipal level and a very strong push to retain the autonomy of local units.

This would seem to leave metropolitan areawide government and functional fragmentation as the best choices for local government in the cities of developing countries. Again, however, there are problems as well as potentials.

The independence of autonomous agencies is both a blessing and a curse. On the one hand, it can produce professionalism in management, remove decisionmaking somewhat from the political arena, and dedicate revenues to the expansion and maintenance of a particular service. On the other hand, it becomes more difficult to coordinate the delivery and financing of services. Professional managers who are unchecked by local governments and who have access to substantial revenues from user charges may overspend on the function involved relative to what is spent on all other local functions. The problem of coordination which arises from functional fragmentation has been dealt with in three ways. One is to create boards with overlapping membership; for example, in Colombia the mayor may serve simultaneously on the boards of all local autonomous agencies. The experience with this approach in Colombia has not been uniformly successful. A second possibility is to limit the number of autonomous agencies and encourage multifunctions, for example, the Bombay Electric Company and Transportation Authority and the public services *empresas* in Cartagena. This provides some fungibility of revenues and reduces the problem of coordination, but only selected functions are covered. A third possibility is to control the operations of the authorities, that is, make them semiautonomous as in Jakarta. This retains the advantage of the professionalism of the separate authority but reintroduces political considerations into the decisionmaking process.

Metropolitan government has two important problems that call for reform. The first is that the management and financing of certain services are beyond the technical abilities of the city administration and need to be separated from the local political process. The creation of autonomous or semiautonomous agencies—some degree of functional fragmentation—seems to have been the answer to this problem. As noted above, the ties between these agencies and the city administration may be made in many ways. The second problem is that a way needs to be found to allow neighborhoods to reveal their preferences for public services and for the city budget to reflect them. There is no shortage of schemes to deal with this issue in developing countries, but we have been unable to find a clearly successful experience.

Summary and Conclusions: The Structure of Local Government and Decentralization

We began this chapter with the question of what is the best way to organize local government to deliver and finance services in developing countries. It will satisfy few that we have concluded with the answer, "It depends." It depends on whether the governments of developing countries are more interested in letting the preferences of people be reflected in the budgets of local governments—which suggests more decentralization—or in creating local governments that operate with maximum efficiency, equalize interregional fiscal capacity disparities, or give the central government maximum flexibility to mobilize and stabilize resources (all of which suggest more centralization). There is some indication as to how governments view these tradeoffs in that they have allowed only a relatively low degree of fiscal decentralization. Subnational governments account for only about 15 percent of all government expenditures, and this proportion has not been increasing.

This 15 percent share could be an overstatement of the fiscal responsibility of subnational governments. This is because there is an important distinction to be drawn between fiscal decentralization on the one hand and moving government closer to the people on the other. Even with more taxing power and expenditure responsibility, and even with the creation of smaller municipalities, local governments in developing countries may not be able to respond to the demands of citizens for different levels and mixes of services and financing. There are a number of constraints: local councils are often appointed rather than elected and therefore may not be representative of the local population; local taxing powers and responsibilities for expenditure are severely circumscribed; there may be administrative constraints on local governments that prohibit either an increase in taxation or an expansion of public services; and the chief officers who carry out the delivery of services are often appointed by a higher level of government. Because all of these constraints hold more or less for most local governments in developing countries, one might guess that the total share of government expenditures which is fully controlled by state and local governments is well below 15 percent.

There is much variation in the fiscal autonomy of local governments within countries. The general rule is: the larger the population, the more fiscal responsibility. The most fiscal latitude is given to large metropolitan areas, where local governments account for a third to a half of total government spending. Moreover, they tend to have more discretion to raise tax rates, broader tax bases, more expenditure responsibilities, and sometimes even the power to borrow from nongovernment sources. Still, these local authorities do not have anything like the same degree of autonomy as do many of their counterparts in industrial countries.

Three systems of horizontal fiscal relations seem to have emerged in the governance of metropolitan areas. The first, jurisdictional fragmentation—many municipalities operating within a single urban area—has the most potential for recognizing differences in preferences and allowing citizen participation. It fails, however, to produce uniformity of service levels and tax burdens within the urban area, to allow for effective planning or coordination of capital investments, or to deal with spillover effects. For this reason, the trend has been toward creating an overlying central tier of government (as in Manila) or a metropolitan development authority (as on the Indian subcontinent).

Many urban areas in developing countries are organized as a metropolitan government overlapped by one or two autonomous agencies (for example, a water company or a bus company). This form of governance has all the advantages of centralization—planning, capturing economies of scale, and internalizing externalities—but it neglects diversity of preferences because government is so large and so far removed from the voter. Some metropolitan governments have attempted to deal with this by creating small subarea administrative units, but mostly the problem seems to have been written off as a "cost" of urbanization. Whether the issue can be ignored as the great metropolitan areas surpass 10 and 20 million people is an interesting question.

The third system, the functional fragmentation model—in which services are delivered by a set of independent public service agencies—is popular in Latin America. It has potentially serious disadvantages of coordination and it leads to a government farther removed from the individual voter than does metropolitan governance. But it has the great advantage of specialized, professional management, and some degree of freedom from the political process. There have been attempts to deal with the problem of coordination by creating interlocking directorates covering all local governments.

The experience with local government in the metropolitan areas of developing countries, then, is one of accommodation. One model emphasizes local control and participation, another central coordination and control, and a third technical efficiency. Although there is an underlying trend toward centralization, each system has been altered to move toward the other two.

Appendix: Application of the Constrained Maximization Model of Local Fiscal Behavior to Developing Countries

There is a well-developed literature in the United States which purports to explain the determinants of local public expenditures. Among other things, this approach has been used to get at the impact of federal grants to state and local governments on their expenditure and taxing decisions. The purpose of this appendix is to consider the applicability of this analysis to developing countries.

Local Public Expenditures

To what extent must the median voter model be bent to be applicable in the developing-country setting? Some insights about patterns of expenditure by local governments in low-income countries might be gained by drawing the distinction between developing and industrial nations in a more formal way. Let us assume that there exists a set of community preferences, I_1, for government goods (G) and private goods (X), and a budget constraint (XG) as shown in figure 12-1. In equilibrium at a, the

Figure 12-1. *The Median Voter Model of Expenditure*

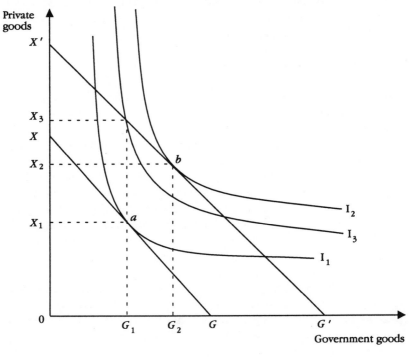

local community would choose $0G_1$ units of government goods and $0X_1$ units of all other goods, and it would pay taxes of X_1X. Now assume that income growth shifts the community budget constraint to $X'G'$. Left to its own devices, the community would move to point b: it would expand public consumption to $0G_2$ and private consumption to $0X_2$, and it would levy taxes of X_2X'.[27] Because the local government is allowed to adjust its tax-expenditure pattern in line with its preferences—the story goes—the community is able to increase its welfare from I_1 to I_2.

This story, however, is based on an industrial-country constrained maximization model and assumes a flexibility in fiscal response that local governments in developing countries do not often have. In developing countries, there are instead three rigidities: constraints on the amount of services that local governments are capable of delivering, constraints on revenue structure, and constraints caused by weak tax administration. A fourth problem is the inability of citizens to reveal their preferences for the provision of public goods and tax levels. Consider first the constraint on delivery. Suppose, as in this example, the community desires to use some of its increase in income to provide better road maintenance (to move from G_1 to G_2) but the skilled labor, raw materials, and equipment needed to get the job done are not available. The community finds itself stuck at G_1 and moves to c, consuming the whole of the increase in personal income in private goods and allowing the tax rate to fall from $(X_1X/0X)$ to $(X_3X'/0X')$. The community ends up at a less preferred level of satisfaction, I_3, because it could not get the increase in government goods it desired. This example suggests why some local governments make a poor revenue effort.

Second, the constraint may be on the revenue side. Suppose the tax administration is so weak that even with the increase in income, and even with the technical ability to expand public service provision to G_2, it cannot raise more than X_1X ($= X_3X'$) in taxes. Residents of the community would prefer a higher tax rate, but the local tax administration simply cannot respond. The community is again "stuck" at c, and the gains in revenue mobilization and efficiency are not realized. Third, taxes may not rise to X_2X' because the tax bases given to the local governments are not income-elastic and the local government is legally prohibited from increasing rates on the taxes to which they do have access. With the second or third constraint, the result is a level of government goods smaller than G_2 (to the left of b), with an underprovided public sector and a citizenry that has an untapped willingness and ability to pay more taxes.

Fourth, the government may fail to recognize citizen demands for an adjustment in the package of public services. The analysis presented above is based on a presumption that there is a community indifference curve which reflects the relative preference for public goods. In industrial countries this may be seen as the preference function of the median voter, as interpreted by the elected officials who make the budgetary decision. The officials, to maximize their chance for reelection, take the median voter's preferences as their own. In developing countries, however, there may be no voters at all. And even if there are, local officials often are not elected and may act on what they see as the preferences of the appointing body—usually the state or central government. Hence, another reason why public goods might not expand from G_1 to G_2 in the face of an increase in income is that local officials are not concerned with citizen preferences. But one should not be too quick to dismiss totally the idea of a preference model in developing countries. Voters and nonvoters alike will show their displeasure with utility rate or bus fare increases, or with what they see to be high property taxes. It would be wrong to assume that even appointed officials are completely insensitive to citizen preferences for public goods and taxes. In conclusion, then, potential efficiency gains do not offer the same impetus for fiscal decentralization in developing countries as in industrial countries.[28]

Tax Effort and Grants in Industrial Countries

To demonstrate the impact of grant design on tax effort in an industrial country, assume a community preference function for government (G)

Figure 12-2. *The Effects of Matching Grants on the Tax Effort*

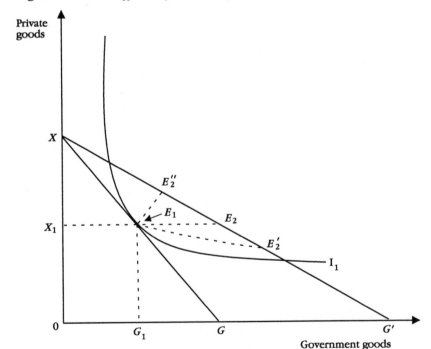

and private goods (X), as shown in figure 12-2. At equilibrium (E_1), the community consumes $0X_1$ private goods and $0G_1$ government goods and pays taxes of X_1X. Now introduce a matching or cost reimbursement grant that lowers the cost of government goods as described by the new budget line XG'. If equilibrium moves to E_2, the entire amount of the grant (E_1E_2) will be used for the consumption of government goods, and taxes will remain at X_1X. No change in tax effort has occurred. If more than the grant amount is spent on government consumption, for example, a solution at E_2', then tax effort will increase. Solutions to the left of E_2, for example E_2'', imply that some of the grant was effectively used to reduce taxes below X_1X.

Now consider the ways in which a grant may be designed to increase or maintain tax effort. A partial cost reimbursement grant would cause the budget line to pivot out toward XG' by lowering the relative price of G. How far it pivots depends on the percentage of cost reimbursed and the importance of the aided function in the local budget. Whether one ends up on XG', hence whether or not tax effort is increased, depends on the income and price-elasticities of demand and on the existence of other binding constraints. Suppose a maintenance-of-effort provision is in the grant design; that is, taxes may not fall below X_1X. If

Figure 12-3. *The Effects of a Lump-Sum Grant on the Tax Effort*

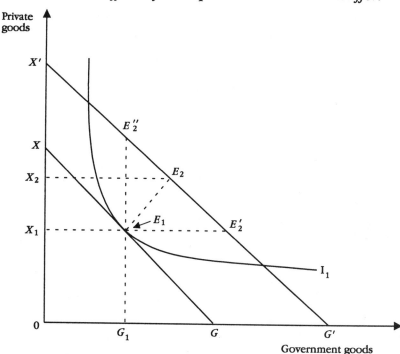

the income- and price-elasticities are such that the community would
have chosen E_2'', a mandated solution at E_2 will distort the local budget
from what it would have been in the absence of a requirement to maintain
effort and will lead to a loss in community welfare.

A second approach is to build a provision for tax effort directly into
the grant formula. The community, assuming that no one else increases
taxes, now sees itself on a new budget line such as XE_1E_2G'. How far
out the budget line pivots for taxation levels above X_1X depends on the
weight given to tax effort in the formula, that is, how much more G can
be obtained for a given increase in taxes (sacrifice in X). Again, the
answer one gets depends on the price- and income-elasticities of demand.

Another possibility is to make use of a lump-sum grant (neither matching nor cost reimbursement) as is shown in figure 12-3. At the pre-grant
equilibrium (E_1) the tax rate is X_1X/OX. After the grant is given, the
tax rate may rise or fall, depending on the income-elasticity of demand.
At a unitary income-elasticity, equilibrium moves to E_2 and the tax rate
is X_2X'/OX', which is equal to the pre-grant rate. At solutions to the
right of E_2, such as E_2', the demand for public goods is income-elastic
and tax effort will increase.

Figure 12-4. *The Effects of Grants in Developing Countries*

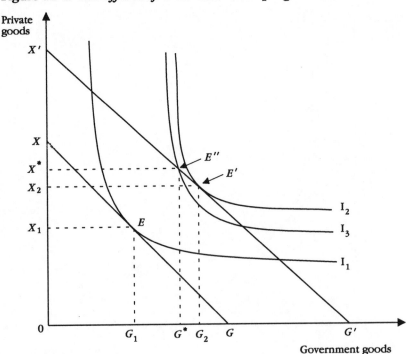

The Application to Developing Countries

The case in the typical developing country is quite different, as is shown in figure 12-4. Assume, for the moment, that there does exist a preference function such as I_1 which somehow drives local budgetary decisions, and that there is an initial equilibrium E at $(X_1 G_1)$. A lump sum grant of amount XX' would have driven public services to point G_2 and changed the tax rate to $X_2 X'/0X'$. The equilibrium at E' would be determined by the income-elasticity of demand for public goods. Such a response is not likely to occur in a developing-country city, however, and public goods are more likely to be underproduced. Consider the possibilities of two cases, A and B.

In case A, the income-elasticity of revenue from local taxes, the regulation of discretionary changes in local tax rate and base, and administrative problems all combine to restrict taxes to a maximum of $X^* X'$. This would imply no increase in government goods beyond G^*. This equilibrium in case A reflects a lower level of utility than I_2. In case B, the ability of the local government to deliver more public goods and services is constrained to G^*, hence local government resource mobilization cannot rise beyond $X^* X'$. In either case A or case B, local government goods will be underproduced by $G^* G_2$.

There is another explanation for the possible underprovision of local public services: the preference function of the higher level of government has been imposed on the local government because local councils are appointed or because the chief operating officers of local government are seconded government officials. Even in the absence of technical or administrative constraints, then, local budgets would not respond to grant incentives.

13 Flows and Effects of Intergovernmental Transfers

ONE WAY to resolve the conflict between central and lower levels of government over the division of taxing authority and expenditure responsibility is a system of transfers from the center—shared taxes and grants—to lower levels. This compromise solution permits central governments to retain the authority to tax productive resource bases but guarantees state and local governments a flow of revenues. A system of grants is a step toward fiscal decentralization in that it finances local government services, but the degree of autonomy it gives local governments to make their budget decisions depends on how it is structured.

It seems axiomatic that a program of intergovernmental transfers should be designed to meet the government's objectives. But which level of government should define the objectives? And because such objectives as equity, revenue-elasticity, and neutrality often conflict, how can priorities be established? These questions point to an important but frequently misunderstood feature of systems of transfers: even the best designed system will have advantages and disadvantages. On the one hand, a formal program of transfers can broaden the resource base of local governments and provide for a growing source of revenue if grant distributions are tied to the growth of an elastic tax base for the central government. Such a program has the added advantage of avoiding the high administrative costs usually associated with tax assessment and collection by local governments. On the other hand, grants can make local governments less accountable for their fiscal decisions (they may now increase spending without increasing taxes); hence, there will be less incentive to improve the efficiency of local government operations and develop innovative methods of delivering public services. Likewise it is alleged that the tax effort of local governments may be dampened because they will have less incentive to search for new sources of revenue or to more efficiently collect taxes from existing bases.

Other advantages and disadvantages are much less clear-cut. For example, an important issue in the design of grant systems is the centralist-decentralist dispute over whether the size of the grant allocations will be more or less controlled by the center. A disadvantage of central control, from the point of view of the local government, is that grant allocations may become political decisions and therefore the amount of funds will be uncertain from year to year. This makes fiscal planning very difficult for local governments. But central control can make the central government's budgeting more flexible, and in that sense is a great advantage. Another example is that some grants carry matching requirements or expenditure mandates which distort the budget choices of local governments. Viewed another way, however, such conditions attached to the receipt of grants may help accomplish national goals. In fact, grant policies are always controversial from some point of view, and the academic search for an optimal grant structure is likely to be no more fruitful than the search for an optimal structure of local government. Indeed, conclusions about the advantages and disadvantages of any program of grants from central to local governments depend on whether a national or local point of view is taken: one level's uncertainty about the regularity and adequacy of grant flows is the other's budgetary flexibility.

To make matters more difficult, it is all but impossible to measure whether a grant program achieves its objective; at best the answer may be known only after the fact. The problem is that it is hard to separate the effect of the grant from that of everything else; an increase in income and employment or an improvement in tax administration may be as responsible for an increase in local tax effort as is the grant. Similar problems arise if we try to measure the extent to which a grant contributes to the equalization of fiscal capacity or to the provision of a basic level of public services.

This, then, is the context for the study of intergovernmental grants in developing countries: conflicting objectives and little possibility for ex post facto evaluation. In this context, this chapter describes and evaluates the range of grant programs used in developing countries and suggests principles which might be used to evaluate the potential successes and failures of these programs. We first discuss the revenue importance of grants for raising revenue and then turn to a taxonomy of the systems of grants most common in developing countries. Another form of grant assistance—the capital subsidy—is given separate treatment. In the final sections we consider the main problems and choices for policy which arise in the design and operation of grant systems.

Our concern here is broader than grants-in-aid strictly defined and is meant to include all transfers between governmental units. Hence, a shared tax between the central and local levels of government is considered a grant if the tax rate and base are determined by the higher level. (A shared tax is a local levy if the local government can freely choose to set a sur-rate on a national tax.) We will also consider loans to local governments as intergovernmental transfers, because these are often substitutes for (or complements to) capital grants, are rationed among local governments in a manner similar to that used for grants, and often have the central government as the principal lender. Because the focus in this book is on local government finance, particularly the financing of large cities, our concern is mostly center-local and state-local relations. We also, however, consider federal grants to states in this

Table 13-1. *The Importance of Intergovernmental Transfers for Local Government Finance*

Subnational government share[a] of total government expenditure	Intergovernmental transfers as a percentage of government revenues[b]
Share of more than 30 percent	
Rio de Janeiro, Brazil, 1967	1.7
Rio de Janeiro, Brazil, 1984	0.4
Ahmadabad, India, 1971	4.2
Ahmadabad, India, 1981	8.6
Bombay, India, 1971	1.0
Bombay, India, 1975	1.0
Bombay, India, 1982	0.7
Calcutta, India, 1970	18.5
Calcutta, India, 1975	19.4
Calcutta, India, 1982	54.9
Madras, India, 1976	25.1
Madras, India, 1979	13.7
Seoul, Rep. of Korea, 1968	23.2
Seoul, Rep. of Korea, 1971	15.8
Seoul, Rep. of Korea, 1975	14.3
Seoul, Rep. of Korea, 1983	22.0
Ibadan, Nigeria, 1982	64.4
Share of 10–30 percent	
Bogotá, Colombia, 1972	12.9
Bogotá, Colombia, 1979	8.8
Cali, Colombia, 1974	2.8
Cartagena, Colombia, 1972	12.8
Mombasa, Kenya, 1975	33.8
Mombasa, Kenya, 1981	32.2
Nairobi, Kenya, 1975	31.6
Nairobi, Kenya, 1982	24.7
Mexico City, Mexico, 1968	8.9
Mexico City, Mexico, 1982	26.3
Karachi, Pakistan, 1975	2.8
Karachi, Pakistan, 1982	3.0

a. In this computation, central grants to state and local governments are netted out of total central government expenditures to avoid double counting.

b. Total local government revenues including borrowing.

chapter because the experience in this area has yielded some principles for grant design and because local budgets in federal countries may be compromised or enhanced by the size and structure of federal-state transfers.

The Importance of Grants for Revenue

The reliance on grants as a source of financing varies widely across cities. To many, the most surprising finding from the cross-section comparison of cities in table 13-1 is likely to be that grants do not show up uniformly as the main source of local revenue; the share of grants in

Subnational government share[a] of total government expenditure	_Intergovernmental transfers as a percentage of government revenues[b]_
Manila,[c] Philippines, 1970	30.0
Manila,[c] Philippines, 1975	30.0
Share of less than 10 percent	
Chittagong, Bangladesh, 1983	41.7
Dhaka, Bangladesh, 1983	34.6
La Paz, Bolivia, 1975	9.0
La Paz, Bolivia, 1985	2.0
Francistown, Botswana, 1972	1.9
Francistown, Botswana, 1986	47.0
Abidjan, Côte d'Ivoire, 1981	67.1
Addis Ababa, Ethiopia, 1973	18.7
Jakarta, Indonesia, 1973	21.1
Jakarta, Indonesia, 1981	39.1
Tehran, Iran, 1974	45.2
Kingston, Jamaica, 1972	67.2
Kingston, Jamaica, 1977	98.2
Dakar, Senegal, 1980	78.7
Colombo, Sri Lanka, 1977	19.0
Colombo, Sri Lanka, 1982	42.6
Bangkok, Thailand, 1968	19.8
Bangkok, Thailand, 1977	39.6
Tunis, Tunisia, 1972	0.7
Tunis, Tunisia, 1985	17.1
Istanbul, Turkey, 1968	28.0
Bukaru, Zaire, 1971	30.1
Kinshasa, Zaire, 1971	73.1
Lumbumbashi, Zaire, 1972	9.5
Mbuji-May, Zaire, 1971	29.8
Kitwe, Zambia, 1975	2.2
Lusaka, Zambia, 1972	6.0

c. Aggregate of all cities and municipalities in Metropolitan Manila.

total local revenue ranges from more than 90 percent to less than 1 percent. The sample was chosen solely on the basis of available information.

One would be hard pressed to pull from these data a general statement about what determines how much large cities in developing countries rely on external resources. Indeed, the two most important observations about the data in table 13-1 have to do with the patterns that do not show up. First, for the dozen or so cities for which data are available for more than one year, the trend does not seem to be in the direction of a growing reliance on intergovernmental transfers—as many cities increased their share of revenues from grants as reduced it. Second, the degree to which expenditure is decentralized in a country does not predict whether its large cities will depend on grants. For example, some cities in decentralized India are relatively less dependent and the cities in centralized Zaire are very dependent. On average, local governments are no more or less dependent in a decentralized federation than in a highly centralized unitary system.

A Typology of Grant Programs

Most studies of the effects of intergovernmental grants have been done in the United States because it has a relatively decentralized federal system in which grant policy is an important national concern and because a substantial amount of comparable data are available for empirical testing.[1] Though the methodology and results of this work are the current state of the art, a taxonomy of grants based on the U.S. grant system would not apply to developing countries.[2] This is because analysts of the U.S. federal grant system are only concerned with interstate distribution, whereas in most countries analysts must be concerned with both the size of the divisible pool of grants and how it is allocated among recipients. Some have referred to the pool size as having to do with the vertical fiscal balance between the central and subnational governments and allocation as having to do with horizontal fiscal balance.

A new taxonomy of grant systems that takes both of these dimensions into account is diagramed in table 13-2. Consider first the determination of the size of the total amount to be distributed in a given year, that is, the divisible pool. The current practice suggests three basic approaches: a specified share of national (or state) government tax revenues, an ad hoc decision (such as an annual appropriation voted by parliament), or reimbursement of approved expenditures. Once the amount of the pool

Table 13-2. *Alternative Forms of Intergovernmental Grant Programs*

Method of allocating the divisible pool among eligible units	Method of determining the total divisible pool		
	Specified share of national or state government tax	*Ad hoc decision*	*Reimbursement of approved expenditures*
Origin of collection of the tax	A	n.a.	n.a.
Formula	B	F	n.a.
Total or partial reimbursement of costs	C	G	K
Ad hoc	D	H	n.a.

n.a. Not applicable.
Note: For definitions of forms A–K, see text.

is determined, allocations among local governments are typically made in four ways: by returning shares to the jurisdictions from which the taxes were collected, that is, using a derivation principle; by formula; ad hoc; or by reimbursing costs.

This two-way classification gives a taxonomy of twelve grant types; the eight of these which seem more or less common in developing countries are displayed in table 13-2. For example, the total national allocation for a type B grant is based on a share of a national tax, but the distribution among local governments is made by formula. Thus in the Philippines, 20 percent of national internal revenue collections are distributed among local governments on the basis of population and land area. A type C grant differs in that the distribution is on the basis of project costs, for example, a fixed percentage of a national tax is distributed among local governments on the basis of the cost of public works projects or teachers' salaries.[3]

Type C, G, and K grants are usually categorical (designated for specific purposes) rather than general purpose: most grants that reimburse costs are designated for specific projects and usually must be approved by the central government. Type K grants may be open-ended in that the total grant fund is determined as the sum of all reimbursable expenditures. Type C and G grants are closed-ended: the degree of reimbursement and the number of projects approved may vary from year to year according to the total funding available.[4]

The remaining five types are all more likely to be general purpose than specified for a particular use, and are all closed-ended. Type A is a shared grant in terms of both the determination of the pool and its allocation among jurisdictions; these funds are usually not earmarked. Types B and D are probably the most common. The pool is determined as a share of a national or state tax and is then allocated by formula or ad hoc. For types F, G, and H the pool is determined in an ad hoc manner (usually on a political basis) as part of the central government's regular budgeting process. For type F the allocation is by formula, whereas for type H it is purely ad hoc.

This taxonomy could easily be expanded, and many more types and subtypes could be identified. To develop a perfect classification system that takes every grant feature into account is not our objective, however. Rather, we will make two uses of the taxonomy in analyzing grants for equity, efficiency, administrative ease, and effectiveness in generating revenue. First, we will be able to pay separate attention to the two dimensions of divisible pool and allocation. Second, we will be able to better understand the importance of how grants are designed for meeting the objectives of a grant system. Indeed, the objectives of a country's system become very murky when (as often is the case) it combines several of the eight types.

The Pure Shared Tax

The purest form of shared tax—type A grants—requires that some proportion of the amount collected in the jurisdiction of a local government be returned to that local government, that is, that a derivation principle of revenue sharing be applied. The higher level of government deducts a fee for collection, usually a specified percentage of total receipts. Under this system, the local government has no control over determination of rate and base. Type A is thus an intergovernmental transfer and not a local tax.

Why would a shared tax be used instead of an outright grant or a local tax? There are three reasons. First, the central government may be pursuing a bona fide program of fiscal decentralization and is intent on guaranteeing the subnational government some share of locally generated revenues. Revenue-productive and income-elastic tax bases are most likely to be devolved in large federal countries in which state and perhaps local governments have substantial political power and diverse preferences. Brazil designates shares of the value added tax (VAT) for state and local governments; Colombia shares beer tax revenues with Bogotá and the departments; Malaysia shares excise taxes on petroleum with the states; and the Chinese central, provincial, and local governments share the revenues from profit and sales taxes with provincial and local governments. Second, the central government may see the need to mobilize more resources from local tax bases but think that local governments do not have the administrative capacity or political will to carry it off. Third, the government may want to retain—through shared taxes rather than independent local taxes—a method of fiscal control while answering some of the calls for a better vertical fiscal balance.

Property Taxes

Perhaps the most common tax sharing arrangement is for property taxes. The motives behind establishing a shared central property tax have some appeal: it is a tax involving local assets and economic activity rather than interstate commerce; local assessment and record-keeping abilities are limited; and rate setting and valuation for the property tax are sensitive political issues. A few examples may help convey the sense of sharing the property tax base. Before 1974 property taxes in Jamaica were shared with the local parishes on the basis of the location of collection—the parochial taxes went to local governments and the general tax was retained by the central government. The rate, base, assessment, and collection were strictly central functions (Bougeon-Maassen and Linn 1977; Risden 1979). After 1974, the central government no longer shared any portion of the tax on a derivation basis. Instead, a general grant was instituted that bore no relation to revenues collected in a particular jurisdiction.

Central governments in other countries continue to share the local property tax on a derivation basis. Such an arrangement has long existed in Indonesia (Linn, Smith, and Wignjowijoto 1976), though the property tax accounts for a very small share of Jakarta's revenues. Property tax sharing is also practiced in many Latin American countries (rural municipalities in Brazil, Colombia, Costa Rica, and Guatemala), where the central government levies and collects the tax on behalf of local governments (De Mello 1977: 14–15).[5] Many other countries have central administration, at least of assessment, but allow local governments to set rates. We do not consider this to be an intergovernmental transfer because the local government is free to set the rate.

Property transfer taxes are also shared with local governments and can be a significant source of revenue. In Bangladesh, a tax of 1 percent of the value of transferred land and buildings is levied by the central government and credited to the accounts of the cities and municipalities. This tax generates about 5 percent of own-source revenues in Dhaka and 8 percent in Chittagong. A number of other property-based, minor taxes are shared with state and local governments; however, these taxes (for example, taxes on vacant and agricultural land) tend to have a quite narrow base and are not very revenue-productive at tax rates that are politically acceptable. Central enforcement of these minor taxes often tends to be lax: why spend a great deal of effort for such a low potential return? Such devolutions do give local governments some additional revenues, but do not provide a financial basis for significant expansion in local services.

Are shared property taxes a successful transfer? They may be for small municipalities in which administrative skills are limited and in which the historical absence of a strong property tax leaves local officials loath to impose a high enough rate or penalize delinquents. The argument for a shared tax versus a local tax is weaker, however, for large cities. Up-to-date valuation of parcels, identification of new improvements and subdivisions, and tracking ownership and land use changes might all be done more efficiently at the local level (see also chapter 4). Even with central administration, there would seem little reason to deny the local population the right and the responsibility to set the tax rate within specified bounds.

Consumption Taxes

All tax sharing with local governments, however, is not based on so small a potential source of revenue as the property tax. Some local governments have been given access to more productive and income-elastic bases. Perhaps the best example is the value added tax in Brazil.[6] Responsibility for administration and all revenues from the VAT on final sales have been assigned to the states, but the federal government has retained the power to define the base and set the rate. In this sense, the VAT is a shared tax for both state and local governments. Moreover, the law guarantees that municipalities must receive 15 percent of state VAT collections within their boundaries. The result is that this shared tax accounts for about a third of total municipal revenues.

Some countries have agreed to share taxes that have consequences for interstate and even international commerce. Especially important, and troublesome, is the issue of whether state and local governments should benefit from the central taxation of natural resources within local areas. There are arguments that the states or local areas with mineral resources ought to be compensated for being dispossessed of their land, suffering from pollution, and perhaps needing to invest in additional development of infrastructure.[7] The counterarguments are that state and local governments should not permanently have their fiscal capacities enlarged by an accident of geography and that grants rather than shared revenues are the best way to compensate governments for social costs incurred by mining activities. Such a debate ensued over the allocation of a share of mineral royalties to Bendel and Rivers states in Nigeria in 1980. Both Malaysia and Papua New Guinea return a share of mineral-based taxes to the states on a derivation basis (see table 13-3). The debate about who should get the fiscal benefits of natural resources is not limited to developing countries. The situations regarding taxation in mineral-rich states and provinces in Australia, Canada, and the United States are other good examples of this problem.[8]

Advantages and Disadvantages

There are three important advantages to pure shared taxes. First, in comparison with allocation by formula or ad hoc arrangement, under sharing the amount of transfer to the local unit is certain and the fiscal planning of local government is improved by this certainty.[9] If ad hoc (type D) methods of distributing earmarked national tax shares are used, there is much room for debate over the proper method of allocation, and for cost-reimbursement allocations (type C). The central government may make ad hoc changes in the costs which are covered or in other conditions for approval. Second, the sharing might give the local government access to an income- and inflation-elastic revenue base, such as consumption or production, and thereby improve the adequacy of the revenue raised by local government. Third, if conditions are not imposed on the use to which the funds are put, local fiscal autonomy might increase significantly.

This third advantage, of course, depends on the central government's willingness not to tamper with the vertical fiscal balance that has been created. This is not always the case. The Brazilian government redefined the base of the state VAT to exclude projects of national interest, hence dampening the flow of revenue. Mahar and Dillinger note the revenue loss to state and local governments, though they doubt São Paulo State's estimate of a one-third reduction in VAT revenues (1983: 22–23). In most cases, however, the sharing arrangements are fixed; for example, in India the Finance Commission works out a new set of sharing percentages every fifth year.

Shared taxes are not without major disadvantages and enthusiastic opponents. The Revenue Allocation Committee's 1978 report to the government of Nigeria stated: "It is our firm belief that the principle of derivation has little or no place in a cohesive fiscal system for national political and social development" (Nigeria 1978: 36). Eventually the Nigerians did away with the derivation principle and installed tax sharing by formula and ad hoc. From the point of view of the central government, sharing arrangements tend to be inflexible because it is politically difficult to change the earmarked percentages—the vertical balance—and because it is difficult to make year-to-year adjustments in the total budget allocation to specific local governments. Such flexibility is important in economies which are exposed to much economic uncertainty because of external events (for example, rising energy costs, declining world prices for minerals, typhoons, and so forth) and which therefore may require stabilization.

An even more important problem with the pure shared tax is that it is not equalizing. The return of revenues on the basis of the location of collection will further enrich the wealthiest urban communities. This may accommodate the government's need to provide resources to meet the pressing expenditure needs of large cities, but it runs counter to the goal of reallocating national resources so as to reduce interregional disparities in fiscal capacity. For example, under Brazil's arrangement of value added tax sharing with municipalities, an industrial city within metropolitan São Paulo received $147 per capita in 1975 whereas a residential suburb received less than $1 per capita (Mahar and Dillinger 1983: 43). Counterequalizing transfers, because they are so visible and can be so extreme, may provoke negative public sentiment, disrupt national unity, and offset the distributional effects of other, equalizing transfers in the system.

The fact that this form of central assistance is effectively a local area tax over which the local government has no control creates both advantages and disadvantages. The advantage is that the lack of local control frees local officials from having to make unpopular decisions about increasing tax rates and enforcing collection. This feature probably makes the tax more productive than would be the case if it were an independent local tax. But the potential disadvantage with any form of central assistance is that separating the pain of taxation from the pleasant benefits of expenditure means that local governments are given less incentive to operate more efficiently, to reallocate expenditures among functions, and to increase the total level of spending or tax effort. The shared tax is better than the other forms of central grant assistance on this count, and

Table 13-3. *Pure Tax Sharing Arrangements with Local and State Governments*

Country	City or other jurisdiction, year	Shared tax	Sharing arrangement
		Shared with local governments	
Bangladesh	Chittagong and Dhaka, 1983	Transfer tax on immovable property	Revenues from a 1 percent rate are returned on the basis of origin
Brazil	States and municipalities, as of 1982	Value added	80 percent of revenues from this state tax are retained by the state government; of the remaining 20 percent, three-fourths is distributed among municipalities on the basis of origin and the remainder at the discretion of the state government
		Minerals	90 percent is distributed among states on the basis of origin; of this amount, 22 percent is distributed among municipalities on the basis of origin
		Property transfer	A state tax, evenly divided between states and municipalities on the basis of origin
		Vehicle registration	45 percent of collections returned to states on the basis of origin; distribution among municipalities at the discretion of states
Brazil	Municipalities, as of 1982	Rural land	80 percent distributed among municipalities on the basis of origin
Colombia	Bogotá, 1984	Beer	40 percent of a 48 percent tax on producer price is returned to the Bogotá District and the departments on the basis of estimated beer consumption
India	Ahmadabad, 1981	Property	One-third of a state government surrate on the local property tax is retained for local use
		Open lands	75 percent of state government collections

Country	Tax	Arrangement
Indonesia (Jakarta, 1981)	Property	100 percent of amount collected
Jamaica (Kingston, before 1974)	Petroleum products	Fixed amount per liter
	Property	50 percent of collections (parochial rates) on the basis of origin
Pakistan (Gujranwala, 1970s)	Vacant land	100 percent of collections on the basis of origin
	Shared property tax with province	50 percent on the basis of origin of collections
Zaire (Kinshasa, 1970s)	Head tax for low-income residents (based on income level)	Origin of collections

Shared with state governments

Country	Tax	Arrangement
Brazil (States, as of 1982)	Education salary	Two-thirds of collections returned to states on the basis of origin (earmarked for education)
Malaysia (States, 1980s)	Import and excise duties on gasoline	30 percent of yield is returned to states on the basis of derivation
	Export duty on tin	10 percent of yield is returned to states on the basis of derivation
	Export duty on timber and other forest products	100 percent is returned on a derivation basis to Sabah and Sarawak
Nigeria (States, 1979)	Rents and royalties on in-shore mining	20 percent are retained by the states
Papua New Guinea (Provinces, 1980)	Export	1.25 percent of the value of exports generated in the province (with a two-year lag and minus any royalties paid to the province)
	Turnover tax on bookmakers	95 percent of collections
	Motor vehicle and driver's license	75–95 percent to provinces

the greater the percentage of the tax to be retained, the more incentive local residents will have to comply. The issue here is the extent to which local taxpayers perceive the shared tax as being "kept at home" to finance local services.[10]

Formula Grants

An alternative to the pure shared tax is to distribute the grant pool among eligible local units on the basis of some formula. Formula grants may be differentiated according to whether the total grant fund is determined as a shared tax (type B), or on an ad hoc basis (type F; see table 13-2).

Determining the Pool

The shared tax or earmarked version of a formula grant requires that the total amount to be distributed among eligible units be determined as a fixed percentage of a national tax but that the allocation among local units be determined by formula. The shared tax-formula grant is probably the most common form of intergovernmental transfer. One may not, however, easily find norms in the practice as to which taxes should be earmarked for state and local governments or what percentage of those taxes should be devolved (see table 13-4). The central taxes that are shared cover the spectrum, for example, income taxes in Turkey, sales taxes in Colombia, and a pool of nearly all central revenues in Nigeria and the Philippines.

The ad hoc version differs in that the total grant pool is determined by political decisions year to year; that is, the national assembly or the president's office makes a budgetary allocation of some amount to each grant program in each budget year, or the amount is determined in some arbitrary way. This distributable pool is then allocated to state and local governments by formula. The ad hoc determination of the pool is not uncommon. Since the mid-1970s, Jamaica and Korea have both changed from a shared tax to an ad hoc method, though both have retained a formula for distribution among local governments.

The choice between the shared tax and ad hoc methods depends on how much control the central (or state) government wants to retain over the division of fiscal resources between central and lower levels of government, and on how much faith the center has in the ability of localities to absorb increased revenues efficiently. Jamaica has little confidence in the ability of local governments to use more revenues productively, whereas Korea—although it makes substantial allocations to the local sector—reserves the power to vary this amount as national needs dictate. In Brazil, India, and Nigeria, where a tax share is used to determine the grant fund, the inclination has been for the size of the share to creep up over time.

Which tax should be shared with subnational governments, and what percentage of the tax should be shared? It depends on the extent to which one wants to guarantee subnational governments a large revenue base with potential for growth. Some countries have given quite income-elastic bases to tax sharing programs, indicating a willingness to allow aggregate local expenditures to grow as fast as central expenditures and to be as susceptible to fluctuations in the business cycle.

Determining the Formula for Allocation

The formula for allocating the pool among local governments also varies widely (table 13-4) but seems to reflect some combination of the desire to equalize fiscal capacity or to reduce disparities in the levels of public service and to encourage local governments to mobilize resources. In almost every country the formula developed is constrained by the availability of data at the state or local level. These constraints are sometimes so severe that the issue becomes less "what would we like to do" than "what can we do."

The desire to balance regional inequities in the ability to finance public services or in the level of public services actually provided is the primary motivation for formula grants. Although the idea of giving more funds to poor jurisdictions is straightforward enough, the practice is disappointing. The problem is to find an operational measure for making an equalizing allocation. Measures of personal income are commonly used for this purpose in advanced countries but are rarely available below the national level in developing countries. There are some exceptions to this general situation; personal income estimates are made for states in some large federal countries. As table 13-4 shows, Brazil and India partially allocate certain grants according to per capita income. Or a certain part of the grant may simply be reserved for those areas of a country that are known to be poor, for example, the Northeast in Brazil.

Allocations intended to respond to needs for public services are plagued by the problem of how to identify indicators of need and by data limitations. Some countries have resorted to very general measures of differences in the cost of providing services with no recognition of differences in financial capacity. Population and land area are common factors in grant formulas, probably more because of data availability than because of the belief that these are rough proxy measures of need. In some countries, grants have been allocated to match the needs for certain services—usually those which are most important in the local budgets. For example, measures of the need for road maintenance are not unusual in grant formulas (road mileage in Jamaica, Kenya, and Tunisia; number of licensed vehicles in Brazil).

Finally, some countries have attempted to build measures of tax effort directly into the formula in order to stimulate local resource mobilization.

(*Text continues on page 446.*)

Table 13-4. *Grants Distributed by Formula or Ad Hoc*

Country	City or other jurisdiction, year	Determination of total grant pool	Eligible units	Method of distribution among eligible units
Brazil	All cities, 1982	23 percent of the industrial production tax and the manufacturers sales tax	10.5 percent to states, 10.5 percent to municipalities, and 2 percent to a special fund for low-income northeastern states	State shares are distributed according to land area (5 percent) and population and inverse per capita income (95 percent). The municipal share is distributed 10 percent to the state capital and 90 percent to other municipalities on a population basis. 20 percent of the municipal share is earmarked for education
		Tax on fuels and lubricants	31 percent to state and 8 percent to municipalities	Weighted according to consumption of imported fuels (40 percent), population (40 percent), and land area (20 percent). Earmarked for transport sector
		Tax on electricity	50 percent to states and 10 percent to municipalities	20 percent by land area, 60 percent by population, 2 percent by production, 15 percent by consumption of electric energy, and 3 percent by area of hydroelectric projects. Earmarked for investment in energy sector
Colombia	Bogotá, 1980	Tax on licensing of vehicles	States and municipalities	Number of vehicles licensed
		15 percent of national current revenues less shared taxes	Decentralized special districts for primary education and public health	In the Bogotá District and the departments, 70 percent is distributed by population and 30 percent by equal shares. Of the amount received by the Bogotá District, 74 percent is allocated to the Education Special District and 26 percent to the Special Health District

	Bogotá, 1980; Cartagena, 1975	30 percent of national sales tax collections	Departments (states), municipalities, Bogotá District	The amount to be distributed among the local governments is divided as follows: 70 percent is shared among the departments in proportion to their population; the remaining 30 percent is shared in equal parts among the departments, regardless of population. The departments distribute 40 percent of their respective shares among municipalities on a per capita basis
India	Ahmadabad, 1981 States, 1970s	Proceeds of a pre-1939 roll tax on vehicles	States	90 percent by population, 10 percent by origin of collection
		85 percent of individual income tax collections less union surcharge, agricultural income tax, and union territory share (1979–84)	States	25 percent by population, 25 percent by the reciprocal of per capita income, 25 percent by the "poverty" ratio, and 25 percent by revenue equalization
		40 percent of excise duties (1979–84)		
		Plan grants determined annually on an ad hoc basis	States	60 percent by population, 10 percent to states whose per capita income is below the national average, 10 percent according to tax effort, 10 percent according to outlays on major irrigation and power projects, 10 percent in discretionary assistance for special problems
Indonesia	Jakarta, 1981	10 percent of foreign currency raised through province exports in 1976 plus 5 percent automatic increase per year		

(Table continues on the following page.)

Table 13-4 (continued)

Country	City or other jurisdiction, year	Determination of total grant pool	Eligible units	Method of distribution among eligible units
Jamaica	Kingston, 1973	50 percent of motor vehicle licenses	Local authorities	Mileage of parochial roads
		Deficit grant; ad hoc distribution	Local authorities	"Approved" deficits
Korea, Rep. of	Seoul, pre- and 1972	Education grant: 11.55 percent of national tax revenues	All local governments providing education services	Fixed amount per school and per class
		Local share grant: 17.6 percent of national tax revenue	All local governments	Approved budget "deficits" defined as the difference between approved costs and 80 percent of "collectable" revenue
	Seoul, post-1972	Local share grant: ad hoc decision, depending on current budget condition of central government	Same as pre-1972	Same formula as pre-1972 except that approximately 20 percent is distributed on an ad hoc basis by the Ministry of Home Affairs
		Subsidy: ad hoc determination	Same as pre-1972	Approved on a project basis
Nigeria	All cities, 1970s	Distribution pool: 50 percent of rents and royalties on inshore mining, 50 percent of excise duties	State governments	50 percent is divided equally among the nineteen states; 50 percent is distributed on the basis of population
Philippines	Manila, 1980	20 percent of national taxes	All local governments	76 percent to cities and provinces and 24 percent to municipalities; 70 percent by population, 20 percent by land area and 10 percent by equal shares
		A share of specific excise taxes on petroleum products		

Country	City, year	Tax or revenue shared	Recipients	Basis of distribution
Tunisia	Tunis, 1972	Common fund: 10 percent of taxes on production, consumption, and services, and 15 percent of taxes on business licenses and nonbusiness profits	Communes and governorates	10 percent of the total divisible pool is distributed to the commune of Tunis. Tunis also shares in the remaining 90 percent as follows: 17.5 percent of the total divisible pool is distributed according to population, 35 percent of the total is prorated according to rental value tax revenues, and 10 percent of the pool is distributed among the four largest communes (including Tunis) on the basis of the size of their ordinary budgets
		Common fuel and tire fund: 10 percent of excise taxes on oil and gas and 15 percent of tax on tires and tubes	Communes and governorates	The commune of Tunis receives 10 percent of the divisible pool and shares another 10 percent with the three other largest municipalities according to size of the ordinary budget. Approximately 53 percent of the pool is divided among communes according to the area of their highway system, and the remaining 17 percent is divided among Governorate Councils according to the area of their highway system
Turkey	Istanbul, 1968	5 percent of national income taxes	Municipalities	Population
		25 percent of property taxes	Municipalities	Population
		Motor vehicle and traffic fines (11 percent), fuel production tax (8 percent), and monopoly revenues (2 percent)	Municipalities	Population
Zaire	Kinshasa, 1970s	15 percent of customs duties	Municipalities	Population
		Central government subsidy determined on an ad hoc basis	All cities	Ad hoc distribution

The Korean system (described below) is one effort to try to hold tax rates at about their present level: if a city drops below the standard tax rate, there is a built-in penalty in the form of a lower allocation. Other programs are more aggressive and even try to reward higher tax efforts in the allocation. For example, Indian Plan Grants include a measure of tax effort in the formula, as does the Nigerian formula for sharing central revenues with the states. Few countries can follow this practice, however, because the common measure of tax effort is the ratio of taxes to personal income and few countries have adequate measures of local personal income.

Grants to Reimburse Costs

A third way to transfer central government resources to local governments is through grants that reimburse costs (types C, G, and K in table 13-2). Under such schemes, the center agrees to reimburse the locality for all or a portion of the cost of an activity (if it is a portion, a matching share from the locality is required). Grants to reimburse costs are typically tied to a particular government expenditure.

Determining the Distributable Pool

There are various methods for determining the total amount of grants for reimbursed costs available for distribution. If a limit on the total is desired, a specified share of a national revenue source or an ad hoc method may be used to fix the size of the pool. A more open-ended method is to reimburse all eligible expenditures. The catch here is that the central government determines what is eligible; the grant is thus always closed-ended. The closed-ended, shared tax method is often used to support current services, and ad hoc determination is more frequent for capital projects.

Determining the Distribution

There is a fine line between distributing a grant amount by formula and distributing to reimburse cost. Both approaches may reflect differences in need and the objectives of equalization, and both may use exact equations to arrive at a final distribution among local governments. Only reimbursement, however, takes the cost of providing the service explicitly into account. This is a very important distinction. No less important is whether reimbursement is complete or partial; the choice suggests two very different sets of consequences.

FULL REIMBURSEMENT. Full reimbursement of costs amounts to central financing of a locally administered service; hence, no incentive is given to the local government for improved efficiency in the delivery of the service. Moreover, full reimbursement is likely to be accompanied by a rigid central government approval process, and local government fiscal choices may be minimized if not eliminated. This is another reason why such a grant is not likely to draw out a great deal of local enthusiasm for improving the quality of the service.

Despite these shortcomings, full reimbursements are used, as described in table 13-5. The idea is to stimulate the provision of certain services by lowering their marginal cost to zero and by mandating a certain level of service. Full reimbursement of teacher salaries is a common form of local grant. This method may promote the equalization of services in different parts of the country and stimulate certain types of activities, but it does not encourage local governments to mobilize additional resources or lead to more efficient operations. For example, grants were made to Calcutta and Colombo to compensate the municipal budget for cost-of-living increases to local government employees, but because the local governments did not bear these costs, there was no incentive to be concerned with the productivity of these workers.

PARTIAL REIMBURSEMENT. Central governments have attempted to overcome the problem of incentives by subsidizing less than 100 percent of costs, that is, by requiring a match from the recipient governments. Such grants to reimburse costs partially can stimulate the tax effort of local government on behalf of the aided function. The amount of stimulation depends on the percentage of reimbursement, which lowers the tax price of the service in question; on the income- and price-elasticity of demand for the service, which determines how the local government will expand provision of the service in the face of the lower tax price; and on the fungibility of local expenditures, that is, whether a dollar of matching funds is simply taken from a nonaided service. (See the appendix to chapter 12 for a more formal presentation of this situation.) Despite its merits, this type of grant imposes important costs on the residents of recipient communities and perhaps on society. The stimulation of expenditure induced by the grant will distort the local budget in favor of the aided service and against other services that local residents would have chosen. Another potential cost is that such grants may be counterproductive to the goal of regional equity. Many of the takers will be wealthy communities, those most able to match the grants.

A big problem in designing a program to reimburse costs partially is choosing the matching share. If the central share of reimbursement is set too high, there will be too few takers and low-income communities will be driven away from the program. If the central share is set too low, the opportunity to stimulate more mobilization of local resources and better management will have been bypassed. In practice, the matching shares appear to have been set without careful quantitative assessment of these possible effects (see table 13-5).

A notable exception to this approach is Korea's local share grant—its largest grant program—which reimburses local governments in the

Table 13-5. *Reimbursement Grants*

Country	City or other jurisdiction, year	Function	Cost eligible for reimbursement
India	Ahmadabad, 1971	Education	25–50 percent of approved expenditures
		Health	50–100 percent of approved expenditures
India	Calcutta, 1972	Employee compensation	State grant covers about 80 percent of inflation compensation of municipal employees
Indonesia	Jakarta, 1981	General	100 percent of approved compensation for approved positions
Korea, Rep. of	Seoul, pre-1972	Education	35 percent of practical training and laboratory fees
		Education	100 percent of primary teachers' salaries
		Capital projects	Varying degrees of reimbursement tied to particular projects
Papua New Guinea	Provinces, 1980	Capital works, maintenance, and rural improvements	Estimated 1976–77 costs, increased annually by the lesser of the consumer price index or changes in tax and loan receipts of the central government
Pakistan	Gujranwala, 1970s	Capital assistance	65–80 percent of project costs
Sri Lanka	Colombo, 1985	Employee compensation	Grant from central government covers the increase in employee compensation

448

amount of the difference between the cost of an estimated standard of public services and the revenue yield from a standard of tax effort. The indicators of need are measures such as the number of voting districts for election expenses, length of road for paving expenses, and population for public health expenditures. In each case an approved unit cost is prescribed by the Ministry of Home Affairs. On the revenue side, the standard for financial ability is 80 percent of local taxes collected at normal rates. The difference between expenditure needs and financial ability defines the cost reimbursement to which that local government is entitled.[11] The amount awarded, then, becomes a form of deficit grant. A similar method is used in Zambia. This type of grant has merit in that it is less likely to reward slack tax effort than is a straight needs allocation, and it may be used to stimulate local public expenditures for targeted services. But it is very complicated to manage; for example, standard unit costs must be updated every year, and data on the many underlying indicators must be gathered annually.

Another problem with grants that partially reimburse costs is that they tend to carry central restrictions on reimbursable costs. The most common restriction is to require that all local governments participate and that reimbursed expenditures be approved by the central government (see table 13-5). The usual procedure is for the central government to provide a list of eligible expenditures, such as number of approved positions, compensation levels, and construction standards. This practice eliminates some of the problems of regional equity in that it mandates a local contribution, but in reducing the option for local fiscal choices it gives up the possibility for a maximum stimulation of tax effort. For example, the possibility that local governments would be willing to raise more taxes to meet their matching share of a teacher's salary grant could be thwarted by placing an upper limit on the number of teachers permitted.

Ad Hoc Grants

Perhaps the extreme case of centralization in grant design is an ad hoc program (type H grants) in which the size of the divisible pool is determined annually by the center and the distribution is made on some subjective basis. For example:

- Virtually all open-ended construction grants which require approval of each project
- That portion of any grant program allocated on a discretionary basis by the state or central government
- Supplementary grants allocated for special purposes during the fiscal year.

The great advantage and disadvantage of ad hoc grants is that they do not mandate a particular vertical fiscal balance between the central and local government. This gives the central government maximum flexibility to redirect resources to sectors of greatest need, but it leaves local governments vulnerable and uncertain about the finances available for them. In many instances, the creation of an ad hoc grant program is motivated by a desire to limit the financial autonomy and importance of subnational governments. Several examples illustrate this point.

The government of Bangladesh abolished the tax of local governments in 1981 and installed a compensatory octroi grant to replace the lost local revenues. In the ensuing two years the divisible grant pool was set at 75–80 percent of previous octroi collections. Two years after establishment of the compensatory grant, the real amount distributed was less than half of 1980 real octroi collections. Moreover, the distribution across local governments, based on 1980 actual octroi collections, did not reflect changes in the relative degree of economic growth in the recipient cities.[12] In Kenya a local wage tax was abolished by the central government and replaced by a compensatory grant. By 1982, this grant to the Nairobi City Council was at about the same nominal level as it had been in 1973. Distributions among eligible local governments are made on the basis of the relative amounts collected from the earnings tax in the early 1970s. Virtually the same story of a declining transfer can be told for Kingston after the replacement of the shared property tax with a compensatory grant (Bougeon-Maassen and Linn 1977). Korea is yet another example. Before 1972, Korea's local tax share grant was fixed at 17.6 percent of national tax collections. An ad hoc determination of the total grant fund was adopted in 1972, and the local share of national tax revenues fell to 10.9 percent by 1977 (Smith and Kim 1979). In 1983, the share was set at 13.27 percent.

Capital Grants and Loans

Local capital projects are financed by a combination of capital grants, loans, and short-term borrowing. Loans are usually allocated to the local governments by the central government, their terms are dictated by central regulations, and their repayment is frequently forgiven. Such loans are in every sense a part of the system of intergovernmental transfers, and are treated as such here.

Capital Grants

Because of the desire to encourage local capital formation, central governments often earmark grants to local governments for capital purposes. The two most common forms are block grants and project grants. (Capital grants may be structured in any of the eight forms given in table 13-2.)

Block grants distribute the funds for capital projects to local governments but allow them to decide which projects to develop. Some monitoring of the use of the funds is usually carried out, but each governmental unit is guaranteed its grant amount by some means other than the inherent worthiness of specific projects. In the Philippines, grants from a shared petroleum tax—distributed by formula—are designated for capital projects and earmarked for the infrastructure funds of local governments. In addition, 20 percent of the general grant to local governments must be transferred from the general to the infrastructure fund (Bahl and Schroeder 1983b: chap. 4). In Tunisia, 10 percent of the receipts from each of the two largest grant programs is earmarked for capital purposes.

Project grants, which depend heavily on an approval process, are most common if the central government is encouraging local governments to invest in particular sectors, for example, housing and water supply. Project grants have some important advantages over block grants. Block grants are allocated without knowledge of how well the local government can absorb the money to carry out and maintain the capital project. This can result in an accumulation of cash balances or in expenditure of the money for ill-conceived projects.[13] Project grants are much more likely to draw out productive investment opportunities. But block grants have some decided advantages over project grants. They are more easily administered and can be implemented more quickly because the approval process does not require a project feasibility study.[14] Moreover, block grants can be distributed by formula on an equalizing basis, whereas project grants are more likely to go to those with more fiscal capacity and stronger capabilities for project design and implementation.

Does either type of capital grant lead local governments to mobilize more revenue or expend more capital? Project grants probably cause capital expenditures to increase more than do block grants because there is less likelihood that if a government applies for a project grant it will be unable to absorb the funds and because funds for project grants are more likely to be additions to planned capital spending. Project grants are also more likely to stimulate an increase in revenue effort because they can be given on a partial reimbursement basis and because their use might be restricted to projects that generate income.

Loans

There is no theoretical or administrative reason why local governments should not finance capital projects with borrowing. Capital assets are long-lived and appropriately paid for over a period of time; and the services produced by these assets can have local zones of benefits that dictate the wisdom of drawing financing from the local area tax base. Thus there is more and more interest in finding institutional credit mechanisms to finance local capital projects. This interest has risen with the growing needs for infrastructure and the capacity of large urban governments to repay loans. Yet local governments in developing countries—even large cities—do not use credit financing extensively. This is in part because their financial ability to carry debt is limited and in part due to central constraints on local borrowing. These constraints include a cumbersome and often lengthy review and approval process, high interest rates, high local capital matching contributions, and short loan maturities. The underlying reason for these constraints, one suspects, is that local governments are not trusted to spend the money wisely or to repay their debt obligations.

Today, then, local borrowing in developing countries is highly regulated and centralized—with a very few exceptions. The central government usually establishes the total amount of credit available, eligible projects, terms of the loan, and the actual distribution among local governments. A central sign-off on local borrowing is required in nearly all countries. Even with this common pattern of central control, however, there are alternatives in designing local government loan programs. And central governments have devised ways to promote credit financing by local governments.

DETERMINING THE POOL. A description of loan programs in developing countries begins with the same questions as a description of grant programs: How is the total divisible pool determined? How is it allocated across local governments? The answer to the first question does not vary greatly across countries. The central bank and the ministry of finance usually set a total credit ceiling for the economy, and this amount is rationed among potential borrowers (including the aggregate local governments) in an ad hoc manner. Borrowing outside this limit is sometimes permitted for larger cities, but not in great amounts and only with consent from the center. Direct external borrowing by local governments is not permitted, though "on-lending" by central governments to local governments is not uncommon.

DETERMINING THE ALLOCATION. Techniques for allocating the total loan among local governments vary widely. The range of possibilities may be illustrated by describing four kinds of practices in various countries. First, the loan program in the Philippines is done project by project, with approval required by the Ministry of Finance (Hubbell 1983: chap. 6). Less than full reimbursement of costs is typically provided because the approved loan always falls short of the total cost. This appears to be a convention rather than a legal requirement. Borrowing is from the government-owned Development Bank and Land Bank, and no formal ceiling is placed on local borrowings. In fact, local governments have not made substantial use of this system. By 1980, the gross outstanding debt of local governments was equivalent to only about 2 percent of their gross revenue.

A second possibility is the system of plan loans in India, which are apportioned among state governments in a more objective manner. The shares of individual states are distributed by a formula which includes population, tax effort, relative low-income status, and commitments to irrigation and power projects. States are required to make matching expenditures for certain kinds of projects as a condition of receiving central assistance.

A third type of lending mechanism establishes a local government loan authority as a central agency, as in Kenya and Tunisia. The Tunisian loan fund is capitalized from a share of the divisible grant pool for local governments, loans raised in the market, and repayments. The loan fund is a source of subsidized credit to local governments but is distributed on an ad hoc basis and involves a complex approval process (Prud'homme 1975).

Fourth, loans to local governments may be disbursed through a specialized credit agency. These have been set up in some Latin American countries, for example, Brazil, Nicaragua, and Venezuela.[15] The agency may be capitalized with grants or loans from the central government, foreign aid, contributions of shares from local governments, and earmarked taxes. This kind of specialized agency can maintain the expertise to help local governments overcome barriers to project preparation and develop proposals for credit financing. But agencies must at least break even in their lending operations; hence there is careful scrutiny of the creditworthiness of applicants. Because large, wealthy local governments tend to have a greater capacity to repay, this mechanism is not likely to lead to an equalizing system of loan distributions.

In most intergovernmental systems, large cities are given some special privileges to finance debt, often including the authority to bypass the usual regulations, to borrow more, and to borrow from sources other than the central government. Case studies in Bombay (Bougeon-Maassen 1976) and Cartagena (Linn 1975) revealed that these city governments borrowed long term from the private sector. The amounts involved were nominal, however, and closely regulated by the central government. Prud'homme (1975) reports that the commune of Tunis may bypass much of the compliance procedure and work directly with the Ministry of the Interior.

Short-Term Borrowing

Surprisingly, some local governments in developing countries are permitted to undertake short-term borrowing. Linn (1975) reports that the municipality of Cartagena and its decentralized agencies can cover budget deficits with overdrafts and other short-term loan arrangements with local banks. Kenyan local authorities have also made use of overdrafts from commercial banks to cover annual shortfalls in revenue. Thimmaiah (1977) reported a problem of states' unauthorized overdrafts from the

Reserve Bank of India because the limits agreed to between the bank
and the state governments were exceeded and because overdrafts were
not repaid.

Evaluating the Alternatives

The design or reform of the system of grants in nearly any developing
country raises a common set of questions:

- What allocative effects will the system have? Will it make local
  governments more accountable for their fiscal decisions, and will
  it induce them to mobilize more resources?
- Will the system equalize differences between rich and poor areas
  in public services?
- Will local governments receive an adequate flow of revenues?
- Will the total fiscal system be planned to operate more efficiently?
- Will local autonomy be improved or compromised by the system?

As we shall see below, the answers to these questions depend very much
on the design of the grant system.

Allocative Effects

The central issue in evaluating the allocative effects of a system of
grants is whether and how it distorts the level and mix of local taxes and
expenditures from what they would have been in its absence. There is
a rich literature on the subject, but with a few exceptions (for example,
Bird 1980, Bahl and Linn 1983, and Hicks 1977), it is focused on the
experience in industrial countries (for example, Break 1980, Oates 1972,
1977a, and Mathews 1980). The model for such analysis is well developed theoretically and has been extensively applied in the United States,
but its applicability to developing countries has not been carefully considered.

In developing nations, however, the allocative concerns are much the
same as in industrial countries: whether the system will make the local
government less accountable and therefore encourage inefficient operations, and whether it will cause the local government to change its allocation of budget resources. Underlying these two concerns is the possibility that central grants are seen by local governments as a substitute
for locally raised taxes. If this is true, an increase in the flow of grants
leads to a one-for-one reduction in local tax effort, and local financing
is removed yet another step from the local population. These three concerns—accountability, distortions in local budgets, and effects on the
local tax effort—are now each discussed.

ACCOUNTABILITY. The fiscal system of a local government can be structured to be an effective instrument for making local decisionmakers and
managers accountable for their operations. This accountability, which

one hopes can make local governments more efficient, can be achieved in three ways. First, local services can be financed by local taxes; hence the accountability is to the local people who pay the taxes. If local councils are elected and local chief officers are appointed (and removed) by the local council, local financing can be a strong incentive for local government to become more efficient. This route to efficiency, however, is often thwarted because local officials and councils are appointed by higher levels of government and may feel less responsibility to local taxpayers than to ministry officials. A good case in point is the Philippines, where local treasurers and assessors are central government employees and not strictly accountable to the local population. A more extreme example is the appointment of local administrators in the aftermath of the imposition of martial law in Bangladesh in 1982. Schroeder comments that "there was often a significant difference in leadership style of the appointed administrators vis-à-vis the popularly elected chairmen. In great part this stemmed from the fact that administrators had no need to establish and maintain political support" (1985a: 19).

Second, the central government can mandate good local management. If the central government strictly regulates local operations, then local officials are accountable to it and not to the local population. This approach is often taken in setting standards for activities such as building highways, setting teacher salaries, and determining user charges. But central governments in developing countries do not have the wherewithal to monitor carefully the activities of all local governments or perhaps the vision to write regulations to cover every set of local conditions. Carried to an extreme, mandates lead to situations such as a two-year takeover by the Jamaican central government of the Kingston–Saint Andrews parish government beginning in 1984.

Third, the central government can finance the local service with a grant rather than a local tax but rely on provisions in the grant to induce local officials to be accountable. The intuitive argument against financing with grants is appealing: local taxpayers do not see grants as costing them anything; hence they will not become agitated if the money is spent with less than maximum efficiency. Neither will there be accountability to the central government if the money is given with no strings attached. This suggests that a part of the responsibility for ensuring good local management could be shifted to the central government. Such a change could be made with appropriate grant design, the principle being that local officials should see a reward (or penalty) associated with the efficiency (or inefficiency) of their operations. This could be done by mandating how the money could be spent and by requiring a match as a condition for receipt of the grant.

This leads to the question of which types of grant referred to in table 13-2 do the best job of promoting accountability and operational efficiency. The general answer is cost reimbursement grants (types C, G, K in the table), but only if there is partial reimbursement, that is, if the local government must match the central contribution and if the receipt of the money is conditional upon some specified use. The greater the match, the more local officials are accountable to their constituents, who must pay the difference. Full cost reimbursement grants, which require strict central approval of expenditures, are especially likely to thwart local initiative, although accountability to the center will be mandated.

A formula grant, with a provision for a tax effort in its determination (types B or F in the table), may also serve the goal of accountability in that the tax creates some pain for taxpayers and that it makes local officials responsible to the taxpayers. The effectiveness of this approach depends, however, on the importance of the tax effort term in the formula, and as noted above, tax effort does not usually weigh heavily in formula grants. Another possibility is that formula grants may be conditional and require monitoring of the disposition of the funds. This is not usually the case, and therefore accountability to the center is limited.

Taxes shared on a derivation basis (type A in the table) provide accountability to local residents if the taxes are seen as local and if local officials are locally elected or appointed. A general principle is the greater the percentage share of the tax returned to the local government and the more easily identifiable the tax, the more the local population will identify with the tax. For example, the return of 100 percent of the property tax is more likely to be seen as local tax revenue than is the return of 10 percent of total central government tax collections.

BUDGET DISTORTIONS. A grant may cause a local community to change its budget priorities. For example, if it receives a grant for education, it may spend more on education than it would have in the absence of the grant. Suppose the community is thought to be spending too little on primary education to satisfy national goals. The result of a conditional education grant could be to stimulate spending on that function, thereby increasing national welfare, but at the cost of a higher tax rate or of reduced community spending for some noneducation purposes. The local community is clearly worse off—it has been deterred from reaching its preferred budget outcome. The nation, however, may be better off if the aided function (education in this case) is characterized by significant external benefits. If the aided function does not have significant spillover benefits, however, the community will suffer a loss in welfare but there will be no commensurate regional or national gains.

The above discussion presupposes that the grant was effective in stimulating local expenditures on the aided function and that the desired increase in expenditures was induced. But not all types of grants are equally effective in stimulating expenditures for a particular purpose. Partial cost reimbursement grants (types C, F, and G), which lower the relative price of one government service in comparison with all others, offer the best possibility for such an effect and are often used to give financial support to services the government wants to encourage. Such grants provide both a price effect (they lower the relative tax price of each unit of the aided function) and an income effect (they increase the flow of funds to the local government) to stimulate spending on the function. Grants for teachers' salaries and public works are examples of such programs (see table 13-5).

Another possibility is that central assistance may carry conditions or mandates. The most obvious case is conditional grants, that is, grants earmarked for a particular service. Indeed, conditionality is an element of most grant programs. The above review uncovered a number of examples: central governments require that a specified percentage of grant receipts be spent on economic development projects (Philippines), be set aside for maintenance of capital projects (Bangladesh, Egypt), or be spent on a designated activity. Does conditionality work as a means of stimulating expenditures for specified purposes? The answer is that it might, but it depends on the income-elasticity of demand for the aided function, whether the local government would have spent something for the aided function in any case, and whether local revenues are fungible.[16]

Consider the Philippines, where a designated percentage of the general grant to local governments is set aside for capital development. Are capital expenditures really stimulated to a level above what they would have been in the absence of the grant? Certainly the relative tax price has not been lowered; that is, capital projects have not been made cheaper relative to other public services. The only inducement is the income effect; the local government will spend some of the grant for capital projects just as it would spend some fraction of any increase in its income for capital projects. But capital expenditures will surely not increase by the full amount of the capital grant.

The central government might take steps to monitor the disposition of the funds to ensure that all of the money is spent for the prescribed purpose. But how could it do this? Local government revenues are fungible, and there is no way to know how much the local government would have spent in the absence of the grant. In the Philippines the central government could only mandate that at least the grant amount be spent for capital purposes.

TAX EFFORT EFFECTS. It is the tax effort issue—the fear that grants may reduce rather than increase local revenue mobilization—that has probably raised the most questions about the allocative aspects of grant design. Many central government policymakers would argue that grants to local governments should be stimulative rather than substitutive; that is, a one dollar grant should have the net effect of increasing total local expenditures by more than one dollar. This implies that to receive an additional one dollar in grants, the local government would have to match it with an additional amount of revenue. Because the tax bases traditionally left to local governments are difficult to tap, it is necessary for them to be quite resourceful in increasing revenues—a factor which argues that the matching incentive ought to be considerable. A more realistic goal might be simply a maintenance-of-effort requirement.

Can grant programs in practice be designed to stimulate local governments to find ways to increase tax effort? Theory does not give us a perfectly clear answer, but it does suggest three possible ways to design programs.[17] First, tax effort can be built directly into the allocation formula; that is, governments willing to tax themselves more heavily will be rewarded by receiving a larger share of the divisible grant pool. The logic here is that an increase in taxes would be rewarded by even greater increases in expenditure benefits and therefore citizens would be less resistant to the higher tax. The price of an increase in taxes, in effect, would fall.

It can be shown that this is a necessary but not sufficient condition to stimulate tax effort. It depends on how high are the income- and price-elasticities of demand for local public goods, how heavily weighted is the tax effort variable in the allocation formula, and whether or not all local governments compete for a larger share of grants by raising taxes. In any case, this method is not widely used in countries we have studied, mostly because of the conceptual and empirical problems of measuring the tax effort of local governments. Even in India, where it is used for state governments, there is a very small weight attached to the tax effort component of the allocation formula.

Second, a grant can be made to reimburse costs partially. Because the government pays a share of the cost, aided local government goods become "cheaper" relative to all other goods and the local population will demand more of the now cheaper public goods. How much more they demand will again depend on the strength of the income- and price-elasticities of demand. However, partial cost reimbursement grants may not stimulate revenue effort. Administrative and legal constraints may simply make it impossible for the local government to mobilize additional resources; that is, the incentive may exist and the population may be willing, but the administrative and legal capacity to increase taxes may not be there. The grant is likely to be fully spent on the aided function, but no new taxes will be raised. The matching share for a public works grant may simply come from what would otherwise have been spent for primary education, or even from what the government would have spent on public works in the absence of the grant. Expenditures on the aided function may or may not be stimulated, but overall tax effort will not.

Third, a general purpose subsidy can be given. These are the most common grants in developing countries. They are not matching and do not contain a tax effort term in the allocation formula. They exert only an income effect, and their stimulative effect on taxes depends on the strength of the income-elasticity of demand for government goods. Can such grants stimulate revenue effort? Theory and empirical studies in industrial countries suggest they cannot. If a community receives an additional peso in grant funds, at least some of it will probably show up as a lower rate of taxation (increased rate of spending on private goods) than otherwise would have existed. Again, there is some evidence to suggest that this might be less the case in developing countries. At least for certain goods, the income-elasticity of demand for public goods is stronger than unity. What we are left with then is an answer that it depends on the package of services which the local government provides: the less income-elastic, the more likely are grants to be substituted for locally raised taxes. Grants may be designed to protect against this outcome by requiring a maintenance of tax effort at current levels. Although this would not stimulate tax effort, it might guarantee that a fiscal substitution would not occur. We could find no country that used such a maintenance-of-effort approach.

Because theory can provide only a framework for analyzing the effects on tax effort of grants in developing countries, we are left to search for an answer in the results of empirical research. Unfortunately, there is little to search. The results of a few econometric analyses do not turn up clear evidence of either stimulation or substitution in the effect of grants on public spending in developing countries. The general approach in these analyses is to estimate, from a cross section of local or state governments, the per capita expenditure (E) responsiveness to per capita grants (G), usually from the functional relation:

$$E = a + b_i X_i + cG$$

where X_i are other variables affecting the level of expenditures. If $c > 1$, then a one dollar increase in grants is associated with an increase in expenditures of more than one dollar, which is a stimulative effect; if $c < 1$, the grant is substitutive by the same reasoning; and if $c = 1$, there is a maintenance of effort.

The results of such studies are quite sensitive to the data, model specification, and estimation technique used as well as to the country or countries studied.[18] Bahl and Pillai (1976) found that total federal government transfers stimulated total and development expenditures of Indian states in the early 1970s. The stimulative effects were attributed to general purpose grants: shared taxes distributed on the basis of needs and nonstatutory grants which are partly (10 percent) distributed on the basis of tax effort. Other studies of the effect of federal grants on expenditures of Indian states have indicated a neutral or stimulative response. Conversely, Bird (1984: chap. 8 and app. 3) estimated a substitutive effect on departmental taxes in a cross-sectional study of Colombia's tax allowance grant.

This question has been studied to some extent for local governments in a few developing countries. Bahl and Schroeder (1983: chap. 9) found a neutral response of tax effort to grants for Philippine local governments. Dillinger's (1981) statistical estimates provide no evidence that municipalities in São Paulo State reduced taxes in response to grant inflows. Bird, however, found a substitutive effect for Colombia's sales tax transfer to municipalities, though the substitution was greater in small municipalities than in larger cities (1984: app. 4).

About the best one can conclude from this meager evidence is that intergovernmental transfer programs do not appear to substitute markedly for locally raised taxes. This result is not unexpected. To the extent the binding constraints on local government tax effort are administrative bottlenecks and central government strictures, one would expect grants to be fully spent (see the appendix to chapter 12).

Equalizing Effects

An important feature of grants is the extent to which they equalize fiscal capacities and levels of public service among local governments. With so much discussion focused on the need to achieve more balanced population and income growth in developing countries, there is much concern about how central grants are distributed across regions and among eligible units of local government. Moreover, the competition among states, regions, and local areas makes distribution an explosive political issue.

There is confusion about the purpose of equalizing grants in developing countries. Although the equalization feature of grant policy rightfully attracts a great deal of attention, much of the discussion is uninformed or pointed more at political issues than at the analytical issues of grant design. Before raising the question of what types of grants seem to do the best job of equalizing, we consider the antecedent issues of why a government would want to have a system of equalizing grants and what are the alternative definitions of equalization.

OBJECTIVES OF EQUALIZATION. Governments of developing countries might want to pursue a policy of equalization for two reasons. The first has to do with the possibility of affecting the size of cities. The argument goes that if public services can be improved in small cities and rural areas, the rapid migration to large cities can be slowed. Because small municipalities and rural local governments have little capacity to support improvements in public service, a system of equalizing grants seems logical. In effect, it is a transfer of resources from urban areas, where most taxes are raised, to the rest of the country.

There are good arguments against equalization for this purpose. An equalizing program from a fixed central pool necessarily means a smaller share will go to urban governments. Such a tradeoff will be inefficient if the rural government does not have the capacity to spend the funds or if there are significant economies of scale in spending by urban governments. Moreover, it might be argued that urban areas have the largest needs for public expenditure, that substantially more interpersonal income redistribution can be achieved in urban areas, and that in any case feasible increases in the relative quality of rural government services brought about by equalizing grants are not apt to affect noticeably the flow of migrants to the cities. Finally, one might argue that the productivity of public investments is much higher in larger urban areas than in the rest of the country.

The second possible goal of equalizing grants is to eliminate some of the disparity in fiscal capacity and the levels of public service among local governments in the country. Again, the idea is to improve the relative levels of services available to residents of poorer jurisdictions—perhaps to satisfy some basic objective of meeting needs. The argument, however, is motivated more by distributional goals—providing better services to poorer people—than by any goals related to a national settlement policy. It is a more defensible argument.

DEFINING EQUALIZATION. A first step in designing an equalizing grant system is to define "equalization." There are at least two views on exactly what a grant system is supposed to equalize. The first is that the intent of the system is to equalize the capacity of local governments to finance a given level of services. The second is that needs for expenditure should guide the distribution of grant monies.

The capacity approach would lead to the inclusion of per capita income in the revenue sharing formula. As is shown in the appendix to chapter 12, however, this program would provide no incentive for the recipient government to increase its tax effort. To adjust for this, we might define the fiscal capacity of a local government in terms of some normative tax effort. A relatively simple and completely equalizing system could be defined as follows:

$$(13\text{-}1) \qquad \left[\sum_1^n t_i/n \right] Y_i = T_i^*$$

where t_i = effective tax rate in the ith of n jurisdictions, Y_i = personal income in the ith jurisdiction, and T_i^* = estimated tax capacity of the ith jurisdiction.

$$(13\text{-}2) \qquad T_i^* - \overline{T}^* = G_i$$

where $\overline{T}^* = \sum_1^n (T_i^*/n)$, average tax capacity, and G_i = equalizing grant to the ith jurisdiction. Assuming this arithmetic average of effective tax rates to be a desirable norm for tax effort, a system of positive and negative transfers will result such that $\sum G_i = 0$ and $(T_i^* + G_i)$ will be equal across all i jurisdictions.

Of course, such notions of full capacity equalization are not realistic. Interjurisdictional disparities in fiscal capacity are simply too large to be offset completely. Moreover, accurate data on personal income are not available to measure differences in financial capacity or to gauge equalization efforts. Perhaps this explains the virtual absence of this approach in the developing countries we have studied.

The second view of the equalization objective focuses on expenditure needs rather than fiscal capacity. That is, the grant formula needs to be structured to channel more funds to areas where needs are greatest. Need, however, is a subjective concept, and most governments have simply chosen what seem to be sensible and objective proxy measures rather than develop more sophisticated needs indicators. The crude indicator of needs most often used is population; that is, equal per capita allocations of assistance from the central government could arguably deal with some variations in local needs. There are, of course, substantial weaknesses in using population size to allocate central grants. It leaves out considerations such as the concentration of poverty, economies and diseconomies of scale, and the possibility that levels of income and population go hand in hand in many developing countries. If the most populous jurisdictions also tend to have the highest income, a straight per capita allocation will not be equalizing. An allocation which gives large cities more per capita probably tends to widen the disparity in financial capacity.

GRANT DESIGN AND EFFECT. In theory, formula grants provide the best opportunity for equalization (types B and F in table 13-2). Ideally, formula grants would include per capita personal income in the allocation. Estimates of local personal income, however, are rarely available in developing countries (we know of none). In practice, formula grants are most often distributed by land area and population (Colombia, Philippines, Tunisia, and Turkey) and hence are not likely to equalize fiscal capacity (see table 13-4).[19] Deficit grants may also be equalizing. If minimum approved expenditure levels and standard revenue yield are used in computing the deficit, communities with higher fiscal capacities will qualify for little if any of the grant. This turns out to be the case in the distribution of Korea's deficit grant. Ad hoc grants (types D and H in table 13-2) are potentially equalizing simply because the grant funds can be arbitrarily directed toward those communities that are thought to have the lowest incomes.

The other forms of central assistance are much less likely to provide a relatively greater share of the total grant fund to the lowest-income communities. Shared taxes distributed on the basis of origin of collection are counterequalizing because they return a greater share to high-income communities. Cost reimbursement schemes often have a similar effect in that they reward high-spending communities by defraying a percentage of the cost incurred. Capital subsidies may be even more counterequalizing in that they award grants to those governments most able to design and implement capital projects.

One cannot easily look to empirical work to verify the equalization features of a grant system. There has been some empirical work, focused mostly on the correlation between actual grant distributions and per capita personal income, and on the share of central grants accruing to large cities. Indian central grants to states (per capita) are significantly and negatively related to state per capita income (Bahl and Pillai 1976). Bahl (1975) found no significant relation between per capita grants of the Gujarat state government and the per capita assessed values of the jurisdictions within the state. Kim's (1977) study of the Korean grant system relates the per capita distribution of central grants to per capita incomes of Seoul City (which has provincial status) and the remaining provinces. He finds that local education grants—allocated according to numbers of students, classes, and approved costs—are highly equalizing. Conversely, he finds the per capita local share grants—also allocated by need—to be unrelated to variations in per capita income.[20] In a statistical analysis of the Colombian sales tax transfer grant to municipalities, Bird finds "the present system tends slightly to favor those municipalities which have less capacity and greater needs (1984: 413)."

One might also study the equalization issue by determining whether grant funds are being diverted from or to large cities. Prud'homme's (1975) study of the allocation of general subsidies between Tunis and other communes in Tunisia suggests a counterequalizing pattern. The allocation formula explicitly favors Tunis by allocating it 10 percent of the fund, before distribution among the remaining eligible local units (see table 13-4). Most of the remainder is distributed according to population, property tax collections, and the size of the budget—all factors which would favor Tunis. The result is that Tunis receives 31 percent of the total national subsidy even though it contains only 22 percent of the population; per capita, it receives nearly twice as much as the average of all local governments in the metropolitan area.[21]

Although the Jakarta metropolitan government receives some preferential treatment as a capital city—it receives an additional grant which amounts to 20–30 percent of the national government's general subsidy—it does not receive a disproportionate share of total national assistance. In fiscal year 1972–73, Jakarta received 3.37 percent of total assistance, compared with its 3.97 percent of total population (Linn, Smith, and Wignjowijoto 1976). In fact, only nine of the remaining twenty-five provinces received smaller per capita amounts. By the mid-1980s, Jakarta's share of total central grants had declined slightly to about 2.5 percent.

Adequacy of Revenue

The most important purpose of the grant system is to provide an adequate source of revenue for local governments. "Adequacy" is difficult to define, but one might begin with two propositions: grants should be large enough to redress the imbalance between the revenue bases and expenditure responsibility assigned to local governments, and grant revenues should grow at least in proportion to the growth in local population and prices. The first goal might be satisfied by the central allocation to the divisible pool and depends almost exclusively on the priority which is assigned to improving the quality of public services assigned by local governments.

The second proposition is more a matter of grant design. Achievement of this goal would allow local governments a better opportunity to hold real per capita expenditures approximately constant. Whether grants are responsive to population and inflation, however, depends on three features of the grant system: how the growth of the pool is determined; how allocations among local governments are made; and whether the central government actually makes the full monetary distributions called for by the system.

A shared tax system of determining the total pool, if the tax shared is income-elastic, is the best method of ensuring adequate revenue. The Colombian and Philippine systems are, in theory, based on income-elastic shared national revenue sources. If these shared taxes are distributed on a derivation basis, or even on a formula basis weighted heavily toward population, the goal of maintaining real per capita expenditures can likely be realized. If the distribution of the shared tax is by origin of collection, then the grant flow will be more adequate for large, high-income cities than for small, poor communities.

Grant distributions which are tied to ad hoc government decisions are the least likely to produce adequate revenue flows to local governments. The temptation to reduce the local share to accommodate other national needs is just too great. There are many examples, but the experiences in Bangladesh, Jamaica, Kenya, and Korea described above are illustrative. In each case the move to an ad hoc determination of the size of the distributive pool foretold a slower rate of growth in local revenue.

Sometimes the very nature of a grant system is altered by changing national priorities. Economic and social changes in the Philippines in the 1970s led the central government actually to distribute only about half the grant entitlements of local governments (Bahl and Schroeder 1983b). A shared tax base system was largely converted to an ad hoc system. Linn (1975) reports a similar situation in Colombia.

Fiscal Planning

The grant system should be structured so as to encourage efficient management and fiscal planning by local governments. Grant revenues should be a part of the local budgeting process, just like any other regular revenue source. Unfortunately, budgeting for grant receipts is much less certain in most developing countries. In some cases this is due to the nature of the grant system itself. The sizes of grants determined on an ad hoc basis can hardly be predicted, and forecasts of cost reimbursement grants depend on speculation about which costs will be eligible and which projects will be approved. At the other end of the spectrum, pure shared taxes and shared taxes distributed by formula offer the best possibilities for designing a grant system which improves local fiscal planning.

Local Autonomy and Decentralization

A final question is whether and by how much the grant system weakens local autonomy, that is, the participation of the local population in fiscal decisionmaking. In raising a given amount of revenue, a locally raised tax would provide more autonomy than would a grant of equal yield. This is because the burden would be placed on the community both to set the tax rate and decide on the level and composition of expenditure. A grant, however, does not necessarily weaken local autonomy severely. It depends again on the structure of the grant system. At one extreme is the pure shared tax, for which the local government does not set the tax rate but receives a return on taxes paid in the local area. In this case, there is not a complete separation of the pain of taxation and the benefits received from the expenditure of those tax monies. Depending on the conditions placed on the disposition of the grant funds, local autonomy may be weakened least with this kind of intergovernmental transfer.

Beyond this point, one might say only that general purpose grants provide more local discretion than do conditional grants (grants designated for a specific purpose, or requiring a matching contribution). In theory, the general purpose or unconditional form does not distort local budgets and—depending on the income-elasticity of demand for public and private goods—will result in some combination of increased spending for various public functions and tax reduction.[22] The conditional form of grant-in-aid, conversely, is designed to stimulate spending for a particular function. For example, if local residents undervalue a government service because full social costs or benefits are not taken into account, a conditional grant may be used to stimulate spending on that function.[23] This is usually done by making the grant-aided good cheaper than it was previously by lowering the price paid by the local government for that good. As a result, such conditional grants are, all other things being equal, thought to change local budgets in favor of the aided good. Conditional grants, then, are the more effective way of imposing the national will on local governments; hence they compromise local fiscal autonomy the most.

Cost reimbursement grants are conditional, and they would seem to limit local autonomy more than any other form. If there is full reimbursement for a particular function, the local government may have little to say about the level or composition of services provided. For example, the central government is not likely to pay all teachers' salaries without playing the principal role in determining the number of teachers and their salary schedules. Nor is it likely to fund capital projects without a say in project design. Projects that partially reimburse costs also impinge on local autonomy (compared with general purpose grants) because the required match (price effect) induces a distortion in the local government budget.

Policy Choices

If there is any clear conclusion to be drawn from the above, it is that no optimal grant structure exists. What is a good feature of a particular type of grant depends on whether one takes a local or a central government view and on which objectives the government most wants to achieve. This review suggests that developing countries are not of one mind about what is most important. Some appear to push fiscal decentralization and local autonomy. Others are more concerned with tax effort, equalization, or the stimulation of local expenditures on particular activities.

The grant systems which have evolved in developing countries are mostly a mixture of the eight grant types discussed above. In light of the different effects of these grant types, it is difficult even to infer the underlying objectives of grant policy, much less to evaluate the net effects on equity, allocation, and so forth. More likely than not, this mixture exerts offsetting as well as reinforcing effects and the net effect on any given objective is uncertain.

Given this state of affairs, it is not surprising that intergovernmental grant systems in developing countries are in a state of flux as each country continues to look for the proper system. What is proper, however, depends on the point of view one takes. Accordingly, it would seem useful to summarize the advantages and disadvantages of the grant types discussed above, recast in terms of the relative preferences of central versus local governments. The policy matrix in table 13-6 enumerates eight important objectives of a grant system.

Maintenance of Control

Both central and local governments wish to maintain as much control as possible over local finances. The central government is always suspicious of the ability of local units to operate efficiently, whereas localities are always seeking more autonomy to meet rising budgetary needs. Central governments can maintain maximum control over local finances if the total grant fund is determined ad hoc and if allocations are made by formula or to reimburse costs (that is, grant types F, G, H, and K in table 13-2). These are noted by P in the first row of table 13-6 to indicate

Table 13-6. *Appropriateness of Various Types of Grants to the Objectives of Governments*

Objective	Grant type[a]							
	A	B	C	D	F	G	H	K
Of central government								
Maintain control over local finances	L	L	—	—	P	P	P	P
Equalize services and fiscal capabilities among localities	L	P	—	P	P	—	P	—
Stimulate expenditures for a particular function or overall tax effort	—	—	P	—	—	P	—	P
Increase local tax effort	—	—	P	P	—	P	—	P
Of local government								
Maintain control over local finances	P	P	—	—	L	L	L	L
Plan efficient budget	P	P	—	—	L	L	L	L
Increase adequacy of local revenue flow	P	P	P	—	L	L	L	P
Joint								
Minimize administrative costs	P	—	L	—	—	L	—	L

Note: P = most preferred; L = least preferred; — = effect is uncertain.
a. See table 13-2 for a description of grant types.

that they are most preferred by the central government, and by L in the fifth row to show that they are least preferred by local governments. Large, wealthy local governments prefer a shared tax redistributed on the basis of derivation (grant type A). Shared taxes distributed by formula (grant type B) also permit a reasonable amount of local control and are favored especially by small municipalities. These again are noted by L and P, respectively, in the table. In many cases covered in the study, the dominant grant types are A and B, indicating a concern for allowing some degree of local autonomy. Type B is relatively more of a compromise, for although the total pool is determined automatically, the distribution among eligible units remains in the hands of the central government.

In two of the cities studied here—Ahmadabad and Jakarta—there was a mixing of the two systems which included both type A and F grants. This indicates the importance of compromise in the development of intergovernmental systems but also shows the potential for creating a grant system with offsetting effects. Of the remaining cities, Cartagena and Tehran had intergovernmental transfer systems which tended toward more local autonomy, although Seoul (especially) faced a more centralized system.

Equalization

Presumably, central governments would like to use the grant system to equalize public services or fiscal capabilities among jurisdictions in the country. At the very least, the central government would want a flexibility to pursue this objective if it so chose. The best grant systems from this perspective are those that distribute ad hoc or by formula (types D, H, B, and F) to recipient units. Especially attractive from a central vantage is type H, which allows the center to make annual changes in both the amount of equalization grants and their distribution across localities. The least preferred by central governments, and by the poorer provincial and local governments, is the pure shared tax (type A), for which the point of origin principle of distribution guarantees a counterequalizing pattern.

Stimulation of Expenditure

The central government may also wish to induce local governments to increase spending on a particular function or to increase overall tax effort. The preferred grants to stimulate expenditure are those that reimburse costs (types C, G, and K). As demonstrated above, these grants allow the central government to influence local government behavior through both an income and a price effect. Formula grants with an inherent tax effort term conceivably have the same effect, but this is not proven by experience in developing countries. Local governments, conversely, see reimbursement grants as compromising their expenditure choices and prefer general purpose grants.

Efficient Budgetary Planning

It is important that local governments be notified of the annual grant amount in time for their budget processes. If the amount is tied to revenues from a national tax and determined by formula or as a percentage of local collections (type A or B), the local government can estimate the anticipated receipt with reasonable accuracy. But if the amount is determined ad hoc by the central government (types D and H) or is dependent on a rather vague definition of approved expenditures (types C, G, and K), the size of the transfer will likely not be certain at the time of local budgeting.

Revenue Adequacy

It is difficult to argue which grant types result in a more or less adequate flow of revenues to local governments. Shared taxes offer the best possibilities if the national tax chosen for sharing is based on income or consumption. Similarly, cost reimbursement grants can improve the income-elasticity of the revenue system, because education finance is a prime candidate for such grants. Grant funds determined ad hoc lead to the slowest revenue growth because central governments seem to view grants to local governments as one area to cut during times of budget crisis.

Administrative Costs

Central and local governments share the objective of minimizing the administrative cost of raising revenue. In one sense, grant funding is better than locally raised taxes, because the ability of the central government to collect taxes is better than that of local governments. Yet the creation of a grant system requires a bureaucracy to monitor the distribution and the disposition of the grants. The more complicated the distribution system and the more elaborate the checks on how the money is spent, the greater the administrative costs.

Cost reimbursement systems are probably the most expensive in that they require the eligibility of costs to be monitored or the design of capital projects to be evaluated. The least costly is the pure shared tax, especially if the base is a national tax levied irrespective of the sharing arrangement. The more complicated the sharing formula, however, the more it will cost to implement a shared tax system.

Tradeoffs

This analysis illustrates the principle that one policy instrument (grants in this case) cannot accomplish all objectives. For example, if the principal objective is to equalize fiscal capacity across jurisdictions, the goals of stimulating local government tax effort, minimizing administrative costs, and promoting local autonomy are not likely to be well served. The matrix in table 13-6 only suggests the degree to which designing a grant system requires first deciding which objectives are essential and which can be sacrificed.

A natural response to this problem is to include various types of grants in the system, for example, formula grants to equalize, pure shared taxes to provide adequate revenues to large cities, and cost reimbursement grants to stimulate tax effort. Although each grant may accomplish its objective, these effects may be offset by the workings of the entire grant system.

14 Epilogue: Lessons for Policy

THEORY, COMPARISON of theory with practice, and analysis of the effects of various local financing and expenditure practices provide some lessons for policy. Several themes recur in the chapters above:

- The right amount of fiscal decentralization in developing countries depends on a difficult tradeoff between maintaining central flexibility to carry out macroeconomic and equalization objectives, on the one hand, and improving the delivery of services in urban areas, on the other.
- The success of a strategy for fiscal decentralization depends on giving local governments some degree of financial autonomy. Large cities are in the best position to use the autonomy to improve service delivery and augment the overall mobilization of resources for the public sector.
- Local government taxes are most effective when focused on the revenue-raising objectives. "Keep it simple" and "Leave allocative and equity objectives to higher levels of government and to the expenditure side of the budget" are good rules of thumb.
- Tax bases which are "natural" for local governments include real property, business licenses, and automobile use. In some cases, consumption and earnings are appropriate.
- User charges for urban services are an excellent source of local revenue. They can usually be structured in a way to meet revenue, efficiency, and equity objectives.
- Intergovernmental transfers are also an appropriate component of local financing systems, but these should be designed so they do not discourage efforts to levy local taxes and user charges. The right balance in financing sources depends on the expenditure responsibilities assigned.
- There is no "optimal" form of local governance in developing countries. It is important to match local government structure to the objectives which the national government most wants to achieve.

These are very current themes. The strengthening of local government finance is an objective that occupies center stage in the policy discussions in most developing countries today, and there are by now few open advocates of increased centralization. This concluding chapter draws together the main lessons for pragmatic local finance policy as they apply in particular to the management of urban finances.

The Importance of Urban Government in Developing Countries

Subnational government in developing countries is of significantly less importance than in industrial countries. Yet in many developing countries, especially in Latin America, the share of subnational government spending in total public spending is comparable to that in the industrial countries (nearly 50 percent). For large cities, local government is particularly important. Per capita expenditures by local authorities in these cities are a large share of total public expenditures. The well-being of urban dwellers in the big cities is as dependent on the fiscal health of the local government as that of the central government. The fiscal and administrative problems of cities deserve more attention than they are usually accorded under the mistaken belief that local government plays only a negligible role.

The Urban Fiscal Gap

Urban governments in developing and industrial countries alike complain about the lack of resources to provide sufficient services to their populations. Any observer of city life in developing countries can quickly see that urban public resources are woefully deficient. The gap between the perceived need for services and the financial resources to provide them can be attributed in many cases to demand for unrealistically high standards of service which are beyond the financing capacity of an urban economy. Efforts by urban governments to provide services at levels which are not affordable commonly result in an inefficient and inequitable allocation of public resources. For example, excessively high standards for urban housing projects, water and sanitation facilities, and investments in transport, health, and education ultimately limit areas of such public services to a few (usually the better-off) segments of the urban population and leave the majority with inadequate service or none at all. A more accurate assessment of the resource constraints under which an urban economy operates would promote a more realistic approach to public investments and allow better service to be provided to more people.

The fiscal gap also may have its origins in the misallocation of functions and revenues to urban governments by higher-level authorities. Urban populations in most developing countries have grown rapidly in recent years and are likely to continue to do so. This growth has led to concomitant increases in the demand for a minimum level of public services for each new urban dweller, which necessitates expenditure by urban authorities. Rising incomes in urban areas have also increased the demand for public services, yet the revenues of local authorities most directly affected have not usually increased commensurately. The primary explanation for this situation is that urban governments are often restricted in their revenue-raising authority to income-inelastic sources such as property taxes, specific excises, fees, and fines, and transfers from higher-level governments. In such cases, the fiscal gap is the result of a mismatch between urban governments' responsibilities to provide services, on the one hand, and their authority to raise revenue, on the other. The allocation of expenditure responsibility and revenue-raising authority to urban governments is therefore an issue of utmost importance.

The Allocation of Urban Government Functions and Revenue Authority

The "fiscal gap"—the difference between the expenditure needs of local governments and the availability of resources to finance these needs—can be redressed, in principle, in four ways: (a) a reduction in responsibilities that require local expenditure; (b) an increase in the local authority to raise revenue; (c) an increase in the amount of revenues transferred from higher-level government; and/or (d) an increase in the local effort to raise revenue in the face of unchanged revenue-raising authority.

The first option—a reduction of local (expenditure) responsibility—is frequently chosen for reasons of political convenience. Such policies are subject to fiscal constraints imposed by the central government. Moreover, when the central government assumes responsibility for providing urban services, it has only limited accountability to the actual or potential beneficiaries of the services, and there is less likelihood that the costs of the service will be recovered through user charges.

Bahl and Linn (1983) developed a simple framework to pinpoint sources of revenue that are appropriate to finance particular types of assigned urban expenditures. First, for publicly provided goods and services that are of measurable benefits to readily identifiable individuals within a jurisdiction, user charges are the most efficient means of financing. Second, local services, such as administration, traffic control, street lighting, and security—which are goods to the general public in the sense that individual beneficiaries are difficult to identify and individual costs and benefits difficult to measure—are most appropriately financed by taxes on local residents. Third, the cost of services for which significant spillovers to neighboring jurisdictions occur, such as health, education, and welfare, should be borne by substantial state or national intergovernmental transfers. Fourth, borrowing is an appropriate source of financing capital outlays on infrastructure services, particularly public utilities and roads.

In practice, the assignment of revenue authority to local governments in many developing countries deviates considerably from this framework. Commonly, local taxes finance substantial shares of services that could be financed by user charges, and intergovernmental transfers finance services that would be more appropriately financed by local taxes or user charges.

In considering fiscal reform in developing countries, say in the context of decentralization efforts, reference to the normative framework set out here would be useful. Given the constraints on fiscal resources at higher levels of government, however, there is likely to be limited scope for closing the urban fiscal gap through increased tax authority or transfers to local governments. More promising avenues appear to be levying user charges and financing major urban infrastructural investments through improved access to capital markets.

Local tax capacity and effort could in fact be strengthened by more careful design and application of certain higher-level interventions. All too often, such interventions restrict local governments in determining the definition, scope, and valuation of the tax base. These interventions include mandated exemptions and prescribed levels for tax rates and user charges. In all these areas, poor design by a higher-level government has contributed to the weakening of the local tax capacity and effort. Merely assigning to a local government the authority to tax or levy a user charge is not sufficient. The local capabilities to use the authority must be actively strengthened by the higher-level government, and deliberate steps must be taken to minimize unnecessary and harmful interventions that limit local efforts.

Issues in Urban Property Taxation

In principle, property taxation is an ideal way to finance many urban services. The property tax base, that is, the value of urban real estate, grows rapidly with urbanization and can be objectively assessed; it reflects the value of many urban services to the extent that they provide site- or area-specific benefits; and ownership of real estate tends to be more concentrated than the distribution of income, thus making the tax generally progressive. Moreover, if properly administered, a property tax will result in only minor distortions in the allocation of resources. Finally, it can be argued that property taxes are most appropriately administered at the local level, because local government will have a better knowledge base for assessing property values and a greater motivation for collecting the property tax than do higher-level governments.

The property tax is the most common and generally the most important of the taxes collected by urban governments in developing countries. However, urban property tax revenue have generally not kept pace with the growth of urban incomes or property values, and often not even with the growth in urban population. Urban property tax systems vary widely among developing countries, but the systems seem to suffer from a number of common problems: assessment practices are inadequate, professional expertise for valuing urban properties is in short supply, the necessary data base to support assessment and enforcement is not in place, collection and enforcement problems abound, and taxpayer resistance is a universal obstacle to more effective property tax administration. Some of these problems can be attributed to the limited technical and administrative capabilities of urban governments. Just as important, however, are a number of other factors: landownership and tenure conditions are often uncertain; higher-level governments interfere with, or limit the use of, property taxes (for example, through the imposition of rent control or limits on tax rates); and higher effective tax rates on urban property are often successfully opposed.

Notwithstanding these practical obstacles, the urban property tax is clearly among the few main sources of local public revenue that can carry a significant share of the financing requirements for urban expenditure. Substantial efforts and ingenuity, however, are required to mobilize the technical and administrative resources to develop accurate urban property registration and property tax valuation rolls, to update them at regular intervals, and to bill and collect property taxes effectively. In order to be politically acceptable, these improvements must be introduced gradually and fairly, and they need to be linked with a major effort to educate the public about the relationships between the provision of essential urban services and the collection of the property tax.

Automotive Taxation

The ownership and use of motor vehicles represent excellent, but much neglected, tax bases for urban governments in developing countries. The growth in the number of automobiles is more rapid than the growth in city population, automobile ownership and use are easily taxable, and such taxes are likely to fall on persons with high incomes. In addition, the growing number of motor vehicles results in larger expenditures for urban roads, and increased congestion and pollution costs. Thus, for purposes of revenue, efficiency, equity, and administration, automotive taxation represents a nearly ideal revenue instrument for urban governments. Annual automobile registration fees, restrictive area licenses, and tolls have been applied with substantial success to some cities in developing countries, for example, Jakarta and Singapore. These, however, are exceptional cases. Although in many cities the main elements required to administer an effective set of automotive taxes—automobile registration, and taxation of gasoline and diesel fuel at the retail levels are in place—much more could be done in most cities to draw more extensively on the significant revenue potential of this set of taxes.

Other Local Taxes

Some local governments in urban areas also draw on income and sales taxes. The major practical problem with these two types of taxes is that their success depends on effective coordination between local and higher-level authorities. Higher-level governments frequently do not accept them as suitable instruments of local taxation, because of the apparent competition with their own tax collection efforts. As a result, local income and sales taxes are not often found in the cities of developing countries, despite their substantial revenue potential. In the absence of such obstacles, however, local sales and income taxes can be effectively integrated into the local revenue structure.

Much more common is another set of local taxes, namely, taxes levied on industry and commerce and sumptuary taxes. The main reason for their existence is that they can raise substantial amounts of revenue in politically acceptable ways and with little need for coordination with higher-level authorities. However, they almost invariably distort the allocation of urban resources. They are quite regressive and result in considerable administrative and compliance costs. In practice, these drawbacks tend to be given little weight by local legislators and administrators, to whom the expanded use of these taxes offers a path of least resistance in meeting their revenue objectives. An interesting example of the dilemma faced by local authorities in the imposition of these types of taxes is the "octroi" tax, levied in many cities of India and Pakistan on goods entering the city boundaries. This tax is highly inefficient because it interferes with intermunicipal trade and imposes substantial administrative costs. However, its use on the Indian subcontinent continues because it is so productive in generating revenue.

Finally, urban governments generally still draw on a wide variety of "nuisance" taxes (selected excises, licenses, stamp duties, and poll taxes), which perform poorly in terms of revenue generation, efficiency, and distributive effects, and have high collection and compliance costs. Nuisance taxes continue to exist despite their drawbacks, again because their use is generally unencumbered by higher-level interference and because they are conventional and thus politically acceptable sources of local revenues.

Overall, these other local taxes show only limited potential for financing urban services, either because they are not likely to be acceptable to higher-level governments (sales tax or income tax), or because they are inappropriate on grounds of their negative efficiency and equity effects and their high administrative costs (industry and commerce taxes, sumptuary taxes, and nuisance taxes).

User Fees and Development Charges

There can be little doubt about the usefulness and desirability of developing broadly based charging systems for urban public services. The application of properly designed service charges, or more generally the recovery of urban service costs from beneficiaries, can contribute to an improvement of resource allocation within and between urban areas. Such charges serve to limit the demand for urban services to efficient levels and to make actual and would-be urban dwellers aware of the social costs of urbanization. As experience has shown, service charges or cost recovery can generate substantial amounts of revenue for urban governments. Because service charges are directly linked to the provision and extension of much-needed services, they are an important element in urban investment policy.

Service charges can also contribute to equitable urban growth. Recouping the costs of public services from beneficiaries is a fair way to finance a service, and windfall gains may be minimized. Under general revenue financing, these windfall gains are often appropriated by high-income groups in the form of increased property values or increased yields from investments that benefit those groups most directly. Therefore, user charges also serve to increase the vertical equity of the urban fiscal system. As practice has shown, user charges can be designed to serve explicitly the redistributive goals of government, although this feature has to be tempered by concern for the efficiency and fiscal viability of the service being provided.

User charges are not only a tool for ensuring efficient use and equitable financing of public services; they also serve as an investment guide, because consumers' willingness to pay for services is in many instances the only way in which the benefits of a service can be ascertained and compared with the cost of providing the service. What is more, the application of service charges, or more generally the requirement of cost recovery, forces decisionmakers to consider beforehand the ability and willingness of beneficiaries to pay and to design standards of service accordingly. Extensive subsidization of services in the past has often contributed to the expectation of unrealistically high standards of urban service.

The most common rule suggested by economists for guiding decisions on the pricing of public services is to set price equal to marginal cost. A review of the applicability of the simple marginal cost pricing rule indicates that at least two precautions are in order. First, various dimensions of service, including use, access, and location, should be captured in pricing if the rule is to serve the goal of efficient resource allocation. For example, water supply tariffs can be structured to cover these three aspects: beneficiaries with the option to hook up to water service by way of an area trunk line could pay (a) an area-specific property tax or development charge, designed to recoup the cost of trunk-line construction and other systemwide capital costs; (b) a recurrent monthly fee to cover the costs of access—the connection from the trunk line to individual properties, as well as metering and billing; and (c) a water-use charge related to actual consumption to cover the marginal cost of supplying water to the user. Second, the rule needs to be amended to take into account externalities, market distortions, and imperfect consumer information; other important objectives, in addition to efficiency, such as financial and fiscal viability, fairness, and equity; and institutional and political constraints. Considerations of equity and externalities, for example, can be simultaneously allowed for in so-called life-line tariffs, by which the use of small amounts of service results in fees below marginal cost. Poor consumers thereby use the service without an undue financial burden. At the same time, high-income cross-subsidies that are derived, for example, by charging above-marginal cost tariffs or access fees to larger or wealthier consumers, ensure the financial viability of the charging system. This approach has been successfully applied to the financing of urban water supply systems in a number of Latin American countries.

Despite these caveats and amendments to the use of the simple marginal cost pricing rule, it provides a good starting point for the analysis of charging systems; refinements can then be made on a service-by-service application. Once an efficient pricing structure is determined, its financial and equity implications and the extent to which it runs counter to established institutional norms can be explored. Often, the various policy objectives stand less in conflict than appears initially, particularly where multi-part tariffs can be employed. However, the common practice of starting the analysis of user charges with objectives other than efficiency in mind almost invariably means that considerations of efficiency are neglected altogether. The result is a greater loss of efficiency than need be the case—a result that developing countries, given their low levels of income, can ill afford.

Development charges are a special form of cost recovery for urban infrastructural projects. Often termed "special assessments," "contributions for betterment," "land readjustment," or "valorization contributions," they serve different purposes and involve different practices in various countries and cities. However, in general they feature lump-sum charges, phased over a payment period of months or years, which are designed to recoup the public costs of infrastructural development from beneficiaries. They may cover limited projects for a particular service, such as a neighborhood road-paving scheme or the construction of a sewerage line, or the full development of new areas of a city or even entire new towns. Property owners, rather than occupants of property or users of a particular service, usually incur such charges in the areas improved by public action.

Two different types of land development charges—land readjustment in Korea and valorization schemes in Colombia—demonstrate the varying role which such charges can play in financing urban development. Although either system is not necessarily directly transferable to other countries, the evidence suggests that serious consideration of similar development charges is appropriate under most circumstances.

Intergovernmental Transfers

There is often a mismatch between urban governments' responsibility for public service provision, on the one hand, and their revenue-raising authority, on the other. The gap is filled with some form of intergovernmental transfer: a grant, a shared tax, or a subsidy. Certainly, there is justification for intergovernmental transfers as part of the urban local financing structure. Transfers from higher-level governments are an appropriate way to finance those local government functions which have regional or national spillover benefits. Moreover, central governments often justify grant financing of local services as part of a policy of regional equalization of standards of living. Typically, big cities are much less dependent on such transfers than are smaller municipalities or rural local governments. The smaller share may be justified on a number of grounds, in particular, that the cities have a greater fiscal capacity and more revenue-raising authority.

Higher-level governments often treat transfers as a residual in their own budgeting process, even where elaborate allocation systems have been devised to distribute grants to local governments. The local share of central revenue can be one of the first casualties in a budget crisis. The commonly severe constraint on national public finances in developing countries partly explains why intergovernmental transfers generally contribute a relatively small share of local government finances. Only in a few countries does the intergovernmental financing system give the local governments an ironclad guarantee.

There are other reasons why central governments pull back on the use of grants as a financing tool for local governments, particularly large cities. Grants may be viewed as a substitute for local tax effort, shared taxes may increase the revenue disparity between the rich and the poor areas of the countries, and local government tax administration may be deficient. But these are less reasons to cut back on the transfers to local governments than they are reasons to structure transfers to better achieve national and local objectives.

A realistic view is that transfers are unlikely to resolve fully the fiscal problems of local authorities in developing countries. To the extent that grant systems are already in existence, however, substantial structural improvements can generally be made to enhance their contribution. These might include provisions to stimulate local revenue-raising efforts, to better equalize interjurisdictional revenue capacity, and to build in a loan component for large cities. Rationalizing grant structures that now consist of a multiplicity of small, ad hoc transfers and putting them on a more predictable basis could permit more effective fiscal planning, especially at the local level.

The Scope and Prospects for Reform

There is no simple rule for determining the appropriate allocation of responsibility to urban governments. Experience, however, suggests that urban governments do a better job of urban management when they have greater authority over their own affairs than when their powers are limited and they must continually coordinate their actions with those of autonomous national or local entities that are also involved in the provision of urban services.

Among the local revenue sources usually available to urban government, the property tax, motor vehicle taxation, and user charges are attractive. The many examples of their successful use in cities of developing countries provide a good indication that increased reliance could be placed on these sources of revenue. Those examples also show, however, the need for effective administration, political will in implementation, and support from the national government, particularly in the form of technical assistance.

How difficult is it for local governments to improve their fiscal structure? Proposals, often major and sweeping, for fiscal reform as a means of alleviating serious problems of urban governments have been put forward in most, if not all, large cities of the world. Although the nature of these reforms has varied with local conditions and with each team of advisers responsible for them, very few such reforms have been accepted in their entirety. Commonly, resistance on the part of the policymakers and citizens facing the prospect of fiscal reform, however much needed, stems from doubts about the unanticipated effects of untested, large-scale changes in the economic environment and about the distribution of the windfall gains and losses associated with reform. Moreover, losses usually threaten to befall urban elites to the gain of larger, broader socioeconomic groups, including the poor, who have less political clout.

Perhaps the biggest problem of all is the resistance of the central government to the increased local authority that is almost always part of these proposals. Ministries of finance are too worried about their next dollar of revenue to get very enthused about giving more money to local budgets. Ministries of public works are loath to give up control over the allocation of infrastructure funding and the direction of local investment. National legislators see fiscal decentralization as an inroad on their ability to distribute resources in return for political points with the home constituency. Local governments should of course be the proponents of reform, but they are hardly in a position to change national laws concerning the powers of local government, and in many cases the local officials are themselves appointed by the central government.

In most cases of major, sweeping reform in the developing world, certain conditions have prevailed: higher-level government took over important sources of revenue previously allocated to local authorities; sweeping political changes resulted in major shifts in national priorities; or fiscal problems were so unmanageable that reform was unavoidable.

Incremental reforms of local finances have found more general acceptance. Examples are the creation of special districts for capital cities, which give them specific responsibilities to expend and raise revenue; enlargement of metropolitan jurisdictions by annexation of adjacent municipalities; phased development of new sources of revenue and reform of existing sources; reassignment of selected expenditure functions; and ad hoc responses to fiscal pressures.

Given this state of affairs, it seems that a top-down approach to far-reaching fiscal decentralization, however preferred it might be, is not a starter in most developing countries. A better route might be the reform of financing systems in the largest cities, with a decided emphasis on the kinds of fiscal reforms that will make these cities more financially self-sufficient and will lead to a generally higher rate of revenue mobilization. The directions suggested by the research summarized in this volume are likely to provide a good start in pursuing such reforms.

Appendix: Data Sources for Tables

Bangladesh

Table 2-1. Dhaka: 1980–83 World Bank data. *Table 2-10*. Dhaka: 1983 World Bank data. *Table 2-11*. Dhaka: 1983 World Bank data. *Table 4-1*. Dhaka: 1980–83 World Bank data. *Table 4-5*. Dhaka: 1984 World Bank data. *Table 4-7* Dhaka: 1980–82 World Bank data. *Table 13-1*. Chittagong and Dhaka: 1983 World Bank data, Bahl (1989). *Table 13-3*. Chittagong and Dhaka: 1983 World Bank data, Bahl (1989).

Bolivia

Table 2-10. La Paz: 1975 and 1985 World Bank data. *Table 2-11*. La Paz: 1975 and 1985 World Bank data. *Table 2-12*. La Paz: 1983–85 World Bank data. *Table 4-1*. La Paz: 1975 and 1985 World Bank data. *Table 5-3*. La Paz: 1976 data, Holland (1979). *Table 13-1*. La Paz: 1975 and 1985 World Bank data.

Botswana

Table 2-3. Francistown: 1974 World Bank data. *Table 2-6*. Francistown: 1972 World Bank data. *Table 2-10*. Francistown: 1972 and 1986 World Bank data. *Table 2-11*. Francistown: 1972 and 1986 World Bank data. *Table 5-3*. Francistown: 1974 World Bank data. *Table 10-4*. 1972 World Bank data. *Table 13-1*. Francistown: 1972 and 1986 World Bank data.

Brazil

Table 2-1. Rio de Janeiro: 1980–84 World Bank data. São Paulo: 1980–84 World Bank data. *Table 2-2*. State of Guabara: 1980–84 World Bank data. Rio de Janeiro: 1967–69 data, Richardson (1973). São Paulo: 1980–84 World Bank data. *Table 2-9*. Rio de Janeiro and São Paulo: 1984 World Bank data. *Table 2-10*. Rio de Janeiro: 1967 data, Richardson (1973); 1984 World Bank data. São Paulo: 1984 World Bank data. *Table 2-11*. Rio de Janeiro: 1967 data, Richardson (1973); 1984 World Bank data. São Paulo: 1984 World Bank data. *Table 2-12*. Rio de Janeiro and São Paulo: 1980–84 World Bank data. *Table 4-1*. Rio de Janeiro and São Paulo: 1980 and 1984 World Bank data. *Table 4-3*. Rio de Janeiro: 1982 data, Dillinger (1989) and Garzon (1989). *Table 5-2*. Selected cities: 1976 data, Richman (1977). *Table 5-3*. Rio de Janeiro: 1975 data, Richman

(1977). Salvador: 1973 data, Richman (1977). São Paulo: 1975 data, Richman (1977). *Table 10-5*. Belo Horizonte and Minas Gerais: 1974 World Bank data. *Table 13-1*. Rio de Janeiro: 1967 data, Richardson (1973); 1984 World Bank data. *Table 13-3*. States, as of 1982: Dillinger and Mahar (1983). States and municipalities, as of 1982: Dillinger and Mahar (1983). Municipalities, as of 1982: Dillinger and Mahar (1983). *Table 13-4*. All cities: Dillinger and Mahar (1983).

Burundi

Table 10-5. Bujumbura: 1966 World Bank data.

Cameroon

Table 10-5. 1975 World Bank data. *Table 10-15*. Northwest and Southwest and Rest of country: 1975 World Bank data.

Taiwan (China)

Table 4-3. Taipei: 1986 data, Riew (1987). *Table 5-3*. All property: 1974 data, Harris (1979).

Colombia

Table 2-1. Bogotá: 1970–72 data, Linn (1980a). Cali: 1975 data, Linn (1980a). Cartagena: 1969–72 data, Linn (1980a). *Table 2-2*. Bogotá: 1963–72 World Bank data. Cali: 1964–74 World Bank data. Cartagena: 1970–72 data, Linn (1975). *Table 2-3*. Bogotá: 1970–72 data, Linn (1980a). Cali: 1975 data, Linn (1980a). *Table 2-4*. Cartagena: 1972 data, Linn (1975). *Table 2-6*. Bogotá: 1972 data, Linn (1980a). Cali: 1974 data, Linn (1980a). Cartagena: 1972 data, Linn (1975). *Table 2-7*. Bogotá: 1972 World Bank data. Cali: 1974 World Bank data. Cartagena: 1972 data, Linn (1975). *Table 2-10*. Bogotá: 1972 World Bank data. Cali: 1974 World Bank data. Cartagena: 1972 data, Linn (1975). *Table 2-11*. Bogotá: 1972 World Bank data. Cali: 1974 World Bank data. Cartagena: 1972 data, Linn (1975). *Table 2-12*. Bogotá: 1963–72 data, Linn (1980a). Cali: 1969–72 data, Linn (1980a). Cartagena: 1969–72 data, Linn (1975). *Table 2-13*. Bogotá: 1972 data, Linn (1980a). Cali: 1975 data, Linn (1980a). Cartagena: 1972 data, Linn (1975). *Table 4-1*. Bogotá: 1972 data, Linn (1980b). Cali: 1975 data, Linn (1980a). Cartagena: 1972 data, Linn (1975). *Table 4-4*. Bogotá: 1971 data, Linn (1980b). Cartagena: 1972 data, Linn (1975); 1980 World Bank data. *Table 4-5*. Bogotá: 1972 data, Linn (1980b). Cartagena: 1972 data, Linn (1975). *Table 4-6*. Bogotá: 1963–72 data, Linn (1980b). Cartagena: 1970–72 data, Linn (1975); 1978–80 World Bank data. *Table 4-7*. Bogotá: 1962–72 data, Linn (1980a). Cartagena: 1961–72 data, Linn (1975). *Table 5-2*. All property: 1961 data, Taylor and others (1965); 1966 data, McLure (1971a); 1970 data, study 8, McLure (1975a); 1970 data, study 9, Bird (1975). Bogotá: 1970 data; Colombia, Republic of (1973). Cali: 1975 data, study 11, Linn

(1979); 1975 data, study 12, Linn (1980a). *Table 5-3*. Bogotá: 1974 data, Linn (1980b). Cali: 1975 data, Linn (1979). Cartagena: 1973 data, Linn (1975). *Table 7-2*. Cartagena: 1972 data, Linn (1975). *Table 10-5*. Bogotá: 1979 World Bank data. Cali: 1978 World Bank data. Cartagena: 1973 data, Linn (1975). *Table 10-4*. Bogotá: 1972 data, Linn (1976c). Cali: 1974 data, Linn (1975). Cartagena: 1972 data, Linn (1976b). *Table 10-15*. Bogotá: 1973 World Bank data, Linn (1976c). Cali: 1978 World Bank data. Cartagena: 1973 data, Linn (1975). *Table 10-16*. Bogotá: 1979 World Bank data. Cali: 1978 World Bank data. Cartagena: 1973 data, Linn (1975). *Table 11-1*. Bogotá: 1978 World Bank data. Cali: 1978 data, Linn and Sebastian (1980a); and Cali, Empresas Municipales de (1975). Cartagena: 1973 data, Linn (1975). *Table 11-3*. Bogotá: 1973 data, Linn (1976c). Cartagena: 1973 data, Linn (1975). *Table 11-5*. Bogotá: 1980 data, Urrutia (1981). *Table 13-1*. Bogotá: 1972 World Bank data; 1979 data, Linn (1980a). Cali: 1974 World Bank data, Linn (1980a). Cartagena: 1972 data, Linn (1975). *Table 13-3*. Bogotá: 1982 data, Linn (1980a); Bird (1984). *Table 13-4*. Bogotá: 1982 data, Linn (1980a); Bird (1984). Cartagena: 1975 data, Linn (1975); Bird (1984).

Côte d'Ivoire

Table 2-11. Abidjan: 1982 World Bank data. *Table 5-3*. All property: 1974 World Bank data. *Table 10-5*. Abidjan: 1975 World Bank data. *Table 10-16*. Abidjan: 1975 data, Julius and Warford (1977). *Table 13-1*. Abidjan: 1981 World Bank data.

Ecuador

Table 10-5. Guayaquil: 1974 World Bank data.

Ethiopia

Table 10-5. Addis Ababa: 1972 World Bank data. *Table 13-1*. Addis Ababa: 1973 World Bank data.

Gabon

Table 10-5. Libreville: 1973 World Bank data.

Ghana

Table 10-5. Accra/Tenna: 1974 World Bank data.

Guatemala

Table 8-1. Guatemala City: 1979 data, Avenarius and others (1975).

Hong Kong

Table 4-4. Hong Kong: 1973 World Bank data; 1985 World Bank data. *Table 4-6*. Hong Kong: 1984–86 World Bank data. *Table 5-3*. All property: 1974 data, Jao (1976).

India

Table 2-1. Ahmadabad: 1965–71 data, Bahl (1975); 1977–81, World Bank data. Bombay: 1963–70 data, Bougeon-Maassen (1976); 1975–82 World Bank Data. *Table 2-2.* Ahmadabad: 1965–71 data, Bahl (1975); 1977–81 World Bank data. Bombay: 1963–72 data, Bougeon-Maassen (1976); 1975–82 World Bank data. Madras (Corp.): 1972–76 and 1977–79 World Bank data. *Table 2-3.* Ahmadabad: 1971 data, Bahl (1975). Bombay: 1972 data, Bougeon-Maassen (1976). Calcutta: 1977 World Bank data. Delhi: 1970 data, Datta and Koshla (1972). *Table 2-4.* Madras: 1976 World Bank data. *Table 2-6.* Ahmadabad: 1971 data, Bahl (1975). Bombay: 1972 data, Bougeon-Maassen (1976); 1982 World Bank data. *Table 2-7.* Ahmadabad: 1971 data, Bahl (1975); 1981 World Bank data. Bombay: 1971/72 data, Bougeon-Maassen (1976); 1981 World Bank data. Calcutta: 1974/75 and 1982 World Bank data. Madras: 1975/76 and 1982 World Bank data. *Table 2-10.* Ahmadabad: 1970/71 data, Bahl (1975); 1981 World Bank data. Bombay: 1970/71 data, Bougeon-Maassen (1976); 1981/82 World Bank data. Calcutta (Corp.): 1974/75 and 1982 World Bank estimates. Madras: 1975/76 and 1979 World Bank data. *Table 2-11.* Ahmadabad: 1971 data, Bahl (1975); 1981 World Bank data. Bombay: 1970 data, Bougeon-Maassen (1976); 1981 World Bank data. Calcutta (Corp.): 1974/75 and 1982 World Bank estimates. Madras: 1975/76 and 1979 World Bank data. *Table 2-12.* Ahmadabad: 1965–71 data, Bahl (1975); 1977–81 World Bank data. Bombay: 1963–71 data, Bougeon-Maassen (1976); 1975–82 World Bank data. *Table 2-13.* Ahmadabad: 1981 World Bank data. Bombay: 1981 World Bank data. *Table 4-1.* Ahmadabad: 1965–71 data, Bahl (1975); 1977–81 World Bank data. Bombay: 1963–72 data, Bougeon-Maassen (1976); 1975–82 World Bank data. Calcutta (Corp.): 1974/75 and 1982 World Bank estimates. Madras (Corp.): 1972–76 and 1977–79 World Bank data. *Table 4-2.* Ahmadabad: 1980 World Bank data. Madras: 1983 data, Nath and Schroeder (1984). *Table 4-4.* Ahmadabad: 1972 data, Bahl (1975). Bombay: 1971 data, Bougeon-Maassen (1976). Calcutta: 1971 World Bank data. *Table 4-5.* Bombay and Calcutta: 1971 data, Mohan (1974). Delhi: 1979 data, Nath and Schroeder (1984). Madras: 1977 data, Nath and Shcroeder (1984). *Table 4-6.* Ahmadabad and Bangalore: 1961–78 World Bank data. Bombay: 1963–72 data, Bougeon-Maassen (1976); 1969–78 World Bank data. Calcutta: 1966–78 World Bank estimates. Delhi: 1961–81 World Bank data. Madras: 1967–77 World Bank data. *Table 4-7.* Ahmadabad: 1961–71 data, Bahl (1975); 1961–78 World Bank data. Bombay: 1961–71 data, Bougeon-Maassen (1976); 1969–78 World Bank data. Calcutta: 1960–71 World Bank data; 1966–78 World Bank estimates. Delhi: 1966–73 and 1961–81 World Bank data. Madras: 1961–71 and 1967–77 World Bank data. *Table 5-3.* Ahmadabad: 1973 data, Bahl (1975). Bombay: 1973 data, Bougeon-Maassen (1976). Calcutta, Delhi, and Madras: 1973 data, Mohan (1974). *Table 7-2.* Ahmadabad: 1972 data, Bahl (1975); 1981 World Bank data. Bombay: 1971 data, Bougeon-Maassen (1976); 1982 World Bank data. *Table 8-1.* Calcutta: 1977 World Bank data. *Table 10- 4.* Ahmadabad: 1971 data, Bahl (1975); 1981 World Bank data. Bombay: 1971–72 data, Bougeon-Maassen (1976). Calcutta: 1974/75 World Bank estimates. Madras: 1975/76 World Bank data. *Table 10-5.* Ahmadabad: 1973 data, Bahl (1975). Bombay: 1978 data, Bougeon-Maassen (1976) and World Bank data. *Table 10-15.* Ahmadabad: 1973 data, Bahl (1975). Bombay: before and including 1973, Bougeon-Maassen (1976); after 1973, World Bank data. *Table 10-16.* Ahmadabad: 1973 data, Bahl (1975). Bombay: 1973 World Bank data. Uttar Pradesh cities: 1975 data, Julius and Warford (1977). *Table 11-1.* Bombay: 1973 data, Bougeon-Maassen (1976). *Table 11-3.* Ahmadabad: 1972 data, Bahl (1975). Bombay: 1974 data, Bougeon-Maassen (1976). *Table 11-5.* Ahmadabad: 1973 data, Bahl (1975). Bombay: 1976 World Bank data. Calcutta: 1980 World Bank data. *Table 13-1.* Ahmadabad: 1971 data, Bahl (1975); 1981 World Bank data. Bombay: 1971 data, Bougeon-Maassen (1976); 1975 and 1982 World Bank data. Calcutta: 1970, 1975, and 1982 World Bank data. Madras: 1976 and 1979 World Bank data. *Table 13-3.* Ahmadabad: 1981 World Bank data. *Table 13-4.* Ahmadabad: 1981 World Bank data. States: 1970s data, Datta (1981); World Bank data. *Table 13-5.* Ahmadabad: 1971 data, Bahl (1975). Calcutta: 1972 World Bank data.

Indonesia

Table 2-1. Jakarta: 1972/73 data, Linn and others (1976); 1980/81 World bank data. *Table 2-2.* Jakarta: 1970–73 and 1981–82 World Bank data. *Table 2-3.* Jakarta: 1972 data, Linn, Smith, and Wignjowijoto (1976). *Table 2-6.* Jakarta: 1972 data, Linn, Smith, and Wignjiowijoto (1976); 1982 World Bank data. *Table 2-8.* Jakarta: 1972/73 data, Linn, Smith, and Wignjowijoto (1976); 1981 World Bank data. *Table 2-10.* Jakarta: 1972/73 data, Linn, Smith, and Wignjowijoto (1976); 1981 World Bank data. *Table 2-11.* Jakarta: 1972–73, Linn, Smith, and Wignjowijoto (1976); 1981–82 World Bank data. *Table 2-12.* Jakarta: 1970–73 data, Linn, Smith, and Wignjowijoto (1976); 1981–1982 World Bank data. *Table 2-13.* Jakarta: 1982 World Bank data. *Table 4-1.* Jakarta: 1970–73 data, Linn, Smith, and Wignjowijoto (1976); 1981–82 World Bank data. *Table 4-3.* Jakarta: 1986 World Bank data. *Table 4-4.* Jakarta: 1972 data, Linn, Smith, and Wignjowijoto (1976). *Table 4-5.* Jakarta: 1985 data, Bastin and Hadiprobowo (1987). *Table 4-6.* Jakarta: 1970–73 data, Linn, Smith, and Wignjowijoto (1976). *Table 5-3.* Jakarta: 1973 data, Linn, Smith, and Wignjowijoto (1976). *Table 7-2.* Jakarta: 1973 data, Linn, Smith and Wignjowijoto (1976); 1982 World Bank data. *Table 10-5.* Jakarta: 1973 data, Linn, Smith and Wignjowijoto (1976). Malang: 1974 World Bank data. *Table 10-15.* Jakarta: 1973 data, Linn, Smith, and Wignjowijoto (1976). *Table 11-3.* Jakarta: 1973 data, Linn, Smith, and Wignjowijoto (1976). *Table 11-5*. Jakarta: 1973 data, Linn, Smith, and Wignjowijoto (1976); 1980 World Bank data. *Table 13-1*. Jakarta: 1973 data, Linn, Smith, and Wignjowijoto (1976); 1981 World Bank data. *Table 13-3*. Jakarta: 1981 World Bank data. *Table 13-4*. Jakarta: 1981 World Bank data. *Table 13-5*. Jakarta: 1981 World Bank data; Devas (1986).

Iran

Table 2-1. Tehran: 1974 World Bank data. *Table 2-5*. Tehran: 1974 World Bank data. *Table 2-10*. Tehran: 1974 World Bank data. *Table 2-11*. Tehran: 1974 World Bank data. *Table 5-3*. Tehran: 1975 World Bank data. *Table 13-1*. Tehran: 1974 World Bank data.

Jamaica

Table 2-1. Kingston: 1967/68–71/72 data, Bougeon-Maassen and Linn (1977). *Table 2-2*. Kingston: 1969–73 data, Bougeon-Maassen and Linn (1977). *Table 2-5*. Kingston: 1973 data, Bougeon-Maassen and Linn (1977). *Table 2-6*. Kingston: 1972 data, Bougeon-Maassen and Linn (1977). *Table 2-8*. Kingston: 1972 data, Bougeon-Maassen and Linn (1977). *Table 2-10*. Kingston: 1971/72 data, Bougeon-Maassen and Linn (1977). *Table 2-11*. Kingston: 1971/72 data, Bougeon-Maassen and Linn (1977). *Table 2-12*. Kingston: 1963–72 data, Bougeon-Maassen and Linn (1977). *Table 2-13*. Kingston: 1973 data, Bougeon-Maassen and Linn (1977). *Table 4-1*. Kingston: 1971 data, Bougeon-Maassen and Linn (1977). *Table 4-4*. Kingston: 1971 data, Bougeon-Maassen and Linn (1977). *Table 4-6*. Kingston: 1969–73 data, Bougeon-Maassen and Linn (1977). *Table 4-7*. Kingston: 1961–72 data, Bougeon-Maassen and Linn (1977). *Table 5-2*. All property: 1963 data, Lovejoy (1963). *Table 5-3*. Kingston: before and including 1974, Bougeon-Maassen and Linn (1977); after 1974, World Bank data. *Table 7-2*. Kingston: 1971 data, Bougeon-Maassen and Linn (1977). *Table 10-4*. Kingston: 1972 data, Bougeon-Maassen and Linn (1977). *Table 10-5*. Kingston: 1975 data, Bougeon-Maassen and Linn (1977). *Table 10-16*. Kingston: 1975 data, Julius and Warford (1977) and Bougeon-Maassen and Linn (1977). *Table 11-3*. Kingston: 1974 data, Bougeon-Maassen and Linn (1977). *Table 13-1*. Kingston: 1972 data, Bougeon-Maassen and Linn (1977); 1977 World Bank data. *Table 13-3*. Kingston: before and including 1974, Bougeon-Maassen and Linn (1977). *Table 13-4*. Kingston: 1973 data, Bougeon-Maassen and Linn (1977).

Kenya

Table 2-1. Nairobi: 1980/81 World Bank data. *Table 2-2*. Nairobi: 1960–76 and 1980/81 World Bank data. *Table 2-3*. Nairobi: 1976 World Bank data. *Table 2-9*. Mombasa and Nairobi: 1981 World Bank data. *Table 2-10*. Mombasa and Nairobi: 1981 World Bank data. *Table 2-11*.

Mombasa and Nairobi: 1981 World Bank data. *Table 2-13*. Nairobi: 1981 World Bank data. *Table 4-1*. Nairobi: 1981 World Bank data. *Table 4-4*. Nairobi: 1971 World Bank data. *Table 5-3*. 1975 World Bank data. *Table 10-5*. Mombasa: 1975 World Bank data. Nairobi: 1975 data, Hubbel (1977). *Table 10-15*. Nairobi: 1978 World Bank data. *Table 10-16*. Nairobi: 1978 World Bank data. *Table 13-1*. Mombasa and Nairobi: 1975 and 1981 World Bank data.

Republic of Korea

Table 2-1. Daegu, Daejeon, and Gwangju: 1976 data, Smith and Kim (1979); 1981–83 World Bank data. Jeonju: 1975 data, Smith and Kim (1979); 1981–83 World Bank data. Seoul: 1965–71 data, Bahl and Wasylenko (1976); 1981–83 World Bank data. *Table 2-2*. Seoul: 1963–72 data, Bahl and Wasylenko (1976); 1981–83 World Bank data. *Table 2-3*. Daegu, Daejeon, Gwangju, and Jeonju: 1975 data, Smith and Kim (1979). Seoul: 1965–71 data, Bahl and Wasylenko (1976). *Table 2-6*. Daegu, Daejeon, Gwangju, and Jeonju: 1975 data, Smith and Kim (1979); 1983 World Bank data. Seoul: 1971 data, Bahl and Wasylenko (1979); 1983 World Bank data. *Table 2-8*. Daegu, Daejeon, and Gwangju: 1976 data, Smith and Kim (1979). Jeonju: 1975 data, Smith and Kim (1979). Seoul: 1970 data, Bahl and Wasylenko (1979). *Table 2-10*. Daegu, Daejeon, Gwangju, and Jeonju: 1983 World Bank data. Seoul: 1971 data, Bahl and Wasylenko (1976); 1983 World Bank data. *Table 2-11*. Daegu, Daejeon, Gwangju, and Jeonju: 1976 data, Smith and Kim (1979); 1983 World Bank data. Seoul: 1971 data, Bahl and Wasylenko (1976); 1983 World Bank data. *Table 2-12*. Seoul: 1969–72 data, Bahl and Wasylenko (1976); 1981–83 World Bank data. *Table 2-13*. Daegu, Daejeon, Gwangju, and Jeonju: 1983 World Bank data. Seoul: 1983 World Bank data. *Table 4-1*. Seoul: 1965–71 data, Bahl and Wasylenko (1976); 1981–83 World Bank data. Pusan: 1971 and 1983 World Bank data. *Table 4-3*. Seoul: 1985 data, Chun, Kim and Lee (1985). *Table 4-4*. Seoul: 1971 data, Bahl and Wasylenko (1976); 1983 World Bank data. *Table 4-6*. Seoul: 1963–72 data, Bahl and Wasylenlo (1976); 1981–83 World Bank data. *Table 4-7*. Seoul: 1968–71 data, Bahl and Wasylenko (1976). *Table 5-2*. Seoul: 1970 data, Bahl and Wasylenko (1976). *Table 5-3*. Seoul: 1973 data, Bahl and Wasylenko (1976). All property: 1975 data, Smith and Kim (1979). *Table 7-2*. Seoul: 1970 data, Bahl and Wasylenko (1976); 1983 World Bank data. *Table 8-1*. Pusan and Seoul: 1977 data, Smith and Kim (1979). *Table 10-4*. Daegu, Daejeon, Gwangju, and Jeonju: 1976 data, Smith and Kim (1979). Seoul: 1970 data, Bahl and Wasylenko (1976). *Table 10-5*. Seoul: 1972 data, Bahl and Wasylenko (1976). *Table 10-15*. Korean medium-size cities: 1976 data, Smith and Kim (1979). Seoul: 1965–71 data, Bahl and Wasylenko (1976). *Table 11-1*. Seoul: 1976 World Bank data. *Table 11-3*. Seoul: 1973 data, Bahl and Wasylenko (1976). *Table 11-5*. Seoul: 1973 data, Bahl and Wasylenko (1976). *Table 13-1*. Seoul: 1968 World Bank data; 1971 and 1975 data, Bahl and Wasylenko (1976); 1983 World Bank data. *Table 13-4*. Seoul: before 1972, 1972, and after 1972, Bahl and Wasylenko (1976), Smith and Kim (1979). *Table 13-5*. Seoul: pre-1972 data, Bahl and Wasylenko (1976), Smith and Kim (1979).

Lebanon

Table 5-2. All property: 1968 data, de Wulf (1972).

Liberia

Table 2-11. Monrovia: 1982 World Bank data.

Malawi

Table 5-2. All property: no date, World Bank data.

Malaysia

Table 10-5. Kuala Lumpur: 1973 World Bank data. Penang: 1973 data, Katzmann (1977). *Table 10-16*. Kuala Lumpur: 1976 data, Julius and Warford (1977). *Table 13-3*. States: 1980s World Bank data.

Mexico

Table 2-1. Mexico City: 1966 and 1980–84 data, Fried (1972). *Table 2-2*. Mexico City: 1980–84 World Bank data. *Table 2-12*. Mexico City: 1980–84 World Bank data. *Table 10-5*. Mexico City: 1973 data, Katzman (1977). *Table 10-16*. Medium-sized cities: 1976 data, Julius and Warford (1977). *Table 13-1*. Mexico City: 1968 and 1982 World Bank data.

Morocco

Table 2-4. Casablanca: 1970s World Bank data.

Nepal

Table 10-5. Kathmandu: 1970s World Bank data.

Nicaragua

Table 2-1. Managua: 1972 data, Lacayo, Wong, and Velasco Arboleda (1976); 1979 World Bank data. *Table 2-6*. Managua: 1974 data, Lacayo, Layman, and Velasco (1976); 1979 World Bank data. *Table 2-10*. Managua: 1979 World Bank data. *Table 2-11*. Managua: 1974 data, Lacayo, Layman, and Velasco (1976); 1979 World Bank data.

Nigeria

Table 2-2. Lagos: 1979/80 World Bank data. *Table 2-5*. Lagos: 1960s data, Williams and Walsh (1968). *Table 2-10*. Lagos: 1980 World Bank data. *Table 2-11*. Ibadan: 1982 World Bank data. Lagos: 1962/63 data, Orewa (1966); 1980 World Bank data. Maknqdi and Onitsha: 1982

World Bank data. *Table 8-1*. Ibadan: 1984 World Bank data. *Table 10-15*. Lagos: 1960s data, Williams and Walsh (1968). *Table 13-1*. Ibadan: 1982 World Bank data. *Table 13-3*. States: 1979 data, Adamolekun and others (1980). *Table 13-4*. All cities: 1960s data, Adamolekun and others (1980).

Pakistan

Table 2-2. Gujranwala: 1971–75 and 1983–85 World Bank data. Karachi: 1972–75 and 1977–82 World Bank data. *Table 2-4*. Karachi: 1976 World Bank data. *Table 2-5*. Gujranwala: 1975 World Bank data. *Table 2-9*. Gujranwala: 1983 World Bank data. Karachi: 1973/74 World Bank data. *Table 2-10*. Gujranwala: 1983 World Bank data. Karachi: 1974/75 data, Kee (1975); 1982 World Bank data. *Table 2-11*. Gujranwala: 1983 World Bank data. Karachi: 1974/75 data, Kee (1975); 1982 World Bank data. *Table 2-12*. Karachi: 1980/81 World Bank data. *Table 4-1*. Gujranwala: 1970/71–74/75 and 1983–85 World Bank data. Karachi: 1972–75 and 1977–81 World Bank data. *Table 5-2*. All property: no date, Azfar (1971). *Table 5-3*. Karachi: 1976 World Bank data. *Table 10-4*. Karachi: 1973–74 World Bank data. *Table 10-5*. Lahore: 1973 data, Turvey and Warford (1974). *Table 10-16*. Lahore: 1976 data, Julius and Warford (1977). *Table 13-1*. Karachi: 1975 data, Kee (1975); 1982 World Bank data. *Table 13-3*. Gujranwala: 1970s World Bank data. *Table 13-5*. Gujranwala: 1970s World Bank data.

Panama

Table 5-2. All property: 1969 data, McLure (1974).

Papua New Guinea

Table 13-3. Provinces: 1980 data, Bird (1983). *Table 13-5*. Provinces: 1980 data, Bird (1983).

Peru

Lima: 1981/82 World Bank data. *Table 2-5*. Lima: 1982 World Bank data. *Table 2-10*. Lima: 1982 World Bank data. *Table 2-11*. Lima: 1982 World Bank data. *Table 4-1*. Lima: 1981/82 World Bank data. *Table 5-2*. All property: 1966 data, Webb (1967).

Philippines

Table 2-1. Manila: 1960–70 data, Bahl, Brigg, and Smith (1976); 1980–85 World Bank data. *Table 2-2*. Manila: 1960–70 data, Bahl, Brigg, and Smith (1976); 1980–85 World Bank data. *Table 2-4*. Manila: 1980 data, Bahl and Schroeder (1983c). *Table 2-5*. Davao: 1980 data, Bahl and Schroeder (1983c). *Table 2-9*. Manila: 1985 World Bank data. *Table 2-10*. Manila: 1970 data, Bahl, Brigg, and Smith (1976); 1985 World Bank data. *Table 2-11*. Manila: 1970 data, Bahl, Brigg, and Smith (1976);

1985 World Bank data. *Table 2-12*. Manila: 1960–70 data, Bahl, Brigg, and Smith (1976); 1980–85 World Bank data. *Table 2-13*. Manila: 1980 data, Bahl and Schroeder (1983c). *Table 4-1*. Manila: 1970 data, Bahl, Brigg, and Smith (1976); 1985 World Bank data. *Table 4-3*. Manila: 1987 data, Dillinger (1988b). *Table 4-4*. Manila: 1972 data, Bahl, Brigg, and Smith (1976); 1984 World Bank data. *Table 4-6*. Manila: 1974–84 World Bank data. *Table 4-7*. Manila: 1974–84 World Bank data. *Table 5-3*. Manila: 1974 data, Bahl, Brigg, and Smith (1976). *Table 7-2*. Manila: 1970 data, Bahl, Brigg, and Smith (1976). *Table 13-1*. Manila: 1970 data, Bahl, Brigg, and Smith (1976); 1975 data, Bahl, Brigg, and Smith (1976). *Table 13-4*. Manila: 1980 data, Bahl and Schroeder (1983c).

Portugal

Table 5-2. All property: 1973 data, Tanzi and de Wulf (1976). *Table 5-3*. All property: 1976 data, Tanzi and de Wulf (1976).

Senegal

Table 2-11. Dakar: 1982 World Bank data. *Table 4-5*. Dakar: 1985 World Bank data. *Table 8-1*. Dakar: 1984 World Bank data. *Table 13-1*. Dakar: 1980 World Bank data.

Singapore

Table 4-1. Singapore: 1971 and 1983 World Bank data. *Table 4-4*. Singapore: 1968 and 1985 World Bank data. *Table 4-6*. Singapore: 1983–85 World Bank data. *Table 5-3*. Singapore: 1974 World Bank data. *Table 11-3*. Singapore: 1974 World Bank data.

Sri Lanka

Table 4-5. Kandy: 1983 data, Schroeder (1985b). *Table 13-1*. Colombo: 1977 and 1982 World Bank data. *Table 13-5*. Colombo: 1985 World Bank data.

Thailand

Table 2-1. Bangkok: 1975–77 World Bank data. *Table 2-4*. Bangkok: 1974 World Bank data. *Table 2-10*. Bangkok: 1977 World Bank data. *Table 2-11*. Bangkok: 1977 World Bank data. *Table 4-1*. Bangkok: 1977 World Bank data. *Table 4-2*. Bangkok: 1980 World Bank data. *Table 5-3*. All property: 1974 World Bank data. *Table 10-5*. Bangkok: 1975 data, Saunders (1976). *Table 13-1*. Bangkok: 1968 and 1977 World Bank data.

Tunisia

Table 2-1. Tunis: 1965–70 data, Prud'homme (1975); 1984/85 World Bank data. *Table 2-2*. Tunis: 1966–72 data, Prud'homme (1975); 1981/82 World Bank data. *Table 2-5*. Tunis: 1982 data, Prud'homme (1975). *Table 2-9*. Tunis: 1985 World Bank data. *Table 2-10*. Tunis: 1972 data,

Prud'homme (1975); 1985 World Bank data. *Table 2-11*. Tunis: 1973 data, Prud'homme (1975); 1985 World Bank data. *Table 2-12*. Tunis: 1966–73 data, Prud'homme (1975); 1984/85 World Bank data. *Table 4-1*. Tunis: 1986 World Bank data. *Table 4-4*. Tunis: 1971 data, Prud'homme (1975). *Table 4-6*. Tunis: 1966–72 data, Prud'homme (1975). *Table 4-7*. Tunis: 1962–72 data, Prud'homme (1975). *Table 5-3*. Tunis: 1978 data, Prud'homme (1975). *Table 7-2*. Tunis: 1973 data, Prud'homme (1975). *Table 10-5*. Tunis: 1973 data, Prud'homme (1975). *Table 10-15*. Tunis: 1974 data, Prud'homme (1975). *Table 10-16*. Tunis: 1975 data, Julius and Warford (1977). *Table 11-1*. Tunis: 1974 data, Prud'homme (1975). *Table 11-3*. Tunis: 1974 data, Prud'homme (1975). *Table 11-5*. Tunis: 1974 data, Prud'homme (1975). *Table 13-1*. Tunis: 1972 data, Prud'homme (1975); 1985 World Bank data. *Table 13-4*. Tunis: 1972 data, Prud'homme (1975).

Turkey

Table 2-2. Istanbul: 1960–70 World Bank data. *Table 5-2*. All property: 1968 data, Krzyaniak and Ozmucur (1968). *Table 5-3*. Istanbul: 1972 data, Keles (1977) and World Bank data. *Table 13-1*. Istanbul: 1968 World Bank data. *Table 13-4*. Istanbul: 1968 World Bank data.

Puerto Rico (United States)

Table 5-2. All property: no date, Mann (1973).

United States

Table 5-2. All property: 1968 data, Musgrave, Case, and Leonard (1974).

Venezuela

Table 2-5. Valencia: 1960s data, Cannon, Foster, and Witherspoon (1973). *Table 2-10*. Valencia: 1968 data, Cannon, Foster, and Witherspoon (1973). *Table 2-11*. Valencia: 1968 data, Cannon, Foster, and Witherspoon (1973). *Table 10-15*. Valencia: 1968 data, Cannon, Foster, and Witherspoon (1973).

Yugoslavia

Table 10-16. Dubrovnic: 1975 data, Julius and Warford (1977). Sarajevo: 1976 data, Julius and Warford (1977).

Zaire

Table 2-5. Bukaru, Kinshasa, Lumbumbashi, and Mbuji-May: 1973 World Bank data. *Table 2-10*. Bukaru and Kinshasa: 1971 World Bank data. Lumbumbashi: 1972 World Bank data. Mbuji-May: 1971 World Bank data. *Table 2-11*. Bukaru and Kinshasa: 1971 and 1986 World Bank data. Mbuji-May: 1971 World Bank data. *Table 5-3*. All property: 1973

World Bank data. *Table 8-1*. All local authorities: 1973 World Bank data. *Table 13-1*. Bukaru and Kinshasa: 1971 World Bank data. Lumbumbashi: 1972 World Bank data. Mbuji-May: 1971 World Bank data. *Table 13-3*. Kinshasa: 1970s World Bank data. *Table 13-4*. Kinshasa: 1970s World Bank data.

Zambia

Table 2-2. Lusaka: 1966–72 World Bank estimates. *Table 2-4*. Kitwe, Lusaka, and Ndola: 1974 World Bank data. *Table 2-8*. Lusaka: 1972 World Bank data. *Table 2-10*. Kitwe: 1975 World Bank data. Lusaka: 1972 World Bank data. *Table 2-11*. Kitwe, Lusaka, and Ndola: 1972 World Bank data. *Table 2-13*. Kitwe, Lusaka, and Ndola: 1974 World Bank data. *Table 4-1*. Lusaka: 1971 World Bank data. *Table 4-4*. Lusaka: 1972 World Bank data. *Table 4-6*. Lusaka: 1966–72 World Bank data. *Table 5-3*. All property: 1976 World Bank data. *Table 8-1*. All local authorities: 1976 World Bank data. *Table 10-4*. Lusaka: 1972 World Bank data. *Table 13-1*. Kitwe: 1975 World Bank data. Lusaka: 1972 World Bank data.

Notes

1. Introduction: Why Study Urban Public Finance?

1. These trends are discussed in Renaud (1982: 12–53). See also U.N. Department of Economic and Social Affairs (1989: 205), U.N. Center for Human Settlements (1987: 21–32), U.N. Department of International and Social Affairs (1987), and U.N. Department of International Economic and Social Affairs (1980).

2. Perhaps the best known of these comparative studies of developing-country provincial and local finances are Hicks (1974); Smith (1974); Bird (1978); Bahl (1979a); Linn (1983); and Davey (1983).

3. These case studies were carried out under the auspices of the World Bank.

4. See Linn and Wetzel (1991) and World Bank (1991a) for a preliminary effort to delineate ways in which private responsibility and financing can support the provision of physical and social infrastructure in the megacities of the developing world.

2. The Expenditure and Revenue Structure of Urban Governments

1. Throughout this book, "urban government" is defined as the lowest level in the governmental structure which comprises national, state (province), and local authorities. Our definition of urban local government includes autonomous government agencies which have only a local franchise. "Subnational government" is defined as the local and state (province) levels of government. In some unitary systems, no intermediate level of government exists, and hence the local government and subnational government sectors are the same. See also chapter 12.

2. The United Nations does compile data on the finances of all subnational governments country by country for its annual *Yearbook of National Accounts Statistics*. The International Monetary Fund compiles fiscal data for provincial and local governments for most countries, but again, no data for individual city governments are presented (IMF, various years, a [1982]; U.N. Statistical Office 1980).

3. Although these figures provide a general impression of the relative importance of various levels of local government, they have to be treated with caution because of problems of data and definition. Most developing countries do not have universal reporting for all subnational authorities, and therefore the completeness of estimates of local and state spending may vary between countries. Also, the definition of the government sector varies between countries and analysts. Of particular importance is whether or not autonomous government agencies and enterprises are defined as part of the public sector.

4. We included only those developing countries for which data were available for both years.

5. This approach begs the issue of the allocation of expenditure benefits. It is clearly as important a question, but benefit estimation is well beyond the scope of this work.

6. For instance, Cali was able to service approximately 95 percent of its urban population with in-house water and sewer connections in 1976, compared with as little as 60 percent a few years earlier. Yet it had not been able to reduce significantly the proportion of neighborhoods not served by paved streets. Unpaved streets in Cali become virtually impassable during the rainy season and thus seriously affect the provision of many other urban services such as garbage collection, transportation, and public utility maintenance (Linn 1980a).

7. These tables, like most of the tables in these chapters, are a snapshot of the prevailing expenditure (or revenue) patterns at particular moments in time. Over time these patterns change, although experience has shown that the structure of urban finance changes slowly.

8. In the United States, for example, common local government functions would include education, police, fire, refuse collection, parks and recreation, road and street maintenance, and public assistance. For a recent review of local government functions and finances in industrial countries, see Karran (1988).

9. For a detailed discussion of the pattern in the United States, see Wright (1988); for the Federal Republic of Germany before reunification with the German Democratic Republic, see Ehrlicher and Hagemann (1976); and for other industrial countries, see Prud'homme (1987) and Karran (1988). A similar pattern of overlapping functional responsibilities has also been observed in the U.S.S.R. (Pavlova 1975).

10. The category "other expenditure" appears very important in Colombian cities because it includes debt service. This debt, however, is linked almost entirely to the provision of public utility services and highway construction. "Other" also includes pensions and fringe benefits for public employees and health care expenditure.

11. Contrary to data presented in Smith (1974: table 6), all of the Colombian cities shown in table 2-7 have expenditures on education, and two out of three on public health services. The data reported here are based on city expenditure accounts analyzed in the field by the authors, whereas Smith had to rely on secondary sources. This underscores the need for case study research in this area. Note also that Smith's table does not include the expenditure of public utilities or other autonomous local public agencies for the Colombian cities because secondary sources do not permit their consideration. This of course results in a completely different picture of the distribution of local public spending.

12. External revenues do not necessarily constitute subsidies from higher-level government since loan financing may be supported by savings within the urban sector and may be fully repaid over time; and higher-level government grants may ultimately draw on national tax revenues generated mainly in the urban sector. This is the case particularly with shared taxes, which are collected by the national government in the city and then wholly or partially remitted to local authorities.

13. A particularly striking phenomenon in Colombian cities has been the success of "valorization" charges, a betterment levy assessed on the beneficiaries of urban street, highway, and sewerage facilities (see chapter 6).

14. Nairobi relied heavily on a local income tax before it was abolished by the central government in 1973. Korean local governments were given the power in 1973 to raise a combination of local head taxes and income taxes (Smith and Kim 1979).

15. These findings confirm the results of some earlier studies (Walsh 1969; Smith 1974: table 9).

16. For a discussion of the role of grants from the central government in industrial countries, see Bird (1986) for a review of federalism, Lotz (1981) for the Scandinavian countries, Prud'homme (1987) and Karran (1988) for the countries that belong to the Organisation for Economic Co-operation and Development, Yonehara (1986) for Japan, and Ehrlicher and Hagemann (1976) for the Federal Republic of Germany before reunification with the German Democratic Republic. A discussion of the declining importance of federal grants in the United States is in Wright (1988, chaps. 4–7).

17. One basis for this hypothesis is that because the automobile is not as common in the rural areas of developing countries as it is in those of industrial countries, people in developing-country rural areas have much less mobility (short of outright migration to the city).

18. Betterment levies are broadly defined to include cost recoupment schemes which are designed to capture part of the increase in land value generated by investments in infrastructure. These levies include, in particular, valorization in Colombia and land adjustment in Korea (see chapter 6).

19. One particular problem with extensive central control over local borrowing is the often excessive paperwork and delays which are encountered when having to apply for permission to borrow even relatively small amounts. This in itself has helped to discourage borrowing by local governments (see Bird 1980 for the example of Cali, Colombia, and Hubbell 1983 for examples in the Philippines).

20. Causality may, however, also run in the opposite direction: urban governments that successfully expand urban services, and thus spending, may be better able to raise more resources as citizens' willingness to pay increases with increased service availability. Even in this case, it is important that local authorities have the appropriate revenue instruments under their control to raise additional revenues as services are expanded.

3. The Urban Fiscal Problem in Developing Countries: Issues and Approaches

1. Indeed, in the United States, the fiscal plight of central cities is a well-documented problem (see Clark and Ferguson 1983). European and Japanese cities also face financial difficulties (see Yonehara 1986). Even in the U.S.S.R., urban finances in large cities have been a problem (Pavlova 1975).

2. Though the concern in this book is with the urban sector, in relative terms, public service shortages are likely to be even greater in the rural areas of developing countries (see Meerman 1979 and Selowsky 1979 for a discussion of this issue in Malaysia and Colombia, respectively).

3. This presentation assumes simple answers to a number of complex questions, such as whether a community indifference function exists and what distinguishes publicly provided goods and services from privately provided goods and services. Nonetheless, this diagrammatic device is useful in highlighting some of the critical issues.

4. For discussions of various theories of expenditure growth, see Musgrave (1969: chap. 3); Bahl, Kim, and Park (1986: chap. 4); Burkhead and Miner (1974: chaps. 2–4); and Larkey, Stoph, and Winer (1984). For a discussion of the measurement issues involved, see the series of essays in Taylor (1983). For a review of government growth from the public choice perspective, see Mueller (1987).

5. Peacock and Wiseman (1961) used the example of the United Kingdom to test the existence of an upward displacement as a result of two world wars which, they argued, led to popular acceptance of higher public expenditures.

6. For a review of studies following this approach for the United States, see Bahl, Johnson, and Wasylenko (1980).

7. This analysis is presented in a more formal way in chapter 13.

8. See Smith (1975) and Smith and Kim (1979) for evidence that the density of automobile ownership is much higher in the major cities of developing countries than in the country as a whole. Data in World Bank (1975c) indicate a positive association between automobile ownership and per capita income for a cross section of cities in developing countries (see also Linn 1983: chap. 5).

9. In the Latin American countries, communal facilities are generally rejected by the population, whereas they have found acceptance in Asian and African countries.

10. For estimates of the income-elasticities of housing demand, see Grimes (1976), Jimenez and Keare (1984), and Mayo and Gross (1987); for water supply and sewerage services, see Hubbell (1977); for education services for the poor in Malaysia, see Meerman (1979).

11. It might be argued that middle- and higher-income citizens demand more redistributive actions as the level of economic development increases because they have more to protect from the dangers of civil unrest. For the basic model, see Hochman and Rodgers (1969).

12. For a detailed review of the evidence on urbanization costs, see Linn (1982).

13. The rates of inflation were substantially higher in developing countries than in industrial countries for the past two decades. The annual rates of percentage increases in prices for a large sample of industrial and developing countries are shown below (World Bank 1988).

	1965–80	1980–86
Industrial countries	5.3	7.6
Developing countries	44.3	16.7

14. In Colombia, for instance, local teachers and health service personnel pushed extremely actively in the 1970s for higher wages, resorting to strikes, protest marches, and sit-ins at the municipal offices.

15. A good example is Korea, where the central government raised local government wages and salaries by 20 percent in 1975 and by a further 30 percent in 1976, both times significantly above inflation levels (Smith and Kim 1979). Similar examples can be cited for India, Kenya, Pakistan, and Turkey. In Pakistan, however, the central government offset the increased salaries it had mandated by providing a special grant to local authorities. There are also cases of local salaries increasing less rapidly than the general price level, as,

for example, the case of municipal teachers in Bogotá, where real salary levels declined between 1971 and 1973.

16. For instance, at any point in time it can be cheaper per unit of water transmitted to lay a pipe with a large diameter, than one with a smaller diameter. The total outlay, however, is significant. It may well be that the local government must choose to lay two pipes of similar diameter parallel to each other in line with the actual growth in the demand for water rather than to build a large pipe well ahead of actual demand.

17. It is possible, however, that what have traditionally been regarded as public functions at all levels of government (including local government) will more and more be privatized. In many areas this would be appropriate in principle (see World Bank 1991), but in practice progress is likely to remain slow. It is therefore reasonable to assume that the balance between public and private responsibility will not change much in the foreseeable future.

18. Where urban government is geographically fragmented into many jurisdictions within a metropolitan area, a particular jurisdiction may be able to exert a more substantial influence over the size of its own economic base.

19. Another option might be to reassign responsibility for urban service provision to private providers. However, the scope of this in practice is likely to be limited, especially for many of the services required by the urban poor. Nonetheless, stronger efforts should be made to involve private providers in what have traditionally been publicly provided goods and services (World Bank 1988: chap. 4).

20. However, opposition from groups influential in national government circles has been known to hamper the development of effective property and motor vehicle taxation because these groups tend to bear the brunt of such taxes.

21. The recently initiated reforms of local government in Colombia represent a major effort to decentralize governmental functions and finances and to strengthen local government institutions (World Bank 1988: 158). Whether this reform can survive the current political strife in the country remains an open question. Nonetheless, the reforms represent an interesting example of far-reaching local government reform based on years of careful analysis and long-term political consensus building.

4. Property Tax Systems: Practice and Performance

1. An earlier version of this chapter appears as Bahl (1979a: 9–51).

2. Some of the data reported in this chapter are based on case studies completed during the 1970s. Where possible, information in these case studies has been updated. Otherwise, the discussion refers to the practice at the time the case studies were carried out.

3. For good examples of national surveys, see Garzón López (1989), Lent (1974), and Yoingco (1971).

4. Another tax on property, the property transfer tax, is discussed in chapter 8.

5. R. V. Paddington, valuation officer, ex parte Peachey Property Corporation, Limited, in the *State Gazette* 19 (1965): 993, as reported in Holland (1979).

6. There is also the issue of multiple leasing or subletting. In theory, the local government has the choice of taking the first lease (that received by the owner) as the standard rent, as has been done in Calcutta, or of taking the final rent, as is done in Madras (Mohan 1974).

7. Examples of declared rate schedules for cities using the annual value system are presented in Bahl (1979a: 17).

8. Although this separation of the general property tax rate suggests a benefits view of equity, it is not otherwise meaningful since property tax receipts are almost always viewed by the city as completely fungible. In no case study were any of these designated portions of the general rate actually earmarked for any particular use.

9. The case studies are dated, and some of the methods used have changed. Still, based on later analysis, it seems clear that most cities using rental value systems apply similar practices.

10. For a good discussion of the evolution of the site valuation system in Kingston, see Risden (1979).

11. All buildings are taxed under the new property tax system in Jakarta, but the first Rp 2 billion ($2,597 in 1989) are exempt.

12. In some West African countries, only improvements are taxed (Lent 1974).

13. For a persuasive argument against a progressive property tax system, see Hicks and Hicks (1955).

14. More detail is given in Bahl (1979a); in Bahl and Wasylenko (1976) for Seoul; in Linn (1980b) for Bogotá; in Linn (1975) for Cartagena; in Linn, Smith, and Wignjowijoto (1976) for Jakarta, and in Dillinger (1989) for Brazilian cities. Garzón López (1989) presents a brief survey of the practice for Latin American and Caribbean countries.

15. For a discussion of the various models of central-local sharing administration, see Dillinger 1988a: 36–41.

16. We use the term "site value" rather than "land value" because the tax base includes the value resulting from development of the site, for example, roads, drainage, topsoil fill, and so forth. In practice, the natural value of the site (unimproved land value) is so difficult to determine that few valuers would even try. For a good discussion of this issue, see Oldman and Teachout (1979).

17. One exception that we know of is Johannesburg, South Africa, which uses a site value system with an annual value base; see McCulloch (1979).

18. For a discussion of the practice in countries using site values, see Lent (1974) and Lindholm (1977).

19. The Committee on Taxation, Resources, and Economic Development (TRED), a group of U.S. and Canadian property tax scholars, has focused on this subject for some years. *The Taxation of Urban Property in Less Developed Countries* (Bahl 1979b), is the tenth volume in the TRED series.

20. An interesting discussion of the advantages and disadvantages of site value taxation in the Jamaican context is in Hicks and Hicks (1955).

21. McCulloch (1979) suggests that ample evidence is available, even for so developed a city as Johannesburg.

22. For a comparison of annual and capital value tax bases under the assumption of different capitalization rates, see Bahl (1978b).

23. Linn has estimated the income-elasticity of the property tax in Cartagena to be 0.81 (Linn 1975), and 0.77 for Bogotá (Linn 1980b).

24. The property tax is levied on owners in the great majority of countries, but in some cases the direct liability is with the occupier.

25. Bogotá in the 1970s and early 1980s was an exception: relatively simple formulas were used to appraise the value of improvements on the basis of standard factors of age, size, and nature of construction and average annual construction cost indexes.

26. One must be very careful about drawing inferences from such measures, however, because the denominator may well be flawed by duplicate records or by accounts that may never be collected. A case in point is that of unpaid property taxes of some former Indian owners, which were carried for many years as taxes due to Kenyan municipalities.

27. For a similar analysis of Delhi and Madras, see Nath and Schroeder (1984).

5. The Incidence of Urban Property Taxation

1. To the degree that the tax is shifted to other factors rather than to consumers, the traditional view remains inaccurate. In small developing countries with large primate cities, the capital stock in the primate city is not likely to be negligible relative to total capital stock in the country, and therefore a property tax increase, although restricted entirely to this city, may have a considerable effect on the nationwide average rate of return on capital.

2. See, for example, U.N. Department of Economic and Social Affairs (1966: 60), where it is argued that reduced foreign investment in Latin America during the postwar period was associated with a reduced spread in rates of return—particularly between Latin America and the United States.

3. Indeed, the consensus now appears to be that tax incentives do not significantly influence foreign investors' decisions (Clark 1971: 248; Guisinger 1985; Thirsk 1990).

4. The increasing costs are associated with successively tougher lines of borrowing such as credits from bilateral and multilateral institutions, commercial bank credits, Eurodollar loans, and suppliers credits. For a discussion of external financing conditions, see World Bank (1981: chap. 5; 1985; 1988: chap. 1).

5. The rapid expansion of urban land area in the cities of developing countries is ex-emplified by the case of Cali, where the urban land area tripled in the period 1952–69 and again between 1969 and 1985.

6. This discussion of market imperfections draws on McLure (1979).

7. Strictly speaking, these conclusions apply only with a perfectly inelastic capital supply; it is assumed here that any shifts resulting from very limited capital mobility in the short run can be neglected.

8. This is calculated on the basis of the usual capitalization formula for less than an infinite number of periods n:

$$PVT_0 = \frac{T}{1 + r} + \frac{T}{(1 + r)^2} + \cdots + \frac{T}{(1 + r)^n},$$

where PVT is the present value of the future stream of annual taxes T, and where r is the discount rate.

9. In cities such as Bogotá and Seoul, however, the income-elasticity of housing expenditure may be relatively low, since their climates tend to be cold and wet (making shelter a necessity) and since squatter settlements are not prevalent.

10. Very little information is available on the distribution of landownership across income classes for developing countries. In countries such as India, Pakistan, and Sri Lanka, where rental is a predominant form of tenancy in urban areas (see Mohan 1974, Lent 1974), the concentration of landownership is likely to be higher than in countries where urban tenancy is predominantly de facto ownership through squatting or illegal sales, as is the case in many Latin American cities (see, for example, Linn 1977b).

11. Mann's study of Puerto Rico (number 17) assumes that the property tax is shifted forward to consumers, with the exception of the tax on land used for business purposes. That portion is distributed according to dividend receipts. The incidence of the property tax under this set of assumptions is progressive for Puerto Rico.

12. Study number 12 is based on study 8 in its estimates of the incidence of the average property tax rate. It goes beyond study 8 only by assessing the direction of the distributive impact of excise effects.

13. Four other studies of incidence (7, 9, 20 and 22) also result in an estimate of progressivity—without, however, specifying explicitly the shifting assumptions.

14. Smith (1979) reports special taxes on vacant urban land for Chile, Colombia, Ecuador, Pakistan, Peru, Senegal, Syria, and Turkey; vacant urban land was not taxed in Bahamas, Egypt, Haiti, Hong Kong, India (except Delhi and Madras), Mauritius, Morocco, eastern Nigeria, Sierra Leone, and Sri Lanka.

15. This approximates the conventional equity argument of the proponents of site-value taxation, except that they usually do not allow for the partial shifting of the improvements tax to land and labor.

16. For example, in the mid-1970s on a visit to a rural Colombian town in the Department of Valle del Cauca, the mayor of that town told one of the authors that the large landowners in the rural section of the municipality failed to pay their property tax bills and that there exists no politically viable mechanism of extracting payment from them. In Abidjan a special resolution countersigned by the president of Côte d'Ivoire was required in 1974 to urge payment of the property tax by government officials. This appears to have only temporarily improved the collection performance in that city.

17. It is assumed here that, when no clear direction of incidence can be assigned to a particular administrative practice, it has an approximately neutral effect.

18. An exception is Aaron (1975), who considered owner-occupants and renters separately in a study of the United States. He provided a summary evaluation of the first four elasticity terms in equation 5-2 without breaking them down into their components.

19. For each of the elasticities in equations 5-2 and 5-3 that relate a ratio (i) of two variables to income (or rent), the effect of incidence associated with each particular elasticity is progressive, neutral, or regressive depending on whether $E(i,Y)$ is greater than, equal to, or less than zero. In contrast, for the effect associated with elasticities that relate a simple value to income (or rent), the incidence is progressive, neutral, or regressive depending on whether the elasticities are greater than, equal to, or less than unity.

20. It is assumed here that owner-occupants bear the entire burden of the tax on their property. This is in line with the short-run and long-run assumptions of the theoretical framework developed above.

21. It is assumed here that the entire property tax on rental property is passed on to renters, in line with the long-run shifting assumptions discussed above.

6. Allocative Effects of Urban Property Taxation

1. Many analysts of urban policy have pointed out that it may be efficient to delay development of a parcel of land temporarily with the objective of permitting more intensive land use at a later stage; see Clawson (1962); Shoup (1978); and Smith (1979).

2. To the extent that high and rising prices lead to a higher rate of squatting and illegal land development, and if such developments involve high public costs, the rapid increases in land prices may indirectly result in losses in efficiency.

3. In Bogotá, for instance, real land values (that is, deflated by the consumer price index) in the central business district remained stagnant or even declined in recent years, according to Mohan and Villamizar (1980).

4. The data on land value increases reported, for example, in Wong (1976) for Asian cities and in U.N. Center for Human Settlements (1987: 131) appear to be based on selective or impressionistic land value information that do not permit estimation of average increases in land prices.

5. See Walters (1983). Unfortunately, this view is based largely on conjecture, since very little is known about the distribution of landownership in cities of developing countries. For Bogotá, data collected by Vernez (1973) and Carroll (1980) indicate that urban landownership is more highly dispersed and that the urban housing construction industry is more competitive than has frequently been assumed.

6. The effect of instruments on objectives also depends on the time frame: in the short run, the direct effects on the distributional goals will be relatively stronger than those on the allocative goals; the reverse is the case in the long run.

7. See Lent (1974) for a summary of the arguments.

8. During the mid-1970s this possibility was actively considered in Kenya, and in the early 1980s in Jamaica.

9. Hong Kong and Singapore follow the British tradition in exempting vacant land and buildings from the annual value rates.

7. Automotive Taxation

1. Smith (1974: 332). Smith also observes that in industrial countries automobile ownership tends to be much less heavily concentrated in urban areas.

2. See, for instance, Garza and Schteingart (1978: 75), who describe the effect of pollution in Mexico City: "Approximately 60 percent of the air pollution is due to the use of motor vehicles, which annually consume three million cubic meters of gasoline and 400,000 cubic meters of diesel fuel. This has produced a noticeable increase in chronic respiratory and cardiovascular disease among the city's inhabitants."

3. The effects of congestion on vehicle operating costs and loss of time have been well documented. See Walters (1968), Churchill (1972), World Bank (1975c, 1986), and Newbery (1988).

4. Automotive taxation is not the only way to raise funds for urban roadways. Property taxes and betterment levies may also be utilized (see chapters 4–6, 11).

5. See Churchill (1972), McLure (1971a), Nanjundappa (1973), and Newbery (1988) for estimates of appropriate levels of fuel taxes in Central America, Colombia, and India, respectively.

6. Linn, Smith, and Wignjowijoto (1976) and Bastin and Hadiprobowo (1987). Another example of unusually aggressive use of automotive taxation is Singapore, where an area licensing scheme has gone a long way in controlling central city congestion and raising significant amounts of revenue. This case is further discussed below.

7. Some local governments impose fees related to motor vehicle operation, such as vehicle inspection and driver's license fees. These are not discussed here because they are usually of minor revenue importance and are raised mainly to cover the costs of a particular service (vehicle inspection or driver's test). In some cities, however, these types of fees, especially an annual inspection fee, might approximate an annual license tax if rates were higher than necessary for cost recovery. This might be an appropriate approach if outright license taxes cannot easily be imposed because of legal or institutional constraints that cannot be overcome without serious delay or major legislative action by higher-level authorities.

8. The local government in Managua in the mid-1970s also levied a municipal gasoline tax, but revenues from this tax are negligible (Lacayo and others 1976).

9. Churchill (1972) estimated that the variable maintenance costs on paved, gravel, and dirt roads are in the ratio of 1:11:33 in Central America. Nanjundappa (1973) reported that variable maintenance costs on cement-paved, bituminous-paved, waterbound macadam, and earth roads in India are in the ratio of 1:4:20:34. Other factors influencing variable maintenance costs are the axle weight of vehicles and the type of tire used, in particular, whether pneumatic or not.

10. Churchill (1972: 109). The percentage of all traffic on unpaved urban roads is likely to be smaller than the percentage on unpaved rural roads.

11. Churchill (1972: 120) observed for Central American cities that congestion is severe throughout the day in the central areas of large cities, and thus there is much less "peakiness" than in cities in the United States and Europe.

12. This policy is prescribed by Walters (1968), Churchill (1972), and McLure (1971a). Smith (1975), however, has argued that national fuel taxes might be set at higher rates because they are an easily administered and socially equitable source of public funds. See also Hughes (1987) and Newbery (1988).

13. This may also lead to a more extensive use of motor vehicles with low power-weight ratios, which may be inefficient on economic grounds and may contribute to even worse urban congestion (Walters 1968).

14. "As fuel and tires represent only a small fraction of total monetized costs of road transport (and even less if imputed time costs are included), the elasticity of road use with respect to variations in charges for fuel and tires tends to be low. It is indicative that recent increases of 50 percent in gasoline prices appear to have reduced consumption by less than 10 percent" (World Bank 1975c: 89).

15. See, for instance, Tanzi and De Wulf (1976) for an estimate of a highly progressive incidence of fuel taxes in Portugal. Conversely, Hughes (1987) points out that while kerosene and diesel fuel are also taxed, the progressivity of fuel taxation quickly disappears.

16. This may not be universally true. Especially in low-income Asian countries, nonmotorized vehicle and pedestrian traffic contribute considerably to urban road congestion (Nanjundappa 1973).

17. The transfer tax rates are fairly high: 10 percent of the value of a new vehicle and 5 percent of the value of a used vehicle. The license tax is larger in Jakarta than in local government areas, but it is roughly equivalent to 2–3 percent of the value of a motor vehicle.

18. In this respect motor vehicle taxation is quite similar to real estate taxation, for which the existence of a good cadastre is essential. The cadastre in turn serves other important purposes besides property taxation.

19. McLure (1974) for Panama; Krzyzaniak and Ozmucur (1968) for Turkey; De Wulf (1972, 1975) for Lebanon; Mann (1973) for Puerto Rico; Tanzi and De Wulf (1976) for Portugal. Typically these studies assume that vehicle taxes are borne in proportion to expenditures on private automobiles or in proportion to automobile ownership.

20. Other potential pricing systems—various types of mechanical metering devices for measuring and charging for road use—are not discussed here, because they have high capital costs and are highly foreign-exchange-intensive, potentially difficult to administer, and largely untried for the purposes of congestion pricing; see Walters (1968: 209); World Bank (1975c: 91). It is worth noting here, however, that Hong Kong has experimented with an electronic metering system to monitor and charge for central city automobiles. This system was apparently judged technically and financially feasible, but it was ultimately rejected in the face of popular opposition aroused by fears of loss of privacy. Also neglected here is the fact that in some cities not only motor vehicles, but also nonmotorized modes of transportation such as bicycles, animal carts, and pedestrians, contribute extensively to urban congestion (see, for example, Nanjundappa 1973). Fiscal measures are not likely to be useful instruments of control for this type of congestion.

21. This section draws extensively on Watson and Holland (1978).

22. This is no minor feat. See, for instance, the following statement by McLure (1971b: 704): "[Congestion] charges would vary by type of automobile, by the hour of the day, by the area of the city in which the vehicle is used, and so forth. It is also generally agreed that such a system is impossible to administer in its pure form and very difficult to approximate, especially in a developing country such as Colombia."

23. The use of the principle of owner-liability was a major help because it is not necessary to stop vehicles entering the restricted zone without the proper licenses. Of course, the existence of an effective motor vehicle registration system is an essential prerequisite.

24. Watson and Holland (1976) estimated that the total cost of the Singapore scheme was no more than the cost of constructing two kilometers of a four-lane urban expressway.

25. This must be qualified to the extent that high-income automobile users appear to have switched over to car pools more readily than low-income users. Car pools do not pay the license fee.

26. In Singapore, fees in public parking lots were increased substantially with the introduction of the area license scheme. At the same time, commercial parking lot operators were required to charge fees equal to those on public lots and to pay the difference between old and new rates to the government. Apparently, no effort was made to tax private parking facilities (Watson and Holland 1978).

27. Presumably the misguided rationale for this policy is to provide an alternative to on-street parking. No consideration, however, seems to have been given to the fact that this policy, if anything, encourages commuting by car and provides a tax relief for high-income garage and vehicle owners. On-street parking, to the extent that it is permitted at all, is not likely to be reduced by this measure because all available spaces will be used as long as they are free.

28. See Walters (1968: 203). In developing countries it is likely to be important to shadow price the foreign exchange requirements for parking meters as well as labor inputs for administration and enforcement; they may affect the cost calculations considerably because of trade and labor market distortions. See also Churchill (1972: 145) for alternatives to parking meters, such as parking cards or disks, for levying on-street parking fees.

29. In Guatemala City, for example, administrative costs amounted to 64 percent of gross revenues from parking meters (Churchill 1972: 111).

8. Other Urban Taxes

1. The redistribution of income between cities or regions, or between the urban and the rural sector, is more properly a concern of the intergovernmental grant system and is taken up in chapter 13.

2. In the United States the local income tax has increased in importance as a source of local government revenue, and a wide variety of practices is employed in various states (see U.S. Advisory Commission on Intergovernmental Relations 1989; Cline 1986). In Japan, local governments levy a progressive (individual and company) income tax, which in recent years has accounted for as much as about two-thirds of all local tax revenue (Ishihara 1986). In Norway, Sweden, and Denmark, local governments have levied flat rate income taxes averaging more than 20 percent (Lotz 1981).

3. In some countries it may be possible to circumvent higher-level government restrictions on local income taxation by wider interpretation of existing tax legislation. Onitsha (Nigeria) has been prohibited from applying a poll tax to those covered under the state income tax and therefore has labeled its levy a "sanitation rate" or "community levy" (1984 World Bank data). Many years ago, Hicks (1974) made a similar suggestion for the extension of the business and professional license fees collected in Indian cities.

4. The rates were structured so as to result in regressive average tax rates across income groups. A later effort by the city government to introduce a set of progressive rates was effectively vetoed by the central government (Avenarius and others 1975).

5. In the United States, a large number of cities rely quite heavily on local sales taxes. For a thorough description of sales tax practices by state and local governments in the United States, see Due and Mikesell (1983).

6. See Due (1988) for an extensive discussion of alternative forms of sales taxation in developing countries.

7. See the discussion in Tait (1988: chap. 8).

8. In Managua, sales tax revenues appeared to have been more stable than most other primary sources of local revenue. Although total recurrent local revenue declined by 13 percent between 1972 and 1973 in the wake of a severe earthquake, sales tax revenues increased by 4 percent (Lacayo, Wong, and Velasco 1976).

9. For example, counties in New York State in the United States choose a retail sales tax rate of up to 3 percent to piggyback onto the 4 percent state rate.

10. A good example of this problem occurred in the Philippines, where the government held back on the local government share of internal revenue collections (Bahl and Schroeder 1983b), and in Korea, where the local government share of internal tax collections has steadily fallen in recent years (Smith and Kim 1979; Chun, Kim, and Lee 1985).

11. Silveira (1989: 21) reports that only 12 percent of registered professionals paid the local service tax in Rio de Janeiro, as compared with 65 percent in Recife.

12. "Octroi" is derived from a French word, and it could best be translated as "impost." Indeed, it may be of interest to note that "octrois" were levied extensively in pre-revolutionary France—Paris was surrounded by legendary customs walls in 1789—and were one of the sources of popular discontent sparking the French Revolution (Schama 1989: 73).

13. It was abolished in Bangladesh, ostensibly in response to the standard criticism that it is a grossly inefficient way to raise revenue for a local government. In fact, the underlying reasons may also have included the central government's desire to control a greater share of the revenue base. In Iran a local tax equivalent to the octroi ("gate tax") was abolished in 1962 (Marshall 1969). In Cali a local statute prescribes a tax on all merchandise imported from abroad whose final destination is Cali. Because of administrative difficulties and lack of effort in collection, however, this tax only contributed 0.6 percent of local government revenue in 1975 (World Bank data).

14. Similar results are shown in McLure and Thirsk (1978) for Jamaica.

15. In 1977 all local governments in Korea lost the authority to tax entertainment (with the exception of horse-racing bets). These taxes were replaced by the national value added tax (Smith and Kim 1979).

16. This phenomenon is not restricted to cities in developing countries. In Belgium, local authorities have traditionally levied more than 100 local taxes (Marshall 1969), and Tokyo also has relied so extensively on numerous nuisance taxes that there have been calls for reform (Hicks 1974).

17. In Colombian cities, for instance, the ordinances governing the minor local taxes were in general not systematically filed and accessible to local tax officials, who therefore frequently were not informed about many of their provisions.

18. Commercial telephones should probably be exempted on efficiency grounds, and the use of public telephones should not be taxed for reasons of equity and efficiency. Furthermore, a tax on connections rather than usage is preferable on efficiency grounds, given the low price-elasticity of demand and the excess demand for connections.

19. Or if administration involves considerable efforts, as with motor vehicle and property taxation, this has important benefits which go beyond the immediate fiscal concerns, as in the case of the preparation of a good cadastre or an effective plan of motor vehicle registration.

9. Issues in Pricing Urban Services

1. Many of the following arguments may also be found in Kahn (1970); Ray (1975); Saunders, Warford, and Mann (1976); Bös (1985); Katz (1987); Heady (1989); Julius and Alicbuson (1989); and World Bank (1989).

2. Bird (1976b: 42). See also Turvey and Anderson (1977), who argue that one should start with the design of efficient electric power tariffs and only then decide on any deviations from the efficient tariffs according to the nature and strength of other objectives. The design of user charges for World Bank–financed projects usually starts with consideration of the efficiency objective (Julius and Alicbuson 1989).

3. For a mathematical proof of this proposition, see Furobotn and Saving (1971: 45–46).

4. In fact, it can be argued that only if price is permitted to vary, so as to ration short capacity, is it possible to derive some guidance for investment decisions from past pricing behavior. Price-smoothing methods (discussed further below), in particular long-run marginal cost pricing, reduce the usefulness of price as a guide for investment decisions.

5. Rising (or falling) block rates occur if users are charged stepwise higher (or lower) unit prices as they consume more units of a service.

6. Externalities will be discussed in detail below.

7. In some Colombian cities water charges were raised monthly by a small proportion during the 1970s. Although this rate of increase was not strictly in line with the rate of

inflation, it was a step in the right direction, assuming that the prices set initially provided an appropriate tradeoff between various conflicting objectives of rate-making (including efficiency).

8. In some cases, once service facilities are provided, connection or use may be made compulsory, which eliminates private decisionmaking.

9. Location cost differentials may occur with respect to all dimensions of service provision, that is, use-related costs, connection-related costs, and costs related to general service provision throughout a particular area. User fees, connection fees, and general location-related jobs may thus have to be differentiated area by area.

10. The reverse, of course, may also happen, if higher urban costs are not reflected in higher urban charges, for example, for road transportation and water supply.

11. For electricity, higher-cost generators may also be used during peak periods, thus raising operating costs.

12. Exceptions might be if the population of an area changes seasonally (for example, because of seasonal migration) or if connection and installation costs differ seasonally because of changing climatic conditions (it may be more costly to dig ditches or lay pipes during the rainy season). But these cases are rare and can be dealt with ad hoc. Note, however, that it would be the price of a connection or of a location which would be changed between periods, not the price of service use.

13. See Mann (1968: 41) for a cogent statement of this point.

14. However, the practice of charging higher utility tariffs to industrial users than to residential consumers may harm the international competitiveness of industry.

15. In the following paragraphs, externalities are assumed to convey benefits. The analysis can proceed in very similar terms for external costs, since one may define external costs merely as negative external benefits. The curves of marginal social valuation in figures 9-2, 9-3, and 9-4 would then be drawn below, instead of above, the individual private demand curves, in which case the price for the service would be set above marginal cost, resulting in a tax, rather than a subsidy, on use or connection.

16. This is the case because each new telephone connection provides all previous connections with the benefit of being able to contact it.

17. This price could therefore be set according to other criteria, such as equity or financial considerations.

18. The feasibility of compulsion as an alternative to pricing for purposes of achieving optimal service use or connection is subject to institutional constraints. If compulsion is applied universally (as, for instance, for primary education or water supply), it may be easy to implement in a technical sense, although there is almost always a very serious problem of evasion. But if compulsion is required to force connection or consumption only selectively, it becomes extremely difficult to decide who should and should not be thus compelled—not to mention the problems with enforcement.

19. See Kahn (1970, vol. 1: 195), for a strong plea for caution along these lines. Regarding external costs it is common to observe the opposite bias in pricing policies. Congestion and pollution, in particular, are rarely priced at efficient levels in both developing and industrial nations. Greater efforts could be made in many cases to improve pricing policies by explicitly allowing for external costs.

20. See, for instance, Kahn (1970) and Furobotn and Saving (1971).

21. See Little and Mirrlees (1974) and Squire and van der Tak (1975) for the theory and practice of shadow pricing in project analysis. See also Munasinghe and Warford (1978) for a discussion of shadow pricing electric power.

22. See Kahn (1970, vol. 1: 196).

23. An alternative would be to compel property owners to connect their properties to the sewage system. This was discussed in the preceding section.

24. In calculating the costs of a refined pricing scheme the inputs, especially nontraded inputs, should be shadow priced to allow for distortions in market prices. Also, one must consider the welfare loss resulting from distortions generated by other charges or taxes which are replacing use-related charges.

25. See especially Turvey and Warford (1974).

26. The extent of capital indivisibility will vary between services and cities depending on a number of circumstances, in particular the type of technology chosen at given levels of demand and natural resources. For instance, if groundwater is abundant, capacity increments in the water supply system are feasible in much smaller steps than if surface water needs to be tapped from distant sources (Saunders, Warford, and Mann 1976: 7).

27. Two other problems are frequently cited: price fluctuations may create awkward revenue streams for the agency, and they may be difficult for the consuming public to accept. These problems will be further discussed below.

28. They, in turn, would have a considerable interest in continued low prices, which would cause political pressures against service rationing prices and in favor of premature extensions in service capacity.

29. Other considerations, such as the higher, more stable revenue generated by alternative pricing systems and the political advantages of more stable prices, will also enter into the selection. In fact, they may be more important than efficiency.

30. In all likelihood this price path would not be a constant price over time.

31. Another case of financial deficits occurs in which externalities prevail and social marginal costs therefore lie below average financial costs.

32. For an early comprehensive treatment of this issue, see Henderson (1947).

33. Another such tax is the head, or poll, tax. But this tax is generally not considered a viable fiscal instrument because it has unacceptable distributive effects.

34. See chapter 5 for an extensive discussion of land taxation.

35. Even if local taxes had no effects on consumer choices, all tax collection is associated with collection and compliance costs which must be compared with those of raising public funds through user charges.

36. Full cost pricing is pricing that recovers total service costs from the beneficiaries of the service, whether through use-related, access, or location charges.

37. See Little (1965); Ray (1975); and Saunders, Warford, and Mann (1976) for examples.

38. See especially Buchanan (1968: 15).

39. This argument neglects the fact that, even with full cost pricing, service beneficiaries as a group will reap a net benefit, as long as total private benefits exceed total costs, that is, as long as there is a fiscal dividend obtained by the beneficiaries. At an equal rate, nonbeneficiaries do not participate in this dividend and thus will have an incentive to pull public investments in their own direction, that is, toward services which they tend to consume more heavily.

40. See Little (1965: 188); Ray (1975: 34).

41. See Little (1965: 188). However, the view that "he who benefits ought to pay" may not be prevalent everywhere and for all services in developing countries. In fact, the exact opposite view may often prevail if free or highly subsidized services are regarded as a quasi-God-given right of the beneficiaries because such services are seen as essential for life or health. See, for example, Shipman (1967: 3) for an account of this view regarding water supply in Latin America during the 1960s.

42. Where congestion is severe, for example in the central city, or where there is significant excess demand for the service, this is quite a relevant concern.

43. Examples are the municipal electricity tax in Delhi (Lal 1976); the municipal telephone tax in Cartagena (Linn 1975); the statutory requirement of a transfer from the autonomous urban service agency to the municipal government in Cali (Bird 1975); the transfers from electricity services to the general account in Francistown, Botswana (World Bank data); the de facto transfers from the water account to the general account in Nairobi (1978 World Bank data); and the transfers from semiautonomous service agencies to the metropolitan government in Jakarta (Linn, Smith, and Wignjowijoto 1976). In industrial countries such transfers have also been encountered frequently, especially in Germany, South Africa, and Sweden (Hicks 1974: 160). Of course, these financing arrangements are likely to reflect a principle of total-cost-plus-tax financing rather than the attempt to siphon off a surplus resulting from the application of a marginal cost pricing criterion. The main point to be made, however, is that intergovernmental transfers of this kind are quite feasible.

44. See, for example, Coase (1970) and Henderson (1947).

45. See Ng and Weisser (1974) for a quantitative formulation of this financing method. They are concerned with a two-part tariff, under which the marginal cost of access is equal to zero but for which financial considerations may make an access charge desirable in addition to a use-related charge. This model is particularly interesting because it considers explicitly the case when the price-elasticity of access demand is greater than zero (in absolute terms).

46. The question of how one may discriminate between rich and poor consumers is further discussed below.

47. A departure from marginal cost pricing is also called for with general fund financing or multipart tariffs whenever these financing arrangements lead to distortions in the allocation of resources, for example, because of the marginal cost of raising (general) public funds or because demand for access to a service is not perfectly inelastic.

48. Certainly it is conventional wisdom in public finance theory that the distributive goal is not a proper concern for local (or subnational) authorities. Of course, it is precisely these authorities who are most frequently and extensively in charge of the provision of urban public services. See Musgrave and Musgrave (1973: 606).

49. See, for example, McLure (1975b); Linn (1980a); Bird (1977a).

50. In Feldstein's model, these are actually embodied in what he calls the "distributional characteristic" of a good or service (Feldstein 1972b: 33).

51. This holds as long as the service is a normal good, that is, the demand for it increases with income (Feldstein 1972a: 178).

52. That is, the income-elasticity of the income or property tax is greater than the income-elasticity of service demand.

53. Munk also introduces the cost of tax collection as a determinant of optimal service price and finds, not surprisingly, that the higher the cost of tax collection, the higher the optimal service price.

54. This is true provided the service faces declining average costs, that is, marginal cost pricing results in a deficit, and provided the marginal consumer uses less than the average consumer.

55. See, for instance, Linn (1980a) for public service demand in Colombia.

56. Complicating matters is the fact that the demand for service use and the demand for output are interrelated. The cross-price-elasticities which Feldstein (1972b) was able to neglect for practical purposes therefore acquire particular relevance in this context.

57. It is possible to assume unrelatedness, for instance, because service connection is compulsory or because location decisions are not affected by use or access prices.

58. See, for example, Saunders, Warford, and Mann (1976) for the case of water supply.

59. The tax (subsidy) is defined here as the price above (below) marginal cost.

60. See, for example, Linn (1977a) for Côte d'Ivoire and Yang (1975) for Yugoslavia; also see Linn (1976a) for a survey of a number of applications in different countries.

61. This pricing structure is frequently referred to as "life-line rates."

62. A rising block tariff, which subsidizes consumers at low levels of consumption but equals marginal cost at higher levels, could approximate a basic need tariff in practice.

63. The importance of past pricing practices will be further discussed below.

64. Indeed, the resurgence of interest in service charges for the financing of urban services in the United States can to a considerable extent be explained by this growing restlessness of local taxpayers.

65. An example of such a typical reaction is the case of the municipal Water and Sewerage Department in Nairobi, whose managers have generally objected to using water surpluses to finance general account deficits in the Nairobi City Council. Another case is the Municipal Public Service Company in Cali, whose managers very much objected to being forced to transfer 4 percent of its gross revenues to the general account. In Bogotá, the arguments between the Municipal Water Company and the Municipal Electric Company regarding the sharing of costs in a joint project were based on very similar motives.

66. Perhaps one of the most important questions in this connection is how the manager can be given an incentive to achieve efficiency in production. This will require appropriate incentive schemes, regulations, and controls, and possibly competition from private service providers. This issue goes beyond the confines of the current study.

67. Examples for such influence by higher-level authorities are Korea (Smith and Kim 1979) and various others cited by Hicks (1974).

68. Examples are the cases of Colombia and Kenya, where national authorities have actively promoted service prices closer in line with costs.

69. The service pricing practices of the Colombian public utility are a case in point.

70. This has occurred, for example, in Korea (Smith and Kim 1979).

10. Charging for Urban Water Services

1. The information in table 10-2, although dated, provides a good indication of the orders of magnitude and degree of variation commonly observed.

2. The purpose of table 10-5 and the accompanying discussion in the text is to familiarize the reader with the types of water charge systems commonly found in developing countries. Of course, water charges are often changed, sometimes quite substantially; therefore, the information contained in table 10-5 should be seen for what it is: a snapshot of common practices, often of some years ago, and not necessarily an accurate description of current water charges in each city.

3. Depending on country usage, these public taps are also referred to as standposts, standpipes, hydrants, or kiosks.

4. In some countries, however, private developers are required to install the retriculation system at their own expense and then hand it over to the water authority for administration. In principle, this is equivalent to a development charge; in practice, however, such regulations are often not enforceable and therefore tend to affect only high-income developments. This has been the case, for example, in Colombia (Linn 1976c).

5. The discussion follows in essence the arguments developed in the preceding chapter. The reader may refer back to it for a more explicit discussion of the general principles underlying the analysis of the present chapter.

6. Very high connection fees have, however, discouraged water connections even by high-income users in some areas of Cameroon (World Bank 1975a).

7. Access to high-quality and reliable services is likely to be much more important than the price charge for services as far as industrial location decisions are concerned. To the extent that higher charges permit provision of better quality services, there may in fact be a positive association between price and location decision.

8. Following Saunders, Warford, and Mann (1977), the precise definition of AIC is:

$$AIC_t = \frac{\displaystyle\sum_{i=1}^{T} \left[\frac{(R_{t+i} - R_t) + I_{t+i-1}}{(1 + i)^{i-1}} \right]}{\displaystyle\sum_{i=1}^{T} \left[\frac{(Q_{t+t} - Q_t)}{(1 + i)^{i-1}} \right]}$$

where R_t = operations and maintenance expenditure in year t, Q_t = water produced in year t, I_t = capital expenditure in year t, T = number of years for which water expenditures and attributable output are forecast, and i = the discount rate. This approach has been used by the World Bank in its appraisal of water supply projects.

9. SRMC pricing is defined to include the rule that when full capacity use is reached, price is adjusted to ration demand in line with available capacity (see chapter 9).

10. Saunders, Warford, and Mann (1977) have extensively explored the AIC price behavior in comparison with other long-run marginal cost (LRMC) concepts.

11. A case of unusually high deposits was encountered in Liberia (Mbi and Campbell 1980).

12. Similar cost differentials were observed for Nairobi.

13. For Tunisia, see Prud'homme (1975); for the Penang region of Malaysia, see Katzman (1977). For a critical discussion of nationally uniform water tariffs, see also Saunders and Warford (1976).

14. Other goals, in particular redistribution between urban and rural areas, may, however, be used to justify cross-subsidization through water tariffs. This is discussed below.

15. The costs of nonprice rationing are further discussed below.

16. According to Warford and Julius (1977), this type of tariff has been adopted in twenty-one of the thirty-six developing countries that have borrowed from the World Bank in the water supply section and have metered connections. See also table 10-5, in which rising block rates are predominant, many of them consisting of two-block tariffs which are in essence life-line tariffs.

17. For a sample of fifty-three low-income households which responded in 1975 to a questionnaire designed for the World Bank by L. K. Hubbell and administered by staff of the Nairobi City Council in the Mathare valley district of Nairobi the average consumption was only 10.4 lcd. All households drew their water from public water taps ("kiosks").

18. Frequently, however, local authorities and utilities are explicitly exempted from paying tariffs on imported capital goods.

19. When, as is suggested here, the border pricing technique is used to shadow price individual inputs, the resulting cost estimate must be converted to a domestic price equiv-

alent by applying the conversion factor for consumption. This is explained in greater detail in Munasinghe (1979).

20. This case arose during the early 1970s in Nairobi, where a number of small private water systems were gradually compelled to yield to the public system because the ground-water on which they drew had unhealthily high levels of fluoride.

21. See Shipman (1967) and Saunders and Warford (1976) for further discussions of these issues.

22. The capital cost of meter and installation was amortized at a 10 percent discount rate over a five-year lifetime and added to the recurrent costs of meter reading, mainte-nance, and so forth.

23. Water charges are potentially more collectable than local taxes because shutting off water services is a relatively quick and easy but quite painful instrument of enforcement, provided water authorities are willing to use it. In Bogotá, for example, accumulated arrears on water service charges in 1972 amounted to only 11 percent of the annual revenues due, whereas accumulated arrears on valorization charges for sewerage works—development charges which were collected by a separate agency without the power to shut off water service—amounted to 130 percent of the annual revenue due. Nonetheless, uncollected water charges are frequently a serious problem for water utilities; see Linn, Smith, and Wignjowijoto (1976) for the case of Jakarta.

24. The exception was a small group of very low-income and low-quantity consumers in Bogotá.

25. The low residential consumption fee in Bombay appears inappropriate for three reasons. First, under the conditions of serious constraints on capacity in Bombay, even AIC pricing is likely to require extensive rationing; prices below AIC will only aggravate this problem and cause further losses in efficiency. Second, given that the poorest segments in Bombay are not even connected to the water distribution network, the distributive benefits of subsidized residential tariffs are highly dubious. Third, the high industrial and commercial tariffs needed to permit subsidized residential fees contribute to high pro-duction costs for the city's firms and thus reduce their competitiveness domestically and internationally.

26. It is worth noting, however, that the flat percentage rate of the water (and sewer) tax in Bombay already results in higher periodic charges for middle- and high-income consumers because they are more likely to live on properties of higher value than the poor.

27. See Linn (1980a) for a more detailed discussion of alternative definitions of subsidy as applied to public utility pricing.

28. The estimate for Cali is based on a survey of household utility consumption carried out by Johannes Linn in 1976 in conjunction with a survey by Marcelo Selowsky reporting incomes for the same households.

29. Saunders (1976) called attention to the problem of multiple-household connections in Bangkok and observed that life-line tariffs will be of limited benefit under these con-ditions.

30. Both pricing measures are examples of application of the Munasinghe-Warford model discussed in the preceding chapter.

31. What is more, because of the failure of the public utility company to obtain accurate, up-to-date information from the cadastral agency, the income-elasticity was considerably lower and the variability considerably higher for the assessed values in the public utility's books than in the official assessment rolls.

32. The extent to which this assumption is appropriate is further investigated below.

33. The marginal consumption charge applies only to consumption in excess of the fixed basic amount of water allocated to each consumer.

34. Of course, this calculation presupposes that all consumers use their full allotment under the fixed charge. In 1976, 26 percent of sampled consumers did not use the full allotment.

35. These results are based on the 1976 household survey conducted by Johannes Linn in Cali.

36. Other cases in which high connection fees appear to have discouraged connection include Monrovia (Mbi and Campbell 1980), Bangkok (Saunders 1976), and Cameroon (World Bank 1975a).

37. The actual connection charge in these neighborhoods in 1975 amounted to only

Col$1,200 payable over five years at no interest rate, whereas during the same year the actual cost to the water company of a hookup was estimated to amount to about Col$2,500.

38. Of course, there are also costs associated with metering which can be avoided under property tax financing.

39. This is the context in which Feldstein (1972b) formulated his model of optimal utility pricing with allowance for distributive considerations.

40. This is a straightforward result of the Munk (1977) model discussed in the preceding chapter.

41. This case approximates the model postulated by Feldstein (1972a), which was reviewed in the preceding chapter.

42. The municipal tax of 4 percent on all gross public utility revenues in Cali in the 1970s was therefore not likely to be justified in the case of water supply.

43. Saunders and Warford (1976) also cite the case of Costa Rica. Its largest city, San Jose, generated surpluses on water account for use as subsidies to water services in rural areas.

44. See World Bank (1980c) for a discussion of appropriate staging and sequencing of investments in water and sewer systems.

45. Financing sewerage networks through development charges is a common practice in the United States (Julius and Warford 1977).

46. The automaticity depends, however, on an effective system of property valuation, which is not common in developing countries (see chapter 4).

47. Such transfers are particularly inappropriate if they are used mainly to finance expansions of sewer systems benefiting wealthy households, as was the case in Cartagena in the early 1970s (Linn 1975).

48. The next chapter will discuss the valorization method in greater detail.

49. Which of the low-cost sanitation systems is most important in any particular city depends on local soil conditions, densities, and culture, to name but a few factors. Kalbermatten, Julius, and Gunnerson (1982) discuss these factors and ways of dealing with possible difficulties of implementing low-cost sanitation techniques.

50. These costs should also be included in the calculation of residential sewerage costs to the extent that they result from residential wastewater effluents.

51. This holds true provided that the development of monopolistic control over the public taps by a few private individuals is effectively eliminated.

11. Charging for Other Urban Services

1. See Jimenez (1987) for a comprehensive discussion of social service financing.

2. In Colombia more sectoral integration for power and telephone services has frequently been suggested in World Bank reports.

3. Industrial consumers may use one hundred times or more electricity per connection than do commercial and residential consumers. For example, in Cali in 1974 average consumption of electricity per industrial connection was 443,600 kilowatt-hours, per commercial connection 3,100 kilowatt-hours, and per residential connection 7,700 kilowatt-hours (Cali 1975). The decision to install time-dependent metering depends on the additional cost of metering as compared with the benefits from reduced peak-hour demand.

4. Because power tariffs are frequently below marginal cost, however, the appropriate approach would most likely consist of raising residential tariffs rather than lowering industrial tariffs.

5. The situation is quite different in rural areas where lump-sum investments in service capacity lead initially to excess capacity and thus to average costs which are greater than marginal (opportunity) cost (World Bank data).

6. The practice of having municipal power companies make contributions to general municipal budgets is quite common in the United States (Strauss and Wertz 1976).

7. According to Munasinghe (1979) the life-line block would appropriately be limited to 100 kilowatt-hours per month.

8. See World Bank (1975b) for other examples.

9. In Colombia in the 1970s, for example, power companies in the major cities increased their tariffs automatically each month by a fixed percentage (commonly 2 percent).

10. This discussion of telephone service pricing draws extensively on Saunders and Warford (1977), Munasinghe, Saunders, and Warford (1978), and Saunders, Warford, and Wellenius (1983).

11. In Germany, however, very low weekend and night calling rates led to periods of considerable congestion during the low-rate hours, which eventually required a significant increase in low rate call tariffs.

12. For the United States it has been estimated that charging per local call, on a nationwide basis, would result in welfare gains on the order of $250 million per year or more, depending on the precise assumptions made (Mitchell 1978).

13. In most Colombian cities during the 1970s, the fixed monthly fee for industrial and commercial consumers was higher than for residential consumers (Colombia 1975).

14. In Colombia fixed monthly charges during the 1970s typically increased with cadastral property value, and in some cities there were also rising block rates for all charges (Colombia 1975).

15. A study by M. I. Gutierrez de Gomez showed that the estimated reduction in the Gini-coefficient for the income distribution in Colombia on account of redistribution through telephone charges amounted only to a minimal drop from 0.5103 to 0.5102 (Linn 1976c).

16. See Munasinghe, Saunders, and Warford (1978) and Saunders, Warford, and Wellenius (1983) for an evaluation of the telephone service cost structure and methods of measuring marginal cost.

17. In the preparation of this section, the authors have benefited from the unpublished work of Alfredo Sfeir-Younis on solid waste disposal practices and policy in Colombia.

18. The slope of log-linear regression of per capita refuse generation on per capita income is 0.29 with an R^2 of 0.77.

19. Whereas mass transit subsidies are thus of dubious value in many developing countries, taxes on public transit are definitely not appropriate. An extreme example until recently existed in Kuala Lumpur, where a bus seat tax accounted for more than 10 percent of annual expenditures of the city's bus companies. A similar tax was in existence until at least the mid-1970s in Bombay.

20. See Linn (1983) for references and further examples regarding public housing in developing countries.

21. Many of the issues involved in the public provision of urban services are discussed in detail in Linn (1983); as regards the scope for improvements in housing finance, an exhaustive United Nations report provides a useful survey of the issues, experience, and possible policies (U.N. Department of International Economic and Social Affairs 1978).

22. Another issue not addressed here relates to the question of whether the lease or sale of public housing is preferable. For a discussion of this issue, see Doebele (1978).

23. Subsidies are defined here, as throughout this and the previous two chapters, as the difference between marginal cost and price.

24. Based on estimates of annual housing subsidies in Valverde and Bamberger (1980) and Zambian national accounts data for 1978 shown in IMF (various years, b).

25. It should be noted, however, that the Zambian subsidy scheme was not explicitly designed to serve low-income groups. Rather, it forms effectively one of the modes of nonwage remuneration for public employees (Valverde and Bamberger 1980).

26. This discussion of rent control draws on Linn (1983); references and further cases are cited there.

27. Selective subsidies for specific urban services, especially life-line rates for water supply, or limited cross-subsidies among program components, may, however, be appropriate; see chapter 10 and Linn (1983).

28. In the context of the discussion of pricing water sewerage services in chapter 10, the role of development charges was described as part of the overall tariff structure.

29. Usually not only urban governments are entitled to use these charges; higher levels of government can also apply these methods, although they tend to rely less on them than do local authorities. Rural development projects have also drawn on development charges of comparable types.

30. See Bahl and Wasylenko (1976) and Doebele and Hwang (1979) for a description of the system in Korea.

31. See International Center for Land Policy Studies (1980) for a series of brief summaries of the experiences in Australia, Germany, Japan, Korea, and Taiwan (China). The data cited in this paragraph are from the same source.

32. Private development was restricted in comparison with, say, the relatively uninhibited albeit illegal private urban development in the so-called pirate developments in Colombia, especially in Bogotá.

33. The names given to the system vary across countries (see Macon and Merino Mañon 1977); however, the term "valorization" is most common. Similar systems for recovering the costs of infrastructure are also found outside of Latin America. "Special assessments" are common in the United States, "betterment levies" are imposed in Indian cities such as Calcutta (Mohan 1974), and improvement charges for drainage works are found in Tunis (Prud'homme 1975).

34. The application of the valorization system in Bogotá has been analyzed in some detail by Doebele, Grimes, and Linn (1979). The presentation here briefly summarizes some of the major findings of that study.

12. The Structure of Urban Governance

1. A good discussion of many of these issues is found in Davey (1989).

2. See Conyers (1984: 187-97) and Bahl and Nath (1986).

3. Musgrave (1959: chap. 1) and Musgrave (1983). Musgrave (1959: 5-17) defines the responsibility of the allocation branch as securing necessary adjustments in the allocation of resources by the market, determining who is to bear the cost of these adjustments, and identifying the revenue and expenditure policies required to achieve the desired objectives.

4. For a survey of the evidence, see Bahl, Johnson, and Wasylenko (1980).

5. See also Bird (1978), Smith (1974), Bahl and Nath (1986), and Wasylenko (1987).

6. Because transfers will be a small portion of the budgets of most subnational governments, expenditures will be approximately equal to purchases of goods and services.

7. See Bahl and Nath (1986), Oates (1972), Pommerehne (1977), and Wasylenko (1986).

8. See Henderson (1980), Bahl and Nath (1986), and Musgrave (1983).

9. It is important to distinguish between governmental decentralization and administrative decentralization. Administrative decentralization refers to central government decisionmaking, which is decentralized to a regional or even local level but without any autonomy for local governments. Governmental or fiscal decentralization refers to local governments with independent taxing and expenditure responsibilities.

10. Population size, of course, is not the only criterion for classification as a municipality, and the rules vary from country to country and even from state to state. For example, the criteria for a "municipal" classification in West Bengal, India, are a minimum population of 10,000, a minimum population density of 2,000 per square mile, three-fourths of the adult male population engaged in nonagricultural occupations, and an "adequate" municipal income from domestic sources. There are, however, no set standards for designation as a municipal corporation except that the general practice in India is to give that classification to cities with a population of more than 500,000. (Datta 1982: 11).

11. For a good discussion of the difference between a political scientist's and an economist's view of federation, see Beer (1977) and Oates (1977a).

12. Excellent discussions of the experience with federalism may be found in Hicks (1978) and Bird (1986).

13. We adopt the convention of referring to the intermediate level of government as a "state" even though it may be labeled differently in many countries, for example, states in Brazil and India, provinces in Korea and the Philippines, departments in Colombia, and parishes in Jamaica.

14. Though under some federal structures, these powers are constitutionally determined with the local government being a residual claimant, that is, receiving those powers not specifically delegated to the central or state governments.

15. This is described in Campbell and Sacks (1967).

16. In effect, cities have the status of both local and provincial governments.

17. The issue of fiscal autonomy is important even if political control is centralized. Even under highly centralized political systems such as those of Korea and China, there is a continuing struggle by metropolitan governments to gain more fiscal and managerial autonomy.

18. For a discussion of this issue, see Bahl and Linn (1983).

19. Here again there is a more subtle distinction. If the central government exerts substantial control over the local council or if it appoints the chief government officer, as in Jakarta, there is little need to have a rigid budget approval exercise. The central government will have made its input at the stage of budget formulation.

20. The amount of revenue raised defines class of city or municipality in the Philippines.

21. The structure of local government in metropolitan Seoul is discussed in Bahl and Wasylenko (1976).

22. These *gu* are further subdivided into more than 300 *dong*.

23. Bougeon-Maassen and Linn (1977). The KSAC was abolished in October 1984 for financial mismanagement. This discussion is concerned with its activities before that time.

24. This analysis refers to the situation before the Aquino administration came into power.

25. This assumes that public (government) goods whose benefits and costs spill over to or from the local area have already been assigned to higher levels of government.

26. For an example from Bogotá, see Linn (1976c).

27. The increase in taxes is XX' (the increase in income) minus X_1X_2 (the increase in consumption of private goods).

28. Of course there are also important constraints in the industrial-country case: voters' preferences are not easily read because they vote on multiple issues, there are legal limitations on tax actions of local governments, and sometimes the finances of local governments are directly managed by higher levels of government (for example, New York City in the late 1970s).

13. Flows and Effects of Intergovernmental Transfers

1. A thorough overview of the U.S. federal grant system is Break (1980).

2. The standard references on classifying grants according to their fiscal effect are Galper and Gramlich (1973) and Gramlich (1977).

3. The distinction between grant types B, C, and D blurs somewhat, for example, because the approval of cost-reimbursable projects can in some cases be ad hoc, or because teacher salary grants may actually be distributed by formula. Still, there are enough pure cases to justify retaining this classification.

4. The term "open-ended" means that there is no fixed limit on the amount of grant funds available; for example, all eligible projects will be funded or all approved teachers' salaries will be paid. A "closed-ended" grant is one in which the total grant fund is fixed. In practice, most grants of this type are closed-ended in that the government only reimburses approved expenditures.

5. A reverse of the normal case may be observed for Ahmadabad, where the state government imposes a sur-rate on the local property tax, then designates one-third of collections for Ahmadabad's education budget (Bahl 1975).

6. Good descriptions of the Brazilian system are in Mahar and Dillinger (1983) and Gandhi (1983).

7. A similar argument might be made for tourism areas.

8. The situation in the United States and Canada is discussed in McLure and Miezkowski (1983).

9. The amount of the transfer to the locality is at least as certain as the total tax yield.

10. The pure shared tax arrangement may, however, induce an overall increase in tax effort. Local residents may view themselves as paying central government taxes, but they will be more likely to comply if they realize that the expenditure benefits from these tax payments will remain within the local area. The greater the percentage of the tax returned to the local area, the more likely is this favorable compliance effect to occur.

11. The Korean system is described in general terms in Smith and Kim (1979: 50–60), and in some detail by the Korean Ministry of Home Affairs (1975).

12. Schroeder (1985a) reports a proposed large increase in the octroi grant for 1984, but he could not find evidence that the proposed increase was actually distributed.

13. Bahl and Schroeder (1983b) found this to be the case for local governments in Iloilo Province in the Philippines, as did Bahl (1989) in Bangladesh.

14. There must be some monitoring, however, to determine whether local governments use the capital grants for capital improvements.

15. For a description of these programs, see De Mello (1977), United Nations (1972), and U.N. Commission on Settlements (1981).

16. The term "fungible" refers to the ease with which monies can be spent for various purposes. For example, if a grant were given for road construction and the full amount of the grant were used to supplement present expenditures on road construction by the local

government, then the grant funds could be termed not fungible. If, conversely, the grant for road construction simply freed up monies to be spent for other functions of government, then the road construction grant funds would be completely fungible. Obviously, the degree of fungibility has a great deal to do with the possibilities for stimulating spending by the local government.

17. These alternatives are analyzed in a more systematic way in the appendix to chapter 12.

18. For a review of the methodological problems, see Bahl, Johnson, and Wasylenko (1980).

19. It is interesting to note, however, that in Brazil the distribution of monies in one grant program favors municipalities with small populations (see table 13-6).

20. The simple correlation between per capita income and per capita education grants is -0.84; that between per capita income and per capita local share grants is 0.05.

21. Data on personal income are not available.

22. The term "distort" is not used in any normative sense here. In the literature on intergovernmental fiscal relations it means only that the grant system has altered relative prices in such a way that the local government chooses a different expenditure mix than it would have in the absence of the grant program. Indeed, distortions in local expenditure choices may be socially desirable in the presence of externalities.

23. This comparison is summarized in a systematic way in Burkhead and Miner (1974).

References and Selected Bibliography

Aaron, Henry J. 1975. *Who Pays the Property Tax? A New View.* Washington, D.C.: Brookings Institution.

Acharya, Shankar N. 1972. "Public Enterprise Pricing and Social Benefit-Cost Analysis." *Oxford Economic Papers* 24, no. 1: 36–53.

Adamolekun, Ladipo, Osa Osemwata, and Dele Olowu. 1980. *Report on the Performance of Local Governments in Bendel, Kwara, Lagos, Ogun, Ondo, and Oyo States: 1976–1980.* Ife, Nigeria: Department of Public Administration, University of Ife.

American Water Works Association, Taxation and Revenue Allocation Committee. 1974. "Taxation and Revenue Allocation for Municipality Owned Water Utilities." *Journal of the American Water Works Association* (Nov.): 623–27.

Anderson, Dennis, and Ralph Turvey. 1974. "Study of Electricity Tariffs in Thailand." Public Utilities Report 4. World Bank, Public Utilities Department, Washington, D.C.

Apel, Hans. 1977. "Wie lange soll Bonn die Zeche zahlen?" *Die Zeit* 29 (15 July): 3.

Archer, R. W. 1972. "Site Value Taxation and Redevelopment in the Brisbane Central Business Area." *The Valuer* (Sidney) 22, no. 2.

Arnott, Richard J., and James G. MacKinnon. 1977. "The Effects of the Property Tax: A General Equilibrium Simulation." *Journal of Urban Economics* 4, no. 4: 389–407.

Austin, Allan G., and Sherman Lewis. 1970. *Urban Government for Metropolitan Lima.* New York: Institute of Public Administration.

Australia, Government of; Department of the Environment. 1976. *Pricing and Demand Management in the Provision of Water and Sewerage.* Canberra: Australian Government Publishing Service.

Avenarius, Hermann, Dieter Oberndörfer, Erich Schmitz, and Jürgen H. Wolff. 1975. *Kommunalverwaltung in Mittelamerika: Eine Studie über die Hauptstädte Guatemalas and El Salvadors.* Freiburg, Germany: Arnold-Bergstraesser Institut.

Azfar, Yawaid. 1971. "The Income Distribution in Pakistan before and after Taxes, 1966–67." Ph.D diss., Harvard University.

Bahl, Roy W. 1971. "A Regression Approach to Tax Effort and Tax Ratio Analysis." *International Monetary Fund Staff Papers* 18, no. 3: 570–612.

———. 1972. "A Representative Tax System Approach to Measuring Tax Effort in Developing Countries." *International Monetary Fund Staff Papers* 19, no. 1: 87–124.

————. 1975. "Urban Public Finances in Developing Countries: A Case Study of Metropolitan Ahmadabad." Urban and Regional Report 77-4. World Bank, Development Economics Department, Washington, D.C.

————. 1978. "Urban Property Taxation in Less Developed Countries: Fiscal and Growth Management Decisions." In George Break, ed., *Metropolitan Financing and Growth Management Policies: Principles and Practice*. Madison: University of Wisconsin Press.

————. 1979a. "The Practice of Urban Property Taxation in Less Developed Countries." In Bahl 1979b.

————, ed. 1979b. *The Taxation of Urban Property in Less Developed Countries*. Madison: University of Wisconsin Press.

————, ed. 1981. *Urban Government Finance: Emerging Trends*. Beverly Hills, Calif.: Sage.

————. 1983. "Strengthening the Fiscal Performance of Philippines Local Governments." In Bahl and Miller 1983.

————. 1989. "Intergovernmental Grants." In Larry Schroeder, ed., *Financing Governmental Decentralization: The Case of Bangladesh*. Boulder, Colo.: Westview.

————, ed. 1990. *The Jamaican Tax Reform*. Cambridge, Mass.: Lincoln Institute of Land Policy.

Bahl, Roy W., Pamela Brigg, and Roger S. Smith. 1976. "Urban Public Finances in Developing Countries: A Case Study of Metropolitan Manila." Urban and Regional Report 77-8. World Bank, Development Economics Department, Washington, D.C.

Bahl, Roy W., and Alan Campbell. 1976. "Local Government Reform: Efficiency, Equity, and Administrative Dimensions." In Campbell and Bahl 1976.

Bahl, Roy, Stephen Coelen, and Jeremy Warford. 1978. "Allocation Inefficiency of Benefit-Cost Applied to Water and Sewerage Supply: Interactions between Time-Series and Cross-Sectional Models." *Journal of Water Supply and Management* (U.K.) 2.

Bahl, Roy W., Richard Gustely, and Michael J. Wasylenko. 1978. "The Determinants of Local Government Police Expenditures: A Public Employment Approach." *National Tax Journal* 31: 67–79.

Bahl, Roy W., Daniel Holland, and Johannes F. Linn. 1983. *Urban Growth and Local Taxes in Less Developed Countries*. Papers of the East-West Population Institute 89. Honolulu, Hawaii: East-West Center.

Bahl, Roy W., Marvin Johnson, and Michael J. Wasylenko. 1980. "State and Local Government Expenditure Determinants: The Traditional View and a New Approach." In Roy W. Bahl, Jesse Burkhead, and Bernard Jump, eds., *Public Employment and State and Local Government Finances*. Cambridge, Mass.: Ballinger.

Bahl, Roy W., Bernard Jump, and Larry Schroeder. 1978. "The Outlook for City Fiscal Performance." In Roy Bahl, ed., *The Fiscal Outlook for Cities: Implications of a National Urban Policy*. Syracuse, N.Y.: Syracuse University Press.

Bahl, Roy W., Chuk Kyo Kim, and Chong Kee Park. 1986. *Public Finances during the Korean Modernization Process*. Cambridge, Mass.: Harvard University Press.

Bahl, Roy W., and Johannes F. Linn. 1983. "The Assignment of Local Government Revenues in Developing Countries." In McLure 1983.

————. 1987. "Intergovernmental Fiscal Relations in Less Developed Countries." In George S. Tolley and Vinod Thomas, eds., *The Economics of Urbanization and Urban Policies in the Developing Countries*. World Bank Symposium. Washington, D.C.

Bahl, Roy W., and Barbara Miller, eds. 1983. *Local Government Finance in the Third World: A Case Study of the Philippines*. New York: Praeger.

Bahl, Roy W., and Shyam Nath. 1986. "Public Expenditure Decentralization in Developing Countries." *Government and Policy* 4: 405–18.

Bahl, Roy W., and Velayudhan Pillai. 1976. "The Allocative Effects of Intergovernmental Flows in Less Developed Countries: A Case Study of India." *Public Finance/Finances Publique* 31, no. 1: 82–84.

Bahl, Roy W., and Larry Schroeder. 1983a. "The Business License Tax." In Bahl and Miller 1983.

————. 1983b. "Intergovernmental Fiscal Relations." In Bahl and Miller 1983.

————. 1983c. "Local Government Structure, Financial Management, and Fiscal Conditions." In Bahl and Miller 1983.

————. 1983d. "The Real Property Tax." In Bahl and Miller 1983.

Bahl, Roy W. and Walter Vogt. 1976. "State and Regional Government Financing of Urban Public Services." In Campbell and Bahl 1976.

Bahl, Roy W., and Michael J. Wasylenko. 1976. "Urban Public Finances in Developing Countries: A Case Study of Seoul, Korea." Urban and Regional Report 77-3. World Bank, Development Economics Department, Washington, D.C.

Bairoch, Paul. 1982. "Employment and Large Cities: Problems and Outlook." *International Labour Review* 121, no. 5: 527–29.

Barlev, Bension, and Joseph May. 1976. "The Effects of Property Taxes on the Construction and Demolition of Houses in Urban Areas." *Economic Geography* 52, no. 2: 304–10.

Bartik, Timothy J. 1989. "Small Business Start-Ups in the United States: Estimates of the Effects of Characteristics of States." *Southern Economic Journal* 55, no. 4: 1004–1018.

Bastin, Johan, and DiDiek Hadiprobowo. 1987. "Report on Advisory Assistance to Bappeda DKI Jakarta for Jabotabek Urban Development Project." World Bank, Water Supply and Urban Development Department, Washington, D.C.

Batchelor, R. A. 1975. "Household Technology and the Domestic Demand for Water." *Land Economics* 51, no. 3: 208–23.

Bauer, Helfried. 1971. "Finanzen." In Egon Matzner, ed., *Wirtschaft und Finanzen Österreichischer Städte*. Wien: Institut für Städteforschung.

Baumol, William J. 1967. "Macroeconomics of Unbalanced Growth: The Anatomy of Urban Crisis." *American Economic Review* 57 (June): 415–26.

Beer, Samuel H. 1977. "A Political Scientist's Views of Fiscal Federalism." In Oates 1977b.

Beier, George, Anthony Churchill, Michael Cohen, and Bertrand Renaud. 1976.

"The Task Ahead for the Cities in the Developing Countries." *World Development* 4 (May): 363–409.

Bird, Richard M. 1970. *Taxation and Development: Lessons from the Colombian Experience.* Cambridge, Mass.: Harvard University Press.

———. 1972. "The 'Displacement Effect': A Critical Note." *Finanzarchiv* 30 (Feb.): 454–63.

———. 1975. "Intergovernmental Fiscal Relations in a Developing Country: The Case of Cali, Colombia." World Bank, Development Economics Department, Washington, D.C.

———. 1976a. "Assessing Tax Performance in Developing Countries: A Critical Review of the Literature." *Finanzarchiv* 34, no. 2: 244–65.

———. 1976b. *Charging for Public Services: A New Look at an Old Idea.* Toronto: Canadian Tax Foundation.

———. 1976c. "The Incidence of the Property Tax: Old Wine in New Bottles?" *Canadian Public Policy–Analyse de Politiques* 2, Supplement: 323–34.

———. 1977a. "Financing Urban Development: A Worldwide Challenge." *Habitat International* 2, no. 5/6: 549–56.

———. 1977b. "Tax Reform and Tax Design in Developing Countries." *Rivista di Ditritto Finanziario e Scienza Delle Finanze* 36, no. 2: 297–306.

———. 1978. *Intergovernmental Fiscal Relations in Developing Countries.* World Bank Staff Working Paper 304. Washington, D.C.

———. 1980. *Central-Local Fiscal Relations and the Provision of Urban Public Services.* Research Monograph 30. Center for Research on Federal Financial Relations. Canberra: Australian National University.

———. 1983. "The Allocation of Taxing Powers in Papua, New Guinea." Discussion Paper 15. Institute of National Affairs, Port Moresby, Papua, New Guinea.

———. 1984. *Intergovernmental Finance in Colombia: Final Report of the Mission on Intergovernmental Finance.* Cambridge, Mass.: International Tax Program, Law School of Harvard University.

———. 1986. *Federal Finance in Comparative Perspective.* Toronto: Canadian Tax Foundation.

Bird, Richard M., and Luc Henry De Wulf. 1973. "Taxation and Income Distribution in Latin America: A Critical Review of Empirical Studies." *International Monetary Fund Staff Papers* 20, no. 3: 639–82.

Bocherdering, T. E., and R. T. Deacon. 1972. "The Demand for the Services of Non-Federal Governments." *American Economic Review* 62, no. 5: 891–901.

Bonin, Joseph, B. W. Finch, and Joseph Water. 1968. "Alternative Test of the Displacement Effect Hypothesis." *Public Finance/Finances Publiques* 24, no. 3: 441–56.

Bös, Dieter. 1985. "Public Sector Pricing." In Alan J. Auerbach and Martin Feldstein, eds., *Handbook of Public Economics*, vol. 1. New York: North Holland.

Boskin, Michael J. 1978. "Taxation, Savings and the Rate of Interest." *Journal of Political Economy* 86, no. 2, pt. 2: S3–S27.

Bougeon-Maassen, Francine. 1976. "Urban Public Finances in Developing Countries: A Case Study of Metropolitan Bombay." Urban and Regional Report 76-13. World Bank, Development Economics Department, Washington, D.C.

Bougeon-Maassen, Francine, and Johannes F. Linn. 1977. "Urban Public Finances in Developing Countries: A Case Study of Metropolitan Kingston, Jamaica." Urban and Regional Report 77-7. World Bank, Development Economics Department, Washington, D.C.

Break, George. 1980. *Financing Government in a Federal System*. Washington, D.C.: Brookings Institution.

Brown, J. Bruce. 1971. "Updating New Zealand's Land Taxing System." Paper presented at the International Association of Assessing Officers Annual Meeting, September, Boston, Mass.

Buchanan, James M. 1968. "A Public Choice Approach to Public Utility Pricing." *Public Choice* 5 (Fall): 1–18.

———. 1973. "Earmarked Taxes." In R. W. Houghton, ed., *Public Finance*. 2d ed. Baltimore, Md.: Penguin.

Burkhead, Jesse, and Jerry Miner. 1974. *Public Expenditure*. Chicago: Aldine.

Burki, Shahid Javed, and Joris J. C. Voorhoeve. 1977. "Global Estimates for Meeting Basic Needs: Background Paper." Basic Needs Paper 1. World Bank, Policy Planning and Program Review Department, Washington, D.C.

Butlin, Noel. 1976. "Manufacturing and All Other Liquid Waste Flows: A Policy Issue." In Australia 1976.

Caille, P. 1971. "Marginal Cost Pricing in a Random Future as Applied to the Tariff for Electrical Energy by Electricité de France." In Trebing 1971.

Cali, Empresas Municipales de. 1975. "Estudio de Tarifas de Energía Eléctrica." Subgerencia Técnica. Cali, Colombia.

Caminos, Horacio, and Reinhard Goethert. 1976. "Urbanization Primer for Design of Sites and Service Projects." World Bank, Urban Projects Department, Washington, D.C.

Campbell, Alan K., and Roy W. Bahl, eds. 1976. *State and Local Government: The Political Economy of Reform*. New York: Free Press.

Campbell, Alan, and Seymour Sacks. 1967. *Metropolitan America*. New York: Free Press.

Cannon, Mark W., R. Scott Foster, and Robert Witherspoon. 1973. *Urban Government for Valencia, Venezuela*. New York: Praeger.

Carroll, Alan. 1980. *Private Subdivisions and the Market for Residential Lots in Bogotá* . World Bank Staff Working Paper 435. Washington, D.C.

Chelliah, Raja. 1971. "Trends in Taxation in Developing Countries." *International Monetary Fund Staff Papers* 28, no. 2: 254–331.

Chelliah, Raja, and Ram N. Lal. 1977. *Incidence of Indirect Taxation in India 1973–74*. New Delhi, India: National Institute of Public Finance and Policy.

Chun, Dong Hoon, Kim Kyung-hwan, and Kyu Sik Lee. 1985. "Financial Performance of Local Governments in the Seoul Region: Implications for Urban

Deconcentration Policies." Discussion Paper UDD-88. World Bank, Water Supply and Urban Development Department, Washington, D.C.

Churchill, Anthony A. 1972. *Road User Charges in Central America.* World Bank Staff Occasional Paper 15. Baltimore, Md.: Johns Hopkins University Press.

Clark, Joel. 1971. "Tax Incentives in Central American Development." *Economic Development and Cultural Change* 19, no. 2: 229–52.

Clark, Terry N., and Lorna C. Ferguson. 1983. *City Money: Political Processes, Fiscal Strain, and Retrenchment.* New York: Columbia University Press.

Clark, W. A. V. 1974. *The Impact of Property Taxation on Urban Spatial Development.* Report 187. Los Angeles: Institute of Government and Public Affairs, University of California, Los Angeles.

Clawson, Marion. 1962. "Urban Sprawl and Speculation in Suburban Land." *Land Economics* 38, no. 2: 99–111.

Clemens, Eli W. 1971. "A Comparison of English, French, and American Electric Residential Rates and Their Significance for Large Scale Integration of American Utilities." In Harry M. Tocbing, ed., *Essays on Public Utility Pricing and Regulation.* East Lansing, Mich.: Institute of Public Utilities, Michigan State University.

Cline, Robert. 1986. "Personal Income Tax." In Steven D. Gold, ed., *Reforming State Tax Systems.* Denver, Colo.: National Conference of State Legislatures.

Coase, Ronald H. 1970. "The Theory of Public Utility Pricing and Its Application." *Bell Journal of Economics and Management Science* 1, no. 1: 113–28.

Cochrane, Glynn. 1983. *Policies for Strengthening Local Government in Developing Countries.* World Bank Staff Working Paper 582. Washington, D.C.

Colombia, Republic of. 1973. "Bogotá Urban Development Study, Phase II, Fiscal Studies." Bogotá, Colombia.

———. 1975. "Resultados de la Información Basica Anual del Servicio Telefónico en las Principales Ciudades del País, 1974." Bogotá, Colombia: Junta Nacional de Tarifas de Servicios Públicos.

———. 1976. *Program Nacional de Aseo Urbano de Colombia.* Bogotá, Colombia: Ministerio de Salud.

———. 1979. *Resolution No. 056.* October 17. Bogotá , Colombia: Junta Nacional de Tarifas de Servicios Públicos.

Conyers, Diana. 1984. "Decentralization and Development: A Review of the Literature." *Public Administration and Development* 4: 187–97.

Courant, Paul, Edward Gramlich, and Daniel Rubinfeld. 1980. "Why Voters Support Tax Limitations Amendments: The Michigan Case. *National Tax Journal* 33, no. 1: 1–20.

Crew, M. A., and G. Roberts. 1970. "Some Problems of Pricing under Stochastic Supply Conditions: The Case of Seasonal Pricing for Water Supply." *Water Resources Research* 6, no. 5: 1272–276.

Cullen, Matthew, and Sharon Woolery, eds. 1982. *World Congress on Land Policy 1980.* Lexington, Mass.: Lexington Books.

———, eds. 1982. *World Congress on Land Policy 1982.* Lexington, Mass.: Lexington Books.

Datta, Abhijit. 1968. *Rent Control and Housing in India.* New Delhi: Indian Institute of Public Administration.

―――. 1981. "Municipal Finances in India." Discussion Paper UDD-18. World Bank, Water Supply and Urban Development Department, Washington, D.C.

―――. 1982. *State-Municipal Fiscal Relations: A Comparative Study of Australia and India.* Research Monograph 37. Canberra: Center for Research on Federal Financial Relations, Australian National University.

Datta, Abhijit, and J. N. Khosla. 1972. "Delhi." In Robson and Regan 1972.

Davey, Ken. 1983. *Financing Regional Government: International Practices and Their Relevance to the Third World.* New York: Wiley.

―――. 1989. "Strengthening Municipal Government." Discussion Paper INU-47. World Bank, Infrastructure and Urban Development Department, Washington, D.C.

Davies, C. J. 1970. "Comparative Local Government as a Field of Study." *Studies in Comparative Local Government* 4, no. 2: 38–44.

Davis, Kingsley. 1969. *World Urbanization 1950–70.* Berkeley: University of California Press.

De Mello, Diogo Lordello. 1977. "Local Administration and National Development Strategies: A Latin American Perspective." Paper presented to the Latin American Studies Association, November 2, Houston, Tex.

Devas, Nick. 1986. "Local Taxation and Related Issues of Central-Local Relations." Papers on Regional Finance for the Government of the Republic of Indonesia: Development Administration Group. Institute of Local Government Studies, Birmingham, England.

De Wulf, Luc. 1972. "First-Order Effect of the Tax Payments by Income Class: The Case of Lebanon 1968." *Proche Orient, Etudes Economiques* 2 (Sept.): 533–53.

―――. 1975. "Fiscal Incidence Studies in Developing Countries: Survey and Critique." *International Monetary Fund Staff Papers* 22, no. 1: 61–131.

Dillinger, William. 1981. "Implicit Spatial Policies: The Case of the Fiscal System in São Paulo State." World Bank, Development Economics Department, Washington, D.C.

―――. 1982. "Regional Aspects of State and Local Finance in Brazil." World Bank, Infrastructure and Urban Development Department, Washington, D.C.

―――. 1988a. "Urban Property Taxation in Developing Countries." Background paper for *World Development Report 1988.* World Bank, Office of the Vice President for Development Economics, Washington, D.C.

―――. 1988b. "Urban Property Tax Reform: The Case of the Philippines' Real Property Tax Administration Project." Report INU-16. World Bank, Infrastructure and Urban Development Department, Washington, D.C.

―――. 1989. "Urban Property Taxation: Lessons from Brazil." Report INU-37. World Bank, Infrastructure and Urban Development Department, Washington, D.C.

Doebele, William A. 1978. "Selected Issues in Urban Land Tenure." In Dunkerley and Associates 1978.

————. 1979. "Land Readjustment as an Alternative to Taxation for the Recovery of Betterment: The Case of South Korea." In Bahl 1979b.

Doebele, William A., Orville F. Grimes, Jr., and Johannes F. Linn. 1979. "Participation of Beneficiaries in Financing Urban Services: Valorization Charges in Bogotá, Colombia." *Land Economics* 55, no. 1: 73–92.

Doebele, William A., and Myong Chan Hwang. 1979. "Land Policies in the Republic of Korea, with Special Reference to Decentralized Development." Urban and Regional Report 79-4. World Bank, Development Economics Department, Washington, D.C.

Downing, Paul B., ed. 1977a. *Local Service Pricing Policies and Their Effect on Urban Spatial Structure*. Vancouver: University of British Columbia Press.

————. 1977b. "Policy Perspectives on User Charges and Urban Spatial Development." In Downing 1977a.

Downing, Paul B., and Richard D. Gustely. 1977. "The Public Service Costs of Alternative Development Patterns: A Review of the Evidence." In Downing 1977a.

Due, John F. 1988. *Indirect Taxation in Developing Economies*. Rev. ed. Baltimore, Md.: Johns Hopkins University Press.

Due, John F., and John L. Mikesell. 1983. *Sales Taxation, State and Local Structure, and Administration*. Baltimore, Md.: Johns Hopkins University Press.

Dunkerley, Harold B. 1983. "Introduction and Overview." In Harold B. Dunkerley, ed., *Urban Land Policies: Issues and Opportunities*. New York: Oxford University Press.

Dunkerley, Harold B., and Associates, eds. 1978. *Urban Land: Policy Issues and Opportunities*, vol. 2. World Bank Staff Working Paper 283. Washington, D.C.

Ehrenberg, R. 1973. "The Demand for State and Local Government Employees." *American Economic Review* 63, no. 3: 366–79.

Ehrlicher, Werner, and Reiner Hagemann. 1976. "Die Öffentlichen Finanzen der Bundesrepublik im Jahre 1974." *Finanzarchiv* (N.F.) 35, no. 2: 322–46.

Farrell, M. J. 1968. "In Defense of Public-Utility Price Theory." In Turvey 1968.

Feldstein, Martin S. 1972a. "Distributional Equity and the Optimal Structure of Public Prices." *American Economic Review* 62, no. 1: 32–36.

————. 1972b. "Equity and Efficiency in Public Sector Pricing: The Optimal Two-Part Tariff." *Quarterly Journal of Economics* 86, no. 2: 175–87.

Findley, Sally. 1977. *Planning for Internal Migration*. Washington, D.C.: U.S. Department of Commerce, Bureau of the Census.

Follain, James, G. C. Gil-Chin, and Bertrand Renaud. 1980. "The Determinants of Home-ownership in a Developing Country: The Case of Korea." *Urban Studies* 17, no. 1: 13–23.

Follain, James, and Emi Miyake. 1986. "Land Versus Property Taxation: A General Equilibrium Analysis." *National Tax Journal* 39 (December): 451–70.

Fox, William. 1984. "Intergovernmental Fiscal Relations in Egypt and Mobilization of Local Revenues." Department of Economics, University of Tennessee, Knoxville.

Frank, Charles R., Jr., and Richard C. Webb, eds. 1977. *Income Distribution and*

Growth in the Less-Developed Countries. Washington, D.C.: Brookings Institution.

Franzen, Thomas, Kerstin Lovgren, and Irma Rosenberg. 1975. "Redistributional Effects of Taxes and Public Expenditures in Sweden." *Swedish Journal of Economics* 77, no. 1: 31–55.

Fried, Robert C. 1972. "Mexico City." In Robson and Regan 1972.

Friedman, Milton. 1976. *Essays in Positive Economics*. Chicago: University of Chicago Press.

Friend, Irwin, and Joel Hasbrouck. 1983. "Savings and After-Tax Rates of Return." *Review of Economics and Statistics* 65, no. 4: 537–43.

Fundación para el Desarrollo Industrial. 1973. "Municipios del Valle del Cauca: Impuesto de Industria y Comercio." Cali, Colombia.

Furobotn, Erik G., and Thomas R. Saving. 1971. "The Theory of the Second Best and the Efficiency of Marginal Cost Pricing." In Trebing 1971.

Gadsden, Christopher H., and Roger W. Schmenner. 1977. "Municipal Income Taxation." In John R. Meyer and John M. Quigley, eds., *Local Public Finance and the Fiscal Squeeze: A Case Study*. Cambridge, Mass.: Ballinger.

Gall, M. Pirie. 1976. *Municipal Development Programs in Latin America*. New York: Praeger.

Gallagher, David R. 1976. "Pricing for Water Demand Management: Possibilities and Limitations." In Australia 1976.

Gandhi, Ved P. 1983. "Tax Assignment and Revenue Sharing in Brazil, India, Malaysia, and Nigeria." In McLure 1983.

Garza, Gustavo, and Martha Schteingart. 1978. "Mexico City: The Emerging Metropolis." In Wayne A. Cornelius and Robert V. Kemper, eds., *Metropolitan Latin America: The Challenge and the Response*. Beverly Hills, Calif.: Sage.

Garzón López, Hernando. 1978. "Estructura y Tendencias de los Ingresos y Gastos de Cali 1966–74." Bogotá, Colombia.

————. 1989. "The Property Tax Systems Applied in Selected Latin American and Caribbean Nations." Occasional Paper 131. Metropolitan Studies Program, Maxwell School, Syracuse University, Syracuse, N.Y.

Gerard, Michele. 1973. "The Brazilian State Value Added Tax." *International Monetary Fund Staff Papers* 20, no. 1: 118–69.

Gillis, Malcolm. 1971. "Reform of Municipal and Direct Taxes, Service Taxation and Stamp Duties." In Musgrave and Gillis 1971.

Goetz, Charles J. 1973. "The Revenue Potential of User-Related Charges in State and Local Governments." In Richard A. Musgrave, ed., *Broad Based Taxes: New Options and Sources*. Baltimore, Md.: Johns Hopkins University Press.

Goffman, E. M., and D. J. Mahar. 1971. "The Growth of Public Expenditures in Selected Developing Nations: Six Caribbean Countries, 1940–1965." *Public Finance/Finances Publiques* 26, no. 1: 57–72.

Gold, Steven D. 1977. "Scandinavian Local Income Taxation: Lessons for the United States? *Public Finance Quarterly* 5, no. 4: 471–88.

Goldstein, Sidney, and David I. Sly. 1977. *Patterns of Urbanization: Comparative*

Country Studies. Working Paper 3. Dolhain, Netherlands: International Union for the Scientific Study of Population, Ordina Editions.

Gomez-Ibanez, Jose Antonio. 1975. "Federal Assistance for Urban Mass Transportation." Ph.D. diss., Harvard University.

Gorman, W. M. 1980. "The Demand for Water." World Bank Transportation, Water, and Telecommunications Department. Washington, D.C.

Gramlich, Edward M. 1977. "Intergovernmental Grants: A Review of the Empirical Literature." In Oates 1977b.

Gramlich, Edward M., and Harvey Galper. 1973. "State and Local Fiscal Behavior and Federal Grant Policy." *Brookings Papers on Economic Activity* 1: 16–65.

Green, Leslie. 1972. "Ibadan." In Robson and Regan 1972.

Greytak, David. 1983. *Local Government Finances in Peru*. Monograph 8. Syracuse, N.Y.: Metropolitan Studies Program, Maxwell School, Syracuse University.

Greytak, David, and Benjamin Diokno. 1983. "Local Government Public Enterprises." In Bahl and Miller 1983.

Greytak, David, and Victor Mendez. 1986. "The Impact of Intergovernmental Grants on Local Governments in Ecuador: A Study of FONAPAR." Metropolitan Studies Program Occasional Paper 106. Local Revenue Administration Project, Maxwell School, Syracuse University, Syracuse, N.Y.

Grieson, Ronald E. 1974. "The Economics of Property Taxes and Land Values: The Elasticity of Supply of Structures." *Journal of Urban Economics* 1, no. 4: 367–81.

Grimes, Orville F., Jr. 1974. *Urban Land and Public Policy: Social Appropriation of Betterment*. World Bank Staff Working Paper 179. Washington, D.C.

——. 1976. *Housing for Low-Income Urban Families: Economics and Public Policy in the Developing World*. Baltimore, Md.: Johns Hopkins University Press.

Guisinger, Stephen. 1985. "A Comparative Study of Country Policies." In Stephen Guisinger and Associates, eds., *Investment Incentives and Performance Requirements*. New York: Praeger.

Gupta, Shibshankar P. 1967. "Public Expenditure and Economic Growth: A Time Series Analysis." *Public Finance/Finances Publiques* 22, no. 4: 423–61.

——. 1971. "Reforms in Urban Property Taxes: A Case Study of Municipal Corporations in Gujarat." *Anvesak* 1, no. 1: 35–55.

Halvorsen, Robert. 1975. "Demand for Electric Energy in the United States." *Review of Economics and Statistics* 57, no. 1: 12–18.

Hamer, Andrew M., and Johannes F. Linn. 1987. "Urbanization in the Developing World: Patterns, Issues and Politics." In Mills 1987.

Hanke, Steve H. 1970. "Demand for Water under Dynamic Conditions." *Water Resources Research* 6, no. 5: 1253–261.

——. 1972. "Pricing Urban Water." In Selma Mushkin, ed., *Public Prices for Public Products*. Washington, D.C.: Urban Institute.

Hanke, Steve H., and Robert K. Davis. 1971. "Demand Management through Responsive Pricing." *Journal of the American Water Works Association* 63 (September): 555–60.

Hansen, Tore. 1977. "The Financial Problems of Swedish Local Government." Paper for European Consortium for Political Research Workshop on the Financial Problems of European Cities, Berlin.

Hansmeyer, Karl Heinrich, and Dietrich Fürst. 1968. *Die Gebühren*. Stuttgart, Germany: Kohlhammer.

Harberger, Arnold C. 1977. "Fiscal Policy and Income Redistribution." In Frank and Webb 1977.

———. 1978. "Basic Needs versus Distributional Weights in Social Cost-Benefit Analysis." University of Chicago, Background notes to a seminar presented at the World Bank, Chicago.

Harris, C. Lowell. 1976. "Property Taxation and Development." In N. T. Wang., ed., *Taxation and Development*. New York: Praeger.

———. 1979. "Land Taxation in Taiwan: Selected Aspects." In Bahl 1979b.

Hazelwood, A. 1968. "Telephone Service." In Turvey 1968.

Heady, Christopher. 1989. "Public Sector Pricing in a Fiscal Context." Policy, Planning, and Research Working Paper 179. World Bank, Country Economics Department, Washington, D.C.

Heckt, Wilhelm. 1975. *Zur Verkoppelung und Begrenzung der Realsteuerhebesätze*, vol. 107. Bonn, Germany: Institut "Finanzen und Steuern."

Heller, Peter, and Alan Tait. 1984. *Government Employment and Pay: Some International Comparisons*. International Monetary Fund Occasional Paper 24. Washington, D.C.

Heller, Walter. 1954. *Taxes and Fiscal Policy in Developing Countries*. New York: United Nations.

Henderson, A. M. 1947. "The Pricing of Public Utility Undertakings." *Manchester School of Economic and Social Studies* 15, no. 3: 223–50.

Henderson, J. Vernon. 1980. "A Framework for International Comparison of Systems of Cities." World Bank, Development Economics Department, Washington, D.C.

Henning, John, and Dale Tussing. 1974. "Income Elasticity of the Demand for Public Expenditures in the United States." *Public Finance/Finances Publiques* 3, no. 4: 325–41.

Hicks, J. R., and Ursula Hicks. 1955. *Report on Finance and Taxation in Jamaica*. Kingston: Government of Jamaica.

Hicks, Ursula K. 1945. *The Incidence of Local Rates in Great Britain*. Occasional Paper 8. National Institute of Economic and Social Research, London.

———. 1961. *Development from Below*. London: Oxford University Press.

———. 1970. "Current Experiments in Budgetary Organization." *United Malaysian Banking Corporation Economic Review* 6, no. 2: 30–41.

———. 1974. *The Large City: A World Problem*. New York: Wiley.

———. 1976a. *Intergovernmental Fiscal Relations in Less Developed Countries*. Occasional Paper 32. Syracuse, N.Y.: Metropolitan Studies Program, Maxwell School, Syracuse University.

———. 1976b. "Intergovernmental Relations with Special Reference to the Less Developed Countries." Paper presented at the Seminar on Development and Finance of Local Government in Thailand, Chiengmai, Feb. 2–3.

————. 1977. "The Development of Budgetary Techniques for Policy Decisions." *United Malayan Banking Corporation Economic Review* 13, no. 1: 42–50.

————. 1978. *Federation: Failure and Success*. New York: Oxford University Press.

Hickson, Warren. 1976. "Pricing as a Means of Demand Control for Sewerage." In Australia 1976.

Hinrichs, Harley. 1966. *A General Theory of Tax Structure Change during Economic Development*. Cambridge, Mass.: Harvard University Law School, International Tax Program.

Hirshleifer, Jack, James C. De Haven, and Jerome W. Milliman. 1960. *Water Supply: Economics, Technology, and Policy*. Chicago: University of Chicago Press.

Hochman, Harold, and James Rodgers. 1969. "Pareto Optimal Redistribution." *American Economic Review* 59, no. 4: 542–57.

Holland, Daniel. 1979. "Adjusting the Property Tax for Growth Equity and Administration Simplicity: A Proposal for La Paz, Bolivia." In Bahl 1979b.

Holland, Daniel, and James Follain. 1990. "The Property Tax in Jamaica." In Bahl, 1990.

Howe, Charles W., and F. P. Lineweaver, Jr. 1967. "The Impact of Price on Residential Water Demand and Its Relation to System Design and Price Structure." *Water Resources Research* 3, no. 1: 13–32.

Hubbell, L. Kenneth. 1974. "Local Government Administration and Finance in Thailand." Urban and Regional Report 74-8. World Bank, Development Economics Department, Washington, D.C.

————. 1977. "The Residential Demand for Water and Sewerage Service in Developing Countries: A Case Study of Nairobi." Urban and Regional Report 77-14. World Bank, Development Economics Department, Washington, D.C.

————. 1983. "Local Government Credit Financing." In Bahl and Miller 1983.

Hughes, Gordon. 1987. "The Indicence of Fuel Taxes: A Comparative Study of Three Countries." In Newbery and Stern 1987.

Humes, Samuel, and Eileen Martin. 1969. *The Structure of Local Government*. The Hague: International Union of Local Authorities.

Ihlanfeldt, Keith R., and Jorge Martinez-Vazquez. 1987. "Why Property Tax Capitalization Rates Differ: A Critical Analysis." In John M. Quigley, ed., *Perspectives on Local Public Finance and Public Policy*, vol. 31. Greenwich, Conn.: JAI Press.

IMF (International Monetary Fund). Various years, a. *Government Finance Statistics Yearbook*. Washington, D.C.

————. Various years, b. *International Financial Statistics*. Washington, D.C.

Ingram, Gregory K. 1982. "Land in Perspective: Its Role in the Structure of Cities." In Cullen and Woolery 1982.

Inman, Robert. 1971. "Towards an Econometric Model of Local Budgeting." *Proceedings of the Sixty-Fourth Annual Conference on Taxation*. Kansas City, Mo.: National Tax Association.

Insfopal (Instituto de Fomento Municipal). 1975. "Methodologia para la Formulacion del Plan Nacional de Acueductos y Alcantarillados." Bogotá, Colombia.

International Center for Land Policy Studies. 1980. "Seminar on Land Readjustment, Taoyuan, Taiwan, June 6–13, 1979." *ICLPS Newsletter* no. 9 (February): 2–6.

Ishihara, Nobuo. 1986. "The Local Public Finance System." In Tokue Shibata, ed., *Public Finance in Japan*. Tokyo: Tokyo University Press.

Jao, Y. C. 1976. "Land Use Policy and Land Taxation in Hong Kong." In Jong Wang, ed., *The Cities of Asia: A Study of Urban Solutions and Urban Finance*. Singapore: Singapore University Press.

Jimenez, Emmanuel. 1987. *Pricing Policy in the Social Sectors: Cost Recovery for Education and Health in Developing Countries*. Baltimore, Md.: Johns Hopkins University Press.

Jimenez, Emmanuel, and Douglas Keare. 1984. "Housing Consumption and Permanent Income in Developing Countries: Estimates from Panel Data in El Salvador." *Journal of Urban Economics* 15 (March): 172–94.

Julius, DeAnne, and Adelaida P. Alicbuson. 1989. "Public Sector Pricing Policies: A Review of Bank Policy and Practice." Policy, Planning, and Research Working Paper 49. World Bank, Office of the Vice President for Development Economics, Washington, D.C.

Julius, DeAnne S., and Jeremy J. Warford. 1977. "Economic Evaluation and Financing of Sewerage Projects." Guidelines Series 13. World Bank, Energy, Water, and Telecommunications Department, Washington, D.C.

Kahn, Alfred E. 1970. *The Economics of Regulation: Principles and Institutions*. 2 vols. New York: Wiley.

Kalbermatten, John M., DeAnne Julius, and Charles G. Gunnerson. 1982. *Appropriate Sanitation Alternatives: A Technical and Economic Appraisal*. Baltimore, Md.: Johns Hopkins University Press.

Karran, Terrence. 1988. "Local Taxation and Local Spending: International Comparisons." In Ronan Paddison and Stephen Bailey, eds., *Local Government Finance: International Perspectives*. New York: Routledge.

Katz, Michael. 1987. "Pricing Publicly Supplied Goods and Services." In Newbery and Stern 1987.

Katzman, Martin T. 1977. "Income and Price Elasticities of Demand for Water in Developing Countries." *Water Resources Bulletin* 13, no. 1: 47–55.

Katzman, Martin. N.d. "Measuring the Consumer Surplus Benefits of Urban Water Supply Extensions in Developing Countries: Some Operational Notes." World Bank, Water Supply and Urban Development Department, Washington, D.C.

Kaufman, George G., and Philip J. Fischer. 1987. "Debt Management." In J. Richard Aronson and Eli Schwartz, eds., *Management Policies in Local Government Finance*. Washington, D.C.: International City Management Association, p. 287–317.

Kee, Woo Sik. 1975. "Government Finances and Resource Mobilization in Pakistan." World Bank Studies in Domestic Finance 8. World Bank, Washington, D.C.

————. 1977. "Fiscal Decentralization and Economic Development." *Public Finance Quarterly* 5 (Jan.): 79–97.

Keles, Rasen. 1972. *Urbanization in Turkey*. International Urbanization Survey. New York: Ford Foundation.

Kelley, Roy. 1986. "Property Taxation in Indonesia: An Analysis of the New Property Tax Law of 1986. Harvard University, Institute for International Development, Cambridge, Mass.

Kim, Wan Soon. 1977. "The Equalizing Effect of Financial Transfers: A Study of Intergovernmental Fiscal Relations." In Kim Chuk Kyo, ed., *Planning Models and Macroeconomic Policy Issues*. 2 vols. Seoul: Korea Development Institute.

Kim, Hyang-Hwan. 1985. "Municipal Finance in Korea." Discussion Paper UDD-64. World Bank, Water Supply and Urban Development Department, Washington, D.C.

King, Wei-Shin. 1988. "Land Value Taxation in Taiwan: Present Status." Paper presented to International Seminar on Real Property and Land as a Tax Base for Development, November 14–17, Taoyuan, China.

Kneese, Allen V., and Charles L. Schultze. 1975. *Pollution, Prices, and Public Policy*. Washington, D.C.: Brookings Institution.

Korea, Republic of; Ministry of Home Affairs. 1975. *The Local Finance Adjustment System of Korea 1973*. Seoul.

Krzyaniak, Marian, and Süleyman Ozmucur. 1968. "The Distribution of Income and the Short-Run Burden of Taxes in Turkey, 1968." Paper 28. Program of Development Studies, William Marsh Rice University, Houston.

Lacayo de Arguello, Rosa D., Guillermo Layman Wong, and Julian Velasco Arboleda. 1976. *Finanzas Publicas Locales de Managua: Estructura de Ingresos*. Managua, Nicaragua: Vice Ministerio de Planificacion Urbana.

Ladd, Helen, and Julie Boatright Wilson. 1982. "Why Voters Support Tax Limitations: Evidence from Massachusetts Proposition 2½." Sloan Working Paper 3-82. University of Maryland, College Park.

Lal, Hira. 1976. "Some Legal Issues and Court Decisions on Levy and Assessment of Property Taxes." *Nagarlok Urban Affairs Quarterly* 8, no. 4: 53–62.

Laquian, Aprodicio. 1980. "Issues and Instruments in Metropolitan Planning." In *The Population and the Urban Future*, Report on an International Conference Held in Rome, Sept. 1–4. New York: U.N. Fund for Population Activities.

Larkey, Patrick, Chandler Stoph, and Mark Winer. 1984. "Why Does Government Grow?" In Trudi C. Miller, ed., *Public Sector Performance: A Conceptual Turning Point*. Baltimore, Md.: Johns Hopkins University Press.

Lemer, Andrew C. 1987. "Role of Rental Housing in Developing Countries: A Need for Balance." Discussion Paper UDD-104. World Bank, Water Supply and Urban Development Department, Washington, D.C.

Lent, George E. 1974. "The Urban Property Tax in Developing Countries." *Finanzarchiv* 33, no. 1: 45–72.

————. 1977. "Taiwan's Land Tax Policy." *Bulletin for International Fiscal Documentation* 31, no. 7: 291–99.

Lerche, Dietrich. 1974. "The Revenue Potential of the Land Tax for Urban

Finance in Indonesia." Paper prepared for an International Seminar on Land Use and Taxation in Asia, Dec. 16–19. Lincoln Institute of Land Policy, Cambridge, Mass.

Lewis, Carol W. 1976. "The Budgetary Process in Soviet Cities." Columbia University, Center for Government Studies, New York.

———. 1977. "Comparing City Budgets: The Soviet Case." *Comparative Urban Research* 5, no. 1: 46–59.

Lichfield, Nathaniel, Ashis K. Choudhury, and Gerald F. Blundell. 1978. "Equity and Efficiency in Utility Services." Nathaniel Lichfield and Partners, London.

Lindholm, Richard M., ed. 1977. *Property Tax Reform: Foreign and U.S. Experience with Site Value Taxation.* Monograph 77-11. Cambridge, Mass.: Lincoln Institute of Land Policy.

Lineweaver, F. P., Jr., John C. Geyer, and Jerome B. Wolff. 1967. "A Study of Residential Water Use." Report prepared for Technical Studies Program of Federal Housing Administration, U.S. Department of Housing and Urban Development, Washington, D.C.

Linn, Johannes F. 1975. "Urban Public Finances in Developing Countries: A Case Study of Cartagena, Colombia." Urban and Regional Report 77-1. World Bank, Development Economics Department, Washington, D.C.

———. 1976a. "Economic and Social Analysis of Projects in the World Bank: Principles and Application." Occasional Paper 1. University of Bradford, Project Planning Center for Developing Countries, Bradford, England.

———. 1976b. "Estimation of Water Supply Costs in Cali, Colombia." Urban and Regional Report 76-14. World Bank, Development Economics Department, Washington, D.C.

———. 1976c. "Public Utilities in Metropolitan Bogotá: Organization, Service Levels, and Financing." Urban and Regional Report 78-2. World Bank, Development Economics Department, Washington, D.C.

———. 1977a. *Economic and Social Analysis of Projects: A Case Study of Ivory Coast.* World Bank Staff Working Paper 253. Washington, D.C.

———. 1977b. *The Incidence of Urban Property Taxation in Developing Countries: A Theoretical and Empirical Analysis Applied to Colombia.* World Bank Staff Working Paper 264. Washington, D.C.

———. 1979a. "Automotive Taxation in the Cities of Developing Countries." *Nagarlok Urban Affairs Quarterly* 11, no. 1: 1–23.

———. 1979b. "The Incidence of Urban Property Taxation in Colombia." In Bahl 1979b.

———. 1980a. "The Distributive Effects of Local Government Finances in Colombia: A Review of the Evidence." In R. Albert Berry and Ronald Soligo, eds., *Economic Policy and Income Distribution in Colombia.* Boulder, Colo.: Westview.

———. 1980b. "Property Taxation in Bogotá, Colombia: An Analysis of Poor Revenue Performance." *Public Finance Quarterly* 8, no. 4: 457–76.

———. 1981. "Urban Finances in Developing Countries." In Bahl 1981.

———. 1982. "The Costs of Urbanization in Developing Countries." *Economic Development and Cultural Change* 30, no. 3: 625–48.

————. 1983. *Cities in the Developing World: Policies for Their Equitable and Efficient Growth*. New York: Oxford University Press.

Linn, Johannes F., Caroline S. Fawcett, David Greytak, and J. H. Wolff. 1984. "Urban Finances in Bogotá, Colombia." Discussion Paper UDD-39. World Bank, Water Supply and Urban Development Department, Washington, D.C.

Linn, Johannes F., Roger S. Smith, and Hartojo Wignjowijoto. 1976. "Urban Public Finances in Developing Countries: A Case Study of Jakarta, Indonesia." Urban and Regional Report 80-7. World Bank, Development Economics Department, Washington, D.C.

Linn, Johannes F., and Deborah L. Wetzel. 1991. "Financing Infrastructure in Developing Country Mega-Cities." Paper prepared for a Symposium on the Mega-City and Mankind's Future, October 1990. United Nations University, Tokyo.

Little, I. M. D. 1965. *A Critique of Welfare Economics*. 2d ed. London: Oxford University Press.

Little, I. M. D., and J. A. Mirrlees. 1974. *Project Appraisal and Planning for Developing Countries*. New York: Basic Books.

Lotz, Jøergen. 1970. "Patterns of Government Spending in Developing Countries." *Manchester School of Economic and Social Studies* (June): 119–44.

————. 1981. "Fiscal Problems and Issues in Scandinavian Cities." In Bahl 1981.

Lovejoy, Robert M. 1963. "The Burden of Jamaican Taxation." *Social and Economic Studies* 2, no. 6: 442–58.

McCallum., J. Douglas. 1974. "Land Values in Bogotá, Colombia." *Land Economics* 50, no. 3: 312–17.

McCulloch, John. 1979. "Site Value Ratings in Johannesburg, South Africa." In Bahl 1979b.

McLure, Charles E., Jr. 1971a. "Automotive Tax Reform." In Musgrave and Gillis 1971.

————. 1971b. "The Incidence of Taxation in Colombia." In Musgrave and Gillis 1971.

————. 1974. "The Distribution of Income and Tax Incidence in Panama, 1969." *Public Finance Quarterly* 2, no. 2: 155–201.

————. 1975a. "The Incidence of Colombian Taxes: 1970." *Economic Development and Cultural Change* 24, no. 1: 155–83.

————. 1975b. *Taxation and the Urban Poor in Developing Countries*. World Bank Staff Working Paper 222. Washington, D.C.

————. 1977. "Average Incremental Costs of Water Supply and Sewerage Services: Nairobi, Kenya." Urban and Regional Report 77-13. World Bank, Development Economics Department, Washington, D.C.

————. 1979. "The Relevance of the New View of the Incidence of the Property Tax in Less Developed Countries." In Bahl 1979b.

————, ed. 1983. *Tax Assignment in Federal Countries*. Canberra: Australian National University Press.

McLure, Charles, and Peter Mieszkowski, eds. 1983. *Fiscal Federalism and the Taxation of Natural Resources*. Lexington, Mass.: Lexington Books.

McLure, Charles E., Jr., and Wayne R. Thirsk. 1978. "The Inequity of Taxing Inequity: A Plea for Reduced Sumptuary Taxes in Developing Countries." *Economic Development and Cultural Change* 26, no. 3: 487–503.

Macon, Jorge, and Jose Merino Mañon. 1977. *Financing Urban and Rural Development through Betterment Levies.* New York: Praeger.

Mahar, Dennis J., and William R. Dillinger. 1983. *Financing State and Local Governments in Brazil: Recent Trends and Issues.* World Bank Staff Working Paper 612. Washington, D.C.

Malhotra, D. D. 1986. "Financing Urban Local Governments for Urban Development: Bases of State Transfers." In K. S. R. N. Sarma, ed., *Financing Urban Development in India.* Delhi: Indian Institute of Public Administration.

Mann, Arthur J. 1973. "Net Fiscal Incidence in Puerto Rico." *Caribbean Studies* (Institute of Caribbean Studies, University of Puerto Rico) 13, no. 1: 5–35.

Mann, Patrick. 1968. "The Application of Users Charges for Urban Public Services." *Reviews in Urban Economics* 1, no. 2: 25–46.

————. 1977. "The Interlocking of Municipalities and Publicly Owned Utilities." In Downing 1977a.

Manning, Harry J. 1970. "Some Observations on Singapore's Property Tax System." Government of Australia, Department of the Interior, Canberra.

————. 1976. "Urban Renewal and Property Taxation: Some Impressions of Practices." In Wong 1976.

Margolis, Julius. 1974. "Public Policies for Private Profits: Urban Government." In Harold Hochman and George Peterson, eds., *Redistribution through Public Choice.* New York: Columbia University Press.

Marshall, A. H. 1969. *Local Government Finance.* The Hague: International Union of Local Authorities.

Martin, Alison, and W. Arthur Lewis. 1956. "Patterns of Public Revenue and Expenditure." *Manchester School of Economic and Social Studies* 24, no. 3: 203–44.

Mathews, Russel. 1980. *Revenue Sharing in Federal Systems.* Research Monograph 31. Center for Research on Federal Financial Relations. Canberra: Australian National University.

Matzner, Egon, ed. 1971. *Wirtschaft und Finanzen Österreichischer Stadte.* Wien: Institut für Stadtforschung.

Mayo, Stephen K., and David J. Gross. 1987. "Sites and Services—and Subsidies: The Economics of Low-Cost Housing in Developing Countries." *World Bank Economic Review* 1, no. 2: 301–36.

Mayo, Stephen, Stephen Malpezzi, and David J. Gross. 1986. "Shelter Strategies for the Urban Poor in Developing Countries." *World Bank Research Observer* 1, no. 2: 183–203.

Mbi, Emmanuel E., and Tim Campbell. 1980. "Liberia: Monrovia Water, Power, and Urban Projects: Analysis and Strategies for Improved Access to Services by the Urban Poor." World Bank, Urban Projects Department, Washington, D.C.

Meerman, Jacob. 1979. *Public Expenditure in Malaysia: Who Benefits and Why.* London: Oxford University Press.

Meroz, Avigdor. 1968. "A Quantitative Analysis of Urban Water Demand in Developing Countries." Working Paper 17. World Bank, Economics Department, Washington, D.C.

Mieszkowski, Peter. 1972. "The Property Tax: An Excise Tax or a Profits Tax." *Journal of Public Economics* 1, no. 1: 73–96.

Mikesell, John L. 1971. "Local Sales Taxes in North America." *Municipal Finance* 43, no. 3: 133–40.

Mills, Edwin S. 1972. *Urban Economics*. Glenview, Ill.: Scott-Foresman.

———. 1987. *Handbook of Regional and Urban Economics*. Vol. 2. New York: North Holland.

Miner, Jerry, and Bob Hall. 1983. *Local Revenue and Service Provision in Upper Volta*. Syracuse, N.Y.: Metropolitan Studies Program, Maxwell School, Syracuse University.

Minford, A. P. L. N.d. "A Model of Tax Incidence for Malawi." Seminar on African Public Sector Economics, Center of African Studies, University of Edinburgh, Scotland.

Mitchell, Bridger M. 1978. "Optimal Pricing of Local Telephone Service." *American Economic Review* 68, no. 4: 517–37.

Mohan, Rakesh. 1974. "Indian Thinking and Practice Concerning Urban Property Taxation and Land Policies." Princeton University, Research Program in Economic Development Discussion Paper 47, Princeton, N.J.

———. 1977. "Urban Land Policy Income Distribution and the Urban Poor." In Frank and Webb 1977.

Mohan, Rakesh, and Rodrigo Villamizar. 1980. "The Evolution of Land Values in the Context of Rapid Urban Growth: A Case Study of Bogotá and Cali, Colombia." In Cullen and Woolery 1980.

Motha, Phillip. 1976. "The Land Value Dilemma in Developing Economies with Special Reference to Singapore." In Wong 1976.

Mouchet, Carlos. 1972. "Buenos Aires." In Robson and Regan 1972.

Mueller, Dennis. 1987. "The Growth of Government: A Public Choice Perspective." *International Monetary Fund Staff Papers* 34, no. 1: 254–331.

Muller, Thomas. 1975. *Growing and Declining Urban Areas: A Fiscal Comparison*. Urban Institute Paper 000-02. Washington, D.C.

Muller, Thomas, and Tilney, J. 1977. "The Pricing and Delivery of Public Services: An Overview and Research Needs." Urban Institute Report 0245-01. Washington, D.C.

Munasinghe, Mohan. 1979. *Electric Power Pricing Policy*. World Bank Staff Working Paper 340. Washington, D.C.

———. 1980. *The Economics of Power System Reliability and Planning: Theory and Case Studies*. Baltimore, Md.: Johns Hopkins University Press.

Munasinghe, Mohan, Robert J. Saunders, and Jeremy J. Warford. 1978. "The Cost Structure of Telecommunications Services and Pricing Policy in Developing Countries." Communications 78: Communications Equipment and Systems, Conference Publication 162. Institution of Electrical Engineers, London.

Munasinghe, Mohan, and Jeremy J. Warford. 1978. *Shadow Pricing and Power Tariff Policy*. World Bank Staff Working Paper 286. Washington, D.C.

Munk, Knud Jørgen. 1977. "Optimal Public Sector Pricing Taking the Distributional Aspect into Consideration." *Quarterly Journal of Economics* 91, no. 4: 639–50.

Musgrave, Richard A. 1959. *The Theory of Public Finance: A Study of Public Economy*. New York: McGraw-Hill.

———. 1969. *Fiscal Systems*. New Haven, Conn.: Yale University Press.

———. 1983. "Who Should Tax, Where, and What?" In McLure 1983.

Musgrave, Richard A., Karl E. Case, and Herman Leonard. 1974. "The Distribution of Fiscal Burdens and Benefits." *Public Finance Quarterly* 2, no. 3 (July): 259–311.

Musgrave, Richard, and Malcolm Gillis. 1971. *Fiscal Reform for Colombia: The Final Report and Staff Papers of the Colombian Commission on Tax Reform*. Cambridge, Mass.: International Tax Program, Law School of Harvard University.

Musgrave, Richard A., and P. B. Musgrave. 1984. *Public Finance in Theory and Practice*. 4th ed. New York: McGraw-Hill.

Mushkin, Selma J. 1972. "An Agenda for Research." In Mushkin, ed., *Public Prices for Public Products*. Washington, D.C.: Urban Institute.

Nanjundappa, D. M. 1973. *Road User Taxation and Road Financing in the Indian Economy*. Bombay: Jawaharal Nehru Memorial Institute of Development Studies.

Nath, Shyam. 1982. "Property Tax Revenue Growth in Two Indian Cities." Occasional Paper 65. Metropolitan Studies Program, Maxwell School, Syracuse University, Syracuse, N.Y.

———. 1983. "The Impact of Standard Rent on the Property Tax Base." Working Paper 10. National Institute of Public Finance and Policy, New Delhi.

Nath, Shyam, and Larry Schroeder. 1984. "Property Tax Growth in Metropolitan Cities in India." *Nagarlok* 16, no. 2: 33–44.

Netzer, Richard. 1966. *The Economics of the Property Tax*. Washington, D.C.: Brookings Institution.

———. 1974. "The Property Tax: Discussion." *American Economic Review* 64, no. 2: 231–32.

"Neue Heimat-Teure Heimat." 1977. *Wirtschaftswoche* 31, no. 12 (March 11): 16–22.

Newbery, David M. 1988. "Charging for Roads." *World Bank Research Observer* 3, no. 2: 119–38.

Newbery, David, and Nicholas Stern, eds. 1987. *The Theory of Taxation for Developing Countries*. New York: Oxford University Press.

Newton, K. 1977. "Financial Trends in the Local Government of England and Wales." Working Document prepared for the Workshop on the Financial Problems of West European Cities, European Consortium for Political Research Workshops, Berlin, March 27–April 2.

Ng, Yew-Kwang, and Mendel Weisser. 1974. "Optimal Pricing with a Budget Constraint–The Case of the Two-Part Tariff." *Review of Economic Studies* 41 (July): 337–45.

Nigeria, Government of. 1978. "Report of the Technical Committee on Revenue Allocation." Lagos.

Oates, W. E. *Fiscal Federalism.* 1972. New York: Harcourt Brace Jovanovich.

―――. 1977a. "An Economist's Perspective on Fiscal Federalism." In Oates 1977b.

―――, ed. 1977b. *The Political Economy of Fiscal Federalism.* Lexington, Mass.: Heath.

Oldman, Oliver, and Mary Teachout. 1979. "Some Administrative Aspects of Site Value Taxation." In Bahl 1979b.

Orewa, G. Oka. 1966. *Local Government Finance in Nigeria.* Ibadan: Oxford University Press.

Organization of American States. 1976a. "Evaluación Presupuestaria." *Tributacion* (Dominican Republic) 2, no. 5: 116–37.

―――. 1976b. "La Tributacion Sobre Plusvalia y Mejoras en Americana Latina." *Tributacion* (Dominican Republic) 2, no. 5: 105–15.

Pavlova, L. P. 1975. "Problems of Planning and of Financing the Urbanization in the U.S.S.R." Paper contributed to the 22d World Congress of International Union of Local Administrations, Tehran, Iran, April 15–19.

Peacock, Alan, and Jack Wiseman. 1961. *The Growth of Public Expenditure in the United Kingdom.* Princeton, N.J.: Princeton University Press.

Peterson, George E. 1972. "The Regressivity of the Residential Property Tax." Urban Institute Working Paper 1207-10. Washington, D.C.

Peterson, George E., G. Thomas Kingsley, and Jeffrey P. Telgarsky. 1991. *Urban Economies and National Development.* Washington, D.C.: U.S. Agency for International Development.

Please, Stanley. 1970. "The Please Effect Revisited." Working Paper. World Bank, Economics Department, Washington, D.C.

Pollock, Richard, and Max Neutze. 1976. "Alternative Methods of Financing Water Supply and Sewerage Services." In Australia 1976.

Pollock, Richard L., and Donald C. Shoup. 1977. "The Effect of Shifting the Property Tax Base from Improvement Value to Land Value: An Empirical Estimate." *Land Economics* 53, no. 1: 67–77.

Pommerehne, Werner W. 1977. "Quantitative Aspects of Federalism. A Study of Six Countries." In Oates 1977b.

Pope, R. M., J. M. Stepp, and J. S. Lytle. 1975. *Effects of Price Change upon the Domestic Use of Water over Time.* Dawson, S.C.: Water Resources Research Institute, Dawson University.

Prest, Alan. 1982. "Land Taxation and Urban Finances in Less-Developed Countries." In Cullen and Woolery 1982.

Price, John A. 1973. *Tijuana: Urbanization in a Border Culture.* Notre Dame, Ind.: University of Notre Dame Press.

Prud'homme, Rémy. 1973. "Sources of Local Finance in Zaire." Urban and Regional Report 73-2. World Bank, Development Economics Department.

―――. 1975. "Urban Public Finances in Developing Countries: A Case Study of Metropolitan Tunis." Urban and Regional Report 77-2. World Bank, Development Economics Department, Washington, D.C.

―――. 1980. "Fiscal Issues of Metropolitan Areas." Paper presented at U.N.

Center for Human Settlements conference, Nagoya, Japan. Paris: Institut l'Urbanisme de Paris.

———. 1987. "Financing Urban Public Services." In Mills 1987.

Pusić, Eugen, and Annmarie H. Walsh. 1968. *Urban Government for Zagreb, Yugoslavia.* New York: Praeger.

Rao, S. Rama, and M. Nagesaro Rao. 1977. *Economics of Urban Local Public Services.* Bangalore, India: Institute for Social and Economic Change.

Ray, Anandarup. 1975. *Cost Recovery Policies for Public Sector Projects.* World Bank Staff Working Paper 206. Washington, D.C.

Renaud, Bertrand. 1981. *National Urbanization Policy in Developing Countries.* New York: Oxford University Press.

Richardson, Harry W. 1977. *City Size and National Spatial Strategies in Developing Countries.* World Bank Staff Working Paper 252. Washington, D.C.

Richardson, Ivan L. 1973. *Urban Government for Rio de Janeiro.* New York: Praeger.

Richman, Raymond L. 1965. "The Theory and Practice of Site-Value Taxation in Pittsburgh." In *Proceedings of the Fifty-Seventh Annual Conference on Taxation* (1964). Harrisburg, Pa.: National Tax Association.

———. 1977. "A tributação dos bens imóveis no Brazil—argumentos para sua malor utilização." *Revista Brasileria de Economia* 31, no. 3: 499–519.

Riew, John. 1987. "Property Taxation in Taiwan: Merits, Issues and Options." *Industry of Free China* 68, no. 1: 1–36.

Risden, O. St. Clare. 1979. "A History of Jamaica's Experience with Site Value Taxation." In Bahl 1979b.

Rivkin, Malcolm. 1978. "Some Perspectives on Land Use Regulation and Control." In Dunkerley and Associates 1978.

Roberts, Polly. 1977. "The Effect of the Pricing of Local Services on Urban Spatial Structure." In Downing 1977a.

Robson, William A., and D. E. Regan. 1972. *Great Cities of the World: Their Government, Politics, and Planning.* London: Allen and Unwin.

Rommel, Manfred. 1977. "Sind die Gemeinden arm dran?" *Die Zeit,* no. 31 (July 29): 5.

Rondinelli, Dennis A., and Kenneth Ruddle. 1977. "Local Organization for Integrated Rural Development: Implementing Equity Policy in Developing Countries." *International Review of Administrative Sciences* 43, no. 1: 20–30.

Roth, Gabriel J. 1973. "Regulation of Buses in Cities." *Highway Research Record* 476: 21–29.

Ruggles, Nancy. 1968. "Recent Developments in the Theory of Marginal Cost Pricing." In Turvey 1968.

Saito, Katrine W. 1977. "The Determinants of Savings Behavior: A Survey of the Evidence." Studies in Domestic Finance 35. World Bank, Development Economics Department, Washington, D.C.

Saunders, Robert J. 1976. "Bangkok Water Supply Tariff Study." World Bank, Energy, Water, and Telecommunications Department, Washington, D.C.

Saunders, Robert J., and Harold Shipman. 1975. "Evaluation of Solid Waste Projects." Public Utilities Note 18. Washington, D.C.

Saunders, Robert J., and Jeremy J. Warford. 1976. *Village Water Supply: Economics and Policy in the Developing World*. Baltimore, Md.: Johns Hopkins University Press.

————. 1977. "Telecommunications Pricing and Investment in Developing Countries." Public Utilities Report 30. World Bank, Energy, Water, and Telecommunications Department, Washington, D.C.

Saunders, Robert J., Jeremy J. Warford, and Patrick Mann. 1976. "The Definition and Role of Marginal Cost in Public Utility Pricing: Problems of Application in the Water Supply Sector." Public Utilities Report 6. Washington, D.C.

————. 1977. *Alternative Concepts of Marginal Cost for Public Utility Pricing: Problems of Application in the Water Supply Sector*. World Bank Staff Working Paper 259. Washington, D.C.

Saunders, Robert J., Jeremy J. Warford, and Bjorn Wellenius. 1983. *Telecommunications and Economic Development*. Baltimore, Md.: Johns Hopkins University Press.

Schama, Simon. 1989. *Citizens: A Chronicle of the French Revolution*. New York: Knopf.

Schroeder, Larry. 1985a. "Bangladesh: Urban Government Finance and Management Issues and Opportunities." Sector Paper. World Bank, South Asia Projects Department, Washington, D.C.

————. 1985b. "Institutional Development Program for Local Authorities in Sri Lanka: Local Resource Mobilization Consultant's Report." World Bank, South Asia Projects Department, Washington, D.C.

Selowsky, Marcelo. 1979. *Who Benefits from Government Expenditure: A Case Study of Colombia*. New York: Oxford University Press.

Sharefkin, Mark. 1975. "Metropolitan Growth and the Public Utility Services." Resources for the Future, Washington, D.C.

Sharma, Jitendra Nath. 1976. "Tax Evasion and Avoidance: A Crucial but Neglected Aspect of Taxation." Studies in Domestic Finance 30. World Bank, Development Economics Department, Washington, D.C.

Sharpe, L. J. 1977. "A Tentative Outline of the Main Financial Problems of West European Urban Government." Paper for European Consortium for Political Research Joint Sessions, Berlin, March.

Shipman, Harold R. 1967. "Water Rate Structures in Latin America." *Journal of American Waterworks Association* 59, no. 1: 3–12.

Shoup, Carl. 1979. "The Taxation of Urban Property in Developing Countries: A Concluding Discussion." In Bahl 1979b.

Shoup, Donald C. 1978. "Land Taxation and Government Participation in Urban Land Markets: Policy Alternatives in Developing Countries." In Dunkerley and Associates 1978.

————. 1983. "Intermediation through Property Taxation and Public Ownership." In Harold B. Dunkerley, ed., *Urban Land Policy: Issues and Opportunities*. New York: Oxford University Press.

Silveira, Ricardo. 1989. "The Local Tax on Services in Brazil." World Bank, Infrastructure and Urban Development Department, Washington, D.C.

Singapore, Government of; Inland Revenue Department. Various years. *Inland Revenue Report.* Singapore. Published annually.

Smith, Roger Stafford. 1972. *Local Income Taxes: Economic Effects and Equity.* Berkeley: Institute of Governmental Studies, University of California.

————. 1974. "Financing Cities in Developing Countries." *International Monetary Fund Staff Papers* 21, no. 2: 329–88.

————. 1975. "Highway Pricing and Motor Vehicle Taxation in Developing Countries: Theory and Practice." *Finanzarchiv* (N.F.), 33, no. 3: 451–74.

————. 1979. "The Effects of Land Taxes on Development Timing and Rates of Change in Land Prices." In Bahl 1979b.

Smith, Roger S., and Chong-In Kim. 1979. "Local Finances in Non-Metropolitan Cities of Korea." Urban and Regional Report 79-1. World Bank, Development Economics Department, Washington, D.C.

Squire, Lyn. 1973. "Some Aspects of Optimal Pricing for Telecommunications." *Bell Journal of Economics and Management Science* 4, no. 2: 515–25.

Squire, Lyn, and Herman van der Tak. 1975. *Economic Analysis of Projects.* Baltimore, Md.: Johns Hopkins University Press.

Standing, Guy. 1984. *Population Mobility and Productive Relations: Demographic Links and Policy Evolution.* World Bank Staff Working Paper 695. Washington, D.C.

Stanford Research Institute. 1968. "Cost of Urban Infrastructure for Industry as Related to City Size in Developing Countries: India Case Study." Stanford, Calif.

Steiner, Peter O. 1971. "Peakload Pricing Revisited." In Trebing 1971.

Stern, Martin O. 1977. "The Use of Urban Roads and Their Effect on the Spatial Structure of Cities." In Downing 1977a.

Stocker, Frederick D. 1976. "Diversification of the Local Revenue System: Income and Sales Taxes, User Charges, Federal Grants." Paper presented at the National Tax Association–Tax Institute of America Symposium on Urban Fiscal Problems, Washington, D.C., June 14 and 15.

Strauss, Robert P., and Kenneth L. Wertz. 1976. "The Impact of Municipal Electric Profits on Local Public Finance." *National Tax Journal* 29, no. 1: 22–30.

Tait, Alan A. 1988. *Value-Added Tax: International Practice and Problems.* Washington, D.C.: International Monetary Fund.

Tanzi, Vito. 1987. "Quantitative Characteristics of the Tax Systems in Developing Countries." In Newbery and Stern 1987.

Tanzi, Vito, and Luc De Wulf. 1976. "The Distribution of Tax Burden by Income Groups in Portugal." Paper presented at Conference on the Portuguese Economy, Lisbon, Oct.

Taylor, Charles Lewis. 1983. *Why Governments Grow: Measuring Public Sector Size.* Beverly Hills, Calif.: Sage.

Taylor, Milton C., Raymond L. Richman, and Carlos Casas Morales. 1965. *Fiscal Survey of Colombia.* Baltimore, Md.: Johns Hopkins University Press.

Thimmaiah, G. 1977. *Burden of Union Loans on the States*. Bangalore, India: Institute for Social and Economic Change.

Thirsk, Wayne. 1990. "Jamaican Tax Incentives." In Bahl 1990.

Thomas, Vinod. 1978. *The Measurement of Spatial Differences in Poverty: The Case of Peru*. World Bank Staff Working Paper 273. Washington, D.C.

Townroe, Peter M. 1979. "Employment Decentralization: Policy Instruments for Large Cities in Less Developed Countries." In Paul B. Downing, ed., *Progress in Planning*, vol. 2. London: Pergamon Press.

Trebing, Harry M., ed. 1971. *Essays on Public Utility Pricing and Regulation*. East Lansing: Institute of Public Utilities, Michigan State University.

Tullio, Giuseppe, and Francesco Contesso. 1986. "Do After-Tax Interest Rates Affect Private Consumption and Savings? Empirical Evidence for Eight Industrial Countries: 1970–83." *Economic Papers, Commission of the European Communities*, no. 51 (Dec.): 1–36.

Turvey, Ralph. 1957. *The Economics of Real Property*. London: Allen and Unwin.

———, ed. 1968. *Public Enterprise*. Baltimore, Md.: Penguin.

———. 1976. "Analyzing the Marginal Cost of Water Supply. *Land Economics* 52, no. 2: 158–78.

Turvey, Ralph, and Dennis Anderson. 1977. *Electricity Economics: Essays and Case Studies*. Baltimore, Md.: Johns Hopkins University Press.

Turvey, Ralph, and Jeremy J. Warford. 1974. "Urban Water Supply and Sewerage Pricing Policy." Public Utilities Note 11. World Bank, Water Supply and Urban Development Department, Washington, D.C.

United Nations. 1967. *Local Government Personnel Systems*. New York.

———. 1972. *Credit Institutions for Local Authorities*. New York.

———. 1980. "Human Settlements Finance and Management." Theme Paper for the Third Session of the U.N. Commission on Human Settlements, Mexico City, May 6–14. New York.

———. 1982. *World Population Trends and Policies: 1981 Monitoring Report*. 2 vols. New York.

U.N. Center for Human Settlements. 1987. *Global Report on Human Settlements*. New York: Oxford University Press.

U.N. Commission on Human Settlements. 1981. "Meetings of the Ad Hoc Group of Experts on Ways and Means of Establishing or Strengthening Financial Institutions for Human Settlements Financing and Investment." Report of the Executive Director, New York.

U.N. Department of Economic and Social Affairs. 1966. "The Growth of Foreign Investments in Latin America." In Marvin D. Bernstein, ed., *Foreign Investment in Latin America*. New York: Knopf.

———. 1970. "Administrative Aspects of Urbanization." New York.

———. 1977. *Handbook on Government Auditing in Developing Countries*. New York.

———. 1982. *Estimates and Projections of Urban and City Populations, 1950–2025: The 1980 Assessment*. New York.

———. 1989. *World Population Prospects, 1988*. New York.

U.N. Department of International Economic and Social Affairs. 1978. *Noncon-ventional Financing of Housing for Low-Income Households*. New York.

————. 1980. *Patterns of Urban and Rural Population Growth*. Population Stud-ies, no. 68. New York.

————. 1987. *The Prospects of World Urbanization, Revised as of 1984–85*. Pop-ulation Studies, no. 101. New York.

U.N. Economic and Social Council. 1971. "Water Administration in the Latin American Experience." Report 71-12-3279. New York.

U.N. Statistical Office. 1980. *Yearbook of National Accounts Statistics*. New York.

U.N. Water Conference. 1977. "Resources and Needs: Assessment of the World Water Situation." Mar de la Plata, Argentina, March.

Urrutia Montoya, Miguel. 1981. "Evaluación del Sistema de Transporte Público en Bogotá." Bogotá, Colombia.

U.S. Advisory Commission on Intergovernmental Relations. 1977. *Trends in Metropolitan America*. Washington, D.C.: U.S. Government Printing Office.

————. 1989. *Significant Features of Fiscal Federalism, 1989 Edition*. Vol. 1. Washington, D.C.: U.S. Government Printing Office.

USAID (U.S. Agency for International Development). 1976. "Guidelines for For-mulating Projects to Benefit the Urban Poor in Developing Countries." Wash-ington, D.C.: PADCO, Inc.

U.S. Department of Health, Education, and Welfare. 1969. *Guidelines and Cri-teria for Community Water Supplies in the Developing Countries*. Rockville, Md.

U.S. Department of the Interior, Federal Water Pollution Control Administra-tion. 1969. "Sewerage Charges." In *The Cost of Clean Water and Its Economic Impact* 3 (January 10).

Valverde, Nelson, and Michael Bamberger. 1980. "Housing Subsidies in the Public Sector in Zambia." World Bank, Development Economics Department, Washington, D.C.

Vernez, Georges. 1973. "Pirate Settlements, Housing Construction by Incre-mental Development, and Low Income Housing Policies in Bogotá, Colom-bia." New York: New York City Rand Institute.

Vickrey, William W. 1963. "General and Specific Financing of Urban Services." *Public Expenditure Decisions in the Urban Community*. Washington, D.C.: Re-sources for the Future.

Vlieger, C. A. de, A. R. Manuel, G. A. Vuerstra, and M. C. Onlandvan Schen-delen. 1975. "Drinking Water Supply by Public Hydrants in Developing Countries. Draft Final Report." International Reference Center for Com-munity Water Supply, The Hague.

Wagner, Adolph. 1890. *Finanzwissenschaft*. Leipzig, 1890.

Walsh, Annmarie Hauck. 1969. *The Urban Challenge to Government: An Inter-national Comparison of Thirteen Cities*. New York: Praeger.

Walters, Alan. 1968. *The Economics of Road User Charges*. World Bank Occasional Paper 5. Baltimore, Md.: Johns Hopkins University Press.

————. 1979. "The Benefits of Mini-Buses." *Journal of Transport Economics and Policies* 13, no. 3: 320–34.

————. 1983. "The Value of Land." In Harold B. Dunkerley, ed., *Urban Land Policies: Issues and Opportunities*. New York: Oxford University Press.

Warford, Jeremy, and DeAnne Julius. 1977. "The Multiple Objectives of Water Rate Policy in Less Developed Countries." *Water Supply and Management* 1: 335–42.

Wasylenko, Michael. 1987. "Fiscal Decentralization and Economic Development." *Public Budgeting and Finance* 7, no. 4: 57–71.

Wasylenko, Michael, Roy W. Bahl, and Daniel Holland. 1980. "The Real Property Tax Administration Project." Monograph 9. Metropolitan Studies Program, Maxwell School, Syracuse University, Syracuse, N.Y.

Wasylenko, Michael, and Therese McGuire. 1985. "Jobs and Taxes: The Effect of Business Climate on States' Employment Growth Rates." *National Tax Journal* 38: 497–512.

Watson, Peter L., and Edward P. Holland. 1978. *Relieving Traffic Congestion: The Singapore Area License Scheme*. World Bank Staff Working Paper 281. Washington, D.C.

Webb, Richard Charles. 1977. *Government Policy and the Distribution of Income in Peru, 1963–73*. Cambridge, Mass.: Harvard University Press.

Wells, Fred J. 1977. "The Effects of Customer Density and Electrical Distribution Costs." In Downing 1977a.

White, Gilbert F. 1974. "Domestic Water Supply: Right or Good?" In *Human Rights in Health*. Ciba Foundation Symposium 23 (New Series). Amsterdam: North Holland.

White, Gilbert F., David J. Bradley, and Anne U. White. 1972. *Drawers of Water*. Chicago: University of Chicago Press.

Williams, Babatunde A., and Anne Marie Hauck Walsh. 1968. *Urban Government for Metropolitan Lagos*. New York: Praeger.

Wong, John, ed. 1976. *The Cities of Asia: A Study of Urban Solutions and Urban Finance*. Singapore: Singapore University Press.

Woodruff, A. M., and L. L. Ecker-Racz. 1969. "Property Taxes and Land Use Patterns in Australia and New Zealand." In Arthur Becker, ed., *Land and Building Taxes: Their Effect on Economic Development*. Madison: University of Wisconsin Press.

World Bank. 1973. "Pricing in Power and Water Supply." Public Utilities Department, Note 5. Washington, D.C.

————. 1975a. "Cameroon: Water Supply and Sewerage Sector Study." WHO/ IBRD Cooperative Program. Washington, D.C.

————. 1975b. "Telecommunications Sector: Colombia." Regional Projects Department, Report 663-CO. Washington, D.C.

————. 1975c. *Urban Transport*. Sector Policy Paper. Washington, D.C.

————. 1979. *World Development Report 1979*. New York: Oxford University Press.

————. 1980a. *Health*. Sector Policy Paper. Washington, D.C.

————. 1980b. *Shelter*. Poverty and Basic Needs Series. Washington, D.C.

————. 1980c. *Water Supply and Waste Disposal*. Poverty and Basic Needs Series. Washington, D.C.

———. 1980d. *World Development Report 1980*. New York: Oxford University Press.

———. 1981. *World Development Report 1981*. New York: Oxford University Press.

———. 1985. *World Development Report 1985*. New York: Oxford University Press.

———. 1986. *Urban Transport*. A World Bank Policy Study. Washington, D.C.

———. 1988. *World Development Report 1988*. New York: Oxford University Press.

———. 1989. *World Development Report 1989*. New York: Oxford University Press.

———. 1991a. *Developing the Private Sector: The World Bank's Experience and Approach*. Washington, D.C.

———. 1991b. *Urban Policy and Economic Development: An Agenda for the 1990s*. Policy Paper. Washington, D.C.

World Health Organization. 1976. "Community Water Supply and Wastewater Disposal (Mid-Decade Progress Report)." Twenty-Ninth World Health Assembly, May 6, Geneva, Switzerland.

Wright, Deil S. 1988. *Understanding Intergovernmental Relations*. 3d ed. Pacific Grove, Calif.: Brooks/Cole.

Yang, Shu-Chin. 1975. *Social Rate of Return for Project Evaluation: An Estimate for Yugoslavia*. World Bank Staff Working Paper 205. Washington, D.C.

Yoingco, Angel O. 1971. *Property Taxation in Asian Countries*. Manila, Philippines: Joint Legislative-Executive Tax Commission.

———. 1988. "Property Taxation in the Philippines." Paper presented to International Seminar on Real Property and Land as a Tax Base for Development. Nov. 14–17, 1988, Taoyuan, Taiwan (China).

Yonehara, J. 1986. "Financial Relations between National and Local Governments." In Tokue Shibata, ed., *Public Finance in Japan*. Tokyo: University of Tokyo Press.

Zahavi, Yacor. 1976. *Travel Characteristics in Cities of Developing and Developed Countries*. World Bank Staff Working Paper 230. Washington, D.C.

Zimmerman, Horst. 1977. "Cushioning the Fiscal Effects of Economic Changes in Cities: West German and U.S. Federal/State-Local Fiscal Relations." Urban Institute Working Paper 0237-01. Washington, D.C.

Index